DICTIONARY OF
GOVERNMENT AND
POLITICS

second edition

Titles in the series

Workbooks

Visit our web site for full details of all our books

www.petercollin.com

DICTIONARY OF
GOVERNMENT AND
POLITICS

second edition

P.H. Collin

PETER COLLIN PUBLISHING

First published in Great Britain 1988
Second edition 1997

reprinted 2001

Published by Peter Collin Publishing Ltd
32-34 Great Peter Street, London, SW1P 2DB

British Library Cataloguing-in-Publication Data

A catalogue record for this book is available from the British Library

ISBN 0-948549-89-0

Text computer typeset by PCP
Printed and bound in Finland by WS Bookwell
Cover artwork by Gary Weston

PREFACE TO THE FIRST EDITION

This dictionary provides the user with the basic vocabulary used in the fields of government and politics, both in Britain and in the United States. The subject matter covers national legislatures, elections, local government, parliamentary and council procedure, international affairs and political parties and theories.

The 5,000 main words and associated phrases are explained in simple English using a vocabulary of about 500 words over and above those words which actually appear in the dictionary as main words. Very many examples are given to show the words and phrases used in context, and many of the more difficult phrases and expressions are themselves defined in clear and simple English. Words which pose particular grammatical problems have short grammar notes attached, giving irregular verb forms and plurals, as well as notes on constructions and differences between British and American usage. Many words also have comments of a more general nature, giving encyclopaedic information about procedures and institutions. At the back of the book a supplement gives information about the political and legislative systems in Britain and the United States, together with reproductions of relevant documents.

We are particular grateful to the following: to Her Majesty's Stationery Office for permission to reproduce documents relating to the British Parliament; to the Chief Executive and Town Clerk of the London Borough of Richmond upon Thames for his assistance in obtaining documents relating to the borough and for permission to reproduce these documents in the supplement; to Mr Toby Jessel, M.P., for his help in obtaining documents relevant to the work of the House of Commons, and to the Government Chief Whip for permission to reproduce the notice of whipping. We would also like to thank various people who helped in the compilation and checking of the dictionary, in particular Derek Beattie, Mrs M.D. Groves and Tony Thorne.

PREFACE TO THE SECOND EDITION

This new edition of the dictionary now includes much more information about national governments and systems, together with a very much expanded coverage of European Union terminology. In addition, phonetic pronunciation is now given for all entries.

We would like to thank again, all the correspondents who have made suggestions for new material, much of which has been incorporated.

In particular we are grateful to Jorge Díaz-Cintas, of Roehampton Institute, for his valuable help in proofreading the text and making a very large number of suggestions, especially regarding European Union terminology.

Aa

A [eɪ] *first letter of the alphabet* **Schedule A** = schedule to the Finance Acts under which tax is charged on income from land *or* buildings; **Table A** = model articles of association of a limited company set out in the Companies Act, 1985

abandon [ə'bændən] *verb* **(a)** to give up *or* not to continue; **to abandon a Bill** *or* **an action** = to give up trying to promote a Bill *or* to give up a court case **(b)** to leave (something *or* a person); *he abandoned his family and went abroad; the crew abandoned the sinking ship*

abeyance [ə'beɪəns] *noun* state of being suspended; **this law is in abeyance** = this law in not being enforced at the present time; (NOTE: no plural)

abide by [ə'baɪd 'baɪ] *verb* to obey (an order *or* a rule); *the government promised to abide by the decision of the High Court; the rebels did not abide by the terms of the agreement*

abjure [æb'dʒʊə] *verb* **(a)** to renounce something, to swear to give up a claim to something **(b)** *US* to swear not to bear allegiance to another country

◊ **abjuration** [æbdʒə'reɪʃn] *noun* act of abjuring

abnormal [æb'nɔːml] *adjective* not normal *or* not usual

abode [ə'bəʊd] *noun* residence *or* place where someone lives; **right of abode** = right to live in a country

abolish [ə'bɒlɪʃ] *verb* to cancel *or* to put an end to *or* to remove (a law *or* a rule); *the Chancellor of the Exchequer refused to ask*

Parliament to abolish the tax on alcohol; the Senate voted to abolish the death penalty

◊ **abolition** [æbə'lɪʃn] *noun* act of abolishing; *to campaign for the abolition of the death penalty; anarchists advocate the abolition of the state*

abrogate ['æbrəgeɪt] *verb* to end *or* to repeal (a treaty *or* a law)

◊ **abrogation** [æbrə'geɪʃn] *noun* ending (of a treaty *or* a law)

absence ['æbsəns] *noun* not being at a meeting *or* hearing; **in the absence of** = when someone is not there; *in the absence of the chairman, his deputy took the chair; the hearing took place in the absence of the main witness; she was sentenced to death in her absence;* **apologies for absence** = names of members of a committee who have apologized for not being able to attend a meeting (read out at the beginning of the meeting by the secretary *or* chairman and listed in the minutes); **leave of absence** = being allowed to be absent from work *or* (of an MP) to be away from the House of Commons; *see also* IN ABSENTIA

◊ **absent** ['æbsənt] *adjective* not at a meeting *or* hearing

◊ **absentee** [æbsən'tiː] *noun* person who does not attend a meeting *or* hearing

absolute ['æbsəluːt] *adjective* complete *or* total; **absolute government** = government by a person *or* group of people, where the ordinary population has no vote and no say in the affairs of state; **absolute majority** = having more votes than all the other candidates *or* parties put together; *in the alternative vote system, if no candidate has an absolute majority at the first count, the second preferences are counted;* **absolute**

privilege = privilege which protects a person from being sued for defamation (such as an MP speaking in the House of Commons, a judge making a statement in judicial proceedings)

◊ **absolutism** [ˈæbsəluːtɪzm] *noun* political theory that any legitimate government should have absolute power

◊ **absolutist** [ˈæbsəluːtɪst] *adjective & noun* (person) who believes in absolutism; (system) where the government has absolute power

---

power tends to corrupt and absolute power corrupts absolutely

Lord Acton

---

absolve [əbˈzɒlv] *verb* to pronounce someone not responsible; *the court absolved him of all responsibility for the accident;* (NOTE: you absolve someone of a crime)

abstain [əbˈsteɪn] *verb* no to do something (especially not to vote); *sixty MPs abstained in the vote on capital punishment*

◊ **abstention** [əbˈstenʃn] *noun* **(a)** refraining from doing something (especially voting); *the motion was carried by 200 votes to 150, with 60 abstentions* **(b)** *US* situation where a federal court refuses to hear a case and passes it to a state court

abstract 1 [ˈæbstrækt] *noun* short form of a report *or* document; *to make an abstract of a report or of the deeds of a property* **2** [əbˈstrækt] *verb* to make a summary

abuse 1 [əˈbjuːs] *noun* **(a)** using something wrongly; *the Chancellor of the Exchequer has introduced a Bill to correct some of the abuses in the present tax system;* **abuse of power** = using legal powers in an illegal *or* harmful way; **abuse of rules** = using the right to introduce a motion into the House of Commons for a wrong purpose (such as to prevent a debate from continuing) **(b)** rude *or* insulting words; *the prisoner shouted abuse at the judge* **(c)** bad treatment (often sexual) of a person; *child abuse or sexual abuse of children;* (NOTE: no plural for (b) or (c)) **2** [əˈbjuːz] *verb* **(a)** to use something wrongly; **to abuse one's authority** = to use authority

in an illegal *or* harmful way **(b)** to say rude words to (someone); *he abused the police before being taken to the cells* **(c)** to treat someone badly (often in a sexual way); *he had abused small children*

ACAS [ˈeɪkæs] = ADVISORY CONCILIATION AND ARBITRATION SERVICE

ACC = ASSOCIATION OF COUNTY COUNCILS

accede [əkˈsiːd] *verb* **(a)** to join a group; *the treaty by which the UK acceded to the EU* **(b)** to become king or queen **(c)** **accede to someone's request** = to agree to a request

accept [əkˈsept] *verb* **(a)** to take something which is being offered **(b)** to say 'Yes' or to agree to something; *she accepted the offer of a job in Australia; he accepted the nomination of the Labour party; the Speaker accepted the suggestion from the Leader of the House;* **to accept an offer conditionally** = to accept provided that certain conditions apply

◊ **acceptable** [əkˈseptəbl] *adjective* which can be accepted; *the offer is not acceptable to both parties*

◊ **acceptance** [əkˈseptəns] *noun* saying 'Yes' to a proposal; **acceptance of an offer** = agreeing to an offer (and therefore entering into a contract); **we have his letter of acceptance** = we have received a letter from him accepting the offer; **speech of acceptance** *or* **acceptance speech** = speech made by someone accepting the nomination of a party to stand for Parliament

◊ **acceptor** [əkˈseptə] *noun* person who accepts an offer

access [ˈækses] **1** *noun* **(a) to have access to something** = to be able to obtain *or* reach something; **to gain access to something** = to reach *or* to get hold of something; **to have access to someone** = to be able to approach and talk to someone; *he always has access to the Prime Minister; people should be allowed access to their medical records; the Local Government Access to Information Act (1985) makes local councils more open*

(b) right of the owner of a piece of land to use a public road which is next to the land; *he complained that he was being denied access to the main road;* (NOTE: no plural) **2** *verb* to call up (data) which is stored in a computer; *the staff in the Housing Department can access records on all properties and tenants*

◊ **accession** [ək'seʃn] *noun* joining something *or* taking up a position; **accession to the throne** = becoming King *or* Queen; **Accession Treaties** = treaties establishing the terms and conditions under which countries become members of the EU; **the Treaty of Accession** = treaty by which the UK joined the EU

accident ['æksɪdənt] *noun* something unpleasant which happens by chance (such as a plane crash); **industrial accident** = accident which takes place at work; **accident insurance** = insurance which will pay when an accident takes place

◊ **accidental** [æksɪ'dentl] *adjective* which happens by accident

accompany [ə'kʌmpni] *verb* to go with; *they sent a formal letter of complaint, accompanied by an invoice;* (NOTE: accompanied by someone or something)

accordance [ə'kɔːdəns] *noun* agreement; **in accordance with** = in agreement with *or* according to; *the government's legal advisers have stated that the action is in accordance with the United Nations resolution; in accordance with your instructions we have deposited the money in your current account; I am submitting the claim for damages in accordance with the advice of our legal advisers*

◊ **according to** [ə'kɔːdɪŋ 'tu] *preposition* as someone says *or* writes; *according to their MP, the Home Secretary has refused to meet the representatives of the immigrants*

◊ **accordingly** [ə'kɔːdɪŋli] *adverb* in agreement with what has been decided; *we have received your letter and have altered the draft contract of employment accordingly*

account [ə'kaʊnt] **1** *noun* **(a)** invoice *or* record of money paid *or* owed; *please send me your account or a detailed or an itemized account* **(b)** notice *or* attention; **to take account of a report** *or* **to take a report into account** = to pay attention to a report; *the Committee will take account of the report of the Royal Commission or will take the Royal Commission's report into account when drafting the Bill* **(c)** *(in a shop)* arrangement which a customer has with the shop to buy goods and pay for them at a later date (usually the end of the month) **(d)** customer who does a large amount of business with a firm and has a credit account with that firm **(e)** **accounts** = detailed record of an organization's financial affairs; *the auditors examined the council's accounts very thoroughly;* **national accounts** = the record of a country's financial affairs **(f)** **bank account** *or* *US* **banking account** = arrangement to keep money in a bank **(g)** *(Stock Exchange)* set period (formerly about ten working days) during which shares can be bought and at the end of which the purchaser must pay for the shares bought **2** *verb* **to account for** = to explain and record a money deal; *the treasurer was asked to account for the loss or the discrepancy; I cannot account for his absence from the meeting*

◊ **accountable** [ə'kaʊntəbl] *adjective* (person) who has to explain what has taken place *or* who is responsible for something; *the minister is accountable to Parliament;* (NOTE: you are accountable to someone for something)

◊ **accountability** [əkaʊntə'bɪlɪti] *noun* being accountable *or* responsible; *the accountability of the elected representatives to the electors who elect them; there have been demands for increased accountability for ministers*

◊ **accounting** [ə'kaʊntɪŋ] *noun* preparing the accounts of a business

the old version of ministerial responsibility held a minister accountable for things that went wrong in his or her department

Canberra Times

accredited [ə'kredɪtɪd] *adjective* **(a)** (person) who is appointed to represented an organization; *an accredited agent* **(b)**

(ambassador) who is appointed by a country to represent it in another country; *he is accredited to the United Nations*

acculturation [əkʌltʃə'reɪʃn] *noun* assimilation of parts of a different culture

achieve [ə'tʃiːv] *verb* to succeed in doing something *or* to do something successfully; *the government has achieved its aim in splitting the opposition vote*

acknowledge [ək'nɒlɪdʒ] *verb* (a) to accept that something is true; **acknowledged and agreed** = words written on an agreement to show that it has been read and approved (b) to confirm that (a letter) has been received; *the office of the Ombudsman has acknowledged receipt of the letter*

◊ **acknowledgement** [ək'nɒlɪdʒmənt] *noun* act of acknowledging; *he wrote to his MP and received a letter of acknowledgement immediately*

acquire [ə'kwaɪə] *verb* to buy *or* to obtain; *the colony was acquired as a result of a treaty in the 19th century*

◊ **acquis communautaire** ['æki: kɒmjuːnə'teə] *French words meaning* 'established community rights': contents, principles and objectives of the EU treaties, developed over a period of time

◊ **acquisition** [ækwɪ'zɪʃn] *noun* (i) thing bought; (ii) act of obtaining *or* buying something

act [ækt] **1** *noun* (a) statute which has been approved by a law-making body (in Great Britain, by Parliament, in the USA by Congress) and which becomes law; **Act of Parliament** = Bill which has been approved by Parliament and so becomes law; **Companies Act** = British Act which rules how companies should do their business; **Finance Act** = annual Act of the British Parliament which gives the government power to raise taxes as proposed in the budget; (NOTE: use **under** when referring to an Act of Parliament: **a creditor seeking a receiving order under the Bankruptcy Act; she does not qualify under section 2 of the 1979 Act**) (b) thing which is done; **hostile act** = unfriendly action which suggests that the country

committing it is an enemy; *we consider the violation of our air space a hostile act;* **act of God** = natural disaster which you do not expect to happen, and which cannot be avoided (such as a storm *or* a flood); *acts of God are usually not covered by an insurance policy* **2** *verb* (a) to work; *to act as an agent for an American company; to act for someone or to act on someone's behalf* (b) to do something; *the lawyers are acting on our instructions; the government lost no time in acting on the recommendations of the report;* **to act on a letter** = to do what a letter asks to be done

COMMENT: before an Act becomes law, it is presented to Parliament in the form of a Bill. See notes at BILL

action ['ækʃn] *noun* (a) thing which has been done; **to take action** = to do something; *the committee decided to take no further action or that no further action should be taken on this matter* (b) **court action** = civil case in a law court where a person sues another person; **to take legal action** = to begin a legal case (such as to instruct a solicitor *or* to sue someone); *action for damages; action for libel or libel action; to bring an action for damages against someone;* **civil action** = case brought by a person *or* company (the plaintiff) against someone who is alleged to have harmed them (the defendant); *US* **class action** = legal action brought on behalf of a group of people; **criminal action** = case brought usually by the state against someone who is charged with a crime

◊ **actionable** ['ækʃənəbl] *adjective* (writing *or* speech *or* act) which could provide the grounds for bringing an action against someone

◊ **active** ['æktɪv] *adjective* working *or* busy; *agitators were active among the students at the meeting*

◊ **actively** ['æktɪvli] *adverb* in a busy way

◊ **activist** ['æktɪvɪst] *noun* person who works actively for a political party (usually a person who is in disagreement with the main policies of the party *or* whose views are more extreme than those of the mainstream of the party); *the meeting was disrupted by an* *argument between the chairman and left-wing activists; party activists have urged the central committee to adopt a more radical approach to the problems of unemployment*

◊ **activity** [æk'tɪvɪti] *noun* (i) being active; (ii) something which has been done; *there has been a lot of diplomatic activity in the Middle East; the leader of the party condemned the activities of some of the younger members; she was accused of activities hostile to the state*

> our role as activists is to help organize people in communities to take and use power
> *New Statesman*

actual ['æktjʊəl] *adjective* real; **actual value** = real value of something if sold on the open market

additional [ə'dɪʃənəl] *adjective* (which is) added *or* extra; **additional member** = electoral system used in Germany, where half the parliament is elected by the first-past-the-post system, and the other half by a party list system, giving additional members to represent each party's national vote

address [ə'dres] **1** *noun* **(a)** details of number, street and town where an office is or where a person lives **(b)** formal speech; *in his address to the meeting, the mayor spoke of the problems facing the town; in his State of the Union address, the president spoke of the problems of terrorism* **(c)** humble **address** = formal communication from one or both Houses of Parliament to the Queen; **address of thanks** = formal speech, thanking someone for doing something (such as thanking a VIP for opening a new building *or* thanking the Queen for reading the Queen's Speech); **debate on the address** = debate after the Queen's Speech at the Opening of Parliament, where the motion is to present an address of thanks to the Queen, but the debate is in fact about the government's policies as outlined in the Queen's Speech **2** *verb* **(a)** to write the details of an address on an envelope, etc.; *an incorrectly addressed package* **(b)** to speak to; *the Leader of the*

Opposition was asked to address the meeting **(c)** to speak about a particular issue; *he then addressed the question of government aid to universities;* to **address oneself to a problem** = to deal with a particular problem; *the government will have to address itself to problems of international trade*

adequate ['ædɪkwət] *adjective* large enough; *the Bill does not make adequate provision for low-income families*

ad hoc [æd'hɒk] *Latin phrase meaning* 'for this particular purpose'; **an ad hoc committee** = a temporary committee set up to study a particular problem; *see also* STANDING

adjoin [ə'dʒɔɪn] *verb (of a property)* to touch another property; *the developers acquired the old post office and two adjoining properties; the fire spread to the adjoining building which was owned by the council*

adjourn [ə'dʒɜːn] *verb* to stop a meeting for a period *or* to put off a legal hearing to a later date; *they adjourned the meeting or the meeting was adjourned; the chairman adjourned the tribunal until three o'clock; the meeting adjourned at midday; the appeal was adjourned while further evidence was being produced;* **the hearing was adjourned sine die** = the hearing was adjourned without saying when it would meet again; **the House stands adjourned** = the sitting of the House of Commons is adjourned and will resume on the following day

◊ **adjournment** [ə'dʒɜːnmənt] *noun* **(a)** act of adjourning; time when a meeting has been adjourned; *the adjournment lasted two hours; the defendant has applied for an adjournment* **(b)** act of ending a sitting of the House of Commons *or* House of Lords *or* House of Representatives *or* Senate, which will reconvene on the following day; **motion for adjournment of the debate** = motion to adjourn a debate (which has the effect of killing the motion being debated); **motion for the adjournment of the House** = motion to adjourn a sitting until the following day; **adjournment debate** *or* **debate on the**

adjournment = debate in the House of Commons on a motion to adjourn the sitting, used by backbench MPs to raise points of particular interest to themselves; **adjournment sine die** = adjournment without fixing a date for the next meeting (used in the US Congress to end a session); *US* **adjournment to a day certain** = motion to adjourn a sitting of Congress to a certain stated day

---

the Commons adjourned until January 18 without taking a vote on the Government's resolution

Toronto Globe & Mail

---

adjudicate [əˈdʒuːdɪkeɪt] *verb* to give a judgment between two parties in law; to decide a legal problem; *to adjudicate a claim; to adjudicate in a dispute; magistrates may be paid expenses when adjudicating;* **he was adjudicated bankrupt** = he was declared legally bankrupt

◊ **adjudication** [ədʒuːdɪˈkeɪʃn] *noun* act of giving a judgment *or* of deciding a legal problem; **adjudication order** *or* **adjudication of bankruptcy** = order by a court declaring someone bankrupt; **adjudication tribunal** = group which adjudicates in industrial disputes

◊ **adjudicator** [əˈdʒuːdɪkeɪtə] *noun* person who gives a decision on a problem; *an adjudicator in an industrial dispute*

adjust [əˈdʒʌst] *verb* (i) to change something to fit new conditions; (ii) to calculate and settle an insurance claim

◊ **adjuster** [əˈdʒʌstə] *noun* person who calculates losses for an insurance company

◊ **adjustment** [əˈdʒʌstmənt] *noun* act of adjusting; slight change

administer [ədˈmɪnɪstə] *verb* (a) to control *or* manage *or* govern; *the state is administered directly from the capital; the affairs of the national airline are being administered by a group of ministry officials* (b) to organize *or* provide; **to administer justice** = to provide justice *or* to carry out the law (c) **to administer an oath** = to make someone swear an oath

◊ **administration** [ədmɪnɪˈstreɪʃn] *noun* (a) organization *or* control *or* management, especially by a bureaucracy; *there has been a lack of effective administration in the province since the riots; the administration of justice is in the hands of the government-appointed justices of the peace; she took up a career in hospital administration* (b) government; *the Act became law under the previous administration; she was Secretary of State for Education in the last administration;* (NOTE: can be used with the name of the leader of the government: **the Nixon Administration**)

◊ **administrative** [ədˈmɪnɪstrətɪv] *adjective* referring to administration; **administrative court** *or* **administrative tribunal** = tribunal which decides in cases where government regulations affect and harm the lives and property of individuals; **administrative law** = laws which regulate how government organizations affect the lives and property of individuals

◊ **administrator** [ədˈmɪnɪstreɪtə] *noun* person who manages government *or* public affairs *or* a business; *the governor of the province has to be a good administrator; the council has appointed too many administrators and not enough ordinary clerical staff; the best administrators come from the civil service training school*

the Admiralty [ðiːˈædmɪrəltɪ] *noun* British government office which is in charge of the Navy; **Admiralty law** = law relating to ships and sailors, and actions at sea

admit [ədˈmɪt] *verb* (a) to allow someone to go in; *children are not admitted to the bank; old age pensioners are admitted at half price* (b) to agree that an allegation is correct *or* to say that something really happened; *he admitted his mistake or his liability; she admitted that the department was at fault; they admitted having connections with the company which had been awarded the contract;* (NOTE: **admitted - admitting**. Note also that you admit **to** something, or admit **having** done something)

◊ **admissibility** [ədmɪsɪˈbɪlɪtɪ] *noun* being admissible; *the court will decide on the admissibility of the evidence*

◊ **admissible** [əd'mɪsɪbl] *adjective* (evidence) which a court will admit *or* will allow to be used

◊ **admission** [əd'mɪʃn] *noun* **(a)** allowing someone to go in; *there is a £1 admission charge; admission is free on presentation of this card; no admission after 5 p.m.* **(b)** making a statement agreeing that certain facts are correct *or* saying that something really happened; *the Opposition called for an admission of error on the part of the Minister*

adopt [ə'dɒpt] *verb* **(a)** to become the legal parent of a child who was born to other parents **(b)** to agree to (something) *or* to accept (something) so that it becomes law; *the report of the subcommittee was received and the amendments adopted; the meeting adopted the resolution; the proposals were adopted unanimously; the council has adopted a policy of positive discrimination* **(c) to be adopted** = to be chosen by the party as a prospective parliamentary candidate for a constituency

◊ **adoption** [ə'dɒpʃn] *noun* **(a)** act of becoming the legal parent of a child which is not your own **(b)** act of agreeing to something so that it becomes legal *or* accepted; *he moved the adoption of the resolution* **(c)** being chosen as a prospective parliamentary candidate; **adoption meeting** = meeting at which a local party adopts someone as its candidate

adult ['ædʌlt *or* ə'dʌlt] *noun* person who has reached the age of majority (18 years in the UK and USA)

ad valorem [æd və'lɔːrəm] *Latin phrase meaning* 'according to value'; **ad valorem duty** *or* **ad valorem tax** = tax calculated according to the value of the goods taxed

> COMMENT: most taxes are 'ad valorem'; VAT is calculated as a percentage of the charge made, income tax is a percentage of income earned, etc.

advance [əd'vɑːns] **1** *noun* **(a)** money paid as a loan *or* as a part of a payment which is to be completed later; *a cash advance; to* receive an advance from the bank; the council has agreed to make an advance of £100 to the organizers of the exhibition **(b) in advance** = early *or* before something happens; *to pay in advance; the MP notified the Speaker in advance that he was planning to raise the matter in the House* **2** *adjective* **(c)** *the MP gave no advance warning of his question to the Minister; no advance payment is needed when booking the flight; you must give seven days' advance notice of withdrawals from the account* **3** *verb* **(a)** to lend (money); *the bank advanced him £10,000 against the security of his house* **(b)** to increase; *prices generally advanced on the stock market* **(c)** to make something happen earlier; *the date of the hearing has been advanced to May 10th*

advantage [əd'vɑːntɪdʒ] *noun* something useful which may help you to be successful; **to learn something to your advantage** = to hear news which is helpful to you (especially to hear that you have been left a legacy)

adversary ['ædvəsri] *noun* opponent *or* the other side (in a court case)

◊ **adversarial politics** [ædvə'seəriəl 'pɒlɪtɪks] *noun* way of conducting political affairs where opposing sides always attack each other, and create an atmosphere of tension; (NOTE: opposite is **consensus politics**)

adverse ['ædvɜːs] *adjective* in disagreement with *or* opposing; *he said he had received a number of adverse comments on the plan; no adverse comments were expressed at the meeting*

advice [əd'vaɪs] *noun* **(a)** opinion as to what action should be taken; **to take legal advice** = to ask a lawyer to advise about a problem in law; **counsel's advice** = opinion of a barrister about a case **(b) advice note** = written notice to a customer giving details of goods ordered and shipped but not yet delivered

advise [əd'vaɪz] *verb* **(a)** to tell someone what has happened *or* what will happen soon; *we are advised that the shipment will arrive next week* **(b)** to suggest to someone what should be done

◊ **advise against** [əd'vaɪz ə'genst] *verb* to suggest that something should not be done; *the Minister advised against raising the matter in the House; the consultants advised against the proposed development plan*

◊ **adviser** *or* **advisor** [əd'vaɪzə] *noun* person who suggests what should be done; **financial adviser** = person *or* company which gives advice on financial matters for a fee

◊ **advisory** [əd'vaɪzəri] *adjective* as an adviser; *he is acting in an advisory capacity;* **an advisory board** = a group of advisers; *GB* **the Advisory Conciliation and Arbitration Service (ACAS)** = body which assists in settling industrial and employment disputes

advocacy ['ædvəkəsi] *noun* (i) skill of pleading a case orally before a court; (ii) support for a cause; *his advocacy of the right of illegal immigrants to remain in the country*

advocate 1 ['ædvəkət] *noun (in Scotland)* barrister; *US* lawyer; **Faculty of Advocates** = legal body to which Scottish barristers belong; **devil's advocate** = person who argues the opposite case, to provoke a discussion **2** ['ædvəkeɪt] *verb* to argue in favour of something; *anarchists advocate the abolition of the state*

◊ **Advocate General** ['ædvəkət 'dʒenərəl] *noun* **(a)** one of the two Law Officers for Scotland **(b)** *(in the European Court of Justice)* officer of the court who summarizes and presents a case to the judges to assist them in coming to a decision

affair [ə'feə] *noun* **(a)** business *or* dealings; *are you involved in the copyright affair? his affairs were so difficult to understand that the lawyers had to ask accountants for advice* **(b)** scandal (often political); *the Watergate affair; the Minister was caught up in the arms smuggling affair* **(c)** **affairs of state** = government business; **foreign affairs** = matters concerning other countries; **the Ministry of Foreign Affairs** = ministry dealing with a country's relations with other countries; NOTE: in the UK, this is **the Foreign Office** in the USA, it is **the State Department)**

affect [ə'fekt] *verb* to influence *or* to have an effect on (something *or* someone); *the new*

government regulations do not affect us; sales in the Far East were seriously affected by the embargo

affiliate [ə'filieɪt] *verb* to link to a larger group; *a Trades Union affiliated to the Labour Party*

◊ **affiliation** [əfɪli'eɪʃn] *noun* link; **the union has no political affiliation** = the union is not linked to any particular political party

affirm [ə'fɜːm] *verb* **(a)** to state that you will tell the truth, but without swearing an oath; *some of the new MPs affirmed, instead of swearing the oath of allegiance* **(b)** to confirm that something is correct

◊ **affirmation** [æfə'meɪʃn] *noun* **(a)** statement in court that you will say the truth, though this is not sworn on oath **(b)** statement by an MP, showing his allegiance to the Queen (when he does not wish to take the Oath of Allegiance on religious or other grounds)

◊ **affirmative** [ə'fɜːmətɪv] *adjective* meaning 'Yes'; **the answer was in the affirmative** = the answer was 'Yes'; *US* **affirmative action** = policy of avoiding discrimination against groups in society who have a disadvantage (such as handicapped people, etc.); (NOTE: the GB equivalent is 'equal opportunity') **affirmative instrument** = form of SI which must be approved by both Houses of Parliament

a fortiori [eɪ fɔːti'ɔːraɪ] *Latin phrase meaning* 'for a stronger reason'

against [ə'genst] *preposition* **(a)** meaning 'not in agreement with'; *the majority voted against the proposal; three were for and twelve were against the resolution;* **against the law** = which breaks the law; *lighting fires in the street is against the law; the company acted against the law in sending dangerous goods through the post; see also* NO **(b)** relating to *or* part of; *to pay an advance against next month's salary; the bank advanced him £10,000 against the security of his house*

agency ['eɪdʒənsi] *noun* **(a)** (i) arrangement where one person *or* company acts on behalf of another person in contractual matters; (ii) office *or* job of representing another company in an area; *they signed an agency agreement or an agency contract* **(b)** branch of government; *the Atomic Energy Agency; a counter-intelligence agency;* **Central Intelligence Agency (CIA)** = department of the US government dealing with counter-espionage

agenda [ə'dʒendə] *noun* list of things to be discussed at a meeting; *the committee agenda or the agenda of the committee meeting; after two hours we were still discussing the first item on the agenda; the Secretary put finance at the top of the agenda*

agent ['eɪdʒənt] *noun* **(a)** person who represents a company *or* another person in matters relating to contracts **(b)** person who helps *or* represents another person, such as a party official who works on behalf of a candidate in an election; *the party has six full-time election agents; the series of meetings was organized by the local agent for the Liberal Democrats* **(c)** person who works for a government agency, especially in secret; **secret agent** = person who tries to find out information in secret about other countries *or* other governments *or* other armed forces

◊ **Agent-General** ['eɪdʒənt 'dʒenərəl] *noun* official representative of a provincial government of a Commonwealth country in another Commonwealth country; *the Agent-General for Quebec in London;* (NOTE: plural is **agents-general** or **agent-generals)**

◊ **agent provocateur** ['æʒɒŋ prɒvɒkə'tɜː] *French words meaning* 'agent who provokes': person who provokes others to start civil disorder *or* to commit a crime (often by taking part himself) in order to start a revolution *or* to find out who is not reliable *or* in order to encourage people to commit crimes for which they will be arrested

aggression [ə'greʃn] *noun* action of attacking another country (either by declaring war, or by using one's own armed forces or paying other armed forces to attack

without a declaration of war); *they accused the neighbouring states of aggression; numerous acts of aggression have been reported to the United Nations;* (NOTE: no plural. For the plural, use **acts of aggression)**

◊ **aggressor** [ə'gresə] *noun* country which attacks another; *the UN resolution condemns one of the superpowers as the aggressor*

agitate ['ædʒɪteɪt] *verb* to protest *or* to make trouble *or* to be active (in demonstrating); *the party is agitating for social reforms*

◊ **agitation** [ædʒɪ'teɪʃn] *noun* protest and disturbance; *there has been widespread agitation in the capital and the northern provinces;* (NOTE: no plural)

◊ **agitator** ['ædʒɪteɪtə] *noun* person who causes political unrest; *the strike was led by left-wing agitators; agitators from the right of the party have tried to disrupt the meetings of the council*

AGM [eɪdʒiː'em] = ANNUAL GENERAL MEETING

agree [ə'griː] *verb* **(a)** to approve; *the figures were agreed between the two parties; terms of the contract are still to be agreed* **(b)** to say 'Yes' *or* to accept; *after some discussion, the committee agreed to the proposal; it has been agreed that the matter should be referred back to the relevant sub-committee; the chairman agreed to stand down; the government will never agree to increase public sector borrowing* to **agree to do something** = to say that you will do something; (NOTE: you agree **to** or **on** a plan or agree **to do** something)

◊ **agree with** [ə'griː 'wɪθ] *verb* **(a)** to say that your opinions are the same as someone else's **(b)** to be the same as; *the tenant's statement does not agree with that of the landlord*

◊ **agreed** [ə'griːd] *adjective* which has been accepted by everyone; *an agreed amount; on agreed terms or on terms which have been agreed*

◊ **agreement** [ə'griːmənt] *noun* document setting out the contractual terms agreed between two or more parties; *written agreement; unwritten or verbal agreement;*

to draw up or to draft an agreement; to break an agreement; to sign an agreement; to witness an agreement; an agreement has been reached or concluded or come to; to reach an agreement or to come to an agreement on something; an international agreement on trade or an international trade agreement; a collective wage agreement **blanket agreement** = agreement which covers many different items; **agreement in principle** = agreement with the basic conditions of a proposal; **gentleman's agreement** = verbal agreement between two parties who trust each other

> COMMENT: a gentleman's agreement is not usually enforceable in law

aid [eɪd] **1** *noun* help (in the form of money); *the government has set aside $20m for aid to under-developed countries; the poorer countries depend on aid from richer nations; the government will allocate 6% of the gross national product for overseas aid;* **foreign aid** = help offered by one country to another; **humanitarian aid** = help in the form of essential basic food and medicines to prevent death from starvation **2** *verb* to help (by giving money); *a government-aided scheme; see also* GRANT

◊ **aid agency** ['eɪd 'eɪdʒənsi] *noun* organization (such as Oxfam, Save The Children Fund) which specializes in sending help to countries which need it

◊ **aider** or **aid worker** ['eɪdə or 'eɪd 'wɜːkə] *noun* person who works for an aid agency

> Since 1960, about $1.4 trillion (in 1988 dollars) of aid has been transferred from rich countries to poor ones
> *Economist*

al. *see* ET AL.

Albion ['ælbiən] *noun* poetic name for Britain; **perfidious Albion** = French term meaning that Britain is untrustworthy

alia ['eɪliə] *see* ET ALIA, INTER ALIA

alien ['eɪliən] **1** *noun* foreigner, person who is not a citizen of a country; *(in the UK)* person who is not a citizen of the UK, not a

citizen of a Commonwealth country and not a citizen of the Republic of Ireland; **undesirable alien** = person who is not a citizen of a country, and who the government considers should not be allowed to stay in that country; *she was declared an undesirable alien and deported* **2** *adjective* foreign, different from what is normal in our country

◊ **alienate** ['eɪliəneɪt] *verb* to make someone stop being friendly towards you; *the government has alienated its main supporters; the terrorist campaign has alienated the public*

align [ə'laɪn] *verb* to establish a political agreement or alliance; **to align oneself with another country** = to adopt a similar policy as another country; *the three neighbouring states aligned themselves with the USA;* **non-aligned countries** = countries which do not form part of one of the superpower blocs

all [ɔːl] *adjective & pronoun* everything or everyone; *all MPs agree that something should be done to bring down the rate of inflation, but there is no consensus on what steps to take*

◊ **all-in** ['ɔːl'ɪn] *adjective* including everything

◊ **all-party** ['ɔːl'pɑːti] *adjective* containing members of all political parties; *an all-party group visited the United Nations; the report of the all-party committee on procedure*

allege [ə'ledʒ] *verb* **(a)** to state (usually in evidence) that something has happened or is true; *the opposition spokesman alleged that the Minister was hiding something from the House* **(b)** to state something without being able to prove it

◊ **allegation** [ælɪ'geɪʃn] *noun* **(a)** statement (usually in evidence) that something has happened or is true **(b)** statement without any proof

allegiance [ə'liːdʒəns] *noun* obedience to the State or the Crown; **oath of allegiance** = oath which is sworn to put the person under the orders or rules of a country or an army, etc.; *he swore an oath of allegiance to the new president*

alliance [ə'laɪəns] *noun* **(a)** two or more countries who are linked by treaties, especially to help each other if attacked **(b)** link between two or more parties *or* countries; *the country has built up a series of alliances with its larger neighbours; see also* ALLY

allocate ['æləkeɪt] *verb* to give a share of something; *out of the total budget, £3,000 was allocated to repairs*

◊ **allocation** [ælə'keɪʃn] *noun* sharing out a sum of money in various ways; *allocation of funds to research*

allot [ə'lɒt] *verb* **(a)** to share out **(b)** to set aside a period of time for something; *each speaker has been allotted only five minutes to state his case; Parliament has twenty-nine allotted days during the year, which are set aside for discussion of Supply Bills;* (NOTE: **allotting - allotted**)

◊ **allotment** [ə'lɒtmənt] *noun* **(a)** sharing out funds by giving money to various departments **(b)** giving some shares in a new company to people who have applied to buy them **(c)** small area of public land rented to a person living in a municipality to use for growing vegetables

allow [ə'lau] *verb* **(a)** to say that someone can do something; *the law does not allow you to drive on the wrong side of the road; the Speaker allowed the debate to continue; visitors are not allowed onto the floor of the House of Commons* **(b)** to give (someone) time; *parents are allowed thirty days to appeal against the committee's decision* **(c)** to agree *or* to accept legally; *the Speaker allowed the objection*

◊ **allow for** [ə'lau 'fɔː] *verb* to give a discount for *or* to add an extra sum to cover something

◊ **allowable** [ə'lauəbl] *adjective* legally accepted; **allowable expenses** = expenses which can be claimed against tax

◊ **allowance** [ə'lauəns] *noun* **(a)** money which is given for a special reason; *travel allowance or travelling allowance; foreign currency allowance;* **cost-of-living allowance** = addition to normal salary to cover increases in the cost of living **(b)** **personal allowances** = part of a person's income which is not taxed; *allowances against tax or tax allowances;* **wife's earned income allowance** = tax allowance to be set against money earned by the wife of the main taxpayer **(c)** proportion of money removed; *to make an allowance for legal expenses or an allowance for exchange loss*

ally 1 ['ælaɪ] *noun* country *or* person *or* party which is linked to another in a friendly way for mutual protection; *as the invasion seemed likely, the President called on his allies for help; the committee has been run by the mayor and his allies in the Workers' Party* **2** [ə'laɪ] *verb* **to ally yourself with** = to become linked to someone *or* another party *or* country, for protection; *he has allied himself to the left wing of the party; the allied forces attacked the invading enemy*

alphabet ['ælfəbet] *noun* the twenty-six letters used to make words

◊ **alphabetical order** [ælfə'betɪkl 'ɔːdə] *noun* arrangement of records (such as files, index cards) in the order of the letters of the alphabet (A,B,C,D, etc.); *the constituencies are listed in alphabetical order*

alter ['ɒltə] *verb* to change; *several of the Bill's clauses were altered in Committee stage*

◊ **alteration** [ɒltə'reɪʃn] *noun* change; *we made some alterations to clause sixteen*

alternative [ɔːl'tɜːnətɪv] **1** *noun* thing which can be done instead of another; **there is no alternative** = there is nothing else which can be done **2** *adjective* other *or* which can take the place of something; *the architect's department produced two alternative plans;* **to find someone alternative employment** = to find someone another job; **alternative vote (AV)** = system of voting used in Australia, where voters show their preferences on the ballot paper by marking candidates with numbers 1, 2, 3, 4, etc.; if a candidate does not get 50% of the votes, the votes for the candidates with the lowest polls are redistributed to the candidates shown as second preferences on their papers, and so on, until a candidate gets 50% *see also* SECOND BALLOT

Althing ['ælθɪŋ] *noun* legislative body in Iceland

a.m. *or* **ante meridiem** ['eɪ'em or ænti məˈrɪdiəm] *Latin phrase meaning* 'in the morning' *or* 'before 12 midday'; *the session begins at 9.30 a.m.; telephone calls before 6 a.m. are charged at the cheap rate*

AMA [eɪem'eɪ] = ASSOCIATION OF METROPOLITAN AUTHORITIES

ambassador [æmˈbæsədə] *noun* diplomat of the highest level, representing his country in another country; *she is the wife of the Spanish ambassador; our ambassador in France; the government has recalled its ambassador for consultations;* **ambassador plenipotentiary** = ambassador with full powers to negotiate and sign treaties on behalf of his country

◊ **ambassadorial** [æmbæsəˈdɔːrɪəl] *adjective* referring to an ambassador; *the ambassadorial Rolls-Royce*

◊ **ambassadress** [æmˈbæsədres] *noun* **(a)** woman ambassador **(b)** ambassador's wife

> an ambassador is an honest man sent to lie abroad for his country
> *Sir Henry Wotton*

ambiguous [æmˈbɪgjuəs] *adjective* (words) which can mean two or more things; (words) which can be misleading; *the wording of the clause is ambiguous and needs clarification*

◊ **ambiguity** [æmbɪˈgjuːti] *noun* **(a)** being ambiguous **(b)** words which are ambiguous; **latent ambiguity** = words in a contract which can mean two or more things, but which do not appear to be misleading at first sight

amend [əˈmend] *verb* to change *or* correct; *please amend your copy of the minutes accordingly*

◊ **amendment** [əˈmendmənt] *noun* **(a)** change made in a document; *to make amendments to the minutes* **(b)** change proposed to a Bill which is being discussed in Parliament *or* Congress; *the amendment was proposed and seconded and put to the vote; the government whips persuaded him to withdraw his amendment* **(c)** *US* additional clause to the constitution

> COMMENT: the first ten amendments to the American Constitution are known as the Bill of Rights. The most important are the First Amendment (which provides for freedom of speech and thought), and the Fifth Amendment (which protects anyone from giving evidence in court which might incriminate himself)

amenity [əˈmiːnɪti] *noun* thing which gives pleasure *or* improves something; *the town's amenities include three swimming pools and several parks; the Recreation and Amenities subcommittee discussed plans for a new leisure centre*

amnesty ['æmnəsti] **1** *noun* pardon, often for political crimes, given by the state to several people at the same time; **general amnesty** = pardon granted to all prisoners; **gun amnesty** = arrangement where any person having a gun illegally can hand the gun in to the police without being prosecuted for it **2** *verb* to grant convicted persons a pardon; *they were amnestied by the president*

◊ **Amnesty International** ['æmnəsti ɪntəˈnæʃənəl] international organization which campaigns for human rights, and good treatment of prisoners

anarchy ['ænəki] *noun* absence of law and order, because the government has lost control *or* because there is no government; *when the president was assassinated, the country fell into anarchy;* (NOTE: no plural)

◊ **anarchic** *or* **anarchical** [əˈnɑːkɪk(l)] *adjective* with no law or order; *the anarchical state of the country districts after the coup*

◊ **anarchism** ['ænəkɪzm] *noun* belief that there should be no government *or* control of people by the state

◊ **anarchist** ['ænəkɪst] **1** *noun* **(a)** person who believes in anarchism **(b)** person who tries to destroy a government by violent means, without planning to replace it in any way **2** *adjective* referring to anarchists; *an anarchist attack on the Prime Minister*

> COMMENT: anarchism flourished in the latter part of the 19th and early part of the 20th century. Anarchists believe that there should be no government, no army, no civil service, no courts, no laws, and that people should be free to live without anyone to rule them

ancillary [æn'sɪləri] *adjective* which gives help *or* support; *ancillary workers in schools including secretaries, cleaners, caretakers, etc.*

annexe *or US* **annex** ['æneks] **1** *noun* document added *or* attached to a contract **2** *verb* **(a)** to attach (a document) **(b)** to take possession of a territory which belongs to another state and attach it to your country, so taking full sovereignty over the territory; *the island was annexed by the neighbouring republic; the war was caused by a dispute over the annexing of a strip of land*

◊ **annexation** [ænek'seɪʃn] *noun* act of annexing a territory

announce [ə'naʊns] *verb* to tell something to the public *or* to a group of people; *the returning officer announced the result of the election; the Foreign Secretary announced that he would be going to Nigeria shortly; the foreman of the jury announced their verdict*

◊ **announcement** [ə'naʊnsmənt] *noun* telling something in public; *the chairman of the council made an announcement about the development plans*

annual ['ænjʊəl] *adjective* once a year; **Annual General Meeting (AGM)** = meeting of the members of a club *or* shareholders of a company which takes place once a year to approve the accounts; *the parent-teacher association discussed the charges at their AGM; the Annual Meeting of the Council takes place in April;* **on an annual basis** = each year

◊ **annually** ['ænjʊəli] *adverb* each year; *the figures are revised annually*

annul [ə'nʌl] *verb* (i) to cancel *or* to stop something having any legal effect; (ii) to

declare that something never existed *or* that something never had legal effect; *the contract was annulled by the court; their marriage has been annulled;* (NOTE: GB English is **annulling - annulled** but US English **annuling - annuled**)

◊ **annullable** [ə'nʌləbl] *adjective* which can be cancelled

◊ **annulling** [ə'nʌlɪŋ] **1** *adjective* which cancels; *an annulling clause* **2** *noun* act of cancelling; *the annulling of a contract*

◊ **annulment** [ə'nʌlmənt] *noun* act of cancelling; **annulment of adjudication** = cancelling of an order making someone bankrupt; **annulment of marriage** = ending of a marriage, by declaring that in law it had never existed

annum ['ænəm] *see* PER ANNUM

another place [ə'nʌðə 'pleɪs] *see* PLACE

answer ['ɑːnsə] **1** *noun* **(a)** reply, letter or conversation coming after someone else has written or spoken; *I am writing in answer to your letter of October 6th; my letter got no answer or there was no answer to my letter; I tried to phone his office but there was no answer* **(b)** **written answer** = formal reply to a question put in writing to a Minister **2** *verb* **(a)** to speak *or* write after someone has spoken or written to you; **to answer a letter** = to write a letter in reply to a letter which you have received; **to answer the telephone** = to lift the telephone when it rings and listen to what the caller is saying **(b)** to reply formally to an allegation made in court; **to answer charges** = to plead guilty *or* not guilty to a charge

◊ **answerable** ['ɑːnsərəbl] *adjective* having to explain why actions have been taken *or* being responsible for one's actions; *he is answerable to Parliament for the conduct of the Armed Forces;* (NOTE: you are answerable to someone for an action)

ante- ['ænti] *prefix* before

◊ **antedate** ['æntɪdeɪt] *verb* to put an earlier date on a document; *the invoice was antedated to January 1st*

anthem ['ænθəm] *see* NATIONAL

anti- ['ænti] *prefix* against; *an anti-drug campaign; the anti-terrorist squad; anti-government posters appeared in the streets;* (NOTE: the opposite is pro-)

◊ **anti-trust** ['ænti'trʌst] *adjective* which attacks monopolies and encourages competition; *anti-trust laws or legislation*

anticipation [æntɪsɪ'peɪʃn] *noun* doing something before it is due to be done *or* before something expected happens; *they sold the house in anticipation of a fall in prices*

◊ **anticipatory** [æntɪsɪ'peɪtəri] *adjective* done before it is due

> COMMENT: it is out of order on grounds of anticipation for a motion to be mentioned or discussed in the House of Commons before the day on which it is scheduled for discussion

AOB [eɪəʊ'biː] = ANY OTHER BUSINESS

apartheid [ə'pɑːtaɪt] *noun* former policy of racial segregation in South Africa

apologize [ə'pɒlədʒaɪz] *verb* to say you are sorry; *the clerk apologized for the delay in answering; she apologized for being late; he apologized to the tenants for the council's delay in repairing the damage*

◊ **apology** [ə'pɒlədʒi] *noun* saying you are sorry; *to write a letter of apology; I enclose a cheque for £10 with apologies for the delay in answering your letter; the writer of the libel was ordered to print a full apology;* **apologies for absence** = list of members of a committee who have apologized for not being able to attend a meeting, read out at the beginning of the meeting by the secretary or chairman

a posteriori [eɪ pɒsteri'ɔːri] *Latin phrase meaning* 'from what comes after'; **a posteriori argument** = argument based on observation; *compare* A PRIORI

apparat [æpə'ræt] *noun (in former Communist countries)* the bureaucracy

◊ **apparatchik** [æpə' rætʃɪk] *noun* **(a)** *(in a Communist country)* bureaucrat **(b)** *(used as criticism)* slow bureaucrat who follows the

letter of the law and tries to tell ordinary people what to do; (NOTE: plural is **apparatchiki** or **apparatchiks**)

apparent [ə'pærənt] *adjective* which can be seen *or* which seems to be real; **heir apparent** = heir who will certainly inherit if a person dies before him

appeal [ə'piːl] **1** *noun* **(a)** challenge to the ruling of the chairman of a meeting; *Senator Brown made an appeal against the ruling of the President of the Senate* **(b)** asking a higher court to change a decision of a lower court *or* asking a government department to change a decision; *the appeal against the planning decision will be heard next month; he lost his appeal for damages against the company;* she won her case on appeal = her case was lost in the first court, but the appeal court found in her favour; **Appeal Committee** = committee set up by the House of Lords to consider petitions to appeal to the House of Lords from the Court of Appeal; **Appeal Court** *or* **Court of Appeal** *or US* **Court of Appeals** = civil or criminal court to which a person may go to ask for a sentence to be changed and of which the decisions are binding on the High Court and lower courts; **Lord of Appeal in Ordinary** = one of the eleven lords who sits as a member of the House of Lords when it acts as a Court of Appeal **2** *verb* to ask a government department to change its decision *or* a high law court to change a sentence *or* a chairman to change a ruling; *the company appealed against the decision of the planning officers; he has appealed to the Supreme Court;* (NOTE: you appeal **to** a court or **against** a decision; an appeal is **heard** and **allowed** or **dismissed**)

> COMMENT: in English law, in the majority of cases decisions of lower courts and of the High Court can be appealed to the Court of Appeal. The Court of Appeal is divided into the Civil Division and the Criminal Division. The Civil Division hears appeals from the County Court and the High Court; the Criminal Division hears appeals from the Crown Court. From the Court of Appeal,

appeal lies to the House of Lords. When the remedies available under English law are exhausted, it is in certain cases possible to appeal to the European Court of Justice. For many countries (especially Commonwealth countries) appeals may be heard from the highest court of these countries by the Privy Council

appear [əˈpɪə] *verb* (a) to seem; *the witness appeared to have difficulty in remembering what had happened* (b) to come to court *or* to a tribunal; *he was summoned to appear before the Select Committee*

appease [əˈpiːz] *verb* to make concessions to (a dictator)

◊ **appeasement** [əˈpiːzmənt] *noun* policy of avoiding conflict by making concessions

appellant [əˈpelənt] *noun* person who appeals *or* who goes to a higher court to ask it to change a decision *or* a sentence imposed by a lower court

appellate [əˈpelət] *adjective* referring to appeal; **appellate committee** = committee of the House of Lords which considers appeals and reports on them to the House; **appellate jurisdiction** = jurisdiction of the House of Lords to hear appeals

appendix [əˈpendɪks] *noun* additional text at the end of a document; *the map showing the properties covered by the proposal is attached as an Appendix; see Appendix B for the list of county councils;* (NOTE: plural is **appendices**)

apply [əˈplaɪ] *verb* (a) to ask for something, usually in writing; *to apply for a job; to apply for shares; to apply in writing; to apply in person; my client wishes to apply for Legal Aid; he applied for judicial review or for compensation or for an adjournment;* to **apply to the Court** = to ask the court to make an order; *he applied to the Court for an injunction* (b) to affect *or* to touch; *this clause applies only to deals outside the EU; the preservation order applies to all trees in the conservation area*

◊ **applicant** [ˈæplɪkənt] *noun* person who applies for something; *applicant for a job or job applicant; there were thousands of applicants for shares in the new company*

◊ **application** [æplɪˈkeɪʃn] *noun* (a) asking for something, usually in writing; *application for shares; shares payable on application; application for a job or job application;* **application form** = form to be filled in when applying; *to fill in an application (form) for a job or a job application (form);* **letter of application** = letter in which someone applies for a job *or* applies for shares in a new company (b) act of asking the court to make an order; *his application for an injunction was refused; solicitors acting for the wife made an application for a maintenance order*

appoint [əˈpɔɪnt] *verb* to choose someone for a job; *to appoint James Smith to the post of manager; the government has appointed a QC to head the inquiry; the council has appointed a race relations adviser;* (NOTE: you appoint a person **to** a job or **to do** a job)

◊ **appointee** [əpɔɪnˈtiː] *noun* person who is appointed to a job

◊ **appointment** [əˈpɔɪntmənt] *noun* (a) arrangement to meet; *to make or to fix an appointment for two o'clock; to make an appointment with someone for two o'clock; he was late for his appointment; she had to cancel her appointment;* **appointments book** = desk diary in which appointments are noted (b) being appointed to a job; **on her appointment as librarian** = when she was made a librarian; **letter of appointment** = letter in which someone is appointed to a job; **by royal appointment** = appointed by a king or queen (as a supplier of goods or services) (c) job; **appointments vacant** = list of jobs which are vacant

approach [əˈprəʊtʃ] **1** *noun* (a) getting in touch with someone with a proposal; *the governor of the province has made an approach to the leaders of the rebels; the council has had an approach from an Australian consortium wishing to redevelop the old market* (b) method of dealing with something; *he has a professional approach to his work* **2** *verb* (a) to get in touch with someone with a proposal; *he approached the bank with a request for a loan; the company was approached by an American publisher with the suggestion of a merger* (b) to come closer to; *the offer does not approach the figure my client seeks*

appropriate 1 [əˈprəʊprɪət] *adjective* suitable *or* which fits; *is a fine an appropriate punishment for sex offences?* **2** [əˈprəʊprɪeɪt] *verb* (a) to take control of (something) for one's own use; *the town council appropriated the land to build the new municipal offices* (b) to take control of money which has been allocated for use in a particular way

◊ **appropriation** [əprəʊprɪˈeɪʃn] *noun* allocating of money for a particular purpose, especially allocating money to be spent by a particular government department; **appropriation bill** = bill in the US Congress which grants money to the government to be used in a way which has been approved in an authorization bill; **appropriations committee** = committee which examines government expenditure; *compare* MISAPPROPRIATION

approve [əˈpruːv] *verb* (a) to approve of = to think something is good (b) to agree to something officially; *they approved the terms of a contract; the proposal was approved by the board; the motion was approved by the committee*

◊ **approval** [əˈpruːvəl] *noun* (a) agreement; *to submit a budget for approval by the committee;* **certificate of approval** = document showing that an item has been approved officially (b) **on approval** = sale where the buyer pays for goods only after they are found to be satisfactory

a priori [eɪ praɪˈɔːri] *Latin phrase meaning* 'from what came before'; **a priori argument** = reasoning based on principles *or* assumptions, not on real examples; *compare* A POSTERIORI

arbitrate [ˈɑːbɪtreɪt] *verb* to settle a dispute between parties by referring it to an arbitrator instead of going to court (usually used in building *or* shipping *or* employment disputes); *to arbitrate in a dispute*

◊ **arbitration** [ɑːbɪˈtreɪʃn] *noun* settling of a dispute by an outside person *or* persons, chosen by both sides; *to submit a dispute to arbitration; to refer a question to arbitration; to take a dispute to arbitration; to go to arbitration;* **arbitration agreement** = agreement by two parties to submit a dispute to arbitration; **arbitration award** = ruling given by an arbitrator; **arbitration board** *or* **arbitration tribunal** = group which arbitrates; **industrial arbitration tribunal** = court which decides in industrial disputes; *to accept the ruling of the arbitration board;* (NOTE: no plural)

◊ **arbitrator** [ˈɑːbɪtreɪtə] *noun* person not concerned with a dispute who is chosen by both sides to try to settle it; *an industrial arbitrator; to accept or to reject the arbitrator's ruling*

archives [ˈɑːkaɪvz] *plural noun* historical records; *minutes of council meetings dating back to the eighteenth century are kept in the borough archives*

◊ **archivist** [ˈɑːkɪvɪst] *noun* **county archivist** *or* **borough archivist** = official who is in charge of the historical records of an area

arena [əˈriːnə] *noun* place where action takes place, such as for sports and fights; *the political arena*

argue [ˈɑːgjuː] *verb* (a) to discuss something about which there is disagreement; *they argued over or about the price; counsel spent hours arguing about the precise meaning of the clause; the union officials argued among themselves over the best way to deal with the ultimatum from the management* (b) to give reasons for something; *the minister argued that the Bill would curtail freedom of speech; the Prime Minister argued forcefully against giving in to threats by terrorists;* (NOTE: you argue with someone about or over something)

◊ **argument** [ˈɑːgjʊmənt] *noun* (a) discussing something without agreeing; *they got into an argument with the chairman over the relevance of the documents to the inquiry; the Speaker asked the MP to withdraw his allegations after an argument* *over a point of order* **(b)** (speech giving) reasons for something; *the House found the argument of the Secretary of State difficult to follow; counsel presented the argument for the prosecution*

arise [ə'raɪz] *verb* to happen *or* to come as a result; *the situation has arisen because neither side is capable of winning the war; the problem arises from the difficulty in understanding the VAT regulations;* **matters arising** = section in an agenda, where problems *or* questions which refer to items in the minutes of the previous meeting can be discussed; (NOTE: **arising - arose - arisen**)

aristocracy [ærɪ'stɒkrəsi] *noun* the nobility, the people of the highest class in society, usually with titles such as Lord, Duke, etc.; *the aristocracy supported the military dictatorship*

◊ **aristocrat** ['ærɪstəkræt] *noun* member of the aristocracy; *many aristocrats were killed during the revolution*

◊ **aristocratic** [ærɪstə'krætɪk] *adjective* like an aristocrat

arm [ɑːm] **1** *noun* **arms** = weapons, such as guns, bombs, etc.; **in arms** = carrying weapons; **up in arms about something** = very angry about something; **arms control** = control of the sale of weapons to countries who do not manufacture them; **arms race** = competition between countries to buy more and better weapons **2** *verb* to equip with weapons

◊ **armed** ['ɑːmd] *adjective* equipped with weapons; *the prisoners were escorted by armed guards;* **armed uprising** = revolt by people who have weapons; **the armed forces** = the army, navy and air force

armada [ɑː'mɑːdə] *noun* fleet of warships

armaments ['ɑːməmənts] *plural noun* heavy weapons

armistice ['ɑːmɪstɪs] *noun* end of hostilities, stopping fighting

armoury *US* **armory** ['ɑːməri] *noun* the arms of a country; *a country's nuclear armoury*

army ['ɑːmi] *noun* soldiers, part of a country's armed forces who fight mainly on land

arrange [ə'reɪndʒ] *verb* **(a)** to put in order; *the office is arranged as an open-plan area with small separate rooms for meetings; the files are arranged in alphabetical order; arrange the documents in order of their dates* **(b)** to organize *or* to plan; *the hearing was arranged for April; we arranged to have the meeting in their offices; she arranged for a car to meet the Minister at the airport;* (NOTE: you arrange **for** someone to do something or you arrange **for** something to be done)

◊ **arrangement** [ə'reɪndʒmənt] *noun* **(a)** way in which something is organized; *the company secretary is making all the arrangements for the AGM* **(b)** settling of a financial dispute, especially by proposing a plan for repaying creditors; *to come to an arrangement with the creditors*

article ['ɑːtɪkl] *noun* **(a)** product *or* thing for sale; *a company specializing in imported articles of clothing* **(b)** section of a legal agreement; *see article 8 of the constitution* **(c)** **articles of association** *or* *US* **articles of incorporation** = document which regulates the way in which a company's affairs are managed

aside [ə'saɪd] *adverb* to one side *or* out of the way; **to put aside** *or* **to set aside** = (i) to say that something no longer applies; (ii) to save money *or* to keep money for a special purpose; *the appeal court set aside the earlier judgment; the council has set aside £200,000 for street improvements*

ask [ɑːsk] *verb* **(a)** to put a question to someone; *MPs from all sides of the House asked the Minister to explain the government's decision* **(b)** to tell someone to do something; *the Speaker asked the MP to withdraw the remark; the police asked the organizers of the demonstration to avoid the centre of the town; she asked her secretary to fetch a file from the managing director's office; the customs officials asked him to open his case; the select committee asked the MP to provide more details*

◊ **ask for** ['ɑːsk 'fɔː] *verb* **(a)** to say that you want *or* need something; *he asked for the file on 1990 debtors; the Minister asked for more time to consult with his officials; the Opposition asked for an emergency debate on the financial crisis; there is a man on the phone asking for Mr Smith* **(b)** to put a price on something for sale; *they are asking £24,000 for the car*

aspect ['æspekt] *noun* way of seeing a plan *or* a problem; *some aspects of the proposal are worrying the planning committee; we must consider this plan from several aspects; the committee has considered the plan from the environmental aspect only*

assemble [ə'sembl] *verb* **(a)** to put something together from various parts; *the police are still assembling all the evidence* **(b)** to come together *or* to gather; *the crowd assembled in front of the President's Palace*

assembly [ə'sembli] *noun* **(a)** coming together in a group; **freedom of assembly** = being able to meet as a group without being afraid of prosecution **(b)** group of people who come together to discuss political problems *or* to pass laws; **the General Assembly of the United Nations** = meeting of all the members of the United Nations to discuss international problems, where each member state has one vote; **Assembly of Deputies** = lower house of the legislature in Romania; **Assembly of the Republic** = single chamber of the legislature in Portugal; **Grand National Assembly** = single chamber of the legislature in Turkey; **People's Assembly** = main body of legislature in Egypt; **Supreme People's Assembly** = main body of legislature in North Korea; *see also* HOUSE OF ASSEMBLY, LEGISLATIVE ASSEMBLY, NATIONAL ASSEMBLY

◊ **assemblyman** [ə'semblimən] *noun* member of an assembly; (NOTE: many national legislatures are called 'National Assemblies' in English)

assent [ə'sent] *noun* agreement to something; **Royal Assent** = formal passing of a Bill into law to become an Act of Parliament

assert [ə'sɜːt] *verb* to state in a strong way *or* to insist; *he asserted that the damage suffered was extremely serious*

◊ **assertion** [ə'sɜːʃn] *noun* strong statement; *the Prime Minister made a series of assertions which were disputed by the Opposition*

assist [ə'sist] *verb* to help; *after his accident, the Prime Minister had to be assisted into the chamber; the government tries to assist small businesses by reducing red tape*

◊ **assistance** [ə'sistəns] *noun* help; **financial assistance** = help in the form of money

◊ **assistant** [ə'sistənt] **1** *noun* person who helps; *the borough treasurer has three assistants* **2** *adjective* deputy; *the assistant librarian is away on holiday*

association [əsəusi'eiʃn] *noun* group *or* groups of people who join together for a common cause or because they have common interests; *the Commonwealth is a loose association of states, formerly governed by Great Britain;* **housing association** = organization subsidized by government, which provides cheap housing for its tenants; **freedom of association** = being able to join together in a group with other people without being afraid of prosecution, provided that no law is broken

◊ **Association of First Division Civil Servants** trade union representing the top grades of civil servant; *see also* CIVIL AND PUBLIC SERVICES ASSOCIATION, PUBLIC SERVICES, TAX AND COMMERCE UNION

assume [ə'sjuːm] *verb* **(a)** to believe something without any proof; *everyone assumed he was guilty* **(b)** to take; *to assume all risks; he has assumed responsibility for marketing*

◊ **assumption** [ə'sʌmpʃn] *noun* **(a)** believing something without proof; *your assumption is quite correct* **(b)** taking; **assumption of office** = taking up an office; *on his assumption of office, he arrested several of the ministers in the former government*

assure [əˈʃʊə] *verb* to insure *or* to have a contract with a company where if regular payments are made, the company will pay compensation if you die *or* suffer harm or damage

◊ **assurance** [əˈʃʊrəns] *noun* insurance *or* agreement that in return for regular payments, one party will pay another party compensation for loss of life

◊ **assurer** *or* **assuror** [əˈʃʊərə] *noun* insurer *or* company which insures

COMMENT: **assure** and **assurance** are used in Britain for insurance policies relating to something which will certainly happen (such as death or the end of a given period of time); for other types of policy use **insure** and **insurance**

asylum [əˈsaɪləm] *noun* safe place; **to ask for political asylum** = to ask to be allowed to remain in a foreign country because it would be dangerous to return to the home country for political reasons; (NOTE: no plural)

atlas [ˈætləs] *noun* book of maps; (NOTE: plural is **atlases**)

attach [əˈtætʃ] *verb* to fasten *or* to join; *I am attaching a copy of my previous letter; attached is a copy of my letter of June 24th*

◊ **attaché** [əˈtæʃeɪ] *noun* person who does specialized work in an embassy; *a military attaché; a cultural attaché; the government ordered the commercial attaché to return home;* **press attaché** = person whose job it is to link with journalists and the media, giving information about the organization he works for

◊ **attachment** [əˈtætʃmənt] *noun* holding a debtor's property to prevent it from being sold until debts are paid; **attachment of earnings** = legal power to take money from a person's salary to pay money, which is owed, to the courts

attack [əˈtæk] **1** *verb* **(a)** to try to hurt *or* harm someone; *the security guard was attacked by three men carrying guns* **(b)** to criticize; *MPs attacked the government for not spending enough money on the police* **2** *noun* **(a)** act of trying to hurt *or* harm someone; *there has been an increase in*

attacks on police or in terrorist attacks on planes **(b)** criticism; *the newspaper published an attack on the government;* (NOTE: you attack someone, but make an attack on someone)

◊ **attacker** [əˈtækə] *noun* person who attacks; *she recognized her attacker and gave his description to the police*

attainder [əˈteɪndə] *noun* **bill of attainder** = obsolete way of punishing a person legally without holding a trial, by passing a law to convict and sentence him

attempt [əˈtempt] **1** *noun* trying to do something; *the company made an attempt to break into the American market; the takeover attempt was turned down by the board; all his attempts to get a job have failed* **2** *verb* to try; *the government attempted to have the motion dropped; he was accused of attempting to contact a member of the banned opposition party*

attend [əˈtend] *verb* to be present at; *the mayor hopes to attend the ceremony*

◊ **attend to** [əˈtend ˈtʊ] *verb* to give careful thought to (something) and deal with it; *the managing director will attend to your complaint personally*

◊ **attendance** [əˈtendəns] *noun* being present

◊ **attention** [əˈtenʃn] *noun* careful thought; *letter for the personal attention of the Managing Director; your orders will have our best attention; the House turned its attention to the final clauses of the Finance Bill*

attorney [əˈtɜːni] *noun* **(a)** person who is legally allowed to act on behalf of someone else; **letter of attorney** = document showing that someone has power of attorney; **power of attorney** = official power giving someone the right to act on someone else's behalf in legal matters; *his solicitor was granted power of attorney* **(b)** *US* lawyer

◊ **Attorney-General** [əˈtɜːnɪˈdʒenrəl] *noun* **(a)** *GB* one of the Law Officers, a Member of Parliament, who prosecutes for the Crown in certain cases, advises government departments on legal problems and decides if major criminal offences should be tried; **(b)** *US* minister of legal affairs in a state or federal government

> COMMENT: in the US Federal Government, the Attorney-General is in charge of the Department of Justice

attribute [ə'trɪbjuːt] *verb* to suggest that something came from a source; *remarks attributed to the Chief Constable; the statement is attributed to Downing Street sources*

◊ **attributable** [ə'trɪbjʊtəbl] *adjective* which can be attributed

audience ['ɔːdiəns] *noun* interview where an important person, such as a king *or* queen, listens to someone; *the Prime Minister has a weekly audience of the Queen;* (NOTE: you have an audience of someone)

audit ['ɔːdɪt] **1** *noun* examination of the books and accounts of an organization; **Audit Commission** = independent body which examines the accounts of local authorities, which ensures that money is spent legally and wisely, and checks for possible fraud and corruption; **National Audit Office** = independent body, headed by the Comptroller and Auditor-General, which examines the accounts of government departments **2** *verb* to examine the books and accounts

◊ **auditor** ['ɔːdɪtə] *noun* person who audits; **Comptroller and Auditor General** = official whose duty is to examine the accounts of ministries and government departments; **District Auditor** = local official of the Audit Commission; **Court of Auditors** = institution which audits the accounts of the EU

Australian Capital Territory

[ɒs'treɪliən 'kæpɪtəl 'terɪtri] *noun* region round the capital, Canberra, which is not part of any of the states

autarchy ['ɔːtɑːki] *noun* situation where a state has total power over itself, and rules itself without outside interference

autarky ['ɔːtɑːki] *noun* situation where a state is self-sufficient, and can provide all it needs without outside help

authority [ɔː'θɒrɪti] *noun* **(a)** official power given to someone to do something; legal right to do something; *he has no authority to act on our behalf; she was acting on the authority of the Borough Treasurer; on whose authority were these typewriters ordered?* **(b)** person *or* book which has the best information; *he is an authority on the benefit system; Erskine May is the authority on parliamentary procedure* **(c)** **local authority** = elected group, forming a government which runs a small area of a country; *a court can give directions to a local authority; a decision of the local authority pursuant to the powers and duties imposed upon it by the statutory code; the Bill aims at giving protection to children in the care of a local authority* **(d)** **the authorities** = the government *or* those who are in control; *the authorities are trying to put down the riots; the prison authorities have complained about the lack of funding*

◊ **authoritarian** [ɔːθɒrɪ'teəriən] *adjective* exercising strict control; **authoritarian regime** = government which rules its people strictly and does not allow anyone to oppose its decisions

◊ **authoritarianism** [ɔːθɒrɪ'teəriənɪzm] *noun* theory that a regime must rule its people strictly in order to be efficient

authorize ['ɔːθəraɪz] *verb* **(a)** to give official permission for something to be done; *to authorize payment of £10,000* **(b)** to give someone the authority to do something; *to authorize someone to act on your behalf*

◊ **authorization** [ɔːθəraɪ'zeɪʃn] *noun* **(a)** official permission *or* power to do something; *do you have authorization for this expenditure? he has no authorization to act on our behalf; US* **authorization bill** = bill in Congress which authorizes the spending of money on a certain project (it may also limit the amount of money which can be spent) **(b)** document showing that someone has official permission to do something; *he showed the bank his authorization to inspect the contents of the safe*

◊ **authorized** [ˈɔːθəraɪzd] *adjective* permitted

autocracy [ɔːˈtɒkrəsi] *noun* **(a)** rule by an autocrat **(b)** country ruled by an autocrat

◊ **autocrat** [ˈɔːtəkræt] *noun (often as criticism)* dictator, a ruler with total personal power over the people he rules

◊ **autocratic** [ɔːtəˈkrætɪk] *adjective* (state) ruled by an autocrat; *the regime became too autocratic and was overthrown by a military coup*

◊ **autocratically** [ɔːtəˈkrætɪkli] *adverb* like an autocrat

automatic [ɔːtəˈmætɪk] *adjective* which works *or* takes place without any special action *or* instruction; *there is an automatic increase in salaries on January 1st*

◊ **automatically** [ɔːtəˈmætɪkli] *adverb* working without a person giving instructions; *unpaid fines are automatically increased by 15%*

autonomy [ɔːˈtɒnəmi] *noun* self-government, independence, freedom from outside control; *the separatists are demanding full autonomy for their state; the government has granted the region a limited autonomy*

◊ **autonomous** [ɔːˈtɒnəməs] *adjective* (region) which governs itself; *an autonomous regional government; the federation is formed of several autonomous republics;* **semi-autonomous** = (state) with a limited amount of autonomy

AV = ALTERNATIVE VOTE

available [əˈveɪləbl] *adjective* which can be used *or* which is ready to be used; *there are no houses available for rent; the right of self-defence is available only against unlawful attack*

average [ˈævərɪdʒ] **1** *noun* number calculated by adding together several figures and dividing by the number of figures added; *the average for the last three months or the last three months' average; sales average or average of sales;* **on average** *or* **on an average** = in general; *on an average, £15*

worth *of goods are stolen every day* **2** *adjective* **(a)** middle (figure); *average cost of expenses per employee; the average figures for the last three months; the average increase in prices* **(b)** not very good; *the company's performance has been only average; he is an average worker* **3** *verb* to produce as an average figure; *price increases have averaged 10% per annum; days lost through sickness have averaged twenty-two over the last four years*

avoid [əˈvɔɪd] *verb* to try not to do something; *the company is trying to avoid bankruptcy; my aim is to avoid paying too much tax; we want to avoid direct interference in another country's affairs;* (NOTE: you avoid something or someone or avoid doing something)

◊ **avoidance** [əˈvɔɪdəns] *noun* trying not to do something; *avoidance of an agreement or of a contract;* **tax avoidance** = trying (legally) to pay as little tax as possible; *see also* EVASION

await [əˈweɪt] *verb* to wait for; *we are awaiting the decision of the planning department; they are awaiting a decision of the court; the solicitor is awaiting our instructions*

award [əˈwɔːd] **1** *noun* decision which settles a dispute; *an award by an industrial tribunal; the arbitrator's award was set aside on appeal;* **arbitration award** = ruling given by an arbitrator **2** *verb* **(a)** to decide the amount of money to be given to someone; *to award someone a salary increase; to award damages; the judge awarded costs to the defendant* **(b)** to award a contract to a **company** = to decide that a company will have the contract to do work for you

ayatollah [aɪəˈtɒlə] *noun* Iranian Muslim leader

aye [aɪ] = YES **the ayes lobby** = division lobby in the House of Commons, where MPs pass if they are voting for the motion; **the Ayes have it** = the motion has been passed; *see also* DIVISION, NO

Bb

B [biː] *second letter of the alphabet*
Schedule B = schedule to the Finance Acts
under which tax is charged on income from
woodlands; **Table B** = model memorandum
of association of a limited company set out in
the Companies Act, 1985

back [bæk] **1** *noun* opposite side to the
front; *the conditions of sale are printed on
the back of the invoice; please endorse the
cheque by signing it on the back* **2** *adjective*
referring to the past; **back interest** = interest
not yet paid; **back rates** = rates which are
owed; **back rent** = rent owed; **back taxes** =
taxes which have not been paid **3** *adverb* as
things were before; in the opposite direction;
*he will pay back the money in monthly
instalments; the House of Lords sent back
the Bill to the Commons for amendment;
the store sent back the cheque because the
date was wrong; the Finance Minister went
back on his promise not to increase taxes*
back to basics = campaign to reinforce
old-fashioned standards of education,
morality, etc. **4** *verb* **(a) to back someone** =
to help someone financially **(b) to back a bill**
= to support a Bill in Parliament

◊ **back benches** [ˈbæk ˈbentʃɪz] *noun*
seats in the House of Commons, behind the
front benches, where ordinary members of
parliament sit

◊ **backbencher** *or* **backbench MP**

[bækˈbenʃə or ˈbækbenʃ emˈpiː] *noun*
ordinary Member of Parliament who does not
sit on the front benches (and is not a
government minister or a member of the
Opposition shadow cabinet)

◊ **backdate** [bækˈdeɪt] *verb* to put an
earlier date on a cheque *or* an invoice; *could*
*you backdate your invoice to April 1st?; the
pay increase is backdated to January 1st*

◊ **background** [ˈbækgraʊnd] *noun* **(a)**
past work *or* experience *or* family connections;
*can you tell us something of the candidate's
family background?* **(b)** past details; *he
explained the background to the claim; the
House asked for details of the background
to the case; I know the contractual situation
as it stands now, but can you fill in the
background details?*

◊ **backwoodsman** [bækˈwʊdzmən] *noun*
(informal) hereditary peer in the House of
Lords who lives in the country, appears only
rarely in the House and has reactionary or
eccentric opinions

bad [bæd] *adjective* not good; **bad debt** =
debt which will never be paid; **in bad faith** =
dishonestly

balance [ˈbæləns] **1** *noun* **(a)** amount in an
account which makes the total debits and
credits equal; **credit balance** = balance in an
account showing that more money has been
received than is owed; **debit balance** =
balance in an account showing that more
money is owed than has been received **(b)**
rest of an amount owed; *you can pay £100
down and pay off the balance over ten years*
(c) balance of payments = the international
financial position of a country, including
invisible as well as visible trade; **bank
balance** = state of an account at a bank at a
particular time **2** *verb* **(a)** to calculate the
amount needed to make the two sides of an
account equal; *I have finished balancing the
accounts for March* **(b)** to plan a budget so
that expenditure and income are equal; *the
Finance Minister is hoping to be able to*

balance the budget for the first time for some years

◊ **balance of power** ['bæləns ʌv 'pauə] *noun* (a) situation where two powerful blocs *or* states are roughly equal in power and so neutralize each other; *the superpowers have achieved a balance of power for the last twenty years; the rise of the military government has threatened the balance of power in the region* (b) *(of a small group)* to **hold the balance of power** = to be in a position where no larger group has a majority and so effectively hold power by being able to ally with another group (provided certain conditions are met); *the balance of power is held by the small Democratic Party; although the Liberals only have two seats on the council, they hold the balance of power because the other two parties have twenty seats each*

◊ **balance sheet** ['bæləns 'ʃiːt] *noun* statement of the financial position of a company at a particular time, such as the end of the financial year or the end of a quarter; *the company balance sheet for 1990 shows a substantial loss; accountants have prepared the balance sheet for the first half-year*

```
the council could try and cut
spending to make a balanced
budget
                    Local Government News
```

ballot ['bælət] **1** *noun* (a) election where people vote for someone by marking a cross on a paper with a list of names; **ballot box** = sealed box into which ballot papers are put; **ballot paper** = paper on which the voter marks a cross to show for whom he wants to vote; **postal ballot** = election where the voters send their ballot papers by post; **secret ballot** = election where the voters vote in secret; **single ballot** = election where only one ballot is held, the winner having the largest number of votes cast (b) selecting by taking papers at random out of a box; *in the House of Commons, private members Bills are placed in order of precedence by ballot; the share issue was oversubscribed, so there was a ballot for the shares* **2** *verb* (a) to take a vote by ballot; *the union is balloting for the post of president* (b) to select by ballot; *MPs balloted for Private Member's Bills*

◊ **ballot-rigging** ['bælətrɪgɪŋ] *noun* (i) illegal arranging of the votes in a ballot, so that a particular candidate *or* party wins; (ii) illegal miscounting *or* losing of votes cast; *the electoral commission accused the government party of ballot-rigging*

ban [bæn] **1** *noun* order which forbids someone from doing something *or* which makes an act against the law; *a government ban on the sale of weapons; a ban on the copying of computer software;* to **impose a ban on smoking** = to make an order which forbids smoking; to **lift the ban on smoking** = to allow people to smoke **2** *verb* to forbid something *or* to make something illegal; *the government has banned any communication with the imprisoned opposition leader; the sale of pirated records and cassettes has been banned;* (NOTE: banning - banned)

banana republic [bə'nɑːnə rɪ'pʌblɪk] *noun* more or less corrupt tropical republic, dependent on fruit exports

banish ['bænɪʃ] *verb* to send (someone) to live a long distance away (usually out of the country, or to a distant part of the country) as a punishment; *he was banished to a small island for ten years*

◊ **banishment** ['bænɪʃmənt] *noun* being banished; (NOTE: no plural)

bank [bæŋk] **1** *noun* business which holds money for its clients, which lends money at interest, and trades generally in money; **central bank** = main government-controlled bank in a country, which controls the financial affairs of the country by fixing main interest rates, issuing currency and controlling the foreign exchange rate; **clearing bank** = bank which clears cheques by transferring money from the payer's account to another account **2** *verb* to deposit money into a bank or to have an account with a bank

◊ **Bank of England** ['bæŋk ɒv 'ɪŋlənd] central British bank, owned by the state, which, together with the Treasury, regulates the nation's finances

COMMENT: the Bank of England issues banknotes (which carry the signatures of its officials). It is the lender of last resort to commercial banks and puts into effect the general financial policies of the government. The Governor of the Bank of England is appointed by the government

◊ **bank holiday** ['bæŋk 'hɒlɪdeɪ] *noun* a weekday which is a public holiday when the banks are closed; *Easter Monday or Independence Day is a bank holiday*

bankrupt ['bæŋkrʌpt] **1** *adjective & noun* (person) who has been declared by a court not to be capable of paying his debts and whose affairs are put into the hands of a trustee; *he was adjudicated or declared bankrupt; a bankrupt property developer; he went bankrupt after two years in business;* **certificated bankrupt** = bankrupt who has been discharged from bankruptcy with a certificate to show he was not at fault; **discharged bankrupt** = person who has been released from being bankrupt; **undischarged bankrupt** = person who has been declared bankrupt and has not been released from that state **2** *verb* to make someone become bankrupt; *the recession bankrupted my father*

COMMENT: a bankrupt cannot serve as a Member of Parliament, a Justice of the Peace, a director of a limited company, and cannot sign a contract or borrow money

◊ **bankruptcy** ['bæŋkrʌptsi] *noun* state of being bankrupt; *the recession has caused thousands of bankruptcies;* **bankruptcy notice** = notice warning someone that he faces bankruptcy if he fails to pay money which he owes; **bankruptcy petition** = petition to the Court asking for an order making someone bankrupt; **adjudication of bankruptcy** *or* **declaration of bankruptcy** = legal order making someone bankrupt; **discharge in bankruptcy** = being released from bankruptcy; **to file a petition in bankruptcy** = to apply to the Court to be made bankrupt *or* to ask for someone else to be made bankrupt

banner ['bænə] *noun* long flag; piece of material with slogan; *the demonstrators carried banners with the words 'Power to the People'*

bar [bɑː] **1** *noun* **(a)** place where you can buy and drink alcohol; *the council members met in the bar after the meeting* **(b)** small shop; **snack bar** = small restaurant where you can get simple meals **(c)** thing which stops you doing something; *government legislation is a bar to foreign trade* **(d)** the **Bar** = (i) the profession of barrister; (ii) all barristers; **to be called to the bar** = to pass examinations and fulfil certain requirements to become a barrister **(e)** the **Bar of the House** = (i) line across the floor of the House of Commons, behind which people who are not members can stand to present petitions *or* to be questioned; (ii) rail across the floor of the House of Lords, behind which people who are not peers can stand *he appeared in person at the Bar of the House; at the State Opening of Parliament MPs go to the House of Lords and stand behind the bar to hear the Queen's Speech* **(f)** rails in a court, behind which the lawyers and public have to stand or sit; **prisoner at the bar** = prisoner being tried in court *or* the accused **2** *verb* to forbid something *or* to make something illegal; *he was barred from attending the meeting; the police commissioner barred the use of firearms*

baron ['bærən] *noun* lowest rank of nobleman in the House of Lords

◊ **baroness** [bærə'nes] *noun* wife of a baron; a female baron

COMMENT: life peers and peeresses are barons and baronesses; barons are addressed as 'Lord' followed by their family name and baronesses as 'Lady'. In some European countries, the word is used as a form of address: so, Baron Smith is addressed as 'Lord Smith', but Baron Schmidt is addressed in that style

baronet ['bærənet] *noun* hereditary knight

COMMENT: baronets are addressed as 'Sir',followed by the Christian name and family name; their wives are addressed as 'Lady' followed by the family name (hence Sir John Smith's wife is addressed as 'Lady Smith'); the title passes to the heir, but does not qualify the holder for a seat in the House of Lords; baronets can be Members of Parliament)

◊ **baronetcy** ['bærənetsi] *noun* title of a baronet; *he inherited the baronetcy when his uncle died*

barony ['bærəni] *noun* title of a baron

barricade [bærɪ'keɪd] **1** *noun* barrier across a street, set up by revolutionaries, resistance fighters, etc. **2** *verb* to block (a street)

barrier ['bæriə] *noun* thing which stops someone from doing something, especially sending goods from one place to another; **customs barriers** *or* **tariff barriers** = customs duty intended to make trade more difficult; **to impose trade barriers on certain goods** = to restrict the import of certain goods by charging high duty; **to lift trade barriers from imports** = to remove restrictions on imports

base [beɪs] **1** *noun* **(a)** lowest or first position; **bank base rate** = basic rate of interest which a bank charges on loans to its customers; **base year** = first year of an index, against which later years' changes are measured **(b)** place where a company has its main office or factory *or* place where a businessman has his office; *the company has its base in London and branches in all European countries; he has an office in Madrid which he uses as a base while he is travelling in Southern Europe* **2** *verb* **(a)** to start to calculate from a position; *we based our calculations on last year's turnover;* **based on** = starting from **(b)** to set up a company *or* a person in a place; *the European manager is based in our London office; our foreign branch is based in the Bahamas; a London-based sales executive*

basic ['beɪsɪk] **1** *adjective* **(a)** normal; **basic pay** *or* **basic salary** *or* **basic wage** = normal salary without extra payments; **basic**

rate tax = lowest rate of income tax **(b)** most important; **basic commodities** = ordinary farm produce, produced in large quantities (such as corn, rice, sugar); **basic industry** = industry on which a country's economy depends **(c)** simple *or* from which everything starts; *he has a basic knowledge of the market; to work at the cash desk, you need a basic qualification in maths*

◊ **basics** ['beɪsɪks] *plural noun* simple and important facts; **to get back to basics** = (i) to start discussing the basic facts again; (ii) to revive traditional values

◊ **basically** [beɪsɪkli] *adverb* seen from the point from which everything starts

basis ['beɪsɪs] *noun* **(a)** point *or* number from which calculations are made; *we have calculated the costs on the basis of a 6% price increase* **(b)** general terms of agreement *or* general principles on which something is decided; **on a short-term** *or* **long-term basis** = for a short *or* long period; *he has been appointed on a short-term basis; we have three people working on a freelance basis*

battle ['bætl] *noun* important fight between political parties, etc.

battlebus ['bætəlbʌs] *noun (informal)* bus used by a candidate in an election campaign to tour the constituency

beat [biːt] *verb* **(a)** to win in a fight against someone; *the main Opposition party was beaten into third place in the election* **(b)** to **beat a ban** = to do something which is going to be forbidden by doing it rapidly before the ban is enforced; (NOTE: **beating - beat - beaten**)

beforehand [bɪ'fɔːhænd] *adverb* in advance; *the terms of the payment will be agreed beforehand*

begin [bɪ'gɪn] *verb* to start; *the passage of a Bill through Parliament begins with the First Reading in the House of Commons; the auditors' report began with a description of the general principles adopted;* (NOTE: **beginning - began - begun**)

behalf [bɪ'hɑːf] *noun* on behalf of = acting for (someone *or* a company); *I am speaking on behalf of constituents who have suffered financial loss; she is acting on my behalf; the chairman wrote on behalf of the committee*

believe [bɪ'liːv] *verb* to think that something is true; *we believe he has offered to buy 25% of the shares; the government is believed to be about to sign a non-aggression treaty*

belli ['beli] *see* CASUS BELLI

belligerent [bə'lɪdʒərənt] **1** *adjective* warlike; at war; *two belligerent states; the UN will try to achieve a ceasefire between the belligerent parties* **2** *noun* country at war with another country; *the UN tried to set up a meeting where the belligerents could discuss an exchange of prisoners*

◊ **belligerency** [be'lɪdʒərənsi] *noun* state of being at war *or* of threatening to start a war

belong [bɪ'lɒŋ] *verb* (a) to belong to = to be the property of; *the park belongs to the municipal council; the patent belongs to the inventor's son* (b) to belong with = to be part of (a group); *those documents belong with the reports of the Boundary Commission*

bench [bentʃ] *noun* long seat; **the back benches** = two rows of seats in the House of Commons, behind the front benches, where ordinary Members of Parliament sit; **the front benches** = two rows of seats in the House of Commons, facing each other with the table between them, where government ministers or members of the opposition Shadow Cabinet sit; **the Opposition front bench** = (i) the seats for the Opposition Shadow Cabinet; (ii) the members of the Shadow Cabinet; **the government front bench** *or* **the Treasury bench** = (i) the seats where the members of the government sit; (ii) the members of the Cabinet; *an Opposition front bench spokesman asked why the Government had been so slow in investigating the affair*

benefit ['benɪfɪt] **1** *noun* **(a)** money *or* advantage gained from something; *the estate was left to the benefit of the owner's grandsons* **(b)** payments which are made to someone under a national or private insurance scheme; *she receives £50 a week as unemployment benefit; the sickness benefit is paid monthly; the insurance office sends out benefit cheques each week;* **death benefit** = money paid to the family of someone who dies in an accident **2** *verb* to **benefit from** *or* **by something** = to be improved by something *or* to gain because of something; *the council tenants will benefit from the new payment arrangements*

Benelux ['benɪlʌks] *noun* Belgium, the Netherlands and Luxembourg

bet [bet] **1** *noun* amount deposited when you risk money on the result of a race *or* of a game **2** *verb* to risk money on the result of something; *he bet £100 on the result of the election; I bet you £25 the Chancellor will increase taxes;* **betting duty** *or* **tax** = tax levied on betting on horses, dogs, etc.

betray [bɪ'treɪ] *verb* to give away a secret; *he betrayed the secret to the enemy;* **to betray one's country** *or* **a friend** = to give away one's country's *or* friend's secrets to an enemy

◊ **betrayal** [bɪ'treɪəl] *noun* act of betraying; **betrayal of trust** = acting against something with which you have been entrusted

beyond [bɪ'jɒnd] *preposition* further than; **it is beyond question** *or* **beyond reasonable doubt that** = it is certain that; **beyond belief** = unbelievable

bi- [baɪ] *prefix* twice; **bi-monthly** = (i) twice a month; (ii) every two months *or* six times a year; **bi-annually** = twice a year; **biennially** = every two years

bias ['baɪəs] *noun* leaning towards *or* favouring one group rather than another; *the government has shown a bias towards big business*

◊ **biased** ['baɪəst] *adjective* (person) who favours one group rather than another *or* one of the parties in a dispute; *he accused the minister of being biased towards the rich and against the poor;* (NOTE: you show a bias towards or against someone)

bicameral [baɪˈkæmərəl] *adjective* (legislature) which has two chambers or houses; *the United States has a bicameral legislative assembly, composed of the House of Representatives and the Senate*

◊ **bicameralism** [baɪˈkæmərəlɪzm] *noun* system of government where there are two houses of parliament, one senior to the other; (NOTE: the two chambers are usually referred to as the Upper and Lower Houses; systems with only one chamber are called unicameral)

Big Ben [ˈbɪg ˈben] *noun* large bell which strikes the hours in the Clock Tower of the Houses of Parliament

bilateral [baɪˈlætərəl] *adjective* (agreement) between two parties *or* countries; *the minister signed a bilateral trade agreement*

◊ **bilaterally** [baɪˈlætərəli] *adverb* between two parties *or* countries; *the agreement was reached bilaterally; see also* MULTILATERAL, TRILATERAL, UNILATERAL

> the Federal Government will try to negotiate with the US to find a bilateral solution for the dispute
> *Toronto Globe & Mail*

bill [bɪl] **1** *noun* **(a)** written list of charges to be paid; *the salesman wrote out the bill; does the bill include VAT? the bill is made out to Smith Ltd; the builder sent in his bill; he left the country without paying his bills;* to foot the bill = to pay the costs **(b)** draft of a new Act which will be discussed in Parliament; *the house is discussing the Noise Prevention Bill; the Finance Bill had its second reading yesterday;* Private Member's Bill = Bill which is drafted and proposed by an ordinary Member of Parliament, not by a government minister; Private Bill = Bill relating to a particular person *or* corporation *or* institution; Public Bill = ordinary Bill relating to a matter applying to the public in general, introduced by a government minister **(c)**

official document; bill of health = document given to the master of a ship showing that the ship is free of disease; bill of indictment = (i) draft of an indictment which is examined by the court, and when signed becomes an indictment; (ii) *US* list of charges given to a grand jury, asking them to indict the accused; bill of lading = list of goods being shipped, which the shipper gives to the person sending the goods to show that the goods have been loaded; Bill of Rights = (i) Act passed in 1689, restating the rights of Parliament and people after the revolution of 1688; (ii) those sections (the first ten amendments) of the constitution of the United States which refer to the rights and privileges of the individual **(d)** written paper promising to pay money; bill of exchange = document which orders one person to pay another person a sum of money **2** *verb* to present a bill to someone so that it can be paid; *the builders billed him for the repairs to his neighbour's house*

> COMMENT: a Bill passes through the following stages in Parliament: **First Reading, Second Reading, Committee Stage, Report Stage** and **Third Reading**. The Bill goes through these stages first in the House of Commons and then in the House of Lords. When all the stages have been passed the Bill is given the Royal Assent and becomes law as an Act of Parliament. In the USA, a Bill is introduced either in the House or in the Senate. Any number of Senators may jointly sponsor a single bill in the Senate; in the House of Representatives, a maximum of 25 members may jointly sponsor a bill. After its introduction, a bill is referred to a committee which examines it in public hearings, then passes it back for general debate in the full House. The Bill is debated section by section in **Second Reading** and after being passed by both House and Senate is engrossed and sent to the President for signature (or veto)

binational [baɪˈnæʃɔnl] *adjective* between two countries

bind [baɪnd] *verb* to tie *or* to attach (someone) so that he has to do something; *the company is bound by its articles of* association; *he does not consider himself bound by the agreement which was signed by his predecessor; High Court judges are bound by the decisions of the House of Lords; the government is bound by the treaties signed by the previous administration* (NOTE: binding - bound)

◊ **binding** ['baɪndɪŋ] *adjective* which legally forces someone to do something; *this document is legally binding or it is a legally binding document;* the agreement is **binding on all parties** = all parties signing it must do what is agreed; **binding precedent** = decision of a higher court which has to be followed by a judge in a lower court

biological [baɪə'lɒdʒɪkl] *adjective* referring to living things; **biological warfare** = warfare using germs

bipartisan [baɪpɑːti'zæn] *adjective* accepted by the opposition as well as by the government; *a bipartisan approach to the problem of municipal finance;* a bipartisan **foreign policy** = a foreign policy agreed between the Government and Opposition

bipartite [baɪ'pɑːtaɪt] *adjective* with two sides taking part

birth [bɜːθ] *noun* being born; **he is British by birth** = he has British nationality because his parents are British; **date and place of birth** = day of the year when someone was born and the town where he was born; **birth certificate** = document giving details of a person's date and place of birth; **concealment of birth** = offence of hiding the fact that a child has been born

bisque [bɪsk] *noun* absence from the House of Commons which is allowed by a whip

Black Rod ['blæk 'rɒd] *noun* **(Gentleman Usher of the) Black Rod** = member of the Queen's staff in the Houses of Parliament, who attends all meetings of the House of Lords, but can only enter the House of Commons with the permission of the Speaker

COMMENT: like the Sergeant at Arms in the Commons, Black Rod is responsible for

keeping order in the House. His best-known duty is to go from the Lords to summon the Commons to attend the opening of Parliament and hear the Queen's Speech

blame [bleɪm] **1** *noun* saying that someone has done something wrong *or* that someone is responsible; *the Opposition got the blame for holding up the Bill* **2** *verb* to say that someone has done something wrong *or* is responsible for a mistake; *the council chairman blamed the opposition for not supporting the amendment; the lack of fire equipment was blamed by the coroner for the deaths; the spokesman blamed the closure of the hospital on the lack of government funds*

◊ **blameworthy** ['bleɪmwɜːði] *adjective* which is likely to attract blame *or* to be blamed

blanche [blɑːntʃ] *see* CARTE

blank [blæŋk] **1** *adjective* with nothing written; **a blank cheque** = a cheque with the amount of money and the payee left blank, but signed by the drawer **2** *noun* space on a form which has to be completed

blanket ['blæŋkɪt] *noun* thick woollen cover for a bed; **blanket agreement** = agreement which covers many items; **blanket refusal** = refusal to accept many different items

bloc [blɒk] *noun* group of countries linked together by having similar regimes *or* ideals; *a power bloc; the Western bloc; the Eastern bloc*

block [blɒk] **1** *noun* **(a)** series of items grouped together; **block vote** = casting of a large number of votes at the same time (such as those of trade union members) by a person who has been delegated by the holders of the votes to vote for them in this way **(b)** series of buildings forming a square with streets on all sides; **a block of offices** *or* **an office block** = a large building which contains only offices **(c)** **block capitals** *or* **block letters** = capital letters (as A,B,C); *write your name and address in block letters on the top of the* *form* **2** *verb* to stop something taking place; *he used his casting vote to block the motion; the planning committee blocked the plan to build a motorway through the middle of the town;* **to block a Bill** = to prevent a Bill being discussed at a sitting of the House of Commons, by objecting to it formally; **blocked currency** = currency which cannot be taken out of a country because of exchange controls

blockade [blɒ'keɪd] **1** *noun* act of preventing goods *or* people going into or out of a place; *the government brought in goods by air to beat the blockade; the enemy lifted the blockade of the port for two months to let in emergency supplies* **2** *verb* to prevent goods *or* food *or* people going into or coming out of a place; *the town was blockaded by the enemy navy*

blue [bluː] *noun* colour traditionally associated with the British Conservative Party; **a true-blue Tory** = person who is a convinced, old-fashioned Conservative

◊ **Blue Book** [ˈbluː ˈbʊk] *noun* government publication bound in a blue paper binding (such as the official report of a Royal Commission)

◊ **blue laws** [ˈbluː ˈlɔːz] *plural noun US* puritanical laws relating to what can *or* cannot be done on a Sunday

◊ **blue pencil** [ˈbluː ˈpensəl] *verb* to censor; *the report was blue pencilled*

blueprint [ˈbluːprɪnt] *noun* outline plan *or* project

board [bɔːd] **1** *noun* group of people who run an organization (a company *or* trust *or* society); **advisory board** = group of advisors; **editorial board** = group of editors; **board of directors** = group of directors elected by the shareholders to run a company; *the government has two representatives on the board of the nationalized industry; he sits on the board as a representative of the bank; two directors were removed from the board at the AGM;* **board of management** = group of people who manage an organization; **board meeting** = meeting of the directors of a company **2** *verb* to go on to

a ship *or* plane *or* train; *customs officials boarded the ship in the harbour*

body [ˈbɒdi] *noun* **(a)** organization *or* group of people who work together; *Parliament is an elected body; the governing body of the university has to approve the plan to give the President a honorary degree* **(b)** large group *or* amount; **body of opinion** = group of people who have a certain idea; *there is a considerable body of opinion which believes that capital punishment should be reintroduced*

◊ **bodyguard** [ˈbɒdɪgɑːd] *noun* person who protects someone; *the minister was followed by his three bodyguards*

◊ **the body politic** [ðə ˈbɒdi ˈpɒlɪtɪk] *noun* the people of a state

bollweevil [ˈbɒl ˈwiːvəl] *noun (informal) US* senator *or* congressman from one of the states of the Deep South

Bolshevik [ˈbɒlʃəvɪk] **1** *adjective* **(a)** referring to the main Communist party in Russia at the time of the Revolution; *Lenin was the leader of the Bolshevik Party* **(b)** Communist (usually referring to the former Soviet Union) **2** *noun* member of a Communist Party, especially the Russian Communist Party

◊ **bolshevism** [ˈbɒlʃəvɪzm] *noun* form of radical Communism

> COMMENT: the word comes from the Russian 'bolshinstvo', meaning majority, because this section of the Communist Party was in the majority at the time of the Russian Revolution

bona fide [ˈbəʊnə ˈfaɪdi] *Latin phrase meaning* 'in good faith'; **a bona fide offer** = an offer which is made honestly *or* which can be trusted

◊ **bona fides** [ˈbəʊnə ˈfaɪdɪz] *Latin phrase meaning* 'good faith'; honesty; *his bona fides was or were accepted by the company*

bond [bɒnd] *noun* **(a)** contract document promising to repay money borrowed by a company *or* by the government; *government bonds or treasury bonds;* **premium bonds** = government bonds, part of a national savings scheme, which do not pay any interest but which give the owner the chance to win a weekly *or* monthly prize **(b)** contract document promising to repay money borrowed by a person; **bearer bond** = bond which is payable to the bearer and does not have a name written on it; **debenture bond** = certificate showing that a debenture has been issued; **mortgage bond** = certificate showing that a mortgage exists and that the property is security for it **(c)** signed legal document which binds one or more parties to do *or* not to do something; **goods (held) in bond** = goods held by the customs until duty has been paid; **entry of goods under bond** = bringing goods into a country in bond; **to take goods out of bond** = to pay duty on goods so that they can be released by the customs

◊ **bonded** ['bɒndɪd] *adjective* held in bond; **bonded goods** = goods which are held by the customs under a bond until duty has been paid; **bonded warehouse** = warehouse where goods are stored in bond until duty is paid

◊ **bondholder** ['bɒndhəʊldə] *noun* person who holds government bonds

book [bʊk] **1** *noun* **(a)** set of sheets of paper attached together; **a company's books** = the financial records of a company; **book value** = value of a company's assets as shown in the company accounts **(b)** **phone book** *or* **telephone book** = book which lists names of people or companies with their addresses and telephone numbers; *see also* BLUE BOOK **2** *verb* to order *or* to reserve something; *to book a room in a hotel or a table at a restaurant or a ticket on a plane; I booked a table for 7.45; he booked a ticket through to Cairo;* **to book someone into a hotel** *or* **onto a flight** = to order a room *or* a plane ticket for someone

◊ **booking** ['bʊkɪŋ] *noun* act of ordering a room *or* a seat

booth [buːð] *noun* small cabin, usually with three sides, where one person can stand or sit; **polling booth** *or* **voting booth** = small enclosed space in a polling station, where the voter goes to mark his ballot paper in private

border ['bɔːdə] *noun* frontier between two countries; *a border town; he was killed by the border guards*

borough ['bʌrə] *noun* town which has been incorporated; **borough council** = representatives elected to run a borough; **borough architect** *or* **borough engineer** *or* **borough treasurer** = officials in charge of the new buildings *or* machinery *or* finances of a borough

COMMENT: a borough is an officially incorporated town, which has a charter granted by Parliament. A borough is run by an elected council, with a mayor as its official head. Most boroughs are represented in Parliament by at least one MP

borrow ['bɒrəʊ] *verb* to take money from someone for a time, possibly paying interest for it, and repaying it at the end of the period; *he borrowed £1,000 from the bank; the government had to borrow on the international market to pay off the interest on its debts; the company had to borrow heavily to repay its debts; they borrowed £25,000 against the security of the factory*

◊ **borrower** ['bɒrəwə] *noun* person who borrows; *borrowers from the bank pay 12% interest*

◊ **borrowing** ['bɒrəwɪŋ] *noun* **(a)** action of borrowing money; *the new factory was financed by bank borrowing;* **borrowing power** = amount of money which a company can borrow; **public sector borrowing requirement (PSBR)** = amount of money which a government has to borrow to pay for its own spending **(b)** **borrowings** = money borrowed; *the company's borrowings have doubled;* **bank borrowings** = loans made by banks

bound [baʊnd] *see* BIND, DUTY

boundary (line) ['baʊndri] *noun* line marking the edge of a certain area of land; *the boundary dispute dragged through the courts for years; the borough boundary is marked by road signs*

◊ **Boundary Commission** ['baʊndri kə'mɪʃən] *noun* committee which examines the area and population of constituencies for the House of Commons or of local municipalities and recommends changes to make all Members of Parliament represent roughly similar numbers of people

bounty ['baunti] *noun* (i) government subsidy made to help an industry; (ii) payment made by government to someone who has saved lives *or* found treasure

bourgeois ['buəʒwɑː] **1** *adjective* **(a)** middle class *or* referring to the class of businessmen and professional people (as opposed to the aristocracy, the clergy, manual *or* clerical workers, the Armed Forces, etc.); **petty bourgeois** = referring to the lower middle class *or* to small shopkeepers, etc. **(b)** *(used as criticism)* traditional and reactionary, not revolutionary; *the Party is trying to reduce its bourgeois image by promoting young activists to the Central Committee* **2** *noun* middle-class person; **the petty bourgeois** = lower middle-class people

◊ **bourgeoisie** [buəʒwɑˈziː] *noun* the middle class (usually the richer upper levels of the middle class, formed of businessmen and professional people); **petty bourgeoisie** = the lower middle class of shopkeepers, minor civil servants, etc.; (NOTE: the word **bourgeois** is used in radical or communist circles to refer to anyone who is a capitalist, or even anyone who is not a communist)

box [bɒks] *noun* **(a)** container; *the goods were sent in thin cardboard boxes; the drugs were hidden in boxes of office stationery;* **envelopes come in boxes of two hundred** = packed two hundred to a box; **box file** = file (for papers) made like a box; **red box** = suitcase covered in red leather in which government papers are sent to Ministers; *see also* DESPATCH BOX **(b) witness box** = place in a courtroom where the witnesses give evidence; (NOTE: American English is **witness stand**) **(c) box number** = reference number used in a post office or an advertisement to avoid giving an address; *please reply to Box No. 209; our address is: P.O. Box 74209, Edinburgh*

boycott ['bɔɪkɒt] **1** *noun* refusal to buy *or* to deal in goods from a certain country *or* company, used as a punishment; *the union organized a boycott against or of imported cars* **2** *verb* to refuse to buy *or* to deal in goods from a certain country *or* company, as a punishment; *the company's products have been boycotted by the main department stores; we are boycotting all imports from that country;* **the government representative has boycotted the meeting** = has refused to attend the meeting

bracket ['brækɪt] **1** *noun* group of items *or* people of a certain type taken together; **income bracket** *or* **tax bracket** = level of income where a certain percentage tax applies **2** *verb* **to bracket together** = to treat several items together in the same way

branch [brɑːntʃ] **1** *noun* **(a)** local office of a bank or large business; local shop of a large chain of shops; *the bank or the store has branches in most towns in the south of the country; the insurance company has closed its branches in South America; he is the manager of our local branch of Lloyds bank; we have decided to open a branch office in Chicago; the manager of our branch in Lagos or of our Lagos branch* **branch manager** = manager of a branch **(b)** section of government; *the three branches of government are the executive, the legislature and the judiciary;* **Executive Branch** = part of government which puts legislation into action; **Legislative Branch** = part of government which passes laws **(c)** part *or* separate section; *the school welfare service is a branch of the county education service; the Law of Contract and the Law of Tort are branches of civil law* **2** *verb* **to branch out** = to start a new (but usually related) type of business; *from lending books, the library has branched out into organizing exhibitions*

breach [briːtʃ] *noun* **(a)** failure to carry out the terms of an agreement; **in breach of** = failing to do something which was agreed; *the Minister is in breach of his statutory duty;* **breach of contract** = failing to do something which is in a contract; **the company is in breach of contract** = the company has failed to carry out what was agreed in the contract; **breach of trust** = failure to act properly on the part of a trustee in regard to a trust **(b)** failure to obey the law; *the soldier was charged with a serious breach of discipline;* **breach of the peace** = creating a disturbance which is likely to annoy *or* frighten people

◊ **breach of privilege** [briːtʃ ʌv ˈprɪvɪlɪdʒ] *noun* acting in a way which may diminish the reputation *or* power of Parliament (by speaking in a defamatory way about an MP or about Parliament itself)

COMMENT: breaches of parliamentary privilege can take the form of many types of action; the commonest are threats to MPs, or insulting language about MPs; speaking in a rude way about Parliament in public; wild behaviour in the public galleries; trying to influence witnesses appearing before parliamentary committees

break [breɪk] **1** *noun* short space of time, when you can rest; *the committee adjourned for a ten-minute break* **2** *verb* **(a)** to do something which is against the law; *if you hit a policeman you will be breaking the law; he is breaking the law by selling goods on Sunday; the company broke section 26 of the Companies Act* **(b)** to fail to carry out the duties of a contract; *the government has broken the contract or the agreement with the trades unions; the guerillas have broken the ceasefire agreement;* **to break an engagement to do something** = not to do what has been agreed **(c)** to cancel (a contract); *the company is hoping to be able to break the contract;* (NOTE: **breaking - broke - broken)**

◊ **break down** [ˈbreɪk ˈdaʊn] *verb* **(a)** to stop working because of mechanical failure; *the two-way radio has broken down; what do you do when your shredder breaks down?* **(b)** to stop; *negotiations broke down after six hours; the ceasefire agreement broke down almost immediately* **(c)** to show the details item by item; *the trade figures are broken down into visible and invisible exports; can you break down this invoice into spare parts and labour?*

◊ **breakdown** [ˈbreɪkdaʊn] *noun* **(a)** stopping work because of mechanical failure; *we cannot communicate with our embassy because of the breakdown of the radio link* **(b)** stopping work *or* discussion; *a breakdown in wage negotiations; the government news agency has reported a breakdown in the ceasefire* **(c)** showing details item by item; *give me a breakdown of the latest figures for clerical staff*

◊ **break off** [ˈbreɪk ˈɒf] *verb* to stop; *we broke off the discussion at midnight; the government has broken off negotiations with the insurgents;* **to break off diplomatic relations with a country** = to recall the ambassador and close down the embassy in a country; *after the military attaché was shot, and bombs thrown at the embassy, the government decided to break off diplomatic relations and recalled all its diplomatic personnel*

◊ **break out** [ˈbreɪk ˈaʊt] *verb* to start (suddenly); *war broke out between the European powers*

◊ **break up** [ˈbreɪk ˈʌp] *verb* **(a)** to split something large into small sections; *the company was broken up and separate divisions sold off* **(b)** to come to an end *or* to make something come to an end; *the meeting broke up at 12.30; the police broke up the protest meeting*

bribe [braɪb] **1** *noun* money offered corruptly to someone to get him to do something to help you; *the minister was dismissed for taking bribes* **2** *verb* to give someone money corruptly to get him to help you; *he bribed a senior civil servant to get the import licence passed*

◊ **bribery** [ˈbraɪbəri] *noun* crime of paying someone money corruptly to get him to do something to help you; *bribery in the security warehouse is impossible to stamp out;* (NOTE: no plural)

brief [briːf] **1** *noun* details of a case, prepared by officials and given to a Minister to study; **to be on top of one's brief** = to know all the facts of a case **2** *adjective* short; *after a brief discussion, the motion was passed unanimously; the chairman asked each speaker to make his remarks brief, as* *there was only a short time available for debate* **3** *verb* to explain something to someone in detail; *the superintendent briefed the press on the progress of the investigation;* **to brief a minister** *or* **officer** = to give a minister *or* officer all the details of the case which he will argue in Parliament *or* on TV *or* in committee

◊ **briefcase** ['bri:fkeɪs] *noun* case with a handle for carrying papers and documents; *he put all the files into his briefcase*

◊ **briefing** ['bri:fɪŋ] *noun* telling someone details; *all the Whitehall journalists attended a briefing given by the minister;* **briefing papers** = documents prepared by officials for a Minister to study

bring [brɪŋ] *verb* to come to a place with someone *or* something; *he brought his documents with him; the inspector brought his secretary to take notes of the meeting;* **to bring a lawsuit** *or* **proceedings against someone** = to sue someone; (NOTE: bringing - brought)

◊ **bring down** ['brɪŋ 'daʊn] *verb* to make a government lose power; *the government was brought down by the scandal about the Prime Minister's wife*

◊ **bring forward** ['brɪŋ 'fɔːwəd] *verb* to make earlier; *to bring forward the date of repayment; the date of the hearing has been brought forward to March*

◊ **bring up** ['brɪŋ 'ʌp] *verb* to refer to something for the first time; *the chairman brought up the question of corruption in the police force*

Brit [brɪt] *noun (informal)* British person

Britain *or* **Great Britain** ['brɪtən] *noun* country formed of an island off the north coast of Europe; (NOTE: Britain is formed of England, Wales and Scotland; together with Northern Ireland it forms the United Kingdom of Great Britain and Northern Ireland)

◊ **British** ['brɪtɪʃ] **1** *adjective* referring to Britain *or* Great Britain **2** *noun* **the British** = inhabitants, or citizens of Britain; (NOTE: the words **Britain** and **British** are often used to refer to the whole of the United Kingdom: **the British Prime Minister; the British government**)

◊ **British Isles** ['brɪtɪʃ 'aɪlz] *noun* group of islands off the north coast of Europe, consisting of the United Kingdom (England, Wales, Scotland and Northern Ireland) plus the Republic of Ireland, the Channel Islands and the Isle of Man

◊ **Briton** ['brɪtən] *noun* native of Great Britain

budget ['bʌdʒɪt] **1** *noun* **(a)** plan of expected spending and income (usually for one year); *the Chief Executive has drawn up the budget for the coming year; the departments have agreed their budgets for next year* **(b)** **the Budget** = the annual plan of taxes and government spending proposed by a finance minister (in the UK, the Chancellor of the Exchequer); **the budget statement** = speech by a Chancellor of the Exchequer presenting his budget to Parliament; *the minister put forward a budget aimed at slowing down the economy; the Chancellor began his budget statement at 3.30; the budget debate* **or** *the debate on the budget lasted for two days;* **to balance the budget** = to plan income and expenditure so that they balance; *the president is planning for a balanced budget* **2** *verb* to plan probable income and expenditure; *the council is budgeting for a 25% increase in expenditure on roads*

◊ **budgetary** ['bʌdʒɪtəri] *adjective* referring to a budget; **budgetary policy** = policy of planning income and expenditure; **budgetary control** = keeping check on spending; **budgetary requirements** = spending or income required to meet the expected budget

◊ **budgeting** ['bʌdʒɪtɪŋ] *noun* preparing of budgets to help plan expenditure and income

the council could refuse to set a legal budget which would result in its being unable to borrow money and pay its employees

Local Government News

buffer ['bʌfə] *noun* something placed between two powerful forces, which prevents clashes between them; *the UN tried to establish a buffer zone between the two warring factions; the small country found it* *had become a buffer state between the two belligerents*

bug [bʌg] **1** *noun* small device which can record conversations radios secretly and send them to a secret radio receiver; *the cleaners planted a bug under the ambassador's desk* **2** *verb* to place a secret device in a place so that conversations can be heard and recorded secretly; *the agents bugged the President's office;* **bugging device** = bug; *police found a bugging device under the minister's desk*

Bundesbank [ˈbʊndəzbænk] *noun* German Central Bank

Bundesrat [ˈbʊndəzrɑːt] *noun* **(a)** upper house of legislature in Austria and Germany **(b)** federal council in Switzerland (the equivalent of the cabinet)

Bundestag [ˈbʊndəztæg] *noun* lower house of legislature in Germany

bunker [ˈbʌŋkə] *noun* underground shelter during war

bureau [ˈbjʊərəʊ] *noun* **(a)** office which specializes; **computer bureau** = office which offers to do work on its computers for companies which do not own their own computers; **employment bureau** = office which finds jobs for people; **information bureau** = office which gives information **(b)** government agency; *the local employment bureau* **(c)** *(in some countries, but not in Britain)* government department; *see also* POLITBURO (NOTE: the plural is **bureaux**)

◊ **bureaucracy** [bjʊəˈrɒkrəsi] *noun (often used as criticism)* **(a)** group of civil servants *or* officials of central or local government; *the investigation of complaints is in the hands of the local bureaucracy; the new president found it difficult to change the way the bureaucracy worked* **(b)** rule by civil servants; slow and complicated way of working; *I am fed up with all this bureaucracy, just to get an export licence;* (NOTE: no plural for this meaning)

◊ **bureaucrat** [ˈbjʊərəkræt] *noun (often as criticism)* person who works in a bureaucracy; *the bureaucrats in the state capital are well-known for the slowness of*

their decision-making; see also EUROCRAT

◊ **bureaucratic** [bjʊərəˈkrætɪk] *adjective* referring to a bureaucracy *or* to bureaucrats; *you have to follow the correct bureaucratic procedures; the investigation has been held up by bureaucratic muddle*

burgermeister [ˈbɜːgəmaɪstə] *noun* mayor of a German town

burgh [ˈbʌrə] *noun* Scottish borough

◊ **burgher** [ˈbɜːgə] *noun* person who lives in a borough

burgomaster [ˈbɜːgəmɑːstə] *noun* mayor of a Dutch or Flemish town

business [ˈbɪznəs] *noun* **(a)** work of buying or selling; **on business** = on commercial work **(b)** commercial company; *he owns a small car repair business; she runs a business from her home; he set up in business as an insurance broker;* **business hours** = time (usually 9 a.m. to 5 p.m.) when a business is open; **business name** = name under which a firm *or* company trades; **business premises** = building used for business purposes, and therefore charged with a business rate; **business rate** = local tax levied on businesses, usually at a higher rate than for householders **(c)** affairs discussed; *the main business of the meeting was finished by 3 p.m.;* **move the business forward** = go on to the next item on the agenda; **any other business (AOB)** = item at the end of an agenda, where any matter can be raised; **the business of the House** *or* **business of the day** = matters for discussion in the House of Commons on a certain day; **business committee** = committee set up by the House of Commons to work out the agenda of business, especially the length of time allocated to discussion of each Bill; **order of business** = agenda of the House of Commons for a certain day *or* order in which items are discussed or dealt with in the House; (NOTE: no plural for meanings (a) and (c); (b) has the plural **businesses**)

COMMENT: the normal order of business of the House of Commons begins with prayers, followed by messages from the Queen or official messages from foreign governments; then motions for writs to hold by-elections; private business; Question Time, when ministers answer questions about the work of their departments. Following this, various matters can be discussed, including debate on motions and public Bills

busy ['bɪzi] *adjective* occupied in doing something *or* in working; *the police were kept busy dealing with the crowds; the Commons has a busy schedule of legislation;* **the line is busy** = the telephone line is being used

by-election ['baɪɪlekʃən] *noun* election for Parliament *or* for a council during a term of office (because of the death *or* retirement of the person first elected)

bylaw *or* **byelaw** *or* **by-law** *or* **bye-law** ['baɪlɔ:] *noun* rule *or* law made by a local authority *or* public body and not by central government; *the bylaws forbid playing ball games in the public gardens; according to the local bylaws, noise must be limited in the town centre*

COMMENT: bylaws must be made by bodies which have been authorized by Parliament, before they can become legally effective

Byzantine [baɪ'zæntaɪn] *adjective* too complicated; *it is difficult to follow the Byzantine discussions between the two countries about the boundary dispute;* compare MACHIAVELLIAN

Cc

C [siː] *third letter of the alphabet* **Schedule C** = schedule to the Finance Acts under which tax is charged on profits from government stock; **Table C** = model memorandum and articles of association set out in the Companies Act 1985 for a company limited by guarantee having no share capital

CAB = CITIZENS' ADVICE BUREAU (NOTE: plural is **CABX**: say 'Citizens' Advice Bureaux')

cabal [kæˈbɑːl] *noun* small group of politicians who plan action in secret (either to overthrow a government *or* to do something illegal)

cabinet [ˈkæbɪnət] *noun* **(a)** piece of furniture for storing records *or* for display; *last year's correspondence is in the bottom drawer of the filing cabinet* **(b)** committee formed from the most important members of the government, chosen by the Prime Minister or President to be in charge of the main government departments; *Cabinet meetings are held in the Cabinet room; the Cabinet meets on Thursday mornings; the Prime Minister held a meeting of the Cabinet yesterday;* **inner cabinet** = group of the most important members of the Cabinet, who meet with the Prime Minister and decide policy; **kitchen cabinet** = private unofficial committee of ministers, advisers and friends who advise the Prime Minister; **Cabinet Committees** = committees which are formed from Cabinet ministers, junior ministers or civil servants, who advise the Cabinet and Prime Minister on certain matters; **Cabinet government** = form of government where a Prime Minister *or* President forms a cabinet of ministers to run various ministries; **Cabinet Minister** = minister who is a member of the Cabinet; **Cabinet Office** = section of the British Civil Service which works for the Prime Minister and the Cabinet; **Cabinet Secretary** *or* **Secretary to the Cabinet** = head of the Cabinet Office (and also of the British Civil Service), who attends Cabinet meetings; (NOTE: the word Cabinet is used both for the group of people and for a meeting of the group: **the Prime Minister held a Cabinet yesterday; the decision was taken at Thursday's Cabinet**)

COMMENT: in most forms of Cabinet government (as in the UK), the Prime Minister or President chooses the members of his Cabinet and can dismiss them if necessary. In some countries, MPs of the ruling party elect the members of the Cabinet, with the result that the Prime Minister has less overall power over the decisions of the Cabinet, and cannot dismiss ministers easily

cadre [ˈkɑːdə] *noun* active member *or* group of key members of a party (especially a Marxist party)

calculate [ˈkælkjʊleɪt] *verb* **(a)** to find the answer to a problem using numbers; *the bank clerk calculated the rate of exchange for the dollar* **(b)** to estimate; *he calculated that the increase in oil revenues would save the government $1bn*

◊ **calculating** [ˈkælkjʊleɪtɪŋ] *adjective (usually as criticism)* (person) who plans clever schemes in a careful way; *the MP called the Home Secretary a cool calculating plotter*

◊ **calculation** [kælkjʊˈleɪʃn] *noun* answer to a problem in mathematics; *I made some rough calculations on the back of an envelope; according to government* *calculations, the inflation rate has increased by 20% over the last six months*

◊ **calculator** [ˈkælkjʊleɪtə] *noun* electronic machine which works out the answers to problems in mathematics

calendar [ˈkælendə] *noun* **(a)** book *or* set of sheets of paper showing the days and months in a year, often attached to pictures; **calendar month** = a whole month as on a calendar, from the 1st to the 28th, 30th or 31st; **calendar year** = year from the 1st January to 31st December **(b)** **Parliamentary calendar** = timetable of events in Parliament, with dates for discussion of each Bill **(c)** *US* list of Bills for consideration by committees of the House of Representatives *or* the Senate; **calendar Wednesday** = Wednesday when the House of Representatives can consider bills from committees during a short debate

COMMENT: the Senate has only one calendar, but the House of Representatives has several: the Consent Calendar for uncontroversial bills; the Discharge Calendar for motions to discharge a committee of its responsibility for a bill; the House Calendar for bills which do not involve raising revenue or spending money; and the Union Calendar for bills which raise revenue or appropriate money for expenditure

call [kɔːl] **1** *noun* **(a)** conversation on the telephone; **local call** = call to a number on the same exchange; **long-distance call** = call to a number in a different zone *or* area; **overseas call** *or* **international call** = call to another country; **person-to-person call** = call where you ask the operator to connect you with a named person **(b)** (i) demand for repayment of a loan by a lender; (ii) demand by a company to pay for shares; **money at call** *or* **money on call** *or* **call money** = money loaned for which repayment can be demanded without notice **(c)** visit; *the salesmen make six calls a day;* **business call** = visit to talk to someone on business **2** *verb* **(a)** to telephone to someone; *I shall call you at your office tomorrow* **(b)** to admit someone to the bar to practise as a barrister; *he was called (to the*

bar) in 1980 **(c)** to call a meeting to order = to start proceedings officially

◊ **call for** [ˈkɔːl ˈfɔː] *verb* to demand something; *the Opposition called for the Minister's resignation*

◊ **call in** [ˈkɔːl ˈɪn] *verb* **(a)** to visit; *the sales representative called in twice last week* **(b)** to ask someone to come to help; *the Department of Trade decided to call in the Fraud Squad to help in the investigation* **(c)** to ask for plans to be sent to the ministry for examination; *the minister has called in the plans for the new supermarket* **(d)** to ask for a debt to be paid; *the Central banks have called in the country's debts*

◊ **call off** [ˈkɔːl ˈɒf] *verb* to ask for something not to take place *or* not to continue; *the search for the missing children has been called off; the visit was called off because the Foreign Minister was ill*

◊ **call on** [ˈkɔːl ˈɒn] *verb* **(a)** to visit someone; *the visiting Swedish Foreign Minister called on the President yesterday for talks* **(b)** to ask someone to do something; *the minister called on community leaders to help prevent street crime*

camera [ˈkæmərə] *see* BICAMERALISM, IN CAMERA

campaign [kæmˈpeɪn] **1** *noun* **(a)** planned method of working; *the government has launched a campaign against drunken drivers* **(b)** **election campaign** = period immediately before an election, when candidates canvass for support; **campaign trail** = series of meeting *or* visits which form part of an election campaign; *she is out on the campaign trail again this week* **2** *verb* **(a)** to try to change something by writing about it *or* by organizing protest meetings *or* by lobbying Members of Parliament; *they are campaigning for the abolition of the death penalty or they are campaigning against the death penalty; she is campaigning for the reintroduction of the death penalty; he is campaigning for a revision of the Official Secrets Act* **(b)** to try to get the voters to vote for you in an election; *she is campaigning on the issue of more money for the school system; he had been campaigning all day from the top of a bus*

◊ **campaigner** ['kæmpeɪnə] *noun* person who is campaigning for a party *or* for a candidate *or* for a cause; *he is an experienced political campaigner; she is a campaigner for women's rights*

Camp David ['kæmp 'deɪvɪd] *noun* official country home of the Presidents of the United States

cancel ['kænsl] *verb* (a) to stop something which has been agreed *or* planned; *to cancel an appointment or a meeting; to cancel a contract* (b) to cancel a cheque = to stop payment of a cheque which you have signed; (NOTE: GB English is **cancelling - cancelled** but US English **canceling - canceled**)

◊ **cancellation** [kænsə'leɪʃn] *noun* stopping something which has been agreed *or* planned; *cancellation of an appointment; cancellation of an agreement;* **cancellation clause** = clause in a contract which states the terms on which the contract may be cancelled

candidate ['kændɪdət] *noun* person who applies for a job *or* person who puts himself forward for election; *there are six candidates for the post of Party secretary; we interviewed ten candidates for the post; all the candidates in the election appeared on television; which candidate are you voting for?*

◊ **candidacy** *or* **candidature** ['kændɪdəsi *or* 'kændɪdətʃə] *noun* state of being a candidate; *the Senator has announced his candidacy for the Presidential election*

canton ['kæntɒn] *noun* one of the administrative divisions of Switzerland

> COMMENT: the cantons are: Appenzell, Aargau, Basel, Berne, Fribourg, Geneva, Glaris, Grisons, Lucerne, Neuchâtel, Saint-Gall, Schaffhausen, Schwyz, Soleure, Tessin, Thurgau, Unterwald, Uri, Valais, Vaud, Zug, Zurich

canvass ['kænvəs] *verb* to visit people to ask them to vote for a certain candidate *or* to say what they think; *party workers are out canvassing voters;* **to canvass support** = to ask people to support you; *he is canvassing*

support for his Bill among members of the Opposition

◊ **canvasser** ['kænvəsə] *noun* person who canvasses

◊ **canvassing** ['kænvəsɪŋ] *noun* action of asking people to vote for a certain party *or* to say what they think

CAP = COMMON AGRICULTURAL POLICY

capable ['keɪpəbl] *adjective* (a) capable of = able *or* clever enough to do something; *she is capable of very fast typing speeds; the government was not capable of preventing a fall in the exchange rate* (b) efficient *or* (person) who works well; *she is a very capable junior minister*

capacity [kə'pæsɪti] *noun* (a) amount which can be produced *or* amount of work which can be done (b) amount of space; **storage capacity** = space available for storing goods *or* information (c) ability; *he has a particular capacity for business* (d) in his capacity as chairman = acting as chairman; **speaking in an official capacity** = speaking officially

capita ['kæpɪtə] *see* PER CAPITA

capital ['kæpɪtl] **1** *noun* (a) money, property and assets used in a business; **capital gains** = money made by selling a fixed asset *or* by selling shares at a profit; **capital gains tax** = tax paid on capital gains; **capital transfer tax** = tax paid on the transfer of capital *or* assets from one person to another; *see also* EXPENDITURE (b) **to make political capital out of something** = to use something to give you an advantage in politics; *the Opposition made a lot of capital out of the Minister's mistake on TV* (c) **capital (city)** = main town in a country *or* province, where the government is; *London is the capital of the United Kingdom, and Washington is the capital of the USA;* **state capital** *or* **provincial capital** = main town in a state *or* province (d) **capital letters** *or* **block capitals** = letters written as A, B, C, D, etc., and not a, b, c, d; *write your name in block capitals at the top of the form;* (NOTE: no plural for (a)) **2** *adjective* **capital crime** *or* offence = crime for which the punishment is death; **capital punishment** = punishment of a criminal by execution

COMMENT: in the UK the only capital crime is now treason

◊ **capitalism** ['kæpɪtəlɪzm] *noun* **(a)** belief in private ownership of money, property and other assets, used to create profits **(b)** economic system, where money, property and other assets are owned by individuals and where the economy is led by demand, with supply and prices being determined by market forces

◊ **capitalist** ['kæpɪtəlɪst] **1** *noun* *(sometimes used as criticism)* person who owns money, property, and other assets which he uses to make profits **2** *adjective* based on capitalism as a system of economy; **capitalist countries** = countries (mainly in the West) whose economies are run on capitalist principles; **the capitalist system** = all capitalist countries working together

◊ **capitalistic** [kæpɪtə'lɪstɪk] *adjective* *(derogatory)* similar to capitalism

◊ **capitalization** [kæpɪtəlaɪ'zeɪʃn] *noun* **market capitalization** = value of a company calculated by multiplying the price of its shares on the Stock Exchange by the number of shares issued

Capitol ['kæpɪtəl] *noun* **(a)** building in Washington, D.C., where the US Senate and House of Representatives meet; **Capitol Hill** = hill on which the Capitol building stands, together with other important government buildings; **on Capitol Hill** = in the US Senate *or* House of Representatives; *the feeling on Capitol Hill is that the President will veto the proposal* **(b)** State Capitol = building in the main city of a State, housing the State legislature

capture ['kæptʃə] *verb* to take *or* to get control of something; *the Opposition captured six seats in the last general election*

card [kɑːd] *noun* piece of stiff paper; **party card** = card which proves that the person whose name is on it is a member of the political party which issues it; **card-carrying**

Communist = real member of the Communist Party, not just a sympathizer; **card vote** = vote taken at meetings (as at the Trades Union Congress), where delegates vote on behalf of their membership by holding up a card showing the total number of votes which they are casting

care ['keə] *noun* **(a)** act of looking after someone; *the boy was put in the care of his grandmother; the children were put in the care of the social services department;* **child in care** = child who has been put into the care of the local social services department; **care order** = order from a juvenile court, putting a child into the care of a local authority; **care proceedings** = action in court to put a child into the care of someone **(b)** making sure that someone is not harmed; **duty of care** = duty which everyone has not to act negligently; **driving without due care and attention** = driving a car in a careless way, so that other people are in danger

careful ['keəfʊl] *adjective* cautious *or* taking care

carefully ['keəfəli] *adverb* with care

◊ **careless** ['keələs] *adjective* without paying attention to other people; **careless driving** = driving without due care and attention

◊ **carelessly** ['keələsli] *adverb* in a careless way

◊ **care of** ['keə 'ɒv] *phrase (in an address)* words to show that the person is at the address, but only as a visitor; *Herr Schmidt, care of Mr W Brown;* (NOTE: usually written Herr Schmidt, c/o Mr Brown)

caretaker ['keəteɪkə] *noun* person whose job is to look after property; **caretaker Prime Minister** *or* **caretaker chairman** = Prime Minister *or* chairman who occupies the office temporarily until a newly elected *or* appointed official arrives

carpetbagger ['kɑːpətbægə] *noun* *(informal)* person who goes to another part of the country to try to get elected in the place of a local candidate

◊ **carpetbagging** ['kɑːpətbægɪŋ] *noun* going to another part of the country to try to get elected in the place of a local candidate

carry ['kæri] *verb* **(a)** to take from one place to another; *to carry goods; the train was carrying a consignment of cars;* **carrying offensive weapons** = offence of holding a weapon or something (such as a bottle) which could be used as a weapon **(b)** to vote to approve; **the motion was carried** = the motion was accepted after a vote; (NOTE: the opposite is **the motion was lost**) **(c)** to win; to keep the support of someone; **the government carried the day** = the government won the vote; **he was not able to carry his supporters with him** = his supporters voted against him **(d)** to be punishable by; *the offence carries a maximum sentence of two years' imprisonment*

◊ **carry out** ['kæri 'aʊt] *verb* to do a job which has been assigned; *the police carried out the raid with great speed; the secret agent was only carrying out orders when he bugged the Prime Minister's office*

carte blanche ['kɑːt 'blɒnʃ] *French phrase meaning* 'white card': permission given by someone to another person, allowing him to do anything *or* to act in any way; *he has carte blanche to act on behalf of the government or the government has given him carte blanche to act on its behalf*

case [keɪs] *noun* **(a)** suitcase *or* box with a handle for carrying clothes and personal belongings when travelling; *the customs made him open his case; she had a small case which she carried onto the plane* **(b)** (i) cardboard or wooden box for packing and carrying goods; (ii) box containing twelve bottles of alcohol **(c) court case** = legal action *or* trial; **the case is being heard next week** = the case is coming to court; **case law** = law as established by precedents, that is by the decisions of courts in earlier cases **(d)** arguments *or* facts put forward by one side in a debate *or* legal proceedings; *the proposer of the motion put forward a very strong case for repealing the statute; the government's case is particularly weak; there is a strong case against the accused;* **the case rests** = all

the arguments for one side have been put forward; **no case to answer** = submission by the defence (after the prosecution has put its case) that the case should be dismissed

COMMENT: a legal case is referred to by the names of the parties, the date and the reference source where details of it can be found: *Smith v. Jones [1990] 2 W.L.R. 250* This shows that the case involved Smith as plaintiff and Jones as defendant, it was heard in 1990, and is reported in the second volume of the Weekly Law Reports for that year on page 250

cast [kɑːst] *verb* **to cast a vote** = to vote; *the number of votes cast in the election was 125,458; under proportional representation, the number of seats occupied by each party is related to the number of votes cast for that party;* **casting vote** = vote used by the chairman in a case where the votes for and against a proposal are equal; *the chairman has a casting vote; he used his casting vote to block the motion;* (NOTE: **casting - cast - has cast**)

caste [kɑːst] *noun* one of the divisions in a society, such as in India, where social classes are strictly divided

COMMENT: the Indian caste system formerly went from the highest caste (or Brahmins) to the lowest (or Untouchables), and intermarriage between people of different castes was impossible. The system has now to a certain extent broken down

casual ['kæʒjʊəl] *adjective* not permanent; **casual labour** = workers who are employed for short periods; **casual vacancy** = vacancy (as on a committee) which is to be filled temporarily until the next full committee elections take place

casus belli ['kɑːzəs 'beli] *Latin phrase meaning* 'case for war': reason which is used to justify a declaration of war

catch [kætʃ] *verb (of an MP)* **to catch the Speaker's eye** = to stand up and ask the Speaker to be allowed to speak in a debate

category ['kætɪgəri] *noun* type *or* sort of item; *does a protest march come into the category of anti-government activity?*

caucus ['kɔːkəs] *noun* **(a)** group of people in a political party who are strong enough to influence policy **(b)** *US* private meeting of powerful members of a political party to make a decision (such as to decide how they will vote in a presidential election); meeting of local party members to chose a candidate for nomination; (NOTE: plural is **caucuses**)

caudillo [kauˈdiːjɔu] *noun (in Spanish-speaking countries)* head of state

cause [kɔːz] **1** *noun* **(a)** thing which makes something happen; *the cause of the riots was the rise in the price of bread* **(b)** legal proceedings; **cause list** = list of cases which are to be heard by a court; **matrimonial causes** = cases referring to the rights of partners in a marriage **2** *verb* to make something happen; *the recession caused hundreds of bankruptcies*

CBI [siːbiːˈaɪ] = CONFEDERATION OF BRITISH INDUSTRY

ceasefire ['siːsfaɪə] *noun* agreement by two sides in a conflict to stop fighting for a time; *the ceasefire is due to come into effect on Christmas Day; the government troops have observed the ceasefire*

cede [siːd] *verb* to pass possession of a territory to another country; *the Philippines were ceded to the USA by Spain in 1898; see also* CESSION

censor ['sensə] **1** *noun* **(a)** official whose job is to say whether books *or* films *or* TV programmes, etc., are acceptable and can be published or shown to the public; *the film was cut or was banned or was passed by the censor* **(b)** official whose duty is to prevent the publishing of secret information *or* of information which may be harmful to the government; *all press reports have to be passed by the censor* **2** *verb* to say that a book *or* film *or* TV programme, etc. cannot be shown or published because it is not considered right to do so; *all press reports are censored by the government; the news of*

the riots was censored; the TV report has been censored and only parts of it can be shown

◊ **censorship** ['sensəʃɪp] *noun* act of censoring; *TV reporters complained of government censorship; the government has imposed strict press censorship or censorship of the press;* (NOTE: no plural)

censure ['senʃə] **1** *noun* criticism; **motion of censure** *or* **censure motion** = proposal from the Opposition to pass a vote to criticize the government; **vote of censure** *or* **censure vote** = vote which criticizes someone, especially a vote in parliament which criticizes the Government; *the meeting passed a vote of censure on the minister* **2** *verb* to criticize; *the Opposition put forward a motion to censure the Government; the Borough Architect was censured for failing to consult the engineers*

central ['sentrəl] *adjective* organized at one main point; **central office** = main office which controls all smaller offices; *the Conservative Central Office staff;* US **Central Intelligence Agency (CIA)** = the government intelligence agency in the USA, specializing in espionage; (NOTE: the British equivalents are MI5, MI6)

◊ **centralism** ['sentrəlɪzm] *noun* political system, where a country is ruled by a central government with no decentralization *or* devolution

◊ **centralization** [sentrəlaɪˈzeɪʃn] *noun* organization of all government activities from a central point

◊ **centralize** ['sentrəlaɪz] *verb* to organize from a central point; *the gathering of all personal records has been centralized in the headquarters of the Department of Health*

◊ **centre** *or US* **center** ['sentə] *noun* **(a)** group or parties whose political position is between right and left, such as the Liberals or Democrats; **left of centre** = tending towards socialism; **right of centre** = tending towards conservatism; *a left-of-centre political group; the Cabinet is formed mainly of right-of-centre supporters of the Prime Minister;* (NOTE: usually used with the: the centre combined with the right to defeat the motion) **(b)** **business centre** = part of a town where the main banks, shops and offices are (c) important town; *an industrial centre; the centre for the shoe industry* (d) office; **Job Centre** = government office which lists and helps to fill jobs which are vacant; **Law Centre** = local office with a staff of full-time lawyers who advise and represent clients free of charge; **Legal Aid Centre** = local office giving advice to clients with legal problems, giving advice on obtaining Legal Aid and recommending clients to solicitors

◊ **centrist** ['sentrɪst] **1** *adjective* in favour of the centre in politics; *the group advocates a return to centrist politics* **2** *noun* person who is in favour of the centre in politics; *compare* LEFTIST, RIGHTIST

ceremony ['serɪməni] *noun* official occasion (such as the State Opening of Parliament); *the mayor presided at the ceremony to open the new council offices; special police were present at ceremonies to mark the National Day*

◊ **ceremonial** [serɪ'məʊniəl] **1** *adjective* referring to a ceremony; *the mayor wore his ceremonial robes for the opening ceremony; the President rode in a ceremonial procession* **2** *noun* official ceremonies; *the book lays out the rules for court ceremonial; there is a lot of ceremonial attached to the job of Lord Mayor*

certain ['sɜːtn] *adjective* (a) sure; *the government is certain that large numbers of people are evading tax* (b) a **certain** = one particular; *a certain number or a certain quantity* = some

◊ **certainty** ['sɜːtənti] *noun* thing which is certain

certificate [sə'tɪfɪkət] *noun* official document which shows that something is true; **birth certificate** = document giving details of a person's date and place of birth; **clearance certificate** = document showing that goods have been passed by customs; **death certificate** = document giving details of a person who has died, including the cause of death; **fire certificate** = document from the municipal fire department to say that a building is properly protected against fire; **land certificate** = document which shows

who owns a piece of land, and whether there are any charges on it; **share certificate** = document proving that you own shares; **certificate of approval** = document showing that an item has been officially approved; **certificate of incorporation** = document showing that a company has been officially registered; **certificate of origin** = document showing where goods were made *or* produced; **certificate of registration** = document showing that an item has been registered

◊ **certificated** [sə'tɪfɪkeɪtɪd] *adjective* **certificated bankrupt** = bankrupt who has been discharged from bankruptcy with a certificate to show that he was not at fault

cession ['seʃn] *noun* giving up possession of a territory to another country; *the cession of the Philippines to the USA in 1898;* (NOTE: the verb is to cede)

CGT = CAPITAL GAINS TAX

chair ['tʃeə] **1** *noun* **(a)** piece of furniture for sitting on **(b)** position of the chairman, presiding over a meeting; *to be in the chair; she was voted into the chair; she is Chair of the Finance Committee; this can be done by Chair's action and confirmed later;* **Mr Jones took the chair** = Mr Jones presided over the meeting; **to address the chair** = in a meeting, to speak to the chairman and not directly to the rest of the people at the meeting; **to ask a question through the chair** = to ask someone a question directly, by speaking to him through the chairman; *may I ask the councillor through the chair why he did not declare his interest in the matter?* **2** *verb* to preside over a meeting; *the meeting was chaired by Mrs Smith*

◊ **chairman** ['tʃeəmən] *noun* **(a)** person who is in charge of a meeting; person who presides over meetings of a Committee of the House of Commons *or* of a local council; *chairman of the magistrates or of the bench; Mr Howard was chairman or acted as chairman;* **Mr Chairman** *or* **Madam Chairman** = way of speaking to the chairman; **Chairman of Ways and Means** = person elected at the beginning of Parliament to be the chairman of the Committee of the

Whole House, also acting as Deputy Speaker **(b)** person who presides over the board meetings of a company; *the chairman of the board or the company chairman*

◊ **chairmanship** ['tʃeəmənʃɪp] *noun* being a chairman; **the committee met under the chairmanship of Mr Jones** = Mr Jones chaired the meeting of the committee

◊ **chairperson** ['tʃeəpɜːsən] *noun* person who is in charge of a meeting

◊ **chairwoman** ['tʃeəwumən] *noun* woman who is in charge of a meeting; (NOTE: the word **chair** is now often used to mean the person, as it avoids making a distinction between men and women)

challenge ['tʃælɪndʒ] **1** *noun* act of objecting to a decision, and asking it to be set aside **2** *verb* **(a)** to ask someone to do something difficult, which he may not be able to do; *he challenged the Prime Minister to a debate on television* **(b)** to question the truth of something *or* to refuse to accept that something is true; *the Leader of the Opposition challenged the government's unemployment statistics* **(c)** to object to *or* to refuse to accept (a juror *or* evidence); *to challenge a sentence passed by magistrates by appeal to the Crown Court*

chamber ['tʃeɪmbə] *noun* **(a)** room where a committee *or* legislature meets; *the meeting will be held in the council chamber* **(b)** part of a parliament where a group of representatives meet; *the British Parliament is formed of two chambers - the House of Commons and the House of Lords;* **the Lower Chamber** = the lower part of a legislature, such as the British House of Commons or the American House of Representatives; **the Upper Chamber** = the upper part of a legislature, such as the British House of Lords or the American Senate; **Chamber of Deputies** = lower house of legislature in many countries, including Argentina, Bolivia, Belgium, Brazil, Chile, Croatia, Czech Republic, Djibouti, Dominican Republic, Greece, Italy, Luxembourg, Mexico, Paraguay, Spain; **Chamber of Representatives** = single body of the legislature in Morocco; *see also* STATE CHAMBER

◊ **Chamber of Commerce** ['tʃeɪmbə əv 'kɒmɜːs] *noun* **(a)** group of local businessmen who meet to discuss problems which they have in common, and to promote business in the town **(b)** official organization representing a country's business interests in another country; *the Spanish Chamber of Commerce in Britain; the British Chamber of Commerce in Spain*

chance [tʃɑːns] *noun* **(a)** being possible; possibility; *is there any chance of the Bill being passed before Parliament rises for the summer recess?* **(b)** opportunity to do something; *the Leader of the Opposition seized his chance and asked the Prime Minister to repeat the Minister's statement*

chancellery ['tʃɑːnsəlri] *noun* **(a)** position of chancellor **(b)** office attached to an embassy

Chancellor ['tʃɑːnsələ] *noun* **(a)** *(in the United Kingdom)* **Chancellor of the Duchy of Lancaster** = member of the British government with no specific responsibilities; **Chancellor of the Exchequer** = chief finance minister in the British government **(b)** head of the government (in Austria); **Federal Chancellor = head of the federal government in Germany** (NOTE: can be used as a title with names: **Chancellor Schmidt**)

◊ **the Lord Chancellor** [lɔːd 'tʃɑːnsələ] *noun* chief minister of justice in the UK

COMMENT: the Lord Chancellor is a member of the Cabinet; he presides over debates in the House of Lords; he is the head of the judicial system and advises on the appointment of judges

channel ['tʃænl] *noun* way in which information or goods are passed from one place to another; **to go through the official channels** = to deal with government officials (especially when making a request); **to open up new channels of communication** = to open new ways of communicating with someone

chaos ['keɪɒs] *noun* disorder *or* disorderly state; *after the coup the country was in chaos; chaos reigned in the centre of the* *town until the police and fire engines arrived*

◊ **chaotic** [keɪˈɒtɪk] *adjective* in a disorderly state; *the situation was chaotic until the police arrived to control the traffic*

chaplain [ˈtʃæplɪn] *noun* priest employed by someone *or* attached to a group; **the Speaker's Chaplain** = priest who reads prayers at the beginning of each sitting of the House of Commons

chapter [ˈtʃæptə] *noun* official term for an Act of Parliament

character [ˈkærəktə] *noun* general qualities of a person which make him different from others; **he is a man of good character** = he is an honest *or* hard-working *or* decent man; **to give someone a character reference** = to say that someone has good qualities

charge [tʃɑːdʒ] **1** *noun* **(a)** in **charge** = in control; **to be in charge of something** = to be responsible for something; *he is in charge of departmental recruitment; she was put in charge of the council reorganization; no one is in charge of council spending* **(b)** money which must be paid *or* price of a service; *to make no charge for delivery; to make a small charge for rental; there is no charge for service or no charge is made for service;* **admission charge** *or* **entry charge** = price to be paid before going into an exhibition, etc.; **scale of charges** = list showing various prices; **free of charge** = free *or* with no payment to be made **(c) charge on land** *or* **charge over property** = mortgage *or* liability on a property which has been used as security for a loan **(d)** official statement accusing someone of having committed a crime *or* of having done something wrong; *the minister tried to answer the Opposition charges of corruption; he appeared in court on a charge of embezzling or on an embezzlement charge; the clerk of the court read out the charges;* **charge sheet** = document listing the charges which a magistrate will hear *or* listing the charges against the accused together with details of the crime committed; **to answer charges** = to appear in court to plead guilty *or* not guilty to

a charge; **the charges against him were withdrawn** *or* **dropped** = the prosecution decided not to continue with the trial; **to press charges against someone** = to say formally that someone has committed a crime **2** *verb* **(a)** to ask someone to pay for services; to ask for money to be paid; *to charge £5 for delivery; how much does he charge?;* he **charges £6 an hour** = he asks to be paid £6 for an hour's work **(b)** to accuse someone formally of having committed a crime *or* of having done something wrong; *the Opposition charged the Minister with acting too slowly; he was charged with embezzling his clients' money;* (NOTE: you charge someone with a crime) **(c)** to give someone the job of doing something; *the committee is charged with the task of examining witnesses; the officials were charged with organizing the ballot*

◊ **chargeable** [ˈtʃɑːdʒəbl] *adjective* which can be charged

charisma [kəˈrɪzmə] *noun* special quality of a public person, showing charm *or* strength of character *or* attraction, that makes him favourably different from *or* better than other people

◊ **charismatic** [kærɪzˈmætɪk] *adjective* showing charisma; *the old leader has been replaced by a charismatic young politician from the north of the country*

chart [tʃɑːt] *noun* diagram showing information as a series of lines *or* blocks, etc.; **flow chart** = diagram showing the order of various work processes in a series; **organization chart** = diagram showing how the senior personnel in a company *or* an office are organized

charter [ˈtʃɑːtə] **1** *noun* **(a)** document from the Crown establishing a town *or* a corporation *or* a university *or* a company; **bank charter** = official government document allowing the establishment of a bank **(b)** official government document itemizing rights; **Citizens' Charter** = document which states what rights a citizen has; **patients' charter** = document stating what patients should get in the way of medical provision, such as treatment times, waiting times, etc. **(c)** hiring transport for a special purpose; **charter flight** = flight in an aircraft which has been hired for that purpose; **charter plane** = plane which has been chartered; **boat on charter to Mr Smith** = boat which Mr Smith has hired for a voyage **2** *verb* to hire for a special purpose; *to charter a plane or a boat or a bus*

◊ **chartered** ['tʃɑːtəd] *adjective* (company) which has been set up by royal charter, and not registered as a company

chauvinism ['ʃəʊvɪnɪzm] *noun (used as criticism)* feeling of excessive pride in one's country, and assuming that other countries are inferior

◊ **chauvinist** ['ʃəʊvɪnɪst] *noun* person who is excessively proud of his country; *compare* PATRIOT

check [tʃek] **1** *noun* **(a)** sudden stop; **to put a check on the sale of firearms** = to stop some firearms being sold **(b) check sample** = sample to be used to see if a consignment is acceptable **(c)** investigation *or* examination; *the auditors carried out checks on council spending; a routine check of the fire equipment* **2** *verb* **(a)** to stop *or* to delay; *to check the entry of contraband into the country* **(b)** to examine *or* to investigate; *to check that an invoice is correct; to check and sign for goods; he checked the computer printout against the invoices* = he examined the printout and the invoices to see if the figures were the same **(c)** *US* to mark with a sign to show that something is correct

◊ **checking** ['tʃekɪŋ] *noun* examination *or* investigation; *the inspectors found some defects during their checking of the building*

Chequers ['tʃekəz] *noun* official country house of the British Prime Minister

chief [tʃiːf] **1** *noun* traditional tribal leader in Africa; **House of Chiefs** = upper consultative council in Botswana **2** *adjective* most important; *he is the chief accountant of an industrial group; GB* **Lord Chief Justice** = chief judge of the Queen's Bench Division of the High Court who is also a member of the Court of Appeal; *US* **Chief Justice** =

main judge in a court; **Chief Constable** = person in charge of a police force; **Assistant Chief Constable** *or* **Deputy Chief Constable** = ranks in the police force below Chief Constable; **Chief Executive** = official permanent administrator of a town, who works under the instructions of the council; **Chief Minister** = head of government in a semi-autonomous region (as in an Indian state), equivalent to a Premier; **Chief Secretary to the Treasury** = British government minister, working under the Chancellor of the Exchequer, dealing especially with budgets and planning; **Chief Officer** = local civil servant who is head of a department in a local authority

> COMMENT: a local authority will have several Chief Officers: Chief Education Officer, Chief Housing Officer, Chief Planning Officer, and so on, all of whom are responsible to the Chief Executive. In some authorities they are called Director: Director of Education, Director of Finance, etc.

Chiltern Hundreds ['tʃɪltən 'hʌndrədz] *noun* former administrative division of the country west of London, in Buckinghamshire; **Stewardship of the Chiltern Hundreds** = nominal government position, which disqualifies a person from being a Member of Parliament; *(formal)* **to apply for the Stewardship of the Chiltern Hundreds** *or (informal)* **to apply for the Chiltern Hundreds** = to apply to resign from Parliament

> COMMENT: as MPs are not allowed to resign from Parliament, the only way in which they can do so is to apply for an office of profit under the crown, such as this or the Stewardship of the Manor of Northstead

Christian Democrat ['krɪstʃən 'deməkræt] *noun* name of a moderate Conservative political party in several European countries

Christmas Day ['krɪsməs 'deɪ] *noun* 25th December, one of the four quarter days when rent is payable

chronic ['krɒnɪk] *adjective* permanently bad; *the Opposition asked the Minister what steps were being taken to deal with the chronic unemployment in the north of the country*

chronological order [krɒnə'lɒdʒɪkl 'ɔːdə] *noun* arrangement of records (files, invoices, etc.) in order of their dates

CIA [siːaɪ'eɪ] = CENTRAL INTELLIGENCE AGENCY

circular ['sɜːkjʊlə] **1** *adjective* (letter) sent to many people; **circular letter of credit** = letter of credit sent to all branches of the bank which issues it **2** *noun* leaflet *or* letter sent to many people; *they sent out a circular offering a 10% discount*

◊ **circularize** ['sɜːkjʊləraɪz] *verb* to send a circular to; *the committee has agreed to circularize the members; they circularized all their customers with a new list of prices*

◊ **circulate** ['sɜːkjʊleɪt] *verb* to send round to a number of people; *they circulated a new list of prices to all their customers*

◊ **circulating** ['sɜːkjʊleɪtɪŋ] *adjective* which is moving about freely

◊ **circulation** [sɜːkjʊ'leɪʃn] *noun* **(a)** movement; *the company is trying to improve the circulation of information between departments;* **free circulation of goods** = movement of goods from one country to another without import quotas or other restrictions **(b)** **to put money into circulation** = to issue new notes to business and the public; *the amount of money in circulation increased more than had been expected* **(c)** *(of newspapers)* number of copies sold; **a circulation battle** = competition between two newspapers to try to sell more copies in the same market

circumstances ['sɜːkəmstənsɪz] *plural noun* situation as it is when something happens; *the Home Secretary described the circumstances leading to the riot in the prison*

CIS = COMMONWEALTH OF INDEPENDENT STATES

cite [saɪt] *verb* **(a)** to summon someone to appear in court; *he was cited to appear before the Select Committee on Defence* **(b)** to quote *or* to refer to something; *the judge cited several previous cases in his summing up*

◊ **citation** [saɪ'teɪʃn] *noun* **(a)** official request asking someone to appear in court; (NOTE: used mainly in the Scottish and US courts) **(b)** quotation of a legal case *or* authority *or* precedent; **citation clause** = clause in a Bill which gives the short title by which it should be known when it becomes an Act **(c)** words used in giving someone an award *or* honour, explaining why the award is being made

citizen ['sɪtɪzn] *noun* **(a)** person who lives in a city; *the citizens of Manchester* **(b)** person who has the nationality of a certain country; *he is a French citizen by birth;* **Citizens' Advice Bureau (CAB)** = office where people can go to get free advice on legal and administrative problems; **citizen's arrest** = arrest of an alleged criminal by an ordinary citizen without a warrant

◊ **citizenship** ['sɪtɪzənʃɪp] *noun* state of being a citizen of a country; *she has applied for British citizenship;* **European citizenship** = being a citizen of one of the EU countries; (NOTE: no plural)

city ['sɪti] *noun* **(a)** large town; *the largest cities in Europe are linked by hourly flights;* **capital city** = main town in a country, where the government and parliament are usually situated **(b)** **the City** = old centre of London, where banks and large companies have their main offices; the London financial centre; (NOTE: also called the **Square Mile**)

COMMENT: in Britain a city is a large town (usually with a cathedral) which has been given the status of a city by the Crown. Where a town has the same name as the country or state in which it is situated, it is sometimes given the title 'city' to distinguish it: Mexico City, Panama City, Quebec City, etc.

civic ['sɪvɪk] *adjective* referring to a city *or* the official business of running a city; *their civic pride showed in the beautiful gardens to be found everywhere in the city;* **civic**

centre = town hall *or* main offices of a city council; **civic dignitaries** = the mayor and other senior officials of a city *or* town; **civic reception** = official reception for someone, organized by the mayor and council of a city

civil ['sɪvl] *adjective* referring to the rights and duties of private persons *or* corporate bodies; **civil defence** = protecting the civilian population during a war or when attacked; **civil disobedience** = form of protest, where protesters refuse to obey certain laws; **civil law** = laws relating to people's rights and agreements between individuals (as opposed to criminal law); **civil liberties** = freedom to act within the law (liberty of the press, liberty of the individual, etc.); **civil marriage** = marriage without a religious ceremony (in many countries, the legal marriage, which has to be performed before the religious ceremony can take place); **civil rights** = rights and privileges of each individual person according to the law; **civil war** = situation in a country where the nation is divided into two or more sections which fight each other; (NOTE: the opposite is **criminal, military, ecclesiastical**)

◊ **civilian** [sɪ'vɪljən] **1** *adjective* referring to the ordinary citizen (as opposed to the armed forces); *civilian rule was restored after several years of military dictatorship; the military leaders called general elections and gave way to a democratically elected civilian government* **2** *noun* ordinary citizen who is not a member of the armed forces; *the head of the military junta has appointed several civilians to the Cabinet*

◊ **civil service** ['sɪvl 'sɜːvɪs] *noun* organization which administers a country; *he has a job in the civil service; you have to pass an examination to get a job in the civil service *or* to get a civil service job*

COMMENT: members of the armed forces, magistrates and judges are not part of the British civil service

◊ **civil servant** ['sɪvl 'sɜːvənt] *noun* person who works in the civil service

Civil and Public Services Association trade union representing civil servants; *see also* ASSOCIATION OF FIRST DIVISION CIVIL SERVANTS, PUBLIC SERVICES, TAX AND COMMERCE UNION

civilization [sɪvɪlaɪ'zeɪʃn] *noun* highly developed social system

claim [kleɪm] **1** *noun* **(a)** (i) assertion of a legal right; (ii) document used in the County Court to start a legal action **(b)** statement that something is a fact; *the insurgents refuted government claims that the town had been captured; the Leader of the Council was asked to comment on press claims that the auditors had found errors in his returns of expenses* **(c)** statement that someone has a right to property held by another person; **legal claim to something** = legal right to own something; statement that you think you own something legally; *he has no legal claim to the property *or* to the car* **(d)** asking for money; **benefit claim** = asking for benefit to be paid; **wage claim** = asking for an increase in wages; **the union put in a 6% wage claim** = the union asked for a 6% increase in wages for its members; *she put in a claim for £250,000 damages against the driver of the council van* **(e)** **insurance claim** = asking an insurance company to pay for damages *or* for loss; **no claims bonus** = reduction of premiums to be paid because no claims have been made against the insurance policy; **to put in *or* submit a claim** = to ask the insurance company officially to pay for damage *or* loss; **claim form** = form which has to be completed when making an insurance claim; *she put in a claim for repairs to the car; he filled in the claim form and sent it to the insurance company;* **to settle a claim** = to agree to pay what is asked for **(f)** **small claim** = claim for less than £500 in the County Court; **Small Claims Court** = court which deals with disputes over small amounts of money **2** *verb* **(a)** to ask for money; *the council claimed £100,000 damages against the builders; she claimed for repairs to the car against her insurance* **(b)** to say that you have a right to something; *the Leader of the Opposition claimed right of reply; he is claiming possession of the house; she can claim supplementary benefits* **(c)** to state that something is a fact;

the government claims that the treaty was never ratified; the party claims 100% success in the ballot; she claims that the shares are her property

◊ **claimant** ['kleɪmənt] *noun* person who claims, especially state benefits; *benefit claimants will be paid late because of the bank holiday; the government will consider the position of claimants of backdated pensions;* **rightful claimant** = person who has a legal claim to something

◊ **claim back** ['kleɪm 'bæk] *verb* to ask for money to be paid back

clarify ['klærɪfaɪ] *verb* to make something clear *or* easy to understand; *the Opposition asked the Minister to clarify his statement*

◊ **clarification** [klærɪfɪ'keɪʃn] *noun* making something clear *or* easy to understand; *the wording of the clause is ambiguous and needs clarification*

class [klɑːs] **1** *noun* **(a)** category *or* group into which things are classified according to quality *or* price *or* size, etc.; **first-class** = top quality *or* most expensive; **second-class** = less expensive, slower service, etc.; **second-class citizen** = citizen who has fewer rights and worse treatment than the majority of citizens; *US* **class action** *or* **class suit** = legal action brought on behalf of a group of people **(b)** **social class** = group of people who have a certain position in society; **upper class** = aristocracy and the richest and most influential business and professional people; **upper middle class** = wealthy professional people and businessmen; **middle class** = professional people and businessmen; **lower middle class** = small businessmen, shopkeepers, minor civil servants, etc.; **working class** = manual workers and people in low-paid jobs; **class war** *or* **class strife** = confrontation between different social classes **2** *verb* to put into a category *or* to classify; *the inspectors classed the food as unfit for sale; the magazine was classed as an obscene publication*

COMMENT: in the UK the population is classified into social classes for statistical purposes. These are: **Class**

A: higher managers, administrators and professionals; **Class B**: intermediate managers, administrators and professionals; **Class C1**: supervisors, clerical workers and junior managers; **Class C2**: skilled manual workers; **Class D**: semi-skilled or unskilled manual workers; **Class E**: pensioners, casual workers, long-term unemployed

◊ **class-conscious** ['klɑːs 'kɒnʃəs] *adjective* aware of distinctions of class

◊ **classless** ['klɑːsləs] *adjective* (society) which has no classes; *over the last twenty years the country has moved towards a classless society*

classify ['klæsɪfaɪ] *verb* **(a)** to put into classes *or* categories; **classified directory** = book which lists businesses grouped under various headings (such as computer shops, newsagents, hairdressers) **(b)** **classified information** = information which is secret and can be told only to certain people

◊ **classification** [klæsɪfɪ'keɪʃn] *noun* (i) way of putting into classes; (ii) making something secret; (NOTE: opposite is **declassify, declassification**)

clause [klɔːz] *noun* (i) section of a contract *or* of the constitution of a country or political party; (ii) part of a Bill being considered by Parliament, which becomes a section of an Act; *there are ten clauses in the contract; according to clause six, certain categories of business will be exempted from tax;* **Clause IV** = clause in the constitution of the British Labour Party which committed the party to support nationalization; **exclusion clause** = clause in an insurance policy *or* contract which says which items are not covered by the policy *or* gives details of circumstances where the insurance company will refuse to pay; **forfeit clause** = clause in a contract which says that goods *or* a deposit will be forfeited if the contract is not obeyed; **liability clause** = clause in the articles of association of a company which states that the liability of its members is limited; **penalty clause** = clause which lists the penalties which will be imposed if the terms of the contract are not fulfilled; **termination**

clause = clause which explains how and when a contract can be terminated

claw back ['klɔː 'bæk] *verb* (i) to take back money which has been allocated; (ii) *(of the Inland Revenue)* to take back money which was previously granted under another heading; *income tax claws back 25% of pensions paid out by the government; of the £1m allocated to the development of the system, the government clawed back £100,000 in taxes*

◊ **clawback** ['klɔːbæk] *noun* (i) money taken back; (ii) loss of tax relief previously granted

clean bill ['kliːn 'bɪl] *noun US* bill made up of the original text, with deletions made and amendments added during Committee, which is presented to the House of Representatives or Senate again as one whole new bill, so as to avoid having to discuss each amendment separately

clear ['klɪə] **1** *adjective* **(a)** easily understood; *he made it clear that he wanted the minister to resign; there was no clear evidence that the government motion would be acceptable* **(b) clear profit** = profit after all expenses have been paid; *we made $6,000 clear profit on the sale;* **to have a clear title to something** = to have a right to something with no limitations *or* charges **(c)** free *or* total period of time; **three clear days** = three whole working days; *allow three clear days for the cheque to be paid into your account* **2** *verb* **(a)** to make sure that something has been accepted *or* is not in contravention of an order; *has he cleared his visit with the Foreign Ministry? the letter was not cleared by the department head before it was sent* **(b) to clear goods through the customs** = to have all documentation passed by the customs so that goods can leave the country; **to clear a cheque** = to pass a cheque through the banking system, so that the money is transferred from the payer's account to another account; *the cheque took four days to clear or the bank took four days to clear the cheque* **(c)** to remove people from a place; *after the demonstration the chairman ordered the public gallery to be cleared* **(d) to clear someone of charges** = to find that

someone is not guilty of the charges against him; *he was cleared of all charges or he was cleared on all counts* **(e) to clear 10% or $5,000 on the deal** = to make 10% or $5,000 clear profit; *we cleared only our expenses* = the sales revenue paid only for the costs and expenses without making any profit

◊ **clearance** ['klɪərəns] *noun* act of clearing; **security clearance** = making sure that a person is acceptable for work under the Official Secrets Act; **customs clearance** = act of clearing goods through the customs; **clearance certificate** = document which shows that goods have been passed by customs; **clearance of land** = removing buildings *or* people from land; *the council said the land was due for clearance early next month so that the building of the new civic centre could start*

◊ **clearing** ['klɪərɪŋ] *noun* **(a)** clearing of a **cheque through the banks** = passing of a cheque through the banking system; **clearing of goods through the customs** = passing of goods through the customs **(b) clearing of a debt** = paying all of a debt

clemency ['klemənsi] *noun* mercy; *as an act of clemency, the president granted an amnesty to all political prisoners;* (NOTE: no plural)

clerical ['klerɪkl] *adjective* **(a)** (work) done in an office *or* done by a clerk; **clerical error** = mistake made in an office; **clerical staff** = staff of an office; **clerical work** = paperwork done in an office; **clerical worker** = person who works in an office **(b)** referring to the church

clerk [klɑːk *US* klɜːk] *noun* **(a)** person who works in an office; *accounts clerk; sales clerk; wages clerk;* **articled clerk** = trainee who is bound by a contract to work in a solicitor's office for some years to learn the law; **chief clerk** *or* **head clerk** = most important clerk; **(b) Town Clerk** = former term for the most important permanent official of the administration of a town, working under the instructions of the town council (the official is now usually referred to as the Chief Executive); **Clerk of the House (of Commons)** = head of the administrative staff which runs the House of Commons and advises the Speaker on points of procedure; **Clerk of the Parliaments** = head of the administrative staff in the House of Lords; *US* **Clerk of the House** = head of the administrative staff which runs the House of Representatives; *see also* SECRETARY OF THE SENATE **clerk to the justices** = official of a magistrates' court (a qualified lawyer) who advises the magistrates on legal questions; *the functions of a justices' clerk include giving advice about law, practice and procedure; the Clerk of the House advised the Speaker that the speech could be considered breach of Parliamentary privilege*

client ['klaɪənt] *noun* person who buys something *or* who uses a service; *the social worker has a close relationship with her clients; clients for the council's Home Help service are usually elderly;* **client country** *or* **client state** = country which depends on another country for such things as defence, trade, etc.

close 1 *noun* [kləʊz] end; *at the close of the debate, the government's majority was only six* **2** *adjective* [kləʊs] **close to** = very near *or* almost; *the treaty was close to being signed; we are close to bringing inflation down to single figures* **3** *verb* [kləʊz] **(a)** to stop doing business for the day; *the office closes at 5.30; we close early on Saturdays* **(b) to close the accounts** = to come to the end of an accounting period and make up the profit and loss account **(c) to close an account** = (i) to stop supplying a customer on credit; (ii) to take all the money out of a bank account and stop the account **(d) the shares closed at \$15** = at the end of the day's trading the price of the shares was \$15

◊ **closed** [kləʊzd] *adjective* **(a)** shut *or* not open *or* not doing business; *the office is closed on Mondays; all the banks are closed on the National Day* **(b)** restricted to a few people; **closed session** = meeting which is not open to the public or to journalists; *the town council met in closed session to discuss staff problems in the Education Department; the public gallery was cleared when the meeting went into closed session*

◊ **closing** ['kləʊzɪŋ] **1** *adjective* **(a)** final *or* coming at the end; **closing speeches** = final speeches for and against a motion in a debate *or* for prosecution and defence at the end of a trial **(b)** at the end of an accounting period **2** *noun* **(a)** shutting of a shop *or* being shut; **Sunday closing** = not opening a shop on Sundays; **closing time** = time when a shop or office stops work; **early closing day** = weekday (usually Wednesday or Thursday) when many shops close in the afternoon **(b) closing of an account** = act of stopping supply to a customer on credit

closure ['kləʊʒə] *noun* **(a)** act of closing **(b)** *(in the House of Commons)* ending of the debate (such as on a clause in a Bill); **closure motion** = proposal to end a debate

> COMMENT: when an MP wishes to end the debate on a motion, he says 'I move that the question be now put' and the Speaker immediately puts the motion to the vote

cloture ['kləʊtʃə] *noun US* motion to end a filibuster in the Senate, requiring sixteen senators to introduce it and a two-thirds majority to pass

Cmnd = COMMAND PAPERS (NOTE: Command Papers are numbered Cmnd 4546, etc.)

c/o = CARE OF

co- [kəʊ] *prefix* working *or* acting together; *his co-conspirators were jailed for life;* **cosponsor** = person who sponsors a bill with another

coalition [kəʊə'lɪʃn] *noun* group of two or more political parties who come together to form a government, when no single party has an absolute majority; *the coalition government fell when one of the parties withdrew support*

> the question of a coalition has arisen because all three parties are within seven points of each other in the polls and the chances are high that the next election will not give any party a majority
> *Toronto Globe & Mail*

> England does not love coali-
> tions
> *Benjamin Disraeli*

coat of arms ['kəʊt ʌv 'ɑːmz] *noun* distinctive decorative shield, usually with a motto, which is given to a noble family, important town, state, province, or country

code [kəʊd] **1** *noun* **(a)** official set of laws *or* regulations; **the Highway Code** = rules which govern the behaviour of people and vehicles using roads; **the penal code** = set of laws governing crime and its punishment; *failure to observe the code does not render anyone liable to proceedings* **(b)** set of laws of a country; *US* **the Louisiana Code** = laws of the state of Louisiana; **Code Napoleon** = civil laws of France (introduced by Napoleon) **(c)** set of semi-official rules; **code of conduct** = informal (sometimes written) rules by which a group of people work; **code of practice** = (i) rules to be followed when applying a law; (ii) rules drawn up by an association which the members must follow when doing business; *the Code of Practice on picketing has been issued by the Secretary of State; the institution has issued its members with a revised code of practice* **(d)** system of signs *or* numbers *or* letters which mean something; *the spy sent his message in code;* **area code** = numbers which indicate an area for telephoning; **machine-readable codes** = sets of signs or letters (such as bar codes *or* post codes) which can be read by computers; **post code** *or US* **zip code** = letters and numbers used to indicate a town *or* street in an address on an envelope **2** *verb* to write (a message) using secret signs; *we received coded instructions from our agent in New York*

◊ **coding** ['kəʊdɪŋ] *noun* act of putting a code on something; *the coding of invoices*

codify ['kəʊdɪfaɪ] *verb* to put (laws) together to form a code

◊ **codification** [kəʊdɪfɪ'keɪʃn] *noun* **(a)** putting all laws together into a formal legal code **(b)** bringing together all statutes and case law relating to a certain issue, to make a single Act of Parliament; *see also* CONSOLIDATION

coexist [kəʊɪg'zɪst] *verb* to exist together

◊ **coexistence** [kəʊɪg'zɪstəns] *noun* act of existing together; **peaceful coexistence** = situation where governments may be in complete disagreement, but exist together without threatening war

cohabitation [kəʊhæbɪ'teɪʃn] *noun* coexistence of different political parties in executive power (especially in France, where the President and Parliament are elected for different periods of time and so may represent different parties)

cold war ['kəʊld 'wɔː] *noun* period of hostility between Eastern and Western countries between 1945 and 1990

collaborate [kə'læbəreɪt] *verb* **(a)** to work together; *we are collaborating with a French firm on building a bridge; they collaborated on the new aircraft* **(b)** to work together with an enemy who is occupying your country

◊ **collaboration** [kəlæbə'reɪʃn] *noun* **(a)** working together; *their collaboration on the development of the computer system was very profitable* **(b)** working with an enemy

◊ **collaborator** [kə'læbəreɪtə] *noun* **(a)** person who works with another; *the head of the research department thanked all his collaborators for their help* **(b)** person who works with an enemy who is occupying his country; *after the war, several people were executed as collaborators*

collapse [kə'læps] **1** *noun* ruin; sudden ending; *the collapse of the former Soviet Union* **2** *verb* to come to an end suddenly; *the trading agreement between the countries has collapsed*

collect [kə'lekt] **1** *verb* **(a)** to make someone pay money which is owed; **to collect a debt** = to go and make someone pay a debt **(b)** to take goods away from a place; *we have to collect the stock from the warehouse; can you collect my letters from the typing pool?;* **letters are collected twice a day** = the post office workers take them from the letter box to the post office so that they can be sent off **2** *adverb & adjective US* (phone call) where the person receiving the call agrees to pay for it; *to make a collect call; he called his office collect*

◊ **collecting** [kə'lektɪŋ] *noun* **collecting agency** = agency which collects money owed to other companies for a commission

◊ **collection** [kə'lekʃən] *noun* **(a)** getting money together *or* making someone pay money which is owed; **debt collection** = collecting money which is owed; **debt collection agency** = company which collects debts for other companies for a commission; **bills for collection** = bills where payment is due **(b)** fetching of goods; *the stock is in the warehouse awaiting collection;* **collection charges** *or* **collection rates** = charge for collecting something; **to hand something in for collection** = to leave something for someone to come and collect **(c)** taking of letters from a letter box or mail room to the post office to be sent off; *there are six collections a day from the letter box*

◊ **collective** [kə'lektɪv] *adjective* working together; **collective leadership** = system of government where several leaders rule the country together, making decisions as a group, without one being in total charge; *see also* **JUNTA, TROIKA collective ownership** = ownership of a business by the workers who work in it; **collective responsibility** = doctrine that all members of a group (such as the British Cabinet) are responsible together for the actions of the group; **collective security** = security of a group of states together (such as the general security of member states in the UN, under the protection of the Security Council)

◊ **collectivity** [kəlek'tɪvɪti] *noun* community, group of people

◊ **collectivism** [kə'lektɪvɪzm *noun* any economic theory where the country's economy is centrally planned and the employers, trade unions and government all work together for the improvement of the economy

◊ **collector** [kə'lektə] *noun* person who makes people pay money which is owed; *collector of taxes or tax collector; debt collector*

college ['kɒlɪdʒ] *noun* **(a)** place where people can study after they have left school;

he is studying at the College of Further Education; **business college** *or* **commercial college** = college which teaches general business methods; **correspondence college** = college where the teaching is done by mail (sending work to the students who then return it to be marked); **secretarial college** = college which teaches shorthand, typing and word-processing **(b)** **electoral college** = group of people elected by larger groups to vote on their behalf in an election; *the President of the USA is elected by an electoral college*

◊ **collegiate** [kə'liːdʒiət] *adjective* referring to a college *or* to a group; **collegiate decisions** = decisions taken by a group of people collectively

colloquium [kə'ləʊkwiəm] *noun* conference or meeting; *a colloquium was held on the future of the EU*

collusion [kə'luːʒn] *noun* illicit co-operation between people *or* agreement between people to cheat another person *or* in order to defraud another person of a right; *he was suspected of (acting in) collusion with the leader of the council;* (NOTE: no plural)

◊ **collusive action** [kə'luːsɪv 'ækʃən] *noun* action which is taken in collusion with another person

colony ['kɒləni] *noun* **(a)** country or area ruled and settled by another country (usually one which is overseas); *Australia was originally a group of British colonies; the Romans established colonies in North Africa* **(b)** group of people from a certain foreign country, settled in a town, who form a separate social group; *there is a large German colony in London; the Japanese colony in Vancouver*

◊ **colonial** [kə'ləʊniəl] **1** *adjective* referring to a colony *or* colonies; *granting of independence ended a period of a hundred years of colonial rule; the colonial government was overthrown by a coup led by the local police force;* **colonial dependency** = colony *or* territory ruled and settled by another country; **colonial powers** = countries which rule colonies; **colonial status** = the legal status of being a colony **2** *noun* person living in a colony; person who was born in a colony

◊ **colonialism** [kə'ləuniəlızm] *noun* theory or practice of establishing colonies in other lands; *the meeting denounced colonialism, and demanded independence; see also* NEO-COLONIALISM

◊ **colonialist** [kə'ləuniəlıst] **1** *adjective* believing in colonialism; *they fought for their colonialist ideals* **2** *noun* person who believes in colonialism

◊ **colonist** ['kɒlənıst] *noun* person who goes abroad (or is sent abroad) to settle in a colony

◊ **colonize** ['kɒlənaɪz] *verb* to take possession of an area or country and rule it as a colony; *the government was accused of trying to colonize the Antarctic Region*

◊ **colonization** [kɒlənaɪ'zeɪʒn] *noun* act of taking a country and turning it into a colony

comity (of nations) ['kɒməti] *noun* custom whereby the courts of a territory acknowledge and apply the laws of another country in certain cases

command [kə'mɑːnd] **1** *noun* **(a)** order; **by Royal Command** = by order of the Queen *or* King; **Command Papers** = papers (such as White Papers *or* Green Papers *or* reports of Royal Commissions) which are presented to Parliament by the responsible government minister (so called because they are printed 'by Command of Her Majesty') **(b)** leadership; *he is in command of the armed forces* **2** *verb* to order someone to do something; *the chairman commanded that the public gallery should be cleared; the President commanded the Chief of Police to arrest the Members of Parliament;* **to command support** = to be good enough to have the support of voters; *the measure commands widespread support in the House; can the Minister command enough support to win the vote?*

commence [kə'mens] *verb* to begin; *in the House of Commons, the business of the day commences with prayers; the proceedings commenced with the swearing-in of witnesses; the committee has*

commenced the examination of the Bill, clause by clause

◊ **commencement** [kə'mensmənt] *noun* beginning; **date of commencement** = date when an Act of Parliament takes effect

comment ['kɒment] **1** *noun* remark *or* spoken *or* written opinion; *the Secretary of State made a comment on the progress of negotiations; the newspaper has some short comments about the Bill;* **fair comment** = remark which is honestly made on a matter of public interest and so is not defamatory **2** *verb* to remark *or* to express an opinion; *the Speaker commented on the lack of respect shown by MPs; the newspapers commented on the result of the vote*

◊ **commentary** ['kɒməntri] *noun* (i) textbook which comments on the law; (ii) brief notes which comment on the main points of a document

◊ **commentator** ['kɒmənteɪtə] *noun* person (journalist *or* broadcaster) who comments on current events; *a report by the political commentator in 'The Times' on unrest on the Government back benches*

commerce ['kɒmɜːs] *noun* business *or* buying and selling of goods and services; *see also* CHAMBER OF COMMERCE

◊ **commercial** [kə'mɜːʃl] **1** *adjective* **(a)** referring to business; **commercial attaché** = diplomat whose main concern is to encourage business between his country and the country where he is stationed; **commercial college** = college which teaches business studies; **commercial course** = course where business skills are studied; **commercial directory** = book which lists all the businesses and business people in a town; **commercial law** = laws regarding business **(b)** profitable; **not a commercial proposition** = not likely to make a profit

commission [kə'mɪʃn] *noun* **(a)** official order to someone, giving him authority and explaining what his duties are; **he has a commission in the armed forces** = he is an officer in the armed forces **(b)** payment (usually a percentage of turnover) made to an agent; *he has an agent's commission of 15% of sales* **(c)** group of people officially appointed to examine some problem; *the government has appointed a commission of inquiry to look into the problems of prison overcrowding; he is the chairman of the government commission on football violence;* **the European Commission** = main executive body of the EU, made up of twenty commissioners nominated by the member states; **Law Commission** = permanent committee which reviews English law and recommends changes to it; **Royal Commission** = group of people specially appointed by a minister to examine and report on a major problem

◊ **commissioner** [kə'mɪʃnə] *noun* **(a)** member of an official commission; person who has an official commission; **the Commissioners of Inland Revenue** = the Board of Inland Revenue; **commissioner for oaths** = solicitor appointed by the Lord Chancellor to administer affidavits which may be used in court **(b) the Parliamentary Commissioner for Administration** = the Ombudsman, the official who investigates complaints by the public against government departments; **the Health Service Commissioners** = the Health Service Ombudsmen, officials who investigate complaints from the public against the Health Service; **the Local Commissioners** = the Local Government Ombudsmen, officials who investigate complaints against local authorities; *see comment at* OMBUDSMAN **(c)** member of the European Commission

COMMENT: the European Commission is the executive body of the European Community; the twenty commissioners are nominated for a five year term by the member states (two each by France, Germany, Italy, Spain and the UK, and one each by the other member states); their appointments are ratified by the European Parliament. Each commissioner is responsible for a particular department

commit [kə'mɪt] *verb* **(a)** to send someone to prison; *he was committed for trial at the Crown Court* **(b)** to carry out a crime; *he was accused of committing perjury*

◊ **commitment** [kə'mɪtmənt] *noun* **(a)** order for sending someone to prison **(b)**

commitments = obligations *or* things which have to be done; **to honour one's commitments** = to do what one is obliged to do; **financial commitments** = money which is owed *or* debts which have to be paid

commitology [kɒmɪ'tɒlədʒi] *noun* EU system of appointing committees to deal with various areas of action

committed [kə'mɪtɪd] *adjective* **(a)** (person) who has strong political views; *she is a committed socialist* **(b)** (money) which has to be spent in a certain way; *half next year's budget is already committed; the government's subsidy has been committed to repairs to the Town Hall* **(c)** obliged to act in a certain way; *the council is committed to a policy of increasing services and reducing property taxes*

committee [kə'mɪti] *noun* **(a)** official group of people who organize or plan for a larger group; *to be a member of a committee or to sit on a committee; he was elected to the Finance Committee; the new plans have to be approved by the committee members; she is attending a committee meeting; he is the chairman of the Planning Committee; she is the secretary of the Housing Committee* to **chair a committee** = to be the chairman of a committee; **steering committee** = committee which works out the agenda for discussion by a main committee *or* conference (and so can influence the way the main committee *or* conference works) **(b)** section of a legislature which considers bills passed to it by the main chamber; *(in the House of Commons)* **Committee Stage** = one of the stages in the discussion of a Bill, where each clause is examined in detail; *the Bill is at Committee Stage and will not become law for several months;* **joint committee** = committee formed of equal numbers of members of the House of Commons and House of Lords; **select committee** = special committee of the House of Commons (with members representing various political parties) which examines the work of a ministry *or* which deals with a particular problem; *see note at* SELECT **standing committee** = permanent committee which deals with matters not given to other committees *or* parliamentary committee which examines Bills not sent to other committees; **Committee of the Whole House** *or US* **Committee of the Whole** = the House of Commons *or* House of Representatives acting as a committee to examine the clauses of a Bill; **the House went into Committee** = the House of Commons became a Committee of the Whole House; **Committee of the Parliamentary Commission** = committee which examines reports by the Ombudsman; **Committee of Privileges** = special committee of the House of Commons which examines cases of breach of privilege; **Committee of Selection** = committee which chooses the members of the other committees in the House of Commons; **Public Accounts Committee** = committee of the House of Commons which examines the spending of each ministry and department, and of the government as a whole **(c)** *(EU)* **Committee of the Regions** = European institution representing local and regional bodies; **Economic and Social Committee** = advisory body to the EU representing various sectors of economic and social life, such as employers, trade unions, consumers, farmers; **Committee of Permanent Representatives (COREPER)** = institution dealing with preparing for meetings of the Council and channelling information between member governments and the Council

common ['kɒmən] **1** *noun* **(a)** land on which anyone can walk, and may have the right to keep animals, pick wood, etc.; (NOTE: now usually used in place names such as Clapham Common) **(b) in common** = together; **to have something in common** = to share some qualities *or* characteristics; *social workers have a lot in common with teachers* **2** *adjective* **(a)** which happens very often; *forgetting to put the date on a cheque is a common mistake; being caught by the customs is very common these days* **(b)** referring to *or* belonging to several different people or to everyone; **the common good** = the interest of all members of society; *the government is working for the common good of the people;* **common land** = land on which anyone can walk and may have the right to keep animals, pick wood, etc.;

common ownership = ownership of a company *or* a property by a group of people who each own a part; **common pricing** = illegal fixing of prices by several businesses so that they all charge the same price; **common seal** = seal which a registered company must possess, and which is used to seal official papers

◊ **commoner** ['kɒmənə] *noun* ordinary citizen, who is not a member of a noble family

◊ **common law** ['kɒmən 'lɔː] *noun* **(a)** law as laid down in decisions of courts, rather than by statute **(b)** general system of laws which formerly were the only laws existing in England, and which in some cases have been superseded by statute; (NOTE: you say at common law when referring to something happening according to the principles of common law)

◊ **common-law** ['kɒmənlɔː] *adjective* according to the old unwritten system of law; **common-law marriage** = situation where two people live together as husband and wife without being married; **common-law wife** = woman who is living with a man as his wife, although they have not been legally married

◊ **Common Market** ['kɒmən 'mɑːkət] *see* EUROPEAN UNION, SINGLE MARKET

◊ **Commons** ['kɒmənz] *plural noun* = HOUSE OF COMMONS *the Commons voted against the Bill; the majority of the Commons are in favour of law reform; he was first elected to the Commons in 1979; the Bill was passed after an all-night Commons sitting*

Commonwealth ['kɒmənwelθ] *noun* **(a) the Commonwealth** = association of independent sovereign states which were once ruled by Britain; **the Old Commonwealth** = the oldest members of the Commonwealth (such as Canada, Australia and New Zealand); **the Commonwealth Secretariat** = office and officials based in London, organizing the links between the member states of the Commonwealth (the office is headed by the Commonwealth Secretary-General) **(b)** *(used in titles)* state where all people are equal; *the Commonwealth of Australia; the*

Commonwealth of Massachusetts (c) *(British history)* the period in the seventeenth century when Cromwell ruled as Lord Protector

◊ **Commonwealth of Independent States (CIS)** *noun* organization formed of the majority of the republics which formerly were part of the USSR

---

a constitutional amendment
that would acknowledge the commonwealth's right to override
the states on matters of economic development
The Age (Melbourne)

---

commune ['kɒmjuːn] *noun* (a) group of people who live and work together, and share their possessions (b) small administrative area in some countries (such as Switzerland or France), usually with its own mayor and council

◊ **communal** [kə'mjuːnəl] *adjective* shared by all the members of a group *or* community; *the offices share a communal kitchen; tenants have the right to use the communal gardens*

communicate [kə'mjuːnɪkeɪt] *verb* to pass information to someone; *the news was communicated to the press by the Prime Minister's Press Secretary; the members of the jury must not communicate with the witnesses*

◊ **communication** [kəmjuːnɪ'keɪʃn] *noun* (a) passing of information; **to enter into communication with someone** = to start discussing something with someone, usually in writing; *we have entered into communication with the relevant government department* (b) official message; *we have had a communication from the local tax inspector;* **privileged communication** = letter which could be libellous, but which is protected by privilege (such as a letter from a client to his lawyer) **(c) communications** = contacts *or* messages between people or organizations; *after the flood all communications with the outside world were broken*

communiqué [kə'mjuːnɪkeɪ] *noun* official announcement; *in a communiqué from the Presidential Palace, the government announced that the President would be going on a world tour*

Communism ['kɒmjʊnɪzm] *noun* (a) classless social system in which all property is owned and shared by society as a whole, with none belonging to individual citizens (b) political and economic system in countries governed by Communist parties

◊ **Communist** ['kɒmjʊnɪst] **1** *adjective* (person who) practises Communism; referring to *or* belonging to a Communist party; *Communist ideals were put into practice in Russia after the revolution* **2** *noun* member *or* supporter of a Communist Party; *Communists have three seats on the city council*

community [kə'mjuːnɪti] *noun* (a) group of people living or working in the same place; **the local business community** = the business people living and working in the area; **community association** = organization in which people from a local area meet socially and attends clubs, classes, etc.; **community charge** = local tax levied on members of the community (i.e. on each adult person living in the community); **community council** = council of a parish *or* group of parishes; **community home** = house which belongs to a local authority, where children in care can be kept; **community policing** = way of policing a section of a town, whereby the people in the area and the local police force act together to prevent crime and disorder; **community politics** = working politically in a community and dealing with individual problems (at local government level, as opposed to national level); *the party is strong in community politics;* **community service** = working on behalf of the local community; **community service order** = punishment by which a criminal is sentenced to do unpaid work in the local community (b) **the European (Economic) Community** = the Common Market; **Community legislation** = regulations *or* directives issued by the EU Council of Ministers *or* the EU Commission; **the Community ministers** = the ministers of member states of the European Union

company ['kʌmpəni] *noun* **(a)** business *or* group of people organized to buy, sell or provide a service **(b)** group of people organized to buy or sell or provide a service, which has been legally incorporated, and so is a legal entity separate from its individual members; **to put a company into liquidation** = to close a company by selling its assets to pay its creditors; **limited (liability) company** = company where a shareholder is responsible for repaying the company's debts only to the face value of the shares he owns; **private (limited) company** = company with a small number of shareholders, whose shares are not traded on the Stock Exchange; **public limited company (plc)** = company whose shares can be bought on the Stock Exchange **(c) insurance company** = company whose business is insurance; **a tractor** *or* **aircraft** *or* **chocolate company** = company which makes tractors *or* aircraft *or* chocolate **(d) company director** = person appointed by the shareholders to run a company; **company law** = laws which refer to the way companies may work; **company secretary** = person responsible for the company's legal and financial affairs; **the Companies Act** = Act of the British parliament which states the legal limits within which a company may do business; **Registrar of Companies** = official who keeps a record of all incorporated companies, the details of their directors and financial state; **register of companies** *or* **companies' register** = list of companies showing details of their directors and registered addresses; **Companies House** = office which keeps details of incorporated companies **(e)** organization in the City of London which does mainly charitable work, and is derived from one of the former trade associations; *the Drapers' Company; the Grocers' Company*

compare [kəm'peə] *verb* to look at several things to see how they differ; *the finance director compared the figures for the first and second quarters; the spokesman for the Opposition compared the promises in the Government's election manifesto and the legislation proposed by the Minister*

◊ **compare with** [kəm'peə 'wɪθ] *verb* to put two things together to see how they differ; *compared with that of some major cities, our crime rate is quite low*

◊ **comparable** ['kɒmprəbl] *adjective* which can be compared; **the two Bills are not comparable in importance** = one Bill is more important than the other; **which is the nearest county comparable to this one in size?** = which county is of a roughly similar size and can be compared with this one?

◊ **comparative** [kəm'pærətɪv] *adjective* which compares one thing with another

◊ **comparison** [kəm'pærɪsən] *noun* way of comparing; *expenditure is down in comparison with last year;* **there is no comparison between export and home sales** = export and home sales are so different they cannot be compared

compatriot [kəm'pætrɪət] *noun* person from the same country

compel [kəm'pel] *verb* to force (someone) to do something; *the Act compels all drivers to have adequate insurance; after the coup the President was compelled to leave the country;* (NOTE: **compelling - compelled**)

compensate ['kɒmpenseɪt] *verb* to pay for damage done; *to compensate a manager for loss of office*

◊ **compensation** [kɒmpen'seɪʃn] *noun* **(a)** payment made by someone to cover the cost of damage *or* hardship which he has been caused; *the council pay adequate compensation to owners of expropriated land; unlimited compensation may be awarded in the Crown Court;* **compensation for damage** = payment for damage done; **compensation for loss of office** = payment to a director who is asked to leave a company before his contract ends; **compensation for loss of earnings** = payment to someone who has stopped earning money *or* who is not able to earn money **(b)** *US* salary *or* payment made to someone for work which he has done; **compensation package** = salary, pension and other benefits offered with a job

◊ **compensatory** [kɒmpən'seɪtəri] *adjective* **compensatory damages** = damages which compensate for loss *or* harm suffered

competence ['kɒmpɪtəns] *noun* being competent in a job; *candidates will be asked to show competence in handling computers*

competent ['kɒmpɪtənt] *adjective* **(a)** able to do something; efficient; *she is a competent secretary or a competent manager* **(b)** legally able to do something; **the court is not competent to deal with this case** = the court is not legally able to deal with the case

competition [kɒmpə'tɪʃn] *noun* commercial rivalry between countries or organizations

complain [kəm'pleɪn] *verb* to say that something is no good *or* does not work properly; *the office is so cold the staff have started complaining; she complained about the service; they are complaining that the service is too slow; if you want to complain about the Housing Department, write to the manager*

◊ **complainant** [kəm'pleɪnənt] *noun* person who makes a complaint *or* who starts proceedings against someone

◊ **complaint** [kəm'pleɪnt] *noun* statement that you feel something is wrong; *when making a complaint, always quote the reference number; she sent her letter of complaint to the managing director;* **to make** *or* **lodge a complaint against someone** = to write and send an official complaint to someone's superior; **complaints procedure** = agreed way for workers to make complaints to the management about working conditions

complete [kəm'pliːt] **1** *adjective* whole *or* with nothing missing; *the application is complete and ready for sending to the Planning Department; the order should be delivered only if it is complete* **2** *verb* **(a)** to finish; *the committee completed the discussion of the bill in two weeks; how long will it take you to complete the job?* **(b)** to **complete a conveyance** = to convey a property to a purchaser, when the purchaser pays the purchase price and the vendor hands over the signed conveyance and the deeds of the property

◊ **completely** [kəm'pliːtli] *adverb* all *or* totally; *the cargo was completely ruined by*

water; the warehouse was completely destroyed by fire*

◊ **completion** [kəm'pliːʃn] *noun* act of finishing something; **completion date** = date when something will be finished; **completion of a conveyance** = last stage in the sale of a property when the solicitors for the two parties meet, when the purchaser pays and the vendor passes the conveyance and the deeds to the purchaser

complex ['kɒmpleks] **1** *adjective* with many different parts *or* difficult to understand; *a complex system of import controls; the regulations governing immigration are very complex* **2** *noun* collection of buildings which make a whole; *the council is planning to construct a new leisure complex or sports complex outside the town*

compliance [kəm'plaɪəns] *noun* agreement to do what is ordered; *the documents have been drawn up in compliance with the provisions of the Act;* **declaration of compliance** = declaration made by a person forming a limited company, that the requirements of the Companies' Act have been met

◊ **compliant** [kəm'plaɪənt] *adjective* which agrees with something; **not compliant with** = not in agreement with; *the settlement is not compliant with the earlier order of the court*

complicated ['kɒmplɪkeɪtɪd] *adjective* with many different parts *or* sections which make things difficult to understand; *the VAT rules are very complicated; the chairman warned the planning committee that the application was a complicated one and discussion might last several hours*

comply [kəm'plaɪ] *verb* **to comply with** = to obey; *the government has decided it will comply with the requirements of the EU Commission; she refused to comply with the social worker's instructions*

compromise ['kɒmprəmaɪz] **1** *noun* agreement between two sides, where each side gives way a little in order to reach a settlement; *management offered £5 an hour, the union asked for £9, and a compromise of*

£7.50 was reached; after some discussion a compromise solution was reached **2** *verb* **(a)** to reach an agreement by giving way a little; *he asked £15 for it, I offered £7 and we compromised on £10* **(b)** to involve someone in something which damages his reputation; *the minister was compromised in the bribery case*

these activists are used to making compromises with their political opponents
New Statesman

comptroller [kən'trəʊlə] *noun* person in charge of accounts; **Comptroller and Auditor-General** = official in charge of the National Audit Office, whose duty is to examine the accounts of ministries and government departments, and to advise the Public Accounts Committee

compulsory [kəm'pʌlsəri] *adjective* which is forced *or* ordered; which has to be done by everyone; *National Service is compulsory in some countries; in Australia, voting in general elections is compulsory;* **compulsory purchase** = buying of a property by the local council *or* the government even if the owner does not want to sell; **compulsory purchase order (CPO)** = official order from the local council *or* from the government ordering an owner to sell his property

computer [kəm'pjuːtə] *noun* electronic machine which calculates *or* stores information *or* processes information automatically; *the Department records are all on computer; the passport office checked the name on their computer; the registration number does not appear on any of the police computer systems*

◊ **computerize** [kəm'pjuːtəraɪz] *verb* to put (information) on to a computer; to process documents using a computer; *the benefit cheques are all computerized; we have computerized the information about council tenants*

comrade ['kɒmreɪd] *noun* **(a)** friend *or* companion; **comrade-in-arms** = person who has fought with someone (usually as a freedom fighter); (NOTE: plural is

comrades-in-arms) **(b)** fellow member of a socialist or communist party **(c)** form of address to a fellow-member of a socialist or communist party; *Comrades, we must fight to establish the right to union membership*

concede [kən'siːd] *verb* to admit (that someone is right); **to concede defeat** = to admit that you have lost; *counsel conceded that his client owed the money; the Minister conceded under questioning that he had not studied the papers; after two recounts the sitting MP had to concede defeat; see also* CONCESSION

concentration [kɒnsən'treɪʃn] *noun* **(a)** bringing resources together into one area; *a concentration of guerrillas in the mountains* **(b) concentration camp** = harsh camp for political prisoners

concern [kən'sɜːn] **1** *noun* **(a)** business *or* company; **his business is a going concern** = the company is working (and making a profit); **sold as a going concern** = sold as an actively trading company **(b)** state of being worried about a problem; *the management showed no concern at all for the workers' safety* **2** *verb* to deal with *or* to be connected with; *the House is not concerned with statements made in the foreign press; the report does not concern itself with the impartiality of the judge; he has been asked to give evidence to the commission of inquiry concerning the breakdown of law and order; the contract was drawn up with the agreement of all parties concerned* **concerned about something** = worried about something; *the doctors are very concerned about the shortage of trained staff*

concession [kən'seʃn] *noun* **(a)** agreement that someone is right *or* agreement to grant something which someone wants; *the government will make no concessions to terrorists; as a concession to the Opposition, the council leader agreed to hold an emergency meeting; the employers have made several concessions in the new wages deal* **(b)** admission of defeat; **concession speech** = speech made by a loser in an election, admitting that he has lost

conciliation [kənsɪlɪ'eɪʃn] *noun* bringing together the parties in a dispute so that the dispute can be settled; **the Conciliation Service** = ADVISORY, CONCILIATION AND ARBITRATION SERVICE

conclude [kən'kluːd] *verb* **(a)** to complete successfully; *a wage agreement was successfully concluded with the council staff; they concluded an electoral pact with the main Opposition party* **(b)** to believe from evidence; *the police concluded that the thief had got into the building through the main entrance*

◊ **conclusion** [kən'kluːʒn] *noun* **(a)** believing *or* deciding from evidence; *the government has come to the conclusion or has reached the conclusion that the Bill will never get past the House of Lords* **(b)** final completion; *the negotiations on the peace treaty have come to a satisfactory conclusion; the conclusion of the Defence Minister's address;* **in conclusion** = finally *or* at the end; *in conclusion, the chairman thanked the members of the committee for their long and patient service*

concordat [kɒn'kɔːdæt] *noun* agreement between the Vatican and a government, which allows the Roman Catholic Church certain rights and privileges

concurrent [kən'kʌrənt] *noun* taking place at the same time; *US* **concurrent resolution** = motion which shows how the House of Representatives feels about a problem

condemn [kən'dem] *verb* **(a)** to sentence someone to punishment; *he was condemned to prison for contempt of court* **(b)** to say that something should not have been done; *conference passed a resolution condemning the government's action; the council was asked to condemn the statement made by the leader*

condition [kən'dɪʃn] *noun* **(a)** term of a contract *or* duty which has to be carried out as part of a contract *or* something which has to be agreed before a contract becomes valid; **conditions of employment** *or* **conditions of service** = terms of a contract of employment;

conditions of sale = agreed ways in which a sale takes place (such as discounts *or* credit terms); **on condition that** = provided that; *they were granted the lease on condition that they paid the legal costs* **(b)** general state; *item sold in good condition; what was the condition of the car when it was sold?*

◊ **conditional** [kən'dɪʃənl] *adjective* provided that certain things take place *or* (agreement) which is dependent on something; **to give a conditional acceptance** = to accept, provided that certain things happen *or* certain terms apply; **the offer is conditional on the council's acceptance** = provided the council accepts; **he made a conditional offer** = he offered to buy, provided that certain terms applied

◊ **conditionally** [kə'dɪʃənli] *adverb* provided certain things take place; **to accept an offer conditionally** = to accept provided certain conditions are fulfilled

condominium [kɒndə'mɪniəm] *noun* **(a)** rule of a colony *or* protected territory by two or more countries together **(b)** *US* system of ownership, where a person owns an apartment in a building, together with a share of the land and common parts (stairs, roof, etc.)

conduct 1 ['kɒndʌkt] *noun* **(a)** way of behaving; *he was arrested for disorderly conduct in the street;* **code of conduct** = informal (sometimes written) rules by which a group of people work **(b)** (usually bad) way of behaving; *the Speaker criticized members for their conduct in the chamber; she divorced her husband because of his conduct;* **conduct conducive to a breach of the peace** = way of behaving (using rude or threatening language in speech or writing) which seems likely to cause a breach of the peace **2** [kən'dʌkt] *verb* to carry on; *to conduct discussions or negotiations; the chairman conducted the proceedings very efficiently*

confederation *or* confederacy

[kənfedə'reɪʃn *or* kən'fedərəsi] *noun* group of independent states *or* organizations working together for common aims; *a loose confederation of states in the area;* **the**

Confederation of British Industry (CBI) = organization representing employers in the UK; **Confédération Helvétique** = official name for Switzerland

> COMMENT: a confederation (as in Switzerland) is a less centralized form of government than a federation (such as Canada)

◊ **Confederacy** or **Confederate States** [kən'fedərəsi or kən'fedərət 'steɪts] *(American History)* group of eleven Southern states which seceded from the Union and fought the North in the American Civil War (1861 - 1865)

◊ **Confederate** [kən'fedərət] **1** *adjective* referring to the Confederacy of Southern states in the American Civil War; *the Confederate Army; the Confederate headquarters; the Confederate States* **2** *noun* supporter of the Confederacy in the American Civil War

confer [kən'fɜ:] *verb* **(a)** to give power or responsibility to someone; *the discretionary powers conferred on the tribunal by statute* **(b)** to discuss; *the Leader of the Council conferred with the Town Clerk*

conference ['kɒnfərəns] *noun* **(a)** meeting of a group of people to discuss something; *the Police Federation is holding its annual conference this week; the Labour Party Annual Conference was held in Brighton this year; he presented a motion to the conference; the conference passed a motion in favour of unilateral nuclear disarmament* **conference agenda** = business which is to be discussed at a conference; **conference papers** = copies of lectures given at a conference, printed and published after the conference has ended; **conference proceedings** = written report of what has been discussed at a conference; **news conference** or **press conference** = meeting where reporters from newspapers and TV are invited to ask a minister questions or to hear the result of a court case, etc.; (NOTE: in some political parties (such as the British Labour Party), the word **Conference** is used without the **to** indicate that it is not simply a meeting, but a decision-making body: **decisions of Conference** are binding on the Executive; **Conference passed a motion in support of trade unions**) **(b)** *US* meeting between representatives of the Senate and House of Representatives (called managers) to discuss differences of opinion over a bill

confidence ['kɒnfɪdəns] *noun* **(a)** feeling sure or being certain or having trust in (someone); *the junior ministers do not have much confidence in their Secretary of State; the majority group has total confidence in the leader of the council;* **confidence vote** or **vote of no confidence** = vote to show that a person or group is or is not trusted; *he proposed a vote of confidence in the government; the chairman resigned after the motion of no confidence was passed at the AGM; after the Commons passed a vote of no confidence in the government, the Prime Minister called a general election* **(b)** trusting someone with a secret; **breach of confidence** = betraying a secret which someone has told you; **in confidence** = in secret; *I will show you the report in confidence*

◊ **confident** ['kɒnfɪdənt] *adjective* certain or sure; *I am confident that unemployment will fall rapidly; are you confident the sales team is capable of handling this product?*

◊ **confidential** [kɒnfɪ'denʃl] *adjective* secret or not to be told or shown to other people; *he was dismissed for sending a confidential report to the newspaper; please mark the letter 'Private and Confidential'*

◊ **confidentiality** [kɒnfɪdenʃɪ'ælɪti] *noun* being secret; **he broke the confidentiality of the discussions** = he told someone about the secret discussions; (NOTE: no plural)

confirm [kən'fɜ:m] *verb* to say that something is certain or is correct; *the Court of Appeal has confirmed the judge's decision; his secretary phoned to confirm the hotel room or the ticket or the agreement or the booking; the appointment of the President's nominee for the Supreme Court has to be confirmed by the Senate* **to confirm someone in a job** = to say that someone is now permanently in the job

◊ **confirmation** [kɒnfə'meɪʃn] *noun* **(a)** being certain or making certain; *his* appointment to the Supreme Court needs confirmation by the Senate; **confirmation of a booking** = checking that a booking is certain **(b)** document which confirms something; *he received confirmation from the bank that the deeds had been deposited*

conflict 1 ['kɒnflɪkt] *noun* disagreement; fighting; *negotiations are taking place to try to end the conflict in the area;* **armed conflict** = war; **conflict of interest** = situation where a person may profit personally from decisions which he takes in his official capacity *or* may not be able to act properly because of some other person or matter with which he is connected; **Conflict of Laws** = section in a country's legal statutes which deals with disputes between that country's laws and those of another country **2** [kən'flɪkt] *verb* not to agree; *the report of the consultant conflicts with that of the council officers; the UK legislation conflicts with the directives of the EU*

conform [kən'fɔːm] *verb* to act in accordance with something; *the proposed Bill conforms to the recommendations of the Royal Commission*

◊ **conformity** [kən'fɔːmɪti] *noun* **in conformity with** = agreeing with *or* acting in accordance with; *he has acted in conformity with the regulations the government proceeded in conformity with the directives of the Commission*

confrontation [kɒnfrʌn'teɪʃn] *noun* meeting between two people *or* groups, usually in a situation where there is likely to be conflict; **confrontation politics** *or* **adversarial politics** = form of political activity, where opposing sides always attack each other and try to weaken each other's popular support, creating an atmosphere of violence; (NOTE: opposite is **consensus politics**)

Congress ['kɒŋgres] *noun* **(a)** elected federal legislative body in many countries, especially in the USA (formed of a lower and upper house, usually called the House of Representatives and the Senate); *the President is counting on a Democrat majority in Congress; he was first elected to*

Congress in 1975; at a joint session of Congress, the President called for support for his plan; (NOTE: often used without the except when referring to a particular legislature: **the US Congress met in emergency session; the Republicans had a majority in both houses of the 1995 Congress** similar to **Parliament** in the UK) **(b)** single body of legislature in Guatemala and Honduras; **Congress of Deputies** = lower house of legislature in Spain; *see also* NATIONAL CONGRESS, NATIONAL PEOPLE'S CONGRESS **(c) Congress Party** = largest political party in India

◊ **Congressional** [kən'greʃənəl] *adjective* referring to Congress; *a Congressional subcommittee;* **the Congressional Record** = printed record of proceedings in the House of Representatives and Senate, with verbatim text of the speeches made

◊ **Congressman** *or* **Congresswoman** ['kɒŋgresmən or 'kɒŋgreswumən] *noun* member of the US Congress; (NOTE: when used with a name, **Congressman Smith**, it refers to members of the House of Representatives)

conquer ['kɒŋkə] *verb* to defeat by force; *the victorious army is engaged in establishing the rule of law in the areas which it has conquered*

◊ **conqueror** ['kɒŋkərə] *noun* person who leads the invasion of a country; **William the Conqueror** = William I, the Duke of Normandy who led the invasion of England in 1066

◊ **conquest** ['kɒŋkwest] *noun* **(a)** act of capturing by force; **the Norman Conquest** = the taking of England by the Norman army under William I in 1066 **(b)** country which has been captured

conscience ['kɒnʃəns] *noun* feeling of guilt about a moral problem; **prisoner of conscience** = person who has been put in prison because of his or her beliefs

conscientious objector [kɒnʃɪ'enʃəs əb'dʒektə] *adjective* person who refuses to join the army when conscripted, because he feels that it is morally wrong

conscript 1 ['kɒnskrɪpt] *noun* person who has to join the services as part of a legal military service; **a conscript army** = army formed of conscripts **2** [kən'skrɪpt] *verb* to order someone to join the armed services

◊ **conscription** [kən'skrɪpʃn] *noun* legal obligation to join the armed services

consensus [kən'sensəs] *noun* general agreement; *there was a consensus between all parties as to the next steps to be taken; in the absence of a consensus, no decisions could be reached;* **consensus politics** = way of government, where the main political parties agree in general on policy; (NOTE: opposite is **adversarial politics, confrontation politics**)

◊ **consensual** [kən'sensjuəl] *adjective* which happens by agreement

consent [kən'sent] **1** *noun* (a) agreement; *the government rules by consent of the governed; planning consent must be obtained before you can extend the building;* US **Consent Calendar** = list of bills which are not controversial (b) **age of consent** = age at which someone can legally agree to have sexual intercourse **2** *verb* to agree; *the Speaker consented to an emergency debate*

conservation [kɒnsə'veɪʃn] *noun* keeping an area *or* building in its present state; *new building is not permitted in the centre of the village which is a conservation area; because of the trees and lake, the council decided to make the estate a conservation area*

conservative [kən'sɜːvətɪv] **1** *adjective* (a) in favour of established ideas and institutions, and against sudden change; *he became more conservative as he grew older* (b) careful and cautious; *the figures in the document are a conservative estimate* (c) **Conservative** = referring to the Conservative Party; *the Conservative government of 1979; the manifesto attacks Conservative policies* **2** *noun* (a) person who believes that society should not change *or* should change only very slowly (b) **a Conservative** = a supporter of the Conservative Party

◊ **Conservative Party** [kən'sɜːvətɪv 'pɑːti] *noun* political party which is in favour of only gradual change in society, and against state involvement in industry and welfare; *see also* TORY

◊ **conservatism** [kə'sɜːvətɪzm] *noun* the ideas and beliefs of Conservatives; (NOTE: to show the difference between the general meaning of the word, and the political meaning, you talk of 'conservative with a small c': **many elderly people, even socialists, are conservative with a small c**)

COMMENT: in most countries, the Conservative Party is one of the two main political parties, though it is not always called 'Conservative'; for instance, in many European countries the Christian Democrat Party is the conservative party

consider [kən'sɪdə] *verb* (a) to think seriously about something; **to consider the terms of a contract** = to examine and discuss whether the terms are acceptable; **the judge asked the jury to consider their verdict** = he asked the jury to discuss the evidence they had heard and decide if the accused was guilty or not (b) to believe; *he is considered to be one of the leading junior ministers; the librarian considers that fines should be increased*

◊ **consideration** [kənsɪdə'reɪʃn] *noun* (a) serious thought; *we are giving consideration to moving the head office to Glasgow;* **to take something into consideration** = to think about something when deciding what to do (b) the price (but not necessarily money) paid by one person in exchange for the other person promising to do something, an essential element in the formation of a contract; **for a small consideration** = for a small fee *or* payment

considerable [kən'sɪdrəbl] *adjective* quite large; *we sell considerable quantities of our products to Africa; they lost a considerable amount of money on the sale of the property*

◊ **considerably** [kən'sɪdrəbli] *adverb* quite a lot; *crime figures are considerably higher than they were last year*

consist of [kən'sɪst 'ɒv] *verb* to be formed of; *the education department consists of advisory and administrative sections, together with the inspectorate; a delegation consisting of all the heads of department concerned*

consistent [kə'sɪstənt] *adjective* which does not contradict *or* which agrees with; *the sentence is consistent with government policy on the treatment of young offenders*

consolidate [kən'sɒlɪdeɪt] *verb* **(a)** to make more solid *or* to make stronger; *three weeks after the coup the leaders had consolidated their power in the main cities* **(b)** to bring together into a single group; **Consolidated Fund** = fund of money formed of all taxes and other government revenues; **Consolidated Fund Bill** = bill in the House of Commons to allow money to be raised for government expenditure; *see also* EXCHEQUER **(c)** to bring several Acts of Parliament together into one act; **Consolidating Act** = Act of Parliament which brings together several previous Acts which relate to the same subject; *see also* CODIFICATION

◊ **consolidation** [kənsɒlɪ'deɪʃn] *noun* bringing together various Acts of Parliament which deal with one subject into one single Act

consort ['kɒnsɔːt] *noun* husband or wife of a ruling monarch; **the Prince Consort** = title given to Prince Albert, the husband of Queen Victoria

conspiracy [kən'spɪrəsi] *noun* secret agreement *or* plan to do something wrong; **conspiracy of silence** = secret agreement to say nothing about an affair

◊ **conspirator** [kən'spɪrətə] *noun* person who is part of a conspiracy; *after the Gunpowder Plot, the conspirators were rapidly arrested*

◊ **conspiratorial** [kənspɪrə'tɔːriəl] *adjective* as in a conspiracy; *he spoke in a conspiratorial whisper*

◊ **conspire** [kən'spaɪə] *verb* to take part in a conspiracy; *they conspired with other political groups to overthrow the government*

constituency [kən'stɪtjuənsi] *noun* **(a)** area of a country which is represented by a Member of Parliament; *he represents one of the northern constituencies; the UK is divided into 650 single-member constituencies;* **a good constituency MP** = an MP who looks after the interests of his constituents well; **constituency party** = branch of a national political party in a constituency **(b)** area of support; *the leader's natural constituency is the working class*

◊ **constituent** [kən'stɪtjuənt] *noun* person who lives in a constituency; *the MP had a mass of letters from his constituents complaining about aircraft noise*

constitute ['kɒnstɪtjuːt] *verb* to make *or* to form; *the documents constitute the government's main evidence to the subcommittee; this Act constitutes a major change in government policy; conduct tending to interfere with the course of justice constitutes contempt of court*

constitution [kɒnstɪ'tjuːʃn] *noun* **(a)** (usually written) laws under which a country is ruled, which give the people rights and duties, and which give the government powers and duties; *the freedom of the individual is guaranteed by the country's constitution; the new president asked the assembly to draft a new constitution* **(b)** written rules *or* regulations of a society *or* association *or* club; *under the society's constitution, the chairman is elected for a two-year period; payments to officers of the association are not allowed by the constitution*

◊ **constitutional** [kɒnstɪ'tjuʃənl] *adjective* **(a)** referring to a country's constitution; *censorship of the press is not constitutional;* **constitutional law** = laws under which a country is ruled *or* laws relating to government and its function; **constitutional lawyer** = lawyer who specializes in constitutional law *or* in drafting or interpreting constitutions; **constitutional right** = right which is guaranteed by a constitution **(b)** according to a constitution;

the re-election of the chairman for a second term is not constitutional; see also MONARCHY, UNCONSTITUTIONAL

> COMMENT: most countries have written constitutions, usually drafted by lawyers, which can be amended by an Act of the country's legislative body. The United States constitution was drawn up by Thomas Jefferson after the country became independent, and has numerous amendments (the first ten amendments being the Bill of Rights). Great Britain is unusual in that it has no written constitution, and relies on precedent and the body of laws passed over the years to act as a safeguard of the rights of the citizens and the legality of government

```
the Constitution guarantees a
very limited number of rights,
including free trade among the
states, no discrimination
against interstate residents,
etc.
```
The Age (Melbourne)

consul ['kɒnsəl] *noun* **(a)** person who represents a country in a foreign city, and helps his country's citizens and business interests there; *the British Consul in Seville; the French Consul in Manchester;* **honorary consul** = person who represents a country in a foreign city, but is not an employee of the country's government; *see also* VICE-CONSUL **(b)** *(in Roman government)* one of two magistrates, elected every year; **First Consul** = title originally taken by Napoleon, before he became Emperor

◊ **consular** ['kɒnsjʊlə] *adjective* referring to a consul; *the consular offices are open every weekday; he spends most of his time on consular duties;* **consular agent** = person with the duties of a consul in a small foreign town

◊ **consulate** ['kɒnsjʊlət] *noun* house *or* office of a consul; *there will be a party at the consulate on National Day*

◊ **consul-general** ['kɒnsəl'dʒenərəl] *noun* consul based in a large foreign city, who is responsible for other consuls in the area;

(NOTE: plural is **consuls-general** or **consul-generals**)

consult [kən'sʌlt] *verb* to ask an expert for advice; *the Prime Minister has consulted the Law Officers about the case; he consulted his MP about the letter; the Education Officer must consult parents about his plans to close the school*

◊ **consultancy** [kən'sʌltənsi] *noun* act of giving specialist advice; *a consultancy firm; he offers a consultancy service*

◊ **consultant** [kən'sʌltənt] *noun* specialist who gives advice; *engineering consultant; management consultant; tax consultant*

◊ **consultation** [kɒnsʌl'teɪʃn] *noun* act of asking for advice; *there must be full consultation with the union on this matter;* **consultation document** = paper which is issued by a government department to people who are asked to comment and make suggestions for improvement

◊ **consultative** [kən'sʌltətɪv] *adjective* being asked to give advice; *the report of a consultative body; he is acting in a consultative capacity;* **consultative document** = paper which is issued by a government department to people who are asked to comment and make suggestions for improvement

◊ **consulting** [kən'sʌltɪŋ] *adjective* referring to a person who gives specialist advice; *consulting engineer*

consumer [kən'sjuːmə] *noun* person *or* company which buys and uses goods and services; *gas consumers are protesting at the increase in prices; the factory is a heavy consumer of water;* **consumer council** = group representing the interests of consumers; **consumer credit** = provision of loans by banks *or* finance companies to help people buy goods; **consumer goods** = goods bought by the general public (and not by businesses to produce other goods); **consumer legislation** = laws which give rights to people who buy goods *or* who pay for services; **consumer protection** = protecting consumers from unfair *or* illegal business practices

◊ **consumerism** [kən'sjuːmərɪzm] *noun* movement for the protection of the rights of consumers

consumption [kən'sʌmpʃn] *noun* buying *or* using goods or services; *a car with low petrol consumption; the factory has a heavy consumption of coal*

contact ['kɒntækt] **1** *noun* **(a)** person you know *or* person you can ask for help or advice; *he has many contacts in the city; who is your contact in the Ministry?* **(b)** act of getting in touch with someone; **I have lost contact with them** = I do not communicate with them any longer; **he put me in contact with the relevant head of department** = he told me how to get in touch with the relevant head of department **2** *verb* to get in touch with someone *or* to communicate with someone; *he tried to contact his office by phone; can you contact the Borough Treasurer's office?*

contain [kən'teɪn] *verb* to hold something inside; *the contract contains some clauses which are open to misinterpretation; some of the clauses contained in the Bill are quite impossible to carry out*

contempt [kən'tempt] *noun* being rude *or* showing lack of respect to a court *or* Parliament; **contempt of Parliament** *or* **contempt of the House** = conduct which may bring the authority of Parliament into disrepute *or* which obstructs the work of Parliament; **to bring Parliament into contempt** = to do something which obstructs the work of Parliament *or* which shows lack of respect for Parliament; **to be in contempt** = to have shown disrespect to a court, especially by disobeying a court order; **contempt of court** = being rude to a court, as by bad behaviour in court, or by refusing to carry out a court order; **to purge one's contempt** = to apologize *or* to do something to show that you are sorry for the lack of respect shown

content ['kɒntent] *noun* the ideas inside a letter, etc.; **the content of the letter** = the real meaning of the letter

◊ **contents** ['kɒntents] *plural noun* things contained *or* what is inside something; *the contents of the bottle poured out onto the floor; the customs officials inspected the contents of the box;* **the contents of the letter** = the words written in the letter

contest 1 ['kɒntest] *noun* competition, especially in an election; *she won the leadership contest easily* **2** [kən'test] *verb* **(a)** to argue that a decision *or* a ruling is wrong; *I wish to contest the claim made by the Leader of the Opposition* **(b)** to fight (an election); *the seat is being contested by five candidates;* **contested takeover** = takeover where the directors of the company being bought do not recommend the bid and try to fight it

context ['kɒntekst] *noun* other words which surround a word or phrase; general situation in which something happens; *the words can only be understood in the context of the phrase in which they occur; the action of the police has to be seen in the context of the riots against the government;* **the words were quoted out of context** = the words were quoted without the rest of the surrounding text, so as to give them a different meaning; (NOTE: an example of words being quoted out of context might be: 'the Minister has said that the government might review the case', when what the Minister actually said was: 'it is true that under certain circumstances the government might review such a case, but the present situation is quite different')

continent ['kɒntɪnənt] *noun* **(a)** one of seven large masses of land which form the earth's surface (Asia, Africa, North America, South America, Europe, Antarctica); *see also* SUBCONTINENT **(b)** Europe, as opposed to the British Isles; *British exports to the continent have increased dramatically*

◊ **continental** [kɒntɪ'nentl] *adjective* **(a)** referring to a continent **(b) Continental Europe** = Europe, excluding the British Isles

contingency [kən'tɪndʒənsi] *noun* possible state of emergency when decisions will have to be taken quickly; **contingency fund** *or* **contingency reserve** = money set aside in case it is needed urgently;

contingency plan = plan which will be put into action if something happens

◇ **contingent** [kən'tındʒənt] *adjective* **contingent expenses** = expenses which will be incurred only if something happens; **contingent policy** = insurance policy which pays out only if something happens (as if the person named in the policy dies before the person due to benefit)

continue [kən'tınjuː] *verb* to go on doing something *or* to continue to do something which was being done earlier; *the new President has promised to continue the land reform begun by his predecessor; the council voted to continue the grant for a further two years*

◇ **continual** [kən'tınjuːəl] *adjective* which happens again and again

◇ **continually** [kən'tınjuuːli] *adverb* again and again; *rubbish is continually being dumped in the park*

◇ **continuation** [kəntınjuˈeıʃn] *noun* act of continuing

◇ **continuous** [kən'tınjuəs] *adjective* with no end *or* with no breaks; *the meeting was in continuous session for twenty-six hours;* **to be in continuous employment** = to work for a period of time (possibly for several different employers) with no time when you are not employed; **continuous feed** = device which feeds continuous stationery into a printer; **continuous stationery** = paper made as one long sheet, used in computer printers

◇ **continuously** [kən'tınjuəsli] *adverb* without stopping; *the meeting discussed the problem of budgets continuously for five hours*

contradict [kɒntrə'dıkt] *verb* not to agree with *or* to say exactly the opposite; *the statement contradicts the report in the newspapers; the witness before the committee contradicted himself several times*

◇ **contradiction** [kɒntrə'dıkʃn] *noun* statement which contradicts; *the witness' evidence was a mass of contradictions; there is a contradiction between the Minister's statement in the House of Commons and the reports published in the newspapers*

◇ **contradictory** [kɒntrə'dıktəri] *adjective* which does not agree; *a mass of contradictory evidence*

contrary ['kɒntrəri] *noun* opposite; **failing instructions to the contrary** = unless different instructions are given; **on the contrary** = quite the opposite; *counsel was not annoyed with the witness - on the contrary, he praised her*

contravene [kɒntrə'viːn] *verb* to break *or* to go against (rules, regulations); *the workshop has contravened the employment regulations; the fire department can close a restaurant if it contravenes the safety regulations*

◇ **contravention** [kɒntrə'venʃn] *noun* act of breaking a regulation; **in contravention of** = which contravenes; *the restaurant is in contravention of the safety regulations; the management of the cinema locked the fire exits in contravention of the fire regulations*

contribute [kən'trıbjuːt] *verb* **(a)** to give money *or* to add to money; *to contribute 10% of the profits; he contributed to the party funds* **(b) to contribute to** = to help something to happen; *the general agreement on both sides of the House contributed to the rapid passing of the bill; the public response to the request for information contributed to the capture of the terrorists*

◇ **contribution** [kɒntrı'bjuːʃn] *noun* money paid *or* service given to add to a sum; *the company has made substantial contributions to the party's funds; he has made a great contribution to the welfare of the elderly;* **employer's contribution** = money paid by an employer towards a worker's pension; **National Insurance contributions** = money paid each month by a worker and the company to the National Insurance; **pension contributions** = money paid by a company or worker into a pension fund

◇ **contributor** [kən'trıbjutə] *noun* person who contributes

◇ **contributory** [kən'trıbjutri] *adjective* referring to a contribution; **contributory pension plan** *or* **scheme** = pension plan where the employee has to contribute a percentage of salary; **contributory causes** = causes which help something to take place; **contributory factor** = something which contributes to a result

control [kən'trəʊl] **1** *noun* **(a)** power *or* being able to direct something; *the company is under the control of three shareholders; the Democrats gained control of the Senate; the rebels lost control of the radio station;* **to gain control of a council** = to have more than 50% of the seats on the council, so that you can direct the business of the council; **to lose control of a council** = to find that you have less than 50% of the seats on the council, and so are not longer able to direct it **(b)** restricting *or* checking something *or* making sure that something is kept in check; **under control** = kept in check; **out of control** = not kept in check; **exchange controls** = government restrictions on changing the local currency into foreign currency; *the government imposed exchange controls to stop the rush to buy dollars;* **price controls** = legal measures to prevent prices rising too fast; **rent controls** = government regulation of rents charged by landlords **(c) control systems** = systems used to check that a computer system is working correctly **2** *verb* **(a) to control a council** = to have a majority on a council and so direct its business; *Senate is controlled by the Conservatives, while the Socialists have a majority in the national Assembly* **(b)** to make sure that something is kept in check *or* is not allowed to develop; *the government is fighting to control inflation or to control the rise in the cost of living*

◊ **controlled** [kən'trəʊld] *adjective* ruled *or* kept in check; **government-controlled** = ruled by a government; **controlled economy** = economy where most business activity is directed by orders from the government

controversy [kən'trɒvəsi] *noun* violent argument about a problem; *there has been a lot of controversy about the government's tax proposals*

◊ **controversial** [kɒntrə'vɜːʃl] *adjective* which causes a lot of argument; *the council has decided to withdraw its controversial proposal to close the sports club; the bill was*

not controversial and was supported by members of both sides of the house

convene [kən'viːn] *verb* to ask people to come together; *to convene a meeting of a subcommittee*

◊ **convener** *or* **convenor** [kən'viːnə] *noun* person who convenes a meeting, especially a trade unionist who organizes union meetings

convenience [kən'viːniəns] *noun* **at your earliest convenience** = as soon as you find it possible; **ship sailing under a flag of convenience** = ship flying the flag of a country which may have no ships of its own but allows ships of other countries to be registered in its ports

◊ **convenient** [kən'viːnjənt] *adjective* suitable *or* handy; *a bank draft is a convenient way of sending money abroad; is 9.30 a.m. a convenient time for the meeting?*

convention [kən'venʃn] *noun* **(a)** general way in which something is usually done, though not enforced by law; *it is the convention for American lawyers to designate themselves 'Esquire'* **(b)** meeting, or series of meetings held to discuss and decide important matters; *the Democratic Party Convention to select the presidential candidate was held in Washington* **(c)** international treaty; *the Geneva Convention on Human Rights; the three countries are all signatories of the convention*

converge [kən'vɜːdʒ] *verb* to come together at a certain place

◊ **convergence** [kən'vɜːdʒəns] *noun* meeting at a certain point; **convergence criteria** = the economic criteria set out in the Maastricht treaty, which members of the EU have to satisfy in order to move to the single European currency

convict 1 ['kɒnvɪkt] *noun* criminal who has been sentenced to prison **2** [kən'vɪkt] *verb* to find (someone) guilty of a crime

conviction [kən'vɪkʃn] *noun* **(a)** being sure that something is true; *it is his conviction that the proposed legislation will result in the sale of council houses being* *delayed;* **conviction politics** = political policies based on firm beliefs, which a politician has by instinct **(b)** being found guilty; *he had three convictions for drunken driving*

convince [kən'vɪns] *verb* to make someone believe something is true; *the government minister tried to convince the strikers that their claims would be heard; the Finance Minister had difficulty in convincing Parliament that the budget deficit would be reduced*

convoy ['kɒnvɔɪ] *noun* group of ships *or* lorries travelling together under protection; *the UN has sent a convoy of medical supplies to the area*

convulsion [kən'vʌlʃn] *noun* political upheaval

cooperate [kəʊ'ɒpəreɪt] *verb* to work together; *the governments are cooperating in the fight against piracy; the two firms have cooperated on planning the computer system*

◊ **cooperation** [kəʊɒpə'reɪʃn] *noun* working together; *the work was completed ahead of schedule with the cooperation of the whole staff*

◊ **cooperative** [kəʊ'ɒprətɪv] **1** *adjective* willing to work together; *the staff have not been cooperative over the management's reorganization plan;* **cooperative society** = society where the customers and workers are partners and share the profits **2** *noun* business run by a group of workers who are the owners and who share the profits; *an industrial cooperative; to set up a workers' cooperative*

co-opt [kəʊ'ɒpt] *verb* **to co-opt someone onto a committee** = to ask someone to join a committee without having been elected; *she is a co-opted member of the education committee*

cope [kəʊp] *verb* to deal with; *the House is having difficulty in coping with the mass of legislation before it; the Chairman of the Finance Committee said that she doubted if the Borough Treasurer's office could cope with the extra workload*

co-principality [kəʊprɪnsɪ'pælɪti] *noun* state ruled by two princes

> COMMENT: the state of Andorra is a co-principality, its two princes being the Bishop of Urgel (in Spain) and the President of the French Republic

copy ['kɒpi] **1** *noun* **(a)** document which looks the same as another; **carbon copy** = copy made with carbon paper; **certified copy** = document which is certified as being exactly the same in content as the original; **file copy** = copy of a document which is filed in an office for reference **(b)** document; **fair copy** *or* **final copy** = document which is written or typed with no changes or mistakes; **hard copy** = printout of a text which is on a computer *or* printed copy of something which is on microfilm; **rough copy** = draft of a document which, it is expected, will have changes made to it before it is complete; **top copy** = first or top sheet of a document which is typed with carbon copies **(c)** a book *or* a newspaper; *have you kept yesterday's copy of 'The Times'? I read it in the office copy of 'Fortune'; where is my copy of the telephone directory? the library does not have a copy of Hansard* **2** *verb* to make a second document which is like the first; *he copied the company report at night and took it home*

◊ **copier** *or* **copying machine** ['kɒpjə or 'kɒpɪŋ mə'ʃiːn] *noun* machine which makes copies of documents

copyright ['kɒpɪraɪt] **1** *noun* legal right (now lasting for seventy years after the death of a person whose work has been published) which a writer *or* film maker *or* musician, etc., has in his own work, allowing him not to have it copied without the payment of royalties **Copyright Act** = Act of Parliament making copyright legal, and controlling the copying of copyright material; **work which is out of copyright** = work by a writer, etc., who has been dead for fifty years, and which anyone can publish; **work still in copyright** = work by a living writer, artist, etc., or by a person who has not been dead for fifty years; **infringement of copyright** *or* **copyright infringement** = act of illegally copying a work which is in copyright; **copyright notice**

= note in a book *or* film showing who owns the copyright and the date of ownership; **copyright owner** = person who owns the copyright in a work **2** *verb* to confirm the copyright of a written work by printing a copyright notice and publishing the work **3** *adjective* covered by the laws of copyright; *it is illegal to take copies of a copyright work*

◊ **copyrighted** ['kɒpɪraɪtɪd] *adjective* in copyright

cordiale [kɔːdiɑːl] *see* ENTENTE

COREPER = COMMITTEE OF PERMANENT REPRESENTATIVES

coronation [kɒrə'neɪʃn] *noun* official ceremony at which a king *or* queen *or* emperor is crowned

corporate ['kɔːpərət] *adjective* referring to a group *or* organization, especially to an incorporated company; **corporate state** = (i) large powerful state, which appears to work without human intervention; (ii) state where large organizations (such as trade unions *or* employers' organizations) run the country and elect members of parliament

◊ **corporation** [kɔːpə'reɪʃn] *noun* legal body (such as a town council) which has been incorporated; **the mayor and corporation** = the mayor and other councillors; **the corporation workmen** = the workmen employed by a town

◊ **corporatism** ['kɔːpərətɪzm] *noun* system of government where large powerful pressure groups (such as trade unions *or* institutions) influence the policies of the government

◊ **corporatist** ['kɔːpərətɪst] *adjective* referring to corporatism; *he holds corporatist views*

corps [kɔː] *see* DIPLOMATIC

corpus ['kɔːpəs] *noun* body (of laws); (NOTE: plural is **corpora**)

◊ **corpus legis** ['kɔːpəs 'ledʒɪs] *Latin phrase meaning* 'body of laws': books containing Roman civil law

correct [kə'rekt] **1** *adjective* accurate *or* right; *the chairman signed the minutes as a*

correct record of the previous meeting; the published accounts do not give a correct picture of the council's financial position; see also POLITICALLY CORRECT **2** *verb* to remove mistakes from something; *the secretary will have to correct all these typing errors before you send the contract; the minister had to make a statement correcting the information given at the press conference the previous day; US* **correcting the record** = recording a change of vote by a senator after the vote has been counted

◊ **correction** [kə'rekʃn] *noun* act of making something correct; change which makes something correct; *he made some corrections to the draft minutes*

correspond [kɒrɪ'spɒnd] *verb* **(a)** to **correspond with someone** = to write letters to someone **(b)** to **correspond with something** = to fit *or* to match something; *these figures do not correspond with those given by the consultant*

◊ **correspondence** [kɒrɪ'spɒndəns] *noun* letters which are exchanged; **business correspondence** = letters concerned with a business; **to be in correspondence with someone** = to write letters to someone and receive letters back; (NOTE: no plural)

◊ **correspondent** [kɒrɪ'spɒndənt] *noun* **(a)** person who writes letters **(b)** journalist who writes articles for a newspaper on specialist subjects; *a financial correspondent; 'The Times' legal correspondent; he is the Paris correspondent of the 'Telegraph';* **a court correspondent** = journalist who reports on the activities of a king *or* queen and the royal family; **a lobby correspondent** = journalist from a newspaper who is part of the lobby which gets private briefings from government ministers

corridors of power ['kɒrɪdɔːz əv 'pauə] *noun* the important offices of the civil service and government, where high-level decisions are discussed and taken

corrigendum [kɒrɪ'dʒendəm] *noun* correction *or* word which is to be corrected; (NOTE: plural is **corrigenda**)

corrupt [kə'rʌpt] **1** *adjective* not honest; **corrupt judge** = judge who takes bribes; **corrupt practices** = illegal practices involving bribes **2** *verb* to bribe someone (to make them act dishonestly)

◊ **corruption** [kə'rʌpʃn] *noun* dishonesty (on the part of officials); *magistrates are investigating corruption in the police force*

Cortes [kɔː'teɪz] *noun* legislature in Spain (equivalent to Parliament)

cosignatory [kəu'sɪgnətri] *noun* country which signs a treaty with another; *the three countries are all cosignatories to the international convention*

cosmopolitan [kɒzmə'pɒlɪtən] *adjective* **(a)** with inhabitants coming from various parts of the world; *London is a cosmopolitan city* **(b)** (person) who travels widely, who has interests in many different parts of the world

cosponsor [kəu'spɒnsə] *noun* person who sponsors something with someone else; *the three cosponsors of the bill*

cost of living ['kɒst əv 'lɪvɪŋ] *noun* money which has to be paid for basic needs, such as food, heating, rent etc.; *to allow for the cost of living in salaries;* **cost-of-living allowance** = special addition to normal salary to cover increases in the cost of living; **cost-of-living increase** = increase in salary to allow it to keep up with the increased cost of living; **cost-of-living index** = way of measuring the cost of living which is shown as a percentage increase on the figure for the previous year

◊ **cost-effective** ['kɒstɪ'fektɪv] *adjective* which gives good value *or* which gives a good result at little cost; *the new scheme was cost-effective as it reduced the number of man-hours worked*

council ['kaunsl] *noun* **(a)** official group chosen to run something *or* to advise on a problem; **consumer council** = group representing the interests of consumers; **Security Council** = permanent ruling body of the United Nations **(b) borough council** *or* **town council** *or* **county council** = representatives elected to run a town *or*

county; **council chamber** = room (in the Town Hall) where a local council meets; **council officers** = employees of a town *or* county council who are in charge of the main departments; **council estate** = area of houses and flats belonging to a council; **council flat** = flat belonging to a council; **council tax** = tax raised on each property, paid by the occupier of the property, and calculated according to the estimated value of the property; **council tenants** = people who live in council property and pay rent to the council **(c)** = PRIVY COUNCIL **Order in Council** = legislation made by the Queen in Council, which is allowed by an Act of Parliament and does not have to be ratified by Parliament **(d)** body of legislature in several states; *see also* LEGISLATIVE COUNCIL, NATIONAL COUNCIL, PEOPLE'S COUNCIL, STATE COUNCIL, SUPREME COUNCIL

◊ **councillor** ['kaunsələ] *noun* member of a council, especially member of a town council; **House of Councillors** = upper house of legislature in Japan; *see also* PRIVY COUNCILLOR

◊ **European Council** [jurə'pɪən 'kaunsɪl] *noun* group formed of the heads of state or of government of the member states of the EU, which meets at least twice a year under the chairmanship of the member state which holds the presidency, to discuss Union matters; the presidency of the council passes from country to country on a six-month basis

◊ **Council of Europe** ['kaunsl əv 'jurəp] *noun* oldest of the European political organizations, with its headquarters in Strasbourg

COMMENT: the Council of Europe was founded in 1949, and currently has 32 members. Its aim is to foster unity of action between European countries in educational, legal and other areas. It created the European Court of Human Rights in 1950

◊ **Council of Ministers** *or* **Council of the European Union** ['kaunsl əv 'mɪnɪstəz *or* əv ðə jurə'piːən 'junɪən] *noun* body made up of ministers of the member states of the EU

COMMENT: the central Council is formed of the Foreign Ministers of the member states, but in fact the membership of the Council of Ministers varies with the subject being discussed; if it is a question of agricultural policy, then the Ministers of Agriculture of each country form the Council under the chairmanship of the minister whose country then holds the presidency of the EU

counsel ['kaʊnsl] **1** *noun* barrister *or* lawyer acting for a party in a case; *in certain cases, people appearing before parliamentary committees may be accompanied by counsel;* **parliamentary counsel** = lawyer responsible for drafting bills going before Parliament **2** *verb* to give advice *or* help; *the job of the student welfare officer is to counsel students on all kinds of problems*

◊ **counselling** ['kaʊnsəlɪŋ] *noun* giving advice *or* help; *students who need counselling should talk to their class teachers; the social services department runs a counselling service for unemployed families*

◊ **counsellor** ['kaʊnsələ] *noun* **(a)** one of the ranks in the diplomatic corps, below Minister **(b)** trained person who gives advice *or* help; *they went to see a marriage guidance counsellor* **(c)** US lawyer who advises a person in a case

count [kaʊnt] **1** *noun* **(a)** act of counting how many items there are; *the count of votes after an election; the count started at ten o'clock and finished just after midnight; see also* RECOUNT **(b)** *(in the House of Commons)* act of counting how many MPs are present (if there are fewer than 40, the sitting is adjourned) **(c)** separate charge against an accused person read out in court in the indictment; *he was found guilty on all four counts* **(d)** noble title, used in European nobility, but not in England; (NOTE: the title is used in French (comte), Spanish (Conde), Italian (Conte), German (Graf), and other countries) **2** *verb* **(a)** to add figures together to make a total; *he counted up the sales for the six months to December* **(b)** to include; *did the*

defence count the accused's theft of money from the till as part of the total theft?

◊ **count on** ['kaʊnt 'ɒn] *verb* **(a)** to expect something to happen; *the government seems to be counting on winning the votes of the floating voters* **(b)** to rely on someone *or* something; *you can count on Mr Jones, he is an excellent committee chairman*

counter ['kaʊntə] **1** *noun* **(a)** long flat surface in a shop for displaying and selling goods; **goods sold over the counter** = retail sales of goods in shops **(b)** something which opposes; *the legislation is seen as a counter to the increasing power of local government* **2** *adverb* **counter to** = against *or* opposite; *the decision of the Commons runs counter to the advice of the Law Officers*

counter- ['kaʊntə] *prefix* against; *counter-insurgency forces*

◊ **counter-demonstration** [kaʊntədemən'streɪʃn] *noun* opposing demonstration in reply to a demonstration

◊ **counter-espionage** *or* **counter-intelligence** ['kaʊnɔespjənɑːʒ or 'kaʊntəɪn'telɪdʒəns] *noun* organization of secret agents whose job is to work against the secret agents of another country; *the offices were bugged by counter-intelligence agents*

◊ **countermand** ['kaʊntəmɑːnd] *verb* to **countermand an order** = to say that an order must not be carried out; *the Chief Officer had to countermand the order given by his assistant*

◊ **counterpart** ['kaʊntəpɑːt] *noun* person who has a similar job *or* is in a similar situation; *the British Minister of Defence wrote to his Spanish counterpart*

◊ **counter-productive** [kaʊntəprə'dʌktɪv] *adjective* which produces the opposite results; *imprisoning the terrorist leaders may be counter-productive; attacking the council on the question of services may prove counter-productive since most of the voters are happy with the services provided*

counter-revolution [kaʊntərevə'luːʃn] *noun* revolt against a revolution

◊ **counter-revolutionary**

[kaʊntərevə'luːʃnri] **1** *adjective* against a revolution **2** *noun* person in revolt against a revolution

countersign ['kaʊntəsaɪn] *verb* to sign a document which has already been signed by someone else; *the payment has to be countersigned by the mortgagor*

countess [kaʊn'tes] *noun* **(a)** *(in European aristocracy)* wife of a count **(b)** *(in the British aristocracy)* wife of an earl

country ['kʌntri] *noun* **(a)** land which is an entity and governs itself; *the contract covers sales in the countries of the European Union; some African countries export oil;* country of origin = country where the goods have been produced or made; to go to the country = to call a general election; *the Prime Minister has decided to go to the country* **(b)** the country *or* the country areas = regions outside large towns; *he has a flat in town and a house in the country;* Country Party = political party which represents the interests of farmers

county ['kaʊnti] *noun* one of the administrative divisions of a country; *it is illegal to transport cattle across the county boundary; the police forces of several counties are cooperating in the search for the missing girl;* county council = group of people elected to run a county; county town = main administrative centre in a county, where the county council offices are situated

COMMENT: rural areas in many countries (such as Britain, New Zealand) and sections of federal states (such as the Provinces of Canada and the States in the USA) are divided into counties. Most counties in Britain are shires (Berkshire, Staffordshire, etc.). Otherwise, the word is used as a title, before the name in Britain (the County of Durham) and after the name in the USA (Marlboro County)

coup (d'état) ['kuː (deɪ'taː)] *noun* rapid change of government which removes one government by force and replaces it by another; *after the coup, groups of students attacked the police stations*

COMMENT: a coup is usually carried out by a small number of people, who already have some power (such as army officers), while a revolution is a general uprising of a large number of ordinary people. A coup changes the members of a government, but a revolution changes the whole social system

course [kɔːs] *noun* **(a)** in the course of = during *or* while something is happening; *in the course of the hearing, several new allegations were made by the witness* **(b)** series of lessons; *he is taking a management course; she has finished her secretarial course; the company has paid for her to attend a course for trainee sales managers* **(c)** course of action = action which has been taken *or* which can be taken; *what is the best course of action the ratepayers should take?;* in the course of employment = done as part of the work of the person concerned **(d)** of course = naturally; *of course the company is interested in profits; are you willing to go on a sales trip to Australia? - of course!*

court [kɔːt] *noun* **(a)** place where a king *or* queen *or* emperor lives and rules from; *the head of the army has a lot of influence at court; at the court of the French King, visitors were allowed to watch the royal family eat;* the Court of St. James = the official residence of the British royal court; *he presented his credentials as Ambassador to the Court of St. James* **(b)** a king *or* queen *or* emperor and their officials and servants; *when war broke out, the court was moved to the north of the country; members of the court plotted to remove the king and replace him with his brother;* court correspondent = journalists who reports on the activities of a king *or* queen and the royal family **(c)** court of law *or* law court = place where a trial is held; *the law courts are in the centre of the town; she works in the law courts as an usher;* to take someone to court = to start legal proceedings against someone; in court = present during a trial; *the defendant was in court for three hours;* in open court = in a courtroom with members of the public present; **a settlement was reached out of court** or **the two parties reached an out-of-court settlement** = the dispute was settled between the two parties privately without continuing the court case; **contempt of court** = being rude to a court, as by bad behaviour in the courtroom or by refusing to carry out a court order; **court order** = legal order made by a court of law, telling someone to do or not to do something; *the court made an order for maintenance or made a maintenance order; he refused to obey the court order and was sent to prison for contempt; the council sought a court order to compel Mr Smith to pay his rates;* **Criminal Court** or **Civil Court** = court where criminal or civil cases are heard; **Court of Appeal** or **Appeal Court** = civil or criminal court to which a person may go to ask for an award or a sentence to be changed; **High Court (of Justice)** = main civil court in England and Wales; **International Court of Justice** = the court of the United Nations, which sits in The Hague, Netherlands; **magistrates' court** = court presided over by magistrates; **Supreme Court (of Judicature)** = (i) highest court in England and Wales (except for the House of Lords), formed of the High Court and the Court of Appeal; (ii) highest federal court in the USA; *(in Scotland)* **Court of Session** = highest civil court in Scotland **(d)** the judges or magistrates in a court; *the court will retire for thirty minutes*

covert ['kəʊvət] *adjective* hidden or secret; **covert action** = action which is secret (such as spying)

CP = COMMUNIST PARTY (NOTE: in other languages, it is often written **PC**: so **PCF** (Parti Communiste Français); **PCI** (Partito Comunista Italiano)

CPO = COMPULSORY PURCHASE ORDER

CPS = CROWN PROSECUTION SERVICE

CPSA = CIVIL AND PUBLIC SERVICES ASSOCIATION

crack down on ['kræk 'daʊn ɒn] *verb (informal)* to use severe measures against something; *the government is cracking down on teenage crime*

create [krɪ'eɪt] *verb* to make something new; *the Prime Minister has created six new life peers; by acquiring small unprofitable companies he soon created a large trading group; the government scheme aims at creating new jobs for young people*

◊ **creation** [krɪ'eɪʃn] *noun* making something new; *the press has criticized the creation of several new life peers;* **job creation scheme** = government-backed scheme to encourage new work for the unemployed

credentials or letters of credence

[krɪ'denʃəlz or 'letəz əv 'kriːdəns] *noun* official documents, proving that an ambassador has really been appointed legally; *(of an ambassador)* **to present his credentials** or **to present his letters of credence** = to visit for the first time the head of the state of the country where he is ambassador, to hand over documents showing that he has been legally appointed

crisis ['kraɪsɪs] *noun* serious state of affairs, when something has to be done; *the President tried to solve the political crisis after the government was defeated in the Assembly; the leader of the council tried to say that the city was not facing a financial crisis;* **crisis measures** = actions taken because of a state of crisis; *we shall have to take crisis measures to deal with the unemployment situation;* (NOTE: plural is **crises** ['kraɪsiːz])

criterion [kraɪ'tɪərɪən] *noun* standard by which something can be judged; *using the criterion of the ratio of cases solved to cases reported, the police force is becoming more efficient;* (NOTE: plural is **criteria**)

critical ['krɪtɪkəl] *adjective* **(a)** which criticizes; *he was critical of the council's action; they issued a report critical of government policy* **(b)** very serious; *the staffing situation is critical*

criticize ['krɪtɪsaɪz] *verb* to say that something *or* someone is wrong *or* is working badly, etc.; *the Opposition criticized the government for the way in which it had handled the financial crisis*

◊ **criticism** ['krɪtɪsɪzm] *noun* words showing that you consider that someone *or* something is wrong; *the leader objected to criticism of his policies; she replied to criticisms of her statement in the press or to press criticism of her statement; the judge made some criticism of the way the application had been presented*

cross [krɒs] *verb* **(a)** to go across; *Concorde takes only three hours to cross the Atlantic; to get to the bank, you turn left and cross the street at the post office; (of a sitting MP)* **to cross the floor (of the House)** = to change political party **(b) to cross a cheque** = to write two lines across a cheque to show that it has to be paid into a bank; **crossed cheque** = cheque with two lines across it to show that it can only be deposited at a bank and not exchanged for cash

◊ **cross benches** ['krɒs 'bentʃɪz] *noun* seats in the House of Commons or House of Lords (some of them running across the chamber) where Lords or MPs sit if they are not members of a political party

◊ **crossbencher** ['krɒs'bentʃə] *noun* MP who is a not a member of one the main political parties *or* who is sitting as an independent *or* who has resigned the party whip

◊ **cross off** ['krɒs 'ɒf] *verb* to remove something from a list; *he crossed my name off his list; you can cross him off our mailing list*

◊ **cross out** ['krɒs 'aut] *verb* to put a line through something which has been written; *she crossed out £250 and put in £500*

cross-examine [krɒsɪg'zæmɪn] *verb* to question witnesses thoroughly, in the hope that you can destroy their evidence; *the Select Committee cross-examined the junior minister*

◊ **cross-examination**
[krɒsɪgzæmɪ'neɪʃn] *noun* questioning of witnesses

crown [kraun] **1** *noun GB* **(a)** ceremonial headdress worn by a king *or* queen *or* emperor **(b) the Crown** = the King *or* Queen as representing the State; *Mr Smith is appearing for the Crown; the Crown submitted that the maximum sentence should be applied in this case; the Crown case or the case for the Crown was that the defendants were guilty of espionage;* (NOTE: in legal reports, the Crown is referred to as Rex *or* Regina (abbreviated to R.) depending on whether there is a King or Queen reigning at the time: **the case of R .v Smith Ltd.) (c)** associate of the Crown Office = official who is responsible for the clerical and administrative work of a court; **Crown Lands** *or* **Crown property** = land *or* property belonging to the King *or* Queen; **Crown copyright** = copyright in government publications **2** *verb* to put a crown on the head of a king *or* queen *or* emperor to confirm that they are legally and according to custom the head of state; *British kings and queens are crowned in Westminster Abbey; see also* CORONATION

◊ **Crown Court** ['kraun 'kɔːt] *noun* court, above the level of the magistrates' courts, which has centres all over England and Wales and which hears criminal cases

> COMMENT: a Crown Court is formed of a circuit judge and jury, and hears major criminal cases

◊ **Crown Prince** ['kraun 'prɪns] *noun* eldest son of a king, who will inherit the throne

◊ **Crown privilege** ['kraun 'prɪvɪlɪdʒ] *noun* right of the Crown *or* the government not to have to produce documents to a court by reason of the interest of the state

◊ **Crown Prosecution Service (CPS)** ['kraun prɒsɪ'kjuːʃn 'sɜːvɪs] *noun* the office of the Director of Public Prosecutions, whose job is to supervise the prosecution of criminals

◊ **Crown prosecutor** ['kraun 'prɒsɪkjuːtə] *noun* official of the Director of Public Prosecution's department who is responsible for prosecuting criminals in a local area

crusade [kruːˈseɪd] **1** *noun* strong action to stop *or* change something; *the government has launched a crusade against drugs* **2** *verb* to take part in a crusade; *he has been crusading for more government action to reduce unemployment*

◊ **Crusades** [kruːˈseɪdz] *noun (historical)* series of expeditions organized by European Christian powers between the 11th and 13th centuries to try to retake the Holy Land which had been captured by Moslem forces

◊ **crusader** [kruːˈseɪdə] *noun* person who takes part in a crusade; *he was a famous crusader for women's right to vote*

crypto- [ˈkrɪptəʊ] *prefix* meaning hidden; **cryptocommunist** = secret communist

◊ **cryptographer** [krɪpˈtɒgrəfə] *noun* person who tries to break a secret code

◊ **cryptography** [krɪpˈtɒgrəfi] *noun* study of codes

culture [ˈkʌltʃə] *noun* a country's civilisation, including art, music, literature, etc.; **culture shock** = shock caused by moving from one type of society to another (as from an Eastern society to a European one)

◊ **cultural** [ˈkʌltʃərəl] *adjective* referring to culture; **cultural attaché** = member of an embassy representing his country's interests in the fields of art, music, literature, etc.

curfew [ˈkɜːfjuː] *noun* ban on movement out of doors; *the government has imposed a dusk-to-dawn curfew in the city*

currency [ˈkʌrənsi] *noun* money in coins and notes which is used in a particular country; **blocked currency** = money which cannot be taken out of a country because of exchange controls; **foreign currency** = currency of another country; **free currency** = currency which a government allows to be bought or sold without restriction; **hard currency** = currency of a country which has a strong economy and which can be changed into other currencies easily; **legal currency** = money which is legally used in a country; **soft currency** = currency of a country with a weak economy, which is cheap to buy and difficult to exchange for other currencies

current [ˈkʌrənt] *adjective* referring to the present time; *the seriousness of the current employment situation; current expenditure is too high;* **current account** = ordinary account in a bank into which money can be deposited and on which cheques can be drawn; **current legislation** = laws which are in effect at the present time; *Parliament will consider a bill to tighten up the current legislation on drugs;* **current liabilities** = debts which a company has to pay within the next accounting period

◊ **currently** [ˈkʌrəntli] *adverb* at the present time; *he is currently director of the research institute; six Bills are currently before Parliament*

curriculum vitae (CV) [kəˈrɪkjʊləm ˈviːtaɪ] *noun* summary of a person's life story showing important details of education and work experience; *candidates should send a letter of application with a curriculum vitae to the administrative office;* (NOTE: often shortened to CV. The plural form is **curricula vitae**. Note the US English is **résumé**)

customs *or* Customs and Excise

[ˈkʌstəmz (ənd ˈeksaɪz)] *plural noun* the government department which organizes the collection of taxes on imports; office of this department at a port *or* airport; **to go through the customs** = to pass through the area of a port *or* airport where customs officials examine goods; *he was stopped by the customs; her car was searched by the customs officers;* **customs barrier** = customs duty intended to prevent imports; **customs clearance** = act of clearing goods through the customs; **customs declaration** = statement showing goods being imported on which duty will have to be paid; **customs union** = agreement between several countries that goods can travel between them without paying duty, while goods from other countries have to pay special duties

cut [kʌt] **1** *noun* **(a)** sudden lowering of a price *or* salary *or* numbers of jobs; *price cuts or cuts in prices; salary cuts or cuts in salaries* **(b)** share in a payment; *he introduces new customers and gets a cut of the salesman's commission* **2** *verb* **(a)** to lower suddenly; *we* *are cutting prices on all our models;* **to cut (back) production** = to reduce the quantity of products made **(b)** to stop *or* to reduce the number of something; **to cut jobs** = to reduce the number of jobs by making people redundant

◊ **cutback** ['kʌtbæk] *noun* reduction in expenditure; *government cutbacks on social security spending*

◊ **cut down** ['kʌt 'daʊn] *verb* to reduce; *the department is trying to cut down on waste*

```
the council could try and cut
spending to make a balanced
budget
```
Local Government News

CV [siː'viː] *noun* = CURRICULUM VITAE *please apply in writing, enclosing a current CV*

Dd

D [diː] *fourth letter of the alphabet* **Schedule D** = schedule to the Finance Acts under which tax is charged on income from trades, professions, interest and other earnings which do not come from employment; **Table D** = model memorandum and articles of association of a public company with share capital limited by guarantee, set out in the Companies Act, 1985

Dáil (Éireann) [ˈdɔɪl ˈeərən] *noun* lower house of parliament in the Republic of Ireland; *the Foreign Minister reported on the meeting to the Dáil;* (NOTE: the upper house is the Seanad Éireann; the members of the Dáil are called **Teachta Dala (TD)**)

danger [ˈdeɪndʒə] *noun* **(a)** possibility of being harmed *or* killed; *there is danger to the workers in using old machinery* **(b)** likelihood *or* possibility; **there is no danger of the government losing the vote** = it is not likely that the government will lose the vote; **in danger of** = which may easily happen; *he is in danger of being in contempt of Parliament*

◊ **danger money** [ˈdeɪndʒə ˈmʌni] *noun* extra money paid to workers in dangerous jobs; *the workers have stopped work and asked for danger money*

◊ **dangerous** [ˈdeɪndʒrəs] *adjective* which can be harmful; **dangerous drugs** = drugs which may be harmful to people who take them, and so can be prohibited from import and general sales

data [ˈdeɪtə] *noun* information (letters *or* figures) which is available on computer; facts used to come to a decision; **data bank** *or* **bank of data** = store of information in a computer; **data processing** = selecting and examining data in a computer to produce

special information; **data protection** = protecting information (such as records about private people) in a computer from being copied or used wrongly; (NOTE: **data** is usually singular: **the data is easily available**)

◊ **database** [ˈdeɪtəbeɪs] *noun* store of information in a large computer; *the government maintains a database of personal records*

date [deɪt] **1** *noun* **(a)** number of day, month and year; **date of commencement** = date when an Act of Parliament *or* other legal document takes effect; **date stamp** = rubber stamp for marking the date on letters received; **date of receipt** = date when something is received **(b) at an early date** = very soon; **up to date** = current *or* recent *or* modern; **to bring something up to date** = to add the latest information to something; **to keep something up to date** = to keep adding information to something so that it is always up to date **(c) to date** = up to now; **interest to date** = interest up to the present time **2** *verb* to put a date on a document; *the draft of the minutes was dated March 24th; he forgot to date the cheque; the Secretary of State's letter was dated June 15th*

day [deɪ] *noun* **(a)** period of 24 hours; *there are thirty days in June; the first day of the month is a public holiday;* **three clear days** = three whole working days; *to give ten clear days' notice; allow four clear days for the cheque to be paid into the account;* **early day motion** = motion proposed in the House of Commons for discussion at an early date (usually used to introduce the particular point of view of the MP proposing the motion, without necessarily going to a full debate) **(b)** period of work during a 24 hour day; *the debate lasted three days*

◇ **day-to-day** ['deɪtədeɪ] *adjective* ordinary *or* which goes on all the time; *the clerk organizes the day-to-day running of the House of Commons*

DC = DISTRICT COUNCIL, DISTRICT OF COLUMBIA

dead [ded] *adjective* **(a)** not alive; *six people were dead as a result of the accident; we inherited the house from my dead grandfather* **(b)** not working; **dead letter** = regulation which is no longer valid; *this law has become a dead letter;* **dead loss** = total loss; *the car was written off as a dead loss*

◇ **deadline** ['dedlaɪn] *noun* date by which something has to be done; **to meet a deadline** = to finish something in time; **to miss a deadline** = not to finish something in time

◇ **deadlock** ['dedlɒk] *noun* point where two sides in a dispute cannot agree; **to break a deadlock** = to find a way to start discussions again

◇ **deadlocked** ['dedlɒkt] *adjective* unable to agree to continue discussing; **talks have been deadlocked for ten days** = after ten days the talks have not produced any agreement

deal [diːl] **1** *noun* **(a)** business agreement *or* affair *or* contract; *to arrange a deal or to set up a deal or to do a deal; to sign a deal;* **to call off a deal** = to stop an agreement; **package deal** = agreement where several different items are agreed at the same time; *the teachers had to accept new conditions of service as part of a package deal agreed by the Secretary of State* **(b)** **a great deal** *or* **a good deal of something** = a large quantity of something; *he has made a good deal of money on the stock market; committee members wasted a great deal of time cross-examining the Parliamentary Under-Secretary* **2** *verb* **to deal with** = to be busy with *or* to have to do with; *the Borough Treasurer's department is dealing with the query*

◇ **dealer** ['diːlə] *noun* person who buys and sells; *a wine dealer or a foreign exchange dealer*

◇ **dealing** ['diːlɪŋ] *noun* **(a)** buying and selling on the Stock Exchange; **fair dealing** = (i) legal trade *or* legal buying and selling of shares; (ii) legal quoting of small sections of a copyright work; **foreign exchange dealing** = buying and selling foreign currencies **(b)** buying and selling goods; **to have dealings with someone** = to do business with someone

debate [dɪ'beɪt] **1** *noun* discussion leading to a vote, especially the discussion of a motion in Parliament; *several MPs criticized the government in or during the debate on the Finance Bill; the Bill passed its Second Reading after a short debate; the debate continued until 3 a.m.* **2** *verb* to discuss a proposal, especially in Parliament; *the MPs are still debating the Data Protection Bill*

debug [diː'bʌg] *verb* to remove hidden microphones from a room; (NOTE: **debugged**)

decade ['dekeɪd] *noun* period of ten years

decent ['diːsənt] *adjective* which does not shock people *or* which conforms to the standards of society in general; *this book should be banned - it will shock any decent citizen*

◇ **decency** ['diːsənsi] *noun* being decent; *the film shocked public decency*

decentralize [diː'sentrəlaɪz] *verb* to move power *or* authority *or* action from a central point to local areas; *the decision-making processes have been decentralized to semi-autonomous bodies*

◇ **decentralization** [diːsentrəlaɪ'zeɪʃn] *noun* transferring of power from the centre to local areas

decide [dɪ'saɪd] *verb* **(a)** to give a judgment in a civil case; *the judge decided in favour of the plaintiff* **(b)** to make up your mind to do something; *the government decided to negotiate with the rebels; we have decided to take our neighbours to court; the tribunal decided against awarding any damages*

◇ **deciding** [dɪ'saɪdɪŋ] *adjective* **deciding factor** = most important factor which influences a decision

◇ **decision** [dɪ'sɪʒn] *noun* **(a)** judgment in a civil court; **the decision of the House of Lords is final** = there is no appeal against a decision of the House of Lords **(b)** making up one's mind to do something; *to come to a decision or to reach a decision;* **decision making** = act of coming to a decision; **the decision-making processes** = ways in which decisions are reached; **decision maker** = person who has to decide **(c)** *(EU)* binding legislation; *see also* DIRECTIVE, RECOMMENDATION, REGULATIONS

COMMENT: a decision is binding in its entirety on those to whom it is addressed; a decision may be addressed to a member state, to an organization or to an individual person (see Article 189 EC)

declare [dɪ'kleə] *verb* to make an official statement *or* to announce to the public; *to declare someone bankrupt; to declare that E. Jones has been elected Member of Parliament for the constituency; (of a country)* **to declare independence** = to state that it is now independent, and no longer ruled by another country which ruled it until that point; **to declare war on a country** = to state that a country considers itself at war with another country; **to declare an interest** = to state in public that you own shares in a company being investigated *or* that you are related to someone who can benefit from your contacts, etc.

◊ **declared** [dɪ'kleəd] *adjective* which has been made public or officially stated; **declared value** = value of goods entered on a customs declaration

◊ **declaration** [deklə'reɪʃn] *noun* **(a)** official statement; **declaration of bankruptcy** = official statement that someone is bankrupt; **declaration of income** = statement declaring income to the tax office; **declaration of independence** = statement from a country making itself independent of another country which ruled it until then; **declaration of war** = statement by a country that it considers itself at war with another country; **statutory declaration** = (i) statement made to the Registrar of Companies that a company has complied with certain legal conditions; (ii) statement made, signed and witnessed for official purposes; **VAT declaration** = statement declaring VAT income to the VAT office **(b)**

official statement that someone has been elected; *the count has been going on since 10 o'clock and we are still waiting for the declaration*

declassify [diː'klæsɪfaɪ] *verb* to make a document *or* piece of information no longer secret, so that it can be made public; *the government papers relating to the war have recently been declassified*

◊ **declassification** [diːklæsɪfɪ'keɪʃn] *noun* making something no longer secret

decline [dɪ'klaɪn] **1** *noun* fall; *the decline in the value of the local currency; a decline in buying power; the last year has seen a decline in real wages* **2** *verb* to refuse to do something; to refuse something which is offered; *the witness declined to take the oath; the chairman refused the invitation to speak at the dinner*

decolonization [diːkɒlənaɪ'zeɪʃn] *noun* process by which a state withdraws from its colonies and grants them independence

decommission [diːkə'mɪʃn] *verb* to get rid of something no longer useful, such as weapons

decontrol [diːkən'trəʊl] *verb* to stop *or* remove controls from something; **to decontrol the price of petrol** = to stop controlling the price of petrol so that a free market price can be reached; (NOTE: **decontrolled - decontrolling**)

decrease 1 ['diːkriːs] *noun* fall (in number); *deaths from cold have shown a sharp decrease* **2** [dɪ'kriːs] *verb* to make smaller *or* to become smaller; *the government proposes to decrease the rate of VAT*

decree [dɪ'kriː] **1** *noun* order made by a head of state, but which is not passed by a parliament; **to govern by decree** = to rule a country by issuing orders without having them debated and voted in a parliament **2** *verb* to make an order; *the President decreed that June 1st should be a National Holiday*

deduct [dɪ'dʌkt] *verb* to remove money from a total; *to deduct £3 from the price; to deduct a sum for expenses; to deduct 5%*

from salaries; **tax deducted at source** = tax which is removed from a salary, interest payment or dividend payment on shares before the money is paid

◊ **deductible** [dɪ'dʌktɪbl] *adjective* which can be deducted; **tax-deductible** = which can be deducted from an income before tax is paid; **these expenses are not tax-deductible** = tax has to be paid on these expenses

◊ **deduction** [dɪ'dʌkʃn] *noun* **(a)** conclusion which is reached by observing something; *by a process of deduction, the investigators came to the conclusion that the leak originated in the Foreign Office* **(b)** removing of money from a total *or* money removed from a total; *net salary is salary after deduction of tax and social security contributions;* **deductions from salary** *or* **salary deductions** *or* **deductions at source** = money which a company removes from salaries to give to the government as tax, national insurance contributions, etc.; **tax deductions** = (i) money removed from a salary to pay tax; (ii) *US* business expenses which can be claimed against tax

deed [diːd] *noun* **(a)** action; *the government will be judged by its deeds, not by its promises* **(b)** legal document which has been signed by the person making it; **deed of covenant** = signed legal agreement to do something (such as to pay someone a sum of money every year); **deed of partnership** = agreement which sets up a partnership; **title deeds** = document showing who owns a property; *we have deposited the deeds of the house in the bank*

◊ **deed poll** ['diːd 'pəʊl] *noun* legal agreement which refers only to one party; **to change one's name by deed poll** = to sign a legal document by which you change your name

deem [diːm] *verb* to believe *or* to consider; *the Speaker deemed it necessary to order the public galleries to be cleared*

deepen ['diːpən] *verb* to become stronger; to become closer; *concern is deepening in Brussels that the convergence targets will not be met; a deepening debate within the*

EU regarding future closer ties with eastern European countries

de facto ['deɪ 'fæktəʊ] *Latin phrase meaning* 'in fact': as a matter of fact, even though the legal title may not be certain; *he is the de facto owner of the property; the de facto government has been recognized;* **de facto authority** *or* **de facto rule** = authority *or* rule of a country by a group because it is actually ruling; **de facto recognition** = recognition of a new government because it is in power, whether it is ruling legally or not; *see also* DE JURE

defame [dɪ'feɪm] *verb* to say *or* write negative things about the character of someone so as to damage his reputation

◊ **defamation** [defə'meɪʃn] *noun* **defamation of character** = act of ruining someone's reputation by maliciously saying *or* writing things about him

> COMMENT: defamation may be libel (if it is in a permanent form, such as printed matter) or slander (if it is spoken)

◊ **defamatory** [dɪ'fæmətri] *adjective* **defamatory statement** = statement which is made to defame someone's character

default [dɪ'fɒlt] **1** *noun* failure to carry out the terms of a contract, especially failure to pay back a debt; **in default of payment** = if no payment is made; **by default** = because no one else will act; **he was elected by default** = he was elected because all the other candidates withdrew *or* because there were no other candidates **2** *verb* to fail to carry out the terms of a contract, especially to fail to pay back a debt; **to default on payments** = not to make payments which are due under the terms of a contract

defeat [dɪ'fiːt] **1** *noun* failure to get a majority in a vote; *the minister offered to resign after the defeat of the motion in the House of Commons* **2** *verb* to beat someone *or* something in a vote; *the bill was defeated in the Lords by 52 to 64; the government was defeated in a vote on law and order*

defect 1 ['diːfekt] *noun* something which is wrong *or* which stops a machine *or* law from working properly **2** [dɪ'fekt] *verb (of a spy or agent or government employee)* to leave your country and go to work for an enemy country; *(of Member of Parliament)* to leave your party and join another

◊ **defection** [dɪ'fekʃən] *noun* going over to work for the enemy; leaving one political party and joining their opponents

◊ **defective** [dɪ'fektɪv] *adjective* **(a)** faulty *or* not working properly; *the machine broke down because of a defective cooling system* **(b)** not legally valid; *his title to the property is defective*

◊ **defector** [dɪ'fektə] *noun* person who defects

defence *or US* **defense** [dɪ'fens] *noun* **(a)** protecting someone *or* something against attack; **Ministry of Defence** *or US* **Defense Department** = government department in charge of the armed forces; **Secretary of State for Defence** *or* **Defence Secretary** *or US* **Secretary for Defense** *or* **Defense Secretary** = government minister in charge of the armed forces **(b)** (i) party in a civil legal case which is sued by the plaintiff; (ii) party in a criminal case which is being prosecuted; (iii) lawyers representing a party being sued *or* prosecuted; **defence counsel** = lawyer who represents the defendant *or* the accused; *compare* PROSECUTION

◊ **defend** [dɪ'fend] *verb* **(a)** to fight to protect someone *or* something which is being attacked; *the company is defending itself against the takeover bid* **(b)** to fight an election to keep the seat which you have been holding; *she is defending a majority of only 2,400; he is defending a safe Labour seat* **(c)** to speak to show that your actions were right; *the Minister defended his decision;* to **defend an action** = to appear in court to state your case when accused of something

◊ **defendant** [dɪ'fendənt] *noun* person who is accused of doing something illegal; person who is sued in a civil law suit

◊ **defender** [dɪ'fendə] *noun* person who defends

defer [dɪ'fɜ:] *verb* to put back to a later date *or* to postpone; *to defer judgment; the*

decision has been deferred until the next meeting; (NOTE: **deferring - deferred**)

◊ **deferment** [dɪ'fɜ:mənt] *noun* postponement *or* putting back to a later date; *deferment of payment; deferment of a decision*

◊ **deferred** [dɪ'fɜ:d] *adjective* put back to a later date; **deferred business** = matters which have been put back to a later meeting; **deferred payment** = payment for goods by instalments over a long period

defiance [dɪ'faɪəns] *noun* acting against (law *or* authority)

◊ **defiant** [dɪ'faɪənt] *adjective* showing resistance to authority

◊ **defiantly** [dɪ'faɪəntli] *adverb* in a defiant way

deficiencies [dɪ'fɪʃənsɪz] *noun US* = SUPPLEMENTAL APPROPRIATIONS

deficit ['defɪsɪt] *noun* amount by which spending is higher than income; *the council is trying to agree on how to reduce its current deficit; the President has promised to reduce the budget deficit;* **trade deficit** = situation where a country imports more goods than it exports

the Deputy Premier rejected the claim that the budget deficit had developed over a number of years

Canberra Times

define [dɪ'faɪn] *verb* to say clearly what a word *or* phrase means; *immigrant persons as defined in Appendix 3; the law makes an attempt to define the word 'obscene'; the judge asked counsel to define what he meant by 'incapable'*

deflation [dɪ'fleɪʃn] *noun* reducing inflation

deflationary [dɪ'fleɪʃənəri] *adjective* which leads to deflation; *the government has introduced some deflationary measures in the budget*

defraud [dɪ'frɔ:d] *verb* to trick someone so as to obtain money illegally; *he defrauded*

the Inland Revenue of thousands of pounds;
(NOTE: you defraud someone of something)

defray [dɪˈfreɪ] *verb* to provide money to
pay (costs); *the council agreed to defray the
expenses of the exhibition*

defy [dɪˈfaɪ] *verb* **(a)** to refuse to obey
(someone, the law); *the protesters have
defied the court order* **(b)** to defy someone
to do something = to challenge someone to
do something

de jure [ˈdeɪ ˈdʒuːreɪ] *Latin phrase
meaning* 'by law': as a matter of law, where
the legal title is clear; *he is the de jure owner
of the property;* de jure recognition =
recognizing a new government because it is
the legal government of the country; *see also*
DE FACTO

delay [dɪˈleɪ] **1** *noun* time when someone *or*
something is later than planned; *there was a
delay of thirty minutes before the hearing
started or the hearing started after a thirty
minute delay* **2** *verb* to be late; *the
government delayed signing the treaty until
the other side had clarified the question of
reciprocal trade; the decision was delayed
while the committee asked for further advice*

delegate 1 [ˈdelɪgət] *noun* person who is
chosen *or* elected by others to put their case at
a meeting; *the management refused to meet
the trade union delegates* **2** [ˈdelɪgeɪt] *verb*
to pass certain limited authority or
responsibility to someone else; *the
committee delegated the appointment of
staff to the chairman;* delegated legislation
= orders, which have the power of Acts of
Parliament, but which are passed by a
minister to whom Parliament has delegated
its authority; delegated powers = powers
which may be legally passed by a council to a
committee or by a committee to a
sub-committee

◊ **delegation** [delɪˈgeɪʃn] *noun* **(a)** group
of delegates; *a Chinese trade delegation; the
management met a union delegation* **(b)** act
of passing limited authority or responsibility
for making decisions to someone else; (NOTE:
no plural for (b))

◊ **delegatus non potest delegare**
[delɪˈgætʌs nɒn pɒtest delɪˈgɑːrɪ] *Latin
phrase meaning* 'the delegate cannot
delegate to someone else'

delete [dɪˈliːt] *verb* to remove words in a
document; *the chairman ordered the
remarks to be deleted from the record; the
lawyers have deleted clause two from the
draft of the Bill*

◊ **deletion** [dɪˈliːʃn] *noun* **(a)** act of
deleting something; *the treasurer asked for
the deletion of paragraph 2B* **(b)** deletions =
parts of a text which have been deleted; *after
the secretary had deleted the remarks about
the chairman from the minutes, the meeting
voted to restore the deletions*

deliberate 1 [dɪˈlɪbərət] *adjective* done on
purpose; *the police suggest that the letter
was a deliberate attempt to encourage
disorder* **2** [dɪˈlɪbəreɪt] *verb* to consider *or* to
discuss a problem; *the committee deliberated
for several hours before reaching a decision*

◊ **deliberately** [dɪˈlɪbərətli] *adverb* on
purpose *or* intentionally; *he was accused of
deliberately setting fire to the shop*

◊ **deliberations** [dɪlɪbəˈreɪʃnz] *plural
noun* discussions; *the result of the
committee's deliberations was passed to the
newspapers*

delimit [dɪˈlɪmɪt] *verb* to define the
boundaries or limits of something; *the terms
of reference of the commission only cover
certain strictly delimited areas*

deliver [dɪˈlɪvə] *verb* to transport goods to a
customer

◊ **delivery** [dɪˈlɪvəri] *noun* **(a)** delivery of
goods = transport of goods to a customer's
address; delivery note = list of goods being
delivered, given to the customer with the
goods; delivery order = instructions given
by the customer to the person holding his
goods, to tell him to deliver them; recorded
delivery = mail service where the letters are
signed for by the person receiving them; cash
on delivery = payment in cash when the
goods are delivered; to take delivery of
goods = to accept goods when they are

delivered **(b)** goods being delivered; *we take in three deliveries a day; there were four items missing in the last delivery*

demagogue ['deməgɒg] *noun (usually as criticism)* leader who is able to get the support of the people by exciting their feelings and prejudices

◊ **demagogy** *or* **demagoguery**
['deməgɒgi *or* 'deməgɒgri] *noun* acting as a demagogue, by appealing to the feelings of the mass of the people

demand ['dɪmɑːnd] **1** *noun* **(a)** asking for payment; **payable on demand** = which must be paid when payment is asked for; **demand bill** = bill of exchange which must be paid when payment is asked for; **final demand** = last reminder from a supplier, after which he will sue for payment **(b)** need for goods at a certain price; **supply and demand** = amount of a product which is available at a certain price and the amount which is wanted by customers at that price; **law of supply and demand** = general rule that the amount of a product which is available is related to the needs of possible customers **2** *verb* to ask for something and expect to get it; *the Leader of the Opposition demanded an apology from the minister; the council is demanding immediate payment of back rent*

démarche ['deɪmɑːʃ] *noun* official diplomatic move (such as a visit to the Foreign Office *or* passing a letter from a head of government)

demise [dɪ'maɪz] *noun* death; **demise of the Crown** = death of a king *or* queen

demo ['deməʊ] *see* DEMONSTRATION

democracy [dɪ'mɒkrəsi] *noun* **(a)** theory or system of government by freely elected representatives of the people; the right to fair government, free elections of representatives and equality in voting; *after the coup, democracy was replaced by a military dictatorship; see also* SOCIAL DEMOCRACY **(b)** country ruled in this way; *the pact was welcomed by western democracies*

◊ **democrat** ['deməkræt] *noun* **(a)** person who believes in democracy **(b) Democrat** = member *or* supporter of the Democratic Party (in the USA); **Christian Democrat** = member of the main conservative party in some European countries; *see also* SOCIAL DEMOCRAT

◊ **democratic** [demə'krætɪk] *adjective* **(a)** referring to a democracy; *after the coup the democratic processes of government were replaced by government by decree* **(b)** free and fair *or* reflecting the views of the majority; *the resolution was passed by a democratic vote of the council; the action of the leader is against the wishes of the party as expressed in a democratic vote at the party conference*

◊ **Democratic Party** [demə'krætɪk 'pɑːti] *noun* one of the two main political parties in the USA, which is in favour of some social change and state help for poor people, together with restrictions on the power of the federal government; *compare* REPUBLICAN PARTY

◊ **democratically** [demə'krætɪkli] *adverb* in a democratic way; *he is the first democratically elected president following the end of military rule*

demonstrate ['demənstreɪt] *verb* **(a)** to show *or* to make clear; *the police demonstrated how the bomb was planted; the MP's comments demonstrated his lack of sympathy for the unemployed* **(b)** to make a public protest about something; *crowds of students were demonstrating against the government*

◊ **demonstration** [demən'streɪʃn] *noun* **(a)** act of showing; *the manager gave a demonstration of the new computer system for recording details of tenants and their rents* **(b)** act of protesting; *police broke up the student demonstration; ratepayers are organizing a demonstration in front of the Town Hall;* (NOTE: in informal speech sometimes shortened to **demo**)

◊ **demonstrator** [demən'streɪtə] *noun* person who demonstrates; *demonstrators have occupied the municipal building*

demur [dɪ'mɜː] *verb* not to agree; *the MP stated that there was a question of privilege,* *but the Speaker demurred;* (NOTE: demurring - demurred)

denuclearize [diː'njuːkliəraɪz] *verb* to get rid of nuclear weapons in an area

deny [dɪ'naɪ] *verb* **(a)** not to allow something; *he was denied the right to see his lawyer* **(b)** to say that you have not done something; *he denied being in the house at the time of the murder;* (NOTE: you deny someone something or deny doing or having done something)

◊ **denial** [dɪ'naɪəl] *noun* **(a)** act of not allowing something; **denial of human rights** = refusing someone a right which is generally accepted as fair; **denial of justice** = situation where justice appears not to have been done **(b)** act of stating that you have not done something; *in spite of his denials he was found guilty*

depart [dɪ'paːt] *verb* **(a)** to leave; *the plane departs at 11.15* **(b)** to depart from normal practice = to act in a different way from the normal practice

◊ **department** [dɪ'paːtmənt] *noun* **(a)** specialized section of an organization; *complaints department; legal department;* **accounts department** = section which deals with money paid or received; **head of department** *or* **department head** *or* **department manager** = person in charge of a department **(b)** section of a large store selling one type of product; **furniture department** = department in a large store which sells furniture **(c) Department of State** = (i) major section of the British government headed by a Secretary of State; (ii) major section of the US government headed by a Secretary; *the Department of Trade and Industry; the Department for Education and Employment;* **State Department** = department in the US government dealing with relations with other countries; *compare* MINISTRY **(d)** one of the administrative divisions of a country, such as France

◊ **departmental** [dɪpaːt'mentəl] *adjective* referring to a department; *if you want to complain, you should first talk to your departmental head*

departure [dɪ'paːtʃə] *noun* **(a)** going away; *the plane's departure was delayed by two hours* **(b)** new type of business; *selling records will be a departure for the local bookshop* **(c)** departure from = thing which is different from what happened before; *this forms a departure from established practice; any departure from the terms and conditions of the contract must be advised in writing*

depend [dɪ'pend] *verb* **(a)** to depend on = to need someone *or* something to exist; *the company depends on efficient service from its suppliers; we depend on government grants to pay the salary bill* **(b)** to happen because of something; *the success of the anti-drug campaign will depend on the attitude of the public;* **depending on** = happening as a result of something; *depending on the circumstances, the Bill may be passed through the House of Lords without amendment, or it may be amended and sent back to the House of Commons for further discussion*

◊ **dependant** *or* **dependent** [dɪ'pendənt] *noun* person who is supported financially by someone else; *he has to provide for his family and dependants out of a very small salary*

◊ **dependent** [dɪ'pendənt] *adjective* (person) who is supported financially by someone else; *tax relief is allowed for dependent relatives*

deplore [dɪ'plɔː] *verb* to disapprove of (an action); *the motion that the council deplores the action of the government was carried; he wrote to the local paper deploring the incorrect reporting of the council meeting*

depoliticize [diːpə'lɪtɪsaɪz] *verb* to remove the party political character from something; *the government wants to depoliticize the debate on crime*

depopulated [diː'pɒpjuːleɪtɪd] *adjective* having fewer inhabitants (because most have moved away)

deport [dɪ'pɔːt] *verb* to send (someone) away from a country; *the illegal immigrants were deported*

◊ **deportation** [diːpɔːˈteɪʃn] *noun* sending of someone away from a country; *the convicts were sentenced to deportation;* **deportation order** = official order to send someone away from a country; *the minister signed the deportation order;* (NOTE: no plural)

depose [dɪˈpəuz] *verb* to remove (a king) from the throne

deposit [dɪˈpɒzɪt] **1** *noun* **(a)** money placed in a bank for safe keeping or to earn interest; **deposit account** = bank account which pays interest but on which notice has to be given to withdraw money; **licensed deposit-taker** = business (such as a bank) which takes deposits from individuals and lends the money to others **(b)** money given in advance so that the thing which you want to buy will not be sold to someone else; *to leave £10 as deposit;* **to forfeit a deposit** = to lose a deposit because you have decided not to buy the item **(c)** money paid by a candidate when nominated for an election, which is forfeited if the candidate does not win enough votes; *he polled only 25 votes and lost his deposit* **2** *verb* **(a)** to put documents somewhere for safe keeping; *we have deposited the deeds of the house with the bank; he deposited his will with his solicitor* **(b)** to put money into a bank account; *to deposit £100 in a current account*

depreciate [dɪˈpriːʃɪeɪt] *verb* to lose value; *the pound has depreciated by 5% against the dollar*

◊ **depreciation** [dɪprɪʃɪˈeɪʃn] *noun* regular loss of value; *the depreciation of the pound against the dollar*

deprive [dɪˈpraɪv] *verb* **to deprive someone of something** = to remove something from someone *or* not to allow someone to have something; *the prisoners were deprived of contact with their families; the new Bill will deprive aliens of the right to appeal*

dept = DEPARTMENT

depute [dɪˈpjuːt] **1** *noun* (*in Scotland*) = DEPUTY **2** *verb* to give someone the job of

doing something; *he was deputed to act as chairman*

deputy [ˈdepjuti] *noun* **(a)** person who takes the place of a higher official *or* who assists a higher official; *he acted as deputy for the chairman or he acted as the chairman's deputy;* **Deputy Mayor** = member of a town council who stands in for a mayor if the latter is absent; **Deputy Prime Minister** = title given to a senior cabinet minister who stands in for the Prime Minister when the latter is unable to act; **Deputy Speaker** = Chairman of Ways and Means, who stands in for the Speaker when the latter is absent **(b)** *US* person who acts for *or* assists a sheriff **(c)** (*in Canada*) **Deputy Minister** = chief civil servant in charge of a ministry; (NOTE: in the UK, this is the **Permanent Secretary**) **(d)** (*in some countries*) member of parliament *or* of a legislative body; *after the Prime Minister resigned, the deputies of his party started to discuss the election of a successor;* **Chamber of Deputies** = lower house of the legislature in some countries (as opposed to the Senate)

◊ **deputize** [ˈdepjutaɪz] *verb* **to deputize for someone** = to take the place of someone who is absent; **to deputize someone** = to appoint someone as a deputy

derecognition [diːrekəgˈnɪʃn] *noun* withdrawing recognition of a government in a country

deregulate [diːˈregjuːleɪt] *verb* to remove government regulations from an industry; *Parliament is considering a Bill to deregulate the airlines*

◊ **deregulation** [dɪregjuːˈleɪʃn] *noun* reducing government control over an industry; *the deregulation of the airlines*

dereliction [derɪˈlɪkʃn] *noun* **dereliction of duty** = failure to do what you ought to do; *he was found guilty of gross dereliction of duty*

derive [dɪˈraɪv] *verb* **(a)** to come from; *this law derives from or is derived from the former Roman law of property* **(b)** to obtain; *he derived financial benefit from the transaction*

derogation [derə'geɪʃn] *noun (EU)* temporary waiver of a regulation or directive

descended from [dɪ'sendɪd 'frɒm] *adjective* having a person as an ancestor; *he is descended from William I*

◊ **descendant** [dɪ'sendənt] *noun* person who is descended from an ancestor; *his wife is a descendant of King Charles II*

◊ **descent** [dɪ'sent] *noun* family ties of inheritance between parents and children; *he is British by descent or he is of British descent* = one (or both) of his parents is British; **lineal descent** = direct descent from parent to child

describe [dɪ'skraɪb] *verb* to say what someone *or* something is like; *she described her attacker to the police; he described the previous speaker as a silly old man*

◊ **description** [dɪs'krɪpʃn] *noun* words which show what something is like; *the police circulated a description of the missing boy or of the wanted man;* **trade description** = description of a product to attract customers; *GB* **Trade Descriptions Act** = Act of Parliament which limits the way in which products can be described so as to protect consumers from wrong descriptions made by the makers

desegregate [diː'segrəgeɪt] *verb* to end segregation *or* stop (schools *or* buses, etc.) being segregated

◊ **desegregation** [diːsegrə'geɪʃn] *noun* ending of segregation

deselect [diːsɪ'lekt] *verb* to decide that a person who had been selected by a political party as a candidate for a constituency is no longer the candidate

◊ **deselection** [diːsɪ'lekʃn] *noun* act of deselecting; *some factions in the local party have proposed the deselection of the candidate*

desert [dɪ'zɜːt] *verb* to leave the armed forces without permission

◊ **deserter** [dɪ'zɜːtə] *noun* person who leaves the armed forces without permission

designate ['dezɪgneɪt] **1** *adjective* person who has been appointed to a job but who has not yet started work; *the chairman designate;* (NOTE: always follows a noun) **2** *verb* to name *or* to appoint officially; *the area was designated a National Park*

despatch [dɪs'pætʃ] *verb* to send; *the letters about the rates were despatched yesterday; the Defence Minister was despatched to take charge of the operation*

◊ **despatch box** [dɪs'pætʃ 'bɒks] *noun* **(a)** red box in which government papers are sent to ministers **(b)** one of two boxes on the centre table in the House of Commons at which a Minister *or* member of the Opposition Front Bench stands to speak; *(of a minister)* **to be at the despatch box** = to be speaking in parliament

despot ['despɒt] *noun* tyrant, dictator who rules a country absolutely

◊ **despotic** [dɪ'spɒtɪk] *adjective* like a dictator

◊ **despotism** ['despətɪzm] *noun* dictatorship by a despot

detail ['diːteɪl] **1** *noun* small part of a description; **in detail** = giving many particulars; *the contract lists all the markets in detail* **2** *verb* **(a)** to list in detail; *the document details the arrangements for maintenance payments; the terms of the licence are detailed in the contract* **(b)** to tell someone to do something; *two council officials were detailed to search the records*

◊ **detailed** ['diːteɪld] *adjective* in detail; **detailed account** = account which lists every item

détente ['deɪtɒnt] *noun* relaxation of tension between two or more countries

determine [dɪ'tɜːmɪn] *verb* **(a)** to fix *or* to arrange *or* to decide; *to determine prices or quantities; the conditions of the contract are still to be determined* **(b)** to bring to an end; *the tenancy was determined by a notice to quit*

deterrent [dɪ'terənt] *noun* thing which discourages; **nuclear deterrent** = nuclear weapon which it is hoped with prevent attacks from other countries

dethrone [diː'θrəʊn] *verb* to remove (a king) from the throne

develop [dɪ'veləp] *verb* **(a)** to plan and produce; *to develop a new product* **(b)** to plan and build an area; *to develop an industrial estate*

◊ **developer** [dɪ'veləpə] *noun* **a property developer** = person who plans and builds a group of new houses *or* new factories

◊ **developing country** *or* **developing nation** [dɪ'veləpɪŋ 'kʌntri *or* dɪ'veləpɪŋ 'neɪʃn] *noun* country which is not yet fully industrialized

◊ **development** [dɪ'veləpmənt] *noun* **(a)** planning the production of a new product *or* new town; **industrial development** = planning and building of new industries in special areas; **development area** *or* **development zone** = area which has been given special help from a government to encourage businesses and factories to be set up there; **development plan** = plan drawn up by a government *or* council to show how an area should be planned over a long period **(b)** change which has taken place; *the lending of tapes is a new development in the library service*

deviate ['diːvɪeɪt] *verb* **to deviate from a course of action** = to do something different *or* to act in a different way

device [dɪ'vaɪs] *noun* small useful machine; way of doing something; *it is simply a device to avoid paying tax or a tax-saving device*

devolve [dɪ'vɒlv] *verb* to pass power to another authority; *power is devolved to regional assemblies*

◊ **devolution** [diːvə'luːʃn] *noun* passing of power from a central government to a local or regional authority

COMMENT: devolution involves passing more power than decentralization. In a devolved state, the regional authorities are almost autonomous

DHA = **DISTRICT HEALTH AUTHORITY**

dialogue ['daɪəlɒg] *noun* official diplomatic contact between two countries

diary ['daɪəri] *noun* book in which you can write notes or appointments for each day of the week and record events which have taken place; **the Parliamentary diary** = list of days of the week, showing what Parliamentary business is due to take place each day

dictate [dɪk'teɪt] *verb* **(a)** to say something with the power to enforce it; *the victorious general was able to dictate conditions to the defeated army; the trades unions attempted to dictate to the government* **(b)** to say something to someone who then writes down your words; **dictating machine** = machine which records what someone dictates, which a secretary can play back and then type out the text

◊ **dictation** [dɪk'teɪʃn] *noun* act of dictating words to someone; **to take dictation** = to write down what someone is saying; **dictation speed** = number of words per minute which a secretary can write down in shorthand

◊ **dictator** [dɪk'teɪtə] *noun* ruler who has complete personal power; *the country has been ruled by a military dictator for six years; the MPs accused the party leader of behaving like a dictator*

◊ **dictatorial** [dɪktə'tɔːrɪəl] *adjective* **(a)** referring to a dictator; *a dictatorial form of government* **(b)** behaving like a dictator; *officials dislike the Minister's dictatorial way of working*

◊ **dictatorship** [dɪk'teɪtəʃɪp] *noun* **(a)** rule by a dictator; *under the dictatorship of Mussolini, personal freedom was restricted;* **the dictatorship of the proletariat** = in Marxist theory, the period after a revolution when the Communist Party takes control until a true classless society develops **(b)** country ruled by a dictator; **a military dictatorship** = country ruled by an army officer as a dictator

diehard ['daɪhɑːd] *noun & adjective* stubborn (person) who resists any form of change; *he's a diehard Conservative;*

diehard Labour supporters criticised the new style of leadership

Diet ['daɪət] *noun* legislative body in Japan (equivalent to Parliament or Congress)

differ ['dɪfə] *verb* not to agree with; *one of the appeal judges differed from the others;* I **beg to differ** = I want to say that I do not agree

◊ **difference** ['dɪfrəns] *noun* way in which two or more things are not the same

◊ **different** ['dɪfrənt] *adjective* not the same

dilatory ['dɪlətri] *adjective* too slow; **dilatory motion** = motion in the House of Commons to put off the debate on a proposal until a later date

diplomat *or (formal)* diplomatist

['dɪpləmæt or dɪ'plomətɪst] *noun* person (such as an ambassador) who is an official representative of his country in another country

◊ **diplomacy** [dɪp'ləuməsi] *noun* **(a)** management of a country's interest in another country, by its diplomats; *the art of diplomacy is to anticipate the next move by the other party;* **gunboat diplomacy** = trying to solve international problems by force *or* by threatening to use force; **quiet diplomacy** = discussing problems with officials of another country in a calm way, without telling the press about it; **secret diplomacy** = discussing problems with another country in secret; **he is a master of diplomacy** = he is very good at negotiating **(b)** quiet and tactful way of persuading people to do what you want *or* of settling problems

◊ **diplomatic** [dɪplə'mætɪk] *adjective* **(a)** referring to diplomats; *his car had a diplomatic number plate; she was using a diplomatic passport;* **the diplomatic bag** = bag containing official government documents which is carried from one country to another by diplomats and cannot be opened by the customs; *he was accused of shipping arms into the country in the diplomatic bag;* **diplomatic channels** = communicating between countries through their diplomats; *the message was delivered by diplomatic*

channels; they are working to restore diplomatic channels between the two countries; **diplomatic corps** = all foreign diplomats in a city *or* country; **diplomatic immunity** = not being subject to the laws of the country in which you are living, because you are a diplomat; *he claimed diplomatic immunity to avoid being arrested;* **diplomatic service** = the government department concerned with relations with other countries, including embassies, consulates, and other representatives; *he has decided on a career in the diplomatic service;* **to grant someone diplomatic status** = to give someone the rights of a diplomat **(b)** quiet and tactful, in dealing with other people

direct 1 [daɪ'rekt] *verb* to order *or* to give an order to (someone); *the council directed the Chief Fire Officer to prepare a survey of fire precautions in schools* **2** ['daɪrekt] *adjective* straight *or* with no interference; **direct debit** = system where a customer allows a company to charge costs to his bank account automatically and where the amount charged can be increased or decreased automatically, the customer being informed of the change by letter **direct elections** = elections where the voters actually vote for the person to represent them (as opposed to election by an electoral college); **direct labour organization (DLO)** = organization of manual workers (builders, maintenance workers, etc.) who are employed by a council as opposed to putting work out to tender; **direct mail** = selling a product by sending advertising material by post to possible buyers; **direct purchasing** = purchasing by a council of goods and equipment directly from the manufacturer, and not from a retailer; **direct selling** = selling a product direct from the manufacturer to the customer without going through a shop; **direct taxation** = tax, such as income tax, which is paid direct to the government **3** [daɪ'rekt] *adverb* straight *or* with no third party involved; *we pay income tax direct to the government; the fine is paid direct to the court*

◊ **direction** [dɪ'rekʃn] *noun* **(a)** way in which something is going; *his speech changed the direction of the debate* **(b)** organizing *or* managing; *he took over the direction of a large bank* **(c) directions** = (i) order which explains how something should be done; (ii) instructions from a judge to a jury; (iii) orders given by a judge concerning the general way of proceeding with a case; *the court is not able to give directions to the local authority*

◊ **directive** [dɪ'rektɪv] *noun* **(a)** order *or* command to someone to do something **(b)** *(EU)* legislation which is binding, but which member states can implement as they wish; *the Commission issued a directive on food prices; see also* DECISION, RECOMMENDATION, REGULATIONS

COMMENT: a directive is binding as to the result to be achieved, but leaves to the national authorities the choice of form and method (Article 189 EC)

◊ **directly** [daɪ'rekli] *adverb* **(a)** immediately; *the summons was served directly after the magistrate had signed the warrant* **(b)** in a straight way; *the Metropolitan Police Commissioner is directly responsible to the Home Secretary*

◊ **director** [dɪ'rektə] *noun* **(a)** person who is in charge of a programme of work, an official institute, etc.; *he is the director of a government institute; she was appointed director of the charity* **(b)** chief officer of a department in a council; **Director of Education** *or* **Housing** *or* **Social Services** = chief officer in a local government administration, in charge of the education *or* housing *or* social services in his area **(c)** person appointed by the shareholders to manage a company; **managing director** = the most senior executive director in a company; **chairman and managing director** = managing director who is also chairman of the board of directors; **board of directors** = all the directors of a company

◊ **director-general** [dɪ'rektə 'dʒenrəl] *noun* person in charge of a large organization, with several directors beneath him;; *(in the EU)* civil servant in charge of one of the directorates-general; **Director-General of Fair Trading** = official in charge of the Office of Fair Trading, dealing with consumers and the law

◊ **directorate** [dɪ'rektərət] *noun* **(a)** group of directors; **directorate-general** = administrative section of the European Commission **(b)** office of a director; *the Directorate of Social Services is advertising for secretaries*

◊ **Director of Public Prosecutions (DPP)** *noun* government official in charge of the Crown Prosecution Service, reporting to the Attorney-General, who advises on criminal cases brought by the police, prosecutes in important cases and advises other government departments if prosecutions should be started *the papers in the case have been sent to the Director of Public Prosecutions*

directory [daɪ'rektəri] *noun* list of people *or* businesses with their addresses and telephone numbers, and sometimes further information about them; **classified directory** = list of businesses grouped under various headings, such as computer shops or newsagents; **commercial directory** *or* **trade directory** = book which lists all the businesses and business people in a town; **street directory** = (i) list of people living in a street; (ii) map of a town which lists all the streets in alphabetical order in an index; **telephone directory** = book which lists all people and businesses who have telephones, in alphabetical order with their addresses and phone numbers

disabled [dɪ'seɪbld] *adjective* (person) who is unable to do some normal activity; *a council home for the elderly disabled*

disadvantage [dɪsəd'vɑːntɪdʒ] **1** *noun* something which makes you less successful; *it is a disadvantage for a tax lawyer not to have studied to be an accountant;* **to be at a disadvantage** = to be in a more awkward position (than another person); *not having studied law puts him at a disadvantage* **2** *verb* to put someone in a more awkward position; *he is disadvantaged by not having the right qualifications for the job;* **the disadvantaged** = people who do not have the right qualifications *or* who are handicapped in some way

disagree [dɪsə'griː] *verb* not to agree; *two of the members of the Royal Commission disagreed with the final report; the Leader of the House disagreed with the Speaker's ruling;* **the jury disagreed and were not able to return a verdict** = there were not enough jurors who were in agreement to be able to form even a majority verdict

◊ **disagreement** [dɪsə'griːmənt] *noun* not agreeing; *there was disagreement among the MPs about how the police should deal with terrorist attacks*

disallow [dɪsə'laʊ] *verb* to reject *or* not to accept; *the chairman disallowed the point of order; he claimed £2,000 for fire damage, but the claim was disallowed*

disapprove [dɪsə'pruːv] *verb* to **disapprove of something** = to show that you do not approve of something *or* that you do not think something is good; *the junta openly disapproves of the judicial system*

◊ **disapproval** [dɪsə'pruːvl] *noun* act of disapproving; *the Speaker showed his disapproval of the MP's behaviour*

disarmament [dɪs'ɑːməmənt] *noun* reducing the number of arms held by a country; **multilateral (nuclear) disarmament** = removing nuclear weapons from several countries all at the same time; **unilateral (nuclear) disarmament** = removing all nuclear weapons from a country, even if other countries keep theirs

disburse [dɪs'bɜːs] *verb* to pay money out of a fund

◊ **disbursement** [dɪs'bɜːsmənt] *noun* payment of money

discharge [dɪs'tʃɑːdʒ] *verb* to let someone go free; to tell someone that he is no longer needed; *the judge discharged the jury; US* **to discharge a committee** = to remove jurisdiction over a bill from a committee (used especially if a committee has not reported on a bill within thirty days); **Discharge Calendar** = list of motions for discharging committees

COMMENT: committees of both House of Representatives and the Senate can

be discharged; the action to discharge a committee in the House of the Representatives is called a 'discharge petition' and in the Senate a 'discharge resolution'

discipline ['dɪsɪplɪn] **1** *noun* orderly way of behaving; *the chairman had difficulty in keeping discipline in the meeting* **2** *verb* to punish (an employee); *the clerk was disciplined for leaking the report to the newspapers*

◊ **disciplinary** [dɪsɪ'plɪnəri] *adjective* **disciplinary procedure** = way of warning a worker officially that he is breaking rules *or* that he is working badly; **to take disciplinary action against someone** = to punish someone

disclaim [dɪs'kleɪm] *verb* to refuse to admit *or* accept; *he disclaimed all knowledge of the bomb; the management disclaims all responsibility for customers' property*

◊ **disclaimer** [dɪs'kleɪmə] *noun* **(a)** legal refusal to accept responsibility *or* to accept a right **(b)** clause in a contract where a party disclaims responsibility for something

disclose [dɪs'kləʊz] *verb* to tell (something); *the bank has no right to disclose details of my account to the tax office*

◊ **disclosure** [dɪs'kləʊʒə] *noun* act of telling details *or* of publishing a secret; *the disclosure of the takeover bid raised the price of the shares; the defendant's case was made stronger by the disclosure that the plaintiff was an undischarged bankrupt*

discrepancy [dɪs'krepənsi] *noun* difference between two sets of figures; *there is a discrepancy between the crime figures released by the Home Office and those of the Metropolitan Police Force*

discretion [dɪs'kreʃn] *noun* freedom to decide correctly what should be done; *the chairman has discretion to make minor staff appointments;* **to exercise one's discretion** = to decide which of several possible ways to act; **the court exercised its discretion** = the court decided what should be done; **I leave it to your discretion** = I leave it for you to decide what to do; **at the discretion of someone** = the decision is left to be made by someone; *membership is at the discretion of the committee; sentencing is at the discretion of the judge; the granting of an injunction is at the discretion of the court*

◊ **discretionary** [dɪs'kreʃənri] *adjective* which can be used if someone wants; **the minister's discretionary powers** = powers which the minister could use if he thought he should do so; **the tribunal has wide discretionary powers** = the tribunal can decide on many different courses of action

discriminate [dɪs'krɪmɪneɪt] *verb* **(a)** to note differences between things and act accordingly; *the planning committee finds it difficult to discriminate between applications which improve the community, and those which are purely commercial;* **to discriminate against someone** = to treat someone unequally; *the council was accused of discriminating against women in its recruitment policy; he claimed he had been discriminated against because of his colour*

◊ **discrimination** [dɪskrɪmɪ'neɪʃn] *noun* **(a)** noting the differences between things; *the arts committee showed discrimination in selecting the design for the new civic centre* **(b)** action which treats different groups of people in different and unequal ways; *racial discrimination is against the law; she accused the council of sexual discrimination in their recruitment policy;* **positive discrimination** = giving more favourable treatment to one group to help them be more equal; *the council's policy of positive discrimination has ensured that more women are appointed to senior posts*

discuss [dɪs'kʌs] *verb* to talk about a problem; *they spent two hours discussing the details of the contract; the inspectors discussed the closing of the building*

◊ **discussion** [dɪs'kʌʃn] *noun* talking about a problem; *after some discussion the committee agreed to an adjournment*

disenfranchise *or* disfranchise

[dɪsɪn'fræntʃaɪz *or* dɪs'fræntʃaɪz] *verb* to take away someone's right to vote; *the*

government tried to disenfranchise some of the immigrant groups

disloyal [dɪs'lɔɪəl] *adjective* not loyal, not true to the ideology of a political party

◊ **disloyalty** [dɪs'lɔɪəlti] *noun* being disloyal

dismantle [dɪs'mæntl] *verb* to take to pieces; *the government is trying to dismantle the labour legislation set up by its predecessors*

dismiss [dɪs'mɪs] *verb* to remove (an employee) from a job; *the President suddenly dismissed the Prime Minister and called for new general elections; the council has dismissed two of its maintenance staff*

◊ **dismissal** [dɪs'mɪsəl] *noun* removing someone from a job; *he went into opposition after his dismissal from office*

disobey [dɪsə'beɪ] *verb* not to obey; *the husband disobeyed the court order to pay maintenance to his children*

◊ **disobedience** [dɪsə'biːdiəns] *noun* not obeying; *the prisoners were put in solitary confinement as punishment for their disobedience of the governor's orders;* **civil disobedience** = disobeying orders by civil authorities (such as the police) as an act of protest; *the group planned a campaign of civil disobedience as a protest against restrictions on immigrants;* (NOTE: no plural)

disorder [dɪs'ɔːdə] *noun* lack of order *or* of control; **civil disorder** *or* **public disorder** *or* **public disorders** = riots *or* disturbances *or* fighting in the streets

◊ **disorderly** [dɪs'ɔːdəli] *adjective* badly behaved *or* wild; *he was charged with disorderly conduct *or* with being drunk and disorderly*

dispense [dɪs'pens] *verb* **(a)** to give out (justice) **(b)** **to dispense with something** = not to use *or* to do without something; *the chairman of the tribunal dispensed with the formality of taking minutes; the Director of Education decided to dispense with the services of a his second assistant*

◊ **dispensation** [dɪspən'seɪʃn] *noun* **(a)** act of giving out justice **(b)** special permission to do something which is normally not allowed or is against the law; *by special dispensation the witness was allowed to bring a lawyer*

disposal [dɪsˈpəʊzl] *noun* getting rid of something; **waste disposal** = getting rid of rubbish; *domestic refuse collection is just one part of the council's waste disposal services*

disqualify [dɪsˈkwɒlɪfaɪ] *verb* to make (someone) not able to do something; *being a judge disqualifies him from being a Member of Parliament; after the accident he was fined £1,000 and disqualified from driving for two years; applicants will be disqualified for canvassing*

◊ **disqualification** [dɪskwɒlɪfɪˈkeɪʃn] *noun* being disqualified from doing something; **disqualification from office** = rule which forces a director to be removed from a directorship if he does not fulfil certain conditions

disrupt [dɪsˈrʌpt] *verb* to interrupt (a meeting) noisily; *the meeting of the committee was disrupted by demonstrators singing*

◊ **disruption** [dɪsˈrʌpʃn] *noun* act of disrupting; *after the disruption had ended the chairman tried to reconvene the meeting*

◊ **disruptive** [dɪsˈrʌptɪv] *adjective* which disrupts; *disruptive behaviour in the public galleries prevented the planning inquiry from taking evidence*

dissent [dɪˈsent] **1** *noun* not agreeing; *the opposition showed its dissent by voting against the Bill* **2** *verb* not to agree with someone; *the motion was carried, three councillors dissented;* **dissenting opinion** = opinion of a member of a committee, showing that he disagrees with the other members

dissident [ˈdɪsɪdənt] **1** *adjective* not in agreement with a ruling political régime; *a dissident writer* **2** *noun* person who is not in agreement with a ruling political régime

dissolve [dɪˈzɒlv] *verb* to bring to an end; *to dissolve a marriage* or *a partnership* or *a company;* **to dissolve Parliament** = to end a session of Parliament, and so force a general election

◊ **dissolution** [dɪsəˈluːʃn] *noun* ending (of a partnership *or* a marriage); **dissolution of Parliament** = ending of a Parliament, so forcing a general election; *the government lost the vote of no confidence, and so the Prime Minister asked for a dissolution of parliament*

COMMENT: the British Parliament can only be dissolved by the Queen, acting on the advice of the Prime Minister

dissuade [dɪˈsweɪd] *verb* **to dissuade someone from something** = to persuade someone not to do something

◊ **dissuasion** [dɪˈsweɪʒn] *noun* persuading someone not to something

distinction [dɪsˈtɪŋkʃn] *noun* **(a)** difference between two things; *there is no distinction between payments to individuals and to organizations; I see no distinction between the two claims* **(b)** thing which makes someone better than others; *he has the distinction of being the longest serving Member of Parliament* **(c)** honour (such as a medal *or* prize) given to someone; *she had received several distinctions from foreign governments*

◊ **distinguish** [dɪsˈtɪŋgwɪʃ] *verb* to state the difference between two things; (NOTE: you distinguish one thing **from** another, or you distinguish **between** two things)

distribute [dɪsˈtrɪbjuːt] *verb* to share out *or* to give out (to various people); *the money in the estate is to be distributed among the members of the deceased's family*

◊ **distribution** [dɪstrɪˈbjuːʃn] *noun* sharing out property in an estate; **distribution of assets** = sharing the assets of a company among the shareholders

district [ˈdɪstrɪkt] *noun* section of a town *or* of a country; **postal district** = area of a town identified by a certain postcode

◊ **district attorney (DA)** ['dɪstrɪkt ə'tɜːni] *noun US* (i) prosecuting attorney in a federal district; (ii) state prosecuting attorney

◊ **district council** ['dɪstrɪkt 'kaʊnsəl] *noun* elected body which runs a local area

COMMENT: there are two kinds of district council: those covering large urban areas or metropolitan districts, which are responsible for all local matters; and non-metropolitan districts which deal with some local matters, but leaving other matters to be dealt with by the county council

◊ **district court** ['dɪstrɪkt 'kɔːt] *noun US* court in a federal district

◊ **District Health Authority (DHA)** ['dɪstrɪkt 'helθ ɔː'θɒrɪti] *noun* administrative unit in the national Health Service which is responsible for all health services in a district, including hospitals and clinics

◊ **District of Columbia (DC)** ['dɪstrɪkt v kə'lʌmbiə] *noun* district of which Washington is the centre, which is not part of any state of the USA and is administered directly by Congress

disturbance [dɪs'tɜːbəns] *noun* riot *or* fighting *or* noisy behaviour in the street; *the police were called out to control the disturbances near the Parliament building*

divide [dɪ'vaɪd] *verb* (a) to cut into separate sections; *the country is divided into six administrative regions; the two departments agreed to divide the work between them* (b) *(in the House of Commons)* to vote; *the House divided at 10.30* (c) not unanimous; **opinion is divided over the question** = people disagree over the problem

division [dɪ'vɪʒn] *noun* (a) section of something which is divided into several sections; *Smith's is now a division of the Brown group of companies* (b) separate section of the High Court (the Queen's Bench Division, the Family Division and the Chancery Division) or the separate sections of the Appeal Court (Civil Division and Criminal Division) (c) vote in the House of Commons; *in the division on the Law and Order Bill, the government had a*

comfortable majority; **division bell** = bell which is rung to warn MPs that a vote is going to be taken; **division bell area** = area round the House of Commons which is near enough for MPs to hear the division bell and run to vote (eight minutes is allowed between the bell and the vote); *he has a flat in the division bell area;* **division lobby** = one of the two corridors beside the House of Commons where MPs pass to vote (the Ayes lobby and the Noes lobby); *US* **division vote** *or* **standing vote** = vote in the House of Representatives, where members stand up to be counted and the vote is not recorded in the record (c) act of dividing *or* of being divided; **to have a division of opinion** = to disagree; **division of responsibility** = act of splitting the responsibility for something between several people

COMMENT: when a division is called in the House of Commons, the Speaker names four MPs as tellers, bells are rung and the doors out of the division lobbies are closed. MPs file through the lobbies and are counted as they pass through the doors and go back into the chamber. At the end of the division, the tellers report the numbers of Ayes and Noes, and the Speaker declares the result by saying 'the Ayes have it' or 'the Noes have it'

◊ **divisional** [dɪ'vɪʒnəl] *adjective* referring to a division; *a divisional education officer*

DLO = DIRECT LABOUR ORGANIZATION

```
a good DLO will subcontract
work to the private sector, if
only to give itself a benchmark
for performance measurement
```
Local Government News

doctrine ['dɒktrɪn] *noun* general principle of law; *US* **the Monroe Doctrine** = the principle that the USA has an interest in preventing outside interference in the internal affairs of other American countries

document ['dɒkjuːmənt] **1** *noun* (a) paper with writing on it; *deeds, contracts and wills are all legal documents* (b) official paper from a government department; **consultation**

document or consultative document = paper which is issued by a government department to people who are asked to comment and make suggestions for improvement **2** *verb* to put in a published paper; *the cases of unparliamentary language are well documented in Hansard*

◊ **documentary** [dɒkjuˈmentri] *adjective* in the form of documents; *documentary evidence; documentary proof*

◊ **documentation** [dɒkjuːmənˈteɪʃn] *noun* all documents referring to something; *please send me the complete documentation concerning the sale;* (NOTE: no plural)

Dod's Parliamentary Companion

[ˈdɒdz] *noun* small reference book, containing details of all MPs, their constituencies, government posts, etc.

domain [dəˈmeɪn] *noun* area of responsibility; **public domain** = land or property or information which belongs to and is available to the public; **publication which is in the public domain** = publication which is no longer in copyright

Domesday Book [ˈduːmzdeɪ bʊk] *noun* record made for King William I in 1086, which recorded lands in England and their owners and inhabitants for tax purposes

domestic [dəˈmestɪk] *adjective* **(a)** referring to a family; **domestic premises** = house or flat, etc., used for private accommodation; **domestic rate** = local tax which is levied on houses and flats **(b)** referring to the home country or to the country where a business is situated; *the remarks by the ambassador were regarded as interference in the country's domestic affairs;* **domestic consumption** = consumption on the home market; **domestic market** = market in the country where a company is based; **domestic production** = production of goods in the home country

domicile [ˈdɒmɪsaɪl] **1** *noun* country where someone is deemed to live permanently or where a company's office is registered (especially for tax purposes); **domicile of origin** = domicile which a person has from birth (usually the domicile of the father);

domicile of choice = country where someone has chosen to live, which is not the domicile of origin **2** *verb* **he is domiciled in Denmark** = he lives in Denmark officially; **bills domiciled in France** = bills of exchange which have to be paid in France

dominion [dəˈmɪnjən] *noun* **(a)** power of control; *to exercise dominion over a country* **(b)** **a Dominion** = an independent state, part of the British Commonwealth; *the Dominion of Canada;* **Dominion Day** = Canadian National Day (1st July)

domino effect [ˈdɒmɪnəʊ ɪˈfekt] *noun* collapse of one party, which provokes the collapse of the next (as in the case of a country falling under the control of an aggressor, so allowing the aggressor to attack its neighbour)

donate [dəʊˈneɪt] *verb* to give money (to a party, charity, etc.

◊ **donation** [dəˈneɪʃn] *noun* money given to a party, charity, etc., to help it to work; *donations have fallen since the split in the party hierarchy*

doorstep [ˈdɔːstep] **1** *noun* step at the entrance to a house; *he spent six nights canvassing on people's doorsteps;* **doorstep poll** = opinion poll carried out by asking people questions at their front doors; *a doorstep poll suggested that the sitting MP might lose his seat* **2** *verb* to canvass at people's doors

dormant [ˈdɔːmənt] *adjective* not active; *the committee decided to let the matter lie dormant for a while;* **dormant account** = bank account which is not used

dossier [ˈdɒsɪə] *noun* collection of relevant papers on a particular subject

double [dʌbl] **1** *adjective* **(a)** twice as large or two times the size; **double taxation** = taxing the same income twice; **double taxation agreement** or **treaty** = agreement between two countries that a person living in one country shall not be taxed in both countries on the income earned in the other country **(b)** which happens twice; **in double figures** = with two figures or 10 to 99;

inflation is in double figures; we have had double-figure inflation for some years; **double jeopardy** = right of a citizen not to be tried twice for the same crime **2** *verb* to become twice as big; to make something twice as big; *our rate of inflation has doubled in the last three years*

dove [dʌv] *noun* person who prefers diplomacy and tries to achieve peace (as opposed to a hawk)

◊ **doveish** ['dʌvɪʃ] *adjective* like a dove; *he was accused of having doveish tendencies*

Downing Street ['daʊnɪŋ striːt] *noun* street in London where the Prime Minister and Chancellor of the Exchequer have their official houses; **10 Downing Street** = house of the Prime Minister, where the cabinet meets and which is the centre of the executive branch of the British government; **No. 11 Downing Street** = official house of the Chancellor of the Exchequer; (NOTE: the words 'Downing Street' are often used to mean 'the Prime Minister' or even 'the British government': a Downing Street spokesman revealed that the plan had still to be approved by the Treasury; Downing Street sources indicate that the Prime Minister has given the go-ahead for the change; Downing Street is angry at suggestions that the treaty will not be ratified. See also NUMBER TEN)

doyen of the diplomatic corps
['dɔɪən] *noun* senior ambassador in a country (that is the ambassador who has been in that country the longest)

DPP = DIRECTOR OF PUBLIC PROSECUTIONS

draconian [drə'kəʊnjən] *adjective* very severe *or* harsh; *the government took draconian measures against the student protesters*

draft [drɑːft] **1** *noun* **(a)** order for money to be paid by a bank; **to make a draft on a bank** = to ask a bank to pay money for you; **bank draft** *or* **banker's draft** = cheque payable by a bank; **sight draft** = bill of exchange which is payable when it is presented **(b)** first rough plan *or* document

which has not been finished; *draft of a contract or draft contract; he drew up the draft agreement on the back of an envelope; the draft minutes were sent to the chairman for approval; the draft Bill is with the House of Commons lawyers; the draft of the press release was passed by the Minister* **rough draft** = plan of a document which may have changes made to it before it is complete **2** *verb* to make a first rough plan of a document; *to draft a contract or a document or a bill; the contract is still being drafted or is still in the drafting stage*

◊ **drafter** ['drɑːftə] *noun* person who makes a draft

◊ **drafting** ['drɑːftɪŋ] *noun* act of preparing the draft of a document; *the drafting of the contract took six weeks; the drafting stage of a parliamentary Bill*

◊ **draftsman** *or* **draughtsman**
['drɑːftsmən] *noun* person who drafts documents; **parliamentary draftsman** = lawyer who drafts Bills going before Parliament

drastic ['dræstɪk] *adjective* severe; *drastic measures were necessary to keep the population under government control*

◊ **drastically** ['dræstɪkli] *adverb* sharply; *the government's popularity has fallen drastically since the election*

draw up ['drɔː 'ʌp] *verb* to write a legal document; *to draw up a contract or an agreement; to draw up a company's articles of association*

drop [drɒp] **1** *noun* fall; *the opinion polls show a drop in support for the government* **2** *verb* **(a)** to fall; *government support has dropped by 10% or has dropped 10%; the pound dropped three points against the dollar* **(b)** to give up; *the opposition have dropped their motion of no confidence; he dropped his plan to build an extension to the garage;* (NOTE: dropping - dropped)

dual ['djuːəl] *adjective* referring to two things; **person of dual nationality** *or* **person who has dual nationality** = person who is a citizen of two countries

ducal ['dju:kl] *adjective* referring to a duke or duchess

duchess ['dʌtʃəs] *noun* wife of a duke; woman who holds the title of a duke

◊ **duchy** ['dʌtʃi] *noun* territory ruled by a duke; *see also* CHANCELLOR

due [dju:] *adjective* **(a)** owed; **to fall due** *or* **to become due** = to be ready for payment; **balance due to us** = amount owed to us which should be paid **(b)** expected to arrive; *the plane is due to arrive at 10.30 or is due at 10.30* **(c)** proper *or* as is right; **in due form** = written in the correct legal form; *receipt in due form; contract drawn up in due form;* **driving without due care and attention** = offence of driving in such a way that other people and property may be harmed; **after due consideration of the problem** = after thinking seriously about the problem; **the due process of the law** = the formal work of a fair legal action **(d) due to** = caused by; *the late completion of the building programme was due to a strike by the construction workers; supplies have been delayed due to bad weather; the council continues to pay the wages of staff who are absent due to illness*

duke [dju:k] *noun* nobleman of the highest rank; **Royal Duke** = prince of the royal house who has been given the title of Duke; *see also* DUCHY (NOTE: the wife of a duke is a duchess)

duly ['dju:li] *adverb* **(a)** properly; *duly authorized representative* **(b)** as was expected; *we duly received his letter of 21st October*

Duma ['dju:mə] *noun* **State Duma** = lower house of the legislature in Russia

dummy ['dʌmi] *noun* paper with the titles of a Bill, presented in the House of Commons for the First Reading when the short title is read out by the clerk

duplicate 1 ['dju:plɪkət] *noun* copy; *he sent me the duplicate of the contract;* **duplicate receipt** *or* **duplicate of a receipt** = copy of a receipt; **in duplicate** = with a copy; **receipt in duplicate** = two copies of a

receipt; *to print an invoice in duplicate* **2** ['dju:plɪkeɪt] *verb* **(a)** *(of entry in accounts)* **to duplicate with another entry** = to repeat another entry *or* to be the same as another entry **(b) to duplicate a letter** = to make a copy of a letter

◊ **duplicating** ['dju:plɪkeɪtɪŋ] *noun* copying; **duplicating machine** = machine which makes copies of documents; **duplicating paper** = special paper to be used in a duplicating machine

◊ **duplication** [dju:plɪ'keɪʃn] *noun* copying of documents; **duplication of work** = work which is done twice without being necessary

◊ **duplicator** ['dju:plɪkeɪtə] *noun* machine which makes copies of documents

duty ['dju:ti] *noun* **(a)** work which a person has to do; *it is the duty of every citizen to serve on a jury if called; the government has a duty to protect its citizens from criminals;* **duty of care** = duty which every citizen has not to act negligently towards others **(b)** official work which you have to do in a job; **to be on duty** = to be doing official work at a special time; **night duty** = work done at night; **duty sergeant** = police sergeant who is on duty at a particular time **(c)** tax which has to be paid; *to take the duty off alcohol; to put a duty on cigarettes;* **ad valorem duty** = duty calculated on the sales value of the goods; **customs duty** *or* **import duty** = tax on goods imported into a country; **excise duty** = tax on the sale of goods (such as alcohol and petrol) which are produced in the country *or* on imports where the duty was not paid on entry into the country; **goods which are liable to duty** = goods on which customs or excise tax has to be paid; **duty-paid goods** = goods where the duty has been paid; **stamp duty** = tax on legal documents (such as the conveyance of a property to a new owner); **estate duty** *or US* **death duty** = tax paid on the property left by a dead person

◊ **duty bound** ['dju:ti 'baʊnd] *adjective* bound to do something because it is your duty; *witnesses under oath are duty bound to tell the truth*

◊ **dutiable** ['djuːtiəbl] *adjective* **dutiable goods** *or* **dutiable items** = goods on which a customs or excise duty has to be paid

dwelling ['dwelɪŋ] *noun* place where someone lives (such as a house *or* flat); *the tax on dwellings has been raised*

dynasty ['dɪnəsti] *noun* (a) family of rulers, following one after the other; *the Ming dynasty ruled China from 1368 to 1644* (b) period of rule by members of the same family

◊ **dynastic** [dɪ'næstɪk] *adjective* referring to a dynasty; *the rules of dynastic succession*

Ee

E [iː] *fifth letter of the alphabet* **Schedule E** = schedule to the Finance Acts under which tax is charged on wages, salaries and pensions; **Table E** = model memorandum and articles of association of an unlimited company with share capital set out in the Companies Act

earl [ɜːl] *noun* peer of middle rank, below a marquess and above a viscount; (NOTE: the wife of an **earl** is a **countess**)

◊ **earldom** [ˈɜːldəm] *noun* title of earl

early [ˈɜːli] *adjective & adverb* **(a)** before the usual time; **early closing day** = weekday, usually Wednesday or Thursday, when most shops in a town close in the afternoon; **at your earliest convenience** = as soon as you find it possible; **at an early date** = very soon; **early day motion** = motion proposed in the House of Commons for discussion at an early date (usually used to introduce a particular point of view without necessarily going to a full debate) **(b)** at the beginning of a period of time; *he took an early train to Paris;* **we hope for an early resumption of negotiations** = we hope negotiations will start again soon

earmark [ˈiːmɑːk] *verb* to reserve for a special purpose; *to earmark funds for a project; the grant is earmarked for computer systems development*

east [iːst] *adjective, adverb & noun* **(a)** one of the directions on the earth's surface, the direction facing the rising sun **(b)** region of a country or the world; **the Far East** = countries to the east of India; **the Middle East** = countries to the east of Egypt and west of Pakistan; **the Near East** = countries at the eastern end of the Mediterranean; *(as opposed to* THE WEST)

Easter [ˈiːstə] *noun* one of the four sittings of the Law Courts; one of the four law terms

easy [ˈiːzi] *adjective* not difficult; **easy terms** = credit terms which are not difficult to accept *or* instalments which are easy to pay; **the loan is repayable in easy payments** = with very small sums paid back regularly

◊ **easily** [ˈiːzɪli] *adverb* **(a)** without any difficulty; *the motion was passed by the Commons easily* **(b)** much *or* by far; *this is easily the most important piece of legislation before the House this session; the firm is easily the biggest in the market; this is easily the largest consignment of drugs to have been seized by the Customs*

EC [iːˈsiː] = EUROPEAN COMMUNITY *EC ministers met today in Brussels; the USA is increasing its trade with the EC;* (NOTE: now referred to as **EU** or **European Union**)

economy [ɪˈkɒnəmi] *noun* **(a)** being careful not to waste money *or* materials; **an economy measure** = action to try to save money *or* materials; **economies of scale** = making a product *or* service more cheaply by producing it *or* buying it *or* offering it in large quantities **(b)** financial state of a country *or* the way in which a country makes and uses its money; **black economy** = work which is paid for in cash *or* goods but not declared to the tax authorities; **free market economy** = system where the government does not interfere in business activity in any way

◊ **economic** [iːkəˈnɒmɪk] *adjective* referring to economy; *the government's economic policy was shown to be working; it would not be economic to open the Council Offices on Sundays;* **economic sanctions** = restrictions on trade with a country in order to influence its political situation *or* in order to make its government change its policy

ECU = EUROPEAN CURRENCY UNIT

edict ['i:dɪkt] *noun* public announcement of a law

editor ['edɪtə] *noun* (i) person in charge of a newspaper or a section of a newspaper; (ii) person who is responsible for a reference book; (iii) person who checks the work of a writer; (iv) computer program used for writing and checking text **political editor** = editor of a British newspaper dealing with political parties and government

◊ **editorial** ['edɪtɔːrɪəl] **1** *adjective* referring to an editor; **editorial board** = group of editors (on a newspaper, etc.) **2** *noun* main article in a newspaper, written by the editor

education [edjʊ'keɪʃn] *noun* teaching of children and students; **the Department for Education and Employment** = British government department which deals with education; **Director of Education** = officer of a local authority who is responsible for schools and colleges in the area; **further education** = teaching of students after they have left school; *the borough's College of Further Education offers a wide range of courses*

COMMENT: although the Department of Education and Science has overall responsibility for education, much of the decision-making is in the hands of the local authorities, their Directors of Education and the schools themselves

Eduskunta [edʊs'kʊntə] *noun* single body of legislature in Finland

EEA = EUROPEAN ECONOMIC AREA

EEC = EUROPEAN ECONOMIC COMMUNITY (NOTE: now simply **EC** or **European Community**)

Eerste Kamer ['eəstə 'kæmə] *noun* upper house of the States-General (or Parliament) in the Netherlands

effect [ɪ'fekt] **1** *noun* **(a)** result; **to put into effect** = to make terms or conditions apply; **terms of a contract which take effect** *or* **come into effect from January 1st** = terms which start to operate on January 1st; **prices are increased 10% with effect from January 1st** = new prices will apply from January 1st; **to remain in effect** = to continue to be applied **(b)** meaning; **clause to the effect that** = clause which means that; **we have made provision to this effect** = we have put into the contract terms which will make this work **(c)** **personal effects** = personal belongings **2** *verb* to carry out; **to effect a payment** = to make a payment; **to effect customs clearance** = to clear something through customs; **to effect a settlement between two parties** = to bring two parties together and make them agree to a settlement

◊ **effective** [ɪ'fektɪv] *adjective* which works well *or* which gives the correct result; *the Finance Department is trying to find an effective means of collecting rent arrears;* **effective date** = date on which a rule *or* a contract starts to be applied; **clause effective as from January 1st** = clause which starts to be applied on January 1st

efficient [ɪ'fɪʃənt] *adjective* working well; *an efficient secretary; the efficient policing of city centres*

◊ **efficiently** [ɪ'fɪʃəntli] *adverb* which works well; *the police coped efficiently with the crowds of protesters*

EFTA = EUROPEAN FREE TRADE AREA

e.g. ['iː'dʒiː] for example *or* such as; *the contract is valid in some countries (e.g. France and Belgium) but not in others*

egalitarianism [iːgælɪ'teərɪənɪzm] *noun* political theory that all members of society have equal rights and should have equal treatment

◊ **egalitarian** [iːgælɪ'teərɪən] **1** *adjective* referring to egalitarianism; *he holds egalitarian views* **2** *noun* person who supports egalitarianism

EGM [ˈiːdʒiːˈem] = EXTRAORDINARY GENERAL MEETING

Éireann [ˈeərən] *see* DAIL, SEANAD

elect [ɪˈlekt] *verb* **(a)** to choose someone by a vote; *a vote to elect the officers of an association; she was elected chair of the committee; he was first elected for this constituency in 1979* **(b)** to choose to do something; *he elected to stand trial by jury*

◊ **-elect** [ɪˈlekt] *suffix* person who has been elected but has not yet started the term of office; *she is the president-elect;* (NOTE: the plural is **presidents-elect**)

◊ **election** [ɪˈlekʃn] *noun* **(a)** act of electing a representative *or* representatives; **general election** = choosing of a parliament by all the voters in a country; **local elections** *or* **municipal elections** = elections to choose representatives for local government *or* for a town *or* county council; **election agent** = agent appointed by a party to organize its campaign in a constituency during an election; *the ruling party lost votes in the general election or in the elections for local councils; the election results are shown on television; see also* BY-ELECTION **(b)** act of choosing; *his election as president of the society; the accused made his election for jury trial*

◊ **electioneer** [ɪlekʃəˈnɪə] *verb (often as criticism)* to try to attract votes in an election; *cutting taxes just before the election is pure electioneering*

◊ **elector** [ɪˈlektə] *noun* person who votes or who is eligible to vote in an election; **register of electors** = official list of names and addresses of people living in a certain area who are eligible to vote in local or national elections

◊ **electoral** [ɪˈlektərəl] *adjective* referring to an election; **electoral roll** *or* **electoral register** = REGISTER OF ELECTORS **electoral college** = group of people elected by a larger group to vote on their behalf in an election

◊ **electorate** [ɪˈlektərət] *noun* all electors taken as a group; (NOTE: **electorate** is a group noun and can take a singular or plural verb: **the electorate is tired of party political broadcasts; the British electorate want a change of government**)

COMMENT: in Britain, a Parliament can only last for a maximum of five years, and a dissolution is usually called by the Prime Minister before the end of that period. The Lord Chancellor then issues a writ for the election of MPs. All British subjects (including Commonwealth and Irish citizens), are eligible to vote in British elections provided they are on the electoral register, are over 18 years of age, are sane, are not members of the House of Lords and are not serving prison sentences for serious crime. In the USA, members of the House of Representatives are elected for a two-year period. Senators are elected for six-year terms, one third of the Senate being elected every two years. The President of the USA is elected by an electoral college made up of people elected by voters in each of the states of the USA. Each state elects the same number of electors to the electoral college as it has Congressmen, plus two. This guarantees that the college is broadly representative of voters across the country. The presidential candidate with an overall majority in the college is elected president. A presidential term of office is four years, and a president can stand for re-election once

eligible [ˈelɪdʒɪbl] *adjective* person who can be chosen; *she is eligible for re-election*

◊ **eligibility** [elɪdʒəˈbɪləti] *noun* being eligible; *the chairman questioned her eligibility to stand for re-election*

élite [eɪˈliːt] *noun* top people in a group or society; *the country is run by an élite of thirty families*

e-mail [ˈiːmeɪl] *noun* electronic mail, a system of sending messages from one computer to another, using the telephone lines

emancipation [ɪmænsɪˈpeɪʃn] *noun* making free, especially making a slave free *or* giving someone the right to vote

embargo [ɪmˈbɑːgəʊ] **1** *noun* government order which stops something, such as a type of trade; **to lay** *or* **put an embargo on trade with a country** = to say that trade with a country must not take place; **to put an embargo on a press release** = to say that the information in the release must not be published before a certain date; **to lift an embargo** = to allow trade to start again; **to be under an embargo** = to be forbidden; (NOTE: plural is **embargoes**) **2** *verb* to stop something *or* not to allow something to take place; *the government has embargoed trade with the Eastern countries;* **the press release was embargoed until 1st January** = the information in the release could not be published until 1st January

embassy ['embəsi] *noun* **(a)** building where an ambassador and other diplomats work in a foreign country; *each embassy is guarded by special police; the embassy cleaners planted bugs in the ambassador's office; the American Embassy is in Grosvenor Square* **(b)** an ambassador and his staff, sent by a government to represent it in another country, usually on a temporary basis; *Queen Elizabeth I sent an embassy to the Tsar Ivan the Terrible*

COMMENT: an embassy is the territory of the country which it represents. The police and armed forces of the country where the embassy is situated are not allowed to enter the embassy without official permission. People seeking asylum can take refuge in embassies, but it is not easy for them to leave, as to do so they have to step back into the country against which they are seeking protection

emblem ['embləm] *noun* object used as the symbol of a country, state, town, etc.; *the leek is the emblem of Wales*

emergency [ɪ'mɜːdʒənsi] *noun* dangerous situation where decisions have to be taken quickly; **the government declared a state of emergency** = the government decided that the situation was so dangerous that the police *or* army had to run the country; **to call for an emergency debate** = to ask for a special debate on a certain subject which is very important (if an MP asks for an emergency debate before 12 noon on a certain day, and if

the subject is considered serious, the House will debate it at 7 p.m. on the following day) **to take emergency measures** = to take action rapidly to stop a serious state of affairs developing; **emergency planning department** = department in a local council which plans for action to be taken in case of major accidents, etc.; **emergency planning officer** = council official who plans and supervises action to deal with crises, such as major accidents, etc.; **emergency powers** = special powers granted by law to a government *or* to a minister to deal with an emergency, usually without going through the normal democratic processes; **emergency reserves** = ready cash held in case it is needed suddenly; **emergency services** = police, fire and ambulance services, which are ready for action if an emergency arises

emergent [ɪ'mɜːdʒənt] *adjective* recently created; still in the process of developing; **emergent countries of Africa** = African countries which have recently become independent; **emergent economies from Asia**

emigrate ['emigreit] *verb* to go to another country to live permanently

◊ **emigration** [emi'greiʃn] *noun* leaving a country to go to live permanently in another country

◊ **emigrant** ['emigrənt] *noun* person who emigrates; (NOTE: an **emigrant** from one country becomes an **immigrant** in his new country)

emissary ['emisri] *noun* envoy, a person who carries a special message from one government to another

emoluments [ɪ'mɒljumənts] *plural noun* pay, salary or fees, or the earnings of directors who are not employees; (NOTE: US English uses the singular **emolument**)

emperor ['emprə] *noun* man who rules an empire; *the Emperor of Japan or the Japanese Emperor; see also* EMPRESS

◊ **empire** ['empaiə] *noun* (i) independent country ruled by an emperor; (ii) large group of countries ruled by one country, usually ruled by an emperor; *the Roman Empire covered most of what is now Europe; the*

British Empire came to an end after the Second World War, and was replaced by the Commonwealth; see also IMPERIAL, IMPERIALISM

employ [ɪm'plɔɪ] *verb* to give someone regular paid work; *the council employs disabled people in its offices; he runs a department employing two hundred people;* **to employ twenty staff** = to have twenty people working for you *or* to give work to twenty people

◊ **employed** [ɪm'plɔɪd] **1** *adjective* **(a)** in regular paid work; **he is not gainfully employed** = he has no regular paid work; **self-employed** = working for yourself; *he worked in a bank for ten years but now is self-employed* **(b)** (money) used profitably; *return against capital employed* **2** *plural noun* people who are working; *the employers and the employed;* **the self-employed** = people who work for themselves

◊ **employee** [emplɔɪ'i:] *noun* worker *or* person employed by someone; *employees of the firm are eligible to join a profit-sharing scheme; relations between management and employees have improved; the council has decided to stop taking on new employees*

◊ **employer** [ɪm'plɔɪə] *noun* person *or* company which has employees and pays them; **employers' organization** *or* **association** = group of employers with similar interests; **employer's contribution** = money paid by an employer towards an employee's pension

◊ **employment** [ɪm'plɔɪmənt] *noun* contractual relationship between an employer and employee; **conditions of employment** = terms of a contract whereby someone is employed; **contract of employment** *or* **employment contract** = contract between an employer and an employee showing all the conditions of work; **employment office** *or* **bureau** *or* **agency** = office which finds jobs for people; **Employment Appeal Tribunal** = court which hears appeals from industrial tribunals; **employment statistics** = government statistics on the numbers of people in work

empower [ɪm'pauə] *verb* to give someone the power to do something; *the agent is*

empowered to sell the property; she was empowered by the company to sign the contract; the government is empowered to call in the army to deal with the crisis

empress ['emprəs] *noun* **(a)** woman who rules an empire; *Queen Victoria was the Empress of India* **(b)** wife of an emperor

enable [ɪ'neɪbl] *verb* to make it possible for something to happen; **enabling legislation** *or* **statute** = Act of Parliament which gives a minister the power to put other legislation into effect

enact [ɪ'nækt] *verb* to make (a law); **enacting clause** *or* **enacting words** = first clause in a bill or act (starting with the words 'be it enacted that') which makes the act lawful

◊ **enactment** [ɪ'næktmənt] *noun* (i) making a law; (ii) an Act of Parliament

enclave ['enkleɪv] *noun* territory which belongs to one country and is totally surrounded by another country

enclose [ɪn'kləuz] *verb* to put something inside an envelope with a letter; *to enclose an invoice with a letter; I am enclosing a copy of the contract; a letter enclosing two cheques; please find the cheque enclosed herewith*

◊ **enclosure** [ɪn'kləuʒə] *noun* document enclosed with a letter

encourage [ɪn'kʌrɪdʒ] *verb* to help someone to do something *or* to help something to happen *or* to stimulate; *the government has set aside grants to encourage new industry to settle in the region; leaving windows open only encourages burglars; some people believe that lenient sentences encourage crime*

endorse [ɪn'dɔːs] *verb* **(a)** to agree with; *the council endorsed the action taken by the Chief Executive* **(b)** to endorse a bill *or* a cheque = to sign a bill *or* a cheque on the back to make it payable to someone else **(c)** to make a note on a driving licence that the holder has been convicted of a traffic offence

◊ **endorsee** [ɪndɔː'siː] *noun* person in whose favour a bill *or* a cheque is endorsed

◊ **endorsement** [ɪn'dɔːsmənt] *noun* **(a)** act of endorsing; signature on a document which endorses it **(b)** note on an insurance policy which adds conditions to the policy **(c)** note on a driving licence to show that the holder has been convicted of a traffic offence

◊ **endorser** [ɪn'dɔːsə] *noun* person who endorses a bill *or* cheque

enemy ['enəmi] *noun* person or country which is hostile to another

energy ['enədʒi] *noun* power used to heat *or* drive machines (such as electricity, oil, gas, etc.); *the department's new energy policy should cut fuel costs;* Department of **Energy** = government department which deals with the production of power for industry and domestic users; **an energy-efficient system** = a system which makes the best use of energy

enforce [ɪn'fɔːs] *verb* to make sure something is done *or* is obeyed; *to enforce the terms of a contract;* **to enforce a debt** = to make sure a debt is paid

◊ **enforceable** [ɪn'fɔːsəbl] *adjective* which can be enforced; *in practice the bylaw was not easily enforceable*

◊ **enforcement** [ɪn'fɔːsmənt] *noun* making sure that something is obeyed; *enforcement of the terms of a contract;* **law enforcement** = making sure that a law is obeyed; **law enforcement officers** = members of the police force, the Drug Squad, etc.; (NOTE: no plural)

enfranchise [ɪn'fræntʃaɪz] *verb* to give (someone) the right to vote

◊ **enfranchisement** [ɪn'fræntʃaɪzmənt] *noun* action of giving someone a vote; **leasehold enfranchisement** = right of a leaseholder to buy the freehold of the property which he is leasing

engage [ɪn'geɪdʒ] *verb* **(a)** to engage someone to do something = to bind someone contractually to do something; *the contract engages the council to purchase minimum annual quantities of goods* **(b)** to employ;

we have engaged the best commercial lawyer to represent us **(c)** to be engaged in = to be busy with; *he is engaged in work on computers; the company is engaged in trade with Africa*

◊ **engagé** [ɒn'gæʒeɪ] *adjective (of artists, writers, etc.)* showing political commitment

◊ **engaged** [ɪn'geɪdʒd] *adjective* busy (telephone); *you cannot speak to the manager - his line is engaged*

◊ **engagement** [ɪn'geɪdʒmənt] *noun* **(a)** agreement to do something; **to break an engagement to do something** = not to do what you have legally agreed to do **(b)** **engagements** = arrangements to meet people; *I have no engagements for the rest of the day; she noted the appointment in her engagements diary*

engross [ɪn'grəʊs] *verb* to draw up a legal document in its final form ready for signature; *US* **engrossed Bill** = Bill which has been passed by either the House of Representatives *or* Senate which is written out in its final form with all amendments to be sent to the other chamber for discussion

◊ **engrossment** [ɪn'grəʊsmənt] *noun* (i) drawing up of a legal document in its final form; (ii) legal document in its final form

enlarge [ɪn'lɑːdʒ] *verb* to make bigger; *several governments proposed to enlarge the EU to include countries of Eastern Europe*

◊ **enlargement** [ɪn'lɑːdʒmənt] *noun* making something larger; *1995 saw the enlargement of the EU to include Austria, Finland and Sweden as new member states*

enlist [ɪn'lɪst] *verb* to join up voluntarily as a member of the armed forces

enquire [ɪŋ'kwaɪə] = INQUIRE

◊ **enquiry** [ɪŋ'kwaɪri] = INQUIRY

enrol [ɪn'rəʊl] *verb* to join and register (as a student)

enrolled bill [ɪn'rəʊld 'bɪl] *noun US* final copy of a bill which has been passed by both House and Senate, and is written out with all its amendments for signature by the Speaker of the House of Representatives, the

President of the Senate and the President of the USA

ensuing [ɪnˈsjuːɪŋ] *adjective* which follows; *in the ensuing argument, MPs shouted and waved their order papers*

entente [ɒnˈtɒnt] *noun* agreement between two or more countries (used especially of the 'Entente Cordiale' between Britain and France in 1904)

enter [ˈentə] *verb* (a) to go in; *they all stood up when the mayor entered the council chamber* (b) to be elected to Parliament for the first time; *he entered Parliament in 1979* (c) to write; *he entered the name on a list; the clerk entered the objection in the minutes;* to enter a bid for something = to offer (usually in writing) to buy something; to enter a caveat = to warn legally that you have an interest in a case or other official matter, and that no steps can be taken without notice to you (d) to enter into = (i) to begin to do something; (ii) to agree to do something; *to enter into relations with someone; to enter into negotiations with a foreign government; to enter into a partnership with a friend; to enter into an agreement or a contract*

enterprise [ˈentəpraɪz] *noun* (a) system of carrying on a business; free enterprise = system of business free from government interference; enterprise zone = area of a country, where the government offers special subsidies to firms to encourage them to set up businesses (b) business which is carried on; *she runs a mail order enterprise*

entitle [ɪnˈtaɪtl] *verb* to give (someone) the right to something; *he is entitled to four weeks' holiday; a Privy Councillor is entitled to be heard in the House of Commons*

◊ **entitlement** [ɪnˈtaɪtəlmənt] *noun* thing to which someone is entitled; holiday entitlement = number of days' holiday to which an employee is entitled

entrenched [ɪnˈtrentʃt] *adjective* fixed or which cannot be moved; *the government's entrenched position on employees' rights;* entrenched clause = clause in a constitution

which stipulates that it cannot be amended except by an extraordinary process

entrust [ɪnˈtrʌst] *verb* to entrust someone with something *or* to entrust something to someone = to give someone the responsibility for looking after something; *the head of department entrusted the ordering of supplies to her secretary*

entry [ˈentri] *noun* (a) act of going into a building *or* onto land; *there is no right of entry through this door* (b) written information entered in a record; *the clerk copied the entries into the report*

◊ **entryism** [ˈentriːɪzm] *noun* way of taking control of a political party *or* elected body, where extremists join or are elected in a normal way, and are able to take over because of their numbers *or* because they are more active than other members

◊ **entryist** [ˈentriːɪst] *adjective* referring to entryism; *the party leader condemned entryist techniques*

environment [ɪnˈvaɪrənmənt] *noun* area *or* surroundings in which people live *or* work; Department of the Environment = British government department concerned with the conditions in which people live, and also is responsible for contacts between central government and certain aspects of local government

◊ **environmental** [ɪnvaɪrənˈmentl] *adjective* referring to the environment; *the Opposition spokesman on environmental issues;* environmental health = the health of the public as a whole; Environmental Health Officer = official of a local council who deals with matters of public health such as air pollution, bad sanitation, noise pollution, etc.

envoy [ˈenvɔɪ] *noun* (a) person who is sent with a message from one government *or* organization to another; *the President's special envoy to the Middle East* (b) senior diplomat with a rank below that of ambassador

equal [ˈiːkwəl] **1** *adjective* exactly the same; *male and female workers have equal pay;* Equal Opportunities Commission =

official committee set up to make sure that men and women have equal chances of employment and to remove discrimination between the sexes; **equal opportunities programme** = policy of avoiding discrimination against groups in society who have a disadvantage (such as handicapped people, etc.); (NOTE: in US English this is **affirmative action program**) **2** *noun* person who is at the same level as another (in rank, social position, etc.) **3** *verb* to be the same as; *production this month has equalled our best month ever;* (NOTE: **equalling - equalled** but US English is **equaling - equaled**)

◊ **equalitarian, equalitarianism** [ɪkwɒlɪ'teərɪən or ekwɒlɪ'teərɪənɪzm] *see* EGALITARIAN

◊ **equality** [ɪ'kwɒlɪti] *noun* **(a)** condition where all citizens are equal, have equal rights and are treated equally by the state **(b) equality of opportunity** = situation where each citizen has the same opportunity to get a job *or* be elected, etc.

◊ **equalization** [iːkwəlaɪ'zeɪʃn] *noun GB* **Exchange Equalization Account** = account with the Bank of England used by the government when buying or selling foreign currency to influence the exchange rate for the pound

◊ **equally** ['iːkwəli] *adverb* in the same way; *costs will be shared equally between the two parties*

> we hold these truths to be sacred and undeniable; that all men are created equal and in- dependent
>
> *Thomas Jefferson*

> all animals are equal, but some animals are more equal than others
>
> *George Orwell*

equivalence [ɪ'kwɪvələns] *noun* being equivalent

◊ **equivalent** [ɪ'kwɪvələnt] *adjective* **to be equivalent to** = to have the same value as *or* to be the same as; *the total dividend paid is equivalent to one quarter of the total profits*

Erskine May ['ɜːskɪn 'meɪ] *noun* book on the procedure and privileges of Parliament

> COMMENT: Erskine May's 'Treatise on the Law, Privileges, Proceedings and Usage of Parliament' was originally published in 1844. The author, Sir Thomas Erskine May, was Clerk of the House of Commons. The book is updated frequently, and is the authority on questions of parliamentary procedure

escalate ['eskəleɪt] *verb* to increase at a constant rate

◊ **escalation** ['eskəleɪʃn] *noun* **escalation of prices** = constant increase in prices

◊ **escalation clause** *or* **escalator clause** ['eskəleɪʃn 'klɔːz or 'eskeleɪtə 'klɔːz] *noun* clause in a contract allowing for regular price increases because of increased costs

espionage ['espiɒnɑːʒ] *noun* spying; *see also* COUNTER-ESPIONAGE

essential [ɪ'senʃəl] *adjective* very important *or* necessary; *it is essential that all the facts should be presented to the Committee as clearly as possible*

establish [ɪs'tæblɪʃ] *verb* **(a)** to set up *or* to make *or* to open; *the company has established a branch in Australia; the business was established in Scotland in 1823;* **established post** = permanent post in the civil service or similar organization; **to establish oneself in business** = to become successful in a new business **(b)** to decide what is correct *or* what is fact; *the Home Office is trying to establish the true numbers of immigrants*

◊ **establishment** [ɪs'tæblɪʃmənt] *noun* **(a)** commercial business; *he runs an important printing establishment* **(b)** *(in the EU)* **right of establishment** = right of an EU citizen to live and work in any EU country **(c)** number of people working in a department *or* company; **establishment charges** = cost of people and property, in a company's accounts; **establishment officer** = civil servant in charge of personnel in a government department; **to be on the**

establishment = to be a full-time employee; **office with an establishment of fifteen** = office with a permanent staff of fifteen **(d) the Establishment** = powerful and important people who run the country and its government; *the judiciary and the old universities form the basis of the Establishment; see also* GREAT

estimate 1 ['estɪmət] *noun* **(a)** calculation of probable cost *or* size *or* time of something; **rough estimate** = very approximate calculation; **at a conservative estimate** = calculation which probably underestimates the final figure; *the cost of street lighting has risen by at least 20% in the last year, and that is a conservative estimate;* **these figures are only an estimate** = these are not the final, accurate figures **(b)** calculation of how much something is likely to cost in the future, given to a client so as to get him to make an order; *before we can give the grant we must have an estimate of the total costs involved; to ask a builder for an estimate for building the new community centre;* **to put in an estimate** = to give someone a written calculation of the probable costs of carrying out a job **(c) estimates** = (i) detailed statements of future expenditure for each government department (divided into Civil Estimates and Defence Estimates) presented to the House of Commons for approval; (ii) detailed statements of future expenditure for each department of a local authority **estimates of expenditure** = calculation of future expenditure prepared for each government department by the minister; (NOTE: in central government departments the word **Estimates** is usually spelt with a capital E) **2** ['estɪmeɪt] *verb* **(a)** to calculate the probable cost *or* size *or* time of something; *he estimates that it will cost £1m or he estimates costs at £1m* **(b)** to estimate for a job = to state in writing the future costs of carrying out a piece of work so that a client can make an order

◊ **estimation** [estɪ'meɪʃn] *noun* judgment; *in my estimation, he is the best commercial lawyer in town*

◊ **estimator** ['estɪmeɪtə] *noun* person whose job is to calculate estimates for the carrying out of work

et al. *or* **et alia** ['et 'æl *or* 'et 'eɪliə] *Latin phrase meaning* 'and others' *or* 'and other things'

etc. *or* **etcetera** [et'setərə] and so on; *the import duty is to be paid on expensive items such as cars, watches, etc.*

ethical ['eθɪkl] *adjective* morally correct

ethnic ['eθnɪk] **1** *adjective* referring to a certain nation *or* race; **ethnic group** = people of a certain nation *or* race; **ethnic minority** = group of people of one race in a country where most people are of another race **2** *noun* person who belongs to a certain ethnic group

etiquette ['etɪket] *noun* conventional formality used in dealing with other people; **diplomatic etiquette** = formal conventions of behaviour between diplomats; **parliamentary etiquette** = formal conventions of behaviour in Parliament

Euratom [juː'rætəm] EUROPEAN ATOMIC ENERGY COMMUNITY

Euro ['juːrəʊ] *noun* name of the common European currency, agreed at the Council meeting held in Madrid in December 1995

Euro- ['juːrəʊ] *prefix* referring to Europe or the European Community; **Euro-constituency** *or* **Euro-seat** = constituency which elects an MEP to the European Parliament; **Euro-MP** = MEP *or* Member of the European Parliament

◊ **Eurocrat** ['juːrəʊkræt] *noun (informal)* bureaucrat working in any of the European Union institutions

◊ **European** [juːrəʊ'piːən] *adjective* referring to Europe; **the European Community *or* the European Union (EU)** = (formerly, the European Economic Community (EEC), the Common Market) a group of European countries linked together by the Treaty of Rome, basing their cooperation on the four fundamental freedoms of movement: of goods, capital, people and services **European Community Law** = law created by the European Community and enforceable in EU states; **European Commission *or* Commission of the European Community** = main executive body of the EU, made up of members nominated by each member state; **European Council** *see under* COUNCIL **European Court of Justice** = court responsible for settling disputes relating to European Community Law, and also acting as a last Court of Appeal against laws in individual countries; **European Court of Human Rights** = court considering the rights of citizens of states which are parties to the European Convention for the Protection of Human Rights; **European Economic Area (EEA)** = treaty to promote free trade between the EU and some European countries; **the European Monetary System** = system of controlled exchange rates between some member countries of the EU; **the European Parliament** = parliament of members (MEPs) elected in each member country of the EU; **Single European Act** = reworking of the basic community treaties, with the aim of creating a free internal market in 1992

◊ **Europol** ['juːrəʊpɒl] *noun* = EUROPEAN POLICE

◊ **European Social Charter** [jʊərə'piːən səʊʃl 'tʃɑːtə] charter for workers, drawn up by the EU in 1989, by which workers have the right to a fair wage, to equal treatment for men and women, a safe work environment, training, freedom of association and collective bargaining, provision for disabled workers, freedom of movement from country to country, guaranteed standards of living both for the working population as well as for retired people, etc. (there is no machinery for enforcing the Social Charter) (NOTE: the Social Charter is not the same as the Social Chapter)

Eurosceptic [juːrəʊ'skeptɪk] *adjective & noun* (person) who is reluctant to see further integration in the EU

evacuate [ɪ'vækjuːeɪt] *verb* to make the inhabitants or residents move from a place, because of the threat of disaster or invasion

evaluate [ɪ'væljuːeɪt] *verb* to calculate a value; *the new plans had arrived but there had not been time to evaluate them properly*

evidence ['evɪdəns] **1** *noun* (i) written or spoken statement of facts which helps to

prove something at a trial; (ii) spoken statement made to a committee of the House of Commons or House of Lords, taken down in shorthand and eventually printed; (iii) spoken or written statement made to a government or other inquiry *the National Association of Teachers of English gave evidence to the committee; the Home Secretary gave evidence before the Select Committee; in evidence presented to the tribunal, the trade union showed how its members' wages had not risen in line with the cost of living* documentary evidence = evidence in the form of documents; (NOTE: no plural; to refer to a single item say **a piece of evidence**) **2** *verb* to show; *the lack of good faith, as evidenced by the minister's refusal to make a statement to the Commons*

ex [eks] *preposition & prefix* **(a)** **share quoted ex dividend** = share price not including the right to receive the next dividend **(b)** former *or* formerly; *two ex-prime ministers attended the meeting; Mr Smith, the ex-chairman of the council; she claimed maintenance from her ex-husband* **(c)** **ex-directory number** = telephone number which is not printed in the list of people having telephone numbers

examine [ɪg'zæmɪn] *verb* to look at someone *or* something very carefully to see if it can be accepted; *the customs officials asked to examine the inside of the car; inspectors from the Department of Trade are examining the papers*

◊ **examination** [ɪgzæmɪ'neɪʃn] *noun* **(a)** asking someone questions to find out facts, such as the questioning of a prisoner by a magistrate **(b)** looking at something very carefully to see if it is acceptable; **customs examination** = looking at goods *or* baggage by customs officials **(c)** test to see if someone has passed a course; *he passed his law examinations; she came first in the final examination for the course; he failed his examination and so had to leave his job; see also* CROSS-EXAMINE, CROSS-EXAMINATION

◊ **examiner** [ɪg'zæmɪnə] *noun* person who conducts a test

example 109 **exchange**

example [ɪgˈzɑːmpl] *noun* **(a)** thing chosen to show something; *these sentences are a good example of the harshness of the military tribunals; new laws on computer copying provide an example of how the law changes to keep in step with new inventions;* **for example (e.g.)** = to show one thing out of many; *the government is taking steps to control drugs, for example by increasing the numbers of policemen in the Drug Squad* **(b)** thing which shows how something ought to be; **to set an example to someone** = to show someone how to behave; *members of the council ought to set an example to the community; the rioters were sentenced to periods of imprisonment as an example to others;* **to make an example of someone** = to punish someone harshly so that others will be warned not to do the same

exceed [ɪkˈsiːd] *verb* to be more than *or* to go beyond; *the car was exceeding the speed limit; the council has exceeded the spending limits set by the government; expenditure on new buildings must not exceed the sum allowed for in the estimates;* **to exceed one's powers** = to act in a way which one is not legally entitled to do; *the minister exceeded his powers in telling the local authority to rescind its decision*

excellency [ˈeksələnsi] *noun* being very good; **His Excellency** *or* **Her Excellency** = way of referring to an ambassador; (NOTE: abbreviated to **HE**)

excellent [ˈeksələnt] *adjective* very good; *the new Director of Education is a person of excellent character*

except [ɪkˈsept] *preposition & conjunction* not including; *VAT is levied on all goods and services except books, newspapers and children's clothes; sales are rising in all markets except the Far East; the rule applies in all cases, except where otherwise stated*

◊ **excepted** [ɪkˈseptɪd] *adverb* not including; **errors and omissions excepted** = note on an invoice to show that the company has no responsibility for mistakes in the invoice

◊ **exception** [ɪkˈsepʃn] *noun* **(a)** thing which is not included with others; *all Liberal MPs attended the meeting with the exception of the Leader* **(b)** objection raised to the ruling of a judge; **to take exception to something** = to object to something *or* to protest against something; *the Defence Minister took exception to the remarks made by his Opposition counterpart; he has taken exception to the reports of the debate in the newspapers*

◊ **exceptional** [ɪkˈsepʃnəl] *adjective* not usual *or* different; **exceptional items** = items in a balance sheet which do not appear there each year; **exceptional needs payment** = payment made by the social services to a claimant who has a particular urgent need (such as for clothes)

◊ **exceptionally** [ɪkˈsepʃnəli] *adverb* in an exceptional way; *the discussion of the item was exceptionally long*

excess [ɪkˈses] *noun* **(a)** amount which is more than what is allowed; **excess alcohol in the blood** = more alcohol in the blood than a driver is permitted to have; **excess fare** = extra fare to be paid (such as for travelling first class with a second class ticket); **excess profits** = profits which are more than is considered to be normal; **excess vote** = vote to approve the spending of more money than was originally authorized; **in excess** = above *or* more than; *quantities in excess of twenty-five kilos* **(b)** amount to be paid by the insured as part of any claim made under the terms of an insurance policy; *he has to pay a £50 excess, and the damage amounted to over £1,000*

◊ **excessive** [ɪkˈsesɪv] *adjective* too large; *we found the bill for costs excessive and applied to have it reduced; the driver had an excessive amount of alcohol in his blood*

exchange [ɪksˈtʃeɪndʒ] **1** *noun* **(a)** giving of one thing for another; **part exchange** = giving an old product as part of the payment for a new one **(b)** **foreign exchange** = (i) exchanging the money of one country for that of another; (ii) money of another country; **foreign exchange market** = dealings in foreign currencies; **rate of exchange** *or* **exchange rate** = price at which one currency is exchanged for another; **exchange controls** = government control over the exchange of the local currency for foreign currency; *the government had to impose exchange controls to stop the rush to buy dollars;* GB **Exchange Equalization Account** = account with the Bank of England used by the government when buying or selling foreign currency to influence the exchange rate for the pound **(c) Stock Exchange** = place where stocks and shares are bought and sold; **commodity exchange** = place where commodities are bought and sold **2** *verb* **(a) to exchange an article for another** = to give one thing in place of something else **(b) to exchange contracts** = to hand over a contract when buying or selling a property (done by both buyer and seller at the same time) **(c)** to change money of one country for money of another

◊ **exchangeable** [ɪksˈtʃeɪndʒəbl] *adjective* which can be exchanged

◊ **exchanger** [ɪksˈtʃeɪndʒə] *noun* person who buys and sells foreign currency

Exchequer [ɪksˈtʃekə] *noun* fund of all money received by the government of the UK from taxes and other revenues; *see also* CHANCELLOR

excise 1 [ˈeksaɪz] *noun* **(a) excise duty** *or* **tax** = tax on certain goods produced in a country (such as alcohol) **(b) Customs and Excise** *or* **Excise Department** = government department which deals with VAT, with taxes on imports, and taxes on certain products, such as alcohol, produced in the country **2** [ɪkˈsaɪz] *verb* to cut out; *the chairman ordered the remarks to be excised from the official record*

◊ **exciseman** [ˈeksaɪzmən] *noun* person who works in the Excise Department

exclude [ɪksˈkluːd] *verb* to keep out *or* not to include; *the amendment will exclude several categories of taxpayer from the provisions of the bill before Parliament*

◊ **excluding** [ɪksˈkluːdɪŋ] *preposition* not including; *the regulations apply to members of the public, excluding those serving in the emergency services;* **not excluding** =

including; *government servants, not excluding judges, are covered by the Bill*

◊ **exclusion** [ɪksˈkluːʒn] *noun* not including; *the council voted for the exclusion of the public before discussing the applications for the post of Chief Executive;* **exclusion clause** = clause in a contract which limits the liability of a party, for example a clause in an insurance policy which says which items are not covered; **to the exclusion of** = not including *or* without including; **exclusion order** = court order in matrimonial proceedings which stops a wife *or* husband from going into the matrimonial home; **exclusion zone** = area (usually an area of sea) near a country, which is forbidden to military forces of other countries

◊ **exclusive** [ɪksˈkluːsɪv] *adjective* **(a) exclusive agreement** = agreement where a person *or* firm is made sole agent for a product in a market; **exclusive licence** = licence where the licensee is the only person to be able to enjoy the licence; **exclusive right to market a product** = right to be the only person to market the product **(b) exclusive of** = not including; *the charge comes to £1,000, exclusive of VAT*

execute [ˈeksɪkjuːt] *verb* to carry out (orders, a plan, etc.)

executive [ɪgˈzekjuːtɪv] **1** *adjective* **(a)** which puts decisions into action; **executive committee** = committee which runs a society *or* a club; **executive director** = director who works full-time in the company; **executive powers** = right to put decisions into actions; *US* **executive session** = meeting of a congressional committee where only committee members, witnesses and other members of Congress may attend, and the public is excluded **(b)** referring to the branch of government which puts laws into effect; **executive document** = document (such as a treaty) sent by the President of the USA to the Senate for ratification; **executive order** = order by the president of the USA *or* of a state governor; **executive privilege** = privilege of the President of the USA not to reveal matters which he considers secret **2** *noun* **(a)** person in an organization who takes decisions *or* manager *or* director; **Chief Executive** = (i) official permanent administrator of a town *or* county council; (ii) executive director in charge of a company **(b) the Executive** = section of a government which puts into effect the laws passed by Parliament (in the USA, this is the president)

---

the principles of a free constitution are lost when the
legislative power is nominated
by the executive
Edward Gibbon

---

exempt [ɪɡ'zempt] **1** *adjective* **(a)** not covered by a law; not forced to obey a law; **exempt from tax** *or* **tax-exempt** = not required to pay tax; **exempt supplies** = sales of goods or services on which VAT does not have to be paid **(b) exempt information** = information which may be kept secret from the public (because if it were disclosed it might be unfair to an individual or harmful to the council); *the council resolved that the press and public be excluded for item 10 (applications for headships) as it involved the likely disclosure of exempt information* **2** *verb* to free something from having tax paid on it *or* from having to pay tax; *non profit-making organizations are exempt(ed) from tax; food is exempt(ed) from sales tax; the government exempted trusts from tax;* **exempted business** = certain types of business in the House of Commons, which cannot be interrupted if started late in the sitting (i.e. after 10 p.m. on weekdays, or after 4 p.m. on Fridays)

◊ **exemption** [ɪɡ'zempʃn] *noun* act of exempting something from a contract *or* from a tax; **exemption clause** = clause in a contract exempting a party from certain liabilities; **exemption from tax** *or* **tax exemption** = being free from having to pay tax; *as a non profit-making organization you can claim tax exemption*

exercise ['eksəsaɪz] **1** *noun* **(a)** use (of a power); *a court can give directions to a local authority as to the exercise of its powers in relation to children in care;* **exercise of an option** = using an option *or* putting an option into action **(b)** test *or* trial to get experience or information; *getting the residents' views on the new road will be a useful exercise; the*

leaflets prepared by the department are just a public relations exercise **2** *verb* to use *or* to put into practice; **to exercise one's discretion** = to decide which of several courses to take; *the governors exercised their discretion and allowed the boy to return to school;* **to exercise an option** = to put an option into action; *not many shareholders exercised their option to buy the new issue of shares;* **to exercise a right** = to do something which you are entitled to do; *he exercised his right to call for a vote on the motion*

exile ['egzaɪl] **1** *noun* **(a)** being sent to live in another country as a punishment; *the ten members of the opposition party were sent into exile;* **government in exile** = government formed outside a country to oppose the government inside it; (NOTE: no plural) **(b)** person who has been sent to live in another country as a punishment; *the new leadership hopes that after the amnesty several well-known exiles will return home* **2** *verb* to send someone to live in another country as a punishment; *he was exiled for life; she was exiled to an island in the North Sea*

exodus ['eksədəs] *noun* movement of a large number of people from a place

ex officio ['eks ə'fɪʃɪəʊ] *Latin phrase meaning* 'because of an office held'; *the mayor is ex officio a member or an ex officio member of the finance committee*

expand [ɪk'spænd] *verb* to increase the boundaries of a country

◊ **expansion** [ɪk'spænʃn] *noun* increasing the territory of a country

◊ **expansionist** [ɪk'spænʃnɪst] *adjective & noun* (person, country) which wants to expand its territory

expatriate 1 [ɪks'pætrɪət] *noun* person who lives in a country which is not his own; *there is a large expatriate community or a large community of expatriates in Geneva* **2** [ɪks'pætrɪeɪt] *verb* to force someone to leave the country where he is living

◊ **expatriation** [ɪkspætrɪ'eɪʃn] *noun* forcing someone to leave the country where he is living; *compare* REPATRIATION

expect [ɪk'spekt] *verb* to hope that something is going to happen; *we are expecting him to arrive at 10.45; some commentators are expecting a bonus from the Finance Minister in the form of tax cuts; the house was sold for more than the expected price*

◊ **expectancy** *or* **expectation**
[ɪk'spektənsi *or* ekspek'teɪʃn] *noun* hope that something good will happen in the future; **expectation of life** *or* **life expectancy** = number of years a person is likely to live

expenditure [ɪk'spendɪtʃə] *noun* amounts of money spent; **capital expenditure** = (i) money spent on assets (such as property or machinery); (ii) major costs of a council *or* central government (such as schools, roads, hospitals, etc.); **revenue expenditure** = day-to-day costs of a council (such as salaries and wages, maintenance of buildings, etc.); (NOTE: no plural in GB English; US English uses **expenditures**)

expense [ɪk'spens] *noun* **(a)** money spent; **at great expense** = having spent a lot of money; **expense account** = money which a businessman is allowed by his company to spend on travelling and entertaining clients in connection with his business **(b)** **at someone's expense** = with the result that someone is hurt *or* loses; *the Conservatives made gains in the local elections at the expense of the centre parties*

◊ **expenses** [ɪk'spensɪz] *plural noun* money paid to cover the cost of travelling *or* entertaining *or* buying equipment, etc.; **all expenses paid** = with all costs paid by the company; **allowable expenses** = business expenses which are allowed against tax; **fixed expenses** = money which is spent regularly (such as rent, electricity, telephone); **incidental expenses** = small amounts of money spent at various times, in addition to larger amounts; **legal expenses** = money spent on fees to lawyers; **overhead expenses** *or* **general expenses** *or* **running expenses** = money spent on the day-to-day

costs of a business; **travelling expenses** = money spent on travelling and hotels for business purposes; **election expenses** = money spent by a candidate *or* political party during an election campaign

COMMENT: in the UK, there is a limit to the amount of money each individual candidate can spend, so as not to favour rich candidates against poor ones. After the election the candidates and their agents have to make a return of expenses to show that they have not overspent. There is no limit to the spending of the political parties on a national level, and most of the campaign expenditure is made in this way, with national TV advertising, advertisements in the national press, etc. In the USA, the government subsidizes election expenses by paying an equivalent sum to that raised by each candidate. The candidates for the main elected positions (especially that of President) have to be rich, or at any rate to have rich supporters

experience [ɪk'spɪəriəns] **1** *noun* **(a)** having lived through various situations and therefore knowing how to make decisions; *he is a constitutional lawyer of considerable experience; she has a lot of experience of dealing with government departments; he gained most of his administrative experience in local government* **(b)** something one has lived through; *the accident was a terrible experience for her;* (NOTE: no plural for (a)) **2** *verb* to live through a situation

◊ **experienced** [ɪk'spɪəriənst] *adjective* person who has lived through many situations and has learnt from them; *he is the most experienced negotiator I know; we have appointed a very experienced person as director of tourism*

expiration *or* **expiry** [ekspɪ'reɪʃn *or* eks'paɪri] *noun* coming to an end; *expiration of an insurance policy; to repay before the expiration of the stated period;* **on expiration of the lease** = when the lease comes to an end; **expiry date** = date when something will end; (NOTE: no plural)

◊ **expire** [ɪk'spaɪə] *verb* to come to an end; *the lease expires in 1999;* **his passport has expired** = his passport is no longer valid

explain [ɪks'pleɪn] *verb* to give reasons for something; *he explained to the customs officials that the two computers were presents from friends; can you explain to the inquiry how you came to be paid the extra sum?*

◊ **explanation** [eksplə'neɪʃn] *noun* reason for something; *the VAT inspector asked for an explanation of the invoices; he could give no explanation of how the building came to be demolished without permission*

◊ **explanatory** [ek'splænətri] *noun* which explains; *read the explanatory notes before filling in the form*

explore [ɪk'splɔː] *verb* to examine carefully; *we are exploring the possibility of opening an office in London; we must explore all possible sources of revenue*

export 1 [ɪk'spɔːt] *verb* to send goods to foreign countries for sale; *we have exported more goods this month than ever before* **2** ['ekspɔːt] *noun* **(a)** sending goods out of a country to be sold; *the export of firearms is forbidden;* **export licence** = permit which allows a company to export a certain type of product **(b) exports** = goods sent abroad for sale; *exports have fallen because the exchange rate is too high;* (NOTE: the opposite is **imports**)

expropriate [eks'prəʊprieɪt] *verb* to take private property for public use (without paying compensation)

◊ **expropriation** [eksprəʊpri'eɪʃn] *noun* **(a)** action of the state in taking private property for public use (without paying compensation) **(b)** *US* action of the state in taking private property for public use (and paying compensation to the former owner); (NOTE: the equivalent in the UK is **compulsory purchase**)

expulse [ɪk'spʌls] *verb* to send someone away from a place

◊ **expulsion** [ɪk'spʌlʃn] *noun* sending someone away from a place

expunge [ɪk'spʌnʒ] *verb* to remove (from a record); *the Chairman ordered the remarks to be expunged from the record*

extend [ɪk'stend] *verb* **(a)** to make available *or* to give; *to extend credit to a customer* **(b)** to make longer; *to extend a contract for two years; the council extended the appeal period;* **extended credit** = credit allowing the borrower a longer time to pay; **extended family** = group of related people, including distant relatives and close friends

◊ **extension** [ɪk'stenʃn] *noun* **(a)** allowing longer time; **to get an extension of credit** = to get more time to pay back; **extension of a contract** = continuing the contract for a further period; **extension of time** = allowing a person more time in which to do something **(b)** *(in an office)* individual telephone linked to the main switchboard; *can you get me extension 21? extension 21 is engaged; the Finance Department is on extension 53* **(c)** *US* **extension of remarks** = additional material which a member of Congress adds to the Congressional Record after a sitting

◊ **extensive** [ɪk'stensɪv] *adjective* very large *or* covering a wide area; *he has an extensive knowledge of drugs; she has extensive contacts in the teaching profession*

◊ **extent** [ɪk'stent] *noun* amount *or* area covered by something; *they are assessing the extent of the damage after the fire;* **to a certain extent** = partly *or* not completely; *he was correct to a certain extent*

exterminate [ɪk'stɜːmɪneɪt] *verb* to kill totally

◊ **extermination** [ɪkstɜːmɪ'neɪʃn] *noun* killing of all

extort [ɪk'stɔːt] *verb* to get money *or* promises *or* a confession from someone, by using threats; *the warlords extorted #20,000 from the local government*

◊ **extortion** [ɪk'stɔːʃn] *noun* getting money by threats

extra- ['ekstrə] *prefix* outside; **extra-authority** *or* **extra-borough** *or* **extra-district payments** = payments made to another authority for services provided by that authority; **extra-territorial waters** = international waters, outside the jurisdiction of a country; **extra-territoriality** = being outside the territory of the country where you are living, and so not subject to its laws (used of diplomats)

extradite ['ekstrədaɪt] *verb* to bring an arrested person from one country to another country because he is wanted for trial for a crime which he committed in that country; *he was arrested in France and extradited to stand trial in Germany*

◊ **extradition** [ekstrə'dɪʃn] *noun* bringing an arrested person from one country to be tried for a crime he committed in another country; *the USA requested the extradition of the leader of the drug gang;* **extradition treaty** = agreement between two countries that a person arrested in one country can be sent to the other to stand trial for a crime committed there

extraordinary [ek'strɔːdɪnəri] *adjective* different from normal; **Extraordinary General Meeting (EGM)** = special meeting of shareholders *or* members of a club, etc., to discuss an important matter which cannot wait until the next Annual General Meeting; **extraordinary items** = items in accounts which do not appear each year; *the auditors noted several extraordinary items in the accounts*

extreme [ɪk'striːm] *adjective* more than usual; very outspoken *or* favouring very strong action, even violence; *the leader is trying to prevent his supporters from making extreme statements; her views are more extreme than those of the other candidates*

◊ **extremism** [ɪk'striːmɪzm] *noun (as criticism)* ideas and practices that favour very strong action, such as the use of violence

◊ **extremist** [ɪk'striːmɪst] **1** *noun (as criticism)* person in favour of very strong *or* sometimes violent methods; *the party has been taken over by left-wing extremists; the meeting was broken up by extremists from the right of the party* **2** *adjective* in favour of strong methods; *the electorate decisively rejected the extremist parties*

Ff

F [ef] *sixth letter of the alphabet* **Schedule F** = schedule to the Finance Acts under which tax is charged on income from dividends

facie ['feɪʃi] *see* PRIMA FACIE

facsimile (copy) [fæk'sɪmɪli] *noun* exact copy of a document

fact [fækt] *noun* something which is true and real, especially something which has been proved by evidence in court; *the chairman of the tribunal asked to see all the facts on the compensation claim;* **in fact** *or* **in point of fact** = really; **matters of fact** = facts relevant to a case which is being tried at court

◊ **fact-finding** ['fækt 'faɪndɪŋ] *adjective* looking for information; **a fact-finding delegation** = group of people who visit to search for information about a problem

faction ['fækʃn] *noun (sometimes as criticism)* group of people within a larger organization such as a political party, who have different views or have special aims; *arguments broke out between different factions at the party conference; the Prime Minister has the support of most factions in the party*

◊ **factional** ['fækʃnəl] *adjective* referring to factions; *factional infighting has weakened the party structure*

facto ['fæktəʊ] *see* DE FACTO, IPSO FACTO

factor ['fæktə] *noun* thing which is important *or* which influences; *the need to encourage tourism is a major factor in increased council spending on amenities; the rise in unemployment is an important factor in the job market;* **cyclical factors** =

way in which a trade cycle affects businesses; **contributory factor** = something which contributes to a result; **deciding factor** = most important factor which influences a decision

fair [feə] **1** *noun* **trade fair** = large exhibition and meeting for advertising and selling a certain type of product **2** *adjective* **(a)** honest *or* correct; **fair comment** = remark which is honestly made on a matter of public interest and so is not defamatory; **fair dealing** = (i) legal buying and selling of shares; (ii) quoting small sections of a copyright work; **fair price** = good price for both buyer and seller; **fair trade** = international business system where countries agree not to charge import duties on certain items imported from their trading partners; **fair trading** *or* **fair dealing** = way of doing business which is reasonable and does not harm the consumer; **Office of Fair Trading** = British government department which protects consumers against unfair *or* illegal business; **fair wear and tear** = acceptable damage caused by normal use; *the insurance policy covers most damage, but not fair wear and tear to the machine* **(b)** **fair copy** = document which is written *or* typed with no corrections or mistakes

faithful ['feɪθfʊl] *noun* **the party faithful** = loyal ordinary members of a party

fall [fɔːl] *verb* **(a)** to happen *or* to take place; *the national holiday falls on a Monday;* **the bill fell due** = the bill was due to be paid; **to fall outside** = not to be part of a list *or* not to be covered by a rule; *the case falls outside the jurisdiction of the local planning authority;* **to fall within** = to become part of a list *or* to be covered by a rule; *the newspaper report falls within the category of* defamation; the case falls within the competence of the local authority **(b)** to lose power; *after the government fell, elections were called;* (NOTE: falling - fell - fallen)

fascism ['fæʃɪzm] *noun* **(a)** extreme right-wing nationalistic ideas, emphasising the power of the state, the army and the leader of the nation, violently opposed to Communism **(b)** *(usually as criticism)* extreme right-wing or ultra-conservative ideas

◊ **fascist** ['fæʃɪst] **1** *adjective* referring to fascism; in favour of fascism; *a fascist dictatorship; the leader of the party has made speeches advocating fascist principles* **2** *noun* supporter of fascism; *see also* NEO-FASCIST

Father of the House ['fɑːðə] *noun* the MP who has been an MP for the longest time without a break (also sometimes used to refer to the oldest peer in the House of Lords)

Fatherland ['fɑːðəlænd] *noun* German word for 'motherland'

fatwa ['fætwɑː] *noun* decree condemning someone under Islamic law

fault [fɒlt] *noun* **(a)** being to blame for something which is wrong; *the witness said the accident was the fault of defective machinery; was it the fault of the local authority if the protest march developed into a riot?* **(b)** wrong working; *the technical staff are trying to correct a fault in the computer; we think there is a basic fault in the construction of the bridge*

◊ **faulty** ['fɒlti] *adjective* which does not work properly *or* which has not been done in the correct way; *the accident was caused by faulty brakes or by faulty repairs to the brakes*

favourite *or US* **favorite** ['feɪvərɪt] *adjective* (candidate, party) which is expected to win an election

FBI = FEDERAL BUREAU OF INVESTIGATION

feasible ['fiːzəbl] *adjective* which can be done; *the Planning Department says it is not feasible to produce draft plans at this stage*

◊ **feasibility** [fiːzə'bɪlɪti] *noun* ability to be done; *feasibility study or* feasibility report = work done to see if something which has been planned is a good idea; *the council asked the planning department to comment on the feasibility of the project; the department has produced a feasibility report on the development project*

federal ['fedərəl] *adjective* **(a)** referring to a system of government in which a group of states are linked together in a federation; **a federal constitution** = constitution (such as that in Germany) which provides for a series of semi-autonomous states joined together in a national federation **(b)** referring especially to the central government of the United States; **federal court** *or* **federal laws** = court *or* laws of the USA, as opposed to state courts *or* state laws

◊ **Federal Assembly** ['fedrəl ə'sembli] *noun* legislature in Russia (equivalent to Parliament or Congress)

◊ **Federal Bureau of Investigation (FBI)** ['fedrəl 'bjuːrəʊ əv ɪnvestɪ'geɪʃn] *noun* section of the US Department of Justice, which investigates crimes against federal law and subversive acts in the USA

◊ **federalism** ['fedrəlɪzm] *noun* type of government, in which the state is a federation of semi-autonomous provinces or states, with a central federal government

◊ **Federal Reserve Bank** ['fedrəl rɪzɜːv 'bæŋk] *noun US* one of the twelve central banks in the USA which are owned by the state and directed by the Federal Reserve Board

◊ **Federal Reserve Board** ['fedrəl rɪzɜːv 'bɔːd] *noun US* government organization which runs the central banks in the USA

COMMENT: the Federal Reserve system is the central bank of the USA. The system is run by the Federal Reserve Board, under a chairman and seven committee members (or 'governors') who are all appointed by the President. The twelve Federal Reserve Banks act as lenders of last resort to local commercial banks. Although the board is appointed by the president, the whole system is relatively independent of the US government

federation [fedə'reɪʃn] *noun* **(a)** group of organizations which are linked together and have a central body which represents their interests; *the American Federation of Labor* **(b)** group of states which have a central government which represents them and looks after their common interests in particular as concerns foreign policy and the armed forces; **Federation Council** = upper house of the legislature in Russia (the lower house is the State Duma)

COMMENT: many federations exist, though they are not often called such: the USA, Russia, Canada, Australia, and Germany are all federations

feminism ['femɪnɪzm] *noun* movement advocating equality of women with men in all social situations

◊ **feminist** ['femɪnɪst] *adjective & noun* referring to feminism; *the feminist movement*

feudal society ['fjuːdəl sə'saɪəti] *noun* society where each class or level has a duty to serve the class above it

◊ **feudalism** ['fjuːdəlɪzm] *noun* medieval system, where land was granted by a king to his aristocracy, and by the aristocrats to the peasants, on condition that each paid a service (or feudal duty) to his superior

Fianna Fáil ['fiːənə 'fɔɪl] *noun* one of the two main political parties in Ireland, the republican party

fide ['faɪdi] *see* BONA FIDE

Fifth Amendment [fɪfθ] *noun* amendment to the constitution of the USA, which says that no person can be forced to give evidence which might incriminate himself; **to plead the Fifth Amendment** *or* **to take the Fifth Amendment** = to refuse to give evidence to a court *or* tribunal *or* committee, because the evidence might incriminate you

fighter ['faɪtə] *see* FREEDOM

figure ['fɪgə] *noun* **(a)** number *or* cost written in numbers; **he put a very low figure on the value of the lease** = he calculated the value of the lease as very low **(b)** **figures** = written numbers; **sales figures** = total sales; **to work out the figures** = to calculate; **his income from government contracts runs into five figures** *or* **he has a five-figure income from government contracts** = his income is more than £10,000; **in round figures** = not totally accurate, but correct to the nearest 10 or 100; *the number of illegal immigrants is 45,000 in round figures* **(c)** **figures** = results for a company; *the figures for last year or last year's figures*

file [faɪl] **1** *noun* **(a)** cardboard holder for documents, which can fit in the drawer of a filing cabinet; *put these letters in the planning applications file; look in the file marked 'Scottish tourism';* **box file** = cardboard box for holding documents **(b)** documents kept for reference; *the social services department keeps a file of missing persons; look up her description in the missing persons' file;* **to place something on file** = to keep a record of something; **to keep someone's name on file** = to keep someone's name on a list for reference; **file copy** = copy of a document which is kept for reference in an office; **card file** = information kept on filing cards **(c)** **computer file** = section of information on a computer (such as a list of addresses *or* of customer accounts); *how can we protect our computer files?* **2** *verb* **(a)** to **file documents** = to put documents in order so that they can be found easily; *the correspondence is filed under 'Complaints'* **(b)** to make an official request; **to file a petition in bankruptcy** = to ask officially to be made bankrupt *or* to ask officially for someone else to be made bankrupt **(c)** to register something officially; *to file an application for a patent; to file a return to the tax office*

◊ **filing** ['faɪlɪŋ] **1** *noun* **(a)** delivering a legal document to court **(b)** documents which have to be put in order; *there is a lot of filing to do at the end of the week; the manager looked through the week's filing to see what* *letters had been sent* **2** *adjective* **filing basket** *or* **filing tray** = container kept on a desk for documents which have to be filed; **filing cabinet** = metal box with several drawers for keeping files; **filing card** = card with information written on it, used to classify information into the correct order; **filing clerk** = clerk who files documents; **filing system** = way of putting documents in order for reference

filibuster ['filibʌstə] *noun* speech which carries on for a long time in a debate, so that the debate cannot be closed and a vote taken; *the Democrats organized a filibuster in the Senate*

◊ **filibustering** ['filibʌstriŋ] *noun* organizing *or* carrying out of a filibuster

COMMENT: filibusters are possible in the US Senate, because the rules of the Senate allow unlimited debate. A filibuster may be ended by a cloture motion; the technique is also used in the UK (see also TALK OUT)

final ['faɪnl] *adjective* last *or* coming at the end of a period; *to pay the final instalment; to make the final payment; to put the final details on a document;* **final date for payment** = last date by which payment should be made; **final demand** = last reminder from a supplier, after which he will sue for payment; **final discharge** = last payment of what is left of a debt; **final dividend** = dividend paid at the end of the year

◊ **finally** ['faɪnəli] *adverb* in the end; *the contract for disposal of refuse was finally signed yesterday; after ten hours of discussions, the House of Commons finally rose at two o'clock in the morning*

finance ['faɪnæns] **1** *noun* public money used by a government *or* local authority; *where will the authority find the finance to pay the higher salaries? he is the secretary of the local authority finance committee;* **Finance Bill and Finance Act** = annual Bill and Act of Parliament which gives the Government the power to raise taxes to produce money for the Exchequer, and which then can be spent as proposed in the Budget;

Finance Minister *or* **Minister of Finance** = government minister responsible for finance (both taxation and expenditure) **2** *verb* to pay for something; *the new building must be financed by the local authority; a government-financed programme of prison construction*

◊ **financial** [fɪ'nænʃəl] *adjective* referring to money *or* finance; *he has a financial interest in the company;* **financial assistance** = help in the form of money; *she receives financial assistance from the local authority;* **financial institution** = bank *or* other company which provides finance; **to make financial provision for someone** = to give someone money to live on; **Financial Secretary to the Treasury** = minister of state in charge of the Treasury, under the Chancellor of the Exchequer; *see also* CHIEF SECRETARY

◊ **financially** [fɪ'nænʃli] *adverb* in the form of money; *he is financially involved in the property company; the company is financially very strong*

COMMENT: in most countries, the government department dealing with finance is called the Finance Ministry, with a Finance Minister in charge. Both in the UK and the USA, the department is called the Treasury, and the minister in charge is the Chancellor of the Exchequer in the UK, and the Treasury Secretary in the USA

findings ['faɪndɪŋz] *noun* decision reached by a court *or* tribunal; **the findings of a commission of inquiry** = the conclusions of the commission

Fine Gael ['fiːnə 'geɪl] *noun* one of the two main political parties in Ireland, more moderate than Fianna Fáil

finlandization [fɪnləndaɪ'zeɪʃn] *noun* policy of neutrality, similar to that adopted by Finland because of its geographical position between the West and Russia

first [fɜːst] *noun* person *or* thing which is there at the beginning *or* earlier than others; *our council was one of the first to employ race relations advisers;* **the First Amendment** = first amendment to the

Constitution of the USA, guaranteeing freedom of speech and religion; **First Lord of the Treasury** = British government post, now combined with that of Prime Minister; **first quarter** = three months' period from January to the end of March; **first half** *or* **first half-year** = six months' period from January to the end of June; **first-past-the-post** = electoral system (as in the UK), where the candidate with most votes wins the election (even if he does not have more than half of all votes cast); *see also* PROPORTIONAL REPRESENTATION **First Reading** = formal introduction of a Bill into the House of Commons, after which it is printed

◊ **first-class** ['fɜːst 'klɑːs] *adjective & noun* top quality *or* most expensive; most expensive and comfortable type of travel *or* type of hotel; *he is a first-class accountant; to travel first class; first-class travel provides the best service; a first-class ticket; to stay in first-class hotels;* **first-class mail** = (i) (in Britain) most expensive mail service, planned to be faster; (ii) (in the USA) mail service for letters and postcards; *a first-class letter should get to Scotland from London in a day*

fiscal ['fiskl] *adjective* referring to tax *or* to government revenue; *the government's fiscal policies;* **fiscal measures** = tax changes made by a government to improve the working of the economy; **fiscal year** = twelve-month period on which taxes are calculated (in the UK, April 6th to April 5th; in the USA from July 1st to June 30th); **Procurator Fiscal** = Scottish law officer who decides whether an alleged criminal should be prosecuted

fix [fiks] *verb* (a) to arrange *or* to agree; *to fix a budget; to fix a meeting for 3 p.m.; the date of the hearing has still to be fixed; the price of gold was fixed at $300; the punishment for drug offences has been fixed by Parliament* (b) to mend; *the maintenance staff are coming to fix the telephone; can you fix the copying machine?*

◊ **fixed** [fikst] *adjective* permanent *or* which cannot be removed; **fixed assets** = property *or* machinery which a company owns

and uses; **fixed capital** = capital in the form of buildings and machinery; **fixed costs** = cost of producing a product, which does not change with the amount of product made (such as rent); **fixed deposit** = deposit which pays a stated interest over a set period; **fixed expenses** = money which is spent regularly (such as rent, electricity, telephone); **fixed income** = income which does not change (such as from an annuity); **fixed-price agreement** = agreement where a company provides a service *or* a product at a price which stays the same for the whole period of the agreement; **fixed scale of charges** = rate of charging which cannot be altered; **fixed term** = period which is fixed when a contract is signed and which cannot be changed afterwards

◊ **fixing** ['fiksiŋ] *noun* (a) arranging; *fixing of charges; fixing of a mortgage rate* (b) **price fixing** = illegal agreement between companies to charge the same price for competing products

◊ **fixture** ['fikstʃə] *noun* (a) item in a property which is permanently attached to it (such as a sink or lavatory) and which passes to a new owner with the property itself (b) permanently arranged meeting; *the council meeting is a fixture on the third Wednesday of every month*

flag [flæg] **1** *noun* (a) piece of coloured cloth which is used to represent a country; **flag of convenience** = flag of a country which may have no ships of its own but allows ships of other countries to be registered in its ports; **flag of truce** *or* **white flag** = flag used to end a conflict temporarily, to allow negotiations to take place; **to fly a flag** = (i) to attach the flag in an obvious position to show that your ship belongs to a certain country; (ii) to act in a certain way to show that you are proud of belonging to a certain country *or* working for a certain company; *ship flying the British flag; ship flying a flag of convenience; the Trade Minister has gone to the World Fair to fly the flag; he is only attending the conference to fly the flag for the company* (b) *(in computer programming or on documents)* marker *or* way of indicating something special in a text *or* database **2** *verb* (a) **to flag a ship**

= to give a ship the right to fly a flag, by registering it; *see also* REFLAG **(b)** *(in computing or on documents)* to set markers *or* to indicate something special in a text *or* database; *the committee clerk flagged all the references to building repairs; will members please note the flagged items which we will consider separately?*

flagrant ['fleɪgrənt] *adjective (used as criticism)* clear and obvious; *a flagrant case of contempt of Parliament; a flagrant violation of human rights*

floating voter ['fləʊtɪŋ 'vəʊtə] *noun* (i) voter who has not decided how to vote; (ii) voter who does not always vote for the same party, but changes from election to election; **the floating vote** = votes of floating voters; *the Opposition is trying to capture the bulk of the floating vote*

floor [flɔː] *noun* in a building, the part on which people stand; **the floor of the House** = the main part of the House of Commons *or* Congress; *debates on the floor of the House are often lively; the Senate majority leader is the floor spokesman for his party in the Senate;* **floor manager** = member (usually the chairman of the reporting committee) who is responsible for getting a bill through the House; (NOTE: in the UK, 'floor' is usually taken to refer to the backbenchers: **the feeling on the floor of the House was that the Minister should resign**)

FO ['ef 'əʊ] = FOREIGN OFFICE

fodder ['fɒdə] *see* LOBBY

foe [fəʊ] *noun* enemy; **common foe** = enemy of two countries or parties

Foggy Bottom ['fɒgi 'bɒtəm] *noun US (informal)* the State Department

Folketing ['fɒlkətɪŋ] *noun* single house of legislature in Denmark

follow ['fɒləʊ] *verb* to act in accordance with (a rule); *the Speaker has followed the precedent set in 1972*

◊ **follower** ['fɒləʊə] *noun* person who follows the ideology of a party, without being

a member of that party; *(pejorative)* **camp follower** = disreputable person who follows the fortunes of a party or leader

◊ **follow up** ['fɒləʊ 'ʌp] *verb* to examine something further; *the tax inspectors are following up several leads;* **to follow up an initiative** = to take action once someone else has decided to do something

forbid [fə'bɪd] *verb* to tell someone not to do something *or* to say that something must not be done; *the contract forbids sale of the goods to the USA; the staff are forbidden to use the front entrance; the government forbade any reference to the case in the book;* (NOTE: **forbidding - forbade - has forbidden**)

force [fɔːs] **1** *noun* **(a)** strength; **to be in force** = to be operating *or* working; *the rules have been in force since 1976;* **to come into force** = to start to operate *or* work; *the new regulations will come into force on January 1st;* **to put into force** = to make something apply; **the new regulations have the force of law** = they are the same as if they had been voted into law by parliament **(b)** group of people; **labour force** = all the workers in a company *or* in an area; *the management has made an increased offer to the labour force; we are opening a new factory in the Far East because of the cheap local labour force;* **the armed forces** = the army, navy and air force; **police force** = group of policemen organized in an area; *members of several local police forces have collaborated in searching for the murderer* **(c) force majeure** = something which happens which is out of the control of the parties who have signed a contract (such as strike, war, storm) and which prevents the contract being fulfilled **2** *verb* to make someone do something; *the government has forced the council to put the building work out to tender*

◊ **forcible** ['fɔːsəbl] *adjective* by force *or* using force; *the new regulations allow forcible repatriation of suspected terrorists*

foreign ['fɒrɪn] *adjective* not belonging to one's own country; *foreign cars have flooded our market; we are increasing our* *trade with foreign countries;* **foreign affairs** = matters concerning other countries; **foreign aid** = help offered by one country to another; **foreign currency** = money of another country; **foreign goods** = goods produced in other countries; **foreign investments** = money invested in other countries; **foreign language** = language spoken in another country (for British people, a language which is not English); **foreign policy** = policy followed by a country when dealing with other countries; **the Foreign Service** = government department responsible for a country's representation in other countries; **foreign trade** = trade with other countries

◊ **foreigner** ['fɒrɪnə] *noun* person from another country; *he doesn't like foreigners; our part of the town is popular with foreigners*

◊ **foreign exchange** ['fɒrɪn ɪk'tʃeɪnʒ] *noun* exchanging the money of one country for that of another; **foreign exchange reserves** = foreign money held by a government to support its own currency and pay its debts

◊ **Foreign (and Commonwealth) Office** ['fɒrɪn 'ɒfɪs] *noun* British government department dealing with relations with other countries

◊ **Foreign Secretary** ['fɒrɪn 'sekrɪtri] *noun* British government minister in charge of relations with other countries

COMMENT: in most countries, the government department dealing with other countries is called the Foreign Ministry, with the Foreign Minister in charge. In the UK, these are the Foreign Office and Foreign Secretary; in the USA, they are the State Department and the Secretary of State

form [fɔːm] **1** *noun* **(a) form of words** = words correctly laid out for a legal document; **receipt in due form** = correctly written receipt **(b)** official printed paper with blank spaces which have to be filled in with information; *you have to fill in form A20; customs declaration form; a pad of order forms;* **application form** = form which has to be filled in to apply for something; **claim form** = form which has to be filled in when

making a claim **2** *verb* to start *or* to organize; *the three MPs have formed a splinter group; the brothers have formed a new company*

◊ **formation** *or* **forming** [fɔː'meɪʃn or 'fɔːmɪŋ] *noun* act of organizing; *the formation of the new splinter group has altered the voting pattern in the assembly*

formal ['fɔːməl] *adjective* clearly and legally written; *to make a formal application; to send a formal order*

◊ **formality** [fɔː'mælɪti] *noun* formal procedure *or* thing which has to be done to obey the law or because it is the custom; *the chairman dispensed with the formality of reading the minutes;* **customs formalities** = declaration of goods by the shipper and examination of them by the customs

◊ **formally** ['fɔːməli] *adverb* in a formal way; *we have formally applied for planning permission for the new shopping precinct*

formulate ['fɔːmjʊleɪt] *verb* to write down *or* state clearly; *the Government's proposals are formulated in a White Paper*

forthcoming [fɔːθ'kʌmɪŋ] *adjective* which will take place soon; *the forthcoming general elections*

forthwith [fɔːθ'wɪθ] *adverb* immediately

fortiori [fɔːti'ɔːraɪ] *see* A FORTIORI

forum ['fɔːrəm] *noun* court *or* place where matters are discussed; *the debate should be carried out in the forum of the council chamber, not on the pages of the local newspaper; the parent-teacher committee is an appropriate forum for this type of discussion*

forward ['fɔːwəd] *verb* to send (a document you have received) on to someone else; *thank you for your letter, which has been forwarded to the appropriate committee; he initialled the papers and forwarded them to the chairman*

founder ['faʊndə] *noun* person who establishes a party, institution, company, etc.; **founder member** = member of a party who has been a member from the beginning

Fourth World ['fɔ:θ 'wɜ:ld] *noun* the poorest countries of the Third World

fragment [fræg'ment] *verb* to divide into small parts; *the party's support is very fragmented*

franchise ['fræntʃaɪz] **1** *noun* **(a)** right granted to someone to do something, especially the right to vote in local *or* general elections; **universal franchise** = right to vote which is given to all adult members of the population; *see also* DISENFRANCHISE, ENFRANCHISE (NOTE: no plural in this meaning) **(b)** licence to trade using a brand name and paying a royalty for it; *he has bought a printing franchise or a hot dog franchise* **2** *verb* to sell licences for people to trade using a brand name and paying a royalty; *his sandwich bar was so successful that he decided to franchise it*

◊ **franchisee** [fræntʃaɪ'zi:] *noun* person who runs a business under a franchise

◊ **franchiser** ['fræntʃaɪzə] *noun* person who licenses a franchise

◊ **franchising** ['fræntʃaɪzɪŋ] *noun* act of selling a licence to trade as a franchise; *he runs his sandwich chain as a franchising operation;* (NOTE: no plural)

◊ **franchisor** ['fræntʃaɪzə] *noun* = FRANCHISER

frank [fræŋk] *noun* privilege of sending official mail free of charge, using the signature of a member of Parliament *or* Congress on the envelope instead of a stamp

free [fri:] **1** *adjective & adverb* **(a)** not costing any money; *he was given a free ticket to the exhibition; the price includes free delivery; goods are delivered free; price list sent free on request;* **free sample** = sample given free to advertise a product; **free trial** = testing of a machine with no payment involved; *to send a piece of equipment for two weeks' free trial;* **free of charge** = with no payment to be made **(b)** not in prison; not controlled by others; *all free people are against dictatorship;* **to set someone free** = to let someone leave prison; *the crowd attacked the police station and set the three prisoners free* **(c)** with no restrictions; **free**

circulation of goods = movement of goods from one country to another without import quotas or other restrictions; **free collective bargaining** = negotiations over wages and working conditions between the management and the workers' representatives without government interference; **free competition** = being free to compete without government interference; **free currency** = currency which is allowed by the government to be bought and sold without restriction; **free elections** = elections which are honest and not rigged by one of the parties or by the government; **free enterprise** = system of business with no interference from the government; **free market economy** = system where the government does not interfere in business activity in any way; **free movement of capital** = ability to transfer capital from one EU country to another; **free port** *or* **free trade zone** = port *or* area where there are no customs duties; **free of tax** *or* **tax-free** = with no tax having to be paid; **interest-free credit** *or* **loan** = credit *or* loan where no interest is paid by the borrower; **free of duty** *or* **duty-free** = with no duty to be paid; **free trade** = system where goods can go from one country to another without any restrictions; **free trade area** = group of countries practising free trade **(d)** not busy *or* not occupied; *are there any tables free in the restaurant? the Chief Executive will be free in a few minutes; the hearing was delayed because there was no committee room free* **2** *verb* to release someone from a responsibility *or* from prison; *will the new law free owners from responsibility to their tenants? the new president freed all political prisoners*

◊ **freely** ['fri:li] *adverb* with no restrictions; *money should circulate freely within the European Union*

freedom ['fri:dəm] *noun* **(a)** being free *or* not being held in custody; *the president gave the accused man his freedom* **(b)** being free to do something without restriction; **freedom of association** = being able to join together in a group with other people without being afraid of prosecution, provided that you do not break the law; **freedom of assembly** *or* **of meeting** = being able to meet as a group without being afraid of prosecution, provided that you do not break the law; **freedom of information** = making official information held by government departments available to citizens; **freedom of the press** = being able to write and publish in a newspaper what you wish without being afraid of prosecution, provided that you do not break the law; **freedom of speech** = being able to say what you want without being afraid of prosecution, provided that you do not break the law **(c) freedom of a city** = highest honour given to a notable person by a town; *in a ceremony at the Town Hall yesterday, Lord Smith was given the Freedom of the City*

◊ **freedom fighter** ['fri:dəm 'faɪtə] *noun* guerilla fighting against an oppressive government

◊ **freeman** ['fri:mən] *noun* person who has received the freedom of a city

front [frʌnt] *noun* political group, usually an alliance of several smaller groups, to meet a perceived threat; **to form a common front** = to join into a group against a threat; **National Front** = right-wing political group, upholding racist principles; **Popular Front** = group of Socialist and Communist parties, formed in 1935 to fight fascism

front benches [frʌnt 'bentʃɪz] *noun* two rows of seats in the House of Commons, facing each other with the table between them, where Government ministers or members of the Opposition Shadow Cabinet sit; **the Opposition front bench** = (i) the seat for the Opposition Shadow Cabinet; (ii) the Shadow Cabinet; **the Government front bench** *or* **the Treasury bench** = the seats where the members of the Government sit; *an Opposition front bench spokesman asked why the Government had been so slow in investigating the affair*

◊ **frontbencher** ['frʌnt 'bentʃə] *noun* Member of Parliament who sits on the front benches (i.e., one who is a government minister or a member of the Opposition shadow cabinet)

◊ **front organization** ['frʌnt ɔ:gənaɪ'zeɪʃn] *noun* organization which appears to be neutral, but is in fact an active supporter of a political party *or* is actively engaged in illegal trade

frontier ['frʌntɪə] *noun* boundary of a country; **frontier guard** = soldier guarding the frontier of a country

fulfil *or US* **fulfill** [fʊl'fɪl] *verb* to do everything which is promised in a contract; *the company has fulfilled all the terms of the agreement*

full [fʊl] *adjective* **(a)** with as much inside it as possible; *prisoners have to share cells because the prisons are too full; the council has a very full programme of business* **(b)** complete *or* including everything; **we are working at full capacity** = we are doing as much work as possible; **full costs** = all the costs of manufacturing a product, including both fixed and variable costs; **full cover** = insurance cover against all types of risk; **in full discharge of a debt** = paying a debt completely *or* paying less than the total amount owed by agreement; **full title** = summary of the contents of an Act of Parliament **(c) in full** = completely; *give your full name and address or your name and address in full; he accepted all our conditions in full; full refund or refund paid in full; he got a full refund when he complained about the service; the clerk read out the charges in full* **full payment** *or* **payment in full** = paying all money owed

◊ **fully** ['fʊlɪ] *adverb* completely

function ['fʌŋkʃn] **1** *noun* **(a)** official ceremony; *at a function held in the council offices, the mayor gave testimonials to two of the library staff; the council offices are closed for an official function* **(b)** job *or* duty; *it is not the function of the clerk to give an opinion on the candidates; the job description lists the various functions of a Chief Education Officer* **2** *verb* to work; *lack of qualified engineers is hindering the functioning of the council's maintenance department*

fund [fʌnd] **1** *verb* to pay for something; *the scheme is funded by the local education committee; redevelopment of the centre of the town has been funded partly by government and partly by local industry* **2** *noun* **(a)** collection of money for a special purpose; *the mayor has opened a fund to* *help poor families* **(b)** funds = money; *the council lacks funds to continue the redevelopment; she is organizing an exhibition to raise funds for the children's club*

◊ **fund-raising** ['fʌnd 'reɪzɪŋ] *noun* getting more money, by asking people *or* organizations to give it; *the mayor launched a fund-raising scheme to get more money for the children's club*

fundamental [fʌndə'mentəl] *adjective* basic, going to the roots of something; *there is a fundamental disagreement between the left and right wings of the party*

◊ **fundamentalism** [fʌndə'mentəlɪzm] *noun* **(a)** extremely traditional religious belief **(b)** government *or* regime based on fundamental religious beliefs

◊ **fundamentalist** [fʌndə'mentəlɪst] **1** *adjective* referring to fundamentalism; *a fundamentalist regime* **2** *noun* person who holds fundamentalist views

fusion ['fjuːʒn] *noun* joining together of one or more groups, such as political parties

Gg

gag [gæg] *verb* to try to stop someone talking or writing; *the government was accused of using the Official Secrets Act as a means of gagging the press;* **gag rule** = rule in the House of Representatives which limits the time for debate

gain [geɪn] **1** *noun* **(a)** increase *or* becoming larger; **gain in experience** = act of getting more experience **(b)** increase in profit *or* price *or* value; **to deal in stolen goods for gain** = to buy and sell stolen goods to make a profit; **capital gains** = money made by selling a fixed asset *or* by selling shares at a profit; **capital gains tax** = tax paid on capital gains **(c)** (i) increase in a share of the vote; (ii) winning a seat in an election; *the latest poll shows a socialist gain of 2%; the Conservatives had 20 gains and 10 losses in the local elections* **2** *verb* **(a)** to get *or* to obtain; *he gained some useful experience working in a bank;* **to gain control of a council** = to win a majority of the seats **(b)** to win (a seat); *the Socialists gained six seats on the council at the expense of the Tories*

◊ **gainful** ['geɪnfʊl] *adjective* **gainful employment** = employment which pays money

◊ **gainfully** ['geɪnfʊli] *adverb* **he is not gainfully employed** = he has no regular paid work

gallery ['gæləri] *noun* seats above and around the benches in the House of Commons and House of Lords, where the public and journalists sit; **the Speaker ordered the galleries to be cleared** = the Speaker asked for all visitors to leave the Chamber; **Members' Gallery** = seats for visitors invited by Members of Parliament; **public gallery** = area where members of the public can sit to listen to debates in a council chamber *or* the House of Commons, etc.; **Strangers' Gallery** = public gallery in the House of Commons or House of Lords

gangway ['gæŋweɪ] *noun* space running across the Chamber, dividing the benches on either side of the House of Commons

COMMENT: members sitting below the gangway (i.e. further away from the Speaker) are more independent and less party-minded than those who sit near the Speaker

gather ['gæðə] *verb* **(a)** to collect together *or* to put together; *he gathered his papers together before the meeting started; she has been gathering information on import controls from various sources* **(b)** to understand *or* to find out; *I gather he has left the office; did you gather who will be at the meeting?*

GATT [gæt] = GENERAL AGREEMENT ON TARIFFS AND TRADE *(replaced by the World Trade Organization)*

gavel ['gævl] *noun* small wooden hammer used by a chairman of a meeting to call the meeting to order; *the chairman banged his gavel on the table and shouted to the councillors to be quiet*

COMMENT: there is no mace in the American Senate. Instead, a ceremonial gavel is placed on the Vice-President's desk when the Senate is in session

GDP ['dʒi: di: 'pi:] = GROSS DOMESTIC PRODUCT

general ['dʒenrəl] *adjective* **(a)** ordinary *or* not special; **general expenses** = all kinds of minor expenses *or* money spent on the day-to-day costs of running a business; **general manager** = manager in charge of the administration of a company; **general office** = main administrative office of a company **(b)** dealing with everything *or* with everybody; **general audit** = examining all the books and accounts of a company; **general election** = election of a parliament by all the voters in a country; **general instrument** = form of SI which does not need approval by both Houses of Parliament; **general meeting** = meeting of all the shareholders of a company; **Annual General Meeting (AGM)** = meeting of all the shareholders *or* all the members of a club, which takes place once a year to approve the accounts and make policy decisions; **Extraordinary General Meeting (EGM)** = special meeting of shareholders *or* members of a club to discuss an important matter which cannot wait until the next Annual General Meeting; **general strike** = strike of all the workers in a country

◊ **General Agreement on Tariffs and Trade (GATT)** *noun* international treaty which aimed to try to reduce restrictions in trade between countries

COMMENT: replaced on 1st January 1995 by the World Trade Organization (WTO)

◊ **General Assembly** ['dʒenrəl ə'sembli] *noun* meeting of all the members of the United Nations, where each country is represented and each has a vote

◊ **Generalitat** [henəræli'tæt] *noun* Parliament in Catalonia

◊ **generally** ['dʒenrəli] *adverb* normally *or* usually; *the office is generally closed between Christmas and the New Year; political crimes are generally dealt with more harshly in the military courts*

◊ **General Purposes Committee** ['dʒenrəl 'pɜːpəsɪz kə'mɪtiː] *noun* council committee which deals with matters which do not come under any other committee

Geneva Convention [dʒə'niːvə kən'venʃən] *noun* international treaty governing the behaviour of countries at war relating to captured prisoners; *the attacking*

army was accused of violating the Geneva Convention

Geneva Protocol [dʒə'niːvə 'prəʊtəkɒl] *noun* international agreement to limit the use of chemical and bacteriological weapons

genocide ['dʒɒnəsaɪd] *noun* killing of an entire racial group (usually a minority group)

gentleman ['dʒentlmən] *noun* **(a)** *(formerly)* man of a higher social class, such as the gentry; usually one who lived on his income from investments or rents and did not have a paid job **(b)** *(polite use)* man; **gentleman's agreement** = verbal agreement between two parties who trust each other

gentry ['dʒentri] *noun* class of people below the aristocracy; **landed gentry** = old families who own estates; *he comes from an old family of the landed gentry*

geopolitics [giːəʊ'pɒlɪtɪks] *noun* political planning referring to a geographical area and influenced by geographical factors within that area

germane [dʒɜː'meɪn] *adjective* relevant, which refers to a question; *the argument is not germane to the motion*

gerrymandering ['dʒerɪmændrɪŋ] *noun* reorganizing parliamentary constituencies *or* electoral districts to get an advantage in the next election

get [get] *verb* **(a)** to receive; *we got a letter from the solicitor this morning; he got a £25 fine or a parking ticket* **(b)** to arrive at a place; *the shipment got to Canada six weeks late; she finally got to the committee room at 10.30;* (NOTE: **getting - got - has got**)

◊ **get out** ['get 'aʊt] *verb* to produce something (on time); *the Royal Commission got out the report in time for the meeting; the party was late in getting out its election manifesto*

◊ **get round** ['get 'raʊnd] *verb* **(a)** to get round to doing something = to start doing something much later than was planned; *when is the planning committee likely to get round to considering my application?* **(b)** to avoid; *we tried to get round the embargo by* *shipping from Canada; can you advise me how we can get round the quota system?*

ghetto ['getəu] *noun* area of a town where people live who are not thought equal to the rest; *the black ghettoes of some American cities*

> COMMENT: originally used to refer to Jewish areas in European towns, but now used for any racial minority

ginger group ['dʒɪndʒə 'gru:p] *noun* group of members within a larger organization which tries to make the main organization more active *or* more radical

give [gɪv] *verb* **(a)** to pass something to someone as a gift; *the office gave him a clock when he retired* **(b)** to pass something to someone; *she gave the documents to the accountant; can you give me some information about the new computer system? do not give any details to the police* **(c)** to organize; *the council gave a reception for the visiting mayor from their twin town in France; the candidates gave a press conference on the morning of the election;* (NOTE: giving - gave - given)

◊ **give away** ['gɪv ə'weɪ] *verb* **(a)** to give something as a free present; *we are giving away a pocket calculator with each £10 of purchases* **(b)** to reveal a secret

◊ **give rise to** ['gɪv 'raɪz tu] *verb* to be the cause of something; *the decisions of the planning committee have given rise to complaints from applicants*

◊ **give way** ['gɪv 'weɪ] *verb* to allow someone else to speak; (NOTE: used frequently in the House of Commons when a Member wants to say something when someone else is speaking will the hon. Gentleman give way? No sir, I will not give way)

glasnost ['glæsnɒst] *noun* openness *or* freedom of information

global ['gləubəl] *adjective* referring to the whole world; **global conflict** = a world war

gloss [glɒs] **1** *noun* note which explains *or* gives a meaning to a word or phrase **2** *verb* to **gloss over** = to cover up a mistake *or* fault; *the*

report glosses over the errors made by the officials in the department

GNP ['dʒi: en 'pi:] = GROSS NATIONAL PRODUCT

go [gəu] *verb* **(a)** to move from one place to another; *the cheque went to your bank yesterday; the plane goes to Frankfurt, then to Rome; he is going to our Lagos office* **(b)** to be placed; *the date goes at the top of the letter;* (NOTE: going - went - has gone)

◊ **go-ahead** ['gəuəhed] *noun* **to give something the go-ahead** = to approve something *or* to say that something can be done; *his project got a government go-ahead; the board refused to give the go-ahead to the expansion plan*

◊ **go back on** ['gəu 'bæk ɒn] *verb* not to do what has been promised; *two months later they went back on the agreement*

◊ **go into** ['gəu 'ɪntu] *verb* **(a)** to go into **business** = to start in business; *he went into business selling cars; she went into business in partnership with her son* **(b)** to examine carefully; *the bank wants to go into the details of the council's loans to the club; the fraud squad is going into the facts behind the property deals*

◊ **go on** ['gəu 'ɒn] *verb* **(a)** to continue; *the staff went on working in spite of the fire; the chairman went on speaking for two hours* **(b)** to use to help find something *or* to decide something; *two bank statements are all the tax investigators have to go on; the Foreign Office has only a report in a Hong Kong newspaper to go on*

God Save the Queen ['gɒd seɪv ðə 'kwi:n] *noun* title of the British national Anthem; *everyone stood up when the band played 'God Save the Queen'*

good [gud] *adjective* **(a)** not bad; **a good buy** = excellent item which has been bought cheaply **(b)** **a good deal of** = a large quantity of; *we wasted a good deal of time discussing the arrangements for the AGM; the council had to pay a good deal of money for the building;* **a good many** = very many; *a good many staff members have joined the union*

◊ **good cause** ['gʊd 'kɔːz] *noun* **(a)** group *or* charity which deserves to be helped; *the money collected by the Mayor's Christmas Fund will go to good causes in the borough* **(b)** reason which is accepted in law; *the court asked the accused to show good cause why he should not be sent to prison*

◊ **good faith** ['gʊd 'feɪθ] *noun* general honesty; **in good faith** = believing something to be legal; **he acted in good faith** = he did it honestly; **to buy something in good faith** = to buy something honestly *or* in the course of a transaction which you believe to be honest; *he bought the car in good faith, not knowing that it had been stolen*

◊ **good neighbour** ['gʊd 'neɪbə] *noun* country which has good relations with its neighbours

◊ **good neighbourliness** ['gʊd 'neɪbəlɪnəs] *noun* good relations with neighbouring countries

◊ **goods** [gʊdz] *plural noun* **(a) goods and chattels** = moveable personal possessions; **household goods** = items which are used in the home **(b)** items which can be moved and are for sale; **capital goods** = machinery, buildings and raw materials which are used to make other goods; **consumer goods** = goods bought by the general public and not by businesses

◊ **good title** ['gʊd 'taɪtl] *noun* title to a property which gives the owner full rights of ownership

◊ **goodwill** [gʊd'wɪl] *noun* **(a)** kind feelings towards someone; *the council has lost the goodwill of the electorate* **(b)** good reputation of a business and its contacts with its customers (such as the name of the product which it sells *or* its popular appeal to customers); *he paid £10,000 for the goodwill of the shop and £4,000 for the stock*

govern ['gʌvən] *verb* **(a)** to rule *or* control a country; *the country is governed by a group of military leaders; the Chief Minister governs in the name of the Federal Government* **(b)** to control *or* to influence; *the rules governing elections to the National Assembly*

◊ **governance** ['gʌvənəns] *noun* theory of governing; act of governing; *the Bill is a threat to the governance of Britain*

◊ **government** ['gʌvənmənt] *noun* **(a)** way of ruling *or* controlling a country; *people want democratic government; the leader of the Opposition is promising to provide effective government* **(b)** organization which administers a country or part of a country; *the government has decided to introduce new immigration laws; the Labour government introduced nationalization; succeeding governments have been unable to deal with the rising crime rate;* **central government** = main organization dealing with the affairs of the whole country; **federal government** = central government of a federal state; **local government** = organizations dealing with the affairs of small areas of the country; **government of national unity** = government formed of a coalition of several parties, usually to cope with a particular emergency, such as a civil war **(c)** coming from the government *or* referring to the government; *government intervention or intervention by the government; a government ban on the import of arms; a government investigation into organized crime; government officials prevented him leaving the country; government policy is outlined in the Green Paper; government regulations state that import duty has to be paid on expensive items* **government contractor** = company which supplies goods or services to the government on contract; (NOTE: government can take a singular or plural verb: **the government have decided to repeal the Act; the government feels it is not time to make a statement.** Note also that the word Government is used, especially by officials, without the article: Government has decided that the plan will be turned down; the plan is funded by central government)

◊ **governmental** [gʌvən'mentl] *adjective* referring to a government

governor ['gʌvnə] *noun* **(a)** person who governs a state *or* province; *Ronald Reagan was Governor of California before becoming President; the governor of Uttar Pradesh* **(b)** person representing the Crown, such as the official in charge of a colony **(c)** person in charge of a prison; *a prison* *governor; the prisoners applied to the governor for parole* (**d**) member of a group responsible for controlling a public institution, such as a hospital *or* school

◊ **Governor-General** [ˈgʌvnə ˈdʒenrəl] *noun* person representing the British Crown in a Commonwealth country which is still a monarchy with the British Queen as head of state; *see also* **LIEUTENANT-GOVERNOR**

grade [greɪd] *noun* level *or* rank; *he has reached the top grade in the civil service; the grades in the civil service are numbered G1, G2, G3, etc.*

graft [grɑːft] *noun informal* corruption of officials; *he was accused of graft when it was learnt that he had tried to bribe the Planning Officer;* (NOTE: no plural)

Grand National Assembly [ˈgrænd ˈnæʃənəl əˈsembli] *noun* single chamber of the legislature in Turkey

grant [grɑːnt] **1** *noun* (**a**) act of giving something to someone (permanently *or* temporarily) by a written document, where the object itself cannot be moved; *he made a grant of land to his son* (**b**) money given by the government *or* local authority *or* other organization to help pay for something; *the institute has a government grant to cover the cost of the development programme; the local authority has allocated grants towards the costs of the scheme; many charities give grants for educational projects;* **grant-aided scheme** = scheme which is backed by funds from the government; **grant-in-aid** = money given by central government to local government to help pay for a project; **Grant-Related Expenditure Assessment (GREA)** = government assessment of what each local authority needs to spend; **block grant** *or* **Rate Support Grant** = grant from central government to a local authority to supplement money received from rates or local taxes; **death grant** = state grant to the family of a person who has died, which is supposed to contribute to the funeral expenses **2** *verb* to agree to give someone something *or* to agree to allow someone to do something; *to grant someone permission to*

build a house or to leave the country; the local authority granted the company an interest-free loan to start up the new factory; he was granted leave to appeal; the government granted an amnesty to all political prisoners

◊ **grantee** [grɑːnˈtiː] *noun* person who receives a grant

◊ **grantor** [grɑːnˈtɔː] *noun* person who makes a grant

grass roots [ˈgrɑːs ˈruːts] *noun* basic ordinary members of a political party *or* of society in general; *what is the grass-roots reaction to the constitutional changes? the party has considerable support at grass-roots level; the Chairman has no grass-root support*

grata [ˈgrætə] *see* **PERSONA**

GREA = **GRANT-RELATED EXPENDITURE ASSESSMENT**

great [greɪt] **1** *adjective* large; **a great deal of** = very much; *he made a great deal of money on the Stock Exchange; there is a great deal of work to be done before the company can be made really profitable* **2** *noun* **the Great and the Good** = important public figures, who are usually found on Royal Commissions, quangos, and other public bodies

◊ **Great Seal** [ˈgreɪt ˈsiːl] *noun* seal, kept by the Lord Chancellor, used for sealing important public documents on behalf of the Queen

green card [ˈgriːn ˈkɑːd] *noun* (**a**) special British insurance certificate to prove that a car is insured for travel abroad (**b**) work permit for a person going to live in the USA

Green Paper [ˈgriːn ˈpeɪpə] *noun* discussion document from the British government on possible proposals for a new law; *compare* **WHITE PAPER**

Green Party *or* **the Greens** [ˈgriːn ˈpɑːti *or* ðə ˈgriːnz] *noun* political party existing in several countries, which is concerned mainly with environmental and health issues

Grit [grɪt] *noun & adjective (in Canada, informal)* Liberal

gross [grəus] *adjective* **(a)** total *or* with no deductions; **gross domestic product** = annual value of goods sold and services paid for inside a country; **gross earnings** *or* **gross income** *or* **gross salary** = total earnings before tax and other deductions; **gross national product** = annual value of goods and services in a country including income from other countries **(b)** serious; *he was accused of gross misconduct;* **gross negligence** = act showing very serious neglect of duty towards other people

grounds [graundz] *noun* basic reasons for believing something *or* for doing something; *he retired on medical grounds; does he have good grounds for complaint? there are no grounds for thinking any misconduct has occurred*

group [gruːp] *noun* several people together; *a group of politicians*
◊ **groupuscule** ['gruːpɔskjuːl] *noun* very small and extreme political group

guard [gɑːd] *noun* person employed to protect someone or something; *security guards checks all visitors' passports;* **Civil Guard** = the militia in Spain; **National Guard** = the state militia in the USA, which can be called on to act under the orders of the federal government
◊ **guardsman** ['gɑːdzmən] *noun* member of a military guard; *US* **National**

Guardsman = member of the National Guard

guerilla *or* **guerrilla** [gə'rɪlə] *noun* person *or* small group fighting an enemy, but not a member of an organized army; *after the defeat of the army, guerilla groups sprang up all over the country; guerillas have attacked government outposts in many parts of the North*

guest country ['gest 'kʌntri] *noun* country invited to an international meeting, without the right to vote

guidelines ['gaɪdlaɪnz] *plural noun* unofficial suggestions from the government or some other body as to how something should be done; *the government has issued guidelines on increases in wages and prices; the National Union of Teachers has issued guidelines to its members on dealing with claims; the Secretary of State can issue guidelines for expenditure; the minister said he was not laying down guidelines for the spending of money which was not earmarked for special projects*

guillotine ['gɪlətiːn] **1** *noun* **(a)** machine used in France for executing criminals by cutting off their heads **(b)** motion in the House of Commons to end a debate on a clause of a Bill at a certain time **2** *verb* **(a)** to execute someone by cutting his head off with a guillotine **(b)** to end (a debate) at a certain time

gunboat ['gʌnbəut] *see* DIPLOMACY

Hh

habitation [hæbɪ'teɪʃn] *noun* being lived in; **house fit for human habitation** = house which is in a good state of repair, so that people can live in it; *the flats were condemned as unfit for human habitation*

Hail to the Chief ['heɪl tə ðə 'tʃiːf] *noun* piece of military music played to salute the President of the United States

hamlet ['hæmlət] *noun* small village

hand [hænd] *noun* (a) **to shake hands** = to hold someone's hand when meeting, to show you are pleased to meet him *or* to show that an agreement has been reached; **to shake hands on a deal** = to shake hands to show that a deal has been agreed (b) **by hand** = using the hands, not a machine; **to send a letter by hand** = to ask someone to carry and deliver a letter personally, not sending it through the post (c) **in hand** = kept in reserve; **balance in hand** *or* **cash in hand** = cash held to pay small debts and running costs (d) **goods left on hand** = goods which have not been sold and are left with the retailer or producer (e) **out of hand** = immediately *or* without taking any further time to think; *the committee dismissed his application out of hand* (f) **to hand** = here *or* present; **I have the invoice to hand** = I have the invoice in front of me (g) **show of hands** = way of casting votes where people show how they vote by raising their hands; *the motion was carried on a show of hands*

◊ **hand down** ['hænd 'daʊn] *verb* (a) to pass (something) from one generation to another; *the house has been handed down from father to son since the nineteenth century* (b) **to hand down a verdict** = to announce a verdict

◊ **hand over** ['hænd 'əʊvə] *verb* to pass something to someone; *she handed over the documents to the lawyer; he handed over to his deputy* = he passed his responsibilities to his deputy

◊ **handwriting** ['hændraɪtɪŋ] *noun* writing done by hand; **send a letter of application in your own handwriting** = written by you with a pen, and not typed; **handwriting expert** = person who is able to identify a person by examining his handwriting

◊ **handwritten** ['hændrɪtən] *adjective* written by hand, not typed; *it is more professional to send in a typed rather than a handwritten letter of application*

Hansard ['hænsɑːd] *noun* official verbatim report of what is said and done in the House of Commons and the House of Lords; **Hansard reporters** = people who take shorthand notes of the debates in Parliament for printing in Hansard; *compare* JOURNAL

COMMENT: these reports were originally published by a Mr Hansard in the 19th century, and are now published by the Stationery Office. Hansard is published daily. Each page is divided into two numbered columns, so a reference to a particular speech in Hansard could read: Vol.120, No.24, 22 July 1987, Col. 370

hard [hɑːd] *adjective* (a) strong *or* not weak; **to take a hard line on something** = not to be flexible; *the council is taking a hard line over tenants who are late with their rent payments; the Home Office is taking a hard line on illegal immigrants* (b) difficult; *the examination for entry into the Civil Service is too hard; there are proposals to make it harder to get a gun licence* (c) solid *or* real; **hard copy** = printout of a text which is on computer *or* printed copy of a document which is on microfilm; **hard currency** = currency of a country which has a strong economy and which can be changed into other currencies easily; **hard disk** = computer disk which has a sealed case and can store large quantities of information **(d)** **hard bargain** = bargain with difficult terms; **to drive a hard bargain** = to be a difficult negotiator; **to strike a hard bargain** = to agree a deal where the terms are favourable to you

◊ **hardliner** [hɑːdˈlaɪnə] *noun* person who is inflexible (especially over policy); *hardliners in the Government are pushing the President to refuse to talk to the rebel leader*

harmonize [ˈhɑːmənaɪz] *verb (EU)* to standardize, to make similar or parallel

◊ **harmonization** [hɑːmənaɪˈzeɪʃn] *noun (EU)* standardization; *harmonization of tax policies is one of the EU priorities*

hat [hæt] *noun* piece of clothing worn on the head

COMMENT: if an MP wishes to speak while a division is taking place, he has to wear a hat, and an old top hat is kept in the House of Commons for this purpose

hatch [hætʃ] *verb* to prepare (a plot); *the plot was hatched in the house of the Chief Whip*

hawk [hɔːk] *noun* person who believes in threatening the use of armed force as a means of settling problems between countries; (NOTE: the opposite is **dove**)

◊ **hawkish** [ˈhɔːkɪʃ] *adjective* acting like a hawk; *the agreement will not satisfy the more hawkish members of the Cabinet*

HE [ˈeɪtʃ iː] = HIS EXCELLENCY, HER EXCELLENCY way of referring to an ambassador

head [hed] **1** *noun* **(a)** most important person; **head of department** *or* **departmental head** = person in charge of a department **(b)** most important *or* main; *head clerk; head porter; head salesman; head*

waiter; **head office** = main office, where the board of directors works and meets **(c)** top part *or* first part; *write the name of the company at the head of the list* **(d)** person; *allow £10 per head for expenses; factory inspectors cost on average £25,000 per head per annum* **(e)** **heads of agreement** = draft agreement containing the most important points but not all the details **2** *verb* **(a)** to be the manager *or* to be the most important person; *to head a department; he is heading a government delegation to China* **(b)** to be first; *the list of Bills to be considered is headed by the Bill on the adoption services; the two largest oil companies head the list of stock market results*

◊ **headed** [ˈhedɪd] *adjective* **headed paper** = notepaper with the name and address of a person *or* business printed on it

◊ **headhunt** [ˈhedhʌnt] *verb* to look for managers and offer them jobs in other companies; **he was headhunted** = he was approached by a headhunter and offered a new job

◊ **headhunter** [ˈhedhʌntə] *noun* person *or* company which looks for top managers and offers them jobs in other companies

◊ **heading** [ˈhedɪŋ] *noun* **(a)** words at the top of a piece of text, especially words at the beginning of a section of a statute; *items are listed under several headings; look at the figures under the heading 'Costs 94-95'* **(b)** **letter heading** *or* **heading on notepaper** = name and address of a business *or* person printed at the top of its notepaper

◊ **head of government** [ˈhed əv ˈgʌvənmənt] *noun* leader of a country's government; *see also* PRIME MINISTER

◊ **head of state** [ˈhed əv ˈsteɪt] *noun* official leader of a country

COMMENT: a head of state may not have much political power, and may be restricted to ceremonial duties (meeting ambassadors, laying wreaths at national memorials, opening parliament, etc.) The head of government is usually the effective ruler of the country, except in countries where the President is the executive ruler, and the head of government is in charge of the administration. In the United Kingdom, the Queen is head of state, and the Prime Minister is head of government. In the United States, the President is both head of state and head of government

◊ **headquarters (HQ)** ['hedkwɔːtəz] *plural noun* main office; **party headquarters** *or* **police headquarters** = central office of a political party *or* police force; *the leader called a meeting of the national committee at the party headquarters; the UN headquarters are situated in New York*

health [helθ] *noun* being well *or* not being ill; *the council said that smoke from the factory was a danger to public health; all cigarette packets carry a government health warning;* **Health and Safety at Work Act** = Act of Parliament which rules how the health of workers should be protected by the companies they work for; **(District) Health Authority (DHA** *or* **HA)** = administrative unit in the National Health Service which is responsible for health services, including hospitals and clinics, in a district; **Regional Health Authority (RHA)** = administrative unit in the National Health Service which is responsible for planning the health service in a region; **National Health Service (NHS)** = British organization which provides medical services free of charge or at a low cost, to the whole population; **Environmental Health Officer** *or* **Public Health Inspector** = official of a local authority who examines the environment and tests for air pollution *or* bad sanitation *or* noise levels, etc.; **the Health Service Commissioners** *or* **Health Service Ombudsmen** = officials who investigate complaints from the public about the National Health Service

hear [hiə] *verb* **(a)** to sense a sound with the ears; *you can hear the printer in the next office; the traffic makes so much noise that I cannot hear my phone ringing* **(b)** to have a letter *or* a phone call from someone; *we have not heard from them for some time; we hope to hear from the lawyers within a few days* **(c)** to listen to the arguments in a court case; *the judge heard the case in chambers; the application will be heard next month; the*

committee has heard the evidence from the Permanent Secretary **(d)** **hear! hear!** = words used in a meeting to show that you agree with the person speaking; (NOTE: **hearing - heard**)

◊ **hearing** ['hiərɪŋ] *noun* **(a)** case which is being heard by a committee *or* tribunal *or* court of law; *the hearing about the planning application lasted ten days;* **hearing in camera** = case which is heard in private with no member of the public present; **open hearing** = case where the public and journalists may attend **(b)** being heard by an official body; *he asked to be given a hearing by the full council so that he could state his case*

hegemony [he'dʒeməni] *noun* leadership by one strong state over a group of neighbouring states

hemicycle ['hemɪsaɪkl] *noun* meeting room with seats in the form of a semicircle; *MEPs meet in the hemicycle*

henceforth [hens'fɔːθ] *adverb* from this time on; *henceforth it will be more difficult to avoid customs examinations*

Her Majesty's pleasure [hɜː 'mædʒəstɪz 'pleʒə] *noun* **detention at** *or* **during Her Majesty's pleasure** = detention for an indefinite period, until the Home Secretary decides that a prisoner can be released

COMMENT: used as a punishment for people under a mental disability and children who commit murder

Her Majesty's Stationery Office (HMSO) [hɜː 'mædʒəstɪz 'steɪʃənri 'ɒfɪs] government department which prints and binds documents for all government departments, produces government stationery, as well a publishing and selling books for the government; (NOTE: also called **The Stationery Office** for short)

here- [hiə] *prefix* this time *or* this point; (NOTE: the following words formed from **here-** are frequently used in government and legal documents)

◊ **hereafter** [hɪə'rɑ:ftə] *adverb* from this time *or* point on

◊ **hereby** [hɪə'baɪ] *adverb* in this way *or* by this letter; *we hereby revoke the agreement of January 1st 1982*

◊ **herein** [hɪə'ɪn] *adverb* in this document; *the conditions stated herein; see the reference herein above*

◊ **hereinafter** [hɪərɪn'ɑ:ftə] *adverb* stated later in this document; *the conditions hereinafter listed*

◊ **hereof** [hɪə'ɒv] *adverb* of this; **in confirmation hereof** = to confirm this

◊ **hereto** [hɪə'tʊ] *adverb* to this; *according to the schedule of payments attached hereto;* **as witness hereto** = as a witness of this fact

◊ **heretofore** [hɪətu'fɔ:] *adverb* previously *or* earlier

◊ **hereunder** [hɪə'ʌndə] *adverb* under this heading *or* below this phrase; *see the documents listed hereunder*

hereditament [herɪ'dɪtəmənt] *noun* property which can be inherited; **mixed hereditaments** = properties which are used for both domestic and business purposes

hereditary [he'redɪtri] *adjective* which is inherited *or* which is passed from one member of a family to another; **hereditary office** = official position which is inherited; **hereditary peer** = member of the House of Lords who has inherited his title

hierarchy ['haɪrɑ:ki] *noun* arrangement of an organization in various ranks *or* grades, with one person *or* very few people at the top; *he started as a local official and rapidly rose through the ranks of the party hierarchy*

high [haɪ] **1** *adjective* **(a)** tall; *the door is not high enough to let us get the machines into the building; they are planning a 30-storey high office block* **(b)** large *or* not low; **highest bidder** = person who offers the most money at an auction; **high flier** = (i) person who is very successful *or* who is likely to get a very important job; (ii) share whose market price is rising rapidly; **high taxation** = taxation which imposes large taxes on wages *or* profits *or* estates, etc. **2** *adverb* prices **are running high** = prices are above their

usual level **3** *noun* point where prices *or* sales are very large; **sales volume has reached an all-time high** = has reached the highest point at which it has ever been

◊ **High Commission** ['haɪ kə'mɪʃn] *noun* **(a)** organization of the office of a High Commissioner **(b)** building where a High Commissioner lives and works; *the British High Commission in Ottawa or the UK High Commission in Ottawa; the High Commission staff were told not to speak to journalists; she is joining the High Commission as an interpreter;* (NOTE: a High Commission is the equivalent of an embassy in a non-Commonwealth country)

◊ **High Commissioner** ['haɪ kə'mɪʃənə] *noun* person who represents a Commonwealth country in another Commonwealth country, having the same rank and the same duties as an ambassador

◊ **High Court (of Justice)** ['haɪ 'kɔ:t] *noun* main civil court in England and Wales

> COMMENT: in England and Wales, the High Court is divided into three divisions: the Queen's Bench, the Chancery and the Family Divisions; the court hears most civil claims where the value exceeds £5,000

◊ **High Court of Justiciary** ['haɪ 'kɔ:t əv dʒʌs'tɪʃəri] *noun* the supreme criminal court of Scotland

◊ **high-rise** ['haɪ 'raɪz] *adjective* (building) with many storeys; *the high-rise flats built in the 1960s have been condemned as unsafe*

◊ **High Sheriff** ['haɪ 'ʃerɪf] *noun* senior representative appointed by the Crown in a county

◊ **highway** ['haɪweɪ] *noun* road *or* path; **highways committee** = committee of a local council with deals with roads and paths; **the Highway Code** = rules which govern the behaviour of people and vehicles using the public roads

Hilary ['hɪləri] *noun* one of the four sittings of the law courts; one of the four law terms, beginning in January

historic [hɪ'stɒrɪk] *adjective* **(a)** old *or* having a long history; *the council is trying to* *redevelop the historic centre of the city; the building is preserved as a historic monument* **(b)** important; *the MP, opening the town's first shopping precinct, said that it was a historic occasion*

HMSO ['eɪtʃ em es 'əʊ] = HER MAJESTY'S STATIONERY OFFICE

hoc [hɒk] *see* AD HOC

hold [həʊld] *verb* **(a)** to own *or* to keep *or* to possess; *he holds 10% of the company's shares; she holds the land under a lease from the property company; he holds fifty acres in south Scotland* **(b)** *(of a party or candidate)* **to hold a seat** = to have a member elected for a constituency of the same party as the previous member; *Labour held the seat with an increased majority* **(c)** to contain; *the tin holds twenty packets; each box holds 500 sheets of paper; a bag can hold twenty kilos of sugar* **(d)** to make something happen; *to hold a meeting or a discussion; the hearings were held in camera; the receiver will hold an auction of the company's assets; the inquiry will be held in London in June* **(e)** to decide *or* to make a judgment; *the tribunal held that there had been a prima facie breach of privilege; the committee held that the head teacher was guilty of gross misconduct;* (NOTE: **holding - held**)

◊ **hold back** ['həʊld 'bæk] *verb* to wait *or* not to go forward; **he held back from signing the lease until he had checked the details** = he delayed signing the lease until he had checked the details; **payment will be held back until the contract has been signed** = payment will not be made until the contract has been signed

◊ **hold down** ['həʊld 'daʊn] *verb* to control strictly *or* to keep in check; *the Government is trying to hold down food prices; the army has been sent to hold down the rebel areas*

◊ **hold out** ['həʊld 'aʊt] *verb* **(a)** to offer; *the negotiators held out the possibility of increased aid; the chairman held out the possibility of rapid promotion* **(b)** to remain in a place *or* position, in spite of being attacked; *the rebels are holding out in the*

government radio station; **to hold out for** = to ask for something and refuse to act until you get what you asked for; *he held out for a 50% discount; the union is holding out for a 10% wage increase*

◊ **hold over** ['həʊld 'əʊvə] *verb* to postpone *or* to put back to a later date; *discussion of item 4 was held over until the next meeting*

◊ **hold to** ['həʊld tʊ] *verb* to keep *or* limit; **we will try to hold him to the contract** = we will try to stop him going against the contract; **the government hopes to hold wage increases to 5%** = the government hopes that wage increases will not be more than 5%

◊ **hold up** ['həʊld 'ʌp] *verb* **(a)** to show *or* display; *the agreement was held up as an example of good management-worker relations* **(b)** to stay at a high level; *share prices have held up well; sales held up during the tourist season* **(c)** to delay; *the shipment has been held up at the customs; payment will be held up until the contract has been signed; the strike will hold up delivery for some weeks*

◊ **hold-up** ['həʊldʌp] *noun* delay; *the strike caused hold-ups in the shipment of goods*

holiday ['hɒlɪdeɪ] *noun* **(a) bank holiday** = weekday which is a public holiday on which the banks are closed; *Easter Monday is a bank holiday;* **public holiday** = day when all workers rest and enjoy themselves instead of working; **statutory holiday** = holiday which is fixed by law **(b)** period when a worker does not work, but rests, goes away and enjoys himself; *to take a holiday or to go on holiday; when is the manager taking his holidays? my secretary is off on holiday tomorrow; he is away on holiday for two weeks;* **the job carries five weeks' holiday** = one of the conditions of the job is that you have five weeks' holiday; **the summer holidays** = holidays taken by the workers in the summer when the weather is good and children are not at school; **holiday entitlement** = number of days' paid holiday which a worker has the right to take; **holiday pay** = salary which is still paid during the holidays **(c) tax holiday** = period when a new business is exempted from paying tax

home [həʊm] *noun* place where a person lives *or* country where a company is based; **home-produced products** = products which are not imported

◊ **Home Office** [ˈhəʊm ˈɒfɪs] *noun* British government ministry dealing with internal affairs, including the police and prisons

◊ **Home Rule** [ˈhəʊm ˈruːl] *noun* the right of an area of a country to rule itself after being governed from outside

◊ **Home Secretary** *or* **Secretary of State for Home Affairs** [ˈhəʊm ˈsekrətri] *noun* minister of the British government, in charge of the Home Office, dealing with law and order, the police and prisons

COMMENT: in most countries the government department dealing with the internal order of the country is called the Ministry of the Interior, with a Minister of the Interior in charge

hon. [hɒn] *see* HONOURABLE

honorary [ˈɒnərəri] *adjective* (person) who is not paid a salary; **honorary treasurer** = treasurer (of a society *or* club) who is not paid a salary; **honorary consul** = person who represents a country but is not paid a salary, and is not a member of the diplomatic corps, although he may be granted diplomatic status

honourable [ˈɒnrəbl] *noun* title used when one MP addresses another; *the hon. Member for London East would do well to remember the conditions in his constituency; will my hon. Friend give way? the hon. Gentleman is perfectly entitled to ask that question;* **Right Honourable** = title given to members of the Privy Council; (NOTE: usually written Hon.: the Hon. Member; the Rt. Hon. William Smith, M.P.)

COMMENT: various conventions are attached to the use of the word in Parliament. In general, MPs can refer to each other as 'the hon. Member for...'; the Speaker will refer to all MPs as 'hon. Members'. To distinguish MPs of one's own party from those on the other side of the House, an MP will say 'my hon. Friend'. To distinguish between women and men MPs, you can say 'the hon. Lady' or 'the hon. Gentleman'. Lawyers may be addressed as 'hon. and learned'

hopper [ˈhɒpə] *noun US* box where bills are put after being introduced in the House of Representatives

horse-trading [ˈhɔːstreɪdɪŋ] *noun* bargaining between political parties *or* politicians *or* members of a committee to obtain a general agreement for something; *after a period of horse-trading, the committee agreed on the election of a member of one of the smaller parties as Chairman*

hostile [ˈhɒstaɪl] *adjective* warlike *or* not friendly; *the proposal was given a hostile reception by the main committee;* **hostile act** = act which shows that a country is unfriendly; *we will consider it a hostile act if political asylum is granted to this criminal*

◊ **hostility** [hɒˈstɪlɪti] *noun* **(a)** unfriendly attitude towards someone; *his proposal was greeted by the rest of the committee with hostility; members of the public showed their hostility by throwing eggs* **(b) hostilities** = armed fighting; *the president is trying to negotiate an end to hostilities in the region*

hot [hɒt] *adjective* **(a)** very warm; *the staff complain that the office is too hot in the summer and too cold in the winter; the drinks machine sells coffee, tea and hot soup; switch off the machine if it gets too hot* **(b)** not safe *or* very bad; **to make things hot for someone** = to make it difficult for someone to work *or* to trade; *customs officials are making things hot for the drug smugglers;* **he is in the hot seat** = his job involves making many difficult decisions

◊ **hot pursuit** [ˈhɒt pəˈsjuːt] *noun* right which is claimed in international law to chase a ship into international waters *or* to chase suspected criminals across an international border into another country

house [haʊs] *noun* **(a)** whole building in which someone lives; **house property** = private houses, not shops, offices or factories; **house agent** = estate agent who deals in buying or selling houses **(b)** one of the two parts of the British Parliament (the House of Commons and the House of Lords); *the minister brought a matter to the attention of the House;* **the Houses of Parliament** = (i) the building where the British Parliament meets, containing the chambers of the House of Commons and the House of Lords; (ii) the British Parliament **(c)** one of the two chambers of Congress; *the bill was passed by both houses and sent to the President for signature; US* **the House** = the House of Representatives; **House Calendar** = list of bills which do not appropriate money or raise revenue **(d)** one of the two chambers of a legislature, usually the lower chamber; **House of Assembly** = legislative body in Barbados, Dominica, Tasmania and Zimbabwe; **House of Chiefs** = upper consultative council in Botswana; **House of Councillors** = upper house of legislature in Japan; **House of Representatives** = legislative body in many countries, including Antigua, Australia, Colombia, Cyprus, the Gambia, Jamaica, Japan, Jordan, Nepal, New zealand, the Philippines, Trinidad and Tobago, Yemen

◊ **household** [ˈhaʊsəʊld] *noun* people living in a house; **household effects** = furniture and other items used in a house, and moved with the owner when he moves house

◊ **householder** [ˈhaʊshəʊldə] *noun* person who occupies a private house

◊ **House leader** [ˈhaʊs ˈliːdə] *noun* **(a)** *(in Britain)* Leader of the House *or* main government minister and member of the cabinet, who is responsible for the administration of legislation in the House of Commons *or* House of Lords, and is the main government spokesman in the House **(b)** *(in the USA)* chief of one of the political parties in the House of Representatives; **the House Republican Leader** = head of the Republican Party in the House of Representatives

◊ **House of Commons** [ˈhaʊs əv ˈkɒmənz] *noun* (i) lower house of the British Parliament, made up of 659 elected members; (ii) lower house of a legislature (as in Canada)

◊ **House of Lords** [ˈhaʊs əv ˈlɔːdz] *noun* upper house of the British Parliament made up of hereditary lords, life peers, leading judges and some bishops; **Judicial Committee of the House of Lords** = highest court of appeal in both civil and criminal cases in England and Wales

COMMENT: as a court, the decisions of the House of Lords are binding on all other courts, and the only appeal from the House of Lords is to the European Court of Justice

◊ **House of Representatives** [ˈhaʊs əv reprɪˈzentətɪvz] *noun* (i) lower house of the Congress of the United States, made up of 435 elected members; (ii) lower house of a legislature (as in Australia)

COMMENT: Members of the House of Commons (called MPs) are elected for five years, which is the maximum length of a Parliament. Bills can be presented in either the House of Commons or House of Lords, and sent to the other chamber for discussion and amendment. All bills relating to revenue must be introduced in the House of Commons, and most other bills are introduced there also. The members of the House of Representatives (called Congressmen) are elected for two years. All bills relating to revenue must originate in the House of Representatives; otherwise bills can be proposed in either the House or the Senate and sent to the other chamber for discussion and amendment.

housing [ˈhaʊzɪŋ] *noun* supply of houses *or* flats for people to live in; *the council provides low-cost housing for families in the borough; the family lives in council housing;* **housing department** = department of a local authority which deals with council houses and flats; **housing list** = list of people waiting to be placed in council housing; *this family has been on the housing list for three years*

HQ ['eɪtʃ 'kjuː] = HEADQUARTERS *the party HQ was surrounded by demonstrators*

Hundred Days ['hʌndrəd 'deɪz] *noun* the first 100 days of a new administration, seen as a benchmark of that administration's competence

COMMENT: originally applied to the first 100 days of President Roosevelt's administration in 1933, and now applied to all new administrations

hung [hʌŋ] *adjective* with no majority; **hung council** *or* **hung parliament** = council *or* parliament in which no single party has enough votes to form a government; **hung jury** = jury which cannot arrive at a unanimous *or* majority verdict

Hural [hʊˈræl] *noun* **Great Hural** = legislative body in Mongolia (the equivalent of Parliament or Congress)

hurdle ['hɜːdl] *noun* thing which makes it difficult for something to happen; *the applicant will have to overcome two hurdles if his appeal is to be successful*

hurry ['hʌri] **1** *noun* doing things fast; *there is no hurry for the figures, we do not need them until next week;* **in a hurry** = very fast **2** *verb* to do something *or* to make something *or* to go very fast; *the government whips are trying to hurry the bill through the committee stages; the chairman does not want to be hurried into making a decision; the directors hurried into the meeting*

hustings ['hʌstɪŋz] *noun* **at the hustings** = at a parliamentary election

COMMENT: the hustings were formerly the booths where votes were taken, or the platform on which candidates stood to speak, but now the word is used simply to mean 'an election'

Hybrid Bill ['haɪbrɪd 'bɪl] *noun* term used to refer to a Public Bill which affects the private interests of a particular person or organization

ID ['aɪ 'diː] = IDENTITY **ID card** = IDENTITY CARD

idem ['ɪdem] *pronoun* the same thing *or* the same person

identity [aɪ'dentɪfaɪ] *noun* who someone is; **identity card** = card carried by citizens of a country *or* members of a group to prove identity

ideology [aɪdi'ɒlədʒi] *noun* set of basic ideas about life and society, such as religious *or* political opinions; *most political parties are based on ideologies; Marxist ideology states that a classless society will be established*

◊ **ideological** [aɪdiə'lɒdʒɪkl] *adjective* referring to ideology; *the two sections of the party have important ideological differences*

◊ **ideologist** *or* **ideologue** [aɪdi'ɒlədʒɪst *or* 'aɪdiəlɒg] *noun (often as criticism)* person who follows *or* advocates a certain ideology

i.e. ['aɪ 'iː] *short for the Latin phrase* 'id est', meaning 'that is'; *the biggest spending departments, i.e. Education and Defence, face the largest cutbacks; the import restrictions apply to expensive items, i.e. items costing more than $2,500*

IGC *(EU)* = INTERGOVERNMENTAL CONFERENCE

illegal [ɪ'liːgəl] *adjective* not legal *or* against criminal law; *the illegal carrying of arms; illegal immigrants are deported;* **illegal contract** = contract which cannot be enforced in law (such as a contract to commit a crime)

◊ **illegality** [ɪlɪ'gælɪtɪ] *noun* being illegal

◊ **illegally** [ɪ'liːgəli] *adverb* against the law; *he was accused of illegally bringing firearms into the country*

illicit [ɪ'lɪsɪt] *adjective* not legal *or* not permitted; *illicit sale of alcohol; trade in illicit alcohol*

ILO ['aɪel'əu] = INTERNATIONAL LABOUR ORGANIZATION

immediate [ɪ'miːdiət] *adjective* happening at once; *he wrote an immediate letter of complaint; the Home Secretary ordered her immediate release*

◊ **immediately** [ɪ'miːdiətli] *adverb* at once; *when she arrived in the country, she was immediately arrested by the airport police; when the government heard the news they immediately recalled the ambassador; can you phone immediately you get the information?*

immigrate ['ɪmɪgreɪt] *verb* to move into a country to live permanently

◊ **immigration** [ɪmɪ'greɪʃn] *noun* moving into a country to live permanently; **Immigration Laws** = legislation regarding immigration into a country

◊ **immigrant** ['ɪmɪgrənt] *noun* person who moves into a country to live permanently; **illegal immigrant** = person who enters a country to live permanently without having the permission of the government to do so; *see also* EMIGRATE, EMIGRANT (NOTE: an emigrant from one country becomes an immigrant in his new country)

immunity [ɪ'mjuːnɪti] *noun* protection against arrest *or* prosecution; **diplomatic immunity** = not being subject to the laws of the country in which you are living because of being a diplomat; **when he offered to give**

information to the police, he was granted immunity from prosecution = he was told he would not be prosecuted

> COMMENT: immunity from prosecution is also granted to magistrates, counsel and witnesses as regards their statements in judicial proceedings. Families and servants of diplomats may be covered by diplomatic immunity. In the USA, immunity is the protection of members of Congress against being sued for libel or slander for statements made on the floor of the House (in the UK this is called **privilege**)

impartial [ɪmˈpɑːʃəl] *adjective* not partial *or* not biased *or* not prejudiced; *a judgment must be impartial; to give someone a fair and impartial hearing*

◊ **impartiality** [ɪmpɑːʃiˈælɪti] *noun* state of being impartial; *the newspapers doubted the impartiality of the Ombudsman*

◊ **impartially** [ɪmˈpɑːʃəli] *adverb* not showing any bias *or* favour towards someone; *ACAS has to act impartially towards the two parties in the dispute*

impeach [ɪmˈpiːtʃ] *verb* (a) formerly, to charge a person with treason *or* other serious crime before Parliament (b) to charge a head of state *or* minister with treason *or* with crimes against the state

◊ **impeachment** [ɪmˈpiːtʃmənt] *noun* charge of treason *or* other serious crime brought against a head of state *or* government minister

impending [ɪmˈpendɪŋ] *adjective* which will happen soon; *the newspapers carried stories about the impending general election*

imperial [ɪmˈpɪərɪəl] *adjective* referring to an empire; *the power of imperial Rome*

◊ **imperialism** [ɪmˈpɪərɪəlɪzm] *noun (often as criticism)* (i) idea or practice of having an empire formed of colonies; (ii) controlling other countries as if they were part of an empire

◊ **imperialist** [ɪmˈpɪərɪəlɪst] **1** *adjective* referring to imperialism **2** *noun* person who is in favour of empires and imperialism

◊ **imperialistic** [ɪmpɪərɪəˈlɪstɪk] *adjective* referring to imperialism

> COMMENT: although imperialism is used to refer to states which have or had colonies (such as Britain, France, Belgium, the Netherlands, etc.,) it is now widely used to refer to states which exert strong influence over other states. This influence can be political, military or commercial

implement 1 [ˈɪmplɪmənt] *noun* tool *or* instrument used to do some work; *he was hit on the head with a heavy implement* **2** [ˈɪmplɪment] *verb* to put into action; *to implement an agreement or a decision; the recommendations of the committee of inquiry have never been implemented*

◊ **implementation** [ɪmplɪmenˈteɪʃn] *noun* putting into action; *the implementation of new rules*

implicate [ˈɪmplɪkeɪt] *verb* to involve in; *several ministers were implicated in the arms-selling scandal*

implicit [ɪmˈplɪsɪt] *adjective* implied; *the new manifesto contains an implicit rejection of the party's former defence policy*

imply [ɪmˈplaɪ] *verb* to suggest (that something may be true); *the Leader of the Opposition implied that the Prime Minister had not in fact read the relevant papers; do you wish to imply that the secret service acted improperly?*

◊ **implied** [ɪmˈplaɪd] *adjective* which is presumed to be true; *the Minister rejected the implied criticism of his department's officials*

import 1 [ˈɪmpɔːt] *noun* bringing foreign goods into a country to be sold; *the import of firearms is forbidden;* import levy = tax on imports, especially in the EU a tax on imports of farm produce from outside the EU; import licence = permit which allows a company to bring a certain type of product into a country **2** [ɪmˈpɔːt] *verb* to bring foreign goods into a country

◊ **imports** [ˈɪmpɔːts] *plural noun* goods brought into a country; *all imports must be* *declared to the customs;* (NOTE: the opposite is exports)

importance [ɪm'pɔːtəns] *noun* having a value *or* mattering a lot; *the bank attaches great importance to the deal*

◊ **important** [ɪm'pɔːtənt] *adjective* which matters a lot; *he left a pile of important papers in the taxi; she has an important meeting at 10.30; he was promoted to a more important position*

impose [ɪm'pəʊz] *verb* to ask someone to pay a fine; to put a tax *or* a duty on goods; *the court imposed a fine of £100; to impose a tax on bicycles; they tried to impose a ban on smoking; the government imposed a special duty on oil; the customs have imposed a 10% tax increase on electrical items; the unions have asked the government to impose trade barriers on foreign cars*

◊ **imposition** [ɪmpə'zɪʃn] *noun* putting a tax on goods or services; putting an extra burden of work on someone; *council officials consider having to attending all-night sittings to be an imposition*

impossible [ɪm'pɒsəbl] *adjective* which cannot be done; *it is impossible for any law to cover every future case; getting skilled staff is becoming impossible; government regulations make it impossible for us to sell our computer parts*

impound [ɪm'paʊnd] *verb* to take something away and keep it until a tax is paid *or* until documents are checked to see if they are correct; *the customs impounded the whole cargo*

◊ **impounding** [ɪm'paʊndɪŋ] *noun* act of taking something and keeping it

improper [ɪm'prɒpə] *adjective* not correct *or* not as it should be

◊ **improperly** [ɪm'prɒpəli] *adverb* not correctly; *the extradition order was improperly made out; the official of the Defence Ministry was accused of acting improperly in buying shares in the company before it was awarded the defence contract*

impunity [ɪm'pjuːnɪti] *noun* **with impunity** = without punishment; *no one can flout the law with impunity*

in absentia ['ɪn əb'sentiə] *adverb* in someone's absence; *the former President was tried and sentenced to death in absentia*

inalienable [ɪn'eɪliənəbl] *adjective* (right) which cannot be taken away *or* transferred

in camera ['ɪn 'kæmərə] *adverb* in private *or* with no members of the public permitted to be present; *the case was heard in camera*

inception [ɪn'sepʃn] *noun* beginning of existence; *since its inception, the scheme has helped thousands of poor families*

incite [ɪn'saɪt] *verb* to encourage *or* persuade *or* advise (someone) to commit a crime

◊ **incitement** [ɪn'saɪtmənt] *noun* crime of encouraging *or* persuading *or* advising someone to commit a crime; **incitement to racial hatred** = offence of encouraging (by words *or* actions *or* writing) people to attack others because of their race

include [ɪn'kluːd] *verb* to count something along with other things; *the charge includes VAT; the total comes to £1,000 including freight; the total is £140 not including insurance and freight; the account covers services up to and including the month of June*

◊ **inclusive** [ɪn'kluːsɪv] *adjective* which counts something in with other things; *inclusive of tax or not inclusive of VAT;* **inclusive sum** *or* **inclusive charge** = charge which includes all costs; **the party conference runs from the 12th to the 16th inclusive** = it starts on the morning of the 12th and ends on the evening of the 16th

income ['ɪŋkʌm] *noun* money which a person receives as salary *or* dividend *or* interest *or* fees; **income tax** = tax on a person's income

incoming [ɪn'kʌmɪŋ] *adjective* **(a)** **incoming call** = phone call coming into the office from someone outside; **incoming mail** = mail which comes into an office **(b)** which has recently been elected *or* appointed; **the incoming government** *or* **Minister** = the new government *or* the Minister who has just been appointed and is about to start working; *the chairman welcomed the incoming committee; the incoming cabinet was sworn in at the Presidential palace*

incompetent [ɪnˈkɒmpɪtənt] *adjective* **(a)** who cannot work well *or* who is not able to do something; *the Finance Minister is quite incompetent, but he is the President's brother-in-law; the company has an incompetent sales director* **(b)** not legally able to do something; *he is incompetent to sign the contract*

◊ **incompetency** [ɪnˈkɒmpɪtənsi] *noun* state of not being legally competent to do something

incorporate [ɪnˈkɔːpəreɪt] *verb* **(a)** to bring something in to form part of a main group *or* to make a document part of another document; *income from the 1994 acquisition is incorporated into the accounts; the list of markets is incorporated into the main contract* **(b)** to form a registered company; *a company incorporated in the USA; an incorporated company; J. Doe Incorporated* **(c)** to set up and give legal status to a town

◊ **incorporation** [ɪnkɔːpəˈreɪʃn] *noun* act of incorporating a company; **articles of incorporation** = document which regulates the way in which a company's affairs are managed; **certificate of incorporation** = certificate issued by the Registrar of Companies showing that a company has been officially incorporated and the date at which it came into existence

incorrect [ɪnkəˈrekt] *adjective* wrong *or* not correct; *the minutes of the meeting were incorrect and had to be changed; the wording of the election notice was incorrect*

◊ **incorrectly** [ɪnkəˈrektli] *adverb* wrongly *or* not correctly; *the amendment was incorrectly worded*

increase 1 [ˈɪŋkriːs] *noun* **(a)** growth *or* becoming larger; *increase in tax* *or* *tax increase; increase in price* *or* *price increase;*

profits showed a 10% increase *or* *an increase of 10% on last year;* **increase in the cost of living** = rise in the annual cost of living index **(b)** higher salary; *increase in pay* *or* *pay increase; increase in salary* *or* *salary increase; the government hopes to hold salary increases to 3%;* **cost-of-living increase** = increase in salary to allow it keep up with the increased cost of living; **merit increase** = increase in pay given to a worker whose work is good **(c) on the increase** = growing larger *or* becoming more frequent; *the use of hard drugs is on the increase* **2** [ɪnˈkriːs] *verb* **(a)** to grow bigger *or* higher; **to increase in price** = to cost more; **to increase in size** *or* **in value** = to become larger *or* more valuable **(b)** *his salary was increased to* **£20,000** = he had a rise in salary to £20,000

◊ **increasing** [ɪnˈkriːsɪŋ] *adjective* which is growing bigger; *increasing profits; the company has an increasing share of the market*

◊ **increasingly** [ɪnˈkriːsɪŋli] *adverb* more and more; *the Minister has come to depend increasingly on the advice of the Permanent Secretary*

incumbent [ɪnˈkʌmbənt] **1** *adjective* **(a)** holding an official position; *the incumbent President* **(b)** it is incumbent upon him = he has to do this, because it is his duty; *it is incumbent on us to check our facts before making an accusation* **2** *noun* person who holds an official position; *there will be no changes in the governor's staff while the present incumbent is still in office*

incursion [ɪnˈkɜːʃn] *noun* hostile raid into another country's territory

indefeasible right [ɪndɪˈfiːzəbl ˈraɪt] *noun* right which cannot be made void

indefinite [ɪnˈdefɪnɪt] *adjective* not defined, especially with no stated end; **for an indefinite period of time** = for a period with no stated termination

indemnification [ɪndemnɪfɪˈkeɪʃn] *noun* promise of payment for loss *or* damage

◊ **indemnify** [ɪnˈdemnɪfaɪ] *verb* to (promise to) pay for damage suffered; *to indemnify someone against* *or* *for a loss*

◊ **indemnity** [ɪn'demnɪti] *noun* (i) statement of liability to pay compensation for a loss *or* for a wrong in a transaction to which you are a party; (ii) *(in general)* compensation for a loss *or* a wrong; *he had to pay an indemnity of £100*

independence [ɪndɪ'pendəns] *noun* **(a)** freedom from rule *or* control *or* influence of others; *the colony struggled to achieve independence; Britain granted her colonies independence in the years after the Second World War; an independence movement grew in the colony;* the American War of Independence = war by the American colonies against Britain (1775-1786) by which the colonies became independent; **Declaration of Independence** = document written by Thomas Jefferson (1776) by which the former American colonies declared their independence from Britain; **Unilateral Declaration of Independence (UDI)** = act whereby a colony declares itself independent without the agreement of the colonial power **(b)** time when a country became independent; *the ten years since independence have seen many changes;* **Independence Day** = day when a country celebrates its independence (July 4th in the USA)

◊ **independent** [ɪndɪ'pendənt] *adjective* free *or* not controlled by anyone; *the council has asked an independent consultant to report on the housing department; the country has been independent since 1956;* **independent school** = private school which is not run by a local educational authority

◊ **independently** [ɪndɪ'pendəntli] *adverb* alone *or* without the help of anyone else; *the two advisers reached the same conclusion independently of each other*

index ['ɪndeks] *noun* **(a)** list of items classified into groups or put into order; *we keep a card index of clients* **(b)** regular report which shows rises and falls in prices, etc.; **cost-of-living index** = way of measuring the cost of living shown as a percentage increase on the figure for the preceding period; (NOTE: the plural for (a) is **indexes** and for (b) **indices**)

◊ **index-linked** ['ɪndeks 'lɪŋkt] *adjective* rising automatically with the percentage increase in the cost of living; *he has an index-linked pension*

indicate ['ɪndɪkeɪt] *verb* to show; *the latest figures indicate a fall in the inflation rate*

◊ **indication** [ɪndɪ'keɪʃn] *noun* act of indicating; **he gave no indication that the government was about to change its policy** = he did not show that the government was about to change its policy

◊ **indicator** ['ɪndɪkeɪtə] *noun* thing which indicates; **government economic indicators** = figures which show how the country's economy is going to perform in the short or long term

individual [ɪndɪ'vɪdjuːəl] **1** *noun* single person; *he was approached by two individuals in white coats* **2** *adjective* referring to a single person *or* thing; *the records are kept in individual files*

industrial [ɪn'dʌstriəl] *adjective* relating to work; **industrial property** = property owned by a company such as patents, trademarks, copyrights; **industrial tribunal** = court which decides in disputes between employers and employees or trade unions

infer [ɪn'fɜː] *verb* to reach an opinion about something; *he inferred from the letter that the chairman was not satisfied with the recent decision;* (NOTE: you **infer** something which someone else has **implied**)

infiltrate ['ɪnfɪltreɪt] *verb* to enter (an organization) secretly, without the officials knowing; *the club has been infiltrated by right-wing agitators*

inflation [ɪn'fleɪʃn] *noun* situation where prices rise to keep up with increased money available to purchase goods; **rate of inflation** *or* **inflation rate** = percentage increase in prices over a period such as one year

influence ['ɪnfluəns] **1** *noun* effect on someone *or* something; *they said the president was acting under the influence of the Ambassador; the decision of the court was not influenced by the speech of the Prime Minister; we are suffering from the* *influence of a high exchange rate;* **undue influence** = pressure put on someone which prevents that person from acting independently **2** *verb* to have an effect on someone *or* something; *the House was influenced in its decision by the gravity of the financial crisis; the price of oil has influenced the price of industrial goods; he was accused of trying to influence the Select Committee*

◊ **influence peddling** ['ɪnfluəns 'pedlɪŋ] *noun* offering to use one's influence, especially political power, for payment, to help a person *or* group achieve something

◊ **influential** [ɪnflu'enʃl] *noun* having the power to influence someone or something; *he is the chairman of the influential Foreign Affairs Committee*

influx ['ɪnflʌks] *noun* continuous flow into; *the influx of immigrant workers into the south of the USA*

inform [ɪn'fɔːm] *verb* to tell someone officially; *I regret to inform you that war has been declared; we are pleased to inform you that we wish to appoint you to the post for which you applied; we have been informed by the Department of Trade that new tariffs are coming into force*

◊ **informant** [ɪn'fɔːmənt] *noun* person who informs *or* who gives information to someone; *is your informant reliable?*

◊ **information** [ɪnfə'meɪʃn] *noun* **(a)** details which explain something; *have you any information on *or* about deposit accounts? I enclose this leaflet for your information; to disclose a piece of information; to answer a request for information; for further information, please write to Department 27* **disclosure of confidential information** = telling someone information which should be secret; **freedom of information** = making government information available to ordinary people *or* making official records about private people available to each person concerned; **information bureau** *or* **information office** = office which gives information to tourists *or* visitors; **information officer** = person whose job is to give information about a company *or* an organization *or* a government department

to the public; person whose job is to give information to other departments in the same organization; (NOTE: no plural: to indicate one item use **a piece of Information**) **(b) information technology** = working with computers and data stored in them; **information retrieval** = finding data in a computer

◊ **informer** [ɪn'fɔːmə] *noun* person who gives information to the police about a crime *or* about criminals

informal [ɪn'fɔːml] *adjective* not formal *or* not strictly official; *the Permanent Secretary in the Home Office had an informal meeting with his French counterpart*

infrastructure ['ɪnfrəstrʌktʃə] *noun* basic installations which are necessary to the economic functioning of a country (rail network, electricity, etc.)

infringe [ɪn'frɪndʒ] *verb* to break a law *or* a right

inhabitant [ɪn'hæbɪtənt] *noun* person who lives in a building, town, country, etc.; *Spain has 39 million inhabitants*

in-house ['ɪn'haʊs] *adverb & adjective* working inside a company's building; *the in-house staff; we do all our data processing in-house;* **in-house training** = training given to staff at their place of work

one of the advantages of keeping services in-house is that
a council has a ready pool of
labour and equipment to call on
in an emergency
Local Government News

initial [ɪ'nɪʃl] **1** *adjective* first *or* starting; **initial capital** = capital which is used to start a business; *he started the business with an initial expenditure or initial investment of £500* **2** *noun* **initials** = first letters of the words in a name; *what do the initials DOE stand for? the chairman wrote his initials by each alteration in the contract he was signing* **3** *verb* to write your initials on a document to show you have read it and approved; *to initial an amendment to a* *contract; please initial the agreement at the place marked with an X*

initiative [ɪ'nɪʃjətɪv] *noun* **(a)** decision to start doing something; *the president took the initiative in asking the rebel leader to come for a meeting; the minister has proposed several initiatives to try to restart the deadlocked negotiations* **(b)** *(in Switzerland and the USA)* move by a group of citizens to propose that something should be decided by a referendum

injunction [ɪn'dʒʌŋkʃən] *noun* court order compelling someone to stop doing something *or* not to do something; *he got an injunction preventing the company from selling his car; the council applied for an injunction to stop the developer from continuing with the demolition;* **interim injunction** = injunction which prevents someone from doing something until a certain date; **interlocutory** *or* **temporary injunction** = injunction which is granted until a case comes to court; **prohibitory injunction** = injunction which prevents someone from doing an illegal act

injustice [ɪn'dʒʌstɪs] *noun* lack of justice; *she complained about the injustice of the system;* (NOTE: no plural)

inland ['ɪnlænd] *adjective* **(a)** inside a country; **inland postage** = postage for a letter to another part of the country; **inland freight charges** = charges for carrying goods from one part of the country to another **(b)** the **Inland Revenue** = British government department dealing with income tax; (NOTE: in the USA the department is called the **Internal Revenue Service**)

inner ['ɪnə] *adjective* inside *or* in the middle; **inner cities** *or* **inner city areas** = central parts of large towns; *the crime rate is increasing in inner city areas; the Minister has been given special responsibility for developing decayed inner cities; inner city families often live in overcrowded conditions*

input ['ɪnpʌt] **1** *noun* material *or* information *or* effort put into something; *the chairman hoped for an input of new ideas from the committee; the council is expecting a substantial input of funds from central government;* **input tax** = VAT paid on goods or services bought **2** *verb* to put information into a computer

inquire [ɪŋ'kwaɪə] *verb* to ask questions about something; *he inquired if anything was wrong; she inquired about the rate of inflation in other European countries; the commission is inquiring into corruption in the customs service*

◊ **inquiry** [ɪŋ'kwaɪrɪ] *noun* official investigation; *there has been a government inquiry into the loss of the secret documents*

inquorate [ɪn'kwɔːreɪt] *adjective* without a quorum; *the meeting was declared inquorate and had to be abandoned*

insane [ɪn'seɪn] *adjective* mentally ill *or* suffering from a state of mind which makes it impossible for you to know that you are doing wrong, and so you cannot be held responsible for your actions

◊ **insanity** [ɪn'sænɪtɪ] *noun* being mad *or* not being sane; (NOTE: no plural)

COMMENT: a person who is insane cannot vote, and cannot be an MP. Where an accused person is found to be insane, a verdict of 'not guilty by reason of insanity' is returned and the accused is ordered to be detained at Her Majesty's pleasure

in-service training (INSET) ['ɪnsɜːvɪs 'treɪnɪŋ] *noun* training offered by an employer to his staff; *the report suggested increasing in-service training facilities in the department*

inside [ɪn'saɪd] **1** *adjective & adverb* in, especially in a company's office or building; **inside job** = crime which has been committed on a company's property by one of the employees of the company; **inside worker** = worker who works in the office or factory (not in the open air, as for example a travelling salesman) **2** *preposition* in; *there was nothing inside the container; we have a contact inside the enemy's defence ministry who gives us very useful information*

◊ **insider** [ɪn'saɪdə] *noun* person who works in an organization and therefore knows its secrets; **insider dealing** *or* **insider trading**

= illegal buying or selling of shares by staff of a company who have secret information about the company's plans

insist [ɪn'sɪst] *verb* to state firmly *or* to demand; *he insisted on something being done or he insisted that something should be done to help the families of the crash victims*

insolvent [ɪn'sɒlvənt] *adjective* not able to pay debts; *the company was declared insolvent*

◊ **insolvency** [ɪn'sɒlvənsi] *noun* not being able to pay debts; **the company was in a state of insolvency** = it could not pay its debts; (NOTE: no plural. **Insolvent** and **insolvency** are general terms, but are usually applied to companies; individuals are usually described as **bankrupt** once they have been declared so by a court)

inspect [ɪn'spekt] *verb* to examine in detail; *to inspect a machine or a factory or a school; to inspect the accounts of a company*

◊ **inspection** [ɪn'spekʃn] *noun* close examination of something; *to make an inspection or to carry out an inspection of a machine or a factory; inspection of a product for defects;* **customs inspection** = examination of a shipment by customs officials; **to carry out a tour of inspection** = to visit various places *or* offices *or* factories to inspect them; **inspection stamp** = stamp placed on something to show it has been inspected

◊ **inspector** [ɪn'spektə] *noun* (a) official who inspects; **inspector of factories** *or* **factory inspector** = government official who inspects factories *or* buildings to see if they are safely run; **inspector of taxes** *or* **tax inspector** = official of the Inland Revenue who examines tax returns and decides how much tax each person should pay; **inspector of weights and measures** = government official who inspects weighing machines and goods sold in shops to see if the quantities and weights are correct (b) (police) **inspector** = rank in the police force above a sergeant and below chief inspector

◊ **inspectorate** [ɪn'spektərət] *noun* all inspectors of one type; **the factory inspectorate** = all inspectors of factories; **the school inspectorate** = all local *or* national inspectors of schools

instalment *or US* installment

[ɪn'stɔːlmənt] *noun* part of a payment which is paid regularly until the total amount is paid; *the first instalment is payable on signature of the agreement; the rates can be paid in ten monthly instalments;* **the final instalment is now due** = the last of a series of payments should be paid now; **to pay #25 down and monthly instalments of #20** = to pay a first payment of #25 and the rest in payments of #20 each month; **to miss an instalment** = not to pay an instalment at the right time

instance ['ɪnstəns] *noun* particular example *or* case; *in this instance we will overlook the delay;* **court of the first instance** = court where a case is heard first

instant ['ɪnstənt] *adjective* (a) at this point; **our letter of the 6th instant** = our letter of the 6th of this current month (b) immediately available; *the banks provide instant credit; do not expect an instant reply from the department concerned*

institute ['ɪnstɪtjuːt] **1** *noun* (a) official organization; **research institute** = organization set up to do research; **institute of further education** = organization which gives education to people over the age of 16 (after they have left school) (b) title of a professional organization; *the Royal Institute of British Architects* **2** *verb* to start; *to institute proceedings against someone*

◊ **institution** [ɪnstɪ'tjuːʃn] *noun* (a) organization *or* society set up for a particular purpose; **financial institution** = bank *or* investment trust *or* insurance company whose work involves lending or investing large sums of money (b) building for a special purpose; **mental institution** = special hospital for patients suffering from mental disorders; **penal institution** = place (such as a prison) where convicted criminals are kept

◊ **institutional** [ɪnstɪ'tjuːʃnəl] *adjective* referring to a financial institution; **institutional buying** *or* **selling** = buying or selling shares by financial institutions;

institutional investors = financial institutions who invest money in securities

◊ **institutionalized** [ɪnstɪ'tjuː:ʃnəlaɪzd] *noun* **(a)** (person) who has been put in a mental institution **(b)** (position) which has become an institution; *the office of US President has become institutionalized*

instrument ['ɪnstruməənt] *noun* **(a)** tool *or* piece of equipment; *the technical staff have instruments to measure the output of the machine* **(b)** legal document; **negotiable instrument** = document (such as a bill of exchange *or* a cheque) which can be exchanged for cash; **statutory instrument (SI)** = order (which has the force of law) made under authority granted by an Act of Parliament; *see also* AFFIRMATIVE, GENERAL, NEGATIVE

insular ['ɪnsjʊlə] *adjective* **(a)** referring to islands **(b)** not interested in anything outside one's immediate surroundings; *the British were considered an insular people*

◊ **insularity** [ɪnsjʊ'lærɪti] *noun* indifference to anything outside one's immediate surroundings; *the insularity of the British*

insure [ɪn'ʃʊə] *verb* to have a contract with a company where, if regular payments are made, the company will pay compensation for loss, damage, injury or death; *to insure a house against fire; to insure someone's life; he was insured for £100,000; to insure baggage against loss; to insure against bad weather; to insure against loss of earnings;* **the life insured** = the person whose life is covered by a life assurance; **the sum insured** = the largest amount of money that an insurer will pay under an insurance policy

◊ **insurable** [ɪn'ʃʊərəbl] *adjective* which can be insured; **insurable interest** = interest which a person taking out an insurance policy must have in what is being insured

◊ **insurance** [ɪn'ʃʊərəns] *noun* **(a)** agreement that in return for regular small payments, a company will pay compensation for loss *or* damage *or* injury *or* death; **to take out an insurance against fire** = to pay a premium, so that if a fire happens, compensation will be paid **(b)** medical

insurance = insurance which pays the cost of medical treatment, especially when travelling abroad; **National Insurance** = state insurance which pays for medical care, hospitals, unemployment benefits, etc.; **third-party insurance** = insurance which pays compensation if someone who is not the insured person incurs loss or injury; **whole-life insurance** = insurance where the insured person pays premiums for all his life and the insurance company pays a sum when he dies

◊ **insurer** [ɪn'ʃʊərə] *noun* company which insures; (NOTE: for life insurance, GB English prefers to use **assurance, assure, assurer**)

insurgency [ɪn'sɜːdʒənsi] *noun* state where many groups fight to try to bring down a government over a long period of time

◊ **insurgent** [ɪn'sɜːdʒənt] *noun* person who fights to bring down a government by force; *the army tried to capture the leaders of the insurgents*

insurrection [ɪnsə'rekʃn] *noun* rebellion against a government; *the insurrection lasted two weeks*

◊ **insurrectionist** [ɪnsə'rekʃnɪst] *noun* person who takes part in an insurrection

integrate ['ɪntɪɡreɪt] *verb* to bring together into one whole; *it took several years for the Eastern parts of Germany to become fully integrated into the West*

◊ **integration** [ɪntɪ'ɡreɪʃn] *noun* beinging together into one whole; *the integration of new member states into the EU*

intelligence [ɪn'telɪdʒəns] *noun* secret information; **intelligence service** = government department which deals in discovering other countries' secrets

intend [ɪn'tend] *verb* to plan *or* to want to do something; *the government intends to privatize the industry; we intend to offer jobs to 250 unemployed young people; the council is intending to rebuild the municipal offices*

◊ **intent** [ɪn'tent] *noun* what is planned; **letter of intent** = letter which states what someone intends to do if a certain thing takes place

◊ **intention** [ɪn'tenʃn] *noun* **(a)** wanting *or* planning to do something; *the council has no intention of raising the rates; there has been a delay in according planning permission with the intention of forcing the planners to increase the office content in the proposed development* **(b)** meaning of the words in a document such as a Bill (which may not be the same as what the maker of the document had actually written)

◊ **intentional** [ɪn'tenʃnəl] *adjective* which is intended; *an act of intentional cruelty*

◊ **intentionally** [ɪn'tenʃnəli] *adverb* on purpose *or* as intended; *he intentionally altered the date on the contract*

inter alia ['ɪntə 'eɪliə] *Latin phrase meaning* 'among other things'

inter- ['ɪntə] *prefix* meaning between; **interstate controls** = controls imposed between one state and another

intercameral [ɪntə'kæmərəl] *adjective* between the two chambers of a bicameral legislature

intercontinental [ɪntəkɒntɪ'nentəl] *adjective* between continents

interdependent [ɪntədɪ'pendənt] *adjective* dependent on each other; *Great Britain and the EU are economically interdependent*

interest ['ɪntrəst] **1** *noun* **(a)** special attention; *the managing director takes no interest in the staff club; the government has shown a lot of interest in the scheme;* **special interest group** = group of people who have the same interest, formed to try to promote that interest; *see also* PRESSURE GROUP **(b)** (i) payment made by a borrower for the use of money, calculated as a percentage of the capital borrowed; (ii) money paid as income on investments or loans; *the bank pays 10% interest on deposits; to receive interest at 5%; the loan pays 5% interest; deposit which yields or gives or produces or bears 5% interest; account which earns interest at 10% or which earns 10% interest;* **simple interest** = interest calculated on the capital only, and not

added to it; **compound interest** = interest which is added to the capital and then itself earns interest; **interest-bearing deposits** = deposits which produce interest **(c)** percentage to be paid for borrowing; **interest charges** = cost of paying interest; **interest rate** *or* **rate of interest** = percentage charge for borrowing money; **interest-free credit** *or* **loan** = credit or loan where no interest is paid by the borrower; *the company gives its staff interest-free loans* **(d)** right *or* title to a property *or* money invested in a company *or* financial share in, and part control over, a company; **conflict of interest** = situation where a person may profit personally from decisions which he takes in his official capacity *or* may not be able to act properly because of some other person or matter with which he is connected; **to declare** *or* **disclose an interest** = to state in public that you own shares in a company which is being investigated *or* that you are connected with someone who may benefit from your contacts; *she resigned from the Council because of a conflict of interest; the Chairman opened the proceedings by declaring an interest, in that his wife was a director of the company concerned in the planning application;* **he has a controlling interest in the company** = he owns more than 50% of the shares and so can direct how the company is run; **life interest** = situation where someone benefits from a property as long as he is alive; **majority interest** *or* **minority interest** = situation where someone owns a majority *or* a minority of shares in a company; *he has a majority interest in a supermarket chain;* **to acquire a substantial interest in the company** = to buy a large number of shares in a company **2** *verb* to attract someone's attention; *he tried to interest several companies in his new invention;* **interested in** = paying attention to; *the government is interested only in reducing the balance of payments deficit; no one is interested in the plight of old manufacturing centres;* **interested party** = person *or* company with a financial interest in a company

◊ **interesting** ['ɪntrəstɪŋ] *adjective* which attracts attention; *they made us a very interesting offer for the factory*

interfere [ɪntə'fɪə] *verb* to get involved *or* to try to change something which is not your concern; **to interfere with witnesses** = to try to get in touch with witnesses to influence their evidence

◊ **interference** [ɪntə'fɪərəns] *noun* the act of interfering; *the local authority complained of continual interference from central government; the ambassador protested about the minister's remarks, saying that they were interference in the internal affairs of his country*

intergovernmental [ɪntəgʌvən'mentl] *adjective* between governments; **intergovernmental communications** = messages passed from one government to another; **Intergovernmental Conference (IGC)** = conference in which many countries take part;; *(EU)* special committee of all the heads of the govenrments of the EU, meeting to consider amendments to the existing treaties

interim ['ɪntrɪm] *adjective* temporary *or* not final; **interim report** = report (from a commission) which is not final *or* financial report given at the end of a half-year; **in the interim** = meanwhile *or* for the time being

interior [ɪn'tɪːrɪə] *noun* what is inside; **Ministry of the Interior** *or* **Interior Ministry** = government department dealing with law and order, usually including the police

COMMENT: in the UK, this ministry is called the Home Office

internal [ɪn'tɜːnəl] *adjective* referring to the inside; **an internal call** = telephone call from one office to another in a building; **an internal memo** = memo from one department in an organization to another; **internal affairs of a country** = way in which a country deals with its own citizens; *it is not usual for one country to criticize the internal affairs of another;* US **Internal Revenue Service (IRS)** = American government department dealing with income tax; (NOTE: in the UK, this is the **Inland Revenue)**

international [ɪntə'næʃnəl] *adjective* between countries; referring to links between countries; **international call** = telephone call to another country; **International Court of Justice** = the court of the United Nations, which sits in the Hague, Netherlands; **international law** = laws governing relations between countries

◊ **Internationale** [ɪntənæʃə'naːl] *noun* the Red Flag, song which has been adopted as an anthem by Socialists and Communists

◊ **internationalism** [ɪntə'næʃnəlɪzm] *noun* idea that different countries should try to work together more closely

◊ **International Labour Organization (ILO)** [ɪntə'næʃənl 'leɪbə 'ɔːgənaɪzeɪʃn] organization of the United Nations which tries to improve working conditions and workers' pay in member countries

◊ **International Monetary Fund (IMF)** [ɪntə'næʃənl 'mʌnɪtrɪ 'fʌnd] organization of the United Nations, a type of bank which helps member states in financial difficulties, gives financial advice to members and encourages world trade

Interpol ['ɪntəpɒl] *noun* international police organization whereby the member countries co-operate in solving crimes; *they warned Interpol that the criminals might be disguised as women* (NOTE: used without **the)**

interpret [ɪn'tɜːprɪt] *verb* **(a)** to say what you think a document *or* law *or* ruling means; *the chairman asked the Chief Executive to interpret the clause in the White Paper* **(b)** to translate orally what someone has said into another language; *my assistant knows Spanish, so he will interpret for us*

◊ **interpretation** [ɪntɜːprɪ'teɪʃn] *noun* **(a)** what someone thinks is the meaning of a document *or* law; **to put an interpretation on something** = to make something have a different meaning; *the Chief Executive's interpretation of the instruction is different from that of the Director of Education; this ruling puts quite a different interpretation on the responsibility of trustees;* **Interpretation Act** = Act of Parliament which rules how words used in other Acts of Parliament are to be understood;

interpretation clause = clause in a contract stating the meaning to be given to terms in the contract **(b)** oral translation from one language into another

◊ **interpreter** [ɪnˈtɜːprɪtə] *noun* person who translates orally what someone has said into another language; *my secretary will act as interpreter; the witness could not speak English and the court had to appoint an interpreter*

interregnum [ɪntəˈregnʌm] *noun* period between the death (or deposition) of one king or ruler and the accession of the next

interrogate [ɪnˈterəgeɪt] *verb* to ask questions in a severe manner

interrupt [ɪntəˈrʌpt] *verb* to try to speak *or* to shout when someone else is talking

COMMENT: in the House of Commons, an MP is allowed to interrupt another MP only if he wants to ask the member who is speaking to explain something or to raise a point of order

intervene [ɪntəˈviːn] *verb* **(a)** to come between people *or* things so as to make a change; **to intervene in a dispute** = to try to settle a dispute **(b)** to become a party to an action

◊ **intervener** [ɪntəˈviːnə] *noun* person who intervenes in an action to which he was not originally a party

◊ **intervention** [ɪntəˈvenʃn] *noun* **(a)** acting to make a change; *the government's intervention in the foreign exchange markets; the central bank's intervention in the banking crisis; the Association's intervention in the labour dispute;* **intervention price** = price at which the EU will buy farm produce which farmers cannot sell, in order to store it **(b)** acting to interfere in another country's affairs; *the Minister of Foreign Affairs said the President's remarks were an intervention in the domestic affairs of his country*

intolerant [ɪnˈtɒlərənt] *adjective* refusing to accept the opinions of other people; *extremist political parties tend to be very intolerant*

intra vires [ˈɪntrə ˈvaɪriːz] *Latin phrase meaning* 'within the permitted powers'; *the minister's action was ruled to be intra vires; see* ULTRA VIRES

intransigent [ɪnˈtrænzɪdʒənt] *adjective* refusing to compromise or negotiate

introduce [ɪntrəˈdjuːs] *verb* to present *or* to put forward; *he is introducing a Bill in Parliament to prevent the sale of drugs; the department has introduced some new evidence to the Committee; the education department has decided to introduce vegetarian meals in schools*

◊ **introduction** [ɪntrəˈdʌkʃn] *noun* presenting *or* putting forward; *the introduction of new evidence into the case;* **introduction of a Bill** = putting forward a Bill for discussion in Parliament

invade [ɪnˈveɪd] *verb* to attack and enter another country's territory

◊ **invasion** [ɪnˈveɪʒn] *noun* attacking and entering the territory of another country

invalid [ɪnˈvælɪd] *adjective* not valid *or* not legal; *he tried to enter the country on an invalid passport; this import permit is invalid; a claim which has been declared invalid*

◊ **invalidate** [ɪnˈvælɪdeɪt] *verb* to make something invalid; *because the company has been taken over, the contract has been invalidated*

◊ **invalidation** [ɪnvælɪˈdeɪʃn] *noun* making invalid

◊ **invalidity** [ɪnvəˈlɪdɪti] *noun* being invalid; *the invalidity of the contract;* (NOTE: no plural)

investigate [ɪnˈvestɪgeɪt] *verb* to examine something which may be wrong; *officials of the Ministry of Defence are investigating reports that the plans of the new aircraft have been lost*

◊ **investigation** [ɪnvestɪˈgeɪʃn] *noun* examination to find out what is wrong; *to conduct an investigation into irregularities in the granting of planning permission;* **preliminary investigation** = examining of the details of a case by a magistrate who then has to decide if the case should be committed to a higher court for trial

◊ **investigator** [ɪn'vestɪgeɪtə] *noun* person who investigates; *government investigators asked to see all the company's papers on the takeover deal*

invite [ɪn'vaɪt] *verb* to ask someone to do something; *to invite someone to a meeting; to invite someone to join the board; to invite shareholders to subscribe to a new issue; to invite tenders for a contract*

◊ **invitation** [ɪnvɪ'teɪʃn] *noun* asking someone to do something; *to issue an invitation to someone to join the board or an invitation to tender for a contract or an invitation to subscribe to a new issue*

ipso facto ['ɪpsəʊ 'fæktəʊ] *Latin phrase meaning* 'by this very fact' *or* 'the fact itself shows'; *the writing of the letter was ipso facto an admission that the Minister knew of the case; he was chairman of the committee at the time of the investigation and ipso facto was seen to be under suspicion*

irredentism [ɪrɪ'dentɪzm] *noun* trying to get back a colony *or* territory which has been lost to another country or which is felt to belong to the country (because of similar language *or* culture, etc.)

◊ **irredentist** [ɪrɪ'dentɪst] *noun* person who wants a territory returned; *the meeting was disrupted by Albanian irredentists*

irregular [ɪ'regjuːlə] *adjective* not correct *or* not done in the correct way; *irregular documentation; this procedure is highly irregular*

◊ **irregularity** [ɪrəgjuː'lærɪti] *noun* (a) not being regular *or* not being on time; *the irregularity of the postal deliveries* (b) **irregularities** = things which are not done in the correct way and which are possibly illegal; *they investigated irregularities in the councillor's dealings with the contractor*

irresponsible [ɪrɪ'spɒnsəbl] *adjective* not responsible *or* wild (behaviour); *the Opposition accused the Minister of making irresponsible statements*

◊ **irresponsibility** [ɪrɪspɒnsɪ'bɪliti] *noun* lack of responsibility *or* not acting in a responsible way

isolate ['aɪsəleɪt] *verb* to make alone; *the leader was isolated when the entire council voted against his proposal; there have been isolated incidents of attacks on council property*

◊ **isolation** [aɪsə'leɪʃn] *noun* (a) being alone *or* not being linked by treaties with other countries; **splendid isolation** = policy where a country refuses to link with other countries in treaties (b) **in isolation** = all alone; *the plans for the new bus station should not be seen in isolation - they are part of a major redevelopment scheme for the town centre*

◊ **isolationism** [aɪsə'leɪʃnɪzm] *noun* political policy where a country refuses to get involved in the affairs of other countries and refuses to sign treaties with them

◊ **isolationist** [aɪsə'leɪʃnɪst] *noun* person who believes that his country should not get involved in the affairs of other countries, especially should not fight wars to protect other countries

issue ['ɪʃuː] **1** *noun* (a) child *or* children of a parent; *he had issue two sons and one daughter; she died without issue; they have no issue;* (NOTE: in this meaning issue is either singular or plural and is not used with the) (b) subject of a dispute *or* discussion; *the speaker was told to deal with the issue being discussed; the sale of the site raises a completely new issue;* **collateral issue** = issue which arises from a plea in a criminal court; **point at issue** = the point which is being disputed; *the point at issue is the ownership of the property* (c) giving out new shares; **bonus issue** *or* **scrip issue** = new shares given free to shareholders; **issue of new shares** *or* **share issue** = selling new shares in a company to the public; **rights issue** = giving shareholders the right to buy more shares **2** *verb* to put out *or* to give out; *the chairman's office issued a statement; the council was forced to issue a denial; to issue a writ against someone; the government issued a report on London's traffic; the Secretary of State issued guidelines for expenditure; the Minister* *issued writs for libel in connection with allegations made in a Sunday newspaper*

◊ **issued** ['ɪʃuːd] *adjective* **issued capital** = amount of capital which is sold as shares to shareholders; **issued price** = price of shares in a new company when they are offered for sale for the first time

◊ **issuing** ['ɪʃuːɪŋ] *noun* which organizes an issue of shares; **issuing bank** *or* **issuing house** = bank which organizes the selling of shares in a new company

item ['aɪtəm] *noun* (a) thing for sale; **cash items** = goods sold for cash (b) piece of information; **extraordinary items** = items in accounts which do not appear each year and need to be noted; **item of expenditure** = goods or services which have been paid for and appear in the accounts (c) matter for discussion; point on a list; **we will now take item four on the agenda** = we will now discuss the fourth point on the agenda

◊ **itemize** ['aɪtəmaɪz] *verb* to make a detailed list of things; *itemizing the sales figures will take about two days;* **itemized account** = detailed record of money paid or owed

Jj

Jerga ['dʒɜːgə] *see* LOYA JERGA

join [dʒɔɪn] *verb* **(a)** to put things together; *the offices were joined together by making a door in the wall; the appendix is joined to the report* **(b)** to become part of; **to join a department** = to start work with a department; **he joined on January 1st** = he started work on January 1st; **to join an association** *or* **a group** = to become a member of an association *or* a group; *when he first joined, the service was run from a small office in the basement of the Town Hall; all the staff have joined the company pension plan; Sweden joined the EU in 1995; Smith Ltd has now applied to join the trade association*

joint [dʒɔɪnt] *adjective* **(a)** with two or more organizations or people linked together; **joint account** = bank account for two people; **joint commission of inquiry** *or* **joint committee** = commission *or* committee with representatives of various organizations on it; *US* **joint committee** = committee with members of both House of Representatives and Senate, usually set up to investigate a serious problem; **joint discussions** = discussions between two groups (such as management and workers) before something is done; **joint management** = management done by two or more people; *US* **joint resolution** = Bill which has to be passed by both House of Representatives and Senate, before being sent to the President for signature; **joint venture** *or US* **joint adventure** = very large business partnership where two or more companies join together as partners for a limited period **(b)** one of two or more people who work together *or* who are linked; *joint beneficiary; joint managing director; joint owner; joint signatory;* **joint**

heir = person who is an heir with someone else

◊ **joint and several** ['dʒɔɪnt nd 'sevrəl] *adjective* as a group together and also separately; **joint and several liability** = situation where someone who has a claim against a group of people can sue them separately or together as a group

◊ **jointly** ['dʒɔɪntli] *adverb* together with one or more other people; *to own a property jointly; to manage a company jointly; they are jointly liable for damages*

journal ['dʒɜːnəl] *noun* **(a)** diary *or* record of something which happens each day; *the chairman kept a journal during the negotiations* **(b)** official record of the proceedings of a legislature, such as the House of Commons, House of Lords, House of Representatives or Senate (but not including verbatim speeches which are recorded in Hansard or in the Congressional Record) *the Official Journal of the European Union*

◊ **journalist** ['dʒɜːnəlɪst] *noun* person who works for a newspaper; *the council chairman asked the journalists to leave the committee room*

JP ['dʒeɪ 'piː] *noun* = JUSTICE OF THE PEACE (NOTE: the plural is **JPs**)

judge [dʒʌdʒ] **1** *noun* official who presides over a court and in civil cases decides which party is in the right; *a County Court judge; a judge in the Divorce Court; the judge sent him to prison for embezzlement;* **judge in chambers** = judge who hears a case in his private room without the public being present and not in open court; **Judges' Rules** = informal set of rules governing how the police may question a suspect **2** *verb* to decide; *he judged it was time to call an end to the discussions*

◊ **Judge Advocate-General** ['dʒʌdʒ 'ædvəkət 'dʒenrəl] *noun* lawyer appointed by the state to advise on all legal matters concerning the Army

◊ **Judge Advocate of the Fleet** ['dʒʌdʒ 'ædvəkət əv ðə 'fliːt] *noun* lawyer appointed by the state to advise on all legal matters concerning the Royal Navy

COMMENT: In England, judges are appointed by the Lord Chancellor. The minimum requirement is that one should be a barrister or solicitor of ten years' standing. The majority of judges are barristers, but they cannot practise as barristers. The appointment of judges is not a political appointment, and judges remain in office unless they are found guilty of gross misconduct. In the USA, state judges can be appointed by the state governor or can be elected; in the Federal courts and the Supreme Court, judges are appointed by the President, but the appointment has to be approved by Congress

judgement *or* **judgment** ['dʒʌdʒmənt] *noun* **(a)** ability to make a good decision; *the officer was criticised for showing lack of judgement; the Minister's judgement is at fault* **(b)** legal decision *or* official decision of a court; **final judgment** = judgment which is given at the end of an action after trial; **interlocutory judgment** = judgment given during the course of an action before full trial; **to pronounce judgment** *or* **to give one's judgment on something** = to give an official *or* legal decision about something; (NOTE: the spelling **judgment** is used for the legal meanings)

judice ['dʒuːdɪsiː] *see* SUB JUDICE

judicial [dʒuːˈdɪʃəl] *adjective* referring to a judge *or* the law; done in a court *or* by a judge; **the Judicial Committee of the House of Lords** = the highest appeal court in England and Wales; **the Judicial Committee of the Privy Council** = the appeal court for appeals from some Commonwealth countries and colonies; **judicial immunity** = safety from prosecution granted to a judge when acting in

a judicial capacity; **judicial precedent** = precedent set by a court decision, which can be reversed only by a higher court; **judicial review** = (i) examination of a case a second time by a higher court because a lower court has acted wrongly; (ii) examination by a court of administrative *or* legislative decisions taken by an authority *or* government

◊ **judiciary** [dʒuːˈdɪʃəri] *noun* **the judiciary** = all judges

junior ['dʒuːniə] **1** *adjective* younger *or* lower in rank; **junior clerk** = clerk, usually young, who has lower status than a senior clerk; **junior executive** *or* **junior manager** = less important manager in a company; **junior minister** = Under-Secretary of State *or* Minister of State in a government department; **junior partner** = person who has a smaller part of the shares in a partnership; **John Smith, Junior** = the younger John Smith (i.e. the son of John Smith, Senior) **2** *noun* **(a)** (i) barrister who is not a Queen's Counsel; (ii) barrister appearing with a leader **(b)** office junior = young man or woman who does all types of work in an office

junta ['dʒʌntə] *noun* ruling group of ministers, a government which has taken power by force; *the junta came to power six years ago and is formed of representatives of each of the armed forces;* (NOTE: used mainly of military governments, and usually in South America; the word is correctly pronounced as ['hʊntə] but this pronunciation is not often used in English)

jurisdiction [dʒʊərɪsˈdɪkʃn] *noun* legal power over someone *or* something; **within the jurisdiction of a body** *or* **outside the jurisdiction of a body** = in the legal power of a body *or* not covered by the legal power of body; **the prisoner refused to recognize the jurisdiction of the court** = the prisoner said that he did not believe that the court had the legal right to try him; *it is within the council's jurisdiction to sell council houses to tenants; the upkeep of major roads, such as motorways, falls outside the borough's jurisdiction*

just [dʒʌst] *adjective* fair *or* right; **to show just cause** = to show a reason which is fair and acceptable in law; **just war** = war which is considered to be morally right

justice ['dʒʌstɪs] *noun* **(a)** fair treatment (in law); **to administer justice** = to make sure that the laws are correctly and fairly applied; **natural justice** = the general principles of justice; *US* **Department of Justice** *or* **Justice Department** = department of the US government responsible for federal legal cases, headed by the Attorney-General; *see also* EUROPEAN COURT OF JUSTICE *see also note at* MINISTRY **(b)** magistrate; **chairman of the justices** = chief magistrate in a magistrates' court; **justices' clerk** *or* **clerk to the justices** = official of a Magistrates' Court who gives advice to the justices on law *or* practice *or* procedure; **Lord Chief Justice** = chief judge of the Queen's Bench Division of the High Court, and second most senior judge after the Lord Chancellor; *US* **Chief Justice** = senior judge in a court **(c)** title given to a High Court judge; *Mr Justice Adams;* **Lord Justice** = title given to a judge who is a member of the House of Lords; (NOTE: usually written as J or LJ after the name: **Adams J; Smith LJ**)

◊ **justice of the peace (JP)** ['dʒʌstɪs əv ðə 'piːs] *noun* magistrate *or* local judge

justiciary [dʒʌs'tɪʃəri] *noun* all judges; **High Court of Justiciary** = supreme criminal court in Scotland

justify ['dʒʌstɪfaɪ] *verb* to give an excuse *or* reason for; **the end justifies the means** = if the result is right, the means used to reach it are acceptable

◊ **justifiable** [dʒʌstɪ'faɪəbl] *adjective* which can be shown to be reasonable; *the item for upkeep of the building is a justifiable expense*

◊ **justification** [dʒʌstɪfɪ'keɪʃn] *noun* showing an acceptable reason for an act; **in justification** = as an acceptable excuse; *in justification, the minister claimed that the tax would affect the higher paid more severely than the lower paid*

Kk

Kamer ['kæmə] *see* EERSTE KAMER, TWEEDE KAMER

kangaroo [kæŋgə'ruː] *noun* system used when discussing a Bill, where some clauses are not discussed at all, but simply voted on, with the discussion then moving on to the next item

Kenesh [kə'neʃ] *see* ULUK KENESH

keep [kiːp] *verb* (a) to go on doing something; *they kept on working, even when the boss told them to stop; the other secretaries complain that she keeps singing when she is typing* (b) to do what is necessary; **to keep an appointment** = to be there when you said you would be; **to keep the books of a company** *or* **to keep a company's books** = to note the accounts of a company; **to keep the law** = to make sure the law is obeyed; **to keep the peace** = to obey the law, to behave well and not to create a disturbance (c) to hold items for sale *or* for information; **we always keep this item in stock** = we always have this item in our warehouse *or* shop; **to keep someone's name on file** = to have someone's name on a list for reference (d) to hold things at a certain level; *we must keep our mailing list up to date; to keep spending to a minimum; the price of oil has kept the pound at a high level; the government is encouraging firms to keep prices low; lack of demand for typewriters has kept prices down* (NOTE: **keeping - kept**)

◊ **keep down** ['kiːp 'daʊn] *verb* to control *or* oppress; *the generals have managed to keep down the country districts by stationing troops in the area*

◊ **keeper** ['kiːpə] *noun* person who keeps something; **Keeper of the Great Seal** = the Lord Chancellor

◊ **keeping** ['kiːpɪŋ] *noun* the action of looking after; **safe keeping** = being looked after carefully; *we put the documents into the bank for safe keeping*

key [kiː] *noun* (a) piece of metal used to open a lock; *he has taken the office keys home with him, so no one can get in; we have lost the keys to the computer room;* **key money** = premium paid when taking over the keys of a flat or office which you are renting (b) part of a computer *or* typewriter which you press with your fingers; *there are sixty-four keys on the keyboard;* **control key** = key on a computer which works part of a program; **shift key** = key which makes a typewriter *or* computer move to capital letters (c) important; *a key witness has disappeared; the meeting of key personnel from each department*

◊ **keyboard** ['kiːbɔːd] *noun* part of a computer *or* typewriter with a series of keys which are pressed to make letters or figures

◊ **keynote address** *or* **keynote speech** ['kiːnəʊt] *noun* main speech at a conference, which is supposed to excite the delegates

kill [kɪl] *verb* to stop discussion of a proposal; *the veto in the Security Council killed the resolution*

king [kɪŋ] *noun* man who rules a monarchy; *Juan Carlos is the King of Spain;* (NOTE: often used with a name as a title: **King Juan Carlos**)

◊ **kingdom** ['kɪŋdəm] *noun* country ruled by a king *or* queen; *the United Kingdom of Great Britain and Northern Ireland; the kingdom of Saudi Arabia*

◊ **kingly** ['kɪŋli] *adjective* suitable for a king *or* like a king; (NOTE: **kingly shows** approval, as opposed to **royal** which does not imply approval or condemnation)

◊ **kingship** ['kɪŋʃɪp] *noun* rule of a king

kitchen cabinet ['kɪtʃən 'kæbɪnət] *noun* private, unofficial committee of ministers, advisers and friends who advise the Prime Minister

Knesset ['knesət] *noun* body of legislature in Israel

knight [naɪt] *noun* (a) medieval mounted soldier (b) man who has received an title of honour from the king or queen 2 *verb* to make someone into a knight; *he was knighted in the Birthday honours list*

◊ **knighthood** ['naɪthʊd] *noun* position of being a knight

knock-on effect ['nɒk'ɒn ɪ'fekt] *noun* indirect effect, following on from something; *the airport strike had a knock-on effect on the tourist industry; the coup had a knock-on effect on the governments of neighbouring states*

know [nəʊ] *verb* (a) to learn *or* to have information about something; *the minister did not know the extent of the problem; the council officials do not know where the Chairman of the Finance Committee is* (b) to have met someone; *do you know Mr Jones, the new Borough Treasurer?;* (NOTE: knowing - known)

◊ **know-how** ['nəʊ 'haʊ] *noun* knowledge about how something works *or* how something is made; *you need some legal know-how to do this job; he needs to acquire computer know-how;* (NOTE: no plural)

◊ **knowingly** ['nəʊɪŋli] *adverb* deliberately *or* on purpose; *it was charged that he knowingly broke the Official Secrets Act by publishing the document in his newspaper*

◊ **knowledge** ['nɒlɪdʒ] *noun* what is known to be true; **the official disclaimed all knowledge of the file** = he said he knew nothing about the file; **he had no knowledge of the contract** = he did not know that the contract existed; **to the best of my knowledge** = I am reasonably certain of the fact; *the medical officer said that to the best of his knowledge no case had occurred in the borough for the last ten years;* (NOTE: no plural)

Kremlin ['kremlɪn] *noun* series of buildings surrounded by a high wall in the centre of Moscow, where the offices of the main ministers of the Russian Federation are situated; (NOTE: often used to mean 'the Russian Government': **a Kremlin spokesman said the letter was helpful**)

◊ **Kremlinologist** *or* **Kremlin-watcher** [kremlɪ'nɒlədʒɪst *or* 'kremlɪnwɒtʃə] *noun* person (not a Russian) who specializes in studying the actions of the Russian political leadership and tries to guess what is really going on in Russia

LI

labour *or US* **labor** ['leɪbə] *noun* **(a)** heavy work; **manual labour** = work done by hand; **to charge for materials and labour** = to charge for both the materials used in a job and also the hours of work involved; **hard labour** = punishment of sending someone to prison to do hard manual work **(b)** workers in general; **casual labour** = workers who are hired for a short period; **cheap labour** = workers who do not earn much money; **local labour** = workers recruited near a factory, not brought in from somewhere else; **organized labour** = workers who are members of trade unions; **skilled labour** = workers who have special knowledge or qualifications; **labour-intensive industry** = industry which needs large numbers of workers *or* where labour costs are high in relation to turnover; **direct labour organization (DLO)** = organization of manual workers (builders, maintenance workers, etc.) who are employed by a council as opposed to putting work out to tender **(c)** **labour disputes** = arguments between management and workers; **labour law** *or* **labour laws** *or* **labour legislation** = laws relating to the employment of workers; **labour movement** = group working for the improvement of working conditions for workers; **labour relations** = relations between management and workers; *US* **labor union** = organization which represents workers who are its members in discussions about wages and conditions of work with management **(d)** **International Labour Organization (ILO)** = section of the United Nations which tries to improve working conditions and workers' pay in member countries

◊ **Labor Day** ['leɪbə deɪ] *noun US* annual holiday to honour workers (similar to May 1st in Europe) celebrated on the first Monday in September

◊ **Labour** *or* **the Labour Party** [ðə 'leɪbə 'pɑːti] *noun* political party, such as one of the main parties in Britain, which is in favour of state involvement in industry and welfare, and is supported by the trades unions; *Labour held two marginal seats; 40% of those questioned said they would vote Labour*

COMMENT: the British Labour Party was founded in 1906 as a fusion of the Independent Labour Party and other workers' groups, including representatives from the Trades Union Congress. The Labour Party has been closely allied to the Trades Union Congress in the past; members of trade unions pay a political levy to support the Party, and some Labour MPs are sponsored by trade unions

labourer ['leɪbrə] *noun* person who does unskilled work; **casual labourer** = worker who can be hired for a short period; **manual labourer** = person who does work with his hands

lack [læk] **1** *noun* not enough; **lack of data** *or* **lack of information** = not having enough information; **lack of funds** = not enough money; *the investigation has been held up by lack of information; approval cannot be given for lack of supporting documents; the decision has been put back for lack of up-to-date information; the project was cancelled because of lack of funds* **2** *verb* not to have enough of something; *the* *government lacks the will to act; the Inland Revenue lacks the necessary staff to undertake the investigation*

lady ['leɪdi] *noun* title given to the wife of a knight or baronet

COMMENT: in most case, the title is used before the family name without the Christian name. Where the title is used to indicate the daughter of a nobleman, the Christian name is used. So the wife of Sir Edwin Smith is Lady Smith; the daughter of the Duke of Northumberland is Lady Jane Percy

Lady Day ['leɪdi 'deɪ] *noun* 25th March, one of the quarter days when rent is paid

laissez-faire *or* **laisser-faire** ['leseɪ 'feə] *noun* political theory where a government does nothing to control the economy; *laissez-faire policies resulted in increased economic activity, but contributed to a rise in imports*

lame duck ['leɪm 'dʌk] *noun* company *or* administration which is in difficulties and which needs support; *the government has promised a rescue package for lame duck companies;* **lame duck president** = president in the last part of his term of office, who cannot stand for re-election, and so lacks political force; *no foreign policy decisions can be made because of the lame duck presidency*

LAMSAC = LOCAL AUTHORITIES MANAGEMENT SERVICES AND COMPUTER COMMITTEE

land [lænd] **1** *noun* **(a)** area of earth; **land certificate** = document which shows who owns a piece of land, and whether there are any charges on it; **land charges** = covenants, mortgages, etc. which are attached to a piece of land; **land reform** = changes in the system of ownership of land (usually involving redistributing land by taking it from large landowners and giving it to small farmers); **land register** = register of land, showing who owns it and what buildings are on it; **land registration** = system of registering land and its owners; **Land Registry** = British

government office where land is registered; **land taxes** = taxes on the amount of land owned by someone **(b) lands** = estate *or* large area of land owned by one owner; **Crown Lands** = estates belonging to a King or Queen **(c)** nation *or* country; *the President welcomed the official delegation from the land of his ancestors;* **native land** = country where someone was born **(d) Land** = one of the semi-autonomous provinces which make up the federal republic of Germany and also Austria; (NOTE: plural is **Länder**) **2** *verb* **(a)** to put goods *or* passengers on to land after a voyage by sea *or* by air; **landed costs** = costs of goods which have been delivered to a port *or* airport, unloaded and passed through customs **(b)** to come down to earth after a flight; *the plane landed ten minutes late*

COMMENT: under English law, the ownership of all land is vested in the Crown; individuals or other legal persons may however hold estates in land, the most important of which are freehold estates (which amount to absolute ownership) and leasehold estates (which last for a fixed period of time). Ownership of land usually confers ownership of everything above and below the land. The process of buying and selling land is 'conveyancing'. Any contract transferring land or any interest in land must be in writing. Interests in land can be disposed of by a will

landlord ['lænlɔːd] *noun* person *or* company which owns a property which is let; **ground landlord** = person *or* company which owns the freehold of a property which is then leased *or* let *or* sublet; *our ground landlord is an insurance company;* **the Landlord and Tenant Act** = Act of Parliament which regulates the letting of property

◊ **landmark** ['lænmɑːk] *noun* important event *or* decision; *the opening of the new bridge is a landmark in the town's history;* **landmark decision** = legal *or* legislative decision which creates an important legal precedent

◊ **landowner** ['lændəʊnə] *noun* person who owns large areas of land

◊ **Lands Tribunal** ['lændz traɪ'bjuːnəl] *noun* court which deals with compensation claims relating to land

◊ **landslide** ['lænslaɪd] *noun* overwheming majority obtained in an election; *the Socialists won in a landslide*

lapse [læps] **1** *noun* **(a) a lapse of time** = a period of time which has passed **(b)** ending of a right *or* a privilege *or* an offer (such as the termination of an insurance policy because the premiums have not been paid) **2** *verb* to stop being valid *or* to stop being active; **to let an offer lapse** = to allow time to pass so that an offer is no longer valid; **lapsed passport** = passport which is out of date; **lapsed (insurance) policy** = insurance policy which is no longer valid because the premiums have not been paid

late [leɪt] **1** *adjective* **(a)** after the time stated or agreed; *we apologize for the late arrival of the plane from Amsterdam;* **there is a penalty for late delivery** = if delivery is later than the agreed date, the supplier has to pay a sum of money **(b)** at the end of a period of time; **latest date for signature of the contract** = the last acceptable date for signing the contract **(c) latest** = most recent; *he always drives the latest model of car; here are the latest unemployment figures* **2** *adverb* after the time stated or agreed; *the hearing started late; the shipment was landed late; the plane was two hours late*

◊ **late-night** ['leɪt 'naɪt] *adjective* happening late at night; *the House of Commons had a late-night sitting; their late-night negotiations ended in an agreement which was signed at 3 a.m.*

launch [lɔːnʃ] *verb* to begin *or* to start; *the meeting was held to launch the party manifesto; the Minister called a press conference to launch the new initiative on jobs*

law [lɔː] *noun* **(a)** rule (which may be written or unwritten) by which a country is governed and the activities of people and organizations controlled; in particular, an Act of Parliament which has received the Royal Assent, or an Act of Congress which has been signed by the President of the USA, or which

has been passed by Congress over the President's veto *a law has to be passed by Parliament; the government has proposed a new law to regulate the sale of goods on Sundays;* **conflict of laws** = section in a country's statutes which deals with disputes between that country's laws and those of another country; **labour laws** = laws concerning the employment of workers **(b) law** = all the statutes of a country taken together; **case law** = law as established by precedents, that is by decisions of courts in earlier cases; **civil law** = laws relating to people's rights, and agreements between individuals; **commercial law** = laws regarding business; **company law** = laws which refer to the way companies may work; **constitutional law** = laws under which a country is ruled *or* laws relating to government and its function; **contract law** *or* **the law of contract** = laws relating to agreements; **copyright law** = laws concerning the protection of copyright; **criminal law** = laws relating to acts committed against the laws of the land and which are punishable by the state; **international law** = laws referring to the way countries deal with each other; **maritime law** *or* **the law of the sea** = laws referring to ships, ports, etc.; **mercantile law** *or* **law merchant** = law relating to commerce; **private law** = law relating to relations between individual persons (such as the law of contract); **public law** = law which refers to people in general (such as administrative and constitutional law); **rule of law** = situation in a country where laws passed by the legislature are put into effect by the police and judicial system, and this situation applies equally to all citizens; **law and order** = situation in which the laws of a country are being obeyed by most people; *there was a breakdown of law and order following the assassination of the president;* **law reform** = continuing process of revising laws to make them better suited to the needs of society; **to take someone to law** = to sue someone; **inside the law** *or* **within the law** = obeying the laws of a country; **against the law** *or* **outside the law** = not according to the laws of a country; *dismissing a worker without reason is against the law; the agents were operating* *outside the law;* in **law** = according to the law; *what are the duties in law of a guardian?;* to **break the law** = to do something which is not allowed by law; *he is breaking the law by selling goods on Sunday; you will be breaking the law if you try to take that computer out of the country without an export licence* (c) general rule; **law of supply and demand** = general rule that the amount of a product which is available is related to the needs of the possible customers

◊ **Law Centre** ['lɔː 'sentə] *noun* local office with full-time staff who advise and represent clients free of charge

◊ **Law Commission** ['lɔː kə'mɪʃn] *noun* permanent committee which reviews English law and recommends changes to it

◊ **law court** ['lɔː 'kɔːt] *noun* place where a trial is held *or* place where a judge listens to cases

◊ **lawful** ['lɔːfʊl] *adjective* permitted by the law; **lawful practice** = action which is permitted by the law; **lawful trade** = trade which is allowed by law

◊ **lawfully** ['lɔːfli] *adverb* acting within the law

◊ **Law Lords** ['lɔː 'lɔːdz] *plural noun* members of the House of Lords who are judges (including the Lord Chancellor, the Lords of Appeal in Ordinary and other peers who are judges)

◊ **lawmaker** ['lɔːmeɪkə] *noun* person who makes *or* passes laws (such as an MP, Congressman, etc.)

◊ **law-making** ['lɔːmeɪkɪŋ] *noun* making of laws; *Parliament is the law-making body in Great Britain*

◊ **Law Officers** ['lɔː 'ɒfɪsəz] *plural noun* members of the British government (but not members of the Cabinet): the Attorney-General and Solicitor-General in England and Wales, and the Lord Advocate and Solicitor-General in Scotland

COMMENT: the Law Officers advise the government and individual ministries on legal matters. The Attorney-General will prosecute in trials for serious crimes

◊ **Law Reports** ['lɔː rɪ'pɔːts] *plural noun* regular reports of new cases and legislation

◊ **lawyer** ['lɔːjə] *noun* person who has studied law and can act for people on legal business; **commercial lawyer** *or* **company lawyer** = person who specializes in company law *or* who advises companies on legal problems; **constitutional lawyer** = lawyer who specializes in constitutional law *or* in interpreting constitutions; **international lawyer** = person who specializes in international law; **maritime lawyer** = person who specializes in the law concerning ships

lay [leɪ] **1** *verb* (a) to put *or* to place; *the report of the planning committee was laid before the council;* **to lay an embargo on trade with a country** = to forbid trade with a country; **to lay (an) information** = to start criminal proceedings in a magistrates' court by informing the magistrate of the offence; **to lay a proposal before the House** = to introduce a new Bill before Parliament for discussion **(b) to lay down** = to state clearly; *the conditions are laid down in the document; the guidelines lay down rules for dealing with traffic offences;* (NOTE: **laying - laid - has laid**) **2** *adjective* not belonging to a certain profession, in particular not a member of the legal profession; *the Committee has a chairman and several lay advisers*

◊ **layman** ['leɪmən] *noun* person who does not belong to a particular profession; *most councillors are laymen, but they have professional officers to advise them;* (NOTE: plural is **laymen**)

LC = LORD CHANCELLOR

lead [liːd] **1** *noun* position of being first; **to be in the lead** = to be first; **to take the lead** = to start to do something before anyone else; *the government has taken the lead in tackling budget deficits; the council was asked to take the lead in recycling waste materials;* **to follow someone's lead** = to do what someone else is already doing; *the other members of the EU have followed the Italian lead in dealing with terrorists* **2** *verb* **(a)** to be the first *or* to be in front; *the company leads the world in waste disposal* **(b)** to be the main person in a group; *the*

Parliamentary delegation is led by J.M. Jones, MP **(c)** to start to do something (especially to start to present a motion for debate); *the Home Secretary will lead for the Government in the emergency debate;* (NOTE: **leading - led - has led**)

◊ **leader** ['liːdə] *noun* **(a)** person who manages *or* directs others; *the leader of the construction workers' union or the construction workers' leader; an employers' leader; she is the leader of the trade delegation to Nigeria; the minister was the leader of the party of lawyers on a tour of American courts* **(b)** main barrister (usually a QC) in a team appearing for one side in a case **(c) party leader** = head of a political party, who usually becomes head of government if the party wins power; **council leader** *or* **leader of a council** = head of the majority party in a local council; *the matter will be referred to the Leader; Councillor Jenkins, Leader of the Council, stated that the report would be examined at the next meeting; see also* MAYOR *US* **majority leader** *or* **minority leader** = spokesmen for the majority or minority party in the House *or* Senate, elected by other members of the party

COMMENT: normally a party leader has a great deal of power when it comes to making appointments and deciding party policy. In Britain, the leader of the a party may feel bound to follow policy decisions laid down by the party conference. This may restrict the leader's room for manoeuvre

◊ **Leader of the House** ['liːdə əv ðə 'haʊs] *noun* senior government minister and member of the cabinet, who is responsible for the administration of legislation in the House of Commons or House of Lords, and is the main government spokesman in the House

COMMENT: both can be referred to as Leader of the House: to be more specific, say Leader of the Commons and Leader of the Lords

◊ **Leader of the Opposition** ['liːdə əv ðə ɒpə'zɪʃn] *noun* head of the largest party opposing the government

◊ **leadership** ['liːdəʃɪp] *noun* **(a)** quality of being a good leader; *he showed leadership in defending the party against attacks by splinter groups* **(b)** position of leader; *there are six candidates for the leadership of the party; the leadership contest is wide open* **(c)** main members of a party *or* group; *none of the party leadership appeared at the meeting*

◊ **leading** ['liːdɪŋ] *adjective* **(a)** most important; *leading businessmen feel the end of the recession is near; leading shares rose on the Stock Exchange; leading members of the party forced a change in government policy; they are the leading company in the field;* **leading counsel** = main barrister (usually a QC) in a team appearing for one side in a case **(b) leading question** = question put by a barrister to a witness which suggests to the witness what his answer ought to be *or* which can only be answered 'Yes' or 'No'

◊ **lead (up) to** ['liːd ʌp tʊ] *verb* to be the cause of; *the discussions led to a big argument between the management and the union; we received a series of approaches leading up to the takeover bid*

leaflet ['liːflət] *noun* sheet of paper advertising something (usually a single sheet, perhaps folded in two); *party workers distributed leaflets to all the householders in the constituency*

league [liːg] *noun* **(a)** people *or* states with similar aims, who come together to form a group and lay down guidelines and take action to further their aims; **the League of Nations** = group of states which joined in a group (similar to the present United Nations) between the First and Second World Wars **(b)** *(usually as criticism)* **in league with** = joined and working with; *he was accused of being in league with the fascists* **(c) in the same league as** = of equal size *or* of equal importance as; *the British Navy is not in the same league as that of the Russian Federation*

leak [liːk] **1** *noun* (i) passing secret information (to newspapers *or* TV stations, etc.); (ii) unofficial passing of information which has not yet been published, by officials *or* MPs *or* councillors (to newspapers *or* TV stations, etc.); *the government is investigating the latest leak of documents relating to the spy trial* **2** *verb* (i) to pass secret information (to the newspapers *or* TV stations, etc.); (ii) to pass information unofficially (to newspapers *or* TV stations, etc.); *information about the government plans has been leaked to the Sunday papers; the details of the plan have been leaked to the press to test public reaction*

leave [liːv] **1** *noun* (a) permission to do something; *the representative of the construction company asked leave of the council to show a detailed plan of the proposed development;* 'by your leave' = with your permission (b) to be away from work; **leave of absence** = being allowed to be away from work *or* (of an MP) to be away from the House of Commons; **maternity leave** = period when a woman is away from work to have a baby; **sick leave** = period when a worker is away from work because of illness; **to go on leave** *or* **to be on leave** = to be away from work; *she is away on sick leave* **or** *on maternity leave* **2** *verb* (a) to go away from; *he left his office early to go to the meeting; the next plane leaves at 10.20* (b) to give something to someone when you die; *he left his house to his wife; I was left £5,000 by my grandmother in her will* (c) to resign; *he left his job and bought a farm;* (NOTE: **leaving - left - has left**)

◊ **leave out** [liːv 'aʊt] *verb* not to include; *she left out the date on the letter; the contract leaves out all details of marketing arrangements*

left [left] *noun* (a) **the left** = socialists and communists, their ideals and beliefs; *the left have demanded political reform; many members of the left have been arrested;* **swing to the left** = movement of support towards socialist principles (b) **the left** = section of a party which is more socialist *or* more radical than the main party; *he is on the left of the Conservative Party; the activists on the Labour left;* (NOTE: usually used with the article **the**, and takes a singular or plural verb)

◊ **leftist** ['leftɪst] **1** *adjective (usually as criticism)* left-wing; *the minister is showing*

leftist tendencies **2** *noun* person with left-wing ideas

◊ **left wing** ['left 'wɪŋ] *noun* part of a party *or* group on the left; *he is on the left wing of the Labour Party*

◊ **left-wing** ['leftwɪŋ] *adjective* favouring the left; *he was criticised for abandoning his left-wing principles; the party caucus has been infiltrated by left-wing activists*

◊ **left-winger** [left'wɪŋə] *noun* person on the left of a party; (NOTE: the opposite is **right, rightist, right-wing, right-winger**)

legal ['liːgl] *adjective* (a) according to the law *or* allowed by the law; *the company's action was completely legal* (b) referring to the law; **to take legal action** *or* **to start legal proceedings** = to sue someone *or* to take someone to court; **to take legal advice** = to ask a lawyer to advise about a problem in law; **legal adviser** = person who advises clients about problems in law; *US* **legal age** = age at which a person can sue *or* can be sued *or* can undertake business; **Legal Aid scheme** = British government scheme where a person with very little money can have legal representation and advice paid for by the state; **Legal Aid Centre** = local office giving advice to clients about applications for Legal Aid and recommending clients to solicitors; **legal currency** = money which is legally used in a country; **legal department** *or* **legal section** = section of a company *or* organization dealing with legal matters; **legal expert** = person who has a wide knowledge of the law; **legal holiday** = day when banks and other businesses are closed; **legal tender** = coins or notes which can be legally used to pay a debt (small denominations cannot be used to pay large debts)

◊ **legality** [lɪ'gælɪti] *noun* being allowed by law; *there is doubt about the legality of the company's action in dismissing him;* (NOTE: no plural)

◊ **legalize** ['liːgəlaɪz] *verb* to make something legal; *a proposal to legalize drugs*

◊ **legalization** [liːgəlaɪ'zeɪʃn] *noun* making something legal; *the campaign for the legalization of abortion*

◊ **legally** ['lɪgəli] *adverb* according to the law; **the contract is legally binding** = according to the law, the contract has to be obeyed; **the directors are legally responsible** = the law says that the directors are responsible

legation [lɪ'geɪʃn] *noun* **(a)** group of diplomats representing their country in another country at a lower level than an embassy **(b)** building in which a group of diplomats works (below the rank of ambassador)

legis ['ledʒɪs] *see* CORPUS

legislate ['ledʒɪsleɪt] *verb* to make a law; *Parliament has legislated against the sale of drugs or to prevent the sale of drugs*

◊ **legislation** [ledʒɪs'leɪʃn] *noun* laws or written rules which are passed by Parliament and implemented by the courts; **labour legislation** = laws concerning the employment of workers; (NOTE: no plural)

◊ **legislative** ['ledʒɪslətɪv] *adjective* used to make laws; *the legislative processes; Parliament has a legislative function;* **Legislative Assembly** = lower house of the legislature in Australian states, Canadian provinces, Costa Rica, Panama, El Salvador; **Legislative Council** = upper house of the legislature in several Australian states; *US* **legislative day** = time from the start of a meeting of one of the Houses of Congress to its adjournment (the House of Representatives usually adjourns at the end of each day, but the Senate may not, so that the Senate's legislative day can last several calendar days) **legislative veto** = clause written into legislation relating to government agencies, which states that the agency cannot act in a way that Congress does not approve

◊ **legislator** ['ledʒɪsleɪtə] *noun* member of a legislature, a person who makes or passes laws (such as an MP, Congressman, etc.)

◊ **legislature** ['ledʒɪsleɪtʃə] *noun* **(a)** body (such as a Parliament) which makes laws; *members of the legislature voted against the proposal; the protesters marched towards the State Legislature* **(b)** building where a Parliament meets

the greatest happiness of the greatest number is the foundation of morals and legislation

Jeremy Bentham

legitimate [lɪ'dʒɪtɪmət] *adjective* (i) who inherits by law; (ii) who rules by law; *the legitimate ruler of the kingdom; the legitimate government*

◊ **legitimacy** [lɪ'dʒɪtɪməsi] *noun* being legitimate

◊ **legitimist** [lɪ'dʒɪtəmɪst] *noun* person who supports the return to the throne of the legitimate king or the legitimate descendant of the last king

◊ **legitimize** [lɪ'dʒɪtəmaɪz] *verb* to make something legitimate; *the support of the Prime Minister has legitimized attacks on the party activists*

Leninism ['lenɪnɪzm] *noun* Communist ideas put forward by Vladimir Ilyich Lenin (1870 - 1924)

◊ **Leninist** ['lenɪnɪst] **1** *adjective* referring to Leninism **2** *noun* person who supports and believes in Leninism

COMMENT: Lenin believed that Marxism could be applied successfully only if the proletariat was led by an intellectual group which formed the main leadership of a governing and authoritarian party

letter ['letə] *noun* **(a)** piece of writing sent from one person or company to another to give information; **business letter** = letter which deals with business matters; **circular letter** = letter sent to many people; **covering letter** = letter sent with documents to say why they are being sent; **follow-up letter** = letter sent to someone after a previous letter or after a visit; **private letter** = letter which deals with personal matters; **standard (form) letter** = letter which is sent without change to various correspondents **(b) letter of acknowledgement** = letter which says that something has been received; **letter of application** = letter in which someone applies for a job or applies for shares in a new company; **letter of appointment** = letter in which someone is appointed to a job; **letter**

of complaint = letter in which someone complains; **letter of credit** = letter from a bank allowing someone credit and promising to repay at a later date; **letter of intent** = letter which states what someone intends to do if something happens; **letters patent** = official document from the Crown, which gives someone the exclusive right to do something (such as becoming a lord *or* making and selling an invention) **(c) air letter** = special thin blue paper which when folded can be sent by air without an envelope; **airmail letter** = letter sent by air; **registered letter** = letter which is noted by the Post Office before it is sent, so that compensation can be claimed if it is lost **(d) to acknowledge receipt by letter** = to write a letter to say that something has been received **(e)** written or printed sign (such as A, B, C); *write your name and address in block letters or in capital letters*

◊ **letterhead** ['letəhed] *noun* name and address of an organization *or* person printed at the top of a piece of notepaper

levy ['levi] **1** *noun* money which is demanded and collected by the government *or* by an agency *or* by an official body; **capital levy** = tax on the value of a person's property and possessions; **import levy** = tax on imports, especially in the EU a tax on imports of farm produce from outside the EU; **training levy** = tax to be paid by companies to fund the government's training schemes **2** *verb* to demand payment of a tax *or* an extra payment and to collect it; *the government has decided to levy a tax on imported cars; to levy a duty on the import of computer parts*

liability [laɪə'bɪlɪti] *noun* **(a)** being legally responsible for paying for damage *or* loss, etc.; *the council has admitted liability but the amount of damages has not yet been agreed;* **to accept** *or* **to admit liability for something** = to agree that you are responsible for something; **to refuse liability for something** = to refuse to agree that you are responsible for something; **contractual liability** = legal responsibility for something as stated in a contract; **limited liability** = principle that by forming a limited liability

company, individual members are liable for that company's debts only to the value of their shares; **limited liability company** = company where a member is responsible for repaying the company's debts only up to the face value of the shares he owns **(b) liabilities** = debts of a business; *the balance sheet shows the company's assets and liabilities;* **current liabilities** = debts which a company should pay within the next accounting period; **long-term liabilities** = debts which are not due to be repaid for some years; **he was not able to meet his liabilities** = he could not pay his debts; **to discharge one's liabilities in full** = to repay all debts **(c) a liability** = something which may make someone less likely to succeed; *the candidate's family problems are likely to prove a liability with the voters*

◊ **liable** ['laɪəbl] *adjective* **(a) liable (for)** = legally responsible (for); *the customer is liable for breakages; the chairman was personally liable for the company's debts; the council was found to be liable for damages* **(b) liable to** = which has an official charge to be paid; *house sales are liable to stamp duty; leaving a car on a yellow line renders you liable to a fine*

libel ['laɪbl] **1** *noun* **(a)** written and published or broadcast statement which damages someone's character (in a permanent form); *he claimed that the newspaper report was a libel* **(b)** act of making a libel; **action for libel** *or* **libel action** = case in a law court where someone says that another person has written a libel about him **2** *verb* to damage someone's character in writing or in a broadcast; *compare* SLANDER (NOTE: **libelling - libelled** but US **libeling - libeled**)

liberal ['lɪbrəl] **1** *adjective* **(a)** allowing freedom to others *or* not controlling others; *the government has adopted a very liberal attitude towards tax reform* **(b) Liberal** = referring to *or* supporting a Liberal Party **(c)** generous; *he has given a liberal donation to party funds* **2** *noun* **(a)** person who believes in individual freedom and the improvement of society **(b) a Liberal** = member of a Liberal Party

◊ **Liberal Party** ['lɪbrəl 'pɑːti] *noun* political party which is in favour of some social change, some involvement of the state in industry and welfare, but less centralization of government, with no fixed connections with either workers or employers

◊ **Liberal Democratic Party** ['lɪbrəl demə'krætɪk 'pɑːti] *noun* British political party formed in 1988 from the old Liberal Party and some members of the former Social Democratic Party; (NOTE: often called **the Lib Dems** for short)

◊ **liberalism** ['lɪbrəlɪzm] *noun* ideals and beliefs of Liberals

---

COMMENT: the British Liberal Party developed from the Whig Party of the 17th and 18th centuries. The name Liberal was applied from the middle of the 19th century onwards. If you need to show the difference between the different meanings of the adjective, you can say 'liberal with a small l'

---

liberation [lɪbə'reɪʃn] *noun* being freed from an oppressive regime; **liberation theology** = religious theory common in Latin America, which involves the church in actively finding solutions to social problems

liberty ['lɪbəti] *noun* being free; **at liberty** = (i) free to do something; (ii) free *or* not in prison; *you are at liberty to complain if you are not satisfied with the service of the department; they are still at liberty while waiting for charges to be brought;* **civil liberties** = freedom for people to work *or* write *or* speak as they want, providing they keep within the law; **liberty of the individual** = freedom for each person to act within the law; **liberty of the press** = freedom of newspapers to publish what they want within the law without censorship; **liberty of the subject** = right of a citizen to be free unless convicted of a crime which is punishable by imprisonment

---

```
liberty  is  the  right  to  do
everything which the laws allow
```

Montesquieu

---

licence *or US* **license** ['laɪsns] *noun* **(a)** official document which allows someone

to do something *or* to use something; permission given by someone to another person to do something which would otherwise be illegal; *he granted his neighbour a licence to use his field;* driving licence = document which shows that you have passed a driving test and can legally drive a car *or* truck, etc.; *applicants for the post should hold a valid driving licence;* gaming licence = document which allows someone *or* a club to organize games of chance, such as roulette; import licence *or* export licence = document which allows goods to be imported *or* exported; licence to sell liquor *or* liquor licence = document given by a Magistrates' Court allowing someone to sell alcohol; *GB* off licence = (i) licence to sell alcohol to be drunk away from the place where it is bought; (ii) shop which sells alcohol to be taken away for drinking elsewhere; on licence = licence to sell alcohol for drinking on the premises (as in a bar *or* restaurant); occasional licence = licence to sell alcohol at a certain place and time only

◊ **license** ['laɪsns] **1** *noun US* = LICENCE **2** *verb* to give someone official permission to do something; *licensed to sell beers, wines and spirits; to license a company to produce spare parts; he is licensed to drive a lorry; she is licensed to run an employment agency;* licensed premises = inn *or* restaurant *or* bar *or* shop which has a licence to sell alcohol

◊ **licensee** [laɪsn'siː] *noun* person who has a licence, especially a licence to sell alcohol *or* to manufacture something

◊ **licensing** ['laɪsnsɪŋ] *noun* which refers to licences; *GB* licensing hours = hours of the day where alcohol can be bought to be drunk on the premises; licensing magistrates = magistrates who grant licences to persons *or* premises for the sale of alcohol

lie upon the table [laɪ] *verb (of a petition)* to have been put before the House of Commons

---

COMMENT: after a petition has been presented by an MP it is said to 'lie upon the table'

---

lieu [lju:] *noun* in lieu of = instead of; **to give someone two months' salary in lieu of notice** = to give an employee money equivalent to the salary for two months' work and ask him to leave immediately

lieutenant [lefˈtenənt] *noun* principal helper *or* adviser of a leader; *the party leader's main lieutenant has decided to quit Parliament*

◊ **Lieutenant-Governor** [lefˈtenənt ˈgʌvnə]] *noun* **(a)** representative of the British Crown in states or provinces of countries which are members of the Commonwealth; *the Lieutenant-Governor of Nova Scotia* **(b)** *US* [luːˈtenənt ˈgʌvnə]] deputy to the governor of a state

life [laɪf] *noun* **(a)** time when a person is alive; **for life** = for as long as someone is alive; *his pension gives him a comfortable income for life;* **life annuity** *or* **annuity for life** = annual payments made to someone as long as he is alive; **life assurance** *or* **life insurance** = insurance which pays a sum of money when someone dies, or at a certain date if he is still alive then; **the life assured** *or* **the life insured** = the person whose life has been covered by the life assurance; **life expectancy** = number of years a person is likely to live; **life peer** *or* **life peeress** = member of the House of Lords who is appointed for life, and whose title is not inherited when he or she dies **(b)** period of time when something is in existence; *the new government is likely to have a short life as it has no overall majority; payments are fixed during the life of the agreement;* **shelf life of a product** = length of time when a product can stay in the shop and still be good to use

lift [lɪft] *verb* to take away *or* to remove; *the government has lifted the ban on imports of technical equipment; the minister has lifted the embargo on the export of firearms*

limit [ˈlɪmɪt] **1** *noun* point at which something ends *or* point where you can go no further; **to set limits to imports** *or* **to impose limits on imports** = to allow only a certain amount of goods to be imported; **age limit** = top age at which you are permitted to do something; **credit limit** = fixed amount of

money which is the most a client can owe; **he has exceeded his credit limit** = he has borrowed more money than is allowed; **lending limit** = restriction on the amount of money a bank can lend; **time limit** = maximum time which can be taken to do something; **weight limit** = maximum permitted weight **2** *verb* to stop something from going beyond a certain point; *the Act limits the power of the tribunals;* **the banks have limited their credit** = the banks have allowed their customers only a certain amount of credit

◊ **limitation** [lɪmɪˈteɪʃn] *noun* **(a)** act of allowing only a certain amount of something; *the contract imposes limitations on the number of cars which can be imported;* **limitation of liability** = (i) making someone liable for only a part of the damage *or* loss; (ii) making shareholders in a limited company liable for the debts of the company only in proportion to their shareholding; **time limitation** = amount of time which is available **(b) limitation of actions** *or* **statute of limitations** = law which allows only a certain amount of time (usually six years) for someone to start legal proceedings to claim property *or* compensation for damage, etc.

◊ **limited** [ˈlɪmɪtɪd] *adjective* restricted *or* not open; *admission to the playground is limited to children between 6 and 12 years of age;* **limited liability** = principle that by forming a limited liability company, individual members are liable for that company's debts only to the value of their shares; **limited liability company** = company where a shareholder is responsible for repaying the company's debts only to the face value of the shares he owns; **private limited company** = company whose shares are not traded on the Stock Exchange; **Public Limited Company** = company whose shares can be bought on the Stock Exchange; (NOTE: a private limited company is called **Ltd** or **Limited** a Public Limited Company is called **Plc** or **PLC** or **plc**)

◊ **limiting** [ˈlɪmɪtɪŋ] *adjective* which limits; *a limiting clause in a contract; the short holiday season is a limiting factor on the hotel trade*

limitrophe ['lɪmɪtrəʊf] *adjective (French)* on the border between countries or areas

lineal ['lɪnɪəl] *see* DESCENT

lingua franca ['lɪŋgwə 'frænkə] *noun* language which serves as the language of communication between different countries or different regions

list [lɪst] **1** *noun* **(a)** several items written one after the other; *a list of debtors; list of products or product list; to add a name to a list; to cross someone's name off a list; he has applied to be put on the list of potential candidates;* **list of members** = annual return made by a company listing its shareholders; **address list** *or* **mailing list** = list of names and addresses of people and companies; **black list** = (i) list of goods *or* companies *or* countries which are banned for trade; (ii) list of persons who should not be appointed to a job *or* with whom one should not do business; *the teacher is on the Department of Education black list; the council is drawing up a black list of suppliers;* **housing list** = list of families waiting to be given council accommodation; **waiting list** = list of people waiting for something; *a bid to shorten waiting lists for council flats; the bill will join a long waiting list of measures to be discussed by the committee* **(b)** catalogue; **list price** = price as shown in a catalogue **2** *verb* **(a)** to write a series of items one after the other; *the catalogue lists products by category; the case is listed to be heard next week* **(b)** **listed building** = building of special interest (usually because it is old), which the owners cannot alter or demolish; **listed company** = company whose shares can be bought *or* sold on the Stock Exchange

lobby ['lɒbɪ] **1** *noun* **(a)** division lobby *or* voting lobby = one of two long rooms at the side of the House of Commons chamber, where MPs go to vote; **lobby fodder** = ordinary MPs who vote as their party tells them, and do not think much about the issues **(b)** group of people *or* pressure group which tries to influence MPs *or* the passage of legislation; **the car lobby** = people who try to persuade MPs that cars should be encouraged and not restricted; **the environmentalist lobby** = group who try to persuade MPs that the environment must be protected, pollution stopped, etc. **(c)** group of journalists attached to the House of Commons, who are given 'off-the-record' briefings by senior ministers or their assistants; **lobby correspondent** = journalist who is a member of the Westminster lobby **2** *verb* to ask someone (such as an MP or local official) to do something on your behalf; *a group of local businessmen has gone to London to lobby their MPs on the problems of unemployment in the area*

◊ **lobbyist** ['lɒbiɪst] *noun* person who is paid to represent a pressure group

local ['ləʊkl] **1** *adjective* relating to a certain area *or* place; **local authority** = section of elected government which runs a certain area (such as a district council); **the Local Commissioners** *or* **Local Government Ombudsmen** = officials who investigate complaints against local authorities; *see comment at* OMBUDSMAN **local court** = court (such as a magistrates' court) which hears cases coming from a certain area; **local government** = system of government of towns and districts by elected councils; *a court can give instructions to a local authority as to the exercise of its powers in relation to children in care; a decision of the local authority pursuant to the powers and duties imposed on it by the Act* **2** *noun* person living in a certain place; *the new postman found he did not get on with the locals*

COMMENT: local government in England and Wales is a two-tier system: county councils, with non-metropolitan district councils under them, and metropolitan district councils which are self-governing large urban areas. In Scotland there are nine large Regional Councils instead of county councils

lodge [lɒdʒ] *verb* to put *or* to deposit (officially); **to lodge caution** = to deposit a document with the Land Registry which prevents land *or* property being sold without notice; **to lodge a complaint against someone** = to make an official complaint about someone; **to lodge money with someone** = to deposit money with someone

Lok Sabha ['lɒk 'sæbə] *noun* lower house of Parliament in India; (NOTE: the upper house is the **Rajya Sabha**)

long [lɒŋ] *adjective* for a large period of time; **long credit** = credit terms which allow the borrower a long time to pay; **in the long term** = over a long period of time; **to take the long view** = to plan for a long period ahead

◊ **long-dated** ['lɒŋ 'deɪtɪd] *adjective* **long-dated bills** *or* **paper** = bills of exchange which are payable in more than three months' time

◊ **longhand** ['lɒŋhænd] *noun* handwriting where the words are written out in full and not typed or in shorthand; *applications should be written in longhand and sent to the recruitment officer*

◊ **long-standing** ['lɒŋ 'stændɪŋ] *adjective* (agreement) which has been arranged for a long time

◊ **long-term** ['lɒŋ 'tɜːm] *adjective* lasting for a long period of time; **on a long-term basis** = for a long period of time; **long-term debts** = debts which will be repaid many years later; **long-term forecast** = forecast for a period of over three years; **long-term loan** = loan to be repaid many years later; **long-term objectives** = aims which will take years to fulfil; *the school building programme has to take account of long-term forecasts for the birth rate; will the long-term objectives be met by the end of the century?*

loophole ['luːphəʊl] *noun* way of escape; **to find a loophole in the law** = to find a means of doing what you want to do, by finding a way of getting round a law which otherwise would prevent you from acting; **to find a tax loophole** = to find a legal means of avoiding the payment of tax

lord [lɔːd] *noun* **(a)** member of the House of Lords; **Lord of Appeal** = member of the House of Lords who sits when the House is acting as a Court of Appeal; **Lord of Appeal in Ordinary** = one of eleven lords who are

appointed to sit as members of the House of Lords when it acts as a Court of Appeal; **Lord Chancellor** = member of the government and cabinet who presides over the debates in the House of Lords and is responsible for the administration of justice and the appointment of judges; **Lord Chief Justice** = chief judge of the Queen's Bench Division of the High Court who is also a member of the Court of Appeal; **Lord Justice** = title given to a judge who is a member of the House of Lords; **Lord Justice General** = chief judge in the Scottish High Court of Judiciary; **Lord Justice Clerk** = second most important judge in the Scottish High Court of Justiciary; (NOTE: written **LJ** after the name: **Smith LJ = Lord Justice Smith**) **(b)** title given to barons and to the sons of dukes or marquesses; (NOTE: almost always used with a capital: **Lord**)

> COMMENT: when used for a baron, the title is given with the family name: Lord Smith; when used for the son of a duke or marquess, the Christian name is used as well: Lord James Stuart

◊ **Lords** [lɔːdz] *plural noun* the House of Lords (as a whole); the members of the House of Lords; *the Bill goes before the Lords next week; the Lords voted to amend the Bill;* **Lords Spiritual** = archbishops and bishops who are members of the House of Lords; **Lords Temporal** = members of the House of Lords who are not bishops; **the Law Lords** = members of the House of Lords who are judges

◊ **Lord Advocate** ['lɔːd 'ædvəkət] *noun* member of the government who is one of the two Law Officers in Scotland

◊ **Lord Lieutenant** ['lɔːd lef'tenənt] *noun* representative of the Crown in a county

◊ **Lord Ordinary** ['lɔːd 'ɔːdɪnri] *noun* judge of the upper house of the Scottish Court of Session

◊ **Lord President** ['lɔːd 'prezɪdənt] *noun* judge of the Scottish Court of Session

◊ **Lord President of the Council** ['lɔːd 'prezɪdənt əv ðə 'kaʊnsəl] *noun* senior member of the government, a member of the House of Lords who is the head of the Privy

Council Office and has other duties allocated by the Prime Minister

◊ **Lord Privy Seal** ['lɔːd prɪvi 'siːl] *noun* senior member of the government, often a member of Cabinet, with duties allocated by the Prime Minister

lose [luːz] *verb* **(a)** not to win (an election *or* a vote *or* legal proceedings); *the government lost the vote of no confidence; the government is going to lose the next election; he lost his appeal to the House of Lords; she lost her case for compensation;* **the motion was lost** = the motion was not passed; (NOTE: the opposite is **the motion was carried**) **(b)** not to have something any more; *he lost his seat at the last election; the Opposition lost several seats in the council election;* **to lose an order** = not to get an order which you were hoping to get; *during the strike, the company lost six orders to American competitors;* **to lose control of a council** = to find that you have less than 50% of the seats on the council and so are no longer able to run it **(c)** to have less money; *he lost £25,000 in his father's computer company;* **the pound has lost value** = the pound is worth less **(d)** to drop to a lower price; *the dollar lost two cents against the pound; gold shares lost 5% on the market yesterday;* (NOTE: losing - lost - has lost)

loss [lɒs] *noun* **(a)** not having something which was had before; not winning something; *the government won seats in the south of the country but had serious losses in the north; the loss of the vote of confidence means that there will have to be new elections;* **compensation for loss of earnings** = payment to someone who has stopped earning money *or* who is not able to earn money; **compensation for loss of office** = payment to a director who is asked to leave a company before his contract ends **(b)** having less money than before *or* not making a profit; **the company suffered a loss** = the company did not make a profit; **to report a loss** = not to show a profit in the accounts at the end of the year; **to cut one's losses** = to stop doing something which was losing money

lower ['ləʊə] *adjective* less important; **lower chamber** *or* **lower house** = less important of the two houses in a bicameral system of government; **lower court** = less important court, one which tries less important cases; (NOTE: the opposite is **upper**)

COMMENT: In a bicameral system, the upper chamber is normally a revising chamber, with some limited powers to delay passing of legislation. Bills normally have to passed by both houses before they can become law. The lower house of the British legislature is the House of Commons, and in many ways it has more power, especially over financial matters, than the House of Lords, which is the upper house.

Loya Jerga ['lɔɪə 'dʒɜːgə] *noun* Grand Council (a type of parliament) in Afghanistan

loyal ['lɔɪəl] *adjective* faithful *or* not treacherous; *he has been loyal to the party, even though the leader criticised him in public*

◊ **loyalist** ['lɔɪəlɪst] *noun* person who is loyal to something, especially to a king *or* country with which he feels a strong link

◊ **loyally** ['lɔɪəli] *adverb* faithfully *or* not working for an opponent; *she has served the council loyally for ten years*

◊ **loyalty** ['lɔɪəlti] *noun* being faithful; *all the members of the government have sworn an oath of loyalty to the President*

Lumpenproletariat
[lʌmpənprəʊləˈteəriæt] *noun* ordinary workers, those who are not particularly interested in the workers' cause

Mm

Maastricht ['mɑːstrɪχt] *noun* town in the southern part of the Netherlands; **the Maastricht Treaty** *or* **the Treaty of Maastricht** = treaty of 1st November 1993, by which the member states of the European Community established the European Union, formed of three pillars: the European Community, and two pillars based on the Council of Ministers, which coordinate foreign and security policies (including defence) and justice and interior policies, such as immigration, international terrorism, drug-smuggling, etc.

mace [meɪs] *noun* large ornamental stick, made of gold or silver, which is the emblem of government and is placed on the table in the House of Commons *or* House of Lords, or in some local council chambers, to show that business can begin

◊ **mace-bearer** ['meɪsbeərə] *noun* official who carries a mace in procession

COMMENT: the significance of the mace in the House of Commons is so great that if it is not on the table, no business can be done. The mace is carried by the Serjeant at Arms in official processions; it is kept under the table in the House of Commons and placed on the table at the beginning of each sitting; it is taken off the table when the House goes into Committee. In the House of Lords, the mace is placed on the Woolsack. Local authorities usually also have maces which are carried in front of the mayor on ceremonial occasions by the mace-bearer, and often placed on the table at full council meetings. In the US House of Representatives, the mace is placed beside the Speaker's chair when the House is in session. There is

no mace in the Senate, but a ceremonial gavel is placed on the vice-president's desk when the Senate is in session

Machiavellian [mækiə'veliən] *adjective* cynically political and devious; *compare* BYZANTINE

COMMENT: called after the Italian writer, Machiavelli, whose book, 'The Prince', is a treatise on government in 15th century Italy

machine [mə'ʃiːn] *noun* **(a)** device which works with power from a motor; **copying machine** *or* **duplicating machine** = machine which makes copies of documents; **dictating machine** = machine which records what someone dictates, which a typist can then play back and type out **(b)** **machine code** *or* **machine language** = instructions and information shown as a series of figures (0 and 1) which can be read by a computer; **machine-readable codes** = sets of signs or letters (such as bar codes *or* post codes) which a computer can read **(c)** organized system of doing something; *the government propaganda machine*

◊ **machinery** [mə'ʃiːnəri] *noun* **(a)** machines; *the inspector found that the machinery in the factory was dangerous* **(b)** organization *or* system *or* method of organizing; *the local government machinery or the machinery of local government; the council administrative machinery seems to have broken down; the machinery for awarding government contracts*

Madam ['mædəm] *noun* formal way of addressing a woman, especially one whom you do not know; **Dear Madam** = beginning of a letter to a woman whom you do not know; **Madam Chairman** = way of addressing a woman who is in the chair at the meeting (now it is more usual to say 'Chairman' or 'Chair')

Magna Carta ['mægnə 'kɑːtə] *noun* the Great Charter, granted by King John in 1215, which gave his subjects certain political and personal freedoms

COMMENT: the Magna Carta is supposed to be the first step taken towards democratic rule, since it gave political power to the aristocracy and reduced the power of the King to override the law. It did not give power to the ordinary people, but confirmed the rights of the individual to own property and receive impartial justice

maiden speech ['meɪdən 'spiːtʃ] *noun* first speech by a new MP in the House of Commons

mail [meɪl] **1** *noun* (a) system of sending letters and parcels from one place to another; **by mail** = using the postal services, not sending something by hand or by messenger; **by surface mail** = by land or sea, not by air; **by sea mail** = by post abroad, using a ship; **by air mail** = by post using a plane; **electronic mail** *or* **e-mail** = system of sending messages from one computer to another, using the telephone lines (b) letters sent or received; *your cheque arrived in yesterday's mail; my secretary opens my mail as soon as it arrives; the receipt was in this morning's mail* (c) **direct mail** = selling a product by sending advertising material to possible buyers through the post; **mail shot** = advertising material sent by mail to possible customers **2** *verb* to send something by post

◊ **mailing** ['meɪlɪŋ] *noun* sending something in the post; **direct mailing** = sending of advertising material by post to possible buyers; **mailing list** = list of names and addresses of people who might be interested in a product *or* list of names and addresses of members of a party *or* society; **to buy a mailing list** = to pay a society, etc., money to hire the list of members so that you can use it to mail advertising material; **mailing piece** = leaflet suitable for sending

by direct mail; **mailing shot** = advertising material sent by mail to possible customers

◊ **mail-order** *noun* system of buying and selling from a catalogue, placing orders and sending goods by mail; **mail-order business** *or* **mail-order firm** *or* **mail-order house** = company which sells a product by mail; **mail-order catalogue** = catalogue from which a customer can order items to be sent by mail

main [meɪn] *adjective* most important; *one of the main pieces of legislation to be presented to this Parliament; he is the main contender for the post of deputy leader*

◊ **mainstream** ['meɪnstriːm] *noun* the majority opinion of a party; *he is in the mainstream of Conservative politics; the manifesto follows mainstream policies*

maintain [meɪn'teɪn] *verb* (a) to keep something going *or* working; *the council tries to maintain good relations with the neighbouring authorities; his duty is to maintain contact with the council outreach workers; the chairman banged his gavel in an attempt to maintain law and order in the council chamber* (b) to keep something working at the same level; *the company has maintained the same volume of business in spite of the recession; to maintain an interest rate at 5%;* **to maintain a dividend** = to pay the same dividend as in the previous year (c) to pay for the food and clothing, etc., for a child *or* a person; *the ex-husband was ordered to maintain his wife and three children* (d) to state something firmly; *he maintains that the government's calculations are wrong*

◊ **maintenance** ['meɪntənəns] *noun* (a) keeping things going *or* working; *the maintenance of law and order is in the hands of the local police force* (b) keeping a machine in good working order *or* a building in good condition; *the council is responsible for the maintenance of school buildings in the borough;* **maintenance contract** = contract by which a company keeps a piece of equipment in good working order; **maintenance department** = department which deals with keeping council property in good condition (c) payment made by a divorced or separated husband *or* wife to the former spouse, to help pay for living expenses and the cost of bringing up the children; **maintenance order** = court order which orders a divorced or separated husband *or* wife to pay maintenance to the former spouse; (NOTE: US English is **alimony**)

majesty ['mædʒəsti] *noun* impressive *or* royal quality or appearance; *the majesty of the State Opening of Parliament*

◊ **Majesty** ['mædʒəsti] *noun* title given to a King or Queen; *His Majesty, the King; Their Majesties, the King and Queen; 'Your Majesty, the Ambassador has arrived';* Her **Majesty's government** = the official title of the British government; **on Her Majesty's Service (OHMS)** = words printed on official letters from government departments; *see also* HER MAJESTY'S PLEASURE, HER MAJESTY'S STATIONERY OFFICE

◊ **majestic** [mə'dʒestɪk] *adjective* impressive and admirable

majeure [mæ'ʒɜː] *see* FORCE MAJEURE

Majlis ['mædʒlɪs] *noun* Consultative Assembly (or Parliament) in Iran, Saudi Arabia, Oman and Turkmenistan

major ['meɪdʒə] *adjective* important; *a major council building project; one of the government's major tasks is to restore the country's infrastructure which has been destroyed in the civil war*

◊ **majority** [mə'dʒɒrɪti] *noun* (a) larger group than any other; **a majority of members** = more than 50% of MPs *or* councillors; **straight majority** *or* **overall majority** = more than half the votes; **the cabinet accepted the proposal by a majority of ten to seven** = ten members of the cabinet voted to accept and seven voted against; *US* **majority leader** = spokesman for the majority party in the House of Representatives *or* Senate, elected by the other members of the party; **majority whip** = assistant to the majority leader, whose responsibility is to see that enough members of the party vote; **majority vote** *or* **majority decision** = decision made after a vote according to the wishes of the larger group;

qualified majority vote = voting system used in the EU Council by which out of a total of 87 votes, 62 are needed to pass a law; *compare* BLOCKING MINORITY **majority shareholding** *or* **majority interest** = group of shares which is more than 50% of the total; **a majority shareholder** = person who owns more than half the shares in a company; **majority system** = system of voting where half the votes plus one more must be cast for a proposal for it to be accepted; **majority verdict** = verdict reached by a jury where at least ten jurors vote for the verdict; *compare* PLURALITY (NOTE: in US English **plurality** is used to indicate a majority over another candidate, and **majority** is used to indicate having more votes than all other candidates put together) **(b)** age at which someone becomes responsible for his actions *or* can sue *or* can be sued *or* can undertake business transactions

COMMENT: the age of majority in the UK and US is eighteen

maladministration

['mælədmɪnɪ'streɪʃn] *noun* incompetent *or* illegal administration; *the ombudsman found the council guilty of maladministration;* (NOTE: no plural)

manage ['mænɪdʒ] *verb* **(a)** to direct *or* to be in charge of; *to manage a department; to manage a branch office* **(b)** to **manage property** = to look after rented property for the owner; *tenants have complained about the conditions in council-managed properties* **(c)** to **manage to** = to succeed (with some difficulty) in doing something; *did you manage to see the housing department? the applicant managed to have the hearing adjourned; she managed to write six orders and take three phone calls all in two minutes*

◊ **manageable** ['mænədʒəbl] *adjective* which can be dealt with easily; *the workload in the department has to be kept to manageable proportions; the government is planning to create two new superministries which we feel will be hardly manageable*

◊ **management** ['mænɪdʒmənt] *noun* **(a)** directing *or* running a business; *to study management; good management* **or** *efficient* *management;* line management = organization of a business where each manager is directly responsible for a stage in the operation of the business; **management accountant** = accountant who prepares specialized information (especially budgets) for managers so that they can make decisions; **management accounts** = financial information (on sales, costs, credit, profitability) prepared for a manager *or* director of a company; **management committee** = committee which manages a non-commercial organization (such as a research institute *or* college); **management by objectives** = way of managing a business by planning work for the managers and testing to see if it is completed correctly and on time; **management team** = a group of managers working together; **management training** = training managers by making them study problems and work out ways of solving them; **management trainee** = young person being trained to be a manager **(b)** group of managers or directors; **top management** = the main directors of a company; **middle management** = the department managers of a company who carry out the policy set by the directors and organize the work of a group of workers; **junior management** = managers of small departments *or* deputies to departmental managers

◊ **manager** ['mænɪdʒə] *noun* **(a)** head of a department; **accounts manager** = head of the accounts department; **area manager** = manager who is responsible for an organization in an area; **general manager** = manager in charge of the administration in a large organization **(b)** person in charge of a branch or shop; **bank manager** = person in charge of a branch of a bank; **branch manager** = person in charge of a branch of a company **(c)** *US* **city manager** = executive appointed by a city council to administer the city; (NOTE: in Britain, this is the **Chief Executive**) **(d)** *US* member of the House of Representatives or Senate, elected to represent the chamber in a conference to discuss differences of opinion over a bill

◊ **manageress** [mænɪdʒə'res] *noun* woman who runs a shop, or a department

◊ **managerial** [mænə'dʒɪərɪəl] *adjective* referring to managers *or* to management; **to be appointed to a managerial position** = to be appointed a manager; **decisions taken at managerial level** = decisions taken by managers

◊ **managing director** ['mænɪdʒɪŋ daɪ'rektə] *noun* director who is in charge of a whole company

mandarin ['mændərɪn] *noun (informal)* **Whitehall mandarin** = top British civil servant

mandate ['mændeɪt] **1** *noun* authority given to a person or group authorizing and requiring them to act on behalf of the person giving the authority (in the case of a democratic government, these are the electors); *the government has a mandate from the people to carry out the plans put forward in its manifesto;* **to seek a new mandate** = to try to be reelected to a position **2** *verb* (i) to give (a government) the authority to carry out certain policies; (ii) to give (a person) authority to vote for a group; *the government has been mandated to revise the tax system; the delegates were mandated to vote on behalf of their membership*

mandatory ['mændətəri] *adjective* which has to be done *or* to take place; **mandatory injunction** = order from a court which compels someone to do something; **mandatory meeting** = meeting which must be held *or* meeting which all members have to attend

manifesto [mænɪ'festəʊ] *noun* written public statement of the aims and policies of a group *or* party; *the Labour Party manifesto was published at the beginning of the election campaign; will the government implement all its manifesto promises?*

manual ['mænjʊəl] *noun* **(a)** book which explains how a piece of machinery works; *the computer manual will tell you how to attach a line printer; the operating manual is of no help with this error* **(b)** *US* book which explains the organization and procedures of the Houses of Congress

Maoism ['mæʊɪzm] *noun* Communist ideas taught by Mao Tse-Tung

◊ **Maoist** ['mæʊɪst] **1** *adjective* referring to Maoism **2** *noun* person who follows the ideas taught by Mao Tse-Tung

COMMENT: Maoism follows a different line from Marxism, because it is based on the wisdom of the people as a whole. Party officials and technical experts can be criticized if they do not follow the line dictated by the people. Maoists also believe that Communist principles may be adapted to different circumstances in different countries, though the basic aim of imposing Communism is most important, and is to be achieved by force if necessary

marchioness [mɑːʃəˈnes] *noun* wife or widow of a marquess

marginal ['mɑːdʒɪnəl] *adjective & noun* **(a)** slight *or* not very large; *the rate increases had only a marginal effect on the council's loan repayments* **(b)** marginal *or* marginal constituency *or* marginal seat = constituency where the sitting MP has a small majority; *the swing in several crucial marginals showed that the government was going to lose the election; MPs representing marginal seats are worried about the government's poor showing in the opinion polls;* (NOTE: the opposite is a **safe seat**)

mark up ['mɑːk 'ʌp] *verb US* **to mark up a bill** = to make changes to a bill as it goes through committee

market ['mɑːkɪt] **1** *noun* **(a)** place (often in the open air) where farm produce is sold; **market day** = day when a market is regularly held; **market dues** = rent for a place in a market; **market town** = town where a regular market is held; **market trader** = person who sells in a market; *all market traders must have licences from the council* **(b)** the **Common Market** = former name given to the European Community, now the European Union **(c)** place where a product might be sold *or* group of people who might buy a product; **home** *or* **domestic market** = market in the country where the selling company is based **(d)** possible sales of a certain type of product *or* demand for a certain type of product; **a growth market** = market where sales are likely to rise rapidly **(e) the black market** = buying and selling goods in a way which is not allowed by law; **to pay black market prices** = to pay high prices to obtain items which are not easily available; *there is a lucrative black market in spare parts for cars; he bought gold coins on the black market* **(f)** a **buyer's market** = market where goods are sold cheaply because there is little demand; **a seller's market** = market where the seller can ask high prices because there is a large demand for the product; **market forces** = economic influence of varying factors, not governed by action of the government; **free market economy** = system where the government does not interfere in business activity in any way **(g) capital market** = place where companies can look for investment capital; **the foreign exchange markets** = places where currencies are bought or sold; **forward markets** = places where foreign currency or commodities can be bought or sold for delivery at a later date **(h) stock market** = place where shares are bought and sold; **to buy shares in the open market** = to buy shares on the Stock Exchange, not privately; **over-the-counter market** = secondary market in shares which are not listed on the main Stock Exchange; **market capitalization** = value of a company calculated by multiplying the price of its shares on the Stock Exchange by the number of shares issued **2** *verb* to sell (products); *the council is spending part of its budget on marketing the town as a tourist resort*

marquess ['mɑːkwɪs] *noun* member of the nobility, the rank below a duke; (NOTE: the wife of a **marquess** is a **marchioness**)

martial ['mɑːʃl] *adjective* relating to the armed services; **martial law** = rule of a country *or* part of a country by the army on the orders of the main government, the ordinary civil law having been suspended; *the president imposed or declared martial law in two provinces; the government lifted martial law*

Marxism ['mɑːksɪzm] *noun* communist philosophy taught by Karl Marx

◊ **Marxist** ['mɑːksɪst] **1** *adjective* referring to Marxism; *the book is an account of Marxist ideology; a Marxist analysis of economic history* **2** *noun* person who supports the ideas of Karl Marx

> COMMENT: Marxism advocates the inevitable overthrow of capitalist governments. The capitalist system will be replaced by a centralized, nationalized system, where land, property and the means of manufacture all belong to the people, and where the state itself will finally disappear, leaving a totally classless society

mass [mæs] *noun* large crowd (of people *or* things); **the masses** = the ordinary people; *he spoke at a mass meeting of party members; their speeches aimed at stirring the masses to revolt*

material [mə'tɪərɪəl] **1** *noun* stuff of which something is made; *building materials; non-inflammable materials; the fire officer's report said that the material used in the ceiling was not fire-proof; the committee asked for details of the materials to be used in the building before giving planning permission* **2** *adjective* relating to; *have you presented all the material facts in this paper?*

matter ['mætə] **1** *noun* **(a)** problem *or* question to be discussed; *the most important matter on the agenda; we shall consider first the matter of last month's fall in prices;* **matter of concern** = question which causes concern; *it is a matter of concern to the* **members of the committee** = the members of the committee are worried about it **(b)** **printed matter** = printed books, newspapers, advertising material, etc.; (NOTE: no plural) **2** *verb* to be important; *does it matter if the council staff are paid a day late?*

maximum ['mæksɪməm] **1** *noun* largest possible number *or* price *or* quantity; **up to a maximum of £10** = no more than £10; (NOTE: plural is **maxima**) **2** *adjective* largest possible; *maximum income tax rate or maximum rate of tax; the maximum permitted increase in rates will not cover the council's projected spending;* **to increase**

production to the maximum level = as much as possible

May Day ['meɪ 'deɪ] *noun* annual celebration of workers, held in many countries on May 1st; *see also* **LABOR DAY**

mayor ['meə] *noun* person who is elected *or* chosen as the official head of a town, city or local council; **Lord Mayor** = Mayor of a very large town (such as London, Liverpool)

◊ **mayoral** ['meərəl] *noun* referring to a mayor; *he is carrying out his mayoral duties; the mayoress went to the ceremony in the mayoral car*

◊ **mayoralty** ['meərəlti] *noun* the position of a mayor; the time for which someone is mayor

◊ **mayoress** ['meəres] *noun* (i) woman mayor; (ii) wife of a mayor

◊ **mayor-making** ['meə'meɪkɪŋ] *noun* ceremony which takes place at a council's Annual Meeting, when the new mayor is invested with his chain of office

> COMMENT: previously, a mayor was the head of the elected government of a town, and the head of the majority party. His governmental responsibilities have now been taken over by the Leader of the Council, and the office of mayor is largely ceremonial. It is an honour often given to a long-serving or distinguished councillor. In Scotland, a mayor is called a Provost. In the USA, mayors are elected by popular vote, and appoint their team to run the various departments in a city. Note also that 'Mayor' is used in English to apply to persons holding similar positions in other countries: **the Mayor of Berlin; the Mayor of Paris; the Mayor of New York**

McCarthyism [mə'kɑːθiɪzm] *noun* policy of persecuting and prosecuting Communists or Communist sympathizers in the USA in the 1950s

means [miːnz] *noun* enough money to do something; *he hasn't the means to go to the hospital by taxi;* **means test** = test to find out how poor someone is, to see if he *or* she is eligible for money from the government *or* other body

measure ['meʒə] **1** *noun* **(a)** way of calculating size *or* quantity; **cubic measure =** volume in cubic feet or metres, calculated by multiplying height, width and length; **square measure =** area in square feet or metres, calculated by multiplying width and length; **inspector of weights and measures =** government inspector who inspects weighing machines and goods sold in shops to see if the quantities and weights are correct **(b)** type of action, especially a law passed by Parliament or statutory instrument; *a government measure to reduce crime in the inner cities; this is one of a series of measures to be introduced in the next session of Parliament;* **to take measures to prevent something happening =** to act to stop something happening; **to take emergency measures =** to act rapidly to stop a dangerous situation developing; **an economy measure =** an action to save money; **fiscal measures =** tax changes made by the government to improve the working of the economy; **as a precautionary measure =** to prevent something taking place; **safety measures =** actions to make sure that something is *or* will be safe **2** *verb* **(a)** to find out the size *or* quantity of something; to be of a certain size *or* quantity; *to measure the size of a package; a package which measures 10cm by 25cm or a package measuring 10cm by 25cm* **(b)** to measure the government's *or* the company's performance = to judge how well the government *or* the company is doing

◊ **measurement** ['meʒəmənt] *noun* **(a)** **measurements =** size (in inches, centimetres, etc.); *to write down the measurements of a package* **(b)** way of judging something; *performance measurement or measurement of performance;* **measurement of profitability =** way of calculating how profitable something is

mediate ['miːdɪeɪt] *verb* to try to make the two sides in an argument come to an agreement; *to mediate between the manager and his staff; the government offered to mediate in the dispute*

◊ **mediation** [miːdɪ'eɪʃn] *noun* attempt by a third party to make the two sides in an argument agree; *the employers refused an offer of government mediation; the dispute was ended through the mediation of union officials*

◊ **mediator** ['miːdɪeɪtə] *noun* **official mediator =** government official who tries to make the two sides in an industrial dispute agree

meet [miːt] *verb* **(a)** to come together with someone; *they appointed representatives to meet the negotiating committee; the candidate arranged to meet his agent at his hotel;* **meet the people =** tour made by a statesman or politician to meet members of the general public **(b)** to be satisfactory for; *the amendment failed to meet the sponsor's requirements; he failed to meet the conditions of the court order; they failed to meet the deadline =* they were not able to complete in time **(c)** to pay for; *the state will meet half your expenses; he was unable to meet his mortgage repayments;* **to meet your obligations =** to pay your debts; (NOTE: meeting - met - has met)

◊ **meeting** ['miːtɪŋ] *noun* **(a)** coming together of a group of people; *a staff meeting will be held next Friday; the last item on the agenda is to agree a time for the next meeting;* **freedom of meeting =** being able to meet as a group without being afraid of prosecution; **to hold a meeting =** to organize a meeting of a group of people; *the meeting will be held in the committee room;* **to open a meeting =** to start a meeting; **to conduct a meeting =** to be in the chair for a meeting; **to close a meeting =** to end a meeting; **to put a resolution to a meeting =** to ask a meeting to vote on a proposal **(b)** **committee meeting =** meeting of the members of a committee; **Annual General Meeting =** meeting of all the members of a society *or* shareholders of a company which takes place once a year to agree the accounts and decide general policy; **Annual Meeting =** meeting of a council, which takes place once a year to approve the accounts, elect a mayor, etc.; **Extraordinary General Meeting =** special meeting of members to discuss an important matter which cannot wait until the next Annual General Meeting

megalomania [megələ'meɪnɪə] *noun* madness which overtakes dictators

◊ **megalomaniac** [megələʊ'meɪnɪæk] *adjective & noun* (dictator) with delusions of grandeur

member ['membə] *noun* **(a)** person who belongs to a group *or* a society; **ordinary member** = person who pays a subscription to belong to a club *or* group; **honorary member** = special person who does not have to pay a subscription **(b)** Member of Parliament; *the member for Oxford; the newly elected member for Windsor;* **members' gallery** = one of the galleries in the House of Commons, where the guests of MPs can sit and listen to the debates **(c)** person elected to a local council; *the members asked for a report from the planning officer; officers must carry out the wishes of members* **(d)** organization or country which belongs to a society; *the member countries or the member states of the EU; the members of the United Nations; the member companies of a trade association*

◊ **Member of Parliament (MP)** ['membə əv 'pɑːləmənt] *noun* person elected to represent a constituency in Parliament; (NOTE: often abbreviated to **MP**. The plural is **MPs**)

COMMENT: any British subject over 21 is eligible for election as an MP, but the following are disqualified: peers, ministers of the Church of Scotland, persons holding an office of profit (such as judges and civil servants), bankrupts, people who are insane, and some categories of prisoners

◊ **Member of the European Parliament (MEP)** ['membə əv ðə jʊərə'piːən 'pɑːləmənt] *noun* person elected to represent a Euro-constituency in the European Parliament

◊ **membership** ['membəʃɪp] *noun* **(a)** belonging to a group; *membership qualifications; conditions of membership; to pay your membership or your membership fees; is Iceland going to apply for*

membership of the European Union? **(b)** all the members of a group; *the membership was asked to vote for the new president;* the **club's membership secretary** = committee member who deals with the ordinary members of a society; **the club has a membership of five hundred** = the club has five hundred members

memorandum *or* **memo** [memə'rændəm or 'meməʊ] *noun* short note; *he sent a memorandum or memo to all the Chief Officers about the new arrangements for weekly meetings; there is a pile of memos from the Chief Executive waiting for you;* **memorandum of association** = legal document setting up a limited company and giving details of its aims, capital structure, and registered office; (NOTE: plural is **memoranda**)

memorial [mɪ'mɔːrɪəl] *noun* **(a)** written statement of facts presented by a group of citizens, asking a legislature (Parliament *or* Congress *or* town council) to do a certain action **(b)** act of remembrance; **war memorial** = construction commemorating people who died during a war; **Memorial Day** = public holiday in the USA to remember those who died in wars (celebrated at the end of May)

mention ['menʃn] *verb* to talk about something for a short time; *the council leader mentioned the need for the sub-committee to examine all the documents; can you mention to the secretary that the date of the next meeting has been changed?*

MEP ['em iː 'piː] = MEMBER OF THE EUROPEAN PARLIAMENT

mercenary ['mɜːsənəri] *noun* soldier who fights on behalf of a foreign country for money

mercy ['mɜːsi] *noun* showing that you forgive; **prerogative of mercy** = power (used by the Home Secretary) to commute or remit a sentence

meritocracy [merɪ'tɒkrəsi] *noun* society governed by people selected for their merit

mesocracy [me'zɒkrəsi] *noun* society governed by the middle class

messenger ['mesəndʒə] *noun* person who carries messages; **Queen's Messenger** *or* **King's Messenger** = person with diplomatic status who carries messages to British embassies abroad

metropolis [mə'trɒpəlis] *noun* very large town, usually the capital of a country

◊ **metropolitan** [metrə'pɒlitən] *adjective* referring to a large city; **Metropolitan District Council** = large administrative area covering an urban area in England or Wales; **the Metropolitan Police** = the police force of Greater London, which is directly responsible to the Home Secretary; **the Metropolitan Police Commissioner** = the head of the Metropolitan Police, appointed directly by the Home Secretary; **solicitor for the Metropolitan Police** = solicitor responsible for prosecutions brought by the Metropolitan Police

> COMMENT: the higher ranks in the Metropolitan Police are Deputy Assistant Commissioner, Assistant Commissioner, and Commissioner. See also POLICE

MFN = MOST-FAVOURED NATION

MI5, MI6 ['em aɪ 'faɪv *or* 'em aɪ 'sɪks] *noun* the British government intelligence agencies, specializing in espionage; (NOTE: the US equivalent is **the Central Intelligence Agency (CIA)**)

> COMMENT: MI5 (or the Security Service) is concerned with national security, in particular counter-terrorism and counter-espionage. MI6 (or the Secret Intelligence Service) is concerned with obtaining information about other countries which may be of use to the government's defence, security, economic and foreign services

Michaelmas ['mɪkəlməs] *noun* **(a)** one of the four sittings of the law courts **(b)** one of the four law terms

◊ **Michaelmas Day** ['mɪkəlməs 'deɪ] *noun* 29th September: one of the quarter days when rent is payable on land

middle-of-the-road ['mɪdl əv ðə 'rəʊd] *adjective (informal)* (policy) of the centre

Midsummer day [mɪd'sʌmə 'deɪ] *noun* 24th June: one of the four quarter days when rent is payable

militant ['mɪlitənt] *adjective & noun* (person) who very actively supports and works for a cause; *the speaker was shouted down by militant union members*

military ['mɪlɪtri] **1** *adjective* referring to the army; **military attaché** = army officer who is based in an embassy and reports on military affairs to his home government; **a period of military rule** = government by the army; *the country was ruled by a military government for nine years; the military dictatorship has agreed to return to civilian rule next year* **2** *noun* the **Military** = the Army

minibudget ['mɪnibʌdʒɪt] *noun* an interim budget

minimize ['mɪnɪmaɪz] *verb* **(a)** to make something seem to be very small and not very important; *do not minimize the risks involved; he always minimizes the difficulty of the projects he undertakes* **(b)** to reduce something to a minimum; *the new traffic system is intended to minimize accidents*

◊ **minimum** ['mɪnɪməm] **1** *noun* smallest possible quantity *or* price *or* number; *to keep expenses to a minimum; to reduce the risk of a loss to a minimum;* (NOTE: plural is **minima**) **2** *adjective* smallest possible; **minimum dividend** = smallest dividend which is legal and accepted by the shareholders; **minimum payment** = smallest payment necessary; **minimum sentence** = shortest possible sentence allowed in law for a certain offence; **minimum wage** = lowest hourly wage which a company can legally pay its workers

minister ['mɪnɪstə] *noun* **(a)** **Minister (of the Crown)** = member of a government who is in charge of a ministry; *a government* *minister; the Minister of Information or the Information Minister; the Minister of Foreign Affairs or the Foreign Minister; the Minister of Justice or the Justice Minister;* **Minister of State** = person who is in charge of a section of a government department **(b)** senior diplomat below the rank of ambassador;

COMMENT: in the USA, heads of government departments are called **secretary: the Secretary for Commerce;** in the UK, heads of government departments (see note below) are called **Secretary of State: the Secretary of State for Defence**

◊ **ministerial** [mɪnɪ'stɪərɪəl] *adjective* referring to a minister; *ministerial responsibilities; the ministerial car was waiting at the airport;* **ministerial tribunal** = tribunal set up by a government minister to hear appeals from local tribunals

◊ **Minister-President** ['mɪnɪstə 'prezɪdənt] *noun* title of the premier in one of the German Länder

◊ **ministry** ['mɪnɪstri] *noun* **(a)** department of state in the government; *he works in the Ministry of Finance or the Finance Ministry; he is in charge of the Ministry of Information or of the Information Ministry; a ministry official or an official from the ministry* **(b)** government; **during the Wilson ministry** = when the government headed by Prime Minister Wilson was in office

COMMENT: in Britain and the USA, important ministries are called **departments: the Department of Trade and Industry; the Commerce Department.** Note also that the UK does not have government departments called the 'Ministry of Justice' or 'Ministry of the Interior', and the duties of supervising the administration of justice and law and order fall to the Lord Chancellor's Office and the Home Office

minor ['maɪnə] **1** *adjective* less important; *minor expenditure; one of the minor departments in the government;* **a loss of minor importance** = not a very serious loss **2** *noun* person less than eighteen years old; *minors cannot vote in a general election*

◊ **minority** [maɪ'nɒrɪti] *noun* **(a)** being less than eighteen years old or time when someone is less than eighteen years old; *a person is not liable for debts contracted during his minority* **(b)** number or quantity which is less than half of the total; *a minority of council members opposed the chairman; two of the members of the Royal Commission disagreed with the others and submitted a minority report;* **minority government** = government which does not command an overall majority in the House of Commons; **minority shareholding** or **minority interest** = group of shares which are less than one half of the shares in a company; **minority shareholder** = person who owns a group of shares but less than half of the shares in a company; **in the minority** = being fewer than half; *the small parties are in the minority on the local council;* **blocking minority** = voting system in the EU Council, by which a proposal can be blocked if 26 out of a total of 87 votes are cast against; *compare* QUALIFIED MAJORITY **(c)** small group of people in a society; **ethnic minority** = group of people of one race in a country where most people are of another race

minute ['mɪnɪt] **1** *noun* **(a)** one sixtieth part of an hour; *the committee members cross-examined the witness for fifty minutes* **(b) minutes** = the record of what happened at a meeting; **to take the minutes** = to write notes of what happened at a meeting; **the chairman signed the minutes of the last meeting** = he signed them to show that they were a correct record of what was said and what decisions were taken; **this will not appear in the minutes of the meeting** = this is unofficial and will not be noted as having been said **(c)** note or document about a certain subject; *have you read his minute about the report? I have asked the Chief Education Officer to prepare a minute about the discussions* **2** *verb* to put something into the minutes of a meeting; *the chairman's remarks about the auditors were minuted;* **I do not want that to be minuted** or **I want that not to be minuted** = do not put that remark into the minutes of the meeting

◊ **minutebook** ['mɪnɪtbʊk] *noun* book in which the minutes of a meeting are kept

miscellaneous [ˌmɪsə'leɪnɪəs] *adjective* various *or* mixed *or* not all of the same sort; *miscellaneous items; a box of miscellaneous pieces of equipment; miscellaneous expenditure*

miscount ['mɪskaʊnt] **1** *noun* mistake in counting **2** [mɪs'kaʊnt] *verb* to count wrongly; *the votes were miscounted, so the ballot had to be taken again*

misgovern [mɪs'gʌvən] *verb* to govern badly

◊ **misgovernment** [mɪs'gʌvənmənt] *noun* governing badly

misinterpret [mɪsɪn'tɜːprɪt] *verb* to understand something wrongly; *the rioters misinterpreted the instructions of the police*

◊ **misinterpretation** [mɪsɪntɜːprɪ'teɪʃn] *noun* wrong interpretation *or* understanding of something; **clause which is open to misinterpretation** = clause which can be wrongly interpreted

mislead [mɪs'liːd] *verb* to make someone understand something wrongly; *the instructions in the document are quite misleading; the wording of the Bill is misleading and needs to be clarified; the minister misled the House in his statement on the affair;* (NOTE: misleading - misled)

misrepresent [mɪsreprɪ'zent] *verb* to report facts *or* statements *or* opinions wrongly; *the Minister complained that the TV news report had misrepresented him*

◊ **misrepresentation** [mɪsreprɪzen'teɪʃn] *noun* making a wrong statement, especially with the intention of persuading someone to enter into a contract

mission ['mɪʃn] *noun* (a) special purpose for which someone is sent somewhere; *his mission was to try to persuade the rebels to accept the government's terms* (b) group of people who go abroad for a special purpose; *a trade mission to Japan; the members of the government mission are staying in the embassy* (c) embassy *or* consulate *or* building where representatives of a foreign country work; *the crowd gathered outside the gates of the British Mission*

mistake [mɪs'teɪk] *noun* wrong action *or* wrong decision; **to make a mistake** = to do something wrong; *the shop made a mistake and sent the wrong items; there was a mistake in the address; she made a mistake in addressing the letter;* **by mistake** = in error *or* wrongly; *they sent the wrong items by mistake; she put my letter into an envelope for the Chairman by mistake*

misunderstanding [mɪsʌndə'stændɪŋ] *noun* mistake; *there was a misunderstanding over the date of the next meeting*

mob [mɒb] *noun* large violent crowd; *the embassy was burned down by a mob of students; the police fired on the mob of demonstrators;* **mob rule** = rule (of a town *or* country) by a mob

mobilize ['məʊbɪlaɪz] *verb* (a) to make civilians join the armed forces (in time of war) (b) to make people take decisions or protest about something; *the opposition is trying to mobilize public opinion against the draft legislation*

moderate 1 ['mɒdərət] *adjective* not extreme *or* not very large; *a moderate increase in government spending; she holds very moderate political views; we had only moderate success in our negotiations* **2** ['mɒdərət] *noun* person with moderate ideas *or* opinions; *the moderates were defeated by the extremists* **3** ['mɒdəreɪt] *verb* to make something less extreme; *the rebels were forced to moderate their demands*

◊ **moderation** [mɒdə'reɪʃn] *noun* (a) avoiding extremes *or* becoming less extreme; *the negotiators practised moderation in their dealings with the enemy* (b) reduction; *a moderation in the speed of political change*

modify ['mɒdɪfaɪ] *verb* to change *or* to make something fit a different use; *the chairman modified the organizational system; this is the new modified agreement; the car will have to be modified to pass the government tests*

◊ **modification** [mɒdɪfɪ'keɪʃn] *noun* change; *to make or to carry out modifications to the plan; we asked for modifications to the contract*

modus vivendi ['məʊdəs vɪ'vendi] *Latin phrase meaning* 'way of living'; informal agreement between parties (as between employers and workers, between Church and State) to exist peacefully together; *after years of confrontation, they finally have achieved a modus vivendi*

monarch ['mɒnək] *noun* royal ruler of a country, such as a king or queen or emperor

◊ **monarchic** *or* **monarchical** [mə'nɑːkɪk *or* mə'nɑːkɪkl] *adjective* referring to *or* in favour of a monarchy

◊ **monarchist** ['mɒnəkɪst] *noun* person who supports *or* believes in rule by a monarch

◊ **monarchy** ['mɒnəki] *noun* **(a)** rule by a king *or* queen; *the monarchy was overthrown in the revolution, and the king replaced by a president* **(b)** country ruled by a king or queen; *Belgium, Sweden and Britain are monarchies;* **constitutional monarchy** = monarchy where the king *or* queen has limited constitutional powers, and most power is in the hands of an elected legislature and the government is headed by a democratically elected Prime Minister

money ['mʌni] *noun* **(a)** coins and notes used for buying and selling; **danger money** = extra salary paid to workers in dangerous jobs; **paper money** = money in notes, not coins **(b) Money Bill** = (i) Bill which authorizes expenditure from the Exchequer; (ii) Bill which authorizes the levy of taxes; **money supply** = amount of money which exists in a country; **money markets** = markets for buying and selling short-term loans; **money rates** = rates of interest for borrowers or lenders **(c) money order** = document which can be bought for sending money through the post; **foreign money order** *or* **international money order** *or* **overseas money order** = money order in a foreign currency which is payable to someone living in a foreign country **(d)**

monies = sums of money; *monies owing to the company; to collect monies due*

◊ **moneylender** ['mʌnɪlendə] *noun* person who lends money at interest

monitor ['mɒnɪtə] **1** *noun* screen (like a TV screen) on a computer **2** *verb* to check *or* to examine how something is working well; *they are monitoring the new system of dealing with import controls; the whips were monitoring the progress of the bill through Parliament*

monopoly [mə'nɒpəli] *noun* situation where one person *or* company controls all the market in the supply of a product *or* right given to one person *or* company to control all the market in the supply of a product; *to have the monopoly of alcohol sales or to have the alcohol monopoly; the company has the absolute monopoly of imports of French wine;* **public monopoly** *or* **state monopoly** = situation where the state is the only supplier of a product or service (such as the Post Office, the Coal Board); **the Monopolies (and Mergers) Commission** = British body which examines takeovers and mergers to make sure that a monopoly is not being created; (NOTE: American English uses **trust** more frequently)

◊ **monopolize** [mə'nɒpəlaɪz] *verb* to create a monopoly *or* to get control of all the supply of a product

◊ **monopolization** [mənɒpəlaɪ'zeɪʃn] *noun* making a monopoly

Monroe doctrine ['mʌnrəʊ 'dɒktrɪn] *noun US* principle that the USA has an interest in preventing outside (especially European) interference in the internal affairs of other American states

> COMMENT: so called because it was first proposed by President Monroe in 1823

monthly ['mʌnθli] *adjective* happening every month; *the monthly council meeting will not be held in December; she paid off the debt in monthly instalments; he was ordered to pay a sum of money to his wife monthly*

moratorium [mɒrə'tɔːriəm] *noun* temporary stop, such as to repayments of money owed; *the banks called for a moratorium on payments; the government has instituted a moratorium on nuclear testing;* (NOTE: plural is **moratoria**)

morning hour ['mɔːnɪŋ 'auə] *noun US* period at the beginning of each day's sitting of Congress, given up to routine business

most-favoured nation (MFN)

['məust 'feɪvəd 'neɪʃn] *noun* country which has the best trade terms; **most-favoured-nation clause** = agreement between two countries that each will offer the other the best possible terms in commercial contracts

Mother of Parliaments ['mʌðə əv 'pɑːləmənts]] *noun* the British Parliament at Westminster

◊ **motherland** *or* **mother country** ['mʌðəlænd *or* 'mʌðə 'kʌntri] *noun* country of one's ancestors, especially a country from which colonists have emigrated

motion ['məuʃn] *noun* (a) moving about; **time and motion study** = study in an office *or* factory of the time taken to do certain jobs and the movements workers have to make to do them (b) proposal which will be put to a meeting for that meeting to vote on (such as a proposal to the House of Commons *or* Congress); *to propose or to move a motion; the meeting voted on the motion; to speak against or for a motion;* **the motion was carried** *or* **was defeated by 220 votes to 196** = the motion was approved *or* not approved; **to table a motion** = to put forward a proposal for discussion by putting details of it on the table at a meeting; **substantive motion** = motion which is complete in itself; **subsidiary motion** = motion which is related to a substantive motion (such as a motion for adjournment) (c) application to a judge in court, asking for an order in favour of the person making the application; **notice of motion** = document telling the other party to a case that an application will be made to the court

mould *or US* **mold** [məuld] *noun* form used to make a solid object by pouring liquid into it, and letting the liquid solidify; **to break the mould** = to reorganize something in a totally new way (as changing a country's political *or* economic system)

move [muːv] *verb* (a) to go from one place to another; *the company is moving from London Road to the centre of town; we have decided to move our factory to a site near the airport* (b) to ask a meeting to vote on a proposal *or* to propose formally that a motion be accepted by a meeting; *she moved the proposal for new street lighting; he moved that the accounts be agreed; I move that the meeting adjourn for ten minutes;* (NOTE: US English uses **move for: Congressman Smith moved for a certain measure to be considered**)

◊ **movable** *or* **moveable** ['muːvəbl] **1** *adjective* which can be moved; **movable property** = belongings and other objects which can be moved (as opposed to land) **2** *plural noun* **movables** = movable property

◊ **movement** ['muːvmənt] *noun* (a) changing position *or* going up or down; *movements in the money markets; cyclical movements of trade;* **movements of capital** = changes of investments from one country to another; **free movement of capital** = ability to transfer capital from country to country without any restrictions (b) group of people working towards the same aim, though not necessarily members of a political party; *the British Labour Movement; he was the founder of the movement for the reunification of his country*

◊ **mover** ['muːvə] *noun* (a) person who proposes a motion; *the mover of this resolution has said that it is a matter of public safety* (b) movers and shakers =; influential people who are actively engaged in changing society

MP [em'piː] = MEMBER OF PARLIAMENT, MILITARY POLICE

multi- ['mʌlti] *prefix* meaning many; *compare* BI-, UNI-

◊ **multilateral** [mʌltɪ'lætərəl] *adjective* (agreement) between more than two parties;

multilateral nuclear disarmament = agreement between several countries to stop making *or* holding nuclear weapons; *see also* BILATERAL, TRILATERAL, UNILATERAL

◊ **multilateralism** [mʌltɪˈlætərəlɪzm] *noun* political theory that nuclear power should only be reduced by several countries acting together

◊ **multilaterally** [mʌltɪˈlætərəli] *adverb* between more than two parties *or* countries; *the group of western nations agreed multilaterally to reduce import tariffs*

◊ **multinational** [mʌltɪˈnæʃnl] **1** *adjective* referring to several countries; *a multinational peacekeeping force* **2** *noun* large company operating in several countries

◊ **multiparty** [mʌltɪˈpɑːti] *adjective* where several political parties exist in the same country; *a multiparty democracy; multiparty elections will be held next year;* (NOTE: the opposite is a one-party system)

municipal [mjuːˈnɪsɪpl] *adjective* **(a)** referring to a town which has its own local g

overnment; *the finance department supervises the collection of municipal taxes; he works in the municipal offices; take your household rubbish to the municipal refuse dump* **(b)** municipal law = law which is in operation within a state, as opposed to international law

◊ **municipality** [mjuːnɪsɪˈpælɪti] *noun* town or city with an area of land round it, and its own local government

mutiny [ˈmjuːtɪni] **1** *noun* rebellion against someone in a position of authority, such as the officers in the army, the government and its ministers, etc. **2** *verb* to rebel against authority; *the soldiers mutinied and captured the castle*

◊ **mutineer** [mjuːtɪˈniːə] *noun* person who takes part in a mutiny

◊ **mutinous** [ˈmjuːtɪnəs] *adjective* rebellious, likely to mutiny; *the army was mutinous after they had not received any pay*

Nn

NAFTA = NORTH AMERICAN FREE TRADE AGREEMENT

name [neɪm] **1** *noun* word used to call a thing *or* a person; **brand name** = name of a particular make of product; **corporate name** = name of a large corporation **2** *verb* **(a)** to give someone a name *or* to mention someone's name; *the Secretary of State was named in the divorce case; (of the Speaker)* **to name a Member (of Parliament)** = to say that an MP has been guilty of misconduct by referring to the member by name (as opposed to the convention by which MPs are normally referred to by their constituency); *see also* SUSPEND **(b)** to appoint someone to a post; *Sir John Smith has been named as the new Ambassador in Paris*

nanny ['næni] *noun* woman employed to look after small children; **nanny state** = extreme welfare state, where the state provides everything for the citizens and tells the citizens how they should behave

nation ['neɪʃn] *noun* country and the people living in it

◊ **national** ['næʃnl] **1** *adjective* referring to a particular country; **National Anthem** = piece of music (sometimes with words which are sung to it) which is used to represent the nation officially, and is played at official ceremonies; *everyone stood up when the National Anthem was played; the British National Anthem is 'God Save the Queen';* **National Assembly** = lower body of legislature in many countries, including Benin, Botswana, Bulgaria, Burkina Faso, Cambodia, Central African Republic, Congo, Côte d'Ivoire, Cuba, Equatorial Guinea, France, Gabon, Guyana, Hungary, Kenya, South Korea, Kuwait, Laos, Lesotho, Mauritania, Mauritius, Namibia, Nicaragua, Pakistan, Quebec, Senegal, Seychelles, South Africa, Tanzania, Thailand, Togo and Vietnam **National Audit Office** = independent body, headed by the Comptroller and Auditor-General, which examines the accounts of government departments; **National Congress** = main body of legislature in Ecuador and Venezuela; **National Council** = upper house of legislature in Namibia, Nepal and Slovakia; **National Front** = right-wing political group, upholding racist principles; **National Guard** = the militia in each state of the USA, under the control of federal army; **National Insurance** = state insurance which pays for medical care, hospitals, unemployment benefits, etc.; **National Insurance contributions (NIC)** = money paid into the National Insurance scheme by the employer and the worker; **National Party** = political party representing the interests of the nation; **National People's Congress** = body of legislature in China; **gross national product (GNP)** = annual value of goods and services in a country including income from other countries; **National Savings** = savings scheme for small investors run by the Post Office (including a savings bank, savings certificates and premium bonds); **National Socialist Party** = the Nazi Party, a political party founded in Germany in 1919, and led by Adolf Hitler; **National State Assembly** = body of legislature in Sri Lanka **2** *noun* person who is a citizen of a state; *the government ordered the deportation of all foreign nationals*

◊ **nationalism** ['næʃnəlɪzm] *noun* **(a)** wanting independence for one's country **(b)** feeling of great pride in one's country

◊ **nationalist** ['næʃənəlɪst] *noun* **(a)**

person who wants his country to be independent; *a Welsh nationalist; the Scottish Nationalist Party* **(b)** person who is very proud of his country *or* feels his country is better than other countries

◊ **nationality** [næʃəˈnælɪti] *noun* being the citizen of a state; **he is of United Kingdom nationality** = he is a citizen of the United Kingdom; **he has dual nationality** = he is a citizen of two countries at the same time

◊ **nationalize** [ˈnæʃnəlaɪz] *verb* to put a privately-owned industry under state ownership and control; **nationalized industry** = industry which was once privately owned, but now belongs to the state

◊ **nationalization** [næʃnəlaɪˈzeɪʃn] *noun* taking over of a private industry by the state

◊ **Nationalrat** [næsɪnˈnælræt] *noun* **(a)** lower house of legislature in Austria **(b)** lower house of the federal legislature in Switzerland

◊ **National Union of Civil and Public Servants** trade union representing civil servants replaced by the Public Services, Tax and Commerce Union; *see also* ASSOCIATION OF FIRST DIVISION CIVIL SERVANTS, CIVIL AND PUBLIC SERVICES ASSOCIATION

◊ **nation-state** [ˈneɪʃn ˈsteɪt] *noun* country which is an independent political unit, usually formed of people with the same language and traditions; *the 19th century saw the rise of many European nation-states*

◊ **nationwide** [ˈneɪʃnwaɪd] *adjective* across all a country; *a nationwide opinion poll suggested that the Opposition is losing support in marginal constituencies*

◊ **native** [ˈneɪtɪv] *noun* **(a)** person who comes originally from a place; *he lives in London, but he is a native of Denmark* **(b)** *(derogative)* original inhabitant of a colony; *the colonists captured the natives and sold them into slavery* **(c)** *(humorous, of British EU officials)* **to go native** = to cease to represent the interests of the United Kingdom, and instead to start to believe in the usefulness of the European Union

NATO [ˈneɪtəʊ] = NORTH ATLANTIC TREATY ORGANIZATION

nature [ˈneɪtʃə] *noun* **(a)** kind *or* type; *what is the nature of the contents of the parcel? the nature of his business is not known* **(b)** the living environment

◊ **natural** [ˈnætʃrəl] *adjective* **(a)** found in the earth *or* not made by man; **natural resources** = raw materials (such as coal, gas, iron) which are found in the earth; **natural fibre** = fibre made from animal hair *or* plants, etc. **(b)** **natural child** = child (especially an illegitimate child) of a particular parent; **natural justice** = the general principles of justice; **natural parents** = actual mother and father of a child (as opposed to step-parents, adoptive parents, foster parents, etc.); **natural right** = general right which people have to live freely, usually stated in a written constitution

◊ **natural-born subject** [ˈnætʃrəlbɔːn ˈsʌbdʒekt] *noun* term formerly applied to a person born in the UK or a Commonwealth country who was a British citizen by birth

◊ **naturalization** [nætʃərəlaɪˈzeɪʃn] *noun* granting of citizenship of a state to a foreigner; *she has applied for naturalization; you must fill in the naturalization papers*

◊ **naturalize** [ˈnætʃərəlaɪz] *verb* to make someone a citizen (of another country)

◊ **naturalized** [ˈnætʃərəlaɪzd] *adjective* (person) who has become a citizen of another country; *he is a naturalized American citizen*

Nazi [ˈnɑːtsi] *adjective & noun* (i) (person) who was a member of the Nazi Party; (ii) *(used as criticism)* (person) with extreme right-wing views

◊ **Nazi Party** [ˈnɑːtsi ˈpɑːti] *noun* National Socialist Party, a political party founded in Germany in 1919, and led by Adolf Hitler

◊ **Nazism** [ˈnɑːtsɪzm] *noun* political ideology of Hitler and the Nazi Party

necessary [ˈnesəsəri] *adjective* which has to be done *or* which is needed; *it is necessary to fill in the form correctly; you must have all the necessary documentation before you apply for a subsidy*

◊ **necessarily** [nesəˈserəli] *adverb* in an unavoidable way; *the imposition of* *sanctions is not necessarily the only course open to the government*

◊ **necessitous** [nə'sesitəs] *adjective* poor; **necessitous clothing allowance** = clothing allowance for poor families

◊ **necessity** [nə'sesiti] *noun* (a) thing which is absolutely important, without which nothing can be done; **the necessities of life** = things which every person needs to live (b) situation which makes it impossible not to do something; **of necessity** = unavoidably; *the decision of the Law Lords must of necessity be impartial*

negative ['negətiv] **1** *adjective* saying 'No'; *his reply was in the negative;* **negative instrument** = form of SI which can be annulled by either House of Parliament **2** *verb* to say 'No' to a motion; **question negatived** = the motion was not carried (as for example at the Second Reading of a Bill); (NOTE: the opposite is **agreed to**)

neglect [nı'glekt] **1** *noun* (i) not doing a duty; (ii) lack of care towards someone *or* something; *the children had suffered from neglect;* **wilful neglect** = intentionally not doing something which it is your duty to do; (NOTE: no plural) **2** *verb* (a) to fail to take care of someone; *he neglected his three children* (b) **to neglect to do something** = to forget *or* omit to do something which has to be done; *he neglected to return his income tax form; she neglected to inform the committee of a possible conflict of interest*

negotiate [nı'gəusieit] *verb* to negotiate with someone = to discuss a problem formally with someone, so as to reach an agreement; *the management refused to negotiate with the union;* to negotiate terms and conditions *or* to negotiate a contract = to discuss and agree the terms of a contract; **negotiating committee** = group of representatives of management or unions who negotiate a wage settlement

◊ **negotiation** [nıgəusı'eıʃn] *noun* discussion of terms and conditions to reach an agreement; **contract under negotiation** = contract which is being discussed; **a matter for negotiation** = something which must be discussed before a decision is reached; to enter into negotiations *or* to start negotiations = to start discussing a problem; **to resume negotiations** = to start discussing a problem again, after talks have stopped for a time; **to break off negotiations** = to refuse to go on discussing a problem; **to conduct negotiations** = to negotiate

◊ **negotiator** [nı'gəusieitə] *noun* person who discusses with the aim of reaching an agreement

neighbour *or* **neighbouring state**
US **neighbor** *or* **neighboring state**
['neibə *or* 'neibəriŋ 'steit] *noun* country which is next to another, sharing a common border

nemine contradicente *or* **nem con**
['nemınei kɒntrædı'senti *or* 'nem'kɒn] *Latin phrase meaning* 'with no one contradicting': phrase used to show that no one spoke against the proposal, although some may have abstained in the vote; *the motion was adopted nem con; compare* UNANIMOUS

neo- ['niːəʊ] *prefix* meaning 'new' *or* 'in a new form'; *a neo-fascist movement; a neo-Nazi organization*

◊ **neocolonialism** [niːəʊkə'ləʊniəlızm] *noun* policy of controlling weaker countries as if they were colonies

net *or* **nett** [net] *adjective & adverb* (total) left after money has been deducted for tax, expenses, etc.; *the company's net profit was £10,000;* **net earnings** *or* **net income** *or* **net salary** = total earnings after tax and other deductions; **net gain** = total number of seats gained after deducting seats lost; *the government lost twenty seats and gained thirty one, making a net gain of eleven;* (NOTE: opposite is **gross**)

neutral ['njuːtrəl] **1** *adjective* (a) not aligned to one or other superpower block; not taking sides in a dispute; *the conference agreed to refer the dispute to a neutral power; the UN sent in neutral observers to observe the elections* (b) (country) which refuses to take part in wars *or* which does not join in a war; *during the Second World War, Switzerland and Sweden remained neutral; the navy was accused of having attacked* *neutral shipping; neutral states in the area have tried to bring an end to the war* **2** *noun* country which is neutral

◊ **neutralism** ['njuːtrəlɪzm] *noun* state of affairs where a country does not belong to one or other of the superpower groupings

◊ **neutrality** [njuˈtrælɪti] *noun* being neutral; **armed neutrality** = condition of a country which is neutral during a war, but maintains armed forces to defend itself

new [njuː] *adjective* recent *or* not old; **under new management** = with a new owner; **new issue** = issues of new shares *or* of new banknotes

◊ **New Democratic Party** ['njuː deməˈkrætɪk 'pɑːti] *noun* one of the main political parties in Canada, representing trade unions and workers' interests

◊ **New Labour** ['njuː 'leɪbə] *noun* the British Labour Party since 1995

◊ **news** [njuːz] *noun* information about things which have happened; **news agency** = office which distributes news to newspapers and television companies; **news release** = sheet giving information about a new event which is sent to newspapers and TV and radio stations so that they can use it

next [nekst] *adjective & adverb* **(a)** coming afterwards in time; *on Wednesday he arrived in London and the next day tried to assassinate the Prime Minister; the first item on the agenda is the minutes of the preceding meeting, and the next item is matters arising; the court's next decision was held to be unconstitutional* **(b)** nearest (in place); *the meeting was adjourned to the next committee room; the Finance Minister sat next to the Prime Minister*

NGO ['en dʒiː əu] = NON-GOVERNMENTAL ORGANIZATION

NIC = NATIONAL INSURANCE CONTRIBUTIONS

1922 Committee ['naɪntiːn twenti 'tuː kəˈmɪti] *noun* committee formed of all backbench Conservative MPs in the British House of Commons, who meet regularly and

question ministers and other party leaders; (NOTE: say 'the nineteen twenty-two committee')

COMMENT: the equivalent in the Labour Party is the Parliamentary Labour Party (PLP)

no [nəu] *noun* vote against a motion; *the proposal received a resounding 'No' vote;* **the Noes have it** = announcement that a motion has been defeated; **the Noes lobby** = lobby in the House of Commons where MPs pass to vote against a motion; *see also* AYE, DIVISION

noble ['nəubl] **1** *noun* person from a titled family **2** *adjective* high-minded, aristocratic; **he is of noble birth** = he comes from a titled family

◊ **nobleman, noblewoman** ['nəublmən *or* 'nəublwumən] *noun* member of a noble family

◊ **nobility** [nəˈbɪlɪti] *noun* all noble families, taken as a group

nod [nɒd] *verb* to move the head forwards (to show agreement); *when the chairman asked him if he would head the subcommittee, the treasurer nodded;* **the proposal went through on the nod** = the motion was carried without any discussion and no formal vote; **to nod through** = to agree that an MP's vote is recorded, even if he has not personally gone through the voting lobby (as when an MP is present in the Houses of Parliament, but is too ill to go into the chamber)

Nomenklatura [nɒmenkləˈtjuːərə] *noun* group of influential members of the party and their families, all holding leading posts in a Communist state

nominate ['nɒmɪneɪt] *verb* to suggest someone *or* to name someone for a job; *he was nominated as Labour candidate;* **to nominate someone to a post** = to appoint someone to a post without an election; **to nominate someone as proxy** = to name someone as your proxy

◊ **nomination** [nɒmɪˈneɪʃn] *noun* **(a)** act of nominating; *he was proposed for nomination as Labour candidate;*

nominations close at 10.00 a.m. = the last time for nominating someone is 10.00; **to lodge** *or* **file nomination papers** = to leave completed papers nominating someone as a candidate with the responsible officer **(b)** person nominated; *there were a number of nominations for the post of Deputy Leader*

◊ **nominee** [nɒmɪ'niː] *noun* person who has been nominated; *he is the Party leader's nominee for the post*

COMMENT: in the UK, a person who is nominated as a candidate for local or national elections, has to have the signatures of local residents as his sponsors, and (in the case of national elections) has to deposit a sum of money which he forfeits if he does not poll enough votes. In the United States, the executive (i.e. the President) nominates people to federal offices such as members of the Supreme Court or the cabinet, but these nominations are subject to confirmation by the Senate. Most nominations are accepted without discussion, but some are debated, and some are not confirmed. If the executive nominates someone to a federal post in one of the states without consulting the senators for that state, they can object to the nominee by saying that he is 'personally obnoxious' to them

---

non- [nɒn] *prefix* meaning not *or* without; **non-aggression** = not using force against another country; **a treaty of non-aggression** *or* **a non-aggression treaty** = treaty between two countries who promise not to attack each other; **non-aligned state** = country which is not part of one of the main superpower blocs; **non-member** = person who is not a member of an organization; *non-members may not vote at the AGM;* **non-proliferation treaty** = treaty to prevent the use of nuclear weapons spreading to countries which do not possess them

◊ **non-governmental organization (NGO)** [nɒngʌvən'mentəl ɔːɡənaɪ'zeɪʃn] *noun* organization (such as a pressure group *or* charity *or* voluntary agency) which is not funded by a government and which works on a local *or* national *or* international level

◊ **non-intervention** [nɒnɪntə'venʃən] *noun* not becoming involved in the internal affairs of another country; *the USA has followed a policy of non-intervention*

normal ['nɔːml] *adjective* usual *or* which happens regularly; *normal deliveries are made on Tuesdays and Fridays; now that the strike is over we hope to resume normal service as soon as possible;* **under normal conditions** = if things work in the usual way

◊ **normalize** ['nɔːməlaɪz] *verb* to make normal; *the government has tried to normalize relations with the coup leaders*

◊ **normally** ['nɔːməli] *adverb* in a normal way; *the House normally starts business at 2.30 in the afternoon*

north [nɔːθ] *adjective, adverb & noun* **(a)** one of the directions on the earth's surface, the direction facing away from the sun at midday and towards the North Pole **(b) the North** = the developed countries of the world; *(as opposed to* THE SOUTH*)* **North-South dialogue** = discussions between the developed nations and the underdeveloped countries

◊ **North American Free Trade Association (NAFTA)** *noun* trade association between Canada, Mexico and the United States

◊ **North Atlantic Treaty Organization (NATO)** *noun* organization set up in 1949 to link various countries in a common political and military alliance to provide mutual defence in the case of attack by Communist countries (the members are currently: Belgium, Canada, Denmark, France, Germany, Greece, Iceland, Italy, Luxembourg, the Netherlands, Norway, Portugal, Spain, Turkey, the UK, and the USA)

Northstead ['nɔːθsted] *see note at* CHILTERN HUNDREDS

note [nəʊt] **1** *noun* **(a)** short document *or* short piece of information; **advice note** = written notice to a customer giving details of goods ordered and shipped but not yet delivered; **cover note** = letter from an insurance company giving details of an insurance policy and confirming that the policy exists; **covering note** = letter sent with documents to explain why you are sending them **(b)** (i) short letter *or* short piece of information; (ii) official letter sent from one country to another; *the chairman of the meeting passed a note to the speaker telling him to hurry up; the chargé d'affaires presented a note to the Foreign Minister;* **to make a note of something** = to write something down in a few words; **to take notes of a meeting** = to write down details of a meeting in a few words, so that the details can be remembered later **(c) to take note of something** = to pay attention to something *or* to take something into account; *the Minister said he had taken note of the question; in reaching their decision, the committee took note of all the evidence* **(d)** bank note *or* currency note = piece of printed paper money **2** *verb* **(a)** to pay attention to something; *members of the House will note that the minister has not said that the tax will be abolished* **(b)** to write down details of something and remember them; *the reporter noted the address of the Minister in his notebook; your complaint has been noted*

◊ **notebook** ['nəutbuk] *noun* book for writing notes

◊ **notepad** ['nəutpæd] *noun* pad of paper for writing short notes

notice ['nəutis] *noun* **(a)** piece of written information; *the company secretary pinned up a notice about the pension scheme;* **copyright notice** = note in a book showing who owns the copyright and the date of ownership **(b)** official passing of information to someone especially warning that something may happen (such as a warning that a contract is going to end *or* that a motion of no confidence will be moved *or* that terms are going to be changed *or* that an employee will leave his job at a certain date *or* that a tenant must leave the property he is occupying) *the Leader of the Opposition has given notice that he will seek an emergency debate on the economy; the Minister asked for notice of the question;* **to give someone notice** *or* **to serve notice on someone** = to give someone a legal notice; **to give a tenant notice to quit** *or* **to serve a tenant with notice to quit** = to inform a tenant officially that he has to leave the premises by a certain

date; **she has handed in** *or* **given her notice** = she has said she will quit her job at a certain date; **period of notice** = time stated in the contract of employment which the worker or company has to allow between resigning or being dismissed and the worker actually leaving his job; **notice of motion** = warning given by an MP that he intends to propose a motion; *the member has given notice of a motion for next week;* **until further notice** = until different instructions *or* information are given; *the library will remain closed until further notice;* **at short notice** = with very little warning; **you must give seven days' notice of withdrawal** = you must ask to take money out of the account seven days before you want it; **to give notice of appeal** = to start official proceedings for an appeal to be heard

◊ **noticeboard** ['nəutisbɔ:d] *noun* board fixed to a wall where notices can be put up; *the list of polling stations is displayed on noticeboards in public libraries*

notify ['nəutifai] *verb* to declare *or* inform officially; *you must notify the council of your plan to demolish the house; he notified the Prime Minister of his intention to resign*

notwithstanding [nɒtwiθ'stændiŋ] *adverb & preposition* in spite of; *the debate proceeded notwithstanding the objections of the Opposition members* or *the objections of Opposition members notwithstanding;* (NOTE: can be used before or after the phrase to which it refers)

nuclear ['nju:kliə] *adjective* referring to nuclei, especially referring to the fission *or* fusion of nuclei; **nuclear bomb** = bomb whose destructive power is produced by nuclear fission *or* fusion; **nuclear energy** = energy created during a nuclear reaction, either fission *or* fusion, which, in a nuclear power station, produces heat which warms water and forms steam which runs a turbine to generate electricity; **nuclear power** = electricity generated by a nuclear power station; power generated by a nuclear reactor; **nuclear test** = test on a nuclear weapon; **nuclear test ban** = ban on testing of nuclear weapons; **nuclear war** = war using nuclear weapons; **nuclear waste** = radioactive waste from a nuclear reactor (including spent fuel rods and coolant); **nuclear weapon** = bomb *or* missile whose destructive power is produced by nuclear fission *or* fusion

◊ **nuclear-free zone** ['njuːkliə 'friː 'zəun] *adjective* area which will not allow the use of nuclear reactors *or* the use of nuclear weapons

null [nʌl] *adjective* with no meaning *or* which cannot legally be enforced; **the contract was declared null and void** = the contract was said to be no longer valid; **to render a decision null** = to make a decision useless *or* to cancel a decision

◊ **nullification** [nʌlɪfɪ'keɪʃən] *noun* act of making something invalid

◊ **nullify** ['nʌlɪfaɪ] *verb* to make something invalid *or* to cancel something *or* to state the something never existed

Number Eleven ['nʌmbə ɪ'levən] *noun* No 11, Downing Street, the official residence of the Chancellor of the Exchequer

Number Ten ['nʌmbə 'ten] *noun* No 10 Downing Street, the official residence of the British Prime Minister; **he is hoping to move into Number Ten after the election** = he is expecting to be elected Prime Minister; (NOTE: used to refer to the Prime Minister or to the government in general: **the plan was turned down by Number Ten; sources close to Number Ten say that the cabinet is near to agreement on the draft legislation; it is rumoured that Number Ten was annoyed at the story**)

numerical order [njuː'merɪkl 'ɔːdə] *noun* arrangement (of records) in order of their numbers; *the documents are filed in numerical order*

nuncio ['nʌnsiəu] *noun* **Papal Nuncio** = ambassador sent by the Pope to a country

Oo

oath [əʊθ] *noun* solemn legal promise that someone will say *or* write only what is true; **he was on oath** *or* **under oath** = he had promised in court to say what was true; **to administer an oath to someone** = to make someone swear an oath; **oath of allegiance** = (i) oath which is sworn to put the person under the orders *or* rules of a country; (ii) oath sworn by all MPs before they can take their seats in the House of Commons (or alternatively they can affirm); **to take the oath** = to swear allegiance to the Queen before taking one's seat as an MP; *after taking the oath, the new MP signs the test roll;* **commissioner for oaths** = solicitor appointed by the Lord Chancellor to administer affidavits which may be used in court; *see also* AFFIRM

obey [ə'beɪ] *verb* to do what someone asks you to do; *the crowd refused to obey the police instructions; he was asked to give an undertaking that he would obey the Speaker's ruling*

◊ **obedience** [ə'biːdiəns] *noun* doing what someone asks you to do; *the army swore obedience to the president; every citizen should show obedience to the laws of the state*

object 1 ['ɒbdʒekt] *noun* purpose; **objects clause** = section in a company's memorandum of association which says what work the company will do **2** [əb'dʒekt] *verb* to refuse to do something *or* to say that you do not accept something; *to object to a clause in a contract; the Opposition objected strongly to the Council's decision; the residents have objected to the siting of the new council offices;* **to object that** = to state reasons for not accepting something; *the Opposition leader objected that there had not been enough time for proper debate;* (NOTE: you object to something or someone)

◊ **objection** [əb'dʒekʃn] *noun* opposition to something; **to raise an objection to something** = to object to something; *the union delegates raised an objection to the wording of the agreement; the development plan has been given the go-ahead in spite of the objections of the residents*

◊ **objector** [əb'dʒektə] *noun* person who objects to something; **conscientious objector** = person who refuses to join the army when conscripted, because he feels that it is morally wrong

obnoxious [ɒb'nɒkʃəs] *see note at* NOMINATE

observe [əb'zɜːv] *verb* **(a)** to obey (a rule or a law); *failure to observe the correct procedure; all members of the association should observe the code of practice* **(b)** to watch *or* to notice what is happening; *officials have been instructed to observe the conduct of the election*

◊ **observance** [əb'zɜːvəns] *noun* doing what is required by a law; *the government's observance of international agreements*

◊ **observation** [ɒbzə'veɪʃn] *noun* **(a)** noticing what is happening **(b)** remark; *the Speaker made some observations about the conduct of the members of the House during the debate*

◊ **observer** [əb'zɜːvə] *noun* (i) person who observes; (ii) person who attends a meeting to listen but not to take part; *United Nations observers were stationed on the ceasefire line; two official observers attended the meeting; international observers were present during the general elections*

obsolete [ˈɒbsəliːt] *adjective* no longer used *or* no longer in force; *the law has been made obsolete by new developments in medicine*

obstruct [əbˈstrʌkt] *verb* to get in the way *or* to stop something progressing; to prevent the business (of the House of Commons) from continuing; *the parked cars are obstructing the traffic; MPs attempted to obstruct the passage of the Bill*

◊ **obstruction** [əbˈstrʌkʃn] **(a)** thing which gets in the way; *the car caused an obstruction to the traffic* **(b)** act of obstructing someone, such as preventing discussion of a Bill in Parliament; *the MPs were successful in their obstruction of the Bill*

◊ **obstructive** [əbˈstrʌktɪv] *adjective* which obstructs; *MPs complained of the obstructive behaviour of some right-wingers*

obtain [əbˈteɪn] *verb* **(a)** to get; *to obtain supplies from abroad; we find these items very difficult to obtain; to obtain an injunction against a company; he obtained control by jailing the Opposition leaders* **(b)** to be a rule *or* to have a legal status; *this right does not obtain in the House of Commons; a rule obtaining in international law*

occupation [ɒkjuˈpeɪʃn] *noun* invasion of a country by an army; **army of occupation** = army which invades a country and then stays there

◊ **occupy** [ˈɒkjupaɪ] *verb* to invade a place or building or country and stay there; *the protesters occupied the radio station; the enemy army occupied the south of the country;* **occupying forces** = armed forces which invade a country and then stay there

office [ˈɒfɪs] *noun* **(a)** British government department; **the Cabinet Office** = section of the British Civil Service which works for the Prime Minister and the Cabinet; **the Foreign Office** = ministry dealing with foreign affairs; **the Home Office** = ministry dealing with the internal affairs of the country, including the police and the prisons; **Office of Fair Trading** = government body which protects consumers against unfair or illegal

business **(b)** post *or* position; *he holds or performs the office of treasurer;* **in office** *or* **out of office** = working *or* not working in a position to which you have been appointed *or* elected; *during his year in office, he reorganized the whole department; the government was thrown out of office after the general election;* **high office** = important position or job; **the high offices of state** = the most important ministerial posts in the British government (the Prime Minister, the Foreign Secretary, the Chancellor of the Exchequer, the Home Secretary); **office of profit (under the Crown)** = government post which disqualifies someone from being a Member of Parliament (such as the Stewardship of the Chiltern Hundreds); **compensation for loss of office** = payment to a director who is asked to leave a company before his contract ends; **public office** = important position in a government department; *he has held public office for twenty years* **(c)** set of rooms where an organization works or where business is done; **branch office** = less important office, usually in a different town from the main office; **head office** *or* **main office** = office building where the board of directors works and meets; **registered office** = in Britain, the office address of a company which is officially registered with the Companies' Registrar and to which certain legal documents must normally be sent **(d)** **office block** *or* **a block of offices** = building which contains only offices; **office hours** = time when an office is open; *complaints can be received during normal office hours;* **office space** *or* **office accommodation** = space available for offices or occupied by offices; **office staff** = people who work in offices **(e)** room where someone works and does business; *come into my office; she has a pleasant office which looks out over the park; the Minister's office is on the third floor;* **information office** = office where someone can answer questions from the public

officer [ˈɒfɪsə] *noun* **(a)** **police officer** = policeman, a member of a police force; (NOTE: used in US English with a name: **Officers Smith and Jones went to the scene of the**

accident; GB English is **constable**) **(b)** person who has an official position, such as a person working in a local government department; *detailing the expenditure will necessitate a high cost in officer time; the report was drawn up by the officers on the instructions of the council; the members ignored the advice of the officers;* **Chief Officer** = person who is head of a department in a local authority (such as a Chief Education Officer, Chief Housing Officer), responsible to the Chief Executive; **customs officer** = person working for the customs; **fire safety officer** = person responsible for fire safety in a building; **information officer** = person who gives information about a company or about a government department to the public; **personnel officer** = person who deals with the staff and their conditions of employment, especially interviewing new workers; **training officer** = person who deals with the training of staff **(c)** official (usually unpaid) of a club *or* society, etc.; *the election of officers of an association*

◊ **Law Officers** [ˈlɔː ˈɒfɪsəz] *plural noun* the posts of Attorney-General and Solicitor-General (in England and Wales) and Lord Advocate and Solicitor-General (in Scotland)

official [əˈfɪʃl] **1** *adjective* **(a)** done because it has been authorized by a government department *or* organization; *on official business; he left official documents in his car; she received an official letter of explanation;* **official secret** = piece of information which is classified as important to the state and which it is a crime to reveal; **Official Secrets Act** = Act of Parliament which governs the publication of secret information relating to the state; **speaking in an official capacity** = speaking officially; **to go through official channels** = to deal with officials, especially when making a request **(b) Official Journal** = publication which lists the regulations, statutory instruments and directives of the EU; **the Official Receiver** = government official who is appointed to close down a company which is in liquidation or to deal with affairs of bankrupts; **official referee** = expert judge appointed by the High Court to try

complicated, usually technical, cases where specialist knowledge is required; **Official Report** = Hansard, the verbatim report of what is said and done in the House of Commons and House of Lords; **Official Solicitor** = solicitor who acts in the High Court for parties who have no one to act for them, usually because they are under a legal disability **(c)** done or approved by a director or by a person in authority; *this must be an official order - it is written on the department's notepaper;* **the strike was made official** = the local strike was approved by the main trade union office **2** *noun* person working in a central or local government department; *airport officials inspected the shipment; government officials stopped the import licence; the council members met with officials to discuss the implementation of the new policy;* **customs official** = person working for the customs; **high official** = important person in a government department; **minor official** = person in a low position in a government department; (NOTE: in GB English, a distinction is made between an official, who is an appointed employee of the government, and elected representatives. In US English, even the President is an official)

◊ **officialdom** [əˈfɪʃəldəm] *noun (usually as criticism)* officials working together in a set way; *the whole plan has been obstructed by officialdom*

◊ **officialese** [əfɪʃəˈliːz] *noun* language used in government documents and which can be difficult to understand

◊ **officially** [əˈfɪʃəli] *adverb* in an official way; *officially he knows nothing about the problem, but unofficially he has given us a lot of advice about it;* (NOTE: the opposite is **unofficial, unofficially**)

officio [əˈfɪsiəʊ] *see* EX OFFICIO

OHMS = ON HER MAJESTY'S SERVICE

Oireachtas [ˈerəxtəs] *noun* national parliament of Ireland, consisting of the president and two chambers, the lower is the Dáil Éireann and the upper, the Seanad Éireann

oligarchy ['ɒlɪɡɑːki] *noun* **(a)** government by a small group of people, who appoint members of their group as rulers **(b)** a small ruling group; *the country is ruled by an oligarchy called the 'fifteen families'* **(c)** state ruled by a small group

◊ **oligarch** ['ɒlɪɡɑːk] *noun* member of an oligarchy

◊ **oligarchical** *or* **oligarchic** ['ɒlɪɡɑːkɪkl or 'ɒlɪɡɑːkɪk] *adjective* referring to an oligarchy

ombudsman ['ɒmbədzmən] *noun* Parliamentary Commissioner, an official who investigates complaints by the public against government departments *or* other large organizations

COMMENT: there are in fact several ombudsmen: the main one is the Parliamentary Commissioner, but there are also others, such as the Health Service Commissioners, who investigate complaints against the Health Service, and the Local Commissioners or Local Government Ombudsmen who investigate complaints against local authorities. Although an ombudsman will make his recommendations to the department concerned, and may make his recommendations public, he has no power to enforce them. The Parliamentary Commissioner may only investigate complaints which are addressed to him through an MP, but the Local Government Ombudsmen can be approached directly, or through a local councillor; the member of the public first brings his complaint to his councillor or MP, and if they cannot get satisfaction from the department against which the complaint is made, then the matter is passed to the Ombudsman

omit [ə'mɪt] *verb* **(a)** to leave something out *or* not to put something in; *the secretary omitted the date when typing the contract* **(b)** not to do something; *the minister omitted to tell the Assembly that he had lost the documents;* (NOTE: **omitting - omitted**)

◊ **omission** [ə'mɪʃn] *noun* thing which has been omitted; **errors and omissions excepted** = words written on an invoice to show that the company has no responsibility for mistakes in the invoice

one minute speech ['wʌn 'mɪnɪt 'spiːtʃ] *noun US* short speech by a member of the House of Representatives on any subject at the beginning of the day's business

◊ **one-party state** ['wʌn 'pɑːti 'steɪt] *noun* country in which only one party is allowed to exist, although voters generally have a choice of candidates from that party at local level

open ['əʊpn] **1** *adjective* **(a)** at work; not closed; *the store is open on Sunday mornings; our offices are open from 9 to 6; they are open for business every day of the week* **(b)** ready to accept something; **the job is open to all applicants** = anyone can apply for the job; **open to offers** = ready to accept a reasonable offer; **the council is open to offers for the empty property** = the council is ready to discuss an offer which is lower than the suggested price **(c)** with no restrictions; **open cheque** = cheque which is not crossed and can be exchanged for cash anywhere; **open credit** = bank credit given to good customers without security up to a certain maximum sum; **open door policy** = trading policy, where a country allows trade on the same terms with all other countries; **open government** = system in which most decisions by government and most government records are available for any citizen to read; **open market** = market where anyone can buy or sell **2** *verb* **(a)** to start a new business working; *they have opened a new information office in the Embassy; we have opened a consulate in London* **(b)** to start work *or* to be at work; *the office opens at 9 a.m.; we open for business on Sundays* **(c)** to begin speaking; *the Minister opened for the Government; counsel for the prosecution opened with a description of the accused's family background;* **to open negotiations** = to begin negotiating **(d)** to start; to allow something to start; *she opened the debate with an attack on the government's record; he opened the discussions with a description of the planned development; the chairman opened the meeting at 10.30;* **to open a new building** = to declare officially that a building is open; *the Prime Minister opened the new tunnel;* **to open Parliament** = to start a new session of Parliament; *the Queen opened the new Parliament yesterday*

◊ **open-ended** * US

◊ **open-end** [ˌəʊpənˈendɪd or ˌəʊpənˈend] *adjective* with no fixed limit *or* with some items not specified; *an open-ended agreement*

◊ **opening** [ˈəʊpnɪŋ] **1** *noun* **(a)** act of starting a new business *or* a new branch *or* a new market *or* a new office; **the State Opening of Parliament** = ceremony when the Queen opens a new session of Parliament and reads the Queen's Speech **(b) opening hours** = hours when a shop *or* business is open **(c) job openings** = jobs which are empty and need filling; *there are openings for social workers in many parts of the country* **2** *adjective* at the beginning *or* first; *the chairman's opening remarks; the opening speech from the Home Secretary was interrupted by Opposition shouts*

◊ **openly** [ˈəʊpənli] *adverb* in an frank *or* open way; *he openly admitted that he had sold drugs; the government openly accused the rebels of taking hostages*

opinion [əˈpɪnjən] *noun* **(a) public opinion** = what people think about something; **to be of the opinion** = to believe *or* to think; *the chairman of the inquiry was of the opinion that if the evidence was doubtful the claim should be dismissed* **(b)** piece of expert advice; *the consultants gave their opinion; to ask an adviser for his opinion on a case; the members asked for the planning officer's opinion on the proposed building*

◊ **opinion poll** *or* **opinion research** [əˈpɪnjən ˈpəʊl or əˈpɪnjən rɪˈsɜːtʃ] *noun* asking a sample group of people what their opinion is, so as to guess the opinion of the whole population; *politicians take very careful note of the opinion polls in the run-up to a general election*

opponent [əˈpəʊnənt] *noun* person who is against you *or* who votes against what you propose; *the pro-nuclear group tried to discredit their opponents in the debate*

oppose [əˈpəʊz] *verb* to try to stop something happening; to be *or* to vote against something; *a minority of committee members opposed the motion; we are all opposed to the government's plan; the Speaker opposed the opposition's application for an adjournment;* **opposed business** = matters for discussion in the House of Commons which an MP objects to; **the police opposed bail** *or* **opposed the granting of bail** = the police said that bail should not be granted to the accused; *compare* UNOPPOSED

◊ **opposition** [ɒpəˈzɪʃn] *noun* **(a)** action of trying to stop something *or* of not agreeing to something; *there was considerable opposition to the plan for reorganizing the local boundaries; the voters showed their opposition to the government by voting against the proposal in the referendum* **(b) the Opposition** = (i) the largest political party which opposes the government; (ii) group of parties which oppose the government; *the Opposition tried to propose a vote of censure on the Prime Minister; the Opposition spokesman* **or** *the spokesman for the Opposition answered the Minister's allegations;* **Leader of the Opposition** *or* **Opposition Leader** = head of the largest political party opposing the government; **Opposition Day** = day on which a debate is held on a subject chosen by the Opposition

oppress [əˈpres] *verb* to rule cruelly and unfairly, especially by limiting the personal freedom of the citizens; *the dictator has stayed in power by using the army and police force to oppress the people*

◊ **oppression** [əˈpreʃn] *noun* cruel and unfair rule and control

◊ **oppressive** [əˈpresɪv] *adjective* cruel, using oppression; *under the dictator's oppressive regime, the ordinary citizens were afraid to speak out against the system*

◊ **oppressor** [əˈpresə] *noun* ruler or enemy country which oppresses; *the people rose in revolution to overthrow their oppressors*

opt out [ˈɒpt ˈaʊt] *verb* to decide not to join a group; *the UK has opted out of some provisions of the Maastricht Treaty*

◊ **opt-out** ['ɒptaʊt] *noun* decision not to take part in something; *the British opt-out of the social chapter*

order ['ɔːdə] **1** *noun* **(a)** general state of calm, where everything is working as planned; *there was a serious breakdown of law and order;* **public order** = situation were the general public is calm *or* where there are no riots **(b)** official command asking someone to do something; *on the orders of the Chief Constable, the demonstrators dispersed; the factory was sold by order of the receiver;* **court order** = command (which has no bearing on the final decision in a case) made by a court for someone to do something; *the prisoner was removed by order of the court;* **interim order** = order of a court which has effect while a case is still being heard; **preservation order** = court order which prevents an old building from being knocked down *or* a tree from being cut down **(c) orders** = legislation made by ministers, under powers delegated to them by Act of Parliament, but which still have to be ratified by Parliament before coming into force; **Order in Council** = legislation made by the Queen in Council, which is allowed by an Act of Parliament and which does not have to be ratified by Parliament **(d)** arrangement of records (filing cards, invoices, etc.); **alphabetical order** = arrangement by the letters of the alphabet (A, B, C, etc.); **chronological order** = arrangement by the order of the dates; **numerical order** = arrangement by numbers **(e)** arrangement of business in the House of Commons; **order book** = list showing the House of Commons business for each day of the rest of the term of Parliament; **order paper** = agenda of business to be discussed each day in the House of Commons; **order of the day** = matter which the House of Commons has decided will be discussed on a certain day **(f) standing orders** = rules *or* regulations governing the way in which a meeting *or* a debate in Parliament *or* a local council is conducted; **to call a meeting to order** = to start proceedings officially; **to bring a meeting to order** = to get a meeting back to discussing the agenda again (after an interruption); **'order! order!'** = call by the Speaker of the House of Commons to bring the meeting to order; **point of order** = question relating to the way in which a meeting is being conducted; *he raised a point of order; on a point of order, Mr Chairman, can this committee approve its own accounts? the meeting was adjourned on a point of order* **(g)** working arrangement; **machine in full working order** = machine which is ready and able to work properly; **the telephone is out of order** = the telephone is not working; **is all the documentation in order?** = are all the documents valid and correct? **(h)** official request for goods to be supplied; *to give someone an order or to place an order with someone for twenty filing cabinets;* **to fill** *or* **to fulfil an order** = to supply items which have been ordered; **purchase order** = official paper which places an order for something; **items available to order only** = items which will be made only if someone orders them **(i)** document which allows money to be paid to someone; *he sent us an order on the Chartered Bank;* **banker's order** *or* **standing order** = order written by a customer asking a bank to make a regular payment; **money order** = document which can be bought for sending money through the post **2** *verb* **(a)** to tell someone to do something; *he ordered the police to search the premises; the government ordered the army to occupy the radio station* **(b)** to ask for goods to be supplied; *to order twenty filing cabinets to be delivered to the warehouse; they ordered a new Rolls Royce for the ambassador* **(c)** to put in a certain way; *the address list is ordered by country; that filing cabinet contains personal records ordered by surname*

ordinance ['ɔːdɪnəns] *noun* **(a)** special decree of a government **(b)** *US* rule made by a municipal authority, and effective only within the jurisdiction of that authority

ordinary ['ɔːdnri] *adjective* normal *or* not special; **ordinary member** = person who pays a subscription to belong to a club *or* group; **ordinary resolution** = resolution which can be passed by a simple majority; **ordinary shares** = normal shares in a company, which have no special benefits or restrictions

◊ **ordinarily** ['ɔːdnrəli] *adverb* normally *or* usually; **ordinarily resident** = usually resident in a certain country

organize ['ɔːɡənaɪz] *verb* to arrange (a meeting *or* a business *or* a demonstration) so that it is run properly and efficiently; **organized labour** = workers who are members of trade unions

◊ **organization** [ɔːɡənaɪˈzeɪʃn] *noun* **(a)** way in which something is arranged; *the organization of a protest meeting; the organization of an appeal to the House of Lords* **(b)** group which is organized for a purpose; *he runs an organization for the rehabilitation of criminals*

Országgyülés [ɒrˈʃæɡjuːlis] *noun* body of legislature in Hungary

outbreak ['aʊtbreɪk] *noun* sudden start; *the outbreak of hostilities in the region*

outcome ['aʊtkʌm] *noun* result; *we are waiting for the outcome of the enquiry; the outcome of the debate was in doubt*

outcry ['aʊtkraɪ] *noun* loud public protest

Outer House ['aʊtə 'haʊs] *noun* part of the Scottish Court of Session, formed of five judges

outgoing [aʊt'ɡəʊɪŋ] *adjective* (person) who is about to leave office; *the outgoing president*

outlaw ['aʊtlɔː] **1** *noun* old term for a person who was thrown out of society as a punishment **2** *verb* to say that something is unlawful; *the government has proposed a bill to outlaw drinking in public*

outline ['aʊtlaɪn] **1** *noun* general description, without giving many details; *they drew up the outline of a plan or an outline plan;* **outline planning permission** = general permission to build a property on a piece of land, but not final because there are no details **2** *verb* to make a general description; *the chairman outlined the association's plans for the coming year*

outreach ['aʊtriːtʃ] *noun* services provided for members of the public outside a local government department offices; **outreach worker** = social worker who visits people in their homes, etc.

outright ['aʊtraɪt] *adverb* & *adjective* completely; **to purchase something outright** *or* **to make an outright purchase** = to buy something completely, including all rights in it

outside [aʊt'saɪd] *adjective* & *adverb* not in a company's office or building; **to send work to be done outside** = to send work to be done in other offices; **outside office hours** = when the office is not open; **outside line** = line from an internal office telephone system to the main telephone exchange

outstanding [aʊt'stændɪŋ] *adjective* **(a)** extremely good; *the mayor presented awards for outstanding services to the community* **(b)** not yet paid *or* completed; **outstanding debts** = debts which are waiting to be paid; **matters outstanding from the previous meeting** = questions which were not settled at the previous meeting

outvote [aʊt'vəʊt] *verb* to defeat in a vote; **the chairman was outvoted** = the majority voted against the chairman

Oval Office ['əʊvl 'ɒfɪs] *noun* room in the White House which is the personal office of the President of the United States; (NOTE: also used to mean the President himself: the Oval Office was not pleased by the attitude of the Senate)

over- ['əʊvə] *prefix* meaning too much

overall [əʊvə'rɔːl] *adjective* covering everything; *the Chief Executive has overall responsibility for running the council's affairs;* **overall majority** = majority of votes *or* seats, which is more than all the opposition put together; *the government had an overall majority of two; after the election, the ruling coalition lost its overall majority*

overestimate [əʊvə'estɪmeɪt] *verb* to think something is larger *or* worse than it really is; *the government tends to* *overestimate the size of the problem; the finance officers have overestimated the budget deficit*

over-populated   [əuvə'pɒpjuleɪtɪd] *adjective* having too many people

overrepresent [əuvəreprɪ'zent] *verb* to give more representation to (someone); *the present system tends to overrepresent the majority party; males are overrepresented in the House of Commons*

override [əuvə'raɪd] *verb* to pay no attention to; to be more important than; *the President vetoed the bill, but Congress overrode his veto; the appeal court overrode the decision of the lower court;* **overriding interest** = interest which comes before that of another party; *his wife established an overriding interest in the property against the bank's charge on it;* (NOTE: **overriding - overrode - has overridden)**

COMMENT: if the President of the USA disapproves of a bill sent to him by Congress for signature, he can send it back with objections within ten days of receiving it. Then if the Congress votes with a two-thirds majority in both Houses to continue with the bill, the bill becomes law and the President's veto is overridden

overrule [əuvə'ru:l] *verb* **(a)** *(in a meeting)* not to allow something; *Mr Smith tried to object, but his objection was overruled by the chairman; the committee overruled the decision made by the officers* **(b)** *(of a higher court)* to set a new precedent by deciding a case on a different principle from one laid down by a lower court

overspend [əuvə'spend] *verb* to spend more money than is allowed; *the government has criticized the councils for overspending;*

the department has overspent its budget by 20%; (NOTE: **overspending - overspent)**

overthrow 1 [əuvə'θrəu] *verb* to remove (a government) suddenly from power; *the regime was overthrown in a military coup* **2** ['əuvəθrəu] *noun* sudden removal of a government; *the army was involved in the overthrow of the president*

overwhelm [əuvə'welm] *verb* to to defeat completely

◊ **overwhelming**   [əuvə'welmɪŋ] *adjective* very large; *the government has an overwhelming majority in the lower house*

own [əun] *verb* to have *or* to possess; **a wholly-owned subsidiary** = a subsidiary which belongs completely to the parent company; **a state-owned industry** = industry which is nationalized

◊ **owner** ['əunə] *noun* person who owns something; **sole owner** = person who owns something alone; **owner-occupier** = person who owns and lives in a house; **goods sent at owner's risk** = situation in which it is the owner of the goods who has to insure them while they are being shipped

◊ **ownership** ['əunəʃɪp] *noun* act of owning something; **collective ownership** = situation in which a business is owned by the workers who work in it; **common ownership** *or* **ownership in common** = ownership of a company *or* of a property by a group of people who each own a part; **joint ownership** = situation in which two or more persons own the same property; **public ownership** *or* **state ownership** = situation in which an industry is nationalized; *the company has been put into state ownership;* **private ownership** = situation in which a company is owned by private shareholders; **the ownership of the banks has passed to the state** = the state has become the owner of the banks; (NOTE: no plural)

Pp

Pacific Ocean [pə'sıfık 'əʊʃn] *noun* large sea between the Americas and Asia and Australasia; **countries of the Pacific Rim** = countries around the edge of the Pacific, such as Japan, Singapore, Malaysia, Australia, New Zealand, Chile

pacifism ['pæsıfızm] *noun* policy that rejects violence and proposes that disputes should be solved by non-violent means

◊ **pacifist** ['pæsıfıst] *noun & adjective* (person) supporting pacifism

◊ **pacify** ['pæsıfaı] *noun* to make (a country) peaceful

pack [pæk] *verb* to fill (a committee) with members who are sympathetic to your views; *the left-wing group packed the general purposes committee with activists*

pact [pækt] *noun* agreement between two parties *or* countries; *the countries in the region signed a non-aggression pact; the two minority parties signed an electoral pact not to oppose each other in certain constituencies*

page [peɪdʒ] *noun* young person employed in the US Congress on junior administrative work

paid-up member ['peɪd ʌp 'membə] *noun* person who has paid the subscription to be a member of a political party *or* other organization; *see also* CARD

pair ['peə] **1** *noun* agreement between two MPs from opposite sides of the House of Commons not to vote on a motion, so allowing them both to be away from the House during a vote; *he was not able to find a pair, so had to come back from Paris to attend the debate* **2** *verb* to arrange for two

MPs from opposite sides of the House of Commons to be away from the House at the same time, so that each one's absence cancels out the other's; *he was paired with Mr Smith*

palace ['pæləs] *noun* large house, where a ruler lives; *the Queen lives in Buckingham Palace; guards surrounded the Presidential Palace;* **the Palace of Westminster** = the Houses of Parliament, together with the area round them

pamphlet ['pæmflət] *noun* small booklet, often about a political issue

pan- [pæn] *prefix* meaning 'covering all'; **pan-African** *or* **pan-American** = covering all Africa *or* all America

papal ['peɪpl] *see* NUNCIO

paper ['peɪpə] *noun* **(a)** thin material for writing on or for wrapping; **carbon paper** = sheet of paper with a black coating on one side used in a typewriter to make a copy; **duplicating paper** = special paper to be used in a duplicating machine; **headed paper** = notepaper with the name and address of a person *or* organization printed on it; **lined paper** = paper with thin lines printed on it; **typing paper** = thin paper for use in a typewriter; (NOTE: no plural) **(b)** outline report; *the Treasurer asked his deputy to write a paper on new funding; the planning department prepared a paper for the committee on the possible uses of the site; see also* GREEN PAPER, WHITE PAPER **(c) order paper** = printed agenda of business to be discussed each day in the House of Commons **(d) papers** = documents (in general); *the councillor sent me the relevant papers on the case; the police have sent the* *papers on the fraud to the Director of Public Prosecutions; he has lost the customs papers; the office is asking for the VAT papers* **(e) on paper** = as explained in writing, but not tested in practice; *on paper the system is ideal, but we have to see it working before we will sign the contract;* **paper loss** = loss made when an asset has fallen in value but has not been sold; **paper profit** = profit made when an asset has increased in value but has not been sold **(f) paper money** *or* **paper currency** = banknotes

◊ **paperwork** ['peɪpəwɜːk] *noun* office work, such as writing memoranda and filling in forms; (NOTE: no plural)

paragraph ['pærəgrɑːf] *noun* group of several lines of writing which makes a separate section; *the first paragraph of your letter or paragraph one of your letter; please refer to the second paragraph in clause three of the Bill; the committee voted to amend the final paragraph in the report*

pardon ['pɑːdn] **1** *noun* official ending of a prison sentence which a criminal is serving for a crime **2** *verb* to end the prison sentence which a criminal is serving; *the political prisoners were pardoned by the President*

Paris ['pærɪs] *see* TREATY

parish ['pærɪʃ] *noun* area which surrounds a church and which is served by that church; **parish council** = smallest unit of local government, representing a group of at least 200 people in a village or small town; **parish meeting** = meeting which must be held once a year in a parish and which all electors in the parish may attend; **parish pump politics** = local politics, concerning only minor local issues and the people in the parish

parliament ['pɑːləmənt] *noun* elected group of representatives who form the legislative body which votes the laws of a country (in the UK formed of the House of Commons and House of Lords); **Act of Parliament** = decision which has been approved by Parliament and has received the Royal Assent and so becomes law; **contempt of Parliament** = conduct which may bring

the authority of Parliament into disrepute; **the Houses of Parliament** = (i) the building where the British Parliament meets, containing the chambers of the House of Commons and the House of Lords; (ii) the British Parliament; **Member of Parliament (MP)** = person elected to represent a constituency in parliament; **Mother of Parliaments** = the British Parliament at Westminster; **the European Parliament** = parliament made up of delegates (MEPs or Euro-MPs) elected by the voters of each member state of the EU; (NOTE: often used without 'the': Parliament voted to abolish the death penalty; this is one of the Bills which will shortly be coming before Parliament)

◊ **parliamentarian** [pɑːləmən'teəriən] *noun* **(a)** *GB* member of one of the Houses of Parliament; *a delegation of British parliamentarians was invited to visit Canada* **(b)** *US* one of two officials of Congress (the House Parliamentarian and the Parliamentarian of the Senate) who attend all debates and advise the presiding officers on procedure, precedents and committee jurisdiction

◊ **parliamentary** [pɑːlə'mentəri] *adjective* referring to parliament; **parliamentary agents** = persons (usually solicitors *or* barristers) who advise private individuals who wish to promote a Bill in Parliament; **Parliamentary Commissioner (for Administration)** = the Ombudsman, the official who investigates complaints by the public against government departments; *see comment at* OMBUDSMAN **parliamentary counsel** *or* **parliamentary draftsman** = lawyer who is responsible for drafting Bills going before Parliament; **Parliamentary Labour Party (PLP)** = group formed of all the Labour backbench MPs (the Conservative equivalent is the 1922 Committee); **Parliamentary Private Secretary (PPS)** = young MP attached personally to a Secretary of State or Prime Minister, who acts as a general helper in Parliament; **Parliamentary privilege** = right of a Member of Parliament *or* Member of the House of Lords to speak freely to the House without possibility of being sued for slander

◇ **Parliamentary Secretary** *or*
Parliamentary Under-Secretary

[pɑːləˈmentəri ˈsektrətri or ˈʌndə ˈsekrətri]
noun government member (an MP *or* a
member of the House of Lords) who works in
a department under a Secretary of State or
Minister of State; (NOTE: to avoid confusion,
they are called Parliamentary Under-Secretaries in
departments where the head of the department is
a Secretary of State)

partisan [pɑːtɪˈzæn] *noun* **(a)** person who
supports a policy forcefully; *she's a partisan
of having more women Members of
Parliament* **(b)** armed supporter of a political
faction, fighting against the ruling
government

partition [pɑːˈtɪʃn] *noun* dividing up of a
country *or* of land

party [ˈpɑːti] *noun* **(a) political party** =
organized group of people who believe a
country should be run in a certain way; **the
party faithful** = loyal ordinary members of a
party; **the party line** = official policy of a
political party, which must be followed by its
members and supporters; **to toe the party
line** = to say what the party expects you to
say *or* not to have a different view from the
official party policy; *he was expelled from
the party for refusing to toe the party line;*
party politics = system in which the political
life of the country is run by large powerful
parties, who make their supporters toe the
party line, and where obedience to the party
is more important than following its
principles; *(in a two-party system)* **third
party** = another, usually smaller, political
party, beside the main two; **a third party
candidate** = candidate for one of the smaller
parties **(b) working party** = group of experts
who study a problem; *the government has
set up a working party to study the problems
of industrial waste; Professor Smith is the
chairman of the working party on drug
abuse* **(c)** organization *or* person involved in a
legal dispute *or* legal agreement *or* crime; *the
council is not a party to the agreement* **(d)**
third party = any third person, in addition to
the two main parties involved in proceedings
or a contract; the other person involved in an
accident; **third party insurance** *or* **third**

party policy = insurance which pays
compensation if someone who is not the
insured person incurs loss or injury

◇ **party list system** [ˈpɑːti ˈlɪst sɪstəm]
noun electoral system in some European
countries;   *see   also*   **ADDITIONAL
MEMBER**

> COMMENT: under the list system, each
> party draws up a list of candidates, and
> the electors vote for the party list, not for
> individual candidates. The Parliament is
> then formed of candidates from each
> party's list in proportion to the total
> number of votes which the party has
> received. Elections to the European
> Parliament are carried out in the same
> way in these countries

pass [pɑːs] **1** *noun* permit to allow someone
to go into a building *or* area; *you need a pass
to enter the Ministry offices; all members of
staff must show a pass* **2** *verb* **(a)** to approve;
to vote to make a law; *Parliament passed the
Bill which has now become law; the
Director of Finance has to pass an invoice
before it is paid; the loan has been passed by
the council; the Congress passed the bill
over the president's veto;* **to pass a
resolution** = to vote to agree to a proposal;
*the meeting passed a resolution that salaries
should be frozen* **(b)** to be successful; *he
passed his typing test; she has passed all her
exams and now is a qualified solicitor*

passage [ˈpæsɪdʒ] *noun* **(a)** act of passing;
*they tried to obstruct the Bill's passage
through the House of Commons* **(b)** piece of
text; *the censor removed several passages
from the newspaper report*

passport [ˈpɑːspɔːt] *noun* official
document proving that you are a citizen of a
country, which you usually have to show
when you travel from one country to another;
*we had to show our passports at the customs
post; his passport is out of date; the passport
officer stamped my passport;* **passport
holder** = person who holds a passport; *she is
a British passport holder*

patent [ˈpeɪtənt] **1** *noun* **(a)** official
document showing that a person has the
exclusive right to make and sell an invention;

to take out a patent for a new type of light bulb; to apply for a patent for a new invention; he has received a grant of patent for his invention; **patent applied for** *or* **patent pending** = words on a product showing that the inventor has applied for a patent for it; **to forfeit a patent** = to lose a patent because payments have not been made; **to infringe a patent** = to make and sell a product which works in the same way as a patented product and not pay a royalty for it; **patent agent** = person who advises on patents and applies for patents on behalf of clients; **to file a patent application** = to apply for a patent; **patent holder** = person who has been granted a patent; **infringement of patent** *or* **patent infringement** = act of illegally using *or* making *or* selling an invention which is patented without the permission of the patentee; **patent number** = reference number given to a patented invention; **Patent Office** = government office which grants patents and supervises them; **patent specification** = full details of an invention which is the subject of a patent application **(b) letters patent** = official document from the Crown, which gives someone the exclusive right to do something (such as when someone is made a peer *or* when someone is granted a patent to make and sell an invention); *he received letters patent creating him Baron Smith* **2** *verb* **to patent an invention** = to register an invention with the patent office to prevent other people from copying it **3** *adjective* obvious *or* clear to see; *the reason for the Chancellor's action is patent*

◊ **patented** ['peɪtəntɪd] *adjective* which is protected by a patent

◊ **patentee** [peɪtən'tiː] *noun* person who has been granted a patent

patently ['peɪtəntli] *adverb* clearly *or* obviously; *he made a patently false statement to the committee*

patrial ['peɪtrɪəl] *noun* person who has the right to live in the UK because he has close family ties with the country (for example, if his grandfather was British)

patriarchy ['peɪtrɪɑːki] *noun* system of government by the eldest male of the ruling group

◊ **patriarchal** [peɪtrɪ'ɑːkl] *adjective* referring to a patriarchy

patriate [pætrɪ'eɪt] *verb* to transfer control to the home country; *the Canadian constitution was formally patriated in 1982; compare* EXPATRIATE, REPATRIATE

patriot ['peɪtrɪət] *noun* person who is very proud of his country

◊ **patriotic** [pætrɪ'ɒtɪk] *adjective* referring to patriotism; *it is every citizen's patriotic duty to learn the words of the National Anthem*

◊ **patriotism** ['peɪtrɪətɪzm] *noun* feeling of great pride in one's country; *compare* CHAUVINISM

patronage ['pætrənɪdʒ] *noun* right to give government posts *or* honours to people; *the Prime Minister has considerable patronage;* **patronage secretary** = official of the Prime Minister's staff who deals with appointments to posts

PC ['piː'siː] = PERSONAL COMPUTER, POLICE CONSTABLE, POLITICAL CORRECTNESS, PRIVY COUNCIL, PRIVY COUNCILLOR

peace [piːs] *noun* **(a)** being quiet *or* calm; calm existence; **breach of the peace** = creating a disturbance which is likely to annoy people **(b)** state of not being at war; *after six years of civil war, the country is now at peace; the peace treaty was signed yesterday; both sides claimed the other side broke the peace agreement*

---

there never was a good war or a bad peace
                              Benjamin Franklin

---

peer ['pɪə] *noun* **(a)** member of one of the five ranks of noblemen in the House of Lords (Duke, Marquess, Earl, Viscount, or Baron); **peer of the realm** *or* **hereditary peer** = member of the House of Lords who has inherited the title and will pass it on to his heir; **life peer** = member of the House of Lords who is appointed for life and whose title does not pass to another member of the family **(b)** person who is in the same group *or* rank as another; **peer group** = group of persons of the same level *or* rank; *the Magna Carta gave every free man the right to be tried by his peers; children try to behave like other members of their peer group*

◊ **peerage** ['pɪərɪdʒ] *noun* **(a)** all peers, taken as a group **(b)** position of being a peer; *three new peerages were created in the New Year's Honours List; he was elevated to the peerage in 1993*

◊ **peeress** ['pɪərəs] *noun* female peer; wife of a peer

COMMENT: a peer is disqualified from standing for election to the House of Commons, but can renounce the peerage in order to be able to stand for election as an MP

---

penal ['pi:nl] *adjective* referring to punishment; **penal code** = set of laws governing crime and its punishment; **penal laws** *or* **the penal system** = system of punishments relating to different crimes

◊ **penalize** ['pi:nəlaɪz] *verb* to punish; to fine; *the government penalized councils for overspending; the contractors were penalized for late delivery*

penalty ['penəltɪ] *noun* punishment (such as a fine) which is imposed if something is not done *or* if a law is not obeyed; *the penalty for carrying an offensive weapon is a fine of £2,000 and three months in prison;* **death penalty** = sentence of a criminal to be executed; *the president has introduced the death penalty for certain crimes against the state;* **penalty clause** = clause which lists the penalties which will be imposed if the terms of the contract are not fulfilled; *the contract contains a penalty clause which fines the company 1% for every week the completion date is late*

pending ['pendɪŋ] **1** *adjective* waiting; being waited for; *the decision on the application is pending;* **patent pending** = words printed on a product to show that its inventor has applied for a grant of patent; **pending file** = file containing documents referring to problems which are waiting for a

decision to be made **2** *adverb* while waiting for; *pending the council's decision, rates should be paid in the normal way; pending advice from our lawyers, we sent a simple letter of acknowledgement*

Pentagon ['pentəgən] *noun* building housing the Department of Defense in Washington; (NOTE: the building has five sides, hence the name, which is also used to mean the Defense Department itself: **Pentagon officials stated that the supply of arms was illegal; sources close to the Pentagon refused to comment on the story**)

people ['pi:pl] *noun* **(a)** persons, men and women; *most people voted for the new constitution* **(b)** all the members of a nation *or* racial group; *the President promised to serve the People; the government of the people, by the people, for the people;* (NOTE: takes a plural verb, though the plural **peoples** does exist, meaning members of several nations: **the peoples of southern Africa**)

◊ **People's Assembly** ['pi:plz ə'semblɪ] *noun* body of legislature in Egypt; **Supreme People's Assembly** = body of legislature in North Korea

◊ **People's Bureau** ['pi:plz 'bjʊərəʊ] *noun* embassy of the Libyan Republic

◊ **People's Council** ['pi:plz 'kaʊnsəl] *noun* body of legislature in Syria

◊ **People's Party** ['pi:plz 'pɑ:tɪ] *noun* name given to some political parties (as in Austria)

per [pɜ:] *preposition* **(a)** as per = according to; **as per invoice** = as stated in the invoice; **as per sample** = as shown in the sample; **as per previous order** = according to the details given in our previous order **(b)** at a rate of; **per hour** *or* **per day** *or* **per week** *or* **per year** = for each hour *or* day *or* week *or* year; *the rate is £5 per hour; he makes about £2,500 per month;* **we pay £10 per hour** = we pay £10 for each hour worked; **per head** = for each person; *allow £15 per head for expenses; reliable staff cost on average £15,000 per head per annum* **(c)** out of; *the rate of imperfect items is about fifteen per hundred; the birth rate has fallen to twenty per thousand*

◊ **per annum** [pə'ænʌm] *adverb* in a year *or* annually; *the rent is £2,500 per annum; what is their turnover per annum?*

◊ **per capita** ['pɜː 'kæpɪtə] *adjective & adverb* per head *or* for each person; **average income per capita** *or* **per capita income** = average income of one person; **per capita expenditure** = total money spent divided by the number of people involved

◊ **per procurationem** *or* **p.p.** ['pɜː prɒkjʊrætsɪ'əʊnəm *or* 'piː 'piː] *Latin phrase meaning* 'with the authority of'

◊ **per se** ['pɜː 'seɪ] *Latin phrase meaning* 'on its own' *or* 'by itself'; *fixing the rates is not per se a matter for the Housing Committee, though they may wish to offer an opinion*

per cent [pə'sent] *adjective & adverb* out of each hundred *or* for each hundred; *eighty per cent (80%) of crimes are solved;* (NOTE: usually written **%** after figures)

◊ **percentage** [pə'sentɪdʒ] *noun* amount shown as a proportion of one hundred; **percentage increase** = increase calculated on the basis of a rate per hundred; **a percentage point** = one per cent; *what is the percentage of Bills which pass through the Commons unopposed? the rate of inflation has fallen by two percentage points over the last three years*

perestroika [perɪ'strɔɪkə] *noun* period of political and economic reform in the former Soviet Union

period ['pɪərɪəd] *noun* (a) length of time; *for a period of time or for a period of months or for a six-year period; to deposit money for a fixed period* (b) **accounting period** = period of time at the end of which the firm's accounts are made up

◊ **periodic** *or* **periodical** [pɪːri'ɒdɪk *or* pɪːri'ɒdɪkl] **1** *adjective* happening regularly from time to time **2** *noun* **periodical** = magazine which comes out regularly

permanent ['pɜːmənənt] *adjective* which will last for a very long time or for ever; *he has found a permanent job; she is in permanent employment; the permanent staff work a thirty-five hour week*

◊ **permanency** ['pɜːmənəsi] *noun* being permanent; (NOTE: no plural)

◊ **permanently** ['pɜːmənəntli] *adverb* for ever; *he was permanently disabled by the accident*

◊ **Permanent Secretary** ['pɜːmənənt 'sekrətri] *noun* chief civil servant in a government department or ministry; (NOTE: in Canada, called **Deputy Minister**)

COMMENT: Permanent Secretaries are appointed by the Prime Minister but are responsible to the Secretary of State in charge of the relevant department

permission [pə'mɪʃn] *noun* being allowed to do something; **written permission** = document which allows someone to do something; **verbal permission** = telling someone that he is allowed to do something; **to give someone permission to do something** = to allow someone to do something; *the club asked for permission to use the City Centre facilities; the Housing Department was given permission to buy five extra computers*

permit 1 ['pɜːmɪt] *noun* official document which allows someone to do something; **building permit** = official document which allows someone to build on a piece of land; **entry permit** = document allowing someone to enter a country; **export permit** *or* **import permit** = official document which allows goods to be exported or imported; **re-entry permit** = official document allowing someone to re-enter a country; **work permit** = official document which allows someone who is not a citizen to work in a country **2** [pə'mɪt] *verb* to allow someone to do something; *this document permits the export of twenty-five computer systems; the ticket permits three people to go into the public gallery*

persecute ['pɜːsɪkjuːt] *verb* to harass someone on political or religious or racial grounds

persecution [pɜːsɪ'kjuːʃn] *noun* political, religious or racial harassment

person ['pɜːsn] *noun* **(a)** someone, a man or woman; *insurance policy which covers a named person;* **the persons named in the contract** = people whose names are given in the contract; **the document should be witnessed by a third person** = someone who is not named in the document should witness it; **in person** = someone himself *or* herself; **this important package is to be delivered to the Chairman in person** = the package has to be given to the Chairman himself (and not to his secretary, assistant, etc.); **he came to see me in person** = he himself came to see me **(b) displaced person** = man or woman who has been forced to leave their home and move to another country because of war

◊ **persona** [pɜːˈsəʊnə] *Latin word meaning* person; **persona grata** = person who is acceptable to a government (used especially of foreign diplomats); **persona non grata** = person who is not acceptable to a government (used especially of foreign diplomats); *the Military Attaché was declared persona non grata and asked to leave the country;* (NOTE: plural is **personae gratae, personae non gratae**)

◊ **personal** ['pɜːsnl] *adjective* **(a)** referring to one person; **personal allowances** = part of a person's income which is not taxed; **Personal Bill** = bill which refers to a single person (such as a bill to change an estate); **personal computer (PC)** = small computer which can be used at home; **personal estate** *or* **personal property** = things which belong to someone (excluding land) which can be inherited by his heirs; **personal income** = income received by an individual person before tax is paid; **personal statement** *or* **personal explanation** = statement made by an MP after Question Time, when he explains his behaviour, apologises to the House, etc. **(b)** private; *I want to see the director on a personal matter;* **personal assistant** = secretary who can take on responsibility in various ways when the boss is not there

◊ **personality** [pɜːsəˈnælɪti] *noun* **(a)** qualities of mind and spirit which make one person different from another; **personality cult** = excessive publicity given to make a political leader into a type of god (found in some, usually autocratic, regimes, where pictures of the leader are everywhere, where the leader's speeches are prominently printed, where the leader is seen to be responsible for everything good which happens in the State) **(b) legal personality** = legal existence *or* status of a person; **corporate personality** = legal existence of an incorporated company which can be treated as a person

◊ **personally** ['pɜːsnəli] *adverb* in person; *he personally opened the envelope; the Prime Minister wrote to me personally*

persuade [pəˈsweɪd] *verb* to talk to someone and get him to do what you want; *after hours of discussion, they persuaded the proposer of the motion to accept the amendment; we could not persuade the French negotiating team to sign the agreement*

◊ **persuasive** [pəˈsweɪzɪv] *adjective* which persuades; *he made a very persuasive speech against restoring the death penalty*

pertain [pəˈteɪn] *verb* **to pertain to** = to refer to *or* to relate to; *the law pertaining to public order*

petition [pəˈtɪʃn] **1** *noun* **(a)** written request accompanied by a list of signatures of people supporting it; written request to the House of Commons *or* local council (presented by a private person through an MP *or* councillor); *they presented a petition with a million signatures to Parliament, asking for the law to be repealed; the councillor presented two petitions which were referred to the appropriate committees* **(b)** written application to a court; **bankruptcy petition** = application to a court asking for an order making someone bankrupt; **to file a petition in bankruptcy** = to apply to the court to be made bankrupt or to ask for someone else to be made bankrupt **(c) right of petition** = right of any EU citizen to forward an official complaint to the European Parliament (any citizen of a member state of the EU can submit a petition, either personally or as the representative of a group) **2** *verb* to make an official request; *he petitioned the government for a special pension; the* *marriage had broken down and the wife petitioned for divorce*

◊ **petitioner** [pə'tɪʃənə] *noun* person who puts forward a petition

> COMMENT: Petitions to the House of Commons are written by hand, and have a set form of words. After a petition is presented in the House of Commons at the beginning of the day's business, it is said to 'lie upon the table' and is placed in a bag behind the Speaker's Chair

pillage ['pɪlɪdʒ] *verb* to destroy buildings, steal treasures, etc.

pillar ['pɪlə] *noun* main supporting column; *the three pillars of the Maastricht Treaty*

place [pleɪs] **1** *noun* **(a)** where something is *or* where something happens; **to take place** = to happen; *the meeting will take place in our offices;* **meeting place** = room *or* area where people can meet; **place of work** = office *or* factory, etc., where people work; **public place** = place (such as a road *or* park) where the public in general have a right to be **(b)** job; *he was offered a place with an insurance company; she turned down three places before accepting the one we offered* **(c)** *(in the House of Commons)* **the other place** *or* **another place** = the House of Lords; (NOTE: the convention is that MPs never refer to the House of Lords in debates, but can only talk of 'the other place': '**following a decision in another place**'; '**will my hon. Friend confirm that that opinion was expressed not only in the other place but also in this House?**') **2** *verb* **(a)** to put; **to place money in an account** = to deposit money; **to place a contract with a company** = to decide that a certain company shall have the contract to do work; **to place an order** = to order something; **to place something on file (b) to place staff** = to find jobs for staff

◊ **placement** ['pleɪsmənt] *noun* finding work for someone

Plaid Cymru ['plaɪd 'kʌmri] *noun* nationalist party of Wales

plan [plæn] **1** *noun* **(a)** organized way of doing something; **contingency plan** = plan which will be put into action if something

happens; **development plan** = plans drawn up by the government *or* by a council, showing how an area will be developed over a long period; *the Development Plan for the town centre is on display in the public library;* **the government's economic plans** = the government's proposals for running the country's economy; **the Five-Year Plan** = proposals for running a country's economy over a five-year period **(b)** drawing which shows how something is arranged *or* how something will be built; **floor plan** = drawing of a floor in a building, showing where different departments are; **street plan** *or* **town plan** = map of a town showing streets and buildings **2** *verb* **(a)** to organize carefully how something should be done; *the devaluation was carefully planned in advance;* **to plan for an increase in bank interest charges** = to change a way of doing things because you think there will be an increase in bank interest charges **(b)** to intend to do something; *he plans to stand for parliament at the next general election*

◊ **planned** [plænd] *adjective* **planned economy** = system where the government plans all business activity

◊ **planner** ['plænə] *noun* **(a)** person who plans; **the government's economic planners** = people who plan the future economy of the country for the government; **town planner** = person who supervises the design of a town *or* the way the streets and buildings in a town are laid out and developed **(b) desk planner** *or* **wall planner** = book or chart which shows days *or* weeks *or* months so that the work of an office can be shown on it clearly

◊ **planning** ['plænɪŋ] *noun* **(a)** organizing how something should be done; **economic planning** = planning the future financial state of the country for the government **(b)** organizing how land and buildings are to be used; **planning authority** = local body which gives permission for changes to be made to existing buildings or for new use of land; **planning department** = section of a local government office which deals with requests for planning permission; **planning inquiry** = hearing before a government inspector relating to the decision of a local authority in planning matters; **planning permission** = official document allowing a person or company to plan new buildings on empty land *or* to alter existing buildings; **outline planning permission** = general permission to build a property on a piece of land, but not the final approval because there are no details given; *to be refused planning permission; we are waiting for planning permission before we can start building; the land is to be sold with outline planning permission for four houses*

plank [plæŋk] *noun* one of the items in an electoral platform; *a proposal to raise taxes is the central plank of the party's platform*

platform ['plætfɔːm] *noun* **(a)** raised part in a hall where important people sit; *the central committee was seated on the platform; the resolution from the platform was passed unanimously* **(b)** **electoral platform** = proposals set out in a manifesto before an election; *the party is campaigning on a platform of lower taxes and less government interference in municipal affairs*

pleasure ['pleʒə] *see* HER MAJESTY'S PLEASURE

plebiscite ['plebɪsɪt] *noun* type of vote, where the whole population of a town *or* region *or* country is asked to vote to decide an important issue; *the province decided by plebiscite to lower the voting age to eighteen;*

> COMMENT: a plebiscite may be of a section of a community only; a referendum applies to the whole electorate of a nation

pledge [pledʒ] **1** *noun* solemn promise; *the voters were impressed by the opposition's pledge to reduce taxes;* **to fulfil an election pledge** = to do what was promised before an election **2** *verb* to promise to do something; *the government has pledged not to raise taxes; he pledged his support to the party leader*

plenary ['pliːnəri] *adjective* complete, covering everything; **plenary session** = meeting of the whole European Parliament

plenipotentiary [plenɪpə'tenʃəri] *noun* **(a)** official person acting on behalf of a government in international affairs; *the treaty was signed by plenipotentiaries on behalf of the three governments* **(b)** **Ambassador Extraordinary and Plenipotentiary** = official title of an ambassador

plenum ['pleɪnəm] *noun* meeting at which all members are present

plot [plɒt] **1** *noun* secret plan (to do something against the law); *Guy Fawkes was a member of a plot to blow up the Houses of Parliament; the police discovered a plot to overthrow the government* **2** *verb* to make a secret plan; *the ex-ministers plotted to overthrow the government or they plotted the overthrow of the government;* (NOTE: you can plot **to do** something or plot **something**)
◊ **plotter** ['plɒtə] *noun* person who takes part in a plot; *the plotters were denounced to the secret police and arrested*

PLP = PARLIAMENTARY LABOUR PARTY

pluralism ['plʊərəlɪzm] *noun* system allowing different political or religious groups to exist in the same society
◊ **pluralist state** ['plʊərəlɪst 'steɪt] *noun* state where various political pressure groups can exist and exert influence over the government
◊ **plurality** [plʊə'rælɪti] *noun* (i) number of votes which a candidate receives more than those for another candidate; (ii) having more votes than another candidate; *the candidate with a simple plurality wins the seat;* (NOTE: **plurality** is more common in US English)

plutocracy [pluː'tɒkrəsi] *noun* system of rule by wealthy people
◊ **plutocrat** ['pluːtəkræt] *noun* person who is a member of a plutocracy

p.m. *or* **post meridiem** [piː'em *or* 'pəʊst mə'rɪdiəm] *Latin phrase meaning* 'after 12 o'clock midday'; *the train leaves at 6.50 p.m.; if you phone New York after 8 p.m. the calls are at a cheaper rate*

PM [piː 'em] = PRIME MINISTER

pocket borough ['pɒkɪt 'bʌrə] *noun* formerly, borough where the votes were controlled by a prominent citizen, so as to ensure the election of the candidate he supported

◊ **pocket veto** ['pɒkɪt 'viːtəu] *noun US* veto by the President over a bill after Congress has adjourned

COMMENT: normally the President has ten days to object to a bill which has been passed to him by Congress; if Congress adjourns during that period, the President's veto kills the bill

point [pɔɪnt] *noun* question *or* statement relating to a matter; *there are two points to be considered; the Chief Executive made the point that the day in question was a Sunday; in answer to the points raised by the Opposition spokesman;* to take a point = to agree that the point made by another speaker is correct; **point taken** *or* **I take your point** = I agree that what you say is valid; **point of fact** = question which has to be decided regarding the facts of a case; **in point of fact** = really *or* actually; **point of law** = question relating to the law as applied to a case; *counsel raised a point of law; the case illustrates an interesting point of legal principle;* **point of order** = question regarding the way in which a meeting is conducted; *he raised an interesting point of order; on a point of order, Mr Smith asked the chairman to give a ruling on whether the committee could approve its own accounts*

COMMENT: when raising a point of order, a member will say: 'on a point of order, Mr. Chairman', and the Chairman should stop the discussion to hear what the person raising the point wishes to say

police [pə'liːs] **1** *noun* group of people who keep law and order in a country *or* town; *the police have cordoned off the town centre;*

the government is relying on the police to keep law and order during the elections; the MPs were arrested up by the police at the demonstration; **military police** = soldiers who act as policemen to keep order among other soldiers; **secret police** = policemen who work in secret, especially dealing with people working against the state; **police cordon** = barriers and policemen put round an area to prevent anyone moving in or out of the area; **police court** = magistrates' court; (NOTE: no plural. Police is usually followed by a plural verb) **2** *verb* **(a)** to keep law and order in a place; *the President used the National Guard to police the capital; the meeting was policed by plainclothes men; the council is debating the Chief Constable's policing methods* **(b)** to make sure that regulations *or* guidelines are carried out; *the department is carefully policing the way the guidelines are being followed*

COMMENT: under English law, a policeman is primarily an ordinary citizen who has certain powers at common law and by statute. The police are organized by area, each area functioning independently with its own police force. London, and the area round London, is policed by the Metropolitan Police Force under the direct supervision of the Home Secretary. Outside London, each police force is answerable to a local police authority, although day-to-day control of operations is vested entirely in the Chief Constable

◊ **police authority** [pə'liːs ɔː'θɒrɪti] *noun* local committee which supervises a local police force

◊ **Police Commissioner** [pə'liːs kə'mɪʃənə] *noun* highest rank in certain police forces; **Metropolitan Police Commissioner** = person in charge of the Metropolitan Police in London

◊ **Police Complaints Board** [pə'liːs kəm'pleɪnts 'bɔːd] *noun* group which investigates complaints made by members of the public against the police

◊ **police force** [pə'liːs 'fɔːs] *noun* group of policemen organized in a certain area; *the members of several local police forces have collaborated in the hunt for the terrorists;*

the London police force is looking for more recruits

◊ **police headquarters** [pə'li:s hed'kwɔ:təz] *noun* main offices of a police force

◊ **police inspector** [pə'li:s ɪn'spektə] *noun* rank in the police force above a sergeant

◊ **policeman** [pə'li:smən] *noun* man who is a member of the police; (NOTE: the plural is policemen)

◊ **police officer** [pə'li:s 'ɒfɪsə] *noun* member of the police

◊ **police precinct** [pə'li:s 'pri:sɪŋkt] *noun* US section of a town with its own police station

◊ **police sergeant** [pə'li:s 'sɑ:dʒənt] *noun* rank in the police force above constable and below inspector

◊ **police state** [pə'li:s 'steɪt] *noun (used as criticism)* a country *or* system in which the government uses the police *or* army to control the people; *after the coup, the generals were accused of operating a police state*

◊ **police station** [pə'li:s 'steɪʃn] *noun* local office of a police force

◊ **policewoman** [pə'li:swʊmən] *noun* woman member of a police force; (NOTE: the plural is policewomen)

◊ **policing** [pə'li:sɪŋ] *noun* keeping law and order in a place, using the police force; **community policing** = way of policing a section of a town, where the members of the local community and the local police force act together to prevent crime and disorder, with policemen on foot patrol, rather than in patrol cars; (NOTE: no plural)

policy ['pɒlɪsi] *noun* **(a)** decisions on the general way of doing something; *government policy on wages or government wages policy; the government's prices policy; the country's economic policy; our policy is to submit all contracts to the legal department; it is not the normal policy of the council to give grants for more than three years* **policy committee** = committee which decides what a council's general way of doing things shall be; **the government made a policy statement** *or* **made a statement of**

policy = the government declared in public what its plans were; **budgetary policy** = policy of expected income and expenditure; *see also* PUBLIC POLICY **(b) insurance policy** = document which shows the conditions of an insurance contract; **comprehensive** *or* **all-risks policy** = insurance policy which covers risks of any kind, with no exclusions; **contingent policy** = policy which pays out only if something happens (as for example if the person named in the policy dies before the person due to benefit); **policy holder** = person who is insured by an insurance company

Politburo [pɒ'lɪtbju:rəʊ] *noun* the Central Committee of a Communist Party, as in North Korea (in fact the governing group in the country)

politic ['pɒlɪtɪk] *see* BODY

politics ['pɒlɪtɪks] *noun* the art and practice of running or governing a country; **local politics** *or* **national politics** = the practice of governing a local area *or* a country; **international politics** = relationships between governments of different political parties and systems; **party politics** = system in which the political life of the country is run by large powerful parties, who make their supporters toe the party line, and where obedience to the party is more important than following its principles; **power politics** = the threat to use economic *or* military force by one powerful country to try to get other countries to do what it wants

◊ **political** [pə'lɪtɪkl] *adjective* referring to a certain idea of how a country should be run; *they are hoping for a political rather than a military solution to the crisis;* **political correctness (PC)** = acting in an exaggerated way to avoid giving offence for racial, sexist or other reasons; **political crime** = crime (such as assassination) committed for a political reason; **political fund** = part of the funds of a trade union which is allocated to subsidize a political party; **political levy** = part of the subscription of a member of a trade union which the union then pays to support a political party; **political officer** = diplomat stationed in a colony, who is concerned mainly with the relations between his government and the colonial administration *or* the governments of the nearby countries; **political party** = group of people who believe a country should be run in a certain way; **political prisoner** = person kept in prison because he is an opponent of the political party in power; **political refugee** = person who flees a country because he is afraid of persecution for his political beliefs

◊ **politically** [pə'lɪtɪkli] *adverb* with reference to politics; **politically correct (PC)** = done in an exaggerated way to avoid giving offence for racial, sexist or other reasons

◊ **politician** [pɒlɪ'tɪʃn] *noun* person involved in politics; **a full-time politician** = person who works full-time in politics, as an elected representative; *I blame the politicians for the mess we're in*

---

the most successful politician is he who says what everybody is thinking most often and in the loudest voice
Theodore Roosevelt

---

politics is the art of possible

R.A. Butler

Never lose your temper with the press or the public is a major rule of political life
Christabel Pankhurst

---

poll [pəʊl] **1** *noun* **(a)** voting to choose something; **to go to the polls** = to vote to choose a Member of Parliament *or* a local councillor; **the polls opened an hour ago** = the voting started officially an hour ago; **the polls close at 10 o'clock** = the voting ends at 10 o'clock **(b)** **opinion poll** = asking a sample group of people what they feel about something, so as to guess the opinion of the whole population; **exit poll** = poll taken outside a polling station, asking people who have just voted how they voted, to get an idea of the result of an election; **straw poll** = rapid poll (especially one taken on voting day), where a few people are asked how they intend to vote *or* have voted; *a straw poll among members of staff shows the government is in the lead* **(c)** **deed poll** = legal agreement which refers only to one person; **she changed her name by deed poll**

= she executed a legal document to change her name **2** *verb* **(a)** to receive a certain number of votes in an election; *he polled only 123 votes in the general election; the centre parties polled 15% of the votes;* **polling booth** = small enclosed place in a polling station, where the elector goes to mark his voting paper in private; **polling day** = day of an election; **polling station** = central public place (such as a library *or* school) which is set aside for the people of the surrounding area to vote in **(b)** **to poll a sample of the population** = to ask a sample group of people what they feel about something; **to poll the members of the club on an issue** = to ask the members for their opinion on an issue

◊ **pollster** ['pəʊlstə] *noun* expert in understanding what polls mean

◊ **poll tax** ['pəʊl 'tæks] *noun* tax levied equally on each adult member of the population; *see also* COMMUNITY CHARGE

polyarchy [pɒlɪ'ɑːki] *noun* rule by many people

populace ['pɒpjʊləs] *noun* the ordinary people in an area *or* country; *the government has hidden its plans from the populace;* (NOTE: no plural)

popular ['pɒpjʊlə] *adjective* **(a)** liked by many people; *this is our most popular model; the South Coast is the most popular area for holidays;* **popular prices** = prices which are low and therefore liked **(b)** referring to the people in general; **popular vote** = vote of the people; **the president is elected by popular vote** = the president is elected by a majority of all the voters in the country (as opposed to being elected by parliament)

COMMENT: note that the President of the USA is elected by an electoral college, not by popular vote

---

◊ **Popular Front** ['pɒpjʊlə 'frʌnt] *noun* **(a)** group of Socialist and Communist parties, formed in 1935 to fight fascism **(b)** left-wing organization formed to fight a ruling government *or* colonial power

◊ **Popular Party** ['pɒpjʊlə 'pɑːti] *noun* name for a political party representing a large number of ordinary people

◊ **populist** ['pɒpjʊlɪst] *adjective & noun* (person) who believes ordinary people should have more say in government

population [pɒpju'leɪʃn] *noun* number of people living in a certain place; *the population of Britain has fallen over the last few years; a city with a population of two million or with a 2 million population*

◊ **populated** ['pɒpjuleɪtɪd] *adjective* (region) where people live; *a heavily populated area or a densely populated area;* **over-populated** = having too many people; **depopulated** = having fewer inhabitants (because most have moved away)

◊ **populous** ['pɒpjʊləs] *adjective* (region) where many people live; *the most populous area of the country is round the capital*

portfolio [pɔːt'fəʊliəʊ] *noun* **(a)** office of a minister in the government; *he was offered the Defence portfolio;* **Minister without Portfolio** = minister who does not have responsibility for any particular department **(b)** all the shares owned by someone; *his portfolio contains shares in the major oil companies*

position [pə'zɪʃn] *noun* **(a)** situation or state of affairs; *what is the position concerning my application for planning permission?;* **bargaining position** = position of one group during negotiations **(b)** job, paid work in a company; *to apply for a position as manager; we have several positions vacant; all the vacant positions have been filled; she retired from her position in the accounts department;* **position of trust** = job where the employee is trusted with money, confidential documents, etc.

positive ['pɒzɪtɪv] *adjective* meaning 'Yes'; *the board gave a positive reply;* **positive discrimination** = giving more favourable treatment to a minority to help them be more equal; *the council's policy is one of positive discrimination to ensure that more women are appointed to senior posts;* **positive vetting** = close examination of a

person working with classified information who may not be reliable

possess [pə'zes] *verb* to own *or* to be in occupation of *or* to be in control of; *the company possesses property in the centre of the town; he lost all he possessed when his company was put into liquidation*

◊ **possession** [pə'zeʃn] *noun* **(a)** control over property; **actual possession** = occupying and controlling land and buildings; **vacant possession** = being able to occupy a property immediately after buying it because it is empty; *the property is to be sold with vacant possession* **(b)** physically holding something (which does not necessarily belong to you); **the documents are in his possession** = he is holding the documents; **how did it come into his possession** *or* **how did he get possession of it?** = how did he acquire it?; **an MP in possession of the House** = an MP who is speaking to the House of Commons (and so cannot be interrupted *or* stopped) **(c)** knowledge; **the Committee was not in full possession of the facts** = the Committee did not know all the facts **(d)** **possessions** = property, things owned; colony owned by another country; *the former British possessions in the Far East; they lost all their possessions in the fire*

post [pəʊst] **1** *noun* **(a)** system of sending letters and parcels from one place to another; *to send an invoice by post; he put the letter in the post; the cheque was lost in the post;* **to send a reply by return of post** = to reply to a letter immediately; **letter post** *or* **parcel post** = service for sending letters or parcels; **post room** = room in an office where the post is sorted and sent to each department or collected from each department for sending **(b)** letters sent or received; *has the post arrived yet? my secretary opens the post as soon as it arrives; the receipt was in this morning's post; the letter did not arrive by first post this morning* **(c)** job, paid work; *to apply for a post as clerical assistant; we have three posts vacant; all our posts have been filled; we advertised three posts in 'The Times'* **2** *verb* **(a)** to send something by post; *to post a letter or to post a parcel* **(b)** to a notice = to put a notice on a wall *or* on a noticeboard; **to post an increase** = to let people know that an increase has taken place

◊ **post-** [pəʊst] *prefix* meaning 'after'; **post-colonial period** = period after a colonial occupation

poster ['pəʊstə] *noun* large printed paper stuck on a surface, announcing something *or* advertising something; *party workers stuck election posters over the front of the town hall*

posteriori [pəʊsterɪ'ɔːraɪ] *see* A POSTERIORI

post mortem ['pəʊst 'mɔːtəm] *noun* (i) examination of a dead body to find out the cause of death; (ii) examining something after it has happened to see why it happened; *after the election, the party chiefs carried out a post mortem on party's performance*

postpone [pəs'pəʊn] *verb* to arrange for something to take place later than planned; *he postponed the meeting until tomorrow; they asked if they could postpone payment until the cash situation was better*

◊ **postponement** [pəs'pəʊnmənt] *noun* arranging for something to take place later than planned; *I had to change my appointments because of the postponement of the board meeting*

power ['paʊə] *noun* (a) strength *or* ability *or* capacity; **bargaining power** = strength of one person or group when discussing prices *or* wages *or* contracts; **borrowing power** = amount of money which a company can borrow; **earning power** = amount of money someone should be able to earn; **power base** = are of powerful support; *he has built up a power base in the unions;* **power bloc** = group of countries linked into a powerful group (b) authority, the legal right to do things *or* to make people do things; *the treasurer has no power to vary the order; the powers of a local authority in relation to children in care; the powers and duties conferred on the tribunal by the statutory code; the President was granted wide powers under the new constitution*

executive power = right to act as administrator or to put decisions into action; **power of attorney** = official power which gives someone the right to act on someone else's behalf in legal matters; **the full power of the law** = the full force of the law when applied; *we will apply the full power of the law to regain possession of our property* (c) powerful country *or* state; *one of the important military powers in the region*

◊ **powerful** ['paʊəfʊl] *adjective* having power; *a powerful argument against military intervention in the area; the party has a powerful publicity department*

◊ **powerless** ['paʊələs] *adjective* having no power; *the government was powerless in the face of the strike campaign*

◊ **power politics** ['paʊə 'pɒlɪtɪks] *noun* the threat to use economic *or* military force by one powerful country to try to get other countries to do what it wants

PPS = PARLIAMENTARY PRIVATE SECRETARY

PR [piː'ɑː] = PROPORTIONAL REPRESENTATION, PUBLIC RELATIONS

practice ['præktɪs] *noun* (a) way of doing things; *his practice was to arrive at work at 7.30 and start opening the mail;* **business practices** or **industrial practices** or **trade practices** = ways of managing or working in business, industry or trade; **restrictive practices** = ways of working which exclude free competition in relation to the supply of goods or labour in order to maintain prices or wages; **code of practice** = rules drawn up by an association which the members must follow when doing business (b) **in practice** = when actually done; *the scheme for dealing with young offenders seems very interesting, but what will it cost in practice?* (c) office and clients (of a professional person); *he has set up in practice as a solicitor or a patent agent; he is a partner in a country solicitor's practice* (d) carrying on of a profession; *he has been in practice for twenty years*

practise *US* **practice** ['præktɪs] *verb* to work (in a profession); *he is a practising solicitor;* **practising certificate** = certificate from the Law Society allowing someone to work as a solicitor

Praesidium *or* **Presidium** [prɪˈsɪdiəm] *noun* main committee of a governing Communist Party

pray [preɪ] *verb* to ask someone to do something; *members pray that action may be taken*

◊ **prayer** [preə] *noun* **(a)** request to the House of Commons to do something *or* not to do something **(b) prayers** = address to God, which begins each sitting of the Houses of Parliament **(c)** motion in the House of Commons asking the Crown to annul a statutory instrument

pre- [prɪ] *prefix* before; *pre-contract discussion; a pre-stocktaking sale; there will be a pre-AGM board meeting*

preamble [priːˈæmbl] *noun* first words in an official document (such as a Bill before Parliament *or* contract) introducing the document and setting out the main points in it

precautions [prɪˈkɔːʃnz] *noun* steps taken to prevent something unpleasant; *the company did not take proper fire precautions; staff must take precautions against theft;* **safety precautions** = actions taken to try to make sure that something is safe

precede [prɪˈsiːd] *verb* to go before *or* to come earlier

◊ **preceding** [prɪˈsiːdɪŋ] *adjective* which comes before; *see the preceding paragraph of my letter; the preceding clause gives details of the agency arrangements*

precedence [ˈpresɪdəns] *noun* right to be first, because of being the most important; **order of precedence** = order of things according to their importance; *the item on finance takes precedence over all other items on the agenda*

◊ **precedent** [ˈpresɪdənt] *noun* something (such as a judgment) which has happened earlier, and which can be a guide as to what should be done in the present case; **to set a precedent** = to make a decision in court which will show other courts how to act in

future; **to follow a precedent** = to decide in the same way as an earlier decision in the same type of case; *the judge's decision sets a precedent for future cases of contempt of court; the tribunal's ruling has established a precedent; the officer said that the committee's decision would set a precedent and would lead to many other similar requests*

precept [ˈpriːsept] *noun* order asking for rates to be paid; **the Metropolitan Police precept** = part of the rates paid by London ratepayers which pays for the Metropolitan Police Force; **precepting body** = organization which levies a precept

precinct [ˈpriːsɪŋkt] *noun* **(a)** general area; **pedestrian precinct** *or* **shopping precinct** = part of a town which is closed to traffic so that people can walk about and shop **(b)** *US* administrative district in a town; (NOTE: the UK equivalent is **ward**) **(c) precincts** = definite area covered by a large building and the grounds round it; *armed rebels have got into the precincts of the Presidential Palace; when a division is called an MP has to be within the precincts of the Palace of Westminster in order to vote*

precise [prɪˈsaɪs] *adjective* clear and with correct details; *the clause gives precise details about the types of goods included in the Act*

preclude [prɪˈkluːd] *verb* to forbid *or* to prevent; *the High Court is precluded by statute from reviewing such a decision; this agreement does not preclude a further agreement between the parties in the future*

predecessor [ˈpriːdɪsesə] *noun* person who has held a job before the present person; *he had to accept the treaty which his predecessor had signed*

pre-empt [prɪˈempt] *verb* to act before someone else can act; *the President pre-empted the call for more democracy by suddenly announcing a general election*

◊ **pre-emption** [prɪˈempʃn] *noun* right of first refusal to purchase something before it is sold to someone else

prefer [prɪ'fɜː] *verb* (a) to like something better than another thing; *the government prefers quiet diplomacy rather than direct confrontation* (b) to bring something before a court; **to prefer charges** = to charge someone with an offence; (NOTE: **preferring - preferred**)

◊ **preferable** ['prefrəbl] *adjective* which is preferred *or* which is better; *of the two redevelopment schemes put forward, the second is preferable for several reasons*

◊ **preference** ['prefrəns] *noun* thing which is preferred; **preference shares** = shares (often with no voting rights) which receive their dividend before all other shares and which are repaid first (at face value) if the company is liquidated; **preference shareholders** = owners of preference shares

◊ **preferential** [prefə'renʃl] *adjective* showing that something is preferred more than another; **preferential treatment** = good treatment given to someone who is in power *or* has a connection with the person giving the treatment; *just because he is a councillor, he should not get preferential treatment on the housing list;* **preferential duty** *or* **preferential tariff** = special low rate of tax

◊ **preferment** [prɪ'fɜːmənt] *noun* promoting someone (especially in the government *or* civil service)

prejudge [priː'dʒʌdʒ] *verb* **to prejudge the issue** = to make a decision before examining the facts of the case

prejudice ['predʒudɪs] **1** *noun* (a) bias, unjust feelings against someone; **racial prejudice** = feelings against someone because of his race; *they investigated the claims of racial prejudice against the Housing Committee chairman* (b) harm done to someone; **without prejudice** = phrase spoken *or* written in letters when attempting to negotiate a settlement, meaning that the negotiations cannot be referred to in court or relied upon by the other party if the discussions fail; *payment for the damage has been made without prejudice to the admission of legal liability;* **to act to the prejudice of a claim** = to do something which may harm a claim **2** *verb* to harm; *to prejudice someone's claim*

◊ **prejudiced** ['predʒudɪst] *adjective* biased, with unjust feelings against someone; *the Prime Minister seemed to be prejudiced against foreigners*

preliminary [prɪ'lɪmɪnəri] *adjective* early, happening before anything else; **preliminary discussion** *or* **preliminary meeting** = discussion or meeting which takes place before the main discussion or meeting starts; **preliminary hearing** = court proceedings where the witnesses and the defendant are examined to see if there are sufficient grounds for the case to proceed *or* court proceedings to try a specific issue rather than the whole case; **preliminary investigation** = first examination of the details of a case by a magistrate who then has to decide if the case should be committed to a higher court for trial; **preliminary ruling** = provisional decision of the European Court

premier ['premiə] *noun* (a) Prime Minister (b) *(in a Federal state)* chief minister of a state *or* province (as opposed to the Prime Minister of the Federal government) (as in the States of Australia, the Provinces of Canada; also in China)

◊ **premiership** ['premiəʃɪp] *noun* period when a Prime Minister governs; *during the premiership of Harold Wilson*

COMMENT: used in Canada and Australia more than in the UK, especially referring to the provincial or state premiers

premises ['premɪsɪz] *noun* building and the land it stands on; **business premises** *or* **commercial premises** = building used for commercial use (as a shop *or* warehouse *or* office, etc.); **licensed premises** = building licensed to sell alcohol (such as a shop *or* bar *or* restaurant)

prerogative [prɪ'rɒɡətɪv] *noun* special right which someone has; **royal prerogative** = right of the king *or* queen to do something; **prerogative order** *or* **writ** = writ which requests a body to do its duty *or* not to do some act *or* to conduct an inquiry into its own actions; **prerogative powers** = special powers used by a government, acting in the name of the King *or* Queen, to do something (such as declare war, nominate judges *or* ministers) without needing to ask Parliament to approve the decision

presence ['prezns] *noun* being present *or* being at a place when something happens; *the will was signed in the presence of two witnesses; (in a royal palace)* **presence chamber** = room where the king *or* queen might receive visitors

present 1 ['preznt] *noun* thing which is given; *these calculators make good presents; the office gave her a present when she got married* **2** ['preznt] *adjective* **(a)** happening now; *the present international situation means that police have been put on the alert; what is the present address of the company?* **(b)** being there when something happens; *only four Opposition MPs were present when the vote was put; only six members were present at the Annual General Meeting* **3** [prɪ'zent] *verb* **(a)** to give someone something; *the mayor presented certificates to members of the public who had helped in the rescue operations; he was presented with a watch on completing twenty-five years' service with the council* **(b)** to bring or send or show a document; **to present a petition** = to bring a petition before a meeting for discussion; *Councillor Smith presented a petition requesting improvements to the hospital bus service;* **to present a bill for payment** = to send a bill to be paid

◊ **presentation** [prezən'teɪʃn] *noun* **(a)** giving something; *they made him a presentation of a watch after twenty-five years' service; at a presentation ceremony in the White House, the President awarded the Medal of Honor to three people* **(b)** demonstration *or* exhibition of a proposed plan; *the developers made a presentation of the proposed new civic centre; we have asked two PR firms to make presentations of advertising campaigns aimed at tourists*

preservation order [prezə'veɪʃn 'ɔːdə] *noun* court order which prevents a building from being knocked down *or* a tree from being cut down

preside [prɪ'zaɪd] *verb* **(a)** to be in the chair *or* to be chairman of a meeting; *to preside over a meeting; the meeting was held in the committee room, Mr Smith presiding* **(b)** to be in control when something happens; *the generals presided over a period of economic decline; the finance minister presided over a run-down of the country's gold reserves*

president ['prezɪdənt] *noun* **(a)** head of a department *or* company *or* court; *he was elected president of the sports club; A.B.Smith has been appointed president of the company;* **President of the Board of Trade** = title given to the minister in charge of the British Department of Trade (equivalent to a Minister of Commerce); **President of the European Commission** = chief executive and civil servant of the EU, elected for a five-year period; **President of the Family Division** = judge who is responsible for the work of the Family Division of the High Court; *US* **President of the Senate** = person who presides over debates in the Senate (usually the Vice-President of the USA, but in his absence a president pro tempore takes the chair) **(b)** head of a republic; *the President of the United States;* (NOTE: as a title of a head of state, President can be used with a surname: **President Ford, President Wilson**)

COMMENT: a president is the head of state of a republic; this may be a ceremonial title, with some executive powers, as in India, while the real power resides in the Prime Minister. In other states (such as the USA), the President is both head of state and head of government. The President of the USA is elected by an electoral college, and holds the executive power under the United States constitution. The legislative power lies with Congress, and the President cannot force Congress to enact legislation, although he can veto legislation which has been passed by Congress

presidency ['prezɪdnsi] *noun* **(a)** position of president; *the presidency of the European Union passes from country to country every six months* **(b)** period when a president is governing; *during Kennedy's presidency or during the Kennedy presidency*

◊ **presidential** [prezɪ'denʃl] *adjective* referring to a president of a country; *the US presidential elections; three presidential candidates have appeared on television; the National Guard has surrounded the Presidential Palace;* **presidential government** = type of government where the head of the executive is a president

◊ **presidential-style** [prezɪ'denʃl 'staɪl] *adjective* working in a similar way to the United States presidency; **presidential-style government** = governing in the same way as a President of the USA, who is not a member of the elected legislature; **presidential-style campaign** = election campaign which concentrates on the person of the leader of the party, and not on the party's policies; *the Prime Minister was accused of running a presidential-style government or a presidential-style election campaign*

presidium [prɪ'sɪdɪəm] *see* PRAESIDIUM

press [pres] **1** *noun* newspapers and magazines; **the local press** = newspapers which are sold in a small area of the country; **the national press** = newspapers which are sold in all parts of the country; **press conference** = meeting where reporters from newspapers are invited to hear news of a new product *or* of a court case *or* of a takeover bid, etc.; **Press Council** = body concerned with regulation of the press; **press coverage** = reports about something in the press; **press gallery** = section of the House of Commons, House of Lords or other council chamber, where journalists sit to report on debates; **press release** = sheet giving news about something which is sent to newspapers and TV and radio stations so that they can use the information; **press secretary** = person responsible for contacts with journalists; *the information was communicated by the President's Press Secretary;* **freedom of the press** = being able to write and publish in a newspaper what you wish without being afraid of prosecution, provided that you do not break the law **2** *verb* **(a)** to ask for something again and again; *he pressed the*

Minister for a reply; the Opposition pressed for a debate **(b)** to press charges against someone = to say formally that someone has committed a crime; *the MP is going to press charges against the newspaper*

◊ **pressing** ['presɪŋ] *adjective* urgent; *there is a mass of pressing business for the committee to consider;* **pressing engagements** = meetings which have to be attended

pressure ['preʃə] *noun* force *or* strong influence to make someone change his opinions *or* course of action; *the army exerts strong political pressure on the President; the Prime Minister gave in to pressure from the backbenchers; the Whips applied pressure on the rebel MPs to vote with the government;* **pressure group** = group of people with similar interests, who try to influence government policies; **pressure politics** = attempting to change the government's policies by political pressure

previous ['priːvɪəs] *adjective* which has happened earlier *or* has been in office earlier; *on the previous occasion, the committee turned down the proposal; the bill was introduced by the previous administration;* **he could not accept the invitation because he had a previous engagement** = because he had earlier accepted another invitation to go somewhere; *(in the House of Commons or Congress)* **to move the previous question** = to propose that the previous motion should be discussed again, so that the debate on the current question is dropped

◊ **previously** ['priːvɪəsli] *adverb* happening earlier

prima facie ['praɪmə 'feɪʃi] *Latin phrase meaning* 'on the face of it *or* as things seem at first'; **there is a prima facie case to answer** = one side in a dispute has shown that there is a case to answer, and so the action should be proceeded with

primary ['praɪməri] **1** *adjective* **(a)** in the first place; **of primary importance** = extremely important, the most important of all; *the question is of primary importance to the security of the country* **(b)** first of several stages; **primary school** = school for children aged from 5 to 11 **2** *noun US* local election in which members of a political party meet to choose a candidate for a national election;

COMMENT: in the USA, primaries are held in some states to choose a candidate for the presidency in advance of the nominating conventions

◊ **primarily** ['praɪmrəli] *adverb* in the first *or* most important place; *it is the government which is primarily responsible for the country's economic condition; see also* SECONDARY, SECONDARILY

prime [praɪm] *adjective* **(a)** most important; **prime time** = most expensive advertising time for TV advertisements **(b) prime rate** = best rate of interest at which a bank lends to its customers

◊ **Prime Minister** ['praɪm 'mɪnɪstə] *noun* head of a government; *the Australian Prime Minister or the Prime Minister of Australia;* **Prime Minister's Questions** = period of 30 minutes on Thursdays when MPs put questions directly to the Prime Minister

◊ **Prime Ministerial** ['praɪm mɪnɪs'tiːriəl] *adjective* referring to a Prime Minister; **Prime Ministerial government** = form of government where a Prime Minister is the head of government

COMMENT: the title Prime Minister is used in most countries to indicate the head of the government, except in countries, such as the USA, where the President is head of government as well as the head of state. The British Prime Minister is not the head of state, but the head of government. The Prime Minister is usually the leader of the party which has the majority of the seats in the House of Commons, and forms a cabinet of executive ministers who are either MPs or members of the House of Lords

primus inter pares ['praɪməs ɪntə 'paːriːz] *Latin phrase meaning* 'first among equals': used to refer to the office of Prime Minister, implying that all ministers are equal, and the PM is simply the most important of them

prince [prɪns] *noun* **(a)** male member of a royal family, usually the son of a king *or* queen; *one of the Saudi royal princes;* **prince consort** = title given to the husband of a ruling queen; *when Queen Victoria reigned as queen, her husband, Albert, was Prince Consort* **(b)** title of the ruler of a small country (such as Cambodia or Monaco); (NOTE: spelt with a capital letter when used as a title: **Prince Charles; Prince Abdullah)**

◊ **princedom** ['prɪnsdəm] *noun* principality, a small country ruled by a prince

◊ **princely** ['prɪnsli] *adjective* **(a)** generous *or* very large; *a princely sum of money; a princely gift* **(b)** like a prince

◊ **Prince of Wales** ['prɪns əv 'weɪlz] *noun* title of the male heir to the British throne

◊ **princess** [prɪn'ses] *noun* female member of a royal family, especially the daughter of a king *or* queen, or the wife of a prince; **Princess Royal** = title given to the eldest daughter of a king *or* queen; (NOTE: spelt with a capital letter as a title: **Princess Anne; the Princess of Wales)**

principal ['prɪnsɪpl] **1** *noun* **(a)** person who is responsible for something (especially person who is in charge of a company *or* person who commits a crime) **(b)** person or company which is represented by an agent; *the agent has come to London to see his principals* **(c)** money invested or borrowed on which interest is paid; *to repay principal and interest* **2** *adjective* most important; *the principal shareholders asked for a meeting; the country's principal products are paper and wood; compare* PRINCIPLE

◊ **principality** [prɪnsɪ'pæliti] *noun* country ruled by a prince; *the Principality of Monaco; see also* CO-PRINCIPALITY (NOTE: the state of Andorra is in fact a co-principality, as it is governed by two princes; in Britain, 'the Principality' is the name given to Wales)

principle ['prɪnsɪpl] *noun* basic point *or* general rule; **in principle** = in agreement with a general rule; **agreement in principle** = agreement with the basic conditions of a proposal; **it is against his principles** = it goes against what he believes to be the correct way to act; *compare* PRINCIPAL

prior ['praɪə] *adjective* coming before; *the minister had no prior notice of the question*

◊ **priority** [praɪ'ɒrɪti] *noun* being most important; **priority area** = area to which government must give extra money because of its needs; **order of priority** = order of things, where the most important comes first; *let us deal with the points on the agenda in order of priority;* **to take priority over something** = to be more important than something; *schools must take priority over the provision of recreational facilities;* **the government has got its priorities wrong** = the government is not doing things in the correct order of priority

prison ['prɪzn] *noun* place where people are kept in captivity, usually after legal sentence passed by a court

◊ **prisoner** ['prɪznə] *noun* person kept in a prison; **prisoner of conscience** = person who has been put in prison because of his or her beliefs; **prisoner of state** *or* **political prisoner** = person kept in prison because he is an opponent of the political party in power; **prisoner of war** = serviceman captured by the other side during a war

private ['praɪvət] *adjective* (a) belonging to a single person, not a company or the state; **letter marked 'private and confidential'** = letter which must not be opened by anyone other than the person to whom it is addressed; **Private Bill** *or* **Private Act** = Bill *or* Act relating to a particular person or corporation or institution; *see below* PRIVATE MEMBER'S BILL **private business** = business dealing with the members of a group *or* matters which cannot be discussed in public; *the committee held a special meeting to discuss some private business; US* **Private Calendar** = list of Private Bills to be discussed in the House of Representatives; **private client** *or* **private customer** = client dealt with by a professional man *or* by a salesman as a person, not as a company; **private law** = law as it refers to individuals;

private member = ordinary backbench MP who is not a member of the Government or on the Opposition front bench; **Private Member's Bill** = Bill which is drafted and proposed in the House of Commons by an ordinary Member of Parliament, not by a government minister on behalf of the government; **private property** = property which belongs to a private person, not to the public; **private prosecution** = prosecution for a criminal act, brought by an ordinary member of the public and not by the police (b) **in private** = away from other people; *he asked to see the managing director in private* (c) **private limited company** = company with a small number of shareholders whose shares are not traded on the Stock Exchange; **private enterprise** = economic system where businesses are owned by private shareholders, not by the state; **the private sector** = all companies which are owned by private shareholders, not by the state

◊ **privately** ['praɪvətli] *adverb* away from other people; *the deal was negotiated privately*

◊ **privatize** ['praɪvətaɪz] *verb* to sell a nationalized industry to private shareholders (usually to members of the public)

◊ **privatization** [praɪvətaɪ'zeɪʃn] *noun* action of privatizing a nationalized industry

privilege ['prɪvɪlɪdʒ] *noun* (a) special advantage attached to a position *or* office; *the office of Mayor carries certain privileges, such as the use of the mayoral car and driver; one of the privileges of the job is being able to use the company helicopter* (b) protection from the law *or* from a duty given in certain circumstances; **absolute privilege** = privilege which protects a person from being sued for defamation (such as an MP speaking in the House of Commons, a judge *or* a lawyer making a statement during judicial proceedings); **breach of parliamentary privilege** = speaking in a defamatory way about Parliament *or* about a Member of Parliament; **Committee of Privileges** = special committee of the House of Commons which examines cases of breach of privilege; **Crown privilege** = right of the Crown *or* of the government not to have to produce documents in court; **qualified privilege** = protection from being sued for defamation which is given to someone only if it can be proved that the statements were made without malice; **question of privilege** = matter which refers to the House or a member of it; *US* **question of personal privilege** = matter referring to a member of Congress (which is usually given priority over other matters) **(c)** *US* order of priority; **motion of the highest privilege** = motion which will be discussed first, before all other motions

◊ **privileged** ['prɪvɪledʒd] *adjective* protected by privilege; **privileged communication** = letter which could be libellous but which is protected by privilege (such as a letter from a client to his lawyer); **privileged meeting** *or* **occasion** = meeting where what is said will not be repeated outside; *US* **privileged questions** = order of priority of motions to be discussed

Privy Council ['prɪvi 'kaʊnsəl] *noun* body of senior advisers who advise the Queen on certain matters and who approve orders in council; **Judicial Committee of the Privy Council** = appeal court for appeals from some Commonwealth countries and the colonies

◊ **Privy Councillor** ['prɪvi 'kaʊnsələ] *noun* member of the Privy Council

COMMENT: the Privy Council is mainly formed of members of the cabinet, and former members of the cabinet. It never meets as a group, but three Privy Councillors need to be present when the Queen signs Orders in Council

pro- [prəʊ] *prefix* meaning in favour of; *a pro-abortion lobby; the president is very pro-British; public opinion is not pro-European;* (NOTE: opposite is **anti-**)

problem ['prɒbləm] *noun* thing to which it is difficult to find a solution; *the department suffers from cash flow problems or staff problems;* **to solve a problem** = to find an answer to a problem; **problem area** = part of work which is difficult to manage; *drug-related crime is a problem area in large cities*

procedure [prəˈsiːdʒə] *noun* way in which something is done, especially steps taken to bring an action to the court; *to follow the proper procedure;* **this procedure is very irregular** = this is not the set way to do something; **complaints procedure** *or* **grievance procedure** = agreed way of presenting complaints formally from a trade union *or* from an employee to the management of a company

◊ **procedural** [prəˈsiːdʒərəl] *adjective* referring to procedure; **procedural law** = rules governing how the civil or criminal law is administered by the courts; **procedural motion** = motion referring to procedure; *the chairman moved a procedural motion so that the committee could discuss the next business;* **procedural problem** *or* **question** = question concerning procedure; *the debate last two hours because councillors argued over procedural problems*

proceed [prəˈsiːd] *verb* to go on *or* to continue; *the negotiations are proceeding slowly; the meeting proceeded after the protesters were removed from the council chamber;* **to proceed against someone** = to start a legal action against someone; **to proceed with something** = to go on doing something; *he proceeded with his speech after the interruption*

◊ **proceedings** [prəˈsiːdɪŋz] *plural noun* **(a) conference proceedings** = written report of what has taken place at a conference **(b) legal proceedings** = legal action *or* lawsuit; *to take proceedings against someone; the court proceedings were adjourned;* **to institute** *or* **to start proceedings against someone** = to start a legal action against someone

◊ **proceeds** ['prəʊsiːdz] *plural noun* **the proceeds of a sale** = money received from a sale after deducting expenses; *the proceeds of the Mayoress' Fund were given to local charities*

process ['prəʊses] **1** *noun* **(a)** way in which something happens; **industrial processes** = processes involved in manufacturing products in factories; **decision-making processes** = ways in which decisions are reached; **the peace process** =

gradual establishing peace, by a process of negotiation between former warring parties **(b) in the process of** = while doing something; *in the process of checking the accounts the auditors discovered the discrepancy* **(c)** (i) way in which a court acts to assert its jurisdiction; (ii) writs issued by a court to summon the defendant to appear in court; (iii) legal procedure; **the due process of the law** = the formal work of a fair legal action **2** *verb* **(a) to process figures** = to sort out information to make it easily understood; *the sales figures are being processed by our accounts department; data is being processed in our computer* **(b)** to deal with something in the usual routine way; *to process an insurance claim; the department is processing complaints received from the public*

◊ **processing** ['prəʊsesɪŋ] *noun* **(a)** sorting of information; *processing of information or of figures;* **data processing** *or* **information processing** = selecting and examining data in a computer to produce information in a special form; **word processing** *or* **text processing** = working with words, using a computer to produce, check and amend texts, contracts, reports, letters, etc. **(b) the processing of a claim for insurance** = putting a claim for compensation through the usual office routine in the insurance company

proclaim [prə'kleɪm] *verb* to make an official announcement; *the colony was proclaimed independent; the 25th of July has been proclaimed a national day of remembrance; the army chief was proclaimed king*

◊ **proclamation** [prɒklə'meɪʃn] *noun* official public statement; *the proclamation of a state of emergency*

Procurator Fiscal ['prɒkjʊreɪtə 'fɪskəl] *noun (in Scotland)* law officer who decides whether an alleged criminal should be prosecuted

profit ['prɒfɪt] *noun* **(a)** money gained from a sale which is more than the money spent on making or buying the item sold; **profit and loss account** = accounts for a company

which show expenditure and income balanced to show a final profit or loss; **profit before tax** *or* **pretax profit** = profit before any tax has been paid; **profit after tax** = profit after tax has been paid **(b) office of profit (under the Crown)** = government post which disqualifies someone from being a Member of Parliament

◊ **profitability** [prɒfɪtə'bɪlɪti] *noun* **(a)** ability to yield a profit **(b)** amount of profit made as a percentage of costs; **measurement of profitability** = way of calculating how profitable something is

◊ **profitable** ['prɒfɪtəbl] *adjective* which makes a profit

◊ **profitably** ['prɒfɪtəbli] *adverb* making a profit

◊ **profiteer** [prɒfɪ'tɪə] *noun* person who makes too much profit, especially when goods are rationed or in short supply

◊ **profiteering** [prɒfɪ'tɪərɪŋ] *noun* making too much profit

programme *or US* program

['prəʊgræm° *US* 'prəʊgrəm] *noun* plan of action, especially a party's plan of political *or* legislative action; **the government's legislative programme** = bills which the government plans to put before the House; **employment programme** *or* **housing programme** = plan to create more jobs *or* build more houses

progress 1 ['prəʊgres] *noun* movement forwards; **to make progress** = to move towards an aim; *the negotiations have not made much progress; we made good progress in the discussions over the extradition treaty;* **motion to report progress** = motion to adjourn a meeting of the House of Commons sitting as a committee until a later date (similar to the motion for adjournment of the debate) **2** [prə'gres] *verb* to move forwards; *the government is progressing towards the completion of its legislative programme*

◊ **progressive** [prə'gresɪv] *adjective* **(a)** which moves forward; **a progressive income tax** = tax which becomes higher as the salary increases; **Progressive Conservative Party**

= one of the main political parties in Canada **(b)** in favour of new (usually left-wing) ideas

project ['prɒdʒekt] *noun* plan to do something *or* to build something; *a redevelopment project; the council's project to rehouse council tenants has run into financial difficulties*

proletariat [prəʊlɪ'teərɪət] *noun* the working class, especially manual and industrial workers and their families; **the urban proletariat** = working people who live in towns; **dictatorship of the proletariat** = in Marxist theory, the period after a revolution when the Communist Party takes control until a classless society develops

◊ **proletarian** [prəʊlɪ'teərɪən] *adjective* referring to the working class; *a proletarian movement for government reform;* **the proletarian revolution** = in Marxist theory, the stage when the proletariat overthrows a capitalist society

proliferation [prəlɪfə'reɪʃn] *noun* increase in numbers; **nuclear proliferation** = the spreading numbers of nuclear weapons

promote [prə'məʊt] *verb* **(a)** to introduce a new Bill into Parliament **(b)** to give someone a more important job; *he was promoted from salesman to sales manager* **(c)** to advertise; **to promote a new product** = to increase the sales of a new product by a sales campaign *or* TV advertising *or* free gifts **(d)** to encourage something to grow; *the United Nations hopes to promote better understanding between countries with different systems of government; the government's campaign to promote increased prosperity in urban centres*

◊ **promoter** [prə'məʊtə] *noun* person who introduces a new Bill into Parliament; **company promoter** = person who organizes the setting up of a new company

◊ **promotion** [prə'məʊʃn] *noun* **(a)** moving up to a more important job; **to earn promotion** = to work hard and efficiently and so be promoted **(b)** encouragement to buy a product or use a service; *the council has spent heavily on tourist promotion*

◊ **promotional** [prə'məʊʃnəl] *adjective* used in an advertising campaign; **promotional budget** = expected cost of promoting a new product *or* service

propaganda [prɒpə'gændə] *noun (usually as criticism)* statements which describe the policies *or* actions of a government in a way which persuades people to believe they are true and correct; *the people have grown used to not believing government propaganda; the leader of the opposition denounced the council's advertising campaign as simple propaganda;* **propaganda radio** = radio which sends out broadcasts aimed at changing people's ideas; **propaganda war** = fight between two parties *or* governments, using radio *or* television *or* newspapers, etc., to publicize their ideas and try to persuade people to believe them; (NOTE: no plural)

◊ **propagandist** [prɒpə'gændɪst] *noun* person who issues propaganda

proportion [prə'pɔːʃn] *noun* part (of a total); *a proportion of the pretax profit is set aside for contingencies; only a small proportion of our sales comes from retail shops;* **in proportion to** = showing how something is related to something else; *grants are given in proportion to people's needs*

◊ **proportional** [prə'pɔːʃnəl] *adjective* directly related; **proportional representation (PR)** = system of electing representatives where each political party is allocated a number of places which is directly related to the number of votes cast for the party

proposal [prə'pəʊzl] *noun* **(a)** suggestion, thing suggested; *to make a proposal or to put forward a proposal;* **to lay a proposal before the House** = to introduce a new Bill before Parliament; **the committee turned down the proposal** = the committee refused to accept what had been suggested **(b)** **proposal form** = official document with details of a property *or* person to be insured which is sent to the insurance company when asking for an insurance

◊ **propose** [prə'pəʊz] *verb* (a) to suggest that something should be done; *the Bill proposes that any party to the proceedings may appeal;* to propose a motion = to ask a meeting to vote for a motion and explain the reasons for this; to propose someone as chairman = to ask a group to vote for someone to become chairman (b) to propose to = to say that you intend to do something; *we propose to repay the loan over a period of four years*

◊ **proposer** [prə'pəʊzə] *noun* person who proposes; *each candidate needs a proposer and seconder; Mr Smith is the proposer of the vote of thanks, but who is seconding him?; see also* SECOND, SECONDER

◊ **proposition** [prɒpə'zɪʃn] *noun* motion to be debated

prorogation [prəʊrəʊ'geɪʃn] *noun* ending of a session of Parliament by the Queen

◊ **prorogue** [prəʊ'rəʊg] *verb* to end a session of Parliament; *Parliament was prorogued for the summer recess*

proscribe [prəʊ'skraɪb] *verb* to ban; a proscribed political party = political party which has been banned

prosecute ['prɒsɪkjuːt] *verb* (a) to bring (someone) to court to answer a criminal charge; *he was prosecuted for embezzlement* (b) to speak against the accused person on behalf of the party bringing the charge; *Mr Smith is prosecuting, and Mr Jones is appearing for the defence*

◊ **prosecution** [prɒsɪ'kjuːʃn] *noun* (a) act of bringing someone to court to answer a charge; *his prosecution for embezzlement;* Crown Prosecution Service (CPS) = the office of the Director of Public Prosecutions, whose job is to supervise the prosecution of criminals; Director of Public Prosecutions (DPP) = government official in charge of the Crown Prosecution Service, reporting to the Attorney-General, who advises on criminal cases brought by the police, prosecutes in important cases and advises other government departments if prosecutions should be started (b) (i) party who brings a criminal charge against someone; (ii) lawyers representing the party who brings a criminal

charge against someone; *the costs of the case will be borne by the prosecution;* prosecution counsel *or* counsel for the prosecution = lawyer acting for the prosecution; *see also* DEFENCE

◊ **prosecutor** ['prɒsɪkjuːtə] *noun* person who brings criminal charges against someone; Crown prosecutor = official of the Director of Public Prosecutions' department who is responsible for prosecuting criminals in a local area; public prosecutor = government official who brings charges against alleged criminals (in the UK, the Director of Public Prosecutions)

prospective [prə'spektɪv] *adjective* which may happen in the future; the prospective candidate for the constituency = person who may be chosen as candidate for the constituency; *we have interviewed six prospective candidates for the post of party secretary*

protect [prə'tekt] *verb* to defend something against harm; *the workers are protected from unfair dismissal by government legislation; the computer is protected by a plastic cover; the cover protects the machine from dust;* to protect an industry by imposing tariff barriers = to stop a local industry from being hit by foreign competition by stopping foreign products from being imported; protected country = independent country which is protected by another, more powerful, country; protected tenancy = tenancy where the tenant is protected from eviction; (NOTE: you protect someone **from** something or **from having** something done to him)

◊ **protection** [prə'tekʃn] *noun* action of protecting; thing which protects; *the country is under the protection of the United States; the minister was given round-the-clock police protection;* consumer protection = protecting consumers against unfair *or* illegal traders; data protection = protecting information (such as records about private people) in a computer from being copied or used wrongly; police protection = services of the police to protect someone who might be harmed; (NOTE: no plural)

◊ **protective** [prə'tektɪv] *adjective* which protects; **protective tariff** = tariff which tries to ban imports to stop them competing with local products; **protective treaty** = treaty by which one country agrees to protect another smaller country

◊ **protector** [prə'tektə] *noun* person *or* country which protects; **Lord Protector** = title taken by Oliver Cromwell during the Protectorate

◊ **protectorate** [prə'tektərət] *noun* **(a)** country which is being protected *or* governed by another more powerful country; *a British protectorate* **(b)** the Protectorate = period from 1653 - 1658 when Oliver Cromwell was Lord Protector

pro tempore *or* **pro tem** [prəʊ 'tempreɪ *or* 'prəʊ'tem] *Latin phrase meaning* for the time; **president pro tempore** = temporary president; (NOTE: often shortened to **pro tem.: he agreed to act as chairman pro tem.**)

protest 1 ['prəʊtest] *noun* statement *or* action to show that you do not approve of something; *to make a protest against high prices;* **sit-down** *or* **sit-in protest** = action by members of the staff who occupy their place of work and refuse to leave; **protest march** = demonstration where protesters march through the streets; **in protest at** = showing that you do not approve of something; *the staff occupied the offices in protest at the low pay offer;* **to do something under protest** = to do something, but say that you do not approve of it **2** [prə'test] *verb* **to protest against something** = to say that you do not approve of something; *the retailers are protesting against the ban on imported goods;* (NOTE: in this meaning GB English is **protest against something**, but US English is **to protest something**)

◊ **protester** [prə'testə] *noun* person who protests; *protesters marched to Downing Street*

protocol ['prəʊtəkɒl] *noun* **(a)** (i) draft memorandum; (ii) list of things which have been agreed; *the negotiators signed the protocol of the treaty* **(b)** correct diplomatic behaviour between officials of different governments; **head of protocol** = diplomat in an embassy who is concerned with relations with the host government and other embassies

provide [prə'vaɪd] *verb* **(a) to provide for something** = to allow for something which may happen in the future; *the contract provides for an annual increase in charges; £10,000 has been provided for in the budget; these expenses have not been provided for; payments as provided in Schedule 6 attached;* **to provide for someone** = to put aside money to give someone enough to live on; *he provided for his daughter in his will* **(b)** to put money aside in accounts to cover expenditure or loss in the future; *£25,000 is provided against bad debts* **(c) to provide someone with something** = to supply something to someone; *the Prime Minister provided the House with a detailed account of his movements; the Bill provides no help to the critics of the government's policies*

◊ **provided that** *or* **providing** [prə'vaɪdɪd ðæt *or* prə'vaɪdɪŋ] *conjunction* on condition that; *the committee will decide on the planning application next week provided (that) or providing the architect's report is received in time;* (NOTE: in legal documents, the form **provided always that** is often used)

province ['prɒvɪns] *noun* **(a)** large administrative division of a country; *the ten provinces of Canada; the premier of the Province of Alberta* **(b)** area of a country away from the capital city; **in the provinces** = in the country outside London **(c) the Province** = Northern Ireland

◊ **provincial** [prə'vɪnʃl] **1** *adjective* referring to a province; *a provincial governor; the company is based in the provincial capital* **2** *noun* person from the provinces

◊ **provincialism** [prə'vɪnʃlɪzm] *noun* way of thinking which is typical of the provinces, as opposed to the main towns

provision [prə'vɪʒn] *noun* **(a)** legal condition; **the provisions of a Bill** = conditions listed in a Bill before Parliament; **we have made provision to this effect** = we have put into the contract terms which will make this work **(b) to make provision for** = to see that something is allowed for in the future; **to make financial provision for someone** = to give someone enough money to live on; **there is no provision for** or **no provision has been made for car parking in the plans for the office block** = the plans do not include space for cars to be parked **(c)** money put aside in accounts in case it is needed in the future; *the council has made a £2m provision for bad debts*

◊ **provisional** [prə'vɪʒnəl] *adjective* temporary or not final or permanent; *provisional budget; they wrote to give their provisional acceptance of the contract*

◊ **provisionally** [prə'vɪʒnəli] *adverb* not finally; *the contract has been accepted provisionally; he was provisionally appointed director*

proviso [prə'vaɪzəʊ] *noun* condition in a contract; *we are signing the contract with the proviso that the terms can be discussed again in six months' time;* (NOTE: the proviso usually begins with the phrase 'provided always that')

provocateur [prɒvɒkə'tɜː] *see* AGENT

provost ['prɒvəst] *noun* official in a Scottish town, with a position similar to that of a mayor in England

proxy ['prɒksi] *noun* **(a)** document which gives someone the power to act on behalf of someone else; *to sign by proxy;* **proxy vote** = vote made by proxy **(b)** person who acts on behalf of someone else, especially a person appointed by a shareholder to vote on his behalf at a company meeting; *to act as proxy for someone*

PSBR = PUBLIC SECTOR BORROWING REQUIREMENT

psephology [se'fɒlədʒi] *noun* study of elections, voting patterns, the influence of the media and opinion polls on voting, etc.

◊ **psephologist** [se'fɒlədʒɪst] *noun* person who makes a study of elections and voting patterns, and analyzes election results

PTA = PASSENGER TRANSPORT AUTHORITY, PARENT TEACHER ASSOCIATION

public ['pʌblɪk] **1** *adjective* **(a)** referring to all the people in general; **Public Bill** = Bill referring to a matter applying to the public in general which is introduced in Parliament by a government minister; **public domain** = land or property or information which belongs to and is available to the public; **work in the public domain** = written work which is no longer in copyright; **public holiday** = day when all workers rest and enjoy themselves instead of working; **public house** = building which has been licensed for the sale of alcohol to be drunk on the premises; **public law** = law which affects the people or the public as a whole (such as administrative and constitutional law); **public library** = library provided for the use of the general public; **public place** = place (such as a road or park or pavement) where the public in general have a right to be; **public policy** = general good of all the people; **public transport** = transport (such as buses, trains) which is used by any member of the public; **Public Trustee** = official who is appointed as a trustee of an individual's property **(b)** referring to the government or the state; **Public Accounts Committee** = select committee of the House of Commons which examines the spending of each department and ministry (including such matters as whether the department was entitled to spend the money in question, and whether the expenditure was a waste of money) **public administration** = (i) means by which government policy is carried out; (ii) people responsible for carrying out government policy; **public expenditure** = spending of money by the local or central government; **public finance** = the raising of money by governments (by taxes or borrowing) and the spending of it; **public funds** = government money available for expenditure; **public office** = important position in a government department; *he has held public office for twenty years;* **public ownership** = situation where an industry is nationalized and run by a board appointed by the government **(c)** taking place in front of many people, as opposed to private; *a public* *appearance by a member of the Royal Family; the public opening of the new park* **(d) public limited company (plc)** = company whose shares can be bought on the Stock Exchange; **the company is going public** = the company is going to place some of its shares for sale on the Stock Exchange so that anyone can buy them **2** *noun* **the public** *or* **the general public** = the people in general; **in public** = in front of everyone

◊ **publication** [pʌblɪ'keɪʃn] *noun* **(a)** (i) making something public (either in speech or writing); (ii) making a libel known to people other than the person libelled; *publication of Cabinet papers takes place after thirty years* **(b)** printed work shown to the public; **obscene publication** = book *or* magazine which is liable to deprave *or* corrupt someone who sees or reads it; *the magazine was classed as an obscene publication and seized by the customs*

◊ **public relations (PR)** ['pʌblɪk rɪ'leɪʃnz] *noun* keeping good links between an organization *or* a company *or* a group and the public so that people know what the organization is doing and approve of it; **public relations department** = section of an organization which deals with relations with the public; **public relations officer** = official who deals with relations with the public

◊ **public sector** ['pʌblɪk 'sektə] *noun* nationalized industries and national or local services; *a report on wage rises in the public sector or on public sector wage settlements;* **public sector borrowing requirement (PSBR)** = amount of money which a government has to borrow to pay for its own spending

◊ **Public Services, Tax and Commerce Union** British trade union representing civil servants; *see also* ASSOCIATION OF FIRST DIVISION CIVIL SERVANTS, CIVIL AND PUBLIC SERVICES ASSOCIATION

publish ['pʌblɪʃ] *verb* to have a document (such as a catalogue *or* book *or* magazine *or* newspaper *or* piece of music) written and printed and then sell or give it to the public; *the society publishes its list of members annually; the government has not published*

the figures on which its proposals are based; the company publishes six magazines for the business market

◊ **publisher** ['pʌblɪʃə] *noun* person or company which publishes

purchase ['pɜːtʃəs] **1** *noun* (i) action of buying something; (ii) thing which has been bought; **purchase order** = official order made out by a purchasing department for goods which a company wants to buy; **compulsory purchase** = buying of a property by a local authority *or* by the government, even if the owner does not wish to sell; **compulsory purchase order** = official order from a local authority *or* from the government ordering an owner to sell his property to them; **hire purchase** = system of buying something by paying a sum regularly each month, where the ownership of the item only passes when the final payment has been made; **hire purchase agreement** = contract to pay for something by instalments **2** *verb* to buy; **to purchase something for cash** = to pay cash for something

◊ **purchaser** ['pɜːtʃəsə] *noun* person or company which purchases something

purge [pɜːdʒ] **1** *noun* removing opponents *or* unacceptable people from a group; *the party has begun a purge of right-wing elements* **2** *verb* **(a)** to remove opponents *or* unacceptable people from a group; *the activists have purged the party of moderates or have purged the moderates from the party* **(b) to purge one's contempt** *or* **to purge a contempt of court** = to do something (such as make an apology) to show that you are sorry for the lack of respect you have shown

purpose ['pɜːpəs] *noun* aim *or* plan; *the purpose of the bill is to tighten up existing legislation;* **General Purposes Committee** = council committee which deals with matters which do not come under any other committee

pursuant to [pə'sjuːənt 'tuː] *adverb* relating to *or* concerning; *matters pursuant to Article 124 of the EU treaty; pursuant to the powers conferred on the local authority; pursuant to Standing Order No. 61*

pursue [pə'sjuː] *verb* to continue with (proceedings in court *or* debate in Parliament, etc.); *we shall pursue this matter at our next meeting*

pursuit [pə'sjuːt] *noun* **in pursuit** = following *or* chasing; *the bank robbers escaped in a car with the police in pursuit; see also* HOT

purview ['pɜːvjuː] *noun* general scope of an Act of Parliament *or* of the duties of a body; *it is within the purview of the Finance Committee to review the council's expenditure*

put [pʊt] *verb* to place; **to put a proposal to the vote** = to ask a meeting to vote for or against the proposal; **he moved that the question be put** = he proposed that the matter be voted on; **to put a proposal to the council** = to ask the council to consider a suggestion; (NOTE: **putting - put - has put**)

◊ **put down** ['pʊt 'daʊn] *verb* **(a)** to stop *or* crush a rebellion; *the Prime Minister ordered the army to put down the revolt* **(b)** to write a motion into the agenda of a meeting; *he put down a motion criticizing the government for its foreign policy* **(c)** to write an item in an account book; *to put down a figure for expenses*

◊ **put forward** ['pʊt 'fɔːwəd] *verb* to propose; *Mr John Smith's name has been put forward as a candidate for Treasurer; the government has put forward ten pieces of legislation for the next session; he put forward the suggestion that council meetings should be held on Saturdays*

◊ **put in** ['pʊt 'ɪn] *verb* to place inside; **to put an ad in a paper** = to have an ad printed in a newspaper; **to put in a bid for something** = to offer (usually in writing) to buy something; **to put in an estimate for something** = to give someone a written calculation of the probable costs of carrying out a job; **to put in a claim for damage** *or* **loss** = to ask an insurance company to pay for damage *or* loss

◊ **put off** ['pʊt 'ɒf] *verb* to arrange for something to take place later than planned; *the hearing was put off for two weeks; he asked if we could put the visit off until tomorrow*

◊ **put on** ['pʊt 'ɒn] *verb* to place on; **to put an item on the agenda** = to list an item for discussion at a meeting; **to put an embargo on trade** = to forbid trade

◊ **put out** ['pʊt 'aʊt] *verb* to send out; *to put work out to freelance workers; we put all our typing out to a bureau;* **to put work out to contract** = to decide that work should be done by a company on a contract, rather than employ members of staff to do it

putsch [pʊtʃ] *noun* armed coup against a government

Qq

QMV = QUALIFIED MAJORITY VOTING

qua [kweɪ] *conjunction* as *or* acting in the capacity of; *a decision of the Lord Chancellor qua head of the judiciary*

quadruplicate [kwɒˈdruːplɪkət] *noun* **in quadruplicate** = with the original and three copies; *the invoices are printed in quadruplicate;* (NOTE: no plural)

Quai d'Orsay [ˈkeɪ dɔːˈseɪ] *noun* street by the river Seine in Paris, where the French Foreign Ministry is; (NOTE: often used to refer to the Foreign Ministry itself, or to its policies)

qualification [kwɒlɪfɪˈkeɪʃn] *noun* **(a)** proof that you have completed a specialized course of study; *to have the right qualifications for the job;* **professional qualifications** = documents which show that someone has successfully finished a course of study which allows him to work in one of the professions **(b) period of qualification** = time which has to pass before something *or* someone qualifies for something; **qualification shares** = number of shares which a person has to hold to be a director of a company **(c)** condition *or* reservation; *the committee approved the plan with certain qualifications*

◊ **qualify** [ˈkwɒlɪfaɪ] *verb* **(a) to qualify for** = to be in the right position for *or* to be entitled to; *he does not qualify for Legal Aid; she qualifies for unemployment pay* **(b) qualify as** = to follow a specialized course and pass examinations so that you can do a certain job; *she has qualified as an accountant; he will qualify as a solicitor next year* **(c)** to change *or* to amend; **the auditors have qualified the accounts** = the auditors have found something in the accounts which they do not agree with, and have noted it

◊ **qualified** [ˈkwɒlɪfaɪd] *adjective* **(a)** having passed special examinations in a subject; *she is a qualified solicitor;* **highly qualified** = with very good results in examinations; *all our staff are highly qualified; they employ twenty-six highly qualified legal assistants* **(b)** with some reservations *or* conditions; *the plan received qualified approval from the council;* **qualified privilege** = protection from being sued for defamation given to someone only if it can be proved that the statements were made without malice **(c) qualified accounts** = accounts which have been noted by the auditors because they contain something with which the auditors do not agree **(d) qualified majority vote** = voting system used in the EU Council by which out of a total of 87 votes, 62 are needed to pass a law

◊ **qualifying** [ˈkwɒlɪfaɪŋ] *adjective* **(a) qualifying period** = time which has to pass before something qualifies for a grant *or* subsidy, etc.; *there is a six-month qualifying period before you can get a grant from the local authority* **(b) qualifying shares** = number of shares which you need to own to get a free issue *or* to be a director of a company

quango [ˈkwɒŋgəʊ] *noun* = QUASI-AUTONOMOUS NON-GOVERNMENTAL ORGANIZATION *GB* group of people appointed by a government with powers to deal with certain problems (such as the Race Relations Board or ACAS); (NOTE: plural is **quangos**)

quarantine [ˈkwɒrəntiːn] *noun* period of time (usually 40 days) when diplomatic relations are broken in order to isolate a country

quarter ['kwɔːtə] *noun* **(a)** period of three months; **first quarter** *or* **second quarter** *or* **third quarter** *or* **fourth quarter** *or* **last quarter** = periods of three months from January to the end of March *or* from April to the end of June *or* from July to the end of September *or* from October to the end of the year; *the instalments are payable at the end of each quarter; the first quarter's rent is payable in advance* **(b)** section of a town; *the old Turkish quarter;* **the Latin Quarter** = the part of Paris formerly inhabited by students

◊ **quarter day** ['kwɔːtə 'deɪ] *noun* day at the end of a quarter, when rents should be paid

COMMENT: in England the quarter days are 25th March (Lady Day), 24th June (Midsummer Day), 29th September (Michaelmas Day) and 25th December (Christmas Day)

◊ **quarterly** ['kwɔːtəli] *adjective & adverb* happening every three months *or* happening four times a year; *there is a quarterly charge for electricity; the bank sends us a quarterly statement; we agreed to pay the rent quarterly or on a quarterly basis*

quash [kwɒʃ] *verb* to annul *or* to make something not exist; *the appeal court quashed the verdict; he applied for judicial review to quash the order*

quasi- ['kweɪzaɪ] *prefix* almost *or* which seems like; *a quasi-official body; a quasi-judicial investigation; a quasi-autonomous non-governmental organization or quango*

queen [kwiːn] *noun* (i) female ruler of a monarchy; (ii) wife of a king; *the queen of the Netherlands;* (NOTE: written with a capital letter when used as a title: **Queen Elizabeth II**)

◊ **Queen Mother** ['kwiːn 'mʌðə] *noun* Queen who is the mother of a reigning King or Queen

◊ **the Queen's Speech** ['kwiːnz 'spiːtʃ] *noun* speech made by the Queen at the opening of a session of Parliament, which outlines the government's plans for legislation; **the Debate on the Queen's Speech** = first debate of a new session of Parliament, the motion being to present an address of thanks to the Queen, but the debate in fact being concerned with the Government's legislative programme as outlined in the speech

COMMENT: the Queen's Speech is not written by the Queen herself, but by her ministers, and she is not responsible for what is in the speech

quell [kwel] *verb* to keep under control; *mounted police were brought in to quell the riots*

query ['kwɪəri] **1** *noun* question; *the Chief Secretary to the Treasury had to answer a mass of queries from MPs* **2** *verb* to ask a question about something *or* to suggest that something may be wrong; *the opposition spokesman queried the statements made by the Cabinet Office officials*

question ['kwestʃn] **1** *noun* **(a)** words which need an answer; *MPs asked the minister questions about the Swiss bank accounts; he said he wished to put three questions to the Permanent Secretary; the managing director refused to answer questions about redundancies; the market research team prepared a series of questions to test the public's attitude to the government's record on law and order* **Question Time** = period in the House of Commons and the European Parliament when members can put questions to ministers about the work of their departments; *see also* PRIME MINISTER'S QUESTIONS **written question** = question submitted in advance in writing; **supplementary question** = spoken question asked after a written question has been answered (usually to try to embarrass the person answering) **(b)** problem; *he raised the question of the cost of the lawsuit; the main question is that of time; the tribunal discussed the question of redundancy payments* **(c)** matter *or* motion to be discussed by Parliament; **to put the question** = to ask MPs to say whether they agree with the motion or not **2** *verb* **(a)** to ask questions; *the inspectors questioned the Minister's staff for four hours; she questioned the chairman about the council's investment policy* **(b)** to query *or* to suggest that something may be wrong; *MPs questioned the reliability of the confidential report; the leader of the council questioned the result of the opinion poll*

COMMENT: the Speaker puts the question to get the opinion of the House. He reads out the motion, then asks those in favour to say 'Aye' and then those against to say 'No'; he then decides which is the majority and declares 'the Ayes have it' or 'the Noes have it'. If an MP disagrees with the Speaker's decision, he can challenge it and force a division (i.e. force a vote)

◊ **questioning** ['kwestʃnɪŋ] *noun* action of asking someone questions; *the man was taken to the police station for questioning; the witness became confused during questioning by the Select Committee*

◊ **questionnaire** [kwestʃən'neə] *noun* printed list of questions, especially used in market research; *to send out a questionnaire to test the opinions of users of the system; to answer or to fill in a questionnaire about problems of inner city violence*

quid pro quo ['kwɪd prəʊ 'kwəʊ] *Latin phrase meaning* 'one thing for another': action done in return for something done or promised

Quirinal [kwɪrɪ'næl] *noun* one of the seven hills of Rome, where the Italian government is based; (NOTE: used as a term for the Italian government)

quisling ['kwɪzlɪŋ] *noun* person who collaborates with an enemy invader

COMMENT: derived from the name of the Norwegian collaborator, Vidkun Quisling

quo [kwəʊ] *see* STATUS QUO

quorum ['kwɔːrəm] *noun* minimum number of people who have to be present at a meeting to make it valid; **to have a quorum** = to have enough people present for a meeting to go ahead; *do we have a quorum? the meeting was adjourned since there was no quorum*

◊ **quorate** ['kwɔːreɪt] *adjective* having a quorum; *the resolution was invalid because the shareholders' meeting was not quorate; see also* INQUORATE

COMMENT: in the House of Commons, the quorum is 40 MPs, and 30 peers are needed for a quorum in the House of Lords. In the US Congress, a majority of members must be present (that is, 51 in the Senate and 218 in the House of Representatives)

quota ['kwəʊtə] *noun* fixed amount of something which is allowed to be sold *or* bought *or* obtained; **import quota** = fixed quantity of a particular type of goods which the government allows to be imported; *the government has imposed a quota on the import of cars; the quota on imported cars has been lifted;* **quota system** = system where imports *or* exports *or* supplies are regulated by fixing maximum amounts

quote [kwəʊt] *verb* **(a)** to repeat words used by someone else; to repeat a reference number; *the Foreign Secretary quoted from the statement made by the Leader of the Opposition; she quoted figures from the annual report; in reply please quote this number: PC 1234* **(b)** to estimate *or* to say what costs may be; *to quote a price for supplying stationery; to quote a price in dollars; their prices are always quoted in dollars; he quoted me a price of £1,026; can you quote for supplying 20,000 envelopes?;* **quoted company** = company whose shares are listed on the Stock Exchange

◊ **quotation** [kwəʊ'teɪʃn] *noun* **(a)** words which have been quoted **(b)** estimate of how much something will cost; *they sent in their quotation for the job; to ask for quotations for building a new municipal office building; his quotation was much lower than all the others; we accepted the lowest quotation* **(c) quotation on the Stock Exchange** *or* **Stock Exchange quotation** = listing of the price of a company's shares on the Stock Exchange; **the company is going** for a quotation on the Stock Exchange = the company has applied to the Stock Exchange to have its shares listed

q.v. *or* **quod vide** [kjuː ˈviː or kwɒd ˈviːdeɪ] *Latin phrase meaning* 'which see' (used to refer to another document); *a similar case appears in the agenda for the Social Services Committee (q.v.)*

Rr

rabble ['ræbl] *noun* **the rabble** = the mob, rough people of the lower classes; **rabble-rouser** = politician who encourages the mob to take violent action; **a rabble-rousing speech** = a speech which encourages the mob to take violent action

race [reis] *noun* **(a)** test to see who can go fastest *or* who will win; *the race is on for the Democratic presidential nomination* **(b)** group of people with distinct physical characteristics or culture who are considered to be separate from other groups; **race relations** = relations between people of different racial groups

◊ **racial** ['reiʃl] *adjective* referring to race *or* races; **racial discrimination** = discrimination against someone because of race

◊ **racism** *or* **racialism** ['reisizm or 'reiʃəlizm] *noun* belief in racist ideas; actions based on racist ideas; *the minority groups have accused the council of racism in their allocation of council houses*

◊ **racist** *or* **racialist** ['reisist or 'reiʃəlist] *(usually as criticism)* **1** *adjective* (comment, publication, person) believing that people from other racial groups are different and should receive different (and usually inferior) treatment **2** *noun* person with racist ideas

radical ['rædikl] **1** *adjective* **(a)** extreme *or* involving great change; *the problem of overcrowding is so great, that only a radical solution can solve it; the new leader has started a radical rethink of the party's policies* **(b)** **Radical Party** = political party in favour of great or rapid change in society **2** *noun* **(a)** person who believes that a complete change should be made to society to reduce social problems **(b)** **Radical** = member *or* supporter of a Radical Party

◊ **radicalism** ['rædiklɔizm] *noun* political ideas of radicals

raise [reiz] **1** *noun* US increase in salary; *he asked the boss for a raise; she is pleased - she has had her raise;* (NOTE: British English is **rise**) **2** *verb* **(a)** to ask a meeting to discuss a question; *to raise a question or a point at a meeting; in answer to the point of order raised by Mr Smith;* **to raise an objection** = to object to something; *the opposition members of the Committee raised a series of objections to the wording of the statement* **(b)** to increase *or* to make higher; *the government has raised the penalties for drug smuggling; the company raised its dividend by 10%* **(c)** to obtain (money); to organize (a loan); *the council is trying to raise the capital to fund its housing programme; the government hopes to raise the money by extra taxation; where will he raise the money from to start up his business?*

raison d'état ['reizɒŋ dei'tæ] *noun* reason for a political action, which says that an action is justified because it is for the common good

COMMENT: raison d'état is open to criticism because it can be used to justify acts such as the abolition of individual rights, if the general good of the people may seem to require it at the time

Raj [rɑ:dʒ] *noun* period of British government of India

Rajya Sabha ['rɑ:ʒæ 'sæbæ] *noun* upper house of Parliament in India; (NOTE: the lower house is the **Lok Sabha**)

rally ['ræli] *noun* mass political meeting

rank [ræŋk] **1** level *or* grade in an organization; *in the Foreign Service, the rank of secretary is lower than that of ambassador; he was promoted to the rank of Chief Superintendent* **2** *verb* to be level with; **to rank higher** *or* **lower than** = to be more *or* less important than; *a Minister of State ranks below a Secretary of State*

rapprochement [ræ'prɒʃmɒŋ] *French word meaning* 'coming closer', used to mean a situation where two states become friendly after a period of tension; *political commentators have noted the rapprochement which has been taking place since the old president died*

rate [reɪt] **1** *noun* **(a)** money charged for time worked *or* work completed; **all-in rate** = price which covers all items in a purchase (such as delivery, tax and insurance, as well as the goods themselves); **fixed rate** = charge which cannot be changed; **flat rate** = charge which always stays the same; **full rate** = full charge, with no reductions; **reduced rate** = specially cheap charge **(b) insurance rates** = amount of premium which has to be paid per £1,000 of insurance; **interest rate** *or* **rate of interest** = percentage charge for borrowing money **(c) exchange rate** *or* **rate of exchange** = rate at which one currency is exchanged for another; **forward rate** = rate for purchase of foreign currency at a fixed price for delivery at a later date; **letter rate** *or* **parcel rate** = postage (calculated by weight) for sending a letter *or* a parcel **(d)** amount *or* number *or* speed compared with something else; **birth rate** = number of children born per 1,000 of the population; **error rate** = number of mistakes per thousand entries or per page **(e)** *GB* **rates** = local taxes on property; *our rates have gone up by 25% this year;* **uniform business rate (UBR)** = tax levied on business property which is the same percentage for the whole country; (NOTE: US English is **local property tax**) **2** *verb* **(a)** **to rate someone highly** = to value someone *or* to think someone is very good **(b) highly-rated part of London** = part of London with high local taxes

◊ **rateable** *or* **ratable** ['reɪtəbl] *adjective*

rateable value = value of a property as a basis for calculating local taxes

◊ **rate-capped** ['reɪt 'kæpt] *adjective* (local authority) whose proposed local tax increases have been blocked by central government; *several rate-capped authorities have complained to the Minister of the Environment*

◊ **rate-capping** ['reɪt 'kæpɪŋ] *noun* action of central government in stopping a local council from increasing rates excessively

◊ **ratepayer** ['reɪtpeɪə] *noun* **business ratepayer** = business which pays local taxes on a shop *or* factory, etc.

ratify ['rætɪfaɪ] *verb* to approve officially (something which has already been agreed); *the treaty was ratified by Congress; the ceasefire agreement has to be ratified by all the parties involved; although the directors had acted without due authority, the company ratified their actions*

◊ **ratification** [rætɪfɪ'keɪʃn] *noun* official approval of something which then becomes legally binding; *the Chair of Finance asked the committee for ratification of his decision*

re [riː] *preposition* about *or* concerning *or* referring to; *re your inquiry of May 29th; re: Smith's memorandum of yesterday; re: the agenda for the AGM;* **in re** = concerning *or* in the case of; *in re Jones & Co. Ltd*

re- [riː] *prefix* again; **to re-elect someone** = to elect someone again

reach [riːtʃ] *verb* to come to *or* to arrive at; *the council reached an agreement on the development plan; the jury was unable to reach a unanimous decision*

react [riː'ækt] *verb* to act in response to something; *the government has not reacted to the petition; the Chairman of the Council reacted angrily when a newspaper reported that his holiday had been paid for with public money*

◊ **reaction** [riː'ækʃn] *noun* **(a)** action taken in response to something; *the reaction of the minister has been to attack the Opposition parties* **(b)** *(as criticism)* extreme conservatism *or* being against any reform; *the* *slogan of the Socialists was 'Defeat the Forces of Reaction'*

◊ **reactionary** [riːˈækʃɒnri] *adjective & noun* (person) who has extreme conservative views *or* who is against all reform; *the newspaper is becoming more and more reactionary; as he grew older, the President's policies became reactionary*

reading [ˈriːdɪŋ] *noun* **First Reading** *or* **Second Reading** *or* **Third Reading** = the three stages of discussion of a Bill (in Parliament *or* in Congress)

> COMMENT: First Reading is the formal presentation of the Bill when the title is read to MPs; Second Reading is the stage when MPs have printed copies of the Bill and it is explained by the Minister proposing it, there is a debate and a vote is taken; the Bill is then discussed in Committee and at the Report Stage; Third Reading is the final discussion of the Bill in the whole House of Commons or House of Lords

realignment [riːəˈlaɪmmənt] *noun* **(a)** change in a system of alliances between political parties in a state *or* between states in an alliance; *a basic realignment of parties on the left; a realignment of Caribbean states* **(b)** changing a system, so that different parts are in a different relationship to each other; **a currency realignment** = a change in the international exchange rates

realm [relm] *noun* **(a)** kingdom **(b)** general area; **it is not beyond the realms of possibility** = it is quite likely

Realpolitik [reɪˈælpɒlɪtɪk] *German word meaning* politics based on real and practical factors and not on theoretical or moral principles

rebate [ˈriːbeɪt] *noun* money returned or deducted from a sum to be paid; **rent rebate** *or* **rate rebate** = state subsidy paid to poor people who do not have enough income to pay their rents *or* rates

rebel 1 [ˈrebəl] *noun* person who fights against the government *or* against people in authority; *anti-government rebels have taken six towns; rebel ratepayers have*

occupied the town hall **2** [rɪˈbel] *verb* to fight against authority; (NOTE: **rebelling - rebelled**)

◊ **rebellion** [rɪˈbeljən] *noun* fight against the government *or* against those in authority; *the army has crushed the rebellion in the southern province*

◊ **rebellious** [rɪˈbeljəs] *adjective* fighting against authority

rebut [rɪˈbʌt] *verb* to contradict *or* to go against; *he attempted to rebut the assertions made by the Opposition spokesman;* (NOTE: **rebutting - rebutted**)

◊ **rebuttal** [rɪˈbʌtəl] *noun* act of rebutting

recall [rɪˈkɔːl] **1** *noun* **(a)** asking someone to come back; *MPs are asking for the recall of Parliament to debate the crisis; after his recall, the Ambassador was interviewed at the airport* **(b)** *US* system of ending the term of office of an elected official early, following a popular vote **2** *verb* **(a)** to ask someone to come back; *MPs are asking for Parliament to be recalled to debate the financial crisis; the witness was recalled to the committee room;* **to recall an ambassador** = to ask an ambassador to return to his country (usually as a way of breaking off diplomatic relations) **(b)** to remember; *the witness could not recall having seen the papers*

recapture [riːˈkæptʃə] *verb* to capture again; *the Conservatives recaptured the seat they had lost in the previous Parliament*

receipt [rɪˈsiːt] **1** *noun* **(a)** paper showing that money has been paid *or* that something has been received; *customs receipt; rent receipt; receipt for items purchased; please produce your receipt if you want to exchange items;* **receipt book** *or* **book of receipts** = book of blank receipts to be filled in when purchases are made **(b)** act of receiving something; *goods will be supplied within thirty days of receipt of order; invoices are payable within thirty days of receipt; on receipt of the notification, the company lodged an appeal;* **to acknowledge receipt of a letter** = to write to say that you have received a letter; *we acknowledge receipt of your letter of the 15th;* **in receipt of** = having received; *we are in receipt of a* *letter of complaint; he was accused of being in receipt of stolen cheques;* (NOTE: no plural in this meaning) **(c) receipts** = money taken in sales; *to itemize receipts and expenditure; receipts are down against the same period of last year* **2** *verb* to stamp *or* to sign a document to show that it has been received *or* to stamp an invoice to show that it has been paid

receive [rɪ'siːv] *verb* **(a)** to get something which has been delivered; *we received the payment ten days ago; the workers have not received any salary for six months; the goods were received in good condition;* **'received with thanks'** = words put on an invoice to show that a sum has been paid **(b)** to accept a report officially; *it was resolved that the reports of the subcommittees be received* **(c) to receive stolen goods** = crime of taking in and disposing of property which you know to be stolen

◊ **receiver** [rɪ'siːvə] *noun* **(a)** person who receives something; **receiver of wrecks** = official of the Department of Trade who deals with legal problems of wrecked ships within his area **(b)** person who is appointed to administer a company for a period until the person who has appointed him has been paid money due; **Official Receiver** = government official who is appointed to administer the liquidation of a limited company after a winding up by the court *or* the affairs of a bankrupt after a receiving order has been made; *the court appointed a receiver for the company; the company is in the hands of the receiver* **(c)** person who receives stolen goods and disposes of them

◊ **receivership** [rɪ'siːvəʃɪp] *noun* administration by a receiver; **the company went into receivership** = the company was put into the hands of a receiver; (NOTE: no plural)

◊ **receiving** [rɪ'siːvɪŋ] *noun* act of taking something which has been delivered; **receiving clerk** = official who works in a receiving office; **receiving department** = section of a company which deals with goods *or* payments which are received by the company; **receiving office** = office where goods *or* payments are received; **receiving stolen property** = crime of taking in and

disposing of goods which are known to be stolen

recess [rɪ'ses] **1** *noun* **(a)** period when Parliament or another body is not sitting; *during August, Parliament is in recess; the council's last meeting before the summer recess will be on 23rd July* **(b)** *(in Congress)* period when the chamber does not meet, but is not adjourned **2** *verb* *(of the US Senate)* not to meet, but without adjourning; *the Senate recessed at the end of the afternoon*

reciprocal [rɪ'sɪprəkl] *adjective* given by one country *or* person *or* company to another and vice versa; (arrangement) where each party agrees to benefit the other in the same way; **reciprocal holdings** = situation where two companies own shares in each other to prevent takeover bids; **reciprocal trade** = trade between two countries, where each agrees to buy goods from the other; *the two countries signed a reciprocal trade agreement*

◊ **reciprocate** [rɪ'sɪprəkeɪt] *verb* to do the same thing to someone as he has just done to you; *the President offered to free political prisoners if the rebels would reciprocate by freeing their hostages*

◊ **reciprocity** [resɪ'prɒsɪti] *noun* arrangement which applies from one party to another and vice versa

recognize ['rekəgnaɪz] *verb* **(a)** to know someone *or* something because you have seen *or* heard them before; *she recognized the man who had attacked her; I recognized his voice before he said who he was; do you recognize the handwriting on the letter?* **(b)** to approve something as being legal; **to recognize a government** = to say that a government which has taken power in a foreign country is the legal government of that country; **the prisoner refused to recognize the jurisdiction of the court** = the prisoner said that he did not believe that the court had the legal right to try him; **to recognize a trade union** = to accept that a union can act on behalf of staff; *although all the staff had joined the union, the management refused to recognize it;* **recognized agent** = agent who is approved by the company for which he acts

◊ **recognition** [rekəg'nıʃn] *noun* act of recognizing; **to grant a government recognition** = to say that a government which has taken power in a foreign country is the legal government of that country; **to grant a trade union recognition** = to recognize a trade union

recommend [rekə'mend] *verb* **(a)** to suggest that something should be done; *the committee recommended the adoption of the amended budget; the government's legal advisers recommended applying for an injunction against the directors of the company; the officers do not recommend the proposed course of action; the board meeting recommended a dividend of 10p a share* **(b)** to say that someone *or* something is good; *I certainly would not recommend Miss Smith for the job; can you recommend a good hotel in Amsterdam?;* (NOTE: you recommend someone **for** a job; you recommend something **to** someone or that someone **should** do something or that something **be** done)

◊ **recommendation** [rekəmen'deıʃn] *noun* **(a)** advising that something should be done; *the government is acting on the recommendations of the Royal Commission; the subcommittee forwarded a recommendation for two new computers to the Finance Committee; the Council will consider the recommendation of the subcommittee that the budget be revised* **(b)** saying that someone *or* something is good; *we appointed him on the recommendation of his former employer* **(c)** *EU* type of legislation that has no binding force; *see also* DECISION, DIRECTIVE, REGULATIONS

recommit [ri:kə'mıt] *verb US* to send a bill back to the committee which reported it, for further discussion

◊ **recommittal** [ri:kə'mıtl] *noun* sending a bill back to a committee for further discussion

reconsider [ri:kən'sıdə] *verb* to think again; *the applicant asked the committee to reconsider its decision to refuse the*

application; US **motion to reconsider a vote** = motion at the end of a discussion of any bill, but especially one passed with a close vote, so that a second vote has to be taken to settle the matter

reconvene [ri:kɒn'vi:n] *verb* to meet again; *the committee has adjourned, and will reconvene tomorrow morning*

record 1 ['rekɔːd] *noun* **(a)** report of something which has happened, especially an official transcript of a court action; *the chairman signed the minutes as a true record of the last meeting;* **a matter of record** = something which has been written down and can be confirmed; **for the record** *or* **to keep the record straight** = to note something which has been done; **on record** = (fact) which has been noted; *the chairman is on record as saying that profits are set to rise;* **off the record** = unofficially *or* in private; *he made some remarks off the record about the rising crime figures in the borough* **(b) records** = documents which give information; *the names of customers are kept in the company's records; we find from our records that our invoice number 1234 has not been paid* **(c)** description of what has happened in the past; *the clerk's record of service or service record; the company's record in industrial relations;* **criminal record** = note of previous crimes for which someone has been convicted; *the councillor has a criminal record stretching back twenty years;* **track record** = success or failure of someone in the past; *he has a good track record as a minister* **(d)** result which is better *or* higher than anything before; **record crime figures** *or* **record losses** *or* **record profits** = crime figures *or* losses *or* profits which are higher than ever before; *1994 was a record year for bankruptcies; road accidents in 1993 equalled the record of 1990; the pound reached record highs against other currencies* **2** [rı'kɔːd] *verb* to note *or* to report; *the company has recorded another year of increased sales; your complaint has been recorded and will be investigated; the Government recorded another defeat over the Opposition; US* **recorded vote** = vote in Congress, where each member's vote is noted (this is always done in the Senate, and recorded votes are required in both Houses to override a presidential veto)

◊ **recording** [rɪ'kɔ:dɪŋ] *noun* making of a note; *the recording of an order or of a complaint*

recount 1 ['ri:kaʊnt] *noun* counting again; *the vote was very close, so the loser asked for a recount; after three recounts, Edward Jones was declared the winner by eleven votes* **2** [ri:'kaʊnt] *verb* to count again

recover [rɪ'kʌvə] *verb* (a) to get back something which has been lost; *he never recovered his money; the government's investment was never recovered; the council is trying to recover damages from the driver of the car; he has started a court action against the council to recover his property* (b) to get better or to rise; *the opinion polls show that the Opposition is recovering from the low point it reached last month; the stock market fell in the morning, but recovered during the afternoon*

◊ **recovery** [rɪ'kʌvərɪ] *noun* (a) getting back something which has been lost or stolen; *we are aiming for the complete recovery of the money invested; to start an action for recovery of property* (b) upward movement of shares or of the economy; *the economy showed signs of a recovery; the recovery of the economy after a recession*

recreation [rekrɪ'eɪʃn] *noun* pleasant way of spending free time; *his main recreations are reading and watching TV; the Parks and Recreation Department looks after the leisure centre; recreation areas are provided on all council estates*

◊ **recreational** [rekrɪ'eɪʃnəl] *adjective* referring to recreation; *the Education Department is recommending expanding recreational activities in the borough*

recurrent [rɪ'kʌrənt] *adjective* which happens again and again; *recurrent items of expenditure*

recycle [ri:'saɪkl] *verb* to take waste material and process it so that it can be used

again; *the council collects waste paper for recycling*

red [red] **1** *adjective* **(a)** colour of blood, also used as the colour symbolizing the Socialist or Communist Parties **(b)** Communist; referring to a Communist Party; **the Red Army** = formerly, the army of the USSR; **the Red Guards** = formerly, a militia in the Chinese People's Republic **2** *noun (usually as criticism)* **the Reds** = Communists

◊ **red box** ['red 'bɒks] *noun* suitcase covered in red leather in which government papers are delivered to ministers

◊ **Red Flag** ['red 'flæg] *noun* (i) symbol of international Communism; (ii) The Internationale, song which symbolizes international Communism

◊ **red tape** ['red 'teɪp] *noun* (i) red ribbon used to tie up a pile of legal documents; (ii) rules which slow down administrative work; *the application was held up by red tape; the agreement with the Australian company has been blocked by red tape*

redeploy [ri:dɪ'plɔɪ] *verb* to make better use of people or equipment, by sending them to another place; *the council is proposing to redeploy staff from other departments to make up the staff vacancies in the Finance Department*

◊ **redeployment** [ri:dɪ'plɔɪmənt] *noun* sending staff or equipment to another place

redistribute [ri:dɪs'trɪbju:t] *verb* to share out again; *in some forms of proportional representation, the votes cast for the losing candidates at the first count are redistributed among the main candidates to ensure an election*

◊ **redistribution** [ri:dɪstrɪ'bju:ʃn] *noun* **(a)** sharing out in a different way; *there is a redistribution of rates in London to help the poorer boroughs* **(b)** action of changing Parliamentary constituencies or electoral districts to make them more representative

reduce [rɪ'dju:s] *verb* to make smaller or lower; *the President is aiming to reduce expenditure on social services; the Appeal Court reduced the fine imposed by the* *magistrates or reduced the sentence to seven years' imprisonment; we have made some staff redundant to reduce costs; the government's policy is to reduce inflation to 5%*

◊ **reduced** [rɪ'djuːst] *adjective* lower; *new businesses pay a reduced rate of tax*

◊ **reduction** [rɪ'dʌkʃn] *noun* lowering (of prices, etc.); *price reductions; tax reductions; staff reductions; reduction of expenditure; reduction in demand*

redundancy [rɪ'dʌndənsi] *noun* (a) state where someone is no longer employed, because the job is no longer necessary; *there will be redundancies among local government workers if the system is reorganized;* redundancy payment = payment made to a worker to compensate for losing his job; voluntary redundancy = situation where the worker asks to be made redundant, usually in return for a payment (b) person who has lost a job because he is not needed any more; *rationalization caused 250 redundancies*

◊ **redundant** [rɪ'dʌndənt] *adjective* (a) more than is needed *or* useless; something which is no longer needed; *the old computer is now redundant since we have acquired a completely new system; a redundant clause in a contract; the new legislation has made clause 6 redundant* (b) to make someone redundant = to decide that a worker is not needed any more; redundant staff = staff who have lost their jobs because they are not needed any more

re-elect [riːɪ'lekt] *verb* to elect again; *the sitting member was re-elected with an increased majority*

◊ **re-election** [riːɪ'lekʃn] *noun* electing someone again; *the committee has opposed the automatic re-election of the chairman*

re-entry [riː'entri] *noun* going back into a place; right of re-entry = right of a person resident in a country to go back into that country after leaving it for a time; re-entry visa = visa which allows someone to re-enter a country

refer to [rɪ'fɜː'tuː] *verb* (a) to mention *or* to deal with *or* to write about something; *we refer to your letter of May 26th; he referred to an article which he had seen in 'The Times'; referring to the court order dated June 4th;* the schedule before referred to = the schedule which has been mentioned earlier (b) to pass a problem on to someone else to decide; *to refer a question to a committee; the report stands referred to the Finance Committee; we have referred your complaint to the tribunal* (c) the bank referred the cheque to drawer = the bank returned the cheque to the person who wrote it because there was not enough money in the account to pay it; 'refer to drawer' = words written on a cheque which a bank refuses to pay; (NOTE: **referring - referred**)

◊ **referee** [refə'riː] *noun* (a) person who can give a report on someone's character *or* ability *or* speed of work, etc.; *to give someone's name as referee; she gave the name of her boss as a referee; when applying please give the names of three referees* (b) person to whom a problem is passed for a decision; *the question of maintenance payments is with a court-appointed referee*

◊ **reference** ['refrəns] *noun* (a) passing a problem to a committee *or* consultant for an opinion; terms of reference = areas which a committee *or* an inspector can deal with; *under the terms of reference of the committee, it cannot investigate complaints from the public; the tribunal's terms of reference do not cover motorway planning permission* (b) mentioning *or* dealing with; *with reference to your letter of May 25th; the minister made no reference to the new agreement with the United States* (c) numbers or letters which make it possible to find a document which has been filed; *our reference: PC/MS 1234; thank you for your letter (reference 1234); please quote this reference in all correspondence; when replying please quote reference 1234* (d) written report on someone's character *or* ability, etc.; *to write someone a reference or to give someone a reference; to ask applicants to supply references;* to ask a company for trade references *or* for bank references = to ask for reports from traders or a bank on the company's financial status and reputation; **letter of reference** = letter in which an employer or former employer recommends someone for a job **(e)** person who reports on someone's character *or* ability, etc.; *to give someone's name as reference; please use me as a reference if you wish*

◊ **referral** [rɪ'fɜːrl] *noun* act of passing a problem on to someone else to decide; *the referral of the complaint to the subcommittee; the referral of a bill to the relevant committee*

referendum [refə'rendəm] *noun* type of vote, where a whole population is asked to vote on a single question; *the government decided to hold a referendum on the abolition of capital punishment; compare* PLEBISCITE (NOTE: plural is referenda or referendums)

reflag [riː'flæg] *verb* to change the place of registration of a ship, so that she flies a different flag

reform [rɪ'fɔːm] **1** *noun* change made to something to make it better; *they have signed an appeal for the reform of the benefit system; the reform in the legislation was intended to make the tribunal procedure more straightforward;* **electoral reform** = changing the electoral system to make it fairer; **law reform** = continuing process of revising laws to make them better suited to the needs of society **2** *verb* to change something to make it better; *the group is pressing for the health service to be reformed*

◊ **reformer** [rɪ'fɔːmə] *noun* person who tries to change society *or* an organization to make it better; *a prison reformer*

refugee [refjuː'dʒiː] *noun* person who has left his country because of war, political or religious persectuion, etc.

refund 1 ['riːfʌnd] *noun* money paid back; **full refund** *or* **refund in full** = refund of all the money paid **2** [ri'fʌnd] *verb* to pay back money; *to refund the cost of postage; travelling expenses will be refunded to witnesses giving evidence to the tribunal; all*

money will be refunded if the goods are not satisfactory

refuse 1 ['refjuːs] *noun* rubbish, especially rubbish from houses *or* shops *or* businesses; **refuse collection** = collecting rubbish from property and taking it to a dump; *refuse collections will stop over the holiday period* **2** [rɪ'fjuːz] *verb* to say that you will not do something *or* will not accept something; *the Speaker refused to allow the motion to be put; the MP refused to take the oath; he was refused permission to build a garage; he asked for a rise but it was refused; the loan was refused by the bank; he was offered the post of Chancellor of the Exchequer, but refused it* (NOTE: you **refuse to do something** or **refuse something**)

◊ **refusal** [rɪ'fjuːzl] *noun* saying 'No'; **his request met with a refusal** = his request was refused; **to give someone first refusal of something** = to allow someone to be the first to decide if they want something or not; **blanket refusal** = refusal to accept many different items

regain [riː'geɪn] *verb* to get back into your possession; *he regained control of the party*

regal ['riːgl] *adjective* (i) like a king *or* queen; (ii) suitable for a king *or* queen

regard [rɪ'gɑːd] *noun* **having regard to** *or* **as regards** *or* **regarding** = concerning *or* referring to something; *having regard to the opinion of the European Parliament; as regards or regarding the second point, the council referred the matter to a later meeting*

◊ **regardless** [rɪ'gɑːdləs] *adverb* **regardless of** = without concerning; *the top jobs in the council are open to all regardless of race or sex; the Speaker takes a serious view of noisy scenes in Parliament, regardless of the seriousness of the question being debated*

regent ['riːdʒənt] *noun* person who governs in place of a king or queen (usually when the king or queen is a child or is ill)

◊ **regency** ['riːdʒənsi] *noun* period of government by a regent; **the Regency** = period between 1811 and 1820 when Britain was ruled by the Prince of Wales in place of his father, King George III, who was insane

regicide ['redʒɪsaɪd] *noun* **(a)** crime of killing a king or queen **(b)** person who has killed a king or queen

regime *or* **régime** [re'ʒiːm] *noun (sometimes as criticism)* **(a)** type of government; *under a military regime, civil liberties may be severely curtailed* **(b)** period of rule; *life was better under the previous regime*

region ['riːdʒən] *noun* large area of a country; *a mountainous region; the Highland regions of Scotland;* **Committee of the Regions** = EU body which allows regional and local authorities to be directly involved in discussions at European Community level

◊ **regional** ['riːdʒənəl] *adjective* referring to a region; **Regional Council** = unit of local government in Scotland, covering a very large area of the country; **Regional Development Plan** = government scheme to bring industry, jobs, etc., to a depressed area

register ['redʒɪstə] **1** *noun* **(a)** official list; *to enter something in a register; to keep a register up to date;* **Companies' Register** *or* **Register of Companies** = list of companies, showing their directors and registered addresses, and statutory information kept at Companies House for public inspection; **register of charges** = index of charges affecting land; **register of directors** = official list of the directors of a company which has to be sent to the Registrar of Companies; **register of electors** *or* **electoral register** = list of names and addresses of all people in an area who are entitled to vote in local or national elections; **Register of Members' Interests** = publication showing special interests, consultancies and sponsorships of MPs; **land register** = list of holdings of land, showing who owns it and what buildings are on it; **Lloyd's Register** = classified list showing details of all the ships in the world **(b)** large book for recording details (as in a hotel, where guests sign in, or in a registry where deaths are recorded) **2** *verb* **(a)** to write something in an official list

or record; *to register a company; to register a property; to register a trademark; to register a birth or marriage or death* **(b)** to make an official statement; *the minority group registered a protest; I wish to register a complaint* **(c)** to arrive at a hotel *or* at a conference, sign your name and write your address on a list; *they registered at the hotel under the name of MacDonald* **(d)** to send (a letter) by registered post; *I registered the letter, because it contained some money*

◊ **registered** ['redʒɪstəd] *adjective* **(a)** which has been noted on an official list; **registered company** = company which has been properly formed and incorporated; **registered land** = land which has been registered with the Land Registry; **a company's registered office** = the address of a company which is officially registered with the Registrar of Companies and to which certain legal documents must normally be sent; **registered trademark** = trademark which has been officially recorded; **registered user** = person *or* company which has been officially given a licence to use a registered trademark **(b)** **registered letter** *or* **registered parcel** = letter *or* parcel which is noted by the Post Office before it is sent, so that compensation can be claimed if it is lost; *to send documents by registered mail or registered post*

◊ **Register Office** ['redʒɪstə 'ɒfɪs] *noun* office where records of births, marriages and deaths are kept and where civil marriages are performed

◊ **registrar** ['redʒɪstrɑː] *noun* **(a)** person who keeps official records; **Registrar of Companies** = official who keeps a record of all companies which have been incorporated, with details of directors and turnover; **registrar of trademarks** = official who keeps a record of all trademarks **(b)** official of a court who can hear preliminary arguments in civil cases **(c)** **Registrar of Births Marriages and Deaths** = local government official who registers births, marriages and deaths in an area

◊ **Registrar-General** ['redʒɪstrɑː 'dʒenərəl] *noun* official who is responsible for register offices and the registering of births, marriages and deaths

◊ **registration** [redʒɪ'streɪʃn] *noun* **(a)** act of having something noted on an official list; *registration of a trademark or of a share transaction;* **certificate of registration** *or* **registration certificate** = document showing that an item has been registered; **registration fee** = money paid to have something registered *or* money paid to attend a conference; **registration number** = official number of something which has been registered (such as the number of a car); **Registration Officer** = official who draws up the register of electors in each constituency **(b) land registration** = system of registering land and its owners

◊ **registry** ['redʒɪstri] *noun* **(a)** place where official records are kept; **Land Registry** = British government office where details of land are kept; **district registry** = office where records of births, marriages and deaths are kept **(b)** registering of a ship; **certificate of registry** = document showing that a ship has been officially registered; **port of registry** *or* **registry port** = port where a ship is registered

regnant ['regnənt] *adjective* ruling *or* reigning

regulate ['regjuleɪt] *verb* **(a)** to adjust something so that it works well *or* is correct **(b)** to change *or* maintain something by law; **prices are regulated by supply and demand** = prices are increased *or* lowered according to supply and demand; **government-regulated price** = price which is imposed by the government; **regulated tenancy** = PROTECTED TENANCY

◊ **regulation** [regju'leɪʃn] *noun* act of making sure that something will work well; *the regulation of trading practices*

◊ **regulations** [regju'leɪʃnz] *plural noun* **(a)** rules made by organizations, clubs, councils, which have to be followed by their members; laws *or* rules made by ministers; *according to council regulations, the outgoing chairman cannot stand for re-election; the manufacturer had not applied the new government regulations on standards for electrical goods; safety regulations which apply to places of work; regulations concerning imports and exports*

are explained in this booklet **fire regulations** = local or national regulations which owners of buildings used by the public have to obey in order to be granted a fire certificate **(b)** rules laid down by the Council of Ministers *or* Commission of the European Union, which are of general application, binding in their entirety and apply directly to all member states; *see also* DECISION, DIRECTIVE, RECOMMENDATION

◊ **regulatory** [regju'leɪtəri] *adjective* which regulates *or* which makes something work according to law; *the independent radio and television companies are supervised by a regulatory body; complaints are referred to several regulatory bodies*

reign [reɪn] **1** *noun* period of time when someone is king or queen; *an Act dating back to the reign of Queen Victoria* **2** *verb* **(a)** to be king or queen; *Queen Victoria reigned for 64 years;* **the reigning monarch** = the king or queen at the time **(b)** to be the most important factor; *chaos reigned in the capital for several days after the revolution; it was half an hour before peace reigned again in the council chamber*

reins [reɪnz] *noun* leather strings attached to a horse's head, to allow the rider to control it; **to take up the reins of government** = to begin to rule; **he holds the reins of power** = he is the ruler of the country

reject [rɪ'dʒekt] *verb* to refuse to accept *or* to say that something is not satisfactory; *the appeal was rejected by the House of Lords; the union rejected the management's proposals; the Speaker rejected a request from the Opposition for an emergency debate;* **the company rejected the takeover bid** = the directors recommended that the shareholders should not accept the bid

◊ **rejection** [rɪ'dʒekʃn] *noun* refusal to accept; *the rejection of the Opposition's request for a debate; the rejection of the appeal by the tribunal*

relate [rɪ'leɪt] *verb* **to relate to** = to refer to *or* to have a connection with something

◊ **related** [rɪ'leɪtɪd] *adjective* connected *or* linked *or* being of the same family; *offences* *related to drugs or drug-related offences; the law which relates to drunken driving*

◊ **relating to** [rɪ'leɪtɪŋ tu] *adverb* referring to or connected with; *documents relating to his application*

◊ **relation** [rɪ'leɪʃn] *noun* **(a)** in relation to = referring to or connected with; *documents in relation to the case; the court's powers in relation to children in care* **(b)** relations = links (with other people or other companies); *after the attack on the Embassy, the government recalled the Ambassador and broke off diplomatic relations;* to enter into relations with someone = to start discussing a business deal with someone; to break off relations with someone = to stop dealing with someone; industrial relations or labour relations = relations between management and workers; public relations = keeping good links between an organization or a group and the public so that people know what the group is doing and approve of it; public relations department = section of an organization which deals with relations with the public; public relations officer = official who deals with relations with the public

◊ **relationship** [rɪ'leɪʃnʃɪp] *noun* connection or link with another person or company; *what is the relationship between inflation and the cost-of-living?; there is no relationship between the two decisions*

release [rɪ'liːs] **1** *noun* **(a)** setting (someone) free or allowing someone to leave prison **(b)** allowing secret documents to become public; *the release of Cabinet papers after thirty years* **(c)** press release = sheet giving news about something which is sent to newspapers and TV and radio stations so that they can use the information in it; *the department sent out or issued a press release about the launch of the new job creation scheme; the architect was asked to write a press release about the new shopping precinct* **2** *verb* **(a)** to free (someone or something) or to allow (someone) to leave prison; *the president released the opposition leader from prison; to release goods from customs; the customs released the goods against payment of a fine;* to release someone from a debt or from a contract = to make someone no longer liable for the debt or

for the obligations under the contract **(b)** to make something public; *Cabinet papers are released after thirty years; the company released information about the new mine in Australia; the government has refused to release figures for the number of unemployed women*

relevance ['relɪvəns] *noun* connection with a subject being discussed; *the Minister argued with the Committee chairman over the relevance of the documents to the inquiry*

◊ **relevant** ['relɪvənt] *adjective* which has to do with what is being discussed; *the question is not relevant to the case; which is the relevant government department? can you give me the relevant papers?*

relief [rɪ'liːf] *noun* help; mortgage relief = allowing someone to pay no tax on the interest payments on a mortgage; tax relief = allowing someone to pay less tax on certain parts of his income; relief road = road which is built to take traffic away from another road or from a town centre

◊ **relieve** [rɪ'liːv] *verb* to make easier; *the new clinic will relieve the pressure on the existing facilities; they are planning a new road to relieve traffic congestion in the centre of town; the grant should relieve some of the tax burden*

remain [rɪ'meɪn] *verb* **(a)** to be left; *half the stock remained on the shelves; we will sell off the old stock at half price and anything remaining will be thrown away* **(b)** to stay; *she remained behind at the office after 6.30 to finish her work*

◊ **remainder** [rɪ'meɪndə] **1** *noun* things left behind; *the remainder of the items on the agenda were dealt with in five minutes; the remainder of the stock will be sold off at half price;* remainders = new books sold cheaply **2** *verb* to remainder books = to sell new books off cheaply

Remembrance [rɪ'membrəns] *noun* remembering; Remembrance Day or Remembrance Sunday = day (11th November, or the nearest Sunday) when the people killed in war are remembered

remind [rɪˈmaɪnd] *verb* to make someone remember; *I must remind the House of the seriousness of the financial situation*

◊ **reminder** [rɪˈmaɪndə] *noun* letter to make a person remember to pay *or* do something; *he paid the rent after several reminders; send her a reminder about the staff meeting*

remit 1 [ˈriːmɪt] *noun* area of responsibility given to someone; *this department can do nothing on the case as it is not part of or beyond our remit* **2** [rɪˈmɪt] *verb* to send (money); *to remit by cheque;* (NOTE: remitting - remitted)

◊ **remittance** [rɪˈmɪtəns] *noun* money which is sent; *please send remittances to the treasurer; the family lives on a weekly remittance from their father in the USA*

renounce [rɪˈnaʊns] *verb* to give up a right *or* a planned action; *the government has renounced the use of force in dealing with international terrorists*

◊ **renunciation** [rɪnʌnsɪˈeɪʃn] *noun* act of giving up a right

reopen [riːˈəʊpən] *verb* to start discussions again *or* to start investigating (a case) again; to start (a hearing) again; *the government has decided to reopen negotiations with the rebels; the hearing reopened on Monday afternoon*

reorganize [riːˈɔːɡənaɪz] *verb* to organize in a new way

◊ **reorganization** [riːɔːɡənaɪˈzeɪʃn] *noun* new way of organizing; *London government reorganization will take years to complete;* the **reorganization of a company** *or* **a company reorganization** = restructuring the finances of a company; **reorganization of a school** = changing by law the ages *or* types of children accepted by the school *or* the type of education given

repatriate [riːˈpætrɪeɪt] *verb* to send someone to leave the country he is living in and go back to his own country, sometimes by force; *if terrorism increases, the government may be forced to repatriate foreigners living in the area*

◊ **repatriation** [riːpætrɪˈeɪʃn] *noun* sending someone back to his own country; *the repatriation of the refugees will take months;* compare DEPORT, DEPORTATION

repeal [rɪˈpiːl] **1** *noun* abolishing a law so that it is no longer valid; *MPs are pressing for the repeal of the Immigration Act* **2** *verb* to abolish *or* to do away with (a law); *the Bill seeks to repeal the existing legislation*

reply [rɪˈplaɪ] **1** *noun* **(a)** answer; *there was no reply to my letter or to my phone call; in reply to your letter of the 24th; the company's reply to the takeover bid;* **reply paid card** *or* **letter** = card or letter to be sent back to the sender with a reply, the sender having already paid for the return postage **(b)** **right of reply** = (i) right of someone to answer claims made by an opponent; (ii) right of the mover of a motion to reply to the arguments of someone who has attacked the motion; *he demanded the right of reply to the newspaper allegations* **2** *verb* **(a)** to answer; *to reply to a letter; the company has replied to the takeover bid by offering the shareholders higher dividends* **(b)** to answer claims made by an opponent; to give an opposing view in a discussion; *the Foreign Secretary opened for the Government and the shadow Foreign Secretary replied for the Opposition*

report [rɪˈpɔːt] **1** *noun* **(a)** statement describing what has happened *or* describing a state of affairs; *to make a report or to present a report or to send in a report; the court heard a report from the probation officer; the chairman has received a report from the insurance company;* the **company's annual report** *or* the **chairman's report** *or* the **directors' report** = document sent each year by the chairman of a company or the directors to the shareholders, explaining what the company has done during the year; **confidential report** = secret document which must not be shown to other than a few named persons; **Law Reports** = collection of reports of cases of special interest and importance and which are legal precedents; **progress report** = document which describes what progress has been made; **the**

treasurer's report = document from the honorary treasurer of a society to explain the financial state of the society to its members **(b)** official document from a committee set up by the government to investigate something; *the committee has issued a report on the problems of inner city violence; the Director of Social Services has prepared a report on children in care* **(c)** a **report in a newspaper** *or* **a newspaper report** = article *or* news item; *can you confirm the report that the minister is going to resign?* **(d)** document in which a committee of the House of Commons *or* Congress explains the discussions which have been held and the amendments which have been made to a bill **2** *verb* **(a)** to make a statement describing something; *the council officers reported on the progress of the development plan; he reported the damage to the insurance company; we asked the bank to report on his financial status;* **reporting restrictions** = restrictions on information about a case which can be reported in newspapers; **reporting restrictions were lifted** = journalists were allowed to report details of the case **(b)** *(of a committee)* **to report a bill** = to send a bill back to the main chamber with amendments and comments **(c) to report to someone** = to be responsible to *or* to be under someone; *he reports direct to the managing director* **(d)** to go to a place *or* to attend; *to report for an interview; please report to our London office for training*

◊ **Report Stage** [rɪˈpɔːt ˈsteɪdʒ] *noun* stage in the discussion of a Bill in the House of Commons, where the amendments proposed at Committee Stage are debated by the whole House of Commons

represent [reprɪˈzent] *verb* **(a)** to be the elected representative of an area (in Parliament *or* on a council); *he represents one of the northern industrial constituencies* **(b)** to act on behalf of someone; *the defendant is represented by his solicitor* **(c)** to describe *or* to show; *he was represented as a man of great honour*

◊ **representation** [reprɪzenˈteɪʃn] *noun* **(a)** statement, especially a statement made to persuade someone to enter into a contract **(b)**

to make representations = to put forward views (sometimes complaints); *the Ratepayers' Association made representations to the council about the state of the footpaths* **(c)** being represented by a lawyer; **the applicant had no legal representation** = he had no lawyer to represent him in court **(d)** system where the people of a country elect representatives to a parliament which governs the country; **the Representation of the People Act** = Act of Parliament which states how elections must be organized; **proportional representation** = system of electing representatives where each political party is allocated a number of places which is directly related to the number of votes cast for each party

◊ **representative** [reprɪˈzentətɪv] *noun* **(a)** person elected to represent a group of people; *the legislature is made up of representatives elected by secret ballot* **(b)** *US* member of the lower house of Congress; **House of Representatives** = lower house of the American Congress; (NOTE: a Representative is also referred to as Congressman) **(c)** diplomat who acts on behalf of a government; *the British representative in the area* **(d)** person who represents another person *or* group of people; *the court heard the representative of the insurance company;* **personal representative** = person who is the executor of a will *or* who is the administrator of the estate of a deceased person

repress [rɪˈpres] *verb* to control by limiting freedom; *dictators try to repress opposition to their regimes; compare* OPPRESS, SUPPRESS

◊ **repression** [rɪˈpreʃn] *noun* restricting freedom and expression of feelings; *the country is recovering from twenty years of repression*

◊ **repressive** [rɪˈpresɪv] *adjective* using repression; *the civil rights demonstrators complained about the government's repressive methods*

republic [rɪˈpʌblɪk] *noun* **(a)** state which is not a monarchy, but which is governed by elected representatives headed by a President; *Singapore was declared a* *republic in 1965; most republics have Presidents as head of state*

◊ **republican** [rɪ'pʌblɪkən] *adjective* **(a)** referring to a republic **(b)** believing in the idea of a republic; *some members of the Opposition have republican sympathies*

◊ **Republican** [rɪ'pʌblɪkən] *noun* **(a)** member *or* supporter of a Republican Party, especially in the USA **(b)** person who believes in a republic as the best form of government

◊ **Republican Party** [rɪ'pʌblɪkən 'pɑːti] *noun* one of the two main political parties in the USA, which supports business and is against too much state intervention in industry and welfare; *compare* DEMOCATRIC PARTY

request [rɪ'kwest] **1** *noun* asking for something; *they put in a request for a government subsidy; his request for an adjournment was turned down by the chairman;* on request = if asked for; *we will send samples on request or 'samples available on request'* **2** *verb* to ask for; *to request assistance from the government; the witness requested permission to give evidence sitting down*

require [rɪ'kwaɪə] *verb* **(a)** to ask for *or* to demand something; *to require a full explanation of expenditure; the law requires you to submit all income to the tax authorities; the Bill requires social workers to seek the permission of the juvenile courts before taking action* **(b)** to need; *the document requires careful study; to write the program requires a computer specialist*

◊ **requirement** [rɪ'kwaɪəmənt] *noun* what is needed; *if you let me know your requirements, I will have some plans prepared for you;* Public Sector Borrowing **Requirement** = amount of money which a government has to borrow to pay for its own spending

requisition [rekwɪ'zɪʃn] *verb* **(a)** to demand *or* request formally; *a special meeting was requisitioned by six members* **(b)** to take (private property) into the temporary ownership of the state for the state

to use; *the army requisitioned all the trucks to carry supplies*

rescind [rɪ'sɪnd] *verb* to annul *or* to cancel; *to rescind a contract or an agreement; the committee rescinded its earlier resolution on the use of council premises*

◊ **rescission** [rɪ'sɪʃn] *noun* **(a)** cancellation of a contract **(b)** *US* item in an appropriation bill which cancels money previously appropriated but not spent

reserve [rɪ'zɜːv] **1** *noun* **(a)** money from profits not paid as dividend, but kept back by an organization in case it is needed for a special purpose; **bank reserves** = cash and securities held by a bank to cover deposits; **cash reserves** = an organization's reserves in cash deposits *or* bills kept in case of urgent need; **contingency reserve** *or* **emergency reserve** = money set aside in case it is needed urgently; *repairing damage after the storm used up part of the council's emergency reserves;* **reserve for bad debts** = money kept by an organization to cover debts which may not be paid; **reserve fund** = profits in a business which have not been paid out as dividend but which can be ploughed back into the business **(b) reserve currency** = strong currency held by other countries to support their own weaker currencies; **currency reserves** = foreign money held by a government to support its own currency and to pay its debts; **a country's foreign currency reserves** *or* **gold reserves** = a country's reserves in currencies of other countries *or* in gold **(c) in reserve** = kept to be used at a later date **2** *verb* **(a) to reserve a room** *or* **a table** *or* **a seat** = to book a room *or* table *or* seat *or* to ask for a room *or* table *or* seat to be kept free for you; *I want to reserve a table for four people; can your secretary reserve a seat for me on the train to Glasgow?* **(b)** to keep back; **to reserve one's defence** = not to present any defence at a preliminary hearing, but to wait until full trial; **to reserve judgment** = not to pass judgment immediately, but keep it back until later so that the judge has time to consider the case more fully; **to reserve the right to do something** = to indicate that you consider that you have the right to do something, and intend to use that right in the future; *he reserved the right to reply to the criticism; we reserve the right to appeal against the tribunal's decision*

◊ **reservation** [rezə'veɪʃn] *noun* **(a)** booking of a room *or* table *or* seat; *he phoned reservations and asked to book a room for four nights* **(b)** doubt; *he expressed reservations about the legality of the action; the plan was accepted by the committee with some reservations*

reshuffle [ri:'ʃʌfl] **1** *noun* changing of positions, especially those of Cabinet ministers; *in the reshuffle, the Secretary of State for Education was moved to the Home Office* **2** *verb* to change the positions of Cabinet ministers; *the President is expected to reshuffle his Cabinet soon*

residence ['rezɪdəns] *noun* **(a)** place where someone lives; *the crowd gathered outside the Governor's residence; he has a country residence where he spends his weekends; the Prime Minister has two official residences: Number 10, Downing Street in London, and Chequers in the country* **(b)** act of living *or* operating officially in a country; **residence permit** = official document allowing a foreigner to live in a country; *he has applied for a residence permit; she was granted a residence permit for one year*

◊ **Residency** ['rezɪdənsi] *noun* house where a colonial governor lives

◊ **resident** ['rezɪdənt] **1** *noun* **(a)** person *or* company living or operating in a place; *fire broke out in the council flats and the residents were brought out as quickly as possible; the warden of the hostel looks after the residents; British residents in the country are advised to leave as soon as possible* **(b)** (i) title of a diplomat of lower rank than an Ambassador, living in a foreign country; (ii) governor of a colony **2** *adjective* living *or* based in a country; *the company is resident in France for tax purposes;* **person ordinarily resident in the UK** = person who normally lives in the UK; **non-resident** = person *or* company which is not officially resident in a place; *he has a non-resident*

account with a French bank; she was granted a non-resident visa

residuary [rɪ'zɪdjuəri] *adjective* remaining; **residuary body** = body set up to administer the ending of a local authority and to manage those of its functions which have not been handed over to other authorities

resign [rɪ'zaɪn] *verb* to leave a job; *he resigned from his post as treasurer; he has resigned with effect from July 1st; she resigned as Education Minister*

◊ **resignation** [rezɪg'neɪʃn] *noun* act of giving up a job; *the newspaper published the Minister's letter of resignation and the Prime Minister's reply; he wrote his letter of resignation to the chairman;* **to hand in** *or* **to give in** *or* **to send in one's resignation** = to resign from a job

COMMENT: MPs are not allowed to resign their seats in the House of Commons. If an MP wants to leave the House, he has to apply for an office of profit under the Crown, such as the Stewardship of the Chiltern Hundreds, which will disqualify him from membership of the House of Commons

resist [rɪ'zɪst] *verb* to fight against something *or* not to give in to something; *parents are resisting the local authority's attempt to close the school; the party moderates were unable to resist the takeover by the extremists; the President's bodyguard resisted the attempted coup*

◊ **resistance** [rɪ'zɪstəns] *noun* **(a)** action which shows that people are opposed to something; *there was a lot of resistance from the local residents to the new plan; the Home Secretary's proposal met with strong resistance from the probation service; after the coup, there were still pockets of resistance in some parts of the country* **(b)** group which fights secretly against an enemy occupying a country; *he was in the French Resistance during the war;* **resistance fighters** = armed soldiers who are fighting against a government *or* an occupying enemy; (NOTE: in this meaning **resistance** can take a plural verb: **the resistance has** *or* **have captured several government outposts**)

resolution [rezə'luːʃn] *noun* **(a)** decision taken by one of the Houses of Parliament *or* Congress to show their opinion of something; *US* **joint resolution** = Bill passed by both House and Senate, sent to the President for signature to become law **(b)** decision taken at the United Nations **(c)** decision taken at a meeting; *the conference passed a resolution condemning the use of force by the police; the resolution from the platform was defeated by a large majority;* **to move a resolution** *or* **to put a resolution to a meeting** = to ask a meeting to approve a resolution; **ordinary resolution** = decision which is taken by a majority vote of members or people present; **extraordinary** *or* **special resolution** = resolution (such as a change of the articles of an organization) which usually requires a larger majority of votes than an ordinary resolution; *the special resolution presented to the conference requires a two-thirds majority to be passed*

resolve [rɪ'zɒlv] *verb* to decide (at a meeting); *the meeting resolved that the reports be received and the amendments adopted; the sub-committee resolved to ask the council to consider using outside labour; the council resolved that the Chief Executive be authorized to make adjustments to the claim; Item 2: RESOLVED: that the surveyor be instructed to inspect the building at once* (NOTE: that a committee resolves that something **be** done or resolves **to** do something)

resource [rɪ'sɔːs] **1** *noun* means of help, especially money; *education takes up a large part of the council's resources; there is a resource centre where social workers can get equipment for needy families; the resources allocated by central government are not sufficient to cover the anticipated expenditure* **resource allocation** *or* **allocation of resources** = sharing out of a council's money for housing, social services, etc.; (NOTE: **resources** is often used in the plural) **2** *verb* to give money to; *the nurseries are well resourced and are full of modern equipment*

respect [rɪ'spekt] **1** *noun* **with respect to** *or* **in respect of** = concerning; *his right to*

supplementary payments in respect of his six children; the council counterclaimed for loss and damage in respect of a work not carried out by the contractor **2** *verb* to pay attention to *or* to follow; *to respect a clause in an agreement; the company has not respected the terms of the contract*

◊ **respectively** [rɪ'spektɪvli] *adverb* referring to each one separately; *council caretakers and cleaners were given increases of 5% and 7% respectively*

respond [rɪ'spɒnd] *verb* to reply *or* to act in answer; *the Minister responded by accusing the opposition of distorting the facts; several countries responded to the appeal for help*

◊ **response** [rɪ'spɒns] *noun* reply; *we asked for further details, but so far there has been no response*

responsibility [rɪspɒnsɪ'bɪlɪti] *noun* **(a)** duty *or* thing which you are responsible for doing; *he finds the responsibilities of being managing director too heavy; keeping the interior of the building in good order is the responsibility of the tenant* **(b)** being responsible; *there is no responsibility on the company's part for loss of customers' property; the Minister accepts full responsibility for the actions of his officials;* **collective responsibility** = doctrine that all members of a group (such as the British cabinet) are responsible together for the actions of that group

◊ **responsible** [rɪ'spɒnsɪbl] *adjective* **(a)** **responsible for** = (i) to blame for; (ii) being in charge of *or* in control of; *the government is responsible for the collapse of the economy; the committee chairman was found to be the person responsible for leaks to the press; Ministers are responsible for the actions of their officials; the caretaker is responsible for the security of the building; she is responsible for twenty junior office staff* **(b)** **responsible to someone** = being under someone's authority; *magistrates are responsible to the Lord Chancellor* **(c)** **responsible government** = form of government which acts in accordance with the wishes of the people and which is accountable to Parliament for its actions; **a responsible job** = job where important decisions have to be taken *or* where the employee has many responsibilities; (NOTE: the opposite is **irresponsible**)

◊ **responsibly** [rɪsˈpɒnsɪbli] *adverb* in a responsible way; *the judge congratulated the jury on acting responsibly*

restitution [restɪˈtjuːʃn] *noun* (a) giving back *or* return (of property) which has been illegally obtained; *the court ordered the restitution of assets to the company;* **restitution order** = court order asking for property to be returned to someone (b) compensation *or* payment for damage or loss; *(in the EU)* **export restitution** = subsidies to European food exporters

restore *verb* to put back something which has been removed; *the military government pledged to restore democracy and hold general elections*

restrict [rɪˈstrɪkt] *verb* to limit *or* to impose controls on; *the government has restricted the release of information about the treaty; we are restricted to twenty staff by the size of our offices; to restrict the flow of trade or to restrict imports; free admission is restricted to children under five* **restricted information** = information which can be given only to certain people

◊ **restriction** [rɪˈstrɪkʃn] *noun* limit *or* act of controlling; *import restrictions or restrictions on imports;* **to impose restrictions on imports** *or* **on credit** = to start limiting imports *or* credit; **to lift credit restrictions** = to allow credit to be given freely; **reporting restrictions** = restrictions on information about a case which can be reported in newspapers *or* on radio or TV; **reporting restrictions were lifted** = journalists were allowed to report details of the case

◊ **restrictive** [rɪˈstrɪktɪv] *adjective* which limits; **restrictive practices** = ways of working which exclude free competition in relation to the supply of goods or labour in order to maintain prices or wages; **Restrictive Practices Court** = court which decides in cases of restrictive practices

result [rɪˈzʌlt] **1** *noun* something which happens because of something else; *what was*

the result of the contract investigation? the council doubled its staff with the result that expenditure rose by 26%; **the job creation scheme has produced results** = has produced more jobs **2** *verb* **(a) to result in** = to produce as a result **(b) to result from** = to happen because of something; *the increase in overtime resulted from implementing the development programme*

resume [rɪˈzjuːm] *verb* to start again; *the discussions resumed after a two hour break*

◊ **resumption** [rɪˈzʌmpʃn] *noun* starting again; **we expect an early resumption of negotiations** = we expect negotiations will start again soon; (NOTE: no plural)

résumé [ˈrezuːmeɪ] *noun* **(a)** summary of a text; *a résumé of the debate was published in yesterday's paper* **(b)** *US* summary of a person's life story showing important details of education and work experience; (NOTE: British English for this is **curriculum vitae**)

retire [rɪˈtaɪə] *verb* **(a)** to stop work and take a pension; *she retired with a £6,000 pension; the chairman of the company retired at the age of 65; the shop is owned by a retired policeman;* **retiring age** = age at which people retire (in the UK usually 65 for men and 60 for women) **(b)** to make a worker stop work and take a pension; *they decided to retire all staff over 50 years of age* **(c)** to come to the end of an elected term of office; *the treasurer retires after six years; two retiring directors offer themselves for re-election* **(d)** to go away from a court for a period of time; *the magistrates retired to consider their verdict; the jury retired for four hours*

◊ **retiral** [rɪˈtaɪrəl] *noun US & Scottish* = RETIREMENT

◊ **retirement** [rɪˈtaɪəmənt] *noun* **(a)** act of retiring from work; **to take early retirement** = to leave work before the usual age; **retirement age** = age at which people retire (in the UK usually 65 for men and 60 for women); **retirement pension** = pension which someone receives when he retires **(b)** *(of a jury)* going out of the courtroom to consider their verdict

retract [rɪ'trækt] *verb* to withdraw a statement because it was erroneous; *the minister was forced to retract his statement about the Leader of the Opposition*

retroactive [retrəʊ'æktɪv] *adjective* which takes effect from a time in the past; *they received a pay rise retroactive to last January*

◊ **retroactively** [retrəʊ'æktɪvli] *adverb* going back to a time in the past

retrospective [retrə'spektɪv] *adjective* going back in time; **retrospective legislation** = Act of Parliament which applies to the period before the Act was passed; **with retrospective effect** = applying to a past period; *the tax ruling has retrospective effect*

◊ **retrospectively** [retrə'spektɪvli] *adverb* in a retrospective way; *the ruling is applied retrospectively*

return [rɪ'tɜːn] **1** *noun* (a) going back or coming back; **return journey** = journey back to where you came from; **return fare** = fare for a journey from one place to another and back again (b) sending back; **he replied by return of post** = he replied by the next post service back; **return address** = address to send back something (c) **official return** = official report or statement; **to make a return to the tax office** or **to make an income tax return** = to send a statement of income to the tax office; **to fill in a VAT return** = to complete the form showing VAT inputs and outputs; **annual return** = form to be completed by each company once a year, giving details of the directors and the financial state of the company; **nil return** = report showing no sales or no income or no tax, etc. (d) election of an MP (e) profit or income from money invested; **return on investment** or **on capital** = profit shown as a percentage of money invested; **rate of return** = amount of interest or dividend produced by an investment, shown as a percentage **2** *verb* (a) to send back; *to return damaged stock to the wholesaler; to return a letter to sender* (b) to make a statement; **to return income of £15,000 to the tax authorities** = to notify the tax authorities that you have an income of

£15,000; *(of a jury)* **to return a verdict** = to state the verdict at the end of a trial; *the jury returned a verdict of not guilty* (c) to elect an MP for a constituency; *he was returned with an increased majority*

◊ **returning officer** [rɪ'tɜːnɪŋ 'ɒfɪsə] *noun* official (usually a High Sheriff or mayor) who superintends a parliamentary election in a constituency, receives the nominations of candidates and announces the result of the vote

> COMMENT: when a writ for an election is issued by the Lord Chancellor, the returning officer for each constituency must give notice of the election, and candidates may be nominated up to eight days after the writs are issued

reunify [riː'juːnɪfaɪ] *verb* to unite again after being separated; *reunified Germany*

◊ **reunification** [riːjuːnɪfɪ'keɪʃn] *noun* being united again after being separated; *the reunification of Germany*

revenue ['revənjuː] *noun* money earned or income; *the purpose of the bill is to raise revenue by imposing a sales tax on luxury goods; the rates provide about 46% of the Council's revenue;* **Inland Revenue** or *US* **Internal Revenue Service** = government department dealing with tax; *to make a declaration to the Inland Revenue;* **revenue officer** = person working in a government tax office; **revenue expenditure** = day to day or current expenditure, such as salaries, maintenance of buildings (not capital expenditure)

review [rɪ'vjuː] **1** *noun* (a) general examination of something again; *the education officer presented the annual review of teaching staff; the coroner asked for a review of police procedures;* **financial review** = examination of an organization's finances; **review body** = organization which reviews the salaries of a group of people; *the independent review body has recommended increases of 6% for the top staff grades* (b) magazine or monthly or weekly journal **2** *verb* to examine something generally; *a committee has been appointed to review civil service salaries; the council has reviewed its* *housing policy and decided to make no major changes*

revise [rɪ'vaɪz] *verb* to change (a text *or* a decision) after considerable thought; *the revised examination procedures have been published; the Speaker revised his earlier decision not to allow an emergency debate*

◊ **revision** [rɪ'vɪʒən] *noun* act of changing something; *the council safety regulations urgently need revision*

◊ **revisionism** [rɪ'vɪʒənɪzm] *noun (used as criticism)* changing *or* trying to change the principles on which a political party is based; *the former Party leader was accused of revisionism*

◊ **revisionist** [rɪ'vɪʒənɪst] *adjective & noun* (person) who wants to change a party's principles

revoke [rɪ'vəuk] *verb* to cancel (a permission *or* right *or* agreement *or* offer *or* will); *to revoke a clause in an agreement; the treaty on fishing rights has been revoked*

◊ **revocable** [rɪ'vəukəbl] *adjective* which can be revoked

◊ **revocation** [revɒ'keɪʃn] *noun* cancelling (of permission *or* right *or* agreement *or* offer *or* will)

revolt [rɪ'vəult] **1** *noun* act of rebelling against authority; *the whips are trying to quell the revolt in the party; the revolt in the army was put down by the President's bodyguard;* in revolt against = rebelling against; *the farmers were in revolt against the tax collectors* **2** *verb* to rebel against an authority; *seventy MPs revolted and voted against the Government; the President's bodyguard revolted and the revolt spread to other parts of the army*

revolution [revə'lu:ʃn] *noun* (a) armed rising against a government; *the government was overthrown by a revolution led by the head of the army;* the American Revolution = the War of Independence (1775-83) by which the former American colonies became independent; the British Revolution *or* the Glorious Revolution = the deposition of King James II (1688) and his replacement by William III and Mary; the French

Revolution = the civil war which overthrew the monarchy (1789) and established a republic; the Russian Revolution = the overthrow of the Russian monarchy in 1917 (b) period of social change, where the previous way of life changes radically; the Industrial Revolution = period in the late 18th and early 19th centuries when industry began to develop

◊ **revolutionary** [revə'lu:ʃnəri] **1** *adjective* (a) referring to a revolution; *revolutionary troops surrounded the President's Palace;* the Revolutionary War = the American War of Independence (b) very new and different; *the minister has proposed a revolutionary new system of collecting tax* **2** *noun* person who takes part in a revolution; *the palace was surrounded by revolutionaries*

rider ['raɪdə] *noun* (a) additional clause (to a contract *or* report) (b) *US* clause attached to a bill, which may have nothing to do with the subject of the bill, but which the sponsor hopes to get passed into law more easily in this way

riding ['raɪdɪŋ] *noun* (a) *(in Yorkshire)* administrative section of a county (b) *(in Canada)* constituency *or* area of the country represented by an MP

rig [rɪg] *verb* to arrange (an election) so that a particular candidate wins; *the Opposition claimed that the election had been rigged; see also* BALLOT-RIGGING

right [raɪt] *noun* (a) legal entitlement to something; *the Minister has the right to be heard by the House; she has a right to the property; he has no right to the patent; the staff have a right to know what the company is doing;* civil rights = rights and privileges of each individual according to the law; constitutional right = right which is guaranteed by the constitution of a country; human rights = rights of individual men and women to basic freedoms, such as freedom of speech, freedom of association; right to strike = general right of workers to stop working (as a means of protest); right of way = legal title to go across someone else's property; *see also* BILL OF RIGHTS (b) people who are political conservatives *or* whose ideas and beliefs are conservative; *the right have opposed the increases in government spending; members on the right of the party oppose the new manifesto;* a move to the right = move to support more conservative policies; *the centre party has shown a noticeable move to the right in recent years;* (NOTE: usually used with **the** and with a singular or plural verb. Opposite is **left**)

◊ **rightful** ['raɪtful] *adjective* legally correct; **rightful claimant** = person who has a legal claim to something; **rightful owner** = legal owner

◊ **rightist** ['raɪtɪst] *(usually as criticism)* **1** *adjective* right-wing **2** *noun* person with right-wing views

◊ **right wing** ['raɪt 'wɪŋ] *noun* part of a party or group which is more conservative than the rest; *the right wing of the Conservative Party*

◊ **right-wing** [raɪt'wɪŋ] *adjective* favouring the right *or* conservative policies; *a right-wing newspaper; right-wing politicians have plotted to bring down the government*

◊ **right-winger** [raɪt'wɪŋə] *noun* person who supports a conservative point of view

Riigikogu ['riːkəuguː] *noun* single body of the legislature in Estonia

Riksdag ['rɪksdæg] *noun* single body of the legislature in Sweden

ringleader ['rɪŋliːdə] *noun* person who organizes as revolt or riot

riot ['raɪət] **1** *noun* violent actions by large numbers of people in public; *riots broke out when the government tried to increase the price of bread;* **riot police** = police force with special equipment to deal with riots **2** *verb* to take part in a riot; *the street was blocked by rioting students*

◊ **rioter** ['raɪətə] *noun* person who takes part in a riot

◊ **rioting** ['raɪətɪŋ] *noun* several riots occurring at the same time; *rioting broke out when the price rises were announced*

◊ **riotous** ['raɪətəs] *adjective* disorderly, as in a riot; *the crowd engaged in riotous behaviour*

rise [raɪz] **1** *noun* **(a)** increase *or* growing high; *a rise in the crime rate or in inflation or in interest rates* **(b)** increase in salary; (NOTE: US English is **raise**) **2** *verb* **(a)** to move upwards *or* to become higher; *prices are rising faster than inflation; the rate of companies going into receivership has risen by 15%* **(b)** to stop sitting; *the House rose at 12.15 a.m.; the court will rise at 5 p.m.* **(c)** to rebel against authority; *the southern states rose against the government;* (NOTE: **rising - rose - has risen**)

◊ **rising** ['raɪzɪŋ] *noun* small rebellion; *the government acted swiftly to put down the rising in the university town;* see also **UPRISING**

rival ['raɪvl] **1** *adjective* opposed to a competitor; *he defected to the rival party* **2** *noun* person who competes; *the two rivals for the chairmanship of the party*

roll [rəul] *noun* **(a)** something which has been turned over and over to wrap round itself; *the desk calculator uses a roll of paper* **(b)** list of names (which used to be written on a long roll); **test roll** = book in which each MP signs his name after taking the oath at the beginning of a new Parliament; **Roll of Solicitors** = list of admitted solicitors; **he was struck off the roll** = he was banned from practising as a solicitor; **Master of the Rolls** = judge who presides over the Court of Appeal, and is also responsible for admitting solicitors to the Roll of Solicitors

◊ **rollcall** ['rəulkɔːl] *noun* reading out a list of names to see if everyone is present; *US* **yea-and-nay rollcall** = vote in Congress, where names are read out and each member says how he is voting

◊ **roll over** ['rəul 'əuvə] *verb* to roll over credit *or* funds = to make credit *or* funds available over a continuing period; *the money earmarked for building in this year's budget can be rolled over to next year*

Rome [rəum] *see* **TREATY**

rostrum ['rɒstrəm] *noun* high desk where a member stands to speak to an assembly; *the representative of one of the Civil Service unions was at the rostrum when the interruption occurred;* (NOTE: plural is **rostra**)

rotation [rəu'teɪʃn] *noun* taking turns; **to fill the post of chairman by rotation** = each member of the group is chairman for a period then gives the post to another member

rotten borough ['rɒtn 'bʌrə]] *noun* formerly, a borough where there were very few eligible voters to elect the MP; *see also* POCKET BOROUGH

round [raund] *noun* series of discussions; *the next round of negotiations will be held in London;* **Uruguay round** = series of discussions over several years leading to the settlement of GATT

royal ['rɔɪəl] **1** *adjective* referring to a king *or* queen; **Royal Assent** = signing of a Bill by the Queen, confirming that the Bill is to become law as an Act of Parliament; **by Royal Command** = by order of the Queen *or* King; **Royal Commission** = group of people specially appointed by a minister to examine and report on a major problem; **the Royal Family** = the family of a king or queen; **Royal pardon** = pardon whereby a person convicted of a crime is forgiven and need not serve a sentence; **Royal prerogative** = special right belonging to a king or queen (such as the right to appoint ministers or to prorogue Parliament) **2** *noun (informal)* **the Royals** = members of a royal family

◊ **royalist** ['rɔɪəlɪst] *noun* person supporting rule by a king or queen

◊ **royalty** ['rɔɪəlti] *noun* members of a royal family; *special security measures are taken if royalty is present;* (NOTE: can take singular or plural verb)

RSVP [ɑːesviː'piː] = REPONDEZ S'IL VOUS PLAIT letters on an invitation showing that a reply is asked for

rubber stamp ['rʌbə 'stæmp] **1** *noun* stamp made of hard rubber, cut to form letters **2** *verb* to approve of something

automatically, without attempting to amend it or reject it; *the council rubber stamped the decisions of the President*

rule [ruːl] **1** *noun* **(a)** way in which a country is governed; *the country has had ten years of military rule;* **the rule of law** = principle of government, that all persons and bodies and the government itself are equal before and answerable to the law and that no person shall be punished without trial **(b)** general order of conduct which says how things should be done (such as an order governing voting procedure in Parliament *or* Congress); *the debate followed the rules of procedure used in the British House of Commons;* **company rules (and regulations)** = general way of working in a company; **to work to rule** = to work strictly according to the rules agreed by the company and union, and therefore to work very slowly as a form of protest; **Judges' Rules** = informal set of rules governing how the police should act in questioning suspects; **Ten Minute Rule** = rule in the House of Commons, where an ordinary MP can introduce a Bill with a short speech, and if the Bill is passed on a vote, it can proceed to the Second Reading stage; *the Bill was proposed under the Ten Minute Rule* **(c)** *US* special decision made by the Rules Committee which states how a particular bill should be treated in the House of Representatives; **closed rule** *or* **gag rule** = rule which limits the time for discussion of a bill **2** *verb* **(a)** to govern (a country); *the country is ruled by a group of army officers; the dictator ruled the country for thirty years* **(b)** to give an official decision; *the Speaker ruled that the question was out of order; the commission of inquiry ruled that the company was in breach of contract* **(c)** to be in force *or* to be current; *prices which are ruling at the moment*

◊ **ruler** ['ruːlə] *noun* person who governs *or* personally controls a country or part of a country

◊ **ruling** ['ruːlɪŋ] **1** *adjective* **(a)** in power *or* in control; *the ruling Democratic Party; the actions of the ruling junta have been criticized in the press* **(b)** most important; in operation at the moment *or* current; *the ruling* *consideration is one of cost; we will invoice at ruling prices* **2** *noun* decision (made by a judge *or* magistrate *or* arbitrator *or* chairman, etc.); *the MPs disputed the Speaker's ruling; according to the ruling of the court, the contract was illegal*

run [rʌn] *verb* **(a)** to control *or* manage; *he ran the department while the chief was away; the question is: who is really running the country, the President or his wife?* **(b)** to offer oneself as a candidate in an election; *he is running for president; he had no hope of winning the nomination, so he decided not to run;* **running mate** = person who stands for election with another more important candidate (as when two candidates offer themselves for two posts, i.e. for President and Vice-President)

◊ **run-up** ['rʌnʌp] *noun* **run-up to an election** = period before an election; *in the run-up to the General Election, opinion polls were forecasting heavy losses for the government*

rural ['ruərəl] *adjective* referring to the countryside, as opposed to the towns; *an MP representing a rural constituency; the party has to win the rural vote;* (NOTE: opposite is urban)

ruthless ['ru:θləs] *adjective* showing no compassion; *a ruthless campaign against the Opposition parties*

Ss

sabotage ['sæbəta:ʒ] *noun* action to destroy buildings or equipment, especially used in wartime, or against an occupying army

◊ **saboteur** [sæbə'tɜ:] *noun* person who commits sabotage

Sabha ['sæbæ] *see* LOK SABHA, RAJYA SABHA

SAE *or* **s.a.e.** = STAMPED ADDRESSED ENVELOPE

Saeima ['saimæ] *noun* legislative body in Latvia

safe [seif] *adjective* not in danger; **safe seat** = seat where the Member of Parliament has a large majority and is not likely to lose the seat at an election; *compare* MARGINAL

◊ **safeguard** ['seifga:d] **1** *noun* protection; *the proposed legislation will provide a safeguard against illegal traders* **2** *verb* to protect; *the embassy acted to safeguard the interests of the tourists*

◊ **safety** ['seifti] *noun* **(a)** being free from danger or risk; **Health and Safety at Work Act** = Act of Parliament which regulates what employers must do to make sure that their employees are kept healthy and safe at work; **safety margin** = time *or* space allowed for something to be safe; **to take safety precautions** *or* **safety measures** = to act to make sure something is safe; **safety regulations** = rules to make a place of work safe for the workers **(b) fire safety** = making a place of work safe for the workers in case of fire; **fire safety officer** = person in an organization responsible for seeing that the staff are safe if a fire breaks out; (NOTE: no plural)

sale [seil] *noun* **(a)** act of selling *or* of transferring an item *or* a property from one owner to another, usually in exchange for money; **sale and lease-back** = situation where an organization sells a property to raise cash and then leases it back from the purchaser; **sale or return** = system where the retailer sends goods back if they are not sold, and pays the supplier only for goods sold; **bill of sale** = (i) document which the seller gives to the buyer to show that a sale has taken place; (ii) document given to a lender by a borrower to show that the lender owns a property as security for a loan; **conditions of sale** *or* **terms of sale** = list of terms under which a sale takes place (such as discounts and credit terms); **Sale of Goods Act** = Act of Parliament which regulates the selling of goods (but not land, copyrights, patents, etc.); *the law relating to the sale of goods is governed by the Sale of Goods Act 1979* **(b) for sale** *or* **on sale** = ready to be sold; **to offer something for sale** *or* **to put something up for sale** = to announce that something is ready to be sold; *the government put the development land up for sale; the guide to the borough is on sale in the local bookshops*

sanction ['sæŋkʃn] **1** *noun* **(a)** official permission to do something; *you will need the sanction of the local authority before you can knock down the old office block; the payment was made without official sanction* **(b)** punishment for an act which goes against what is normally accepted behaviour; **(economic) sanctions** = restrictions on trade with a country in order to influence its political situation *or* in order to make its government change its policy; *to impose sanctions on a country or to lift sanctions; the imposition of sanctions has had a* *marked effect on the country's economy* **2** *verb* to approve *or* to permit (officially); *the council sanctioned the expenditure of £1.2m on the development plan*

satellite state ['sætəlaɪt 'steɪt] *noun* country which is economically or politically dependent on another

satisfaction [sætɪs'fækʃn] *noun* **(a)** (i) acceptance of money *or* goods by an injured party who then cannot make any further claim; (ii) payment *or* giving of goods to someone in exchange for that person's agreement to stop a claim **(b)** feeling of being happy *or* good feeling; **job satisfaction** = a worker's feeling that he is happy in his place of work and pleased with the work he does; (NOTE: no plural)

◊ **satisfy** ['sætɪsfaɪ] *verb* **(a)** to convince someone that something is correct; *the Minister had to satisfy the House of Commons that he was pursuing the matter with great urgency* **(b)** to make someone pleased; **to satisfy a client** = to make a client pleased with what he has purchased; **a satisfied customer** = a customer who has got what he wanted **(c)** to fulfil *or* to carry out fully; *does the treaty satisfy all the conditions for ratification by Congress? the company has not satisfied all the conditions laid down in the agreement; we cannot produce enough to satisfy the demand for the product*

schedule ['ʃedjuːl *US* 'skedʒuːl] **1** *noun* **(a)** timetable *or* plan of time drawn up in advance; **to be ahead of schedule** = to be early; **to be on schedule** = to be on time; **to be behind schedule** = to be late; *the Bill is on schedule; the Second Reading was completed ahead of schedule; I am sorry to say that we are three months behind schedule; the MP has a busy schedule of appointments; his secretary tried to fit me into his schedule* **(b)** additional documents attached to a Bill before Parliament *or* to an agenda *or* minutes *or* a contract; *schedule of markets to which a contract applies; see the attached schedule or as per the attached schedule; the schedule before referred to;* **tax schedules** = six types of income as classified in the Finance Acts for British tax;

Schedule A = schedule under which tax is charged on income from land *or* buildings; **Schedule B** = schedule under which tax is charged on income from woodlands; **Schedule C** = schedule under which tax is charged on profits from government stock; **Schedule D** = schedule under which tax is charged on income from trades *or* professions, interest and other earnings not derived from being employed; **Schedule E** = schedule under which tax is charged on income from salaries *or* wages *or* pensions; **Schedule F** = schedule under which tax is charged on income from dividends **(c)** list; *the schedule of charges is revised annually* **2** *verb* **(a)** to list officially; *scheduled prices or scheduled charges are subject to change without notice; the house is scheduled as an ancient monument* **(b)** to plan the time when something will happen; *the building is scheduled for completion in May*

scope [skəʊp] *noun* limits covered by something; *the question does not come within the scope of the minister's competence; the Bill plans to increase the scope of the tribunal's authority*

seal [siːl] **1** *noun* **(a)** piece of wax *or* red paper attached to a document to show that it is legally valid; stamp printed *or* marked on a document to show that it is valid; **common seal** *or* **company's seal** = metal stamp which every company must possess, used to stamp documents with the name of the company to show they have been approved officially; *to attach the company's seal to a document;* **contract under seal** = contract which has been signed and legally approved with the seal of the company *or* the person entering into it; **the Great Seal** = seal used by the monarch on state documents, to show approval; **the Keeper of the Seal** = the Lord Chancellor **(b)** piece of paper *or* metal *or* wax attached to close something, so that it can be opened only if the paper *or* metal *or* wax is removed or broken; *the seals on the ballot box had been tampered with;* **customs seal** = seal attached by customs officers to a box, to show that the contents have passed through the customs **2** *verb* **(a)** to close something tightly; *the computer disks were sent in a* *sealed container;* **sealed envelope** = envelope where the back has been stuck down to close it; **sealed tenders** = tenders sent in sealed envelopes, which will all be opened together at a certain time; *the government has asked for sealed bids for the surplus army stock* **(b)** to attach a seal *or* to stamp something with a seal; *the customs sealed the shipment;* **sealed instrument** = document which has been signed and sealed

Seanad Éireann ['ʃenəð 'eərən] *noun* upper house of the legislature in Ireland (the equivalent of the Senate); (NOTE: the lower house is the Dáil Éireann)

seat [siːt] *noun* **(a)** chair; *seats have been placed on the platform for the members of the council; Opposition MPs left their seats and walked out of the chamber in protest* **(b)** (i) membership of the House of Commons *or* being an MP; (ii) constituency; (iii) membership of a committee; *he lost his seat in the general election; this is a safe Tory seat; marginal seats showed a swing away from the government; the union has two seats on the general council; see also* EUROSEAT, UNSEAT

COMMENT: in the British House of Commons, the seats are arranged in rows facing each other across the chamber, with the table in between the front benches and the Speaker's chair at the end. In other legislative chambers (as in the French National Assembly), the seats are arranged in a semi-circle facing the rostrum with the seat of the President of the Assembly behind it

secede [sɪˈsiːd] *verb* to break away from an organization *or* a federation; *the American colonies seceded from Great Britain in 1776 and formed the USA*

◊ **secession** [sɪˈseʃn] *noun* act of seceding

◊ **secessionist** [sɪˈseʃnɪst] **1** *noun* person who is in favour of secession **2** *adjective* which has seceded or is proposing to secede; *a secessionist state*

second ['sekənd] **1** *adjective* coming after the first; *he came second in the contest for deputy leader; we will now deal with the second item on the agenda* **2** *verb* to second

a motion *or* a candidate = to agree to support a motion after it has been proposed by the proposer, but before a vote is taken; *the motion is proposed by Mr Smith, seconded by Mr Jones; the name of Mr Brown has been proposed for the post of treasurer, who is going to second him?*

◊ **seconder** ['sekəndə] *noun* person who seconds a proposal; *Mr Brown has been proposed by Mr Jones, and Miss Smith is his seconder; the motion could not be put, because the proposer could not find a seconder for it*

◊ **second ballot** ['sekənd 'bælət] *noun* electoral system used in France and other countries, in which if a candidate does not get 50% of the votes, a second ballot is held a short time later, with the lowest candidate or candidates removed from the list

◊ **Second Reading** ['sekənd 'riːdɪŋ] *noun* detailed presentation of a Bill in the House of Commons by the responsible minister, followed by a discussion and vote; *US* detailed examination of a Bill in the House, before it is passed to the Senate

secondary ['sekəndri] *adjective* **(a)** second in importance; *Mr Smith raised a further objection, which he said was of secondary importance to the first;* **secondary banks** = companies which provide money for hire-purchase deals **(b)** at a second stage; **secondary school** = school for children aged 11 and over

◊ **secondarily** ['sekəndrəli] *adverb* in second place; *see also* PRIMARY, PRIMARILY

secret ['siːkrət] **1** *adjective* (something) which is hidden *or* not known by many people; *the chief negotiator kept the report secret from the rest of the government team; they signed a secret deal with their main competitor;* **secret agent** = person who tries to find out information in secret about other countries *or* other governments *or* other armed forces; **secret ballot** = election in which the voters vote in secret; *the new act stipulates that elections to union office shall be by secret ballot of members;* **secret service** = government service which spies on other countries; **in secret** = without telling anyone;

the rebel leader met the chief of police in secret; he photographed the plans of the new missile in secret; **in secret session** = meeting when only members are allowed to be present, with no journalists, and sometimes with no officials; *the Committee met in secret session; the Council went into secret session to discuss the appointment of the new Chief Executive* **2** *noun* something which is kept hidden from most people; **to keep a secret** = not to tell someone a secret which you know; **official secret** = piece of information which is classified as important to the state, and which it is a crime to reveal; **Official Secrets Act** = Act of Parliament governing the publication of secrets relating to the state

◊ **secretly** ['siːkrətli] *adverb* without telling anyone; *the treaty was signed secretly by the Prime Minister and the President; he offered to copy the plans secretly and sell them to another country*

◊ **the Secret Intelligence Service (MI6)** ['siːkrət ɪn'telɪdʒəns 'sɜːvɪs] British government agency concerned with obtaining information about other countries which may be of use to the government's defence, security, economic and foreign services

secretarial [sekrə'teəriəl] *adjective* referring to the work of a secretary; *she is taking a secretarial course; he is looking for secretarial work; we need extra secretarial help to deal with the mailings;* **secretarial college** = college which teaches typing, shorthand, word-processing and office practice

◊ **secretariat** [sekrə'teəriæt] *noun* important office and the officials who work in it, usually headed by a Secretary or Secretary-General; *the United Nations secretariat; the Commonwealth secretariat;*

secretary ['sekrətəri] *noun* **(a)** person who types letters *or* files documents *or* arranges meetings, etc., for someone; *the Minister's secretary and personal assistant; my secretary deals with visitors; his secretary phoned to say he would be late* **(b)** Secretary of State *or* member of the government in charge of a department; *the*

Education Secretary; the Foreign Secretary; UK **Chief Secretary to the Treasury** = senior member of the government under the Chancellor of the Exchequer; US **Secretary of the Treasury** *or* **Treasury Secretary** = senior member of the government in charge of financial affairs **(c)** senior civil servant; **Permanent Secretary** = chief civil servant in a government department or ministry; **the Cabinet Secretary** *or* **Secretary to the Cabinet** = head of the Cabinet Office (and also of the British Civil Service), who attends cabinet meetings; **Private Secretary** = civil servant attached personally to a Secretary of State or Prime Minister, who acts as the link between the minister and the department; **Parliamentary Private Secretary (PPS)** = young MP attached personally to a Secretary of State or Prime Minister, who acts as a general helper in Parliament; US **Secretary to the Senate** = head of the administrative staff in the Senate **(d)** official of a company *or* society; **company secretary** = person who is responsible for a company's legal and financial affairs; **honorary secretary** = person who keeps the minutes and official documents of a committee *or* club, but is not paid a salary

◊ **Secretary-General** ['sekrətri 'dʒenrəl] *noun* main administrator in a large organization (such as the United Nations or a political party); *the main power in the country is held by the Secretary-General of the ruling party*

◊ **Secretary of State** ['sekrətri əv 'steɪt] *noun* **(a)** GB member of the government in charge of a department; *the Secretary of State for Education and Employment* **(b)** US senior member of the government in charge of foreign affairs; *see also notes at* FOREIGN, MINISTER **(c)** *(in Canada)* government minister with general responsibilities for publications, broadcasting and the arts

COMMENT: the uses of the words **Secretary** and **Secretary of State** are confusing: **1.** In the UK, a Secretary of State is the head of a government department, usually a Cabinet Minister. Other members of the government, though not in the Cabinet, are Parliamentary Secretaries or Parliamentary Under-Secretaries of State, who are junior ministers in a department. Finally the Parliamentary Private Secretary is a minister's main junior assistant in Parliament **2.** In the USA, the Secretary of State is the person in charge of the Department of State, which is concerned with foreign policy. The equivalent in most other countries is the Foreign Minister (Foreign Secretary in the UK). Other heads of department in the US government are called simply Secretary: Secretary for Defense or Defense Secretary **3.** In the British civil service, a government department is headed by a Permanent Secretary, with several Deputy Secretaries and Under-Secretaries. They are all government employees and are not MPs. Also a civil servant is a minister's Private Secretary, who is attached to the minister personally, and acts as his link with the department. The British Civil Service formerly used the titles Permanent Secretary, Deputy Secretary, Assistant Secretary and Principal Secretary as grades, but these have now been replaced by a system of numbers (G1, G2, G3, etc.) **4.** Both in the UK and USA, the word Secretary is used in short forms of titles with the name of the department. So, the Secretary of State for Education and Employment in the UK, and the Secretary for Education in the USA are both called Education Secretary for short. In the USA, the word Secretary can be used as a person's title: Secretary Smith

section ['sekʃn] *noun* **(a)** department in an office; **passport section** = part of an embassy which deals with passport enquiries; **legal section** = department dealing with legal matters in a company **(b)** part of an Act of Parliament *or* bylaw; *he does not qualify for a grant under section 2 of the Act*

sector ['sektə] *noun* general area of business; **private sector** = all companies which are owned by private shareholders, not by the state; **public sector** = government departments and the nationalized industries

and services; **public sector borrowing requirement** = amount of money which a government has to borrow to pay for its own spending

security [sɪ'kjuərɪti] *noun* **(a)** being safe *or* not likely to change; **security of employment** *or* **job security** = feeling by a worker that he has the right to keep his job until he retires; **security of tenure** = right to keep a position *or* rented accommodation, provided that certain conditions are met **(b)** being protected; **airport security** = actions taken to protect aircraft and passengers against attack; **security guard** = person whose job is to protect money *or* valuables *or* an office against possible theft or damage; **the Security Services** = government organizations which protect the secrets of the country against spies; **office security** = protecting an office against theft of equipment *or* personal property *or* information **(c)** being secret; **security in this office is nil** = nothing can be kept secret in this office; **security printer** = printer who prints paper money, secret government documents, etc. **(d) social security** = money *or* help provided by the government to people who need it; *he lives on social security payments;* **Department of Health and Social Security** = civil service department which is in charge of the National Health Service, state benefits, insurance and pensions **(e)** guarantee that someone will repay money borrowed; **to stand security for someone** = to guarantee that if the person does not repay a loan, you will repay it for him; *to give something as security for a debt; to use a house as security for a loan; the bank lent him £20,000 without security*

◊ **Security Council** *noun* permanent ruling body of the United Nations, with the responsibility for preserving international peace

COMMENT: the Security Council has fifteen members, five of which (USA, Russia, UK, France and China) are permanent members, the other ten being elected by the General Assembly for periods of two years. The five permanent members each have a veto over the decisions of the Security Council

◊ **the Security Service (MI5)** British government agency concerned with national security, in particular counter-terrorism and counter-espionage

sedition [sə'dɪʃn] *noun* crime of doing acts *or* speaking or publishing words which bring the royal family or the government into hatred or contempt and encourage civil disorder; (NOTE: no plural)

◊ **seditious** [sɪ'dɪʃəs] *adjective* which provokes sedition; **seditious libel** = offence of publishing a libel with seditious intent

COMMENT: sedition is a lesser crime than treason

seek [si:k] *verb* **(a)** to ask for; *they are seeking damages for loss of revenue; the applicant sought help from the Housing Officer; the Bill requires a social worker to seek permission of a juvenile court; a creditor seeking a receiving order under the Bankruptcy Act* to seek an interview = to ask if you can see someone; *she sought an interview with the minister* **(b)** to try to do something; *the local authority is seeking to place the girl in accommodation;* (NOTE: seeking - sought - has sought)

◊ **seeker** ['si:kə] *noun* person who is looking for something; *an asylum seeker*

segregate ['segrɪgeɪt] *verb* to separate *or* keep apart, especially to keep different races in a country apart; *single-sex schools segregate boys from girls*

◊ **segregation** [segrɪ'geɪʃn] *noun* keeping apart; **racial segregation** = keeping different races apart

◊ **segregationist** [segrɪ'geɪʃnɪst] *adjective & noun* (person) who supports a policy of racial segregation

Seimas ['seɪməs] *noun* legislative body in Lithuania

seize [si:z] *verb* to take hold of something *or* to take possession of something; *the customs seized the shipment of books; his case was seized at the airport; the court ordered the company's funds to be seized*

◊ **seizure** ['si:ʒə] *noun* taking possession of something; *the court ordered the seizure of the shipment or of the company's funds;* (NOTE: no plural)

Sejm [seɪm] *noun* lower house of the legislature in Poland

select [sɪ'lekt] **1** *adjective* of top quality *or* specially chosen; *our customers are very select; a select group of clients* **2** *verb* to choose; *three members of the committee have been selected to speak at the AGM; he has been selected as a candidate for a Northern constituency*

◊ **Select Committee** [sɪ'lekt kə'mɪtiː] *noun (in the House of Commons)* special committee (with members representing various political parties) which examines the work of a ministry *or* a particular problem in the House of Commons; *(in Congress)* committee set up for a special purpose, usually to investigate something; **ad hoc Select Committee** = Select Committee set up to examine a special case *or* problem; **departmental Select Committee** = Select Committee set up to examine the work of a government department; **sessional Select Committee** = Select Committee set up at the beginning of each session of parliament; *the Select Committee on Defence or the Defence Select Committee*

COMMENT: the main non-departmental Select Committees are: **the Committee of Privileges** which considers breaches of parliamentary privilege; **the Committee of the Parliamentary Commissioner** which considers the reports of the Ombudsman; **the Public Accounts Committee** which examines government expenditure. The departmental select committees are: **Agriculture, Defence, Education, Employment, Environment, Foreign Affairs, Health, Home Affairs, National Heritage, Northern Ireland, Science and Technology, Scottish Affairs, Social Services, Trade and Industry, Transport, Treasury, Welsh Affairs**

selection [sɪ'lekʃn] *noun* (i) choice; (ii) person *or* thing which has been chosen; **selection board** *or* **selection committee** = committee which chooses a candidate for a job; **selection procedure** = general method of choosing a candidate for election *or* for a job; *see also* DESELECT, DESELECTION

self-determination [selfdɪtɜ:mɪ'neɪʃn] *noun* free choice by the people of a country as to which country (including their own) should govern them; *countries with powerful neighbours have to fight for the right to self-determination*

◊ **self-government** *or* **self-rule** [self'gʌvənmənt or self'ru:l] *noun* control of a country by its own government, free from foreign influence

◊ **self-sufficiency** [selfsə'fɪʃənsi] *noun* being self-sufficient; *we aim to achieve self-sufficiency in energy by the year 2000*

◊ **self-sufficient** [selfsə'fɪʃənt] *adjective* able to provide for oneself; *the country is self-sufficient in oil*

senate ['senət] *noun* **(a)** upper house of a legislative body; *France has a bicameral system: a lower house or Chamber of Deputies and a upper house or Senate* **(b)** the upper house of the American Congress; *the US Senate voted against the proposal; the Secretary of State appeared before the Senate Foreign Relations Committee*

◊ **senator** ['senətə] *noun* member of a senate; (NOTE: written with a capital letter when used as a title: **Senator Jackson**)

◊ **senatorial** [senə'tɔːriəl] *adjective* referring to the senate *or* to senators; **senatorial courtesy** = acknowledgement of the importance of the Senate (as in the convention that the President consults senators about appointments to federal posts in their states)

COMMENT: the senate is the upper house of legislature in many countries, including Antigua, Argentina, Australia, Belgium, Bolivia, Brazil, Canada, Chile, Colombia, Congo, Czech Republic, Dominican Republic, France, Italy, Jamaica, Mauritania, Mexico, Paraguay, the Philippines, Poland,

Romania, South Africa, Spain, Thailand, Trinidad and Tobago, the USA, Uruguay, Venezuela. The US Senate has 100 members, each state electing two senators by popular vote. Bills may be introduced in the Senate, with the exception of bills relating to finance. The Senate has the power to ratify treaties and to confirm presidential appointments to federal posts

senior ['siːnjə] *adjective* older; more important; (worker) who has a more important job *or* who has been employed longer than another; *senior ministers have gathered at 10 Downing Street for a meeting with the Prime Minister; senior civil servants are annoyed at the decision of the committee; she is senior to him in the department;* **senior manager** *or* **senior executive** = manager *or* director who has a higher rank than others; **John Smith, Senior** = the older John Smith (i.e. the father of John Smith, Junior)

◊ **seniority** [siːnɪ'ɒrɪti] *noun* being older *or* more important; being a member of a group longer; **the members were listed in order of seniority** = the member who had been on the committee the longest was put at the top of the list

separate 1 ['seprət] *adjective* being apart; *the constitution of the United States keeps the executive and legislative branches of government quite separate* **2** ['sepəreɪt] *verb* to keep apart; *the constitution separates the power of the executive, legislative and judicial branches of government; the Finance Director was asked to separate the two sets of figures*

◊ **separation** [sepə'reɪʃn] *noun* keeping separate; **separation of powers** = system in which the power in a state is separated between the legislative body which passes laws, the judiciary which enforces the law, and the executive which runs the government

COMMENT: in the USA, the three parts of the power of the state are kept separate and independent: the President does not sit in Congress; Congress cannot influence the decisions of the Supreme Court, etc. In the UK, the powers are not separated, because Parliament has both legislative powers (it makes laws) and judicial powers (the House of Lords acts as a court of appeal); the government (the executive) is not independent and is responsible to Parliament which can outvote it and so cause a general election. In the USA, members of government are not members of Congress, though their appointment has to be approved by Senate; in the UK, members of government are usually Members of Parliament, although some are members of the House of Lords

◊ **separatism** ['sepərətɪzm] *noun* belief that a part of a country should become separate and independent from the rest

◊ **separatist** ['seprətɪst] **1** *adjective* referring to separatism; *the rise of the separatist movement in the south of the country* **2** *noun* person who believes that part of the country should become separate and independent

Serjeant ['sɑːdʒənt] *noun* **Serjeant at Arms** = official of the House of Commons who keeps order in the House, makes sure that no one enters the chamber unless invited to do so, and ejects members if asked to do so by the Speaker; he also carries the mace in procession, and places it on the table at the beginning of each sitting (NOTE: the spelling **Sergeant at Arms** used in the US House of Representatives)

servant ['sɜːvənt] *noun* **(a)** person who is employed by someone; **civil servant** = person who works in the government service; **master and servant** = employer and employee; **the law of master and servant** = employment law **(b)** person who is paid to work in someone's house

serve [sɜːv] *verb* **(a)** to spend time as a member of a committee *or* as Member of Parliament; *he served six years on the Foreign Relations Committee; she has served two terms as chairman;* **to serve on a jury** = to be a juror **(b)** to deal with (a customer) *or* to do a type of work; **to serve a customer** = to take a customer's order and provide what he wants; **to serve in a shop** *or*

in a restaurant = to deal with customers' orders **(c) to serve someone with a writ** *or* **to serve a writ on someone** = to give someone a writ officially, so that he has to obey it

service ['sɜːvɪs] *noun* **(a)** duty to do work for someone; **conditions of service** = terms set out in a contract of employment *or* contract of service; **contract of service** *or* **service contract** = contract between employer and employee showing all conditions of work; **community service order** = punishment where a convicted person is sentenced to do unpaid work in the local community; **jury service** = duty which each citizen has of serving on a jury if asked to do so; **service charge** = charge made by a landlord to cover general work done to the property (cleaning of the stairs, collection of rubbish, etc.) *or* charge made in a restaurant for serving the customer; *see also* IN-SERVICE **(b) civil service** = organization and personnel which administer a country under the direction of the government **(c)** delivery of a document (such as a writ *or* summons) to someone in person *or* to his solicitor; **to acknowledge service** = to confirm that a legal document (such as a writ) has been received

session ['seʃn] *noun* **(a)** meeting *or* period when a group of people meets; *the morning session or the afternoon session will be held in the conference room;* **opening session** *or* **closing session** = first part *or* last part of a conference; **closed session** = meeting which is not open to the public or to newspaper reporters; *see also* SECRET **(b)** period when Parliament is meeting (usually about 12 months long); *the government is planning to introduce the Bill at the next session of Parliament; the first session of the new Parliament opened with the reading of the Queen's Speech* **(c) Court of Session** = highest civil court in Scotland, consisting of the Inner House and Outer House

◊ **sessional** ['seʃnl] *adjective* referring to a session

◊ **sessions** ['seʃnz] *plural noun* court; **petty sessions** = Magistrates' Court; **special sessions** = Magistrates' Court for a district which is held for a special reason (such as to deal with terrorists)

COMMENT: the Parliamentary session starts in October with the Opening of Parliament and the Queen's Speech. It usually lasts until August. In the USA, a new congressional session starts on the 3rd of January each year

set [set] *verb* to put; to arrange; *the debate is set to last several hours*

◊ **set aside** ['set ə'saɪd] *verb* to decide not to apply a decision; *the arbitrator's award was set aside on appeal*

◊ **set-aside** ['setəsaɪd] *noun (EU policy)* using a piece of formerly arable land for another use (such as for recreational use *or* for woodland *or* to lie fallow);

COMMENT: under the Common Agricultural Policy, set-aside allows farmers to be paid compensation for taking part of their land out of cultivation for at least five years

◊ **set forth** ['set 'fɔːθ] *verb* to put down in writing; *the argument is set forth in the document from the European Court*

◊ **set out** ['set 'aʊt] *verb* (a) to put down in writing; *the claim is set out in the enclosed document; the figures are set out in the tables at the back of the book* (b) to try to do something; *the Government has set out to discredit the Opposition*

settle ['setl] *verb* (a) to go to live in an area where no one lived before; *in the 18th century, thousands of people left the country to settle in North America* (b) to put an end to an argument; *the decision of the arbitration board settled the dispute; the matter was settled by an agreement to change the working hours*

◊ **settlement** ['setlmənt] *noun* (a) group of homes built where no one has lived before; *a British settlement on the coast of India* (b) agreement which ends a dispute; *the Department for Education reached a settlement with the teachers' union*

◊ **settler** ['setlə] *noun* person who goes to colonize a country; *settlers built up colonies along the banks of the river*

severe [sə'vɪə] *adjective* bad *or* serious; *severe weather has caused disruption to the council's services; special grants are available for people with severe disabilities*

shadow ['ʃædəʊ] *adjective* the Shadow Cabinet = senior members of the Opposition who cover the areas of responsibility of the actual Cabinet, and will form the Cabinet if their party is elected to government; *the shadow Minister for the Environment; the shadow spokesman on energy matters*

shanty town ['ʃænti 'taʊn] *noun* area of badly built huts around a large city

share ['ʃeə] **1** *noun* (a) part of something; *the party's share of the vote fell in the last local elections* (b) one of many parts into which a company's capital is divided, owned by shareholders; *shares fell on the London market; the company offered 1.8m shares on the market;* ordinary shares = normal shares in a company, which have no special benefits or restrictions; preference shares = shares (often with no voting rights) which receive their dividend before all other shares and are repaid first (at face value) if the company is liquidated; share capital = value of the assets of a company held as shares; share certificate = document proving that someone owns shares; a share-owning electorate = an electorate made up of people who own shares **2** *verb* (a) to own *or* use something together with someone else; *to share a telephone; to share an office* (b) to divide something among several people; *the Cabinet posts have been shared between the two parties in the coalition; the cost of the new development is shared between central government, the local council and the property developers;* to share information *or* to share data = to allow someone to use information which you have

◊ **shareholder** ['ʃeəhəʊldə] *noun* person who owns shares in a company; small shareholder = person who has a few shares in a company; majority *or* minority shareholder = person who owns more than *or* less than half the shares in a company

◊ **shareholding** ['ʃeəhəʊldɪŋ] *noun* group of shares in a company owned by one person; a majority shareholding *or* a minority

shareholding = group of shares which are more *or* less than half the total

sharp [ʃɑːp] *adjective* **(a)** sudden; *a sharp rise in unemployment; sharp drop in inflation* **(b) sharp practice** = way of doing business which is not honest, but not illegal

◊ **sharply** ['ʃɑːpli] *adverb* suddenly; *the rate of inflation has risen sharply over the last few years*

sheikh [ʃeɪk] *noun* chief *or* prince in an Arab country

◊ **sheikhdom** ['ʃeɪkdəm] *noun* state ruled by a sheikh; *many of the Gulf sheikhdoms export oil*

sheriff ['ʃerɪf] *noun* **(a)** *US* official in charge of justice in a county **(b) (High) Sheriff** = official appointed as the government's representative in a county **(c)** *(in Scotland)* chief judge in a district; **Sheriff Court** = court presided over by a sheriff

◊ **sheriffdom** ['ʃerɪfdəm] *noun* district in Scotland with a Sheriff Court

sherpa ['ʃɜːpə] *noun (informal)* civil servant who prepares documents, final communiqués, etc. for summit meeting

shire ['ʃaɪə] *noun* former name for a county in Britain (still used in the county names: Buckinghamshire, Berkshire, etc.); **the shires** = the rural counties in the centre of England; *the Tory Party is very strong in the shires; we have to make sure that we do not lose the support of the shire voters*

shortcoming ['ʃɔːtkʌmɪŋ] *noun* defect; *the government plan has many shortcomings*

shorthand ['ʃɔːthænd] *noun* system of taking notes quickly by writing signs instead of letters; *the court proceedings were taken down in shorthand; the reporters could take notes in shorthand;* **shorthand writer** = person who takes down in shorthand reports of proceedings in Parliament, courts of law, etc.

short title ['ʃɔːt 'taɪtl] *noun* usual shortened name by which an Act of Parliament is known; **short title clause** = clause in a Bill which gives the short title by which the Act will be known

show [ʃəʊ] **1** *noun* **(a)** exhibition *or* display of goods or services for sale; *motor show; computer show* **(b) show of hands** = way of casting votes in which people show how they vote by raising their hands; *the motion was carried on a show of hands* **2** *verb* to make something be seen; *to show a gain or a fall; to show a profit or a loss*

SI = STATUTORY INSTRUMENT

sign [saɪn] *verb* to write your name in a special personal way on a document to show that you have written it or approved it; *to sign a letter or a contract or a document or a cheque; the treaty was signed by the two Presidents; letter is signed by the managing director; the cheque is not valid if has not been signed by the finance director*

◊ **signatory** ['sɪgnətri] *noun* person who signs a contract, etc.; country which signs a treaty *or* convention; *you have to get the permission of all the signatories to the agreement if you want to change the terms; Britain is a signatory to the Geneva Convention*

◊ **signature** ['sɪgnətʃə] *noun* name written in a special way by someone, which identifies that person; *the treaty has been negotiated and is now waiting for signature; Bills waiting for the President's signature; all the company's cheques need two signatures*

sine die ['sɪni 'diːeɪ] *Latin phrase meaning* 'without a day'; **adjournment sine die** = adjournment of a meeting, without giving a date when it will meet again

sine qua non ['sɪni kwɑː 'nɒn] *Latin phrase meaning* 'without which not': condition without which something cannot work; *agreement by the management is a sine qua non of all employment contracts*

single ['sɪŋgl] *adjective* one alone; *the councillor has not attended a single meeting; not a single Opposition MP spoke against the proposal;* **in single figures** = less than ten; *inflation has been reduced to single figures;* **Single European Act** =

reworking of the basic community treaties, with the aim of creating a free internal market in 1992; **Single (European) Market** = the EU considered as one single market, with no tariff barriers between its member states

◊ **single chamber** ['sɪŋgl 'tʃeɪmbə] *noun* legislature with only one chamber (as in New Zealand and Nebraska); *see also* UNICAMERAL

◊ **single transferable vote (STV)** ['sɪŋgl træns'fɜrəbl 'vəʊt] *noun* electoral system used in Northern Ireland for district councils, where all the candidates are listed, and the elector gives them numbers according to his preference. The total votes are counted to show how many votes a candidate needs to be elected (the electoral quota). Candidates with more than the electoral quota of first preference votes are automatically elected, and their second preference votes are passed to other candidates, and so on until the full number of candidates have the required quota and so are elected

sinking fund ['sɪŋkɪŋ 'fʌnd] *noun* fund built up out of amounts of money put aside regularly to meet a future need

Sir [sɜː] *noun* title given to a baronet or knight

COMMENT: the title is always used with the man's Christian name, and in a formal address, with the surname as well: 'good morning, Sir George'; 'may I introduce Sir George Carey?'; 'Sir George and Lady Carey attended the dinner'

sit [sɪt] *verb* (a) to meet; *no one can enter the Council Chamber when the committee is sitting; the court sat from eleven to five o'clock* (b) to be an MP; *she sat for a London constituency for ten years; the sitting MP was re-elected with a comfortable majority* (c) to sit on the bench = to be a magistrate

◊ **sitting** ['sɪtɪŋ] *noun* (a) meeting of Parliament *or* of a court *or* of a tribunal (b) **sittings** = periods when courts sit

COMMENT: a Parliamentary sitting usually starts at 2.30 p.m. (11 a.m. on Fridays) and lasts until about midnight. All-night sittings happen occasionally, usually when Parliament is discussing very important or controversial matters

slander ['slɑːndə] **1** *noun* untrue spoken statement which damages someone's character; **action for slander** *or* **slander action** = case in a law court where someone says that another person had slandered him **2** *verb* **to slander someone** = to damage someone's character by saying untrue things about him; *compare* LIBEL

slate [sleɪt] *noun* list of candidates for a position; *the Democratic slate in the state elections*

slip law ['slɪp 'lɔː] *noun US* law published for the first time after it has been approved, printed on a single sheet of paper, or as a small separate booklet

slogan ['sləʊgn] *noun* short phrase which shows the beliefs of a party, used to attract voters; *the party's slogan is 'More Power to the People'; the party campaigned under the slogan 'Responsibility and Trust'*

slum [slʌm] *noun* crowded dirty area of dwellings inside a large town; *the children were brought up in the slums of Glasgow;* **slum clearance** = organized demolishing of slum areas to replace them with modern blocks of flats

snap [snæp] *adjective* sudden *or* unexpected; *the Prime Minister called a snap election; the Committee will discuss the matter fully and will not reach a snap decision*

SO = STANDING ORDER

soapbox ['səʊpbɒks] *noun* wooden crate used as a stand by a public speaker; **soapbox oratory** = form of public speaking which is aimed at attracting the general public in a simple straightforward way

social ['səʊʃl] *adjective* referring to society in general; *the government dealt carefully*

with many of the social problems of the day;
Social Charter *see* EUROPEAN SOCIAL
CHARTER **Social Chapter** = protocol to
the Maastricht Treaty which commits
signatory states to the promotion of
employment, improved working conditions,
dialogue between management and labour,
development of human resources, and the
fight against exclusion; **social ownership** =
public ownership *or* situation where an
industry is nationalized and run by a board
appointed by the government; **social security**
= money *or* help provided by the government
to people who need it; **social services** =
department of a local *or* national government
which provides services, such as health care,
advice, money, for people who need help;
social worker = person who works in a social
services department, visiting and looking
after people who need help

◊ **Social Credit** ['səʊʃl 'kredɪt] *noun*
system of monetary reform, founded in
Canada

◊ **social democracy** ['səʊʃl de'mɒkrəsi]
noun belief that changes should be made to
the structure of society to make it more
egalitarian, with some state involvement in
industry and welfare, without removing
private capitalism

◊ **social democrat** ['səʊʃl 'demɒkræt]
noun **(a)** person who believes in some social
change and some state involvement in
industry and welfare **(b) Social Democrat** =
person who supports or belongs to a Social
Democratic Party; *the Social Democrats are
in the majority in some areas of the country*

◊ **Social Democratic** ['səʊʃl
demə'krætɪk] *adjective* referring to a Social
Democratic Party

◊ **Social Democratic Party** ['səʊʃl
demə'krætɪk 'pɑːti] *noun* political party
which is in favour of some social change and
some state intervention in industry and
welfare, all achieved by democratic means

◊ **socialism** ['səʊʃəlɪzm] *noun* ideas and
beliefs of socialists, that in a state the means
of production, distribution and exchange
should be controlled by the people, that the
people should be cared for by the state and
that wealth should be shared equally

◊ **Socialist** ['səʊʃəlɪst] **1** *adjective* **(a)** in
favour of social change, wider sharing of
wealth, and of state-run industry and welfare
(b) referring to *or* supporting a Socialist Party
2 *noun* **(a)** person who believes that society
should be changed so that wealth is shared
more widely, and that the state should run the
banks, industry and the welfare services **(b) a
Socialist** = person who supports *or* is a
member of a Socialist Party

◊ **Socialist Party** ['səʊʃəlɪst 'pɑːti] *noun*
(a) political party, such as those in France,
Spain, Portugal, which follows socialist
policies and beliefs **(b) National Socialist
Party** = the Nazi Party, political party
founded in Germany in 1919, and led by
Adolf Hitler

society [sə'saɪɪti] *noun* **(a)** group of people
who live together and have the same laws and
customs; *British society has changed since
the Second World War; all Western societies
have the same social problems;* (NOTE: not
used with the) **(b)** organization of people with
the same interests or jobs; *a political society;
a debating society; the Society of Education
Officers*

socio-economic ['səʊʃɪəʊiːkə'nɒmɪk]
adjective referring to social and economic
conditions; *the socio-economic system in
capitalist countries;* socio-economic groups
= groups in society divided according to
income and position

socio-political ['səʊʃɪəʊpə'lɪtɪkl]
adjective combining social and political
factors

solemn ['sɒləm] *adjective* **solemn and
binding agreement** = agreement which is
not legally binding, but which all parties
promise to obey

solicitor [sə'lɪsɪtə] *noun (in England and
Wales)* lawyer who has passed the
examinations of the Law Society and has a
valid certificate to practise and who gives
advice to members of the public and acts for
them in legal matters; **to instruct a solicitor**
= to give orders to a solicitor to act on your
behalf; **the Official Solicitor** = solicitor who
acts in the High Court for parties who have

no one to act for them, usually because they are under an official disability

◊ **Solicitor-General** [sə'lɪsɪtə 'dʒenrəl] *noun* one of the law officers, a Member of the House of Commons and deputy to the Attorney-General; **Solicitor-General for Scotland** = junior law officer in Scotland

solidarity [sɒlɪ'dærɪti] *noun* expression of unity between people with common interests

sought [sɔːt] *see* SEEK

source [sɔːs] *noun* place where something starts *or* comes from; *source of income; you must declare income from all sources to the Inland Revenue; she refused to reveal her source of information;* **income which is taxed at source** = where the tax is removed before the income is paid

South [sauθ] *adjective, adverb & noun* **(a)** one of the directions on the earth's surface, the direction facing towards the sun at midday and towards the South Pole **(b)** region of a country, especially the part of the USA to the south of Washington; **the Deep South** = group of states in the southern USA (such as Alabama, Georgia, Louisiana) **(c)** **the South** = the underdeveloped countries of the world; *(as opposed to* THE NORTH)

sovereign ['sɒvrɪn] **1** *noun* king *or* queen; *the sovereign's head appears on coins and stamps* **2** *adjective* having complete freedom to govern itself; **sovereign state** = independent country which governs itself

◊ **sovereignty** ['sɒvrɪnti] *noun* power to govern; **to have sovereignty over a territory** = to have power to govern a territory; *two neighbouring states claimed sovereignty over the offshore islands;* **the sovereignty** *or* **supremacy of Parliament** = right of Parliament to make or undo laws; (NOTE: no plural)

soviet ['səuviət] **1** *noun* **(a)** formerly, an elected local, regional or national council in the USSR **(b) the Supreme Soviet** = the legislative body of Tajikistan **2** *adjective & noun* referring to the former Soviet Union

◊ **Soviet Union** ['səuviət 'juːniən] *noun* the former Union of Soviet Socialist Republics (USSR), now split into the Russian Federation and various independent states, some of which have joined the Russian Federation in the Commonwealth of Independent States (CIS)

Speaker ['spiːkə] *noun* person who presides over a meeting of a parliament; **discussions held behind the Speaker's chair** = informal discussions between representatives of opposing political parties meeting on neutral ground away from the floor of the House; (NOTE: MPs address the Speaker as **Mr Speaker** or **Madam Speaker**)

COMMENT: in the House of Commons, the Speaker is an ordinary Member of Parliament chosen by the other members; the speaker in the House of Lords is the Lord Chancellor. In the US Congress, the Speaker of the House of Representatives is an ordinary congressman, elected by the other congressmen; the person presiding over meetings of the Senate is usually the Vice-President

special ['speʃəl] *adjective* different *or* not normal *or* referring to one particular thing; *he offered us special terms; the car is being offered at a special price;* **special agent** = (i) person who represents someone in a particular matter; (ii) person who does secret work for a government; **special committee** = committee set up by Congress to investigate something; **special deposits** = large sums of money which banks have to deposit with the Bank of England in order to reduce the money supply; **special resolution** = resolution to change the articles of a company, which has to be passed by 75% of the shareholders; **special sessions** = magistrates' courts held for a particular reason (such as to deal with terrorists); *US* **special session** = session of Congress convened by the President to discuss an important matter, after Congress has been adjourned sine die

◊ **specialist** ['speʃəlɪst] *noun* person *or* organization which is an expert in one particular type of product or one subject; *you should go to a specialist in local government* *cases* or *to a local government specialist for advice*

◊ **specialize** ['speʃəlaɪz] *verb* **to specialize in something** = to be particularly interested or expert in a certain subject; *a government department specializing in questions of race discrimination; a QC who specializes in international contract cases*

speech [spiːtʃ] *noun* **(a)** speaking or ability to talk; **freedom of speech** = being able to say what you want without being afraid of prosecution, provided that you do not break the law **(b)** talk given in public; *to make a speech in Parliament; counsel's closing speech to the jury; the Chancellor's Budget Speech lasted two hours;* **Queen's Speech** = speech made by the Queen at the opening of a session of Parliament which outlines the government's plans for legislation; **the Debate on the Queen's Speech** = first debate of a new session of Parliament, the motion being to present an address of thanks to the Queen, but the debate in fact being concerned with the Government's legislative programme as outlined in the speech

spend [spend] *verb* **(a)** to pay money; *the government feels that local authorities are spending more than they need; the Defence Department spends millions of pounds on research* **(b)** to use time; *the House of Lords spent two weeks debating the clauses of the Bill; the chairman spent yesterday afternoon with the legal advisers;* (NOTE: **spending - spent - has spent**)

sphere of influence ['sfɪə əv 'ɪnfluəns] *noun* area of the world where a very strong country can exert powerful influence over other states; *some Latin American states fall within the USA's sphere of influence*

spiritual ['spɪrɪtʃuəl] *adjective* **Lords Spiritual** = archbishops and bishops sitting in the House of Lords

splinter group ['splɪntə 'gruːp] *noun* small group which breaks away from a main political party, while usually still remaining close to the main group

spoil [spɔɪl] *verb* to ruin or to make something bad; *half the shipment was spoiled by water; the company's results were spoiled by the last quarter;* **spoilt ballot paper** = voting paper which has not been filled in correctly by the voter and therefore cannot be counted; (NOTE: **spoiling - spoiled** or **spoilt**)

◊ **spoils of war** ['spɔɪlz əv 'wɔː] *plural noun* goods or valuables taken by an army from an enemy

spokesman ['spəuksmən] *noun* man who speaks in public on behalf of a group; *a White House spokesman denied the news report; a government spokesman in the House of Lords revealed that discussions had been concluded on the treaty;* (NOTE: plural is **spokesmen**)

◊ **spokesperson** ['spəukspɜːsən] *noun* person who speaks in public on behalf of a group

◊ **spokeswoman** ['spəukswuːmən] *noun* woman who speaks in public on behalf of a group; (NOTE: plural is **spokeswomen**)

sponsor ['sponsə] **1** *noun* **(a)** person or group (such as a trades union) which sponsors an MP **(b)** MP who proposes a Bill in the House of Commons **2** *verb* **(a)** to **sponsor an MP** = to pay part of the election expenses of an MP, and contribute to his local party's funds (for which the MP is expected to represent the sponsor's interests in Parliament) **(b)** to propose a Bill in the House of Commons

◊ **sponsorship** ['sponsəʃɪp] *noun* act of sponsoring; *sponsorship of two MPs cost the union several thousand pounds*

spy [spaɪ] **1** *noun* person who watches secretly to get information about another country; *half the embassy staff are spies; the government asked the military attaché to leave the country, as they had evidence that he was a spy* **2** *verb* **(a)** to watch another country secretly to get information **(b)** to see; **I spy strangers** = words said by an MP when he wants to tell the Speaker to clear the public galleries

◊ **spying** ['spaɪɪŋ] *noun* action of a spy; *he was sentenced to death for spying for the enemy*

◊ **spymaster** ['spaɪmɑːstə] *noun* man in charge of spies

Square Mile ['skweə 'maɪl] *noun* the City (of London), the British financial centre

squire ['skwaɪə] *noun* (a) formerly, a young man who was an attendant on a great lord (b) country landowner

◊ **squirearchy** ['skwaɪərɑːki] *noun* country society dominated by local landowners

Stalinism ['stɑːlɪnɪzm] *noun* political system advocating the centralized authority of the Communist party and an oppressive totalitarian state (as in the former Soviet Union under Stalin)

stamp [stæmp] **1** *noun* (a) (i) device for making marks on documents; (ii) mark made in this way; *the invoice has the stamp 'Received with thanks' on it; the customs officer looked at the stamps in his passport;* date stamp = stamp with rubber figures which can be moved, used for marking the date on documents; *see also* RUBBER STAMP (b) small piece of gummed paper which you buy from a post office and stick on a letter *or* parcel to pay for the postage; *a postage stamp; a £1 stamp* (c) stamp duty = tax on legal documents (such as the conveyance of a property to a new owner *or* the contract for the purchase of shares) **2** *verb* (a) to mark a document with a stamp; *to stamp an invoice 'Paid'; the documents were stamped by the customs officials* (b) to put a postage stamp on (an envelope, etc.); stamped addressed envelope (s.a.e.) = envelope with your own address written on it and a stamp stuck on it to pay for the return postage

stand [stænd] **1** *noun* (a) active campaign against something; *the government's stand against racial prejudice; the police chief criticized the council's stand on law and order* (b) position of a member of Congress on a question (either for or against) **2** *verb* (a) to offer oneself as a candidate in an election; *he stood as a Liberal-Democrat candidate in the General Election; he is standing against the present deputy leader in the leadership contest; she was persuaded to stand for*

parliament; he has stood for office several times, but has never been elected (NOTE: US English uses the word run in this meaning) (b) to exist *or* to be in a state; *the House stands adjourned; the report stood referred to the Finance Committee;* (NOTE: stands - stood)

◊ **stand down** ['stænd 'daʊn] *verb* to withdraw your name from an election; *the wife of one of the candidates is ill and he has stood down*

◊ **stand in for** ['stænd 'ɪn fɔː] *verb* to take the place of someone; *Mr Smith is standing in for the chairman who is away on holiday*

◊ **stand over** ['stænd 'əʊvə] *verb* to adjourn; *the case has been stood over to next month*

standard ['stændəd] **1** *noun* (a) normal quality *or* normal conditions against which other things are judged; *the new design will set the standard for the future;* up to standard = of acceptable quality; *this report is not up to your usual standard;* British Standards Institute = official body which makes rules about standards of quality, safety, etc.; standards officer = council officer who deals with standards of quality in a borough (b) quality; *the materials used in the building are of high standard; the report blamed the poor standard of workmanship for the accident;* standard of living *or* living standards = quality of personal home life (such as amount of food or clothes bought, size of family car) **2** *adjective* normal *or* usual; *the standard emergency payment is £50; television sets are now standard equipment in schools; the consultant's standard fee is £250;* standard agreement *or* standard contract = normal printed contract form; standard letter = letter which is sent with only minor changes to various correspondents; standard rate = basic rate of income tax which is paid by most taxpayers *or* basic rate of VAT which is levied on most goods and services

Ständerat ['ʃtendərɑːt] *noun* States Council, the upper house of legislature in Switzerland

standing ['stændɪŋ] **1** *adjective* (a) permanent; standing committee = (i) permanent committee which always examines the same problem; (ii) committee of Members of Parliament which examines in detail Bills which are not passed to other committees; *see also* AD HOC **(b)** *US* **standing vote** = vote in the House of Representatives, where members stand up to be counted **2** *noun* **(a) long-standing conflict** *or* **conflict of long standing** = conflict which has been going on for many years **(b)** reputation; *the financial standing of a company;* **company of good standing** = very reputable company

◊ **standing order** ['stændɪŋ 'ɔːdə] *noun* **(a)** order written by a customer asking a bank to pay money regularly to an account; *I pay my subscription by standing order; compare* DIRECT DEBIT **(b) standing orders** = rules *or* regulations which regulate conduct in any body, such as the House of Commons *or* a council *or* the armed forces; *the Council's standing orders require members to obey instructions from the Chair*

Star Chamber ['staː 'tʃeɪmbə] *noun* **(a)** formerly, a royal court which tried cases without a jury **(b)** cabinet committee which examines the spending proposals of government departments

Stars and Stripes ['staːz n 'straɪps] *noun* national flag of the USA

◊ **Star-spangled Banner** ['staː 'spæŋgəld 'bænə] *noun* national anthem of the USA; *compare* HAIL TO THE CHIEF

state [steɪt] **1** *noun* **(a)** independent country; **to turn State's evidence** = to confess to a crime and then act as a witness against the other criminals involved in the hope of getting a lighter sentence; **head of state** = official leader of a country (such as a queen *or* President), though not necessarily the head of the government; **State Opening of Parliament** = ceremony when the Queen opens a new session of Parliament and reads the Queen's Speech; **state visit** = ceremonial visit paid by a head of state to another country; *see also* HEAD, SECRETARY OF STATE **(b)** government of a country; **offence against the State** = act of attacking the lawful government of a country; **State**

enterprise = company run by the State; *the bosses of State industries are appointed by the government;* **State ownership** = situation in which an industry is nationalized; **state school** = school run by a local authority and paid for with public money **(c)** semi-independent section of a federal country (such as the USA); **state capital** = capital city of an American state **(d)** condition; *the Prime Minister is due to make a speech on the state of the economy; in his state of the EU address, the President said that only by working together could the countries of the union tackle the problem of unemployment;* **State of the Union message** = annual speech by the President of the USA which summarizes the political situation in the country **2** *verb* to say clearly; *the document states that all revenue has to be declared to the tax office*

◊ **State Chamber** ['steɪt 'tʃeɪmbə] *noun* lower house of the legislature in Slovenia

◊ **state-controlled** ['steɪt kən'trəʊld] *adjective* run by the State; *state-controlled television*

◊ **State Council** ['steɪt 'kaʊnsəl] *noun* upper house of the legislature in Slovenia

◊ **State Department** ['steɪt dɪ'paːtmənt] *noun* US government department dealing with relations between the USA and other countries; *see note at* FOREIGN

◊ **stateless person** ['steɪtləs 'pɜːsən] *noun* person who is not a citizen of any state

◊ **State-owned** ['steɪt 'əʊnd] *adjective* owned by the State

◊ **States-General** ['steɪts 'dʒenərl] *noun* legislative body in the Netherlands (equivalent to Parliament or Congress)

◊ **statewide** ['steɪtwaɪd] *adjective* across all a state

statement ['steɪtmənt] *noun* **(a)** saying something clearly; **to make a statement** = to give details of something to the press *or* to the police; *(of a Member of Parliament)* **to make a statement to the House** = to tell the House of Commons that you have done something wrong *or* to explain your actions to the House; **to make a false statement** = to give wrong details **(b)** written document containing information; **bank statement** = written document from a bank showing the balance of an account; **financial statement** = document which shows the financial situation of a company; *the accounts department have prepared a financial statement for the shareholders*

statesman ['steɪtsmən] *noun* important political leader or representative of a country; *several statesmen from Western countries are meeting to discuss defence problems;* (NOTE: plural is **statesmen**)

◊ **statesmanlike** ['steɪtsmənlaɪk] *adjective* wise and skilful, like a good statesman

◊ **statesmanship** ['steɪtsmənʃɪp] *noun* ability of being a good statesman

stationery ['steɪʃnəri] *noun* office supplies for writing, such as paper, typewriter ribbons, pens, etc.; *legal stationery supplier; shop selling office stationery;* **continuous stationery** = paper made as a long sheet used in computer printers; **Her Majesty's Stationery Office (HMSO)** *or* **The Stationery Office** = government department which prints and binds documents for all government departments, produces government stationery, as well a publishing and selling books for the government; (NOTE: no plural)

statistics [stə'tɪstɪk] *plural noun* study of facts in the form of figures; *he asked for the birth statistics for 1992; council statistics show that the amount of rented property in the borough has increased; government trade statistics show that exports to the EU have fallen over the last six months;* **vital statistics** = figures dealing with births, marriages and deaths in a district

◊ **statistical** [stə'tɪstɪkl] *adjective* referring to statistics *or* based on figures; **statistical discrepancy** = amount by which two sets of figures differ

◊ **statistician** [stætɪs'tɪʃn] *noun* person who prepares and analyzes statistics

status ['steɪtəs] *noun* **(a)** importance *or* position in society; **loss of status** = becoming less important in a group; **status inquiry** = checking on a customer's credit rating **(b)**

legal status = legal identity of a person *or* body (such as a company *or* partnership); **what is the legal status of the person making the inquiry?** = what legal right has the person to make the inquiry?; (NOTE: no plural)

◊ **status quo** ['steɪtəs 'kwəʊ] *noun* state of things as they are now; *the contract does not alter the status quo;* **status quo ante** = the situation as it was before

statute ['stætʃuːt] *noun* established written law, especially an Act of Parliament; **statute book** = all laws passed by Parliament which are still in force; *the Act is still on the statute book, and has never been repealed;* **Statute of Limitations** = law which prevents a plaintiff from bringing proceedings after a certain period of time (usually six years); *US* **statutes at large** = printed list of statutes passed in each session of Congress, arranged in chronological order

◊ **statute-barred** ['stætʃuːt 'bɑːd] *adjective* which cannot take place because the time laid down in the Statute of Limitations has expired

◊ **statutorily** ['stætʃutərɪli] *adverb* by statute; **a statutorily protected tenant** = tenant protected by law

◊ **statutory** ['stætʃutri] *adjective* fixed by law *or* by a statute; *there is a statutory period of probation of thirteen weeks; the authority has a statutory obligation to provide free education to all children; powers conferred on an authority by the statutory code;* **statutory books** = official registers which a company must keep, such as the register of shareholders, minute books of board meetings, etc.; **statutory declaration** = (i) statement made to the Registrar of Companies that a company has complied with certain legal conditions; (ii) declaration signed and witnessed for official purposes; **statutory duty** = duty which someone must perform and which is laid down by statute; **statutory holiday** = holiday which is fixed by law; **statutory instrument (SI)** = order (which has the force of law) made under authority granted to a minister by an Act of Parliament; *see also* AFFIRMATIVE, GENERAL, NEGATIVE **statutory**

undertakers = bodies formed by statute and having legal duties to provide services (such as gas, electricity, water)

stay [steɪ] **1** *noun* **(a)** length of time spent in one place; *the tourists were in town for only a short stay* **(b)** temporary stopping of an order made by a court; **stay of execution** = temporary prevention of someone from enforcing a judgment; *the court granted the company a two-week stay of execution;* **stay of proceedings** = stopping of a case which is being heard **2** *verb* **(a)** to stop at a place; *the chairman is staying at the Hotel London; inflation has stayed high in spite of the government's efforts to bring it down* **(b)** to stop (an action) temporarily; *an application to stay a hearing in the House of Lords*

stenographer [stə'nɒgrəfə] *noun* official person who can write in shorthand and so take records of what is said in Parliament *or* in court

step [step] *noun* **(a)** type of action; *the first step taken by the new government was to remove the head of the armed forces;* **to take steps to prevent something happening** = to act to stop something happening; *what steps does the council propose to take to avoid setting an illegal budget?* **(b)** movement; *becoming Parliamentary Private Secretary is a step up the promotion ladder for an MP;* **in step with** = moving at the same rate as; *the pound rose in step with the dollar;* **out of step with** = not moving at the same rate as; *the pound was out of step with other European currencies; wages are out of step with the cost of living*

◊ **step down** ['step 'daʊn] *verb* to resign; *he stepped down as Chair of the Finance Committee*

◊ **step up** ['step 'ʌp] *verb* to increase; *the government has stepped up its grants to small businesses;* (NOTE: **stepping - stepped**)

sterling ['stɜːlɪŋ] *noun* standard currency used in the United Kingdom; *to quote prices in sterling or to quote sterling prices;* **pound sterling** = official term for the British currency; **sterling area** = area of the world where the pound sterling is the main trading currency; **sterling balances** = a country's

trade balances expressed in pounds sterling; **sterling crisis** = fall in the exchange rate of the pound sterling; (NOTE: no plural)

stipulate ['stɪpjʊleɪt] *verb* to demand that a condition be put into a contract or agreement, etc.; *the government stipulated that the applicants should take a means test*

◊ **stipulation** [stɪpjʊ'leɪʃn] *noun* special condition; *he failed to meet the stipulation that only native-born citizens are eligible for election*

Stormont ['stɔːmɒnt] *noun* palace in Belfast, which formerly was the seat of the Northern Ireland government

Storting ['stɔːtɪŋ] *noun* legislative body in Norway (equivalent of Parliament or Congress)

stranger ['streɪnʒə] *noun* person who is not an MP but is allowed into the public gallery *or* the press gallery as a visitor; **strangers' gallery** = gallery for visitors in the House of Commons or House of Lords; *see also* SPY

strategy ['strætədʒi] *noun* plan of action; *the Opposition's electoral strategy was to attack the government's record on unemployment*

◊ **strategic** [strə'tiːdʒɪk] *adjective* based on a plan of action; **strategic planning** = planning for the future work of a government

strife [straɪf] *noun* violent public arguments and disorder; *the new rules are intended to lessen racial strife;* **civil strife** = trouble when groups of civilians fight each other

strike [straɪk] **1** *noun* **(a)** stopping of work by the workers (because of lack of agreement with management *or* because of orders from a union); **general strike** = strike of all the workers in a country; **official strike** = strike which has been approved by the union; **protest strike** = strike in protest at a particular grievance; **token strike** = short strike to show that workers have a grievance; **unofficial strike** = strike by local workers, which has not been approved by the union as a whole **(b) to take strike action** = to go on strike; **strike ballot** *or* **strike vote** = vote by workers to decide if a strike should be held; **strike call** = demand by a union for a strike; **no-strike agreement** *or* **no-strike clause** = (clause in an) agreement where the workers say that they will never strike; **strike fund** = money collected by a trade union from its members, used to pay strike pay; **strike pay** = money paid to striking workers by their trade union during a strike **(c) to come out on strike** *or* **to go on strike** = to stop work; *the local government workers are on strike for higher pay;* **to call the workers out on strike** = to tell the workers to stop work **2** *verb* **(a)** to stop working because there is no agreement with management; *to strike for higher wages or for shorter working hours; to strike in protest against bad working conditions; to strike in sympathy with the postal workers* = to strike to show that you agree with the postal workers who are on strike **(b)** to hit (someone); *two policemen were struck by bottles; he was struck on the head by a flying brick* **(c) to strike off** *or* **out** = to delete *or* to remove (a word from a text *or* a name from a list); **to strike someone off the rolls** = to stop a solicitor *or* doctor from practising by removing his name from the list of solicitors *or* doctors; *US* **to strike out the last word** = way of getting permission of the chair to speak on a question, by moving that the last word of the amendment *or* section being discussed should be deleted; **to strike from the record** = to remove words from the written minutes of a meeting because they are incorrect *or* offensive; *the chairman's remarks were struck from the record;* (NOTE: **striking - struck**)

STV = SINGLE TRANSFERABLE VOTE

sub- [sʌb] *prefix* meaning less important

◊ **sub-clause** ['sʌbklɔːz] *noun* part of a clause in a Bill being considered by Parliament, which will become a sub-section when the Bill becomes an Act

◊ **subcommittee** ['sʌbkəmɪti] *noun* committee which is formed to advise a larger committee; *the Schools Subcommittee makes recommendations to the Education Committee*

◊ **subcontinent** [sʌb'kɒntɪnənt] *noun* very large landmass, attached to a continent; **the (Indian) Subcontinent** = India, Pakistan and Bangladesh

subject 1 ['sʌbdʒɪkt] *noun* **(a)** what something is concerned with; *the subject of the report was poverty in the inner cities* **(b)** person who is a citizen of a country and bound by its laws; *he is a British subject; British subjects do not need visas to visit European Union countries;* **liberty of the subject** = right of a citizen to be free unless convicted of a crime which is punishable by imprisonment **2** *adjective* **subject peoples** = races ruled by another power

◊ **subject to 1** ['sʌbdʒɪkt 'tuː] *adjective* **(a)** depending on; *the contract is subject to government approval* = the contract will be valid only if it is approved by the government; **agreement** *or* **sale subject to contract** = agreement *or* sale which is not legal until a proper contract has been signed; **offer subject to availability** = the offer is valid only if the goods are available **(b)** which can receive; **these articles are subject to import tax** = import tax has to be paid on these articles **2** [sʌb'dʒekt 'tuː] *verb* to make someone suffer something; *he was subjected to torture; the MP subjected the committee to a boring list of figures*

sub judice ['sʌb 'dʒuːdəsi] *Latin phrase meaning* 'under the law': being considered by a court (and so not to be mentioned in the media or in Parliament); *the papers cannot report the case because it is still sub judice*

submit [sʌb'mɪt] *verb* to ask for something to be considered by a committee *or* meeting; *he submitted six planning applications to the committee*

subpoena [sʌb'piːnə] **1** *noun* court order requiring someone to appear before a Parliamentary Committee *or* a court of law **2** *verb* to order someone to appear before a parliamentary committee *or* a court of law; *she was subpoenaed to appear before the Commons committee on Defence*

subscribe [sʌb'skraɪb] *verb* **to subscribe to something** = (i) to sign something, showing that you agree to it; (ii) to support a policy or proposal

sub-section ['sʌbsekʃn] *noun* part of a section of a document, such as an Act of Parliament; *you will find the information in sub-section 3 of Section 47*

subsidiarity [sʌbsidi'æriti] *noun (in the EU)* principle that decisions should be taken at the lower possible effective level, so major decisions would be taken at governmental level, and not at the level of the Commission

subsidiary motion [sʌb'sidjəri 'məuʃn] *noun* motion which is attached to a substantive motion

subsidy ['sʌbsidi] *noun* money given by a government to an organization to help it continue to work; *the club relies on council subsidies for its finance*

◊ **subsidize** ['sʌbsidaiz] *verb* to give money to an organization to help it continue to work; *the youth theatre is subsidized by the council; the government has refused to subsidize the construction work*

substantive ['sʌbstəntiv] *adjective* real *or* actual; **substantive law** = all laws including common law and statute law which deal with legal principles (as opposed to procedural law which refers to the procedure for putting the law into practice); **substantive motion** = motion in a debate which is complete in itself

substitute ['sʌbstitjuːt] **1** *noun* **(a)** person *or* thing which takes the place of someone *or* something else; *the Mayor was ill so she sent the Deputy Mayor as substitute* **(b)** *US* motion introduced in place of the business being discussed, which has the effect of killing the original motion **2** *verb* to put in the place of something else; *he proposed to amend the motion by deleting the words 'the Council' in line three and substituting 'the Council Officers'; please substitute 'school' for 'college' on page 4*

suburb ['sʌbɜːb] *noun* area on the edge of a city or town, which is mainly used for dwellings and not for commerce; *a residential suburb;* **the suburbs** = the whole

suburban area round a town; *they moved to the suburbs to be nearer the countryside*

◊ **suburban** [sə'bɜːbən] *adjective* referring to suburbs

◊ **suburbia** [sə'bɜːbiə] *noun* suburban areas of a city; middle-class districts; *life in suburbia is very different from life in a high-rise flat in the town centre*

subvert [sʌb'vɜːt] *verb* to act secretly against a government; *he was accused of trying to subvert the State*

◊ **subversion** [sʌb'vɜːʃn] *noun* secret acts against a government; *the government stated that the power of the State was being undermined by enemy subversion*

◊ **subversive** [sʌb'vɜːsiv] **1** *adjective* which acts secretly against the government; *the police are investigating subversive groups in the student organizations* **2** *noun* person who acts secretly against the government; *the police have arrested several known subversives*

succeed [sək'siːd] *verb* to follow, especially to take the place of someone who has retired *or* died; *George V succeeded his father Edward VII; Mrs Jones is expected to succeed Mr Smith as Chair;* **to succeed to a title** = to become a peer by inheriting the title from someone who has died

◊ **succession** [sək'seʃn] *noun* acquiring property *or* title from someone who has died; **law of succession** = laws relating to how property shall pass to others when the owner dies

◊ **successor** [sək'sesə] *noun* person who takes over from someone; *Mr Smith's successor as chairman will be Mr Jones*

suffrage ['sʌfridʒ] *noun* right to vote in elections; **universal suffrage** = right of all citizens to vote; (NOTE: no plural)

◊ **suffragette** [sʌfrə'dʒet] *noun* woman who campaigned for women to be granted the right to vote (in the early part of the 20th century)

suggest [sə'dʒest] *verb* to put forward a proposal; *the chairman suggested (that) the next meeting should be held in October; we* *suggested Mr Smith for the post of treasurer*

◊ **suggestion** [sə'dʒestʃn] *noun* proposal *or* idea which is put forward; *the Committee voted to accept the suggestion from the Secretary that meetings should start at 2.30 in future*

suitable ['suːtəbl] *adjective* convenient *or* which fits; *Wednesday is the most suitable day for the hearing; we had to advertise the job again because there were no suitable candidates*

sultan ['sʌltən] *noun* hereditary ruler of an Arab country

◊ **Sultanate** ['sʌltəneɪt] *noun* Arab country ruled by a sultan

summary ['sʌməri] **1** *noun* short account of what has happened *or* of what has been written; *the chairman gave a summary of his discussions with the German delegation; the Home Secretary gave a summary of events leading to the arrest of the terrorists* **2** *adjective* which happens immediately; **summary arrest** = arrest without a warrant; **summary conviction** = conviction by a magistrate sitting without a jury; **summary dismissal** = dismissal of an employee without giving the notice stated in the contract of employment; **summary offence** = minor crime which can be tried only in a magistrates' court

◊ **summarily** ['sʌmərəli] *adverb* immediately; *magistrates can try a case summarily or refer it to the Crown Court*

◊ **summarize** ['sʌməraɪz] *verb* to make a short account of something; *the council's discussions were summarized in the evening papers*

summit ['sʌmɪt] *noun* **(a)** top of a mountain **(b)** meeting between heads of state *or* between superpower leaders; *the summit conference or summit meeting was held in Geneva; the matter will be discussed at next week's summit of the EU leaders; see also* SHERPA

◊ **summitry** ['sʌmɪtri] *noun* diplomacy as carried on in summit meetings

summon ['sʌmən] *verb* to ask someone to come; *he was summoned to appear before the committee*

◊ **summons** ['sʌmənz] *noun* official command from a court requiring someone to appear in court to be tried for a criminal offence *or* to defend a civil action

superpower ['suːpəpauə] *noun* very large state, with great economic strength, large armed forces and great influence in world politics; **superpower diplomacy** = diplomatic moves between superpowers

supplemental [sʌplɪ'mentl] *adjective* which is additional to something; *US* **supplemental appropriations** = extra appropriation of money passed later than the normal appropriation bill, but still within the same fiscal year

supplementary [sʌplɪ'mentri] *adjective* which is additional; **supplementary questions** *or* **supplementaries** = questions asked by an MP *or* councillor after a main written question has been answered, used to try to catch a Minister *or* council committee chairman by surprise or to embarrass him

supply [sə'plaɪ] **1** *noun* **(a)** providing something which is needed; **money supply** = amount of money which exists in a country; **Supply Bill** = Bill for providing money for government requirements; **Supply Days** *or* **allotted days** = twenty nine days set aside in each session of Parliament for discussion of Supply Bills and other finance matters; **supply price** = price at which something is provided; **supply and demand** = amount of a product which is available at a certain price and the amount which is wanted by customers at a certain price; **the law of supply and demand** = general rule that the amount of a product which is available is related to the needs of the possible customers **(b) in short supply** = not available in large enough quantities to meet the demand; *spare parts are in short supply because of the strike* **(c)** stock of something which is needed; *the factory is running short of supplies of coal; supplies of coal have been reduced;* **office supplies** = goods needed to run an office (such as paper, pens, printer ribbons) **(d) supplies** = goods *or* services provided; **exempt supplies** = sales of goods *or* services which are exempt from VAT **2** *verb* to provide something which is needed; *to supply a factory with spare parts; the prosecution supplied the court with a detailed map of the area where the crime took place; details of staff addresses and phone numbers can be supplied by the personnel department*

◊ **supplier** [sə'plaɪə] *noun* person *or* company which supplies something

support [sə'pɔːt] **1** *noun* **(a)** giving money to help; *the government has provided support to the computer industry; we have no financial support from the banks;* **rate support grant** = money given by central government to a local authority to be spent in addition to money raised by the rates **(b)** agreement *or* encouragement; *the chairman has the support of the committee;* **support price** = price (in the EU) at which a government will buy farm produce to stop the price from falling **2** *verb* **(a)** to give money to help; *the government is supporting the computer industry to the tune of $2m per annum; we hope the banks will support us during the expansion period* **(b)** to encourage *or* to agree with; *she hopes the other members of the committee will support her; the electorate will not support another increase in income tax*

◊ **supporter** [sə'pɔːtə] *noun* person who agrees with and encourages someone; *Socialist supporters or supporters of the Socialist party were very pleased with the result*

suppress [sə'pres] *verb* **(a)** to stop something from being made public; *the government tried to suppress the news about the riots* **(b) to limit something, such as a person's freedom to act** *the peasants' revolt was suppressed by the army*

◊ **suppression** [sə'preʃn] *noun* act of suppressing; *the suppression of the truth about the Minister's resignation*

supranational [suːprə'næʃnl] *adjective* above nations; having power over national governments

supremacy [su'preməsi] *noun* being in an all-powerful position; **the supremacy of Parliament** = situation of the British Parliament which can both pass and repeal laws

supreme [su'priːm] *adjective* most powerful *or* important

◊ **Supreme Council** [su'priːm 'kaʊnsəl] *noun* body of legislature in the Ukraine

◊ **supreme court** [su'priːm 'kɔːt] *noun* **(a) Supreme Court (of Judicature)** = highest court in England and Wales, consisting of the Court of Appeal and the High Court of Justice **(b)** highest federal court in the USA and other countries

◊ **Supreme Kenges** [su'priːm 'keŋgɪz] *noun* legislative body in Kazakhstan

◊ **Supreme Soviet** [su'priːm 'səʊviət] *noun* the legislative body of Tajikistan

surcharge ['sɜːtʃɑːdʒ] *verb* to levy a charge on a member of a council for having failed to set a legal rate; *ten councillors were surcharged and disqualified*

surrender [sə'rendə] *verb* **(a)** to give in to an enemy; *the town surrendered to the guerrilla forces* **(b)** to hand over something to someone; *he surrendered his seal of office*

survive [sə'vaɪv] *verb* **(a)** to live longer than another person; *he survived his wife; she is survived by her husband and three children;* he left his estate to his surviving **relatives** = to the relatives who were still alive **(b)** to continue to exist after something has happened; *the club will not survive all these changes; the government survived the vote of no confidence*

◊ **survivor** [sə'vaɪvə] *noun* someone who lives longer than another person; someone who lives after something has happened

suspend [sə'spend] *verb* **(a)** to stop (something) for a time; *the sitting of the House was suspended because there was no further business to be transacted; we have suspended payments while we are waiting for news from our agent; the hearings have been suspended for two weeks; work on the preparation of the investigation has been* *suspended; the government decided to suspend negotiations on the treaty* **suspended sentence** = sentence of imprisonment which a court orders shall not take effect unless the offender commits another crime; *US* **motion to suspend the rules** = motion to speed up the passage of a bill, by limiting debate on it and not allowing any amendments **(b)** to stop (someone) working for a time; *he was suspended on full pay while the police investigations were proceeding* **(c)** to punish an MP *or* council member by refusing to allow him to attend sittings *or* meetings; to punish a student by refusing to allow him to attend school *or* college; *John Brown, MP, was named by the Speaker and suspended; three boys were suspended from school for fighting*

◊ **suspension** [sə'spenʃn] *noun* stopping something for a time; stopping an MP *or* council member from attending sittings *or* meetings for a time; *suspension of a sitting; the suspension of an MP*

> COMMENT: when an MP is 'named' by the Speaker, the House will vote to suspend him. Suspension is normally for five days, though it may be for longer if the MP is suspended twice in the same session of Parliament

swear ['sweə] *verb* to make an oath *or* to promise that what you will say will be the truth; *he swore to tell the truth;* **'I swear to tell the truth, the whole truth and nothing but the truth'** = words used when a witness takes the oath in court; (NOTE: **swearing - swore - has sworn**)

◊ **swear in** ['sweə 'ɪn] *verb* to make someone take an oath before taking up a position; *he was sworn in as a Privy Councillor;* **swearing-in** = act of making someone take an oath before taking up a position; *five hundred guests attended the swearing-in of the President*

swing [swɪŋ] *noun* percentage change in votes from one election to another; *a 10% swing away from the government or to the Opposition; he needs a 5% swing to recapture the seat which he lost at the last election*

sympathizer ['sɪmpəθaɪzə] *noun* person who agrees in general with the policies of a political party, without being a party member; *the government is formed of communists and communist sympathizers*

syndicalism ['sɪndɪkəlɪzm] *noun* type of socialism, where property and control of industry is in the hands of the trades unions in each industry (as opposed to strict socialism, where the control of industry is in the hands of the state)

system ['sɪstəm] *noun* **(a)** arrangement *or* organization of things which work together; *the British legal system has been taken as the standard for many other legal systems;* **filing system** = way of putting documents in order for easy reference; **to operate a quota system** = to regulate supplies by fixing quantities which are allowed **(b) computer system** = set of programs, commands, etc., which make a computer work; **control system** = system used to check that a computer system is working correctly; **systems analysis** = using a computer to suggest how an organization should work by analyzing the way in which it works at present; **systems analyst** = person who specializes in systems analysis

◊ **systematic** [sɪstə'mætɪk] *adjective* in order *or* using method; *the Prime Minister ordered a systematic report on the security services*

Tt

table ['teɪbl] **1** *noun* **(a)** piece of furniture for working at; **conference table** *or* **negotiating table** = table around which people sit to negotiate; **round table conference** = conference with a round table, showing that each party at the meeting is of equal status with the rest; *the government is trying to get the rebel leaders to come to the conference table* **(b)** long table in the centre of the House of Commons between the two front benches (the Serjeant at Arms places the mace on the table when the business of the House begins. The two despatch boxes for main speakers from either party are also on the table) **(c) to lay a bill on the table** = (i) to present a bill to the House of Commons for discussion; (ii) *US* to kill debate on a bill in the House of Representatives; *US* **to let a bill lie on the table** = not to proceed with discussion of a bill, but to hold it over to be debated later **(d)** list of figures *or* facts set out in a list; **table of contents** = list of contents in a book; **actuarial tables** = lists showing how long people of certain ages are likely to live, used to calculate life assurance premiums **2** *verb* to put items of information on the table before a meeting; *the report of the finance committee was tabled;* **to table a motion** = to put forward a proposal for discussion by putting details of it on the table at a meeting

tacit ['tæsɪt] *adjective* agreed but not stated; *he gave the proposal his tacit approval; the committee gave its tacit agreement to the proposal*

tactic ['tæktɪk] *noun* way of doing something, so as to achieve success; *the main Opposition tactic is to try to embarrass the Government front bench; their election tactics were wrong, and they only succeeded in alienating the voters*

◊ **tactical** ['tæktɪkl] *adjective* done as part of a tactic to try to achieve success; **tactical voting** = way of voting, which aims not at voting for the candidate you want to win, but at voting in such a way as to prevent the candidate whom you do not want to win from being elected

> COMMENT: in a case where the three candidates A, B and C, have 47%, 33% and 20% of the vote according to an opinion poll, C's supporters might all vote for B, to prevent A winning

take [teɪk] *verb* **(a)** to do a certain action; **to take action** = to do something; *you must take immediate action if you want to stop thefts;* **to take the chair** = to be chairman of a meeting; *in the absence of the chairman his deputy took the chair;* **to take someone to court** = to sue someone *or* to start civil proceedings against someone **(b)** to need (a time *or* a quantity); *it took the committee six hours to debate the motion or the committee took six hours to debate the motion; it will take her all morning to type my letters; it takes six men to guard the building;* (NOTE: **taking - took - has taken**)

◊ **take out** ['teɪk 'aut] *verb* **to take out a patent for an invention** = to apply for and receive a patent; **to take out insurance against theft** = to pay a premium to an insurance company, so that if a theft takes place the company will pay compensation

◊ **take over** ['teɪk 'əuvə] *verb* **(a)** to take control of something (a factory *or* an organization); *during the uprising, the rebels took over the Post Office and radio station; the party has been taken over by an activist group* **(b)** to start to do a job in place of someone else; *the new leader of the party takes over on May 1st; Ambassador Brown* *took over from Ambassador Green last April* **(c) to take over a company** = to buy (a business) by offering to buy most of its shares; *the company was taken over by a large international corporation*

◊ **takeover** ['teɪkəʊvə] *noun* **(a)** act of taking over; *after the takeover by the military, the radio station started broadcasting military music; the takeover of power by the President's brother was greeted with pleasure by the people;* **the takeover period is always difficult** = the period when one person is taking over work from another is always difficult **(b)** buying a business; **takeover bid** *or* **offer** = offer to buy all or a majority of the shares in a company so as to control it; **Takeover Panel** = body which supervises and regulates takeovers

talk out ['tɔːk 'aʊt] *verb* to go on talking in a debate, so that the time runs out before the vote can be taken; *the bill was talked out and so fell*

◊ **talking shop** ['tɔːkɪŋ 'ʃɒp] *noun* place where people talk, but not much action takes place; *the Council Chamber is just a talking shop*

Tammany Hall ['tæməni 'hɔːl] *noun* most powerful Democratic Party Committee in New York; *(as criticism)* **Tammany Hall politics** = old-fashioned corrupt politics (so called after the corrupt Tammany Hall Society in the 19th century)

Tánaiste ['tænɪst] *noun* Deputy Prime Minister (in the Republic of Ireland)

Taoiseach ['tiːʃək] *noun* Prime Minister of the Republic of Ireland

target ['tɑːgɪt] *verb* to try to hit a person, organization, building, etc.; *the terrorists targeted military and political figures; the advertising campaign is targeting floating voters*

tariff ['tærɪf] *noun* **(a)** customs tariffs = tax to be paid for importing *or* exporting goods; **tariff barriers** = customs duty intended to make imports more difficult; *to impose tariff barriers on* or *to lift tariff barriers from a product;* **protective tariff** = tariff which

aims to ban imports to prevent competition with local products **(b)** rate of charging for electricity, hotel rooms, train tickets, etc.; *the electricity industry is planning to raise domestic tariffs*

task force ['tɑːsk 'fɔːs] *noun* **(a)** group organized for a special purpose; *a government task force on inner-city problems* **(b)** *(EU)* group which coordinates a mission affecting more than one Directorate-General

tax [tæks] **1** *noun* **(a)** money taken compulsorily by the government *or* by an official body to pay for government services; **capital gains tax** = tax on capital gains; **capital transfer tax** = tax on the transfer of capital *or* assets from one person to another; **excess profits tax** = tax on profits which are higher than what is thought to be normal; **income tax** = tax on salaries and wages; **land tax** = tax on the value of land owned; **sales tax** = tax paid on each item sold; **Value Added Tax (VAT)** = tax on goods and services, added as a percentage to the invoiced sales price **(b)** ad valorem tax = tax calculated according to the value of the goods taxed; **back tax** = tax which is owed; **basic rate tax** = lowest rate of income tax; **to levy a tax** *or* **to impose a tax** = to make a tax payable; *the government has imposed a 15% tax on petrol;* **to lift a tax** = to remove a tax; **tax adviser** *or* **tax consultant** = person who gives advice on tax problems; **tax allowances** *or* **allowances against tax** = part of one's income which a person is allowed to earn and not pay tax on; **tax avoidance** = trying (legally) to minimize the amount of tax to be paid; **tax code** = number given to indicate the amount of tax allowances a person has; **tax concession** = allowing less tax to be paid; **tax credit** = part of a dividend on which the company has already paid tax, so that the shareholder is not taxed on it again; **tax deductions** = (i) money removed from a salary to pay tax; (ii) *US* business expenses which can be claimed against tax; **tax deducted at source** = tax which is removed from a salary, interest payment or dividend payment before the money is paid out; **tax evasion** = illegally trying not to pay tax; **tax exemption** = (i) being free from payment of tax; (ii) *US* part of income which a person is allowed to earn and not pay tax on; **tax haven** = country where taxes levied on foreigners *or* foreign companies are low; **tax holiday** = period when a new business is exempted from paying tax; **tax inspector** *or* **inspector of taxes** = official of the Inland Revenue who examines tax returns and decides how much tax someone should pay; **tax loophole** = legal means of not paying tax; **tax planning** = planning one's financial affairs so that one pays as little tax as possible; **tax relief** = allowing someone not to pay tax on certain parts of his income; **tax return** *or* **tax declaration** = completed tax form, with details of income and allowances; **double tax treaty** = treaty between two countries so that citizens *or* businesses pay tax in one country only; **tax year** = twelve month period on which taxes are calculated (in the UK, 6th April to 5th April of the following year) **2** *verb* **(a)** to make someone pay a tax *or* to impose a tax on something; *to tax businesses at 50%; income is taxed at 27%; these items are heavily taxed* **(b)** to assess the bill presented by a Parliamentary agent *or* to have the costs of a legal action assessed by the court; **taxing officer** = person appointed by the House of Commons to assess the charges presented by a Parliamentary agent

◊ **taxable** ['tæksəbl] *adjective* which can be taxed; **taxable items** = items on which a tax has to be paid; **taxable income** = income on which a person has to pay tax

◊ **taxation** [tæk'seɪʃn] *noun* act of taxing; **direct taxation** = taxes (such as income tax) which are paid direct to the government out of earnings *or* profit; **double taxation** = taxing the same income twice; **double taxation treaty** = treaty between two countries that citizens *or* businesses pay tax in one country only; (NOTE: no plural)

◊ **tax-deductible** ['tæksdɪ'dʌktɪbl] *adjective* which can be deducted from an income before tax is calculated; **these expenses are not tax-deductible** = tax has to be paid on these expenses

◊ **tax-exempt** ['tæksɪg'zempt] *adjective* (person *or* organization) not required to pay

tax; (income *or* goods) which are not subject to tax

◊ **tax-free** ['tæks'friː] *adjective* on which tax does not have to be paid

◊ **taxpayer** ['tækspeɪə] *noun* person *or* company which has to pay tax; *basic taxpayer or taxpayer at the basic rate; corporate taxpayers*

◊ **tax point** ['tæks 'pɔɪnt] *noun* (i) time when goods are supplied and when a tax such as VAT may be charged; (ii) time at which a tax begins to be applied

TD = TEACHTA DALA

Teachta Dala ['tɪæχtə 'dælə] *noun* member of the Irish Dáil

technical ['teknɪkl] *adjective* referring to a specific procedural point *or* using a strictly legal interpretation; *the motion was rejected on a technical point*

◊ **technicality** [teknɪ'kælɪti] *noun* special interpretation of a legal point; *the Appeal Court rejected the appeal on a technicality*

◊ **technocrat** ['teknəkræt] *noun* technical expert or administrator

teller ['telə] *noun* **(a)** member who counts the votes in the House of Commons *or* House of Representatives **(b)** bank clerk

COMMENT: when a division is called in the House of Commons, the Speaker appoints four MPs as tellers, two for the motion and two against. They do not vote, but check the other MPs as they pass through the division lobbies

tem [tem] *see* PRO TEMPORE

temporal ['temprəl] *see* LORDS

temporary ['temprəri] *adjective* which lasts only a short time; *the council was granted a temporary injunction; the police took temporary measures to close the street to traffic; she has a temporary job or temporary post with the borough rating office; he has a temporary job as a filing clerk or he has a job as a temporary filing clerk* **temporary employment** = full-time work which does not last for more than a few days or months; **temporary injunction** =

injunction which is granted until a case comes to court; **temporary staff** = staff who are appointed for a short time

◊ **temporarily** ['temprərəli] *adverb* lasting only for a short time; *he was temporarily out of town and so missed the vote*

tenancy ['tenənsi] *noun* (i) agreement by which a person can occupy a property; (ii) period during which a person has an agreement to occupy a property

◊ **tenant** ['tenənt] *noun* person *or* company which rents a house *or* flat *or* office in which to live or work; *council tenants are not allowed to have dogs in their flats; the tenant is liable for repairs;* **sitting tenant** = tenant who is living in a house when the freehold or lease is sold

tender ['tendə] **1** *noun* **(a)** offer to work for a certain price; **to put a project out to tender** *or* **to ask for** *or* **to invite tenders for a project** = to ask contractors to give written estimates for a job; **to put in a tender** *or* **to submit a tender** = to make an estimate for a job; **sealed tenders** = tenders sent in sealed envelopes which will all be opened together at a certain time **(b)** **legal tender** = coins or notes which can be legally used to pay a debt (small denominations cannot be used to pay large debts); (NOTE: no plural in this meaning) **2** *verb* **(a)** **to tender for a contract** = to put forward an estimate of cost for work to be carried out under contract; *to tender for the construction of a hospital* **(b)** to offer; **to tender one's resignation** = to give in one's resignation

◊ **tenderer** ['tendərə] *noun* person *or* company which tenders for work; *the company was the successful tenderer for the project*

Ten Minute Rule ['ten 'mɪnɪt 'ruːl] *noun* standing order in the House of Commons, where an ordinary MP can introduce a Bill with a short speech, and if the Bill is passed on a vote, it can proceed to the Second Reading stage; *the Bill was proposed under the Ten Minute Rule*

tense [tens] *adjective* (situation) in which two groups seem likely to attack each other; *the situation in the area is still tense; as the*

situation became more tense, the Defence Department sent troops to nearby bases

◊ **tension** ['tenʃn] *noun* period when relations between states are strained and they may take action against each other; *the Security Council resolution is aimed at reducing tension in the area; the attack on the ship increased tension in the area; the debate in council showed the tension between the two factions*

tentative ['tentətɪv] *adjective* not certain; *they reached a tentative agreement over the proposal; we suggested Wednesday May 10th as a tentative date for the next meeting*

◊ **tentatively** ['tentətɪvli] *adverb* not certainly; *we tentatively suggested Wednesday as the date for our next meeting*

tenure ['tenjə] *noun* **(a)** right to hold property *or* a position; **security of tenure** = right to keep a job *or* rented accommodation provided certain conditions are met; **land tenure** = way in which land is held (such as leasehold) **(b)** time when a position is held; *during his tenure of the office of chairman;* (NOTE: no plural)

term [tɜːm] *noun* **(a)** period of time; *the term of a lease; the term of the loan is fifteen years; to have a loan for a term of fifteen years; during his term of office as chairman;* **term of years** = fixed period of several years (of a lease); **fixed term** = period which is fixed when a contract is signed and which cannot be changed afterwards; **short-term** = for a period of months or only a few years; *short-term planning often causes problems for the future;* **long-term** = for a long period of time; **medium-term** = for a period of one or two years **(b)** **term** *or* **terms** = conditions *or* duties which have to be carried out as part of a contract *or* arrangements which have to be agreed before a contract is valid; *he refused to agree to some of the terms of the lease; by or under the terms of the contract, the contractor is responsible for all damage to the property;* **terms of payment** *or* **payment terms** = conditions for paying something; **terms of sale** = agreed ways in which a sale takes place (such as discounts and credit terms); **implied terms and conditions** = terms and conditions which are not written in a contract, but which are legally taken to be present in the contract **(c)** (i) length of a Parliament before new elections are called; (ii) part of a university *or* college *or* school year; *the autumn* or *winter term starts in September* **(d) terms of employment** = conditions set out in a contract of employment; **terms of reference** = areas which a committee *or* an inspector can deal with; *under the terms of reference of the committee it can only investigate complaints from the public; the tribunal's terms of reference do not cover traffic offences*

terminate ['tɜːmɪneɪt] *verb* to end (something) *or* to bring (something) to an end *or* to come to an end; *to terminate an agreement; his employment was terminated; an offer terminates on the death of the person who makes it*

◊ **terminable** ['tɜːmɪnəbl] *adjective* which can be terminated

◊ **termination** [tɜːmɪˈneɪʃn] *noun* **(a)** bringing to an end; *the termination of an offer* or *of a lease; to appeal against the termination of a foster order* **(b)** US leaving a job (resigning, retiring, or being fired or made redundant)

territory ['terɪtri] *noun* area of land (ruled by a government); *their government has laid claim to part of our territory*

◊ **territorial** [terɪˈtɔːriəl] *adjective* referring to land; **territorial claims** = claims to own land which is part of another country; **territorial waters** = sea water near the coast of a country, which is part of the country and governed by the laws of that country; **outside territorial waters** = in international waters, where a single country's jurisdiction does not run

terror ['terə] *noun* being extremely frightened; **Reign of Terror** = (i) period of repression and violence, when people live in a continual state of fear; (ii) period during the French Revolution, when the Jacobins under Robespierre were all-powerful (1793-94)

◊ **terrorism** ['terərɪzm] *noun* using acts of public violence to achieve political change

◊ **terrorist** ['terərɪst] *adjective & noun* (person) who tries to achieve political change by acts of public violence; *the government has had to face a series of terrorist attacks on post offices and police stations; three terrorists seized the Minister and held him hostage*

test [test] **1** *noun* **(a)** examination to see if something works well *or* is possible; **test certificate** = certificate to show that something has passed a test; **feasibility test** = test to see if something is possible; **means test** = test to see how poor someone is, to see if he *or* she is eligible for a government grant **(b) test case** = legal action where the decision will fix a principle which judges in other cases can follow; **test roll** = book in which each MP signs after having taken the oath at the beginning of a new Parliament **2** *verb* to examine something to see if it is working well; *to test a computer system*

testimonial [testɪˈməʊniəl] *noun* written document praising someone's good qualities, often one which is presented at a ceremony; *at a function in the Town Hall, the mayor presented testimonials to six members of the staff of the municipal offices*

text [tekst] *noun* written part of something; *he wrote notes at the side of the text of the agreement;* **text processing** = working with words, using a computer to produce, check and change documents, contracts, reports, letters, etc.

◊ **textbook** ['tekstbʊk] *noun* book which is used for studying; book of legal commentary which can be cited in court; **textbook case** = problem which is exactly the same as one presented in a textbook; *it is a textbook case of inefficiency caused by lack of financial control*

there- ['ðeə] *prefix* that thing; (NOTE: the following words formed from **there-** are frequently used in government and legal documents)

◊ **thereafter** [ðeərˈɑːftə] *adverb* after that

◊ **thereby** [ðeəˈbaɪ] *adverb* by that

◊ **therefor** [ðeəˈfɔː] *adverb* for that

◊ **therefore** ['ðeəfɔ:] *adverb* as a result of that

◊ **therefrom** [ðeə'frɒm] *adverb* from that

◊ **therein** [ðeə'ɪn] *adverb* in that

◊ **thereinafter** [ðeərɪn'ɑ:ftə] *adverb* afterwards listed in that document

◊ **thereinbefore** [ðeərɪnbɪ'fɔ:] *adverb* before mentioned in that document

◊ **thereinunder** [ðeərɪn'ʌndə] *adverb* mentioned under that heading

◊ **thereof** [ðeə'ɒv] *adverb* of that; **in respect thereof** = regarding that thing

◊ **thereto** [ðeə'tu:] *adverb* to that

◊ **theretofore** [ðeətu:'fɔ:] *adverb* before that time

◊ **therewith** [ðeə'wɪð] *adverb* with that

think tank ['θɪŋk 'tæŋk] *noun* group of advisers who are appointed by the government to discuss important problems and suggest how they should be solved; *Professor Smith is a member of the government's economic think tank*

third [θɜ:d] *noun* part of something which is divided into three equal parts; **to sell everything at one third off** = to sell everything at a discount of 33.3%

◊ **third party** ['θɜ:d 'pɑ:ti] *noun* (a) any person other than the two main parties involved in proceedings *or* contract; the other person involved in an accident; **third-party insurance** = insurance which pays compensation if someone who is not the insured person incurs loss or injury (b) *(in a two-party system)* another political party, beside the main two; **a third party candidate** = candidate for one of the smaller parties

> COMMENT: most political systems have two large parties, and any other party is called a 'third party'

◊ **Third Reading** ['θɜ:d 'ri:dɪŋ] *noun* final discussion and vote on a Bill in Parliament

◊ **Third World** ['θɜ:d 'wɜ:ld] *noun* countries who are not aligned to one or other of the main superpower blocs; *see also* FOURTH WORLD

throne [θrəʊn] *noun* special chair for a king *or* queen; **Speech from the Throne** = QUEEN'S SPEECH, KING'S SPEECH

throw out ['θrəʊ 'aʊt] *verb* (a) to reject *or* to refuse to accept; *the proposal was thrown out by the planning committee; the board threw out the draft contract submitted by the union* (b) to get rid of (something which is not wanted); *we threw out the old telephones and put in a computerized system; the AGM threw out the old board of directors;* (NOTE: throwing - threw - has thrown)

ticket ['tɪkɪt] *noun* US a party's list of candidates for election to political office; *he ran for governor on the Republican ticket*

tier ['tɪə] *noun* one of a series of grades *or* levels; *there is a two-tier system of local government in the counties - the county council and the district councils; the education department has two second-tier officers and three third-tier officers; see note at* LOCAL GOVERNMENT

time [taɪm] *noun* (a) period when something takes place (such as one hour, two days, fifty minutes); **computer time** = time when a computer is being used (paid for at an hourly rate); **real time system** = system whose processing time is within that of the problem, so that it can influence the source of the data (b) hour of the day (such as 9.00, 12.15, ten o'clock at night); *the time of arrival or the arrival time is indicated on the screen; departure times are delayed by up to fifteen minutes because of the volume of traffic;* **on time** = at the right time; *the plane was on time; you will have to hurry if you want to get to the meeting on time or if you want to be on time for the meeting* (c) system of hours on the clock; **Summer Time** *or* **Daylight Saving Time** = system where clocks are set back one hour in the summer to take advantage of the longer hours of daylight; **Standard Time** = normal time as in the winter months (d) hours worked; **he is paid time and a half on Sundays** = he is paid the normal rate with an extra 50% when he works on Sundays (e) period before something happens; **time limit** = period during which something should be done; **to**

keep within the time limits *or* within the time schedule = to complete work by the time stated

◊ **timetable** ['taɪmteɪbl] **1** *noun* **(a)** list showing times of arrivals *or* departures of buses *or* trains *or* planes, etc.; *according to the timetable, there should be a train to London at 10.22; the bus company has brought out its new timetable for the next twelve months* **(b)** list of appointments *or* events; *Mr Smith has a very full timetable, so I doubt if he will be able to see you today; it will be difficult to fit the emergency debate into the crowded Parliamentary timetable;* conference **timetable** = list of speakers *or* events at a conference **2** *verb* to make a list of times of forthcoming events (so that there is enough time for each to take place); *the amount of legislation to be debated makes timetabling difficult for the next session of Parliament*

title ['taɪtl] *noun* **(a)** (i) right to hold goods *or* property; (ii) document proving a right to hold a property; *she has no title to the property; he has a good title to the property;* **title deeds** = document showing who is the owner of a property; **to have a clear title to something** = to have a right to something with no limitations *or* charges **(b)** name given to a person in a certain job; *he has the title 'Chief Executive'* **(c)** honourable name given to someone (such as Lady Smith, Mr Justice Jones); name given to a member of the House of Lords; *he inherited his title from his uncle* **(d)** name of a bill which comes before Parliament *or* name of an Act of Parliament; **full title** *or* **long title** = summary of the contents of an Act of Parliament, printed at the beginning of the Act; **short title** = usual title of an Act of Parliament

◊ **titled** ['taɪtəld] *adjective* (person) with a noble name (such as a lord, etc.)

titular ['tɪtjʊlə] *adjective* holding a title; *he is the titular head of state*

token ['təʊkən] *noun* **(a)** thing which acts as a sign *or* symbol; **token strike** = short strike to show that workers have a grievance **(b)** one person among a group of others apparently nominated as a concession to a

minority; *a token woman on a board of directors*

◊ **tokenism** ['təʊkənɪzm] *noun* giving concessions to minority groups

toll [təʊl] *noun* payment made for using a road *or* bridge *or* ferry

topple *verb* to bring down *or* to make a government lose power or a person lose his position; *the scandal toppled the minister; the smaller parties voted together and succeeded in toppling the government*

Tory ['tɔːri] **1** *adjective* referring to a Conservative Party **2** *noun* member or supporter of a Conservative Party; (NOTE: used of the British Conservative Party, but also of other Conservatives, as in Canada)

totalitarian [təʊtælɪ'teəriən] *adjective (often as criticism)* having total power and not allowing any opposition or any personal freedom; *a totalitarian state; the totalitarian regime of the junta*

◊ **totalitarianism** [təʊtælɪ'teəriənɪzm] *noun (usually as criticism)* political system in which the state has total power over the citizens; *many extreme right-wing or left-wing governments have been accused of practising totalitarianism*

town [taʊn] *noun* place where people live and work, with houses and other buildings; **county town** = main administrative centre in a county, where the county council offices are situated; **market town** = town where a regular market is held; **Town Clerk** = formerly the title of the chief administrator of a town, now usually replaced by Chief Executive; **town council** = representatives elected to run a town; **town councillor** = member of a town council; **town planner** = person who supervises the design of a town *or* the way the streets and buildings in a town are laid out and the land in a town used; **town planning** = supervising the design of a town *or* the use of land in a town

◊ **townspeople** *or* **townsfolk** ['taʊnzpiːpl *or* 'taʊnzfəʊk] *noun* people who live in a town

◊ **township** ['taʊnʃɪp] *noun (in North America)* small town which is a local government centre; *(in South Africa)* town outside the main urban areas, inhabited especially by blacks during the apartheid era

◊ **town-twinning** ['taʊn'twɪnɪŋ] *noun see* TWINNING

trade [treɪd] **1** *noun* **(a)** business of buying and selling; **export trade** *or* **import trade** = the business of selling to other countries *or* buying from other countries; **home trade** = trade in the country where a company is based; **Department of Trade and Industry** = government department dealing with commercial firms, exports, etc. **(b) fair trade** = international business system where countries agree not to charge import duties on certain items imported from their trading partners; **free trade** = system where goods can go from one country to another without any restrictions; **free trade area** = group of countries practising free trade; **trade agreement** = international agreement between countries over general terms of trade; **trade description** = description of a product to attract customers; **Trade Descriptions Act** = Act of Parliament which limits the way in which products can be described so as to protect customers from misleading or wrong descriptions made by the makers of the products; **trade directory** = book which lists all the businesses and business people in an area **2** *verb* to buy and sell *or* to carry on a business; *to trade with another country; to trade on the Stock Exchange; the company has stopped trading; he trades under the name or as 'Eeziphitt'*

◊ **trademark** *or* **trade mark** *or* **trade name** *noun* particular name, design, etc., which identifies the product, has been registered by the maker, and which cannot be used by other makers; *you cannot call your beds 'Softn'kumfi' - it is a registered trademark*

◊ **trader** ['treɪdə] *noun* person who does business; **free trader** = person who is in favour of free trade; **sole trader** = person who runs a business, usually by himself, but has not registered it as a company

◊ **trade union** *or* **trades union** ['treɪd 'juːnɪən *or* 'treɪdz 'juːnɪən] *noun* organization which represents workers, who are its members, in discussions about wages and conditions of employment with employers; *they are members of a trade union or they are trade union members; he has applied for trade union membership or he has applied to join a trade union;* **Trades Union Congress (TUC)** = central organization for all British trade unions; (NOTE: although **Trades Union Congress** is the official name for the organization, **trade union** is commoner than **trades union**)

◊ **trade unionist** ['treɪd 'juːnɪənɪst] *noun* member of a trade union

◊ **trading** ['treɪdɪŋ] *noun* carrying on a business; **fair trading** = way of doing business which is reasonable and does not harm the consumer; **Office of Fair Trading** = government department which protects consumers against unfair *or* illegal business practices; **Trading Standards Department** = department of a council which deals with weighing and measuring equipment used by shops, and other consumer matters; (NOTE: also called the **Weights and Measures Department**) **trading standards officer** = official in charge of a council's Trading Standards Department

traitor ['treɪtə] *noun* person who betrays his country, especially by giving secret information to the enemy

transact [træn'zækt] *verb* to **transact business** = to meet and discuss items on an agenda, and take decisions; to carry out a business activity; *Council will meet next week to transact the following business; Parliament transacted its last piece of business as the enemy forces entered the town*

◊ **transaction** [træn'zækʃn] *noun* **(a) transaction of business** = discussion of matters on an agenda and taking decisions (by a committee); *the council met for the transaction of normal business* **(b) business transaction** = piece of business *or* buying or selling; **cash transaction** = transaction paid for in cash; **a transaction on the Stock Exchange** = purchase *or* sale of shares on the Stock Exchange

transcript ['trænskrɪpt] *noun* record (written out in full) of something noted in shorthand or recorded; *the Committee's report gives a full transcript of the evidence presented to it; transcripts of cases are available in the Supreme Court Library*

transfer 1 ['trænsfə] *noun* moving someone *or* something to a new place; **transfer of property** *or* **transfer of shares** = moving the ownership of property *or* shares from one person to another; **bank transfer** = moving money from a bank account to another account; **capital transfer tax** = tax on the transfer of capital *or* assets from one owner to another; **credit transfer** *or* **transfer of funds** = moving money from one account to another 2 [træns'fɜ:] *verb* (a) to move someone *or* something to a new place; *he has been transferred from the Defence Ministry to the Treasury; the accountant was transferred to our Scottish branch; he transferred his shares to a family trust; she transferred her money to a deposit account;* **transferred charge call** = phone call where the person receiving the call agrees to pay for it (b) to change from one type of travel to another; *when you get to London airport, you have to transfer onto an internal flight;* (NOTE: **transferring - transferred**)

◊ **transferable** [træns'fɜ:rəbl] *adjective* which can be passed to someone else; **the season ticket is not transferable** = the ticket cannot be given or lent to someone else to use; **single transferable vote** = voting system in proportional representation where each voter votes for the candidates in order of preference, and his vote is transferred to the next candidate if his first choice is not elected; *see also* SINGLE

transitional period [træn'zɪʃnəl 'pɪ:rɪəd] *noun (EU)* period during which new members state of the EU can introduce EU legislation gradually, which to introduce it immediately might cause difficulties

transnational [trænz'næʃənl] *adjective* going beyond the borders of one state

transparency [træns'pærənsi] *noun (EU)* being clear when making decisions, and

being open to the public about the actions of the EU

treason ['tri:zn] *noun* crime of betraying one's country, usually by helping the enemy in time of war; *he was accused of treason; three men were executed for treason; the treason trial lasted three weeks;* **high treason** = formal way of referring to treason; (NOTE: no plural)

◊ **treasonable** ['tri:znəbl] *adjective* which may be considered as treason; *he was accused of making treasonable remarks*

treasure ['treʒə] *noun* gold *or* silver *or* jewels, especially when found or stolen; *thieves broke into the palace and stole the king's treasure;* **treasure trove** = treasure which has been hidden by someone in the past and is now discovered

> COMMENT: formerly, treasure which was found was declared to the coroner, who decided if it is treasure trove. If it was not treasure trove, it belonged to the finder or to the person on whose land it was found. Now, all treasure found belongs to the state

◊ **treasurer** ['treʒərə] *noun* (a) person who looks after the money *or* finances of a club or society, etc.; **honorary treasurer** = treasurer who does not receive any fee (b) main financial director of a large organization; *the County Treasurer handles the county's finance*

◊ **treasury** ['treʒri] *noun* **the Treasury** = government department which deals with the country's finance; **the Treasury Bench** = front bench in the House of Commons where the government ministers sit; **Treasury Bill** = bill of exchange which does not give any interest and is sold by the government at a discount; **treasury bonds** = bonds issued by the Treasury of the USA; **Treasury counsel** = barrister who pleads in the Central Criminal Court on behalf of the Director of Public Prosecutions; **Treasury Solicitor** = in England, the solicitor who is head of the government's legal department; *US* **Secretary to the Treasury** *or* **Treasury Secretary** = member of the government in charge of finance

COMMENT: in most countries, the government's finances are the responsibility of the Ministry of Finance, headed by the Finance Minister. In the UK, the Treasury is headed by the Chancellor of the Exchequer

treaty ['triːti] *noun* (a) written legal agreement between countries; *the treaty was signed but never ratified; the minister negotiated a commercial treaty or a cultural treaty with the French* (b) *(EU)* **Treaty of Accession** = treaty by which a new member state joins the European Union, such as that by which the UK joined the European Community in 1972; **Treaty of Maastricht** *or* **Treaty on European Union** = treaty which established the European Union in 1993; **Treaty of Paris** = treaty which established the European Coal and Steel Community in 1951; **Treaty of Rome** = treaty which established the European Economic Community and the European Atomic Energy Community in 1957; *see also* MAASTRICHT (c) agreement between individual persons; **to sell (a house) by private treaty** = to sell (a house) to another person direct and not by auction (c)

trend [trend] *noun* general way things are going; *there is a trend away from old-fashioned party politics; a downward trend in inflation; the report points to upwards trends in reported cases of international terrorism;* **economic trends** = way in which a country's economy is moving

triarchy ['traɪɑːki] *noun* government by three rulers; (NOTE: also called **triumvirate**)

tribunal [traɪ'bjuːnl] *noun* a court; especially a specialist court outside the judicial system which examines special problems and makes judgments; **industrial tribunal** = court which can decide in disputes between employers and employees; **Lands Tribunal** = court which deals with compensation claims relating to land; **military tribunal** = court made up of army officers; **rent tribunal** = court which adjudicates in disputes about rents, and can award a fair rent

Tribune group ['trɪbjuːn 'gruːp] *noun* group of Labour MPs advocating left-wing policies

tricolour ['trɪkələ] *noun* flag with three bands of colours, such as the French flag

trilateral [traɪ'lætrəl] *adjective* involving three states; *trilateral negotiations; see also* BILATERAL, MULTILATERAL, UNILATERAL

tripartism [traɪ'pɑːtɪzm] *noun* division into three political groups

◊ **tripartite** [traɪ'pɑːtaɪt] *adjective* formed of three groups or political parties

triplicate ['trɪplɪkət] *noun* **in triplicate** = with an original and two copies; *to print an invoice in triplicate;* **invoicing in triplicate** = preparing three copies of invoices

triumvirate [traɪ'ʌmvɪrət] *noun* group of three men, especially three leaders running a country together; (NOTE: also called **triarchy**)

troika ['trɔɪkə] *noun* (a) group of three leaders running a country *or* a party; (NOTE: originally used with reference to Russia, but now used for three leaders in any country) (b) *(EU)* three member group consisting of the current president of the Council of the Union, together with his predecessor and successor

Trotskyism ['trɒtskɪɪzm] *noun* political theory opposed to the centralized authority of the Communist party (as in the former Soviet Union), but advocating a continual state of world revolution giving power to smaller individual groups of activists

◊ **Trotskyite** ['trɒtskɪaɪt] *noun* person who supports the ideas of Trotskyism; (NOTE: also informally called a **Trot**)

trouble ['trʌbl] *noun* (a) problem *or* difficult situation; *the police are expecting trouble at the football match; there was some trouble in the council chamber when the vote was taken* (b) **troubles** = riots *or* disturbances

◊ **troubleshooter** ['trʌblʃuːtə] *noun* person whose job is to solve problems

trove [trəʊv] *see* TREASURE

true [truː] *adjective* correct *or* accurate; **true copy** = exact copy; *I certify that this is a true copy; certified as a true copy; see also* BLUE

trust [trʌst] **1** *noun* **(a)** being confident that something is correct, will work, etc.; **we took his statement on trust** = we accepted his statement without examining it to see if it was correct **(b)** duty of looking after goods *or* money *or* property which someone (the beneficiary) has passed to you (the trustee); *he left his property in trust for his grandchildren;* **breach of trust** = failure on the part of a trustee to act properly in regard to a trust; **position of trust** = job where an employee is trusted by his employer to look after money *or* confidential information, etc. **(c)** management of money *or* property for someone; *they set up a family trust for their grandchildren;* **trust fund** = assets (money, securities, property) held in trust for someone; **investment trust** = company whose shares can be bought on the Stock Exchange and whose business is to make money by buying and selling stocks and shares; **unit trust** = organization which takes money from investors and invests it in stocks and shares for them under a trust deed **(d)** *US* small group of companies which control the supply of a product; (NOTE: no plural for (a) and (b)) **2** *verb* **to trust someone with something** = to give something to someone to look after; *can he be trusted with all that cash?*

◊ **trustee** [trʌsˈtiː] *noun* **(a)** person who has charge of money *or* property in trust *or* person who is responsible for a family trust; *the trustees of the pension fund;* **trustee in bankruptcy** = person who is appointed by a court to run the affairs of a bankrupt and pay his creditors; **Public Trustee** = official who is appointed as a trustee of a person's property **(b)** country appointed by the United Nations to administer another country

◊ **trusteeship** [trʌsˈtiːʃɪp] *noun* position of being a trustee; *the territory is under United Nations trusteeship*

◊ **trustworthy** [ˈtrʌstwɜːðɪ] *adjective* (person) who can be trusted; *the staff who deal with cash are completely trustworthy*

TUC [tiːjuːˈsiː] = TRADES UNION CONGRESS

turn [tɜːn] **1** *noun* movement in a circle *or* change of direction; **U-turn** = change in policy to do exactly the opposite of what was done before; *the government made a U-turn and decided to recognise the new regime* **2** *verb* to change direction *or* to go round in a circle; **to turn Queen's evidence** *or* *US* **to turn State's evidence** = to confess to a crime and then act as witness against the other criminals involved in the hope of getting a lighter sentence

◊ **turn down** [ˈtɜːn ˈdaʊn] *verb* to refuse; *the Speaker turned down the Opposition's request for an emergency debate; the bank turned down their request for a loan; the application for a licence was turned down*

◊ **turn out** [ˈtɜːn ˈaʊt] *verb* **(a)** to go to vote; *voters turned out in thousands to vote for their sitting MP* **(b)** to throw out a government; *the ruling party was turned out in the election; vote for the Opposition and help to turn the government out!*

◊ **turnout** [ˈtɜːnaʊt] *noun* number of people who vote in an election; *there was a very low turnout (only 26%) at the municipal elections; in general elections, the turnout is usually higher than in local elections; we can expect a very high turnout in this constituency*

◊ **turnover** [ˈtɜːnəʊvə] *noun* **(a)** *GB* amount of sales; *the company's turnover has increased by 235%; we based our calculations on last year's turnover* **(b)** **staff turnover** *or* **turnover of staff** = changes in staff, when some leave and others join

Tweede Kamer [ˈtweɪdə ˈkæmə] *noun* lower house of the States-General (or Parliament) in the Netherlands

twin [twɪn] *verb* **to twin a town with another town** = to arrange a special relationship between a town in one country and a similar town in another country; *Richmond is twinned with Fontainebleau*

◊ **twinning** [ˈtwɪnɪŋ] *noun* special arrangement between a town in one country and one of similar size or situation in another country; *the district council's town-twinning committee decided that Epping should be twinned with Eppingen in Germany*

two-party system ['tuː'paːti 'sɪstəm] *noun* political system in many countries, where there are only two political parties (or only two very large parties), with the result that any smaller party finds it impossible to get enough votes to form a government; *see also* ONE-PARTY

tyranny ['tɪrəni] *noun (usually as criticism)* **(a)** the use of force and fear to rule a country; *to arrest so many students on minor charges was an act of tyranny* **(b)** government system which relies on force and fear to enable it to rule

◊ **tyrannical** *or* **tyrannous** [tɪ'rænɪkl *or* 'tɪrənəs] *adjective* cruel and unjust; *the people rose up against the tyrannical dictator*

◊ **tyrant** ['taɪrənt] *noun (used as criticism)* ruler who rules by force and fear

Uu

UDI [juːdiːˈaɪ] = UNILATERAL DECLARATION OF INDEPENDENCE

UK [juːˈkeɪ] = UNITED KINGDOM

ultimatum [ˌʌltɪˈmeɪtəm] *noun* final demand *or* proposal to someone that unless he does something within a period of time, action will be taken against him; *unless the ultimatum is accepted, the country will be at war; the Opposition parties argued among themselves over the best way to deal with the ultimatum from the government;* (NOTE: plural is **ultimatums** or **ultimata**)

ultra [ˈʌltrə] *noun* person who holds extremist political views

ultra- [ˈʌltrə] *prefix* meaning extreme *or* extremely; **ultra-leftist** = extremely left-wing; *the ultra-nationalists*

ultra vires [ˈʌltrə ˈvaɪriːz] *Latin phrase* meaning 'beyond powers'; **their action was ultra vires** = they acted in a way which exceeded their legal powers; *the minister's action was ruled to be ultra vires; see* INTRA VIRES

Uluk Kenesh [ˈuːlʌk ˈkeneʃ] *noun* legislative body in Kyrgyzstan

umpire [ˈʌmpaɪə] *noun* person called in to decide when two parties to a dispute cannot come to an agreement

UN [ˈjuːˈen] = UNITED NATIONS

unable [ʌnˈeɪbl] *adjective* not able; *the meeting was unable to come to a decision because one side asked for more time to prepare its evidence; the Housing Department was unable to repair all the houses before they were sold*

unanimity [ˌjuːnəˈnɪmɪti] *noun* being unanimous

unanimous [juˈnænɪməs] *adjective* where everyone votes in the same way; *there was a unanimous vote against the proposal; they reached unanimous agreement;* **unanimous consent** = passage of a motion in Congress without a vote; **unanimous verdict** = verdict agreed by all the jurors; *the jury reached a unanimous verdict of not guilty*

◊ **unanimously** [juˈnænɪməsli] *adverb* with everyone agreeing; *the proposals were adopted unanimously; the House voted unanimously to condemn the action by the rebels; compare* NEM. CON.

unavoidable [ˌʌnəˈvɔɪdəbl] *adjective* which cannot be avoided; *planning applications are subject to unavoidable delays*

◊ **unavoidably** [ˌʌnəˈvɔɪdəbli] *adverb* in a way which cannot be avoided; *the hearing was unavoidably delayed*

unchallenged [ʌnˈtʃælənʒd] *adjective* (evidence) which has not been challenged; *the Opposition will not allow the Minister's statement to go unchallenged*

unconstitutional [ˌʌnkɒnstɪˈtjuːʃənl] *adjective* which is in conflict with a constitution *or* which is not allowed by the rules *or* laws of a country *or* organization; *the chairman ruled that the meeting was unconstitutional; the Appeal Court ruled that the action of the Attorney-General was unconstitutional*

uncontested [ˌʌnkənˈtestɪd] *adjective* (election) which is not contested *or* defended; *he was elected Secretary in an uncontested election*

uncontroversial [ʌnkɒntrə'vɜːʃl] *adjective* which does not cause disagreement

undemocratic [ʌndemə'krætɪk] *adjective* not democratic; *everyone must agree that the first-past-the-post system is undemocratic, because a candidate can be elected who has only a minority of the votes cast*

under ['ʌndə] *preposition* **(a)** lower than *or* less than; *the interest rate is under 10%; under 20% of MPs voted in the division; children under the age of 18 cannot vote* **(b)** controlled by *or* according to; *regulations under the Police Act; under the terms of the agreement, the goods should be delivered in October; he is acting under rule 23 of the union constitution; she does not qualify under section 2 of the 1979 Act*

◊ **undercover agent** ['ʌndəkʌvə 'eɪdʒənt] *noun* secret agent *or* agent acting in disguise

◊ **undermentioned** [ʌndə'menʃənd] *adjective* mentioned lower down in a document

◊ **underrepresent** [ʌndərepri'zent] *verb* to give less representation to; *women are underrepresented in the House of Commons; the present system tends to underrepresent minority parties*

◊ **Under-Secretary (of State)** [ʌndə'sekrətri] *noun* **Parliamentary Under-Secretary (of State)** = junior member of a government working in a government department under the Secretary of State and Ministers of State

◊ **undersheriff** [ʌndə'ʃerɪf] *noun* person who is second to a High Sheriff and deputizes for him

◊ **undersigned** ['ʌndəsaɪnd] *noun* person who has signed a letter; **we, the undersigned** = we, the people who have signed below; (NOTE: can be singular or plural)

◊ **understanding** [ʌndə'stændɪŋ] *noun* private agreement; *the two parties came to an understanding about the division of the estate;* **on the understanding that** = on condition that *or* provided that; *we accept the terms of the contract, on the understanding that it has to be ratified by the full board*

◊ **undertake** [ʌndə'teɪk] *verb* to promise to do something; *the department will undertake an investigation of the fraud; the members of the jury have undertaken not to read the newspapers; he undertook to report to the Commons on the progress of negotiations;* (NOTE: **undertaking - undertook - has undertaken**)

◊ **undertaking** ['ʌndəteɪkɪŋ] *noun* **(a)** business; *a commercial undertaking* **(b)** (legally binding) promise; *they have given us a written undertaking that they will not infringe our patent; the House accepted the Minister's undertaking to reveal the terms of the agreement at a later date*

undesirable [ʌndɪ'zaɪərəbl] *adjective* not wanted; *the object of the motion is to prevent undesirable changes to the constitution of the society;* **undesirable alien** = person who is not a citizen of the country, and who the government considers should not be allowed to stay in the country; *he was deported as an undesirable alien*

undischarged bankrupt [ʌndɪs'tʃɑːʒd 'bæŋkrʌpt] *noun* person who has been declared bankrupt and has not been released from that state (and so cannot be elected an MP)

undue influence ['ʌndjuː 'ɪnfluəns] *noun* wrong pressure put on someone which prevents that person from acting independently; *the government was accused of putting undue influence on the board of the nationalized industry*

unemployed [ʌnɪm'plɔɪd] *adjective & noun* (person) with no paid work; **the unemployed** = people with no paid work

◊ **unemployment** [ʌnɪm'plɔɪmənt] *noun* absence of work; *the unemployment figures or the figures for unemployment are rising;* **unemployment benefit** = money paid by the government to someone who is unemployed

unenforceable [ʌnɪn'fɔːsəbl] *adjective* (contract *or* right) which cannot be enforced

unequivocal [ˌʌnɪ'kwɪvəkl] *adjective* clear *or* not ambiguous; *when questioned, she gave an unequivocal answer; the MP received an unequivocal statement of support from his party leader*

unfit [ʌn'fɪt] *adjective* **(a)** not suitable; *the flats were declared unfit for human habitation* **(b)** not well enough; **unfit to plead** = not mentally capable of standing trial

uni- ['juːni] *prefix* meaning single

unicameral [juːnɪ'kæmərəl] *adjective* (system of parliament) where there is only one legislative chamber; *see also* BICAMERAL

COMMENT: unicameral legislatures exist in many countries and states, including Denmark, Ecuador, Estonia, Finland, Gabon, Greece, Guatemala, Honduras, Hungary, Iceland, Israel, Kenya, Latvia, Lebanon, Lithuania, Malta, Mongolia, Morocco, Nebraska, New Zealand, Panama, Sweden and Turkey

unilateral [juːni'lætərəl] *adjective* on one side only *or* done by one party only; *they took the unilateral decision to cancel the contract;* **unilateral declaration of independence (UDI)** = decision by a colony to become independent, without the approval of the governing colonial power; **unilateral nuclear disarmament** = decision by one country to stop storing *or* making nuclear weapons, regardless of what other countries may do; *compare* BILATERAL, MULTILATERAL, TRILATERAL

◊ **unilateralism** [juːni'lætərəlɪzm] *noun* political doctrine which supports unilateral nuclear disarmament

◊ **unilaterally** [juːni'lætrəli] *adverb* by one party only; *they cancelled the contract unilaterally*

union ['juːniən] *noun* **(a)** state of being linked together *or* act of joining; *we support the union of the environmental pressure groups into a federation* **(b)** group of independent states or organizations which have linked into a federation; **Act of Union** = act of 1801, by which the parliaments of

Great Britain and Ireland were joined to form the United Kingdom; **Treaty of Union** = treaty of 1707 by which Scotland and Britain were joined to form Great Britain; **Treaty on European Union** *or* **Treaty of Maastricht** = treaty which established the European Union in 1993 **(c)** the group of states which formed the United States of America; **the States of the Union** = the states joined together to form the United States of America; **State of the Union message** = annual speech by the President of the USA which summarizes the political situation in the country; **Union Calendar** = list of bills for debate in the House of Representatives which deal with the appropriation of money or raising revenue **(d)** **trade union** *or* **trades union** *or* **US labor union** = organization which represents workers who are its members in discussions with management about wages and conditions of work; **union agreement** = agreement between a management and a trade union over wages and conditions of work; **union dues** *or* **union subscription** = payment made by workers to belong to a union; **union recognition** = act of agreeing that a union can act on behalf of staff in a company **(e)** **customs union** = agreement between several countries that goods can go between them without paying duty, while goods from other countries have special duties charged on them

◊ **unionist** ['juːniənɪst] *noun* **(a)** member of a trade union **(b)** person who supports a political union of states *or* parties

◊ **unionized** ['juːniənaɪzd] *adjective* (company) where the members of staff belong to a trade union

◊ **Union Jack** *or* **Union Flag** ['juːniən 'dʒæk *or* 'juːniən 'flæg] *noun* national flag of the United Kingdom

unite [juː'naɪt] *verb* to join together into a single body; *workers of the world, unite!*

◊ **united** [juː'naɪtɪd] *adjective* joined together to form a single unit

◊ **United Kingdom (UK)** [juː'naɪtɪd 'kɪŋdəm] *noun* independent country, formed of England, Wales, Scotland and Northern Ireland; *he came to the UK to study; does she* *have a UK passport? is he a UK citizen?; see also* BRITISH ISLES, GREAT BRITAIN

◊ **United Nations** *or* **United Nations Organization (UN** *or* **UNO)** [juːˈnaɪtɪd ˈneɪʃnz] *noun* international organization including almost all sovereign states in the world, where member states are represented at meetings; *see also* GENERAL ASSEMBLY, SECURITY COUNCIL

◊ **United States of America (USA)** [juːˈnaɪtɪd ˈsteɪts ʌv əˈmerɪkə] *noun* independent country, a federation of states (originally thirteen, now fifty) in North America; **the United States Code** = book containing all the permanent laws of the USA, arranged in sections according to subject, and revised from time to time

COMMENT: the federal government (based in Washington D.C.) is formed of a legislature (the Congress) with two chambers (the Senate and House of Representatives), an executive (the President) and a judiciary (the Supreme Court). Each of the fifty states making up the USA has its own legislature and executive (the Governor) as well as its own legal system and constitution

universal [juːnɪˈvɜːsəl] *adjective* which applies everywhere *or* to everyone; **universal franchise** *or* **suffrage** = right to vote which is enjoyed by all adult members of the population

unlawful [ʌnˈlɔːfəl] *adjective* (act) which is against the law; *unlawful trespass on property; unlawful sexual intercourse;* **unlawful assembly** = offence when three or more people come together to commit a breach of the peace or other crime

◊ **unlawfully** [ʌnˈlɔːfəli] *adverb* illegally *or* in an unlawful way; *he was charged with unlawfully carrying firearms*

unofficial [ʌnəˈfɪʃl] *adjective* not official; **unofficial strike** = strike by local workers which has not been approved by the union as a whole

◊ **unofficially** [ˈʌnəˈfɪʃəli] *adverb* not officially; *the Foreign Office told the Ambassador, unofficially, that the cultural*

attaché would be declared persona non grata unless he left the country immediately

unopposed [ʌnəˈpəʊzd] *adjective* (motion) with no one voting against; (proceedings) which have not been opposed; *the Bill had an unopposed second reading in the House*

unpaid [ʌnˈpeɪd] *adjective* (person) who does not receive a payment for the work he does; *local councillors are unpaid, though they can claim for expenses*

unparliamentary [ʌnpɑːlɪˈmentəri] *adjective* not suitable for Parliament; **unparliamentary language** = words used in Parliament which are considered to be rude, and which the Speaker may ask the MP to withdraw

COMMENT: various terms of abuse are considered unparliamentary, in particular words which suggest that an MP has not told the truth. In a recent exchange in the House of Commons, a Member called others 'clowns' and 'drunks'; the Deputy Speaker said: 'Order. That is unparliamentary language, and I must ask the hon. Member to withdraw'. Another recent example occurred when an MP said: 'if the hon. Member were honest, I suspect that he would have to do the same'. *Mr. Speaker:* 'Order. All hon. Members are honest.'

unpolitical [ʌnpəˈlɪtɪkl] *adjective* not political *or* not concerned with politics; *the protest group is entirely unpolitical*

unprecedented [ʌnˈpresɪdentɪd] *adjective* which has no precedent *or* which has not happened before; *in an unprecedented move, the government asked the Opposition to join in the discussions*

unreported [ʌnrɪˈpɔːtɪd] *adjective* **(a)** not reported to the police; *there are thousands of unreported cases of theft* **(b)** not reported in the Law Reports; *counsel referred the judge to a number of relevant unreported cases*

unseat [ʌnˈsiːt] *verb* to make a sitting MP lose his seat in an election; *she only needs a* *small swing to have a good chance of unseating the present MP*

unsuccessful [ʌnsək'sesfəl] *adjective* without any success; *the council has been unsuccessful in its search for a new Chief Executive; your application for the job was unsuccessful*

unwritten [ʌn'rɪtən] *adjective* **unwritten agreement** = agreement which has been reached orally (such as in a telephone conversation) but has not been written down; **unwritten law** = rule which is established by precedent

upcoming ['ʌpkʌmɪŋ] *adjective* which will take place soon; *the upcoming general elections*

upheaval [ʌp'hiːvəl] *noun* sudden and violent change (in social system, political system, etc.)

uphold [ʌp'həʊld] *verb* to keep in good order; **to uphold the law** = to make sure that laws are obeyed; **to uphold a sentence** = to reject an appeal against a sentence; *the Appeal Court upheld the sentence;* (NOTE: upholding - upheld)

upper ['ʌpə] *adjective* higher *or* more important; **upper house** *or* **upper chamber** = more important of the two houses *or* chambers in a bicameral system; *after being passed by the legislative assembly, a bill goes to the upper house for further discussion;* (NOTE: opposite is **lower**)

uprising ['ʌpraɪzɪŋ] *noun* rebellion; *the left-wing uprising was crushed by the army*

urban ['ɜːbən] *adjective* referring to a town *or* city; **urban decay** = condition where a part of a town becomes old *or* dirty *or* ruined, because businesses and wealthy families have moved away from it; **urban redevelopment** *or* **urban renewal** = rebuilding old parts of a town to build modern houses and new factories and offices; **urban guerrilla** = guerrilla fighter who fights in a town; (NOTE: opposite is **rural**)

urge [ɜːdʒ] *verb* to suggest something strongly to someone; *he urged the*

government to spend more money on hospitals; the lawyers urged the council to be careful and avoid breaking the law

urgent ['ɜːdʒənt] *adjective* which has to be done quickly; *the leader of the council called an urgent meeting to discuss the new rate; the government has been pressed to take urgent action to calm the situation*

◊ **urgently** ['ɜːdʒəntli] *adverb* immediately; *the Opposition said that action had to be taken urgently to deal with the financial crisis*

US *or* **USA** [juː'es *or* juːes'eɪ] = UNITED STATES OF AMERICA

usage ['juːsɪdʒ] *noun* **(a)** custom *or* way in which something is usually done; *it is the usage of the council for all members to stand when the mayor enters the council chamber* **(b)** use *or* how something is used; *with normal usage, the chairs should last for ten years*

use 1 [juːs] *noun* **(a)** way in which property may be used; **change of use** = order allowing a property to be used in a different way (such as a dwelling house to be used as a business office, a shop to be used as a factory); **land zoned for industrial use** = land where planning permission has been given to build factories **(b)** way in which something can be used; **directions for use** = instructions on how to run a machine; **to make use of something** = to use something; **items for personal use** = items which a person will use for himself, not on behalf of his employer; **he has the use of the mayoral car** = he can use the mayor's official car for private use **2** [juːz] *verb* to take a machine *or* a company *or* a process, etc., and work with it; *the government used the courts to uphold the Official Secrets Act; we use second-class mail for all our correspondence; the office computer is being used all the time; they use freelance typists for most of their work*

◊ **user** ['juːzə] *noun* person who uses something; **end user** = person who actually uses a product; **user's guide** *or* **handbook** = book showing someone how to use something; **registered user** = person *or* company which has been given official permission to use a registered trademark

◊ **user-friendly** ['juːzə'frendli] *adjective* which a computer user finds easy to work; *these programs are really user-friendly*

usher ['ʌʃə] *noun* person who guards the door leading into a courtroom and maintains order in court

usual ['juːʒuəl] *adjective* normal *or* ordinary; *our usual terms or usual conditions are thirty days' credit; the usual practice is to have the contract signed by a director of the company; the usual hours of work are from 9.30 to 5.30*

usurp [juː'zɜːp] *verb* to take and use a right which is not yours (especially to take the throne from a rightful king); *Henry IV usurped the throne from Richard II; the councils complained that the new Education Bill would usurp their powers*

◊ **usurpation** [juːzɜː'peɪʃn] *noun* taking and using a right which is not yours

◊ **usurper** [juː'zɜːpə] *noun* person who usurps power; *the army killed the usurper and placed the king back on his throne again*

utopia [ju'təupiə] *noun* ideal political state, which does not exist in reality, but which can be discussed in theory

◊ **utopian** [ju'təupiən] *adjective* ideal, and also not practical; *his utopian ideal of a state was impossible to put into practice*

U-turn ['juː'tɜːn] *noun* change of policy to do exactly the opposite of what was done before; *the Opposition was surprised at the Government's U-turn on defence expenditure; the council did a U-turn and passed the development plan for the town centre*

Vv

vacant ['veɪkənt] *adjective* empty *or* not occupied; **vacant possession** = being able to occupy a property immediately after buying it because it is empty; *the house is for sale with vacant possession;* **situations vacant** *or* **appointments vacant** = list (in a newspaper) of jobs which are available; **vacant seat** = constituency which has no MP at the moment; *the seat became vacant when Mr Smith was made a life peer*

◊ **vacancy** ['veɪkənsi] *noun* (a) place which is not occupied; *there are two vacancies on the committee* (b) job which needs to be filled; *we have two vacancies for clerks*

vacate [və'keɪt] *verb* to leave; *the rules say that she must vacate the position of vice-chairman after three years in office;* **to vacate the chair** = to leave the position of chairman during a meeting; **to vacate the premises** = to leave a building, so that it becomes empty

◊ **vacation** [və'keɪʃn] *noun* (a) *GB* period when the courts are closed between sittings; period of university holidays (b) *US* holiday, a period when people are not working

valid ['vælɪd] *adjective* (a) which is acceptable because it is true *or* reasonable; *that is not a valid argument or excuse* (b) which can be used lawfully; *the contract is not valid if the signing of it has not been witnessed; ticket which is valid for three months; he was carrying a valid passport*

◊ **validate** ['vælɪdeɪt] *verb* (a) to check to see if something is correct; *the document was validated by the bank* (b) to make (something) valid; *the import documents have to be validated by the customs officials*

◊ **validation** [vælɪ'deɪʃn] *noun* act of making something valid

◊ **validity** [və'lɪdɪti] *noun* being valid; **period of validity** = length of time for which a document is valid; (NOTE: no plural)

valorem [və'lɔːrəm] *see* AD VALOREM

value ['væljuː] **1** *noun* amount of money which something is worth **2** *verb* to estimate how much money something is worth; *the council owns property valued at £6.5m*

◊ **Value Added Tax (VAT)** ['væljuː 'ædɪd tæks] *noun* tax imposed as a percentage of the invoice value of goods and services

◊ **valuation** [væljuː'eɪʃn] *noun* estimate of how much something is worth; *the council asked for a valuation of the property before buying it*

◊ **valuer** ['væljuə] *noun* person who estimates the value of something, especially the value of property; **the Borough Valuer** = official who estimates the value of property, especially where the owner is applying for a grant or where the council is considering buying the property

vary ['veəri] *verb* to change; *the court has been asked to vary the conditions of the order; demand for social services varies according to the weather*

◊ **variable** ['veəriəbl] *adjective* which changes; **variable costs** = costs of producing a product *or* service which change according to the amount produced

◊ **variance** ['veəriəns] *noun* difference; **budget variance** = difference between the cost as estimated for the budget and the actual cost incurred

◇ **variation** [veəri'eɪʃn] *noun* amount by which something changes; **seasonal variations** = changes which take place because of the seasons

VAT [væt or viːeɪ'tiː] = VALUE ADDED TAX

venue ['venjʊ] *noun* place for a meeting; *the venue for next year's party conference will be Brighton*

verbatim [vɜ:'beɪtɪm] *adjective & adverb* in the exact words; *Hansard provides a verbatim account of the proceedings of the House of Commons*

verify ['verɪfaɪ] *verb* to check to see if something is correct

◇ **verification** [verɪfɪ'keɪʃn] *noun* checking if something is correct; *the shipment was allowed into the country after verification of the documents by the customs*

versa ['vɜːsə] *see* VICE VERSA

version ['vɜːʃn] *noun* one person's description of what happened which may differ from someone else's; *the tenant's version of the incident was different from the landlord's;* **she disputed the Minister's version of events** = she argued that the Minister's description of what happened was wrong

vest [vest] *verb* to transfer to someone a legal right *or* duty *or* the legal ownership and possession of land; *the property was vested in the trustees;* (NOTE: you vest something **in** *or* **on** someone)

◇ **vested interest** ['vestɪd 'ɪntrest] *noun* **(a)** interest in a property which will come into a person's possession when the interest of another person ends **(b)** special interest in keeping an existing state of affairs; **she has a vested interest in keeping the business working** = she wants to keep the business working because, for example, she will make more money if it does

vet [vet] *verb* to examine someone *or* a document carefully to see if there is any breach of security; *all applications are vetted by the Home Office;* **positive vetting** = close

examination of a person working with classified information who may not be reliable; (NOTE: **vetting - vetted**)

veto ['viːtəʊ] **1** *noun* right to refuse to allow something to be accepted or to become law, even if it has been passed by a parliament; *the President has the power of veto over Bills passed by Congress; the UK used its veto in the Security Council* **2** *verb* to ban something; to order something not to become law; *the resolution was vetoed by the president; the council has vetoed all plans to hold protest marches in the centre of town;* (NOTE: plural is **vetoes**)

COMMENT: in the United Nations Security Council, each of the five permanent members has a veto. In the USA, the President may veto a bill sent to him by Congress, provided he does so within ten days of receiving it. The bill then returns to Congress for further discussion, and the President's veto can be overridden by a two-thirds majority in both House of Representatives and Senate

---

vice ['vaɪsɪ] *Latin word meaning* 'in the place of'; *was present: Councillor Smith (vice Councillor Brown)*

vice- [vaɪs] *prefix* deputy *or* second in command; *he is the vice-chairman of an industrial group; she was appointed to the vice-chairmanship of the committee*

◇ **vice-consul** ['vaɪs'kɒnsəl] *noun* diplomat with a rank below consul

◇ **vice-president** ['vaɪs'prezɪdənt] *noun* deputy to a president; *when President Kennedy was assassinated, Vice-President Johnson became president;*

COMMENT: in the USA, the Vice-President is the president (i.e. the chairman) of the Senate. He also succeeds a president if the president dies in office (as Vice-President Johnson succeeded President Kennedy)

---

viceroy ['vaɪsrɔɪ] *noun* person who represents a king or queen in an overseas area of empire, and governs on the king's behalf;

in the nineteenth century, India was ruled by viceroys

◊ **viceregal** [vaɪsˈriːgl] *adjective* referring to a viceroy; *the reception was held at the Viceregal Palace*

◊ **vicereine** [vaɪsˈreɪn] *noun* wife of a viceroy

vice versa [ˈvaɪsi ˈvɜːsə] *Latin phrase meaning* 'reverse position': the other way round; **the responsibilities of the employer towards the employee and vice versa** = the responsibilities of the employer to the employee and of the employee to the employer

videlicet [vɪˈdelɪket] *Latin word meaning* 'that is' *or* 'namely'; (NOTE: usually abbreviated to **viz.**: **the Education Committee has three sub-committees, viz. Schools, Further Education and Training)**

village [ˈvɪlɪdʒ] *noun* group of houses and shops in a country area, smaller than a town, but larger than a hamlet

◊ **villager** [ˈvɪlɪdʒə] *noun* person who lives in a village

violate [ˈvaɪəleɪt] *verb* to break a rule *or* a law; *the council has violated the planning regulations; the action of the government violates the international treaty on commercial shipping*

◊ **violation** [vaɪəˈleɪʃn] *noun* act of breaking a rule; *the number of traffic violations has increased; the court criticized the violations of the treaty on human rights;* **in violation of a rule** = breaking a rule; *the government has acted in violation of its agreement*

VIP [viːaɪˈpiː] = **VERY IMPORTANT PERSON** *seats have been arranged for the VIPs at the front of the hall*

virement [ˈvaɪəmənt] *noun* transfer of money from one account to another *or* from one section of a budget to another; *the council may use the virement procedure to transfer money from one area of expenditure to another*

vires [ˈvaɪriːz] *see* INTRA VIRES, ULTRA VIRES

virtute officio [vɜːˈtuːteɪ ɒˈfɪsɪəʊ] *Latin phrase meaning* 'by virtue of his office'

visa [ˈviːzə] *noun* special document *or* special stamp in a passport which allows someone to enter a country; *you will need a visa before you go to the USA; he filled in his visa application form;* **entry visa** = visa allowing someone to enter a country; **multiple entry visa** = visa allowing someone to enter a country many times; **tourist visa** = visa which allows a person to visit a country for a short time on holiday; **transit visa** = visa which allows someone to travel through a country on the way to another country

viscount [ˈvaɪkaʊnt] *noun* member of the peerage, ranking between an earl and a baron

◊ **viscountess** [ˈvaɪkaʊntes] *noun* woman who is the wife of a viscount, or who holds the rank of viscount

visit [ˈvɪzɪt] *noun* journey to see someone; **state visit** = ceremonial visit paid by a head of state to another country

◊ **visitor** [ˈvɪzɪtə] *noun* person who goes to see someone for a short time; *the Speaker ordered all visitors to leave the chamber;* **visitor's visa** = visa which allows a person to visit a country for a short time; **prison visitor** = member of a board of visitors appointed by the Home Secretary to visit, inspect and report on conditions in a prison

vital [ˈvaɪtl] *adjective* very important for life or death; *the stolen documents are of vital national interest;* **vital statistics** = statistics dealing with births, marriages and deaths in a town or district

viz [vɪz or ˈneɪmlɪ] *see* VIDELICET

volume [ˈvɒljuːm] *noun* large book; one book out of a set of books; *Volume 13 of the Law Reports; look in the January 20th 1994 volume of Hansard*

voluntary [ˈvɒləntrɪ] *adjective* **(a)** done in a free way, without being forced; *he made a voluntary contribution to the fund* **(b)**

unpaid; *Community Care is a voluntary organization which helps people in need; many retired people do voluntary work;* **voluntary services** = organizations within an area which give unpaid services or help

◊ **volunteer** [vɒlən'tɪə] *noun* person who offers unpaid help *or* work; *the information desk is manned by volunteers*

vote [vəʊt] **1** *noun* **(a)** marking a paper, holding up your hand, etc., to show your opinion *or* to show who you want to be elected; **to take a vote on a proposal** *or* **to put a proposal to the vote** = to ask people present at a meeting to say if they agree or do not agree with the proposal; **to cast a vote** = to vote; *the number of votes cast in the election was 125,458; under proportional representation, the number of seats occupied by each party is related to the number of votes cast for that party;* **block vote** = casting of a large number of votes at the same time (such as of trade union members) by a person who has been delegated by the holders of the votes to vote for them in this way; **card vote** = vote taken at meetings of the Trades Union Congress, where union representatives vote for their membership by holding up a card showing the total votes which they are casting; **casting vote** = vote used by the chairman in the case where the votes for and against a proposal are equal; *the chairman has the casting vote; he used his casting vote to block the motion;* **one man one vote** = democratic principle that each person eligible to vote has a single vote, equal to all the others (as opposed to a block vote); **popular vote** = vote of the majority of the people in a country; *the French President is elected by popular vote* = he is elected by a majority vote of all the people in France; **postal vote** = election where the voters send in their voting papers by post; **voice vote** = vote in Congress where the members shout Aye or No; **vote of**

censure *or* **censure vote** = vote which criticizes someone, especially a vote which criticizes the government in the House of Commons; **vote of no confidence** = vote to show that a person *or* group is not trusted; *the chairman resigned after the vote of no confidence in him was passed by the AGM* **(b)** the right to vote in elections; *women were given the vote in 1928* **(c)** total number of votes cast; **the vote was up on the last election** = more votes were cast this time than the time before **2** *verb* to show an opinion by marking a paper *or* by holding up your hand at a meeting; *the meeting voted to close the factory; 52% of the members voted for Mr Smith as Chairman;* **to vote for a proposal** *or* **to vote against a proposal** = to say that you agree *or* do not agree with a proposal; **she was voted on to the committee** = she was elected a member of the committee; **he was voted into the chair** = he was elected chairman

◊ **vote down** ['vəʊt 'daʊn] *verb* to defeat a motion; *the proposal was voted down*

◊ **vote in** ['vəʊt 'ɪn] *verb* **to vote someone in** = to elect someone; *the Tory candidate was voted in*

◊ **vote out** ['vəʊt 'aʊt] *verb* **to vote someone out** = to make someone lose an election; *the government was voted out of office within a year*

◊ **voter** ['vəʊtə] *noun* person who votes; *voters stayed away from the polls because of the bad weather*

◊ **vote through** ['vəʊt 'θru:] *verb* to vote to accept; *the proposal was voted through by a large majority*

◊ **voting** ['vəʊtɪŋ] *noun* act of making a vote; **voting card** *or* **voting paper** = paper on which the voter puts a cross to show for whom he wants to vote; **voting patterns** = tendency of voters to vote in a certain way; **voting rights** = rights of shareholders to voting at company meetings

Ww

waive [weɪv] *verb* to give up (a right); *he waived his claim to the estate*

◊ **waiver** ['weɪvə] *noun* voluntarily giving up (a right); removing the conditions (of a rule); *if you want to work without a permit, you will have to apply for a waiver;* **waiver clause** = clause in a contract giving the conditions under which the rights in the contract can be given up

war [wɔː] *noun* situation where one country fights another; *the two countries are at war;* **to declare war on a country** = to state officially that a state of war exists between the two countries; **civil war** = situation inside a country where groups of armed people fight against each other *or* fight against the government; **prisoner of war** = member of the armed forces captured by the enemy in time of war

◊ **warring** ['wɔːrɪŋ] *adjective* fighting; *the warring factions on the town council*

ward [wɔːd] *noun* **(a)** division of a town or city for administrative purposes; **an electoral ward** = area of a town represented by a councillor on a local council; *Councillor Smith represents Central Ward on the council;* (NOTE: the US equivalent is **precinct**) **(b)** minor protected by a guardian *or* by a court; **ward of court** = minor under the protection of the High Court; *the High Court declared the girl a ward of court, to protect her from her uncle who wanted to take her out of the country*

◊ **wardship** ['wɔːdʃɪp] *noun* being in charge of a ward *or* the power of a court to take on itself the rights and responsibilities of parents in the interests of a child; (NOTE: no plural)

warden ['wɔːdən] *noun* (i) person who is in charge of an institution; (ii) person who sees that rules are obeyed; *the block of flats have a warden who helps elderly residents;* **traffic warden** = official whose duty is to regulate the traffic under the supervision of the police, especially to deal with cars which are illegally parked

waste [weɪst] *noun* rubbish, things which are no longer needed; **waste disposal** = getting rid of household rubbish

watchdog (body) ['wɒtʃdɒg] *noun* body which watches something (especially government departments *or* commercial firms) to see that regulations are not being abused; *the Post Office Users Council acts as a watchdog*

water authority ['wɔːtə ɔː'θɒrɪti] *noun* regional body set up to administer the supply of water to an area

way [weɪ] *noun* **(a)** act of going; **right of way** = right to go lawfully along a path on another person's land; (NOTE: no plural) **(b)** manner of doing something; **Ways and Means resolution** = Supply Bill, especially the annual budget proposals

weights and measures department ['weɪts nd 'meʒəz] *noun* council department dealing with weighing and measuring machines used in shops, and other consumer matters; (NOTE: usually called the **Trading Standards Department**)

welfare ['welfeə] *noun* comfort, being well cared for; *it is the duty of the juvenile court to see to the welfare of children in care;* **education welfare officer** = social worker who looks after schoolchildren, and deals with attendance and family problems; **welfare state** = state which spends a large amount of money to make sure that its citizens all have adequate housing, education, public transport and health services

West [west] *adjective, adverb & noun* **(a)** one of the directions on the earth's surface, the direction facing the setting sun **(b)** region of a country (as opposed to the East) **(c) the West** = the democratic countries of Europe and North America (as opposed to the former Communist countries)

Western European Union (WEU)

['westən 'juːrəpiːən 'juːniən] *noun* union formed in 1954, now formed of Belgium, France, Germany, Greece, Italy, Luxembourg, the Netherlands, Portugal, Spain, United Kingdom as full members, and Bulgaria, the Czech Republic, Denmark, Estonia, Hungary, Iceland, Ireland, Latvia, Lithuania, Norway, Poland, Romania, the Slovak Republic and Turkey as associate members, with the aim of harmonizing defence and security in the region

Westminster ['westmɪnstə] *noun* borough in London, where the Houses of Parliament are situated; **the Palace of Westminster** = the Houses of Parliament, the building where the Commons and Lords meet; (NOTE: often used to mean Parliament in general: the news was greeted with surprise at Westminster; MPs returned to Westminster after the summer recess; rumours are current in Westminster that the plan will be defeated)

WEU = WESTERN EUROPEAN UNION

whatever *or* **whatsoever** [wɒt'evə or wɒtsəʊ'evə] *adjective* of any sort; *there is no substance whatsoever in the report; the police found no suspicious documents whatsoever; there is nothing whatsoever to suggest that he intends to leave the country;* (NOTE: always used after a noun and after a negative)

wheeling and dealing ['wiːlɪŋ nd 'diːlɪŋ] *noun* bargaining between political parties *or* factions *or* members of a committee to obtain a general agreement for something;

after some wheeling and dealing, the subcommittee members were selected; see also HORSE-TRADING

where- ['weə] *prefix* which thing; (NOTE: the following words formed from **where-** are frequently used in government and legal documents)

◊ **whereas** [weər'æz] *conjunction* as the situation is stated *or* taking the following fact into consideration; *whereas the contract between the two parties stipulated that either party may withdraw at six months' notice*

◊ **whereby** [weə'baɪ] *adverb* by which; *a deed whereby ownership of the property is transferred*

◊ **wherein** [weər'ɪn] *adverb* in which; *a document wherein the regulations are listed*

◊ **whereof** [weə'ɒv] *adverb* of which; **in witness whereof I sign my hand** = I sign as a witness that this is correct

◊ **whereon** [weə'ɒn] *adverb* on which; *land whereon a dwelling is constructed*

◊ **wheresoever** [weəsəʊ'evə] *adverb* in any place where; *the insurance covering jewels wheresoever they may be kept*

Whig [wɪg] *noun* old name for a member of a political party which later became the Liberal Party in Britain

whip [wɪp] *noun* **(a)** long thin piece of leather, used for beating animals to make them work **(b)** MP who controls the attendance of other MPs of his party at the House of Commons, who makes sure that all MPs vote: **Chief Whip** = main whip, who organizes the other whips; *the Government Chief Whip made sure the MPs were all present for the vote; US* **majority whip** *or* **minority whip** = assistants to majority *or* minority leaders in the House or Senate, whose responsibility is to make sure the members of their party vote **(c)** instruction given by a whip to other MPs, telling them which business is on the agenda and underlining items where a vote may be taken; **three line whip** = strict instructions to MPs to vote as the whips tell them (by underlining the item on the agenda three times)

Whitehall ['waɪthɔːl] *noun* street in London, where several ministries are situated; (NOTE: used to refer to the Government or more particularly to the civil service: **Whitehall sources suggest that the plan will be adopted; there is a great deal of resistance to the idea in Whitehall**)

◊ **White House** ['waɪt 'haʊs] *noun* building in Washington D.C., where the President of the USA lives and works; *see also* CAMP DAVID, OVAL OFFICE (NOTE: also used to mean the President himself, or the US government: **White House officials disclaimed any knowledge of the letter; the White House press secretary has issued a statement**)

White Paper ['waɪt 'peɪpə] *noun GB* report issued by the government as a statement of government policy on a particular problem, often setting out proposals for changes to legislation for discussion before a Bill is drafted; *compare* GREEN PAPER

whole [həʊl] *adjective* complete *or* total; *GB* **Committee of the Whole House** = the House of Commons acting as a committee to examine the clauses of a Bill; *US* **Committee of the Whole** = committee formed of at least one hundred members of the House of Representatives, which discusses a bill which has already been debated in Committee

> COMMENT: in both the House of Commons and House of Representatives, when the House becomes a Committee of the Whole the speaker leaves the chair and his place is taken by a chairman

wind up ['waɪnd 'ʌp] *verb* (a) to end (a meeting *or* a debate); *he wound up the meeting with a vote of thanks to the committee; the Home Secretary wound up for the government* (b) to wind up a company = to put a company into liquidation; *the court ordered the company to be wound up;* (NOTE: winding - wound - has wound)

◊ **winding up** ['waɪndɪŋ 'ʌp] *noun* (a) ending of a meeting; *in his winding-up speech the Home Secretary warned the Commons of the seriousness of the situation* (b) liquidation, closing of a company and selling its assets; **compulsory winding-up order** = order from a court saying that a company must be wound up; **voluntary winding up** = situation where a company itself decides it must close down; **winding-up petition** = application to a court for an order that a company be put into liquidation

wise man ['waɪz 'mæn] *noun* man (or sometimes woman) who has a lot of experience and is appointed to advise a government on matters of state

withdraw [wɪθ'drɔː] *verb* (a) to take (money) out of an account; *to withdraw money from the bank or from your account; you can withdraw up to £50 from any bank on presentation of a banker's card* (b) to take back (an offer); *to withdraw a takeover bid* (c) to take back a charge *or* an accusation *or* a statement *or* a motion; *the prosecution has withdrawn the charges against him; the opposition MPs forced the minister to withdraw his statement; the chairman asked him to withdraw the remarks he had made about the Director of Finance* (d) to leave (a place); *the mayor withdrew from the chair, and the deputy mayor presided;* (NOTE: withdrawing - withdrew - has withdrawn)

◊ **withdrawal** [wɪθ'drɔːl] *noun* removing money from an account; **withdrawal without penalty at seven days' notice** = money can be taken out of a deposit account, without losing any interest, provided that seven days' notice has been given

withhold [wɪθ'həʊld] *verb* to keep back *or* not to give; *he was charged with withholding information from the police; approval of any loan will not be unreasonably withheld*

within [wɪ'ðɪn] *preposition* inside; *the case falls within the jurisdiction of the court; he was within his rights when he challenged the Chairman's ruling*

without [wɪ'ðaʊt] *preposition* **without prejudice** = phrase spoken *or* written in letters when attempting to negotiate a settlement, meaning that the negotiations cannot be referred to in court *or* relied upon by the other party if the discussions fail; **without reservation** = fully; *I support her candidature without reservation*

witness ['wɪtnəs] *noun* person who appears before a court *or* committee to give evidence; *the secretary appeared as a witness before the Commons Defence Committee*

Woolsack ['wʊlsæk] *noun* seat of the Lord Chancellor in the House of Lords

COMMENT: it is really a large cushion stuffed with wool, dating from the time when the wool trade was very important

word [wɜːd] **1** *noun* separate item of speech *or* writing; **word processing** = working with words, using a computer to produce, check and change texts, letters, contracts, etc.; **to give one's word** = to promise; *he gave his word that the matter would remain confidential* **2** *verb* to put something into words; *the contract was incorrectly worded*

◊ **wording** ['wɜːdɪŋ] *noun* series of words; *did you understand the wording of the contract?;* (NOTE: no plural)

works [wɜːks] *noun* building; **clerk of works** = official who superintends the construction of a building

World Trade Organization (WTO)

['wɜːld 'treɪd ɔːgənaɪ'zeɪʃn] *noun* international treaty which aims to try to reduce restrictions in trade between countries

COMMENT: formed on 1st January 1995 to replace the General Agreement on Tariffs and Trade (GATT)

writ [rɪt] *noun* **(a)** legal document which begins an action in the High Court; *the company issued a writ to prevent the trade union from going on strike; he issued writs for libel in connection with allegations made in a Sunday newspaper;* **to serve someone with a writ** = to give someone a writ officially, so that he has to defend it *or*

allow judgment to be taken against him; **writ of habeas corpus** = writ to obtain the release of someone who has been unlawfully held in prison or in police custody *or* to make the person holding a prisoner appear in court to explain why he is being held **(b)** legal action to hold an election *or* a by-election; **to move a writ** = to propose in the House of Commons that a by-election should be held; **writ of summons** = notice from the Lord Chancellor asking a peer to attend the House of Lords

write in ['raɪt 'ɪn] *verb US* to vote for a candidate whose name does not appear on the ballot paper, by writing the name there; **write-in candidate** = candidate whose name has been written by the voters on their voting papers

wrong [rɒŋ] **1** *adjective* not right *or* not correct *or* not legal; *copying computer data is wrong; the total in the last column is wrong; the driver gave the wrong address to the policeman; I tried to phone you, but I got the wrong number* **2** *noun* act against natural justice; act which infringes someone else's right; *civil wrongs against persons or property are called 'torts'*

◊ **wrongdoer** ['rɒŋduːə] *noun* person who commits an offence

◊ **wrongdoing** ['rɒŋduːɪŋ] *noun* bad behaviour; actions which are against the law; (NOTE: no plural)

◊ **wrongful** ['rɒŋfʊl] *adjective* unlawful; **wrongful dismissal** = removing someone from a job for a reason which does not justify dismissal and which is in breach of the contract of employment

◊ **wrongfully** ['rɒŋfʊli] *adverb* in an unlawful way; *he claimed he was wrongfully dismissed; she was accused of wrongfully holding her clients' money*

◊ **wrongly** ['rɒŋli] *adverb* not correctly, badly; *the item was wrongly minuted; he wrongly invoiced the council for £250, when he should have credited them with the same amount*

WTO = WORLD TRADE ORGANIZATION

Xx Yy Zz

xenophobe ['zenəfəub] *noun* person who hates foreigners

◊ **xenophobia** [zenə'fəubiə] *noun* hatred of foreigners

◊ **xenophobic** [zenə'fəubɪk] *adjective* showing hatred of foreigners

Yang di-Pertuan Agong ['jæŋ dɪ'pɜːtwæn 'ægɒŋ] *noun* title given to the head of state of the Malaysian Federation (elected for five years by the rulers of the thirteen states which make up the federation)

yea and nay [jeɪ nd 'neɪ] *noun* old forms of 'yes' and 'no'; **yea and nay vote** = vote in a legislature where members say 'yes' or 'no'

year [jɜː] *noun* period of twelve months; **calendar year** = year from January 1st to December 31st; **financial year** = the twelve month period for a firm's accounts; **fiscal year** *or* **tax year** = twelve month period on which taxes are calculated (in the UK it is from April 6th to April 5th of the following year); **Parliamentary year** = year of a session of Parliament, running from the Opening of Parliament in September to the summer recess in August; **year end** = the end of the financial year, when a company's accounts are prepared; *the accounts department has started work on the year-end accounts*

zero ['zɪərəu] *noun* nought *or* number 0; *the code for international calls is zero one zero (010);* **zero inflation** = inflation at 0%

◊ **zero-rated** ['zɪərəu'reɪtɪd] *adjective* (item) which has a VAT rate of 0%

◊ **zero-rating** ['zɪərəu'reɪtɪŋ] *noun* rating an item at 0% VAT

zone [zəun] *verb* to order that land in a district shall be used only for one type of building; *the land is zoned for industrial use*

◊ **zoning** ['zəunɪŋ] *noun* order by a local council that land shall be used only for one type of building; (NOTE: no plural)

SUPPLEMENT

Local Government Act 1987

1987 CHAPTER 44

An Act to amend Part VIII of the Local Government, Planning and
Land Act 1980; to make further provision about the adjustment
of block grant in connection with education; and for connected
purposes.   [15th May 1987]

BE IT ENACTED by the Queen's most Excellent Majesty, by and
with the advice and consent of the Lords Spiritual and Temporal,
and Commons, in this present Parliament assembled, and by the
authority of the same, as follows:—

Capital expenditure

1. Part VIII of the Local Government, Planning and Land Act 1980
(capital expenditure of local authorities etc.) shall have effect in relation
to the year beginning with 1st April 1987 and subsequent years, and shall
be deemed to have had effect in relation to the year beginning with 1st
April 1986—

Payments in
respect of capital
expenditure.
1980 c.65.

(a) with the insertion after section 80 of the sections set out in Part I
of the Schedule to this Act; and

(b) with the further amendments set out in Part II of that Schedule
(being amendments consequential on the insertion of those
sections).

Block grant: education

2.—(1) Schedule 10 to the 1980 Act (block grant adjustment for
education) shall be amended as follows—

Adjustments
between England
and Wales.

(a) in paragraphs 1(2), (3)(a) and (b) and (4) for "education
expenditure" there shall be substituted "qualifying education
expenditure",

(b) in paragraph 1(3)(a) and (b) the words "(after taking account of
recoupment)" shall be omitted, and

(c) paragraph 3(4) shall be omitted.

A

B I L L

INTITULED

An Act to secure that local and other public authorities undertake
certain activities only if they can do so competitively; to regulate
certain functions of local and other public authorities in
connection with public supply or works contracts; to authorise
and regulate the provision of financial assistance by local
authorities for certain housing purposes; to make provision
about local authorities' publicity, local government
administration, land held by public bodies, direct labour
organisations, arrangements under the Employment and
Training Act 1973, the Commission for Local Authority
Accounts in Scotland, the auditing of accounts of local
authorities in Scotland, and dog licences; and for connected
purposes.

BE IT ENACTED by the Queen's most Excellent Majesty, by and
with the advice and consent of the Lords Spiritual and Temporal,
and Commons, in this present Parliament assembled, and by the
authority of the same, as follows:—

5   PART I

COMPETITION

Preliminary

1.—(1) For the purposes of this Part each of the following is a defined   Defined
authority—   authorities.

10   (a) a local authority,

        (b) an urban development corporation established by an order
            under section 135 of the Local Government, Planning and Land   1980 c. 65.
            Act 1980,

        (c) a development corporation established for the purposes of a new
15   town,

        (d) the Commission for the New Towns,

HL Bill 35   A   50/1

1987 No. 2003 (C.62)

LOCAL GOVERNMENT, ENGLAND AND WALES
LOCAL GOVERNMENT, SCOTLAND

The Local Government Act 1986 (Commencement) Order 1987

Made -   -   -   -   23rd November 1987

The Secretary of State, in exercise of the powers conferred on him by section 12(2) of the Local Government Act 1986(**a**) and of all other powers enabling him in that behalf, hereby makes the following Order:

1. This Order may be cited as the Local Government Act 1986 (Commencement) Order 1987.

2. Section 5 of the Local Government Act 1986 comes into force on 1st April 1988.

23rd November 1987

Nicholas Ridley
One of Her Majesty's Principal Secretaries of State

EXPLANATORY NOTE

(This note is not part of the Order)

This Order brings into force on 1st April 1988 section 5 of the Local Government Act 1986, which requires local authorities to keep separate accounts of their expenditure on publicity. It extends to England and Wales and Scotland.

The remainder of the Act is already in force in accordance with section 12(2).

(**a**) 1986 c.10.

Notice of Whipping

On MONDAY, 14th May, 1973, the House will meet at 2.30 p.m.

Consideration in Committee of the Government New Clause to the Northern Ireland (Emergency Provisions) Bill.

There will be a FREE VOTE.

Motions on the Civil Authorities (Special Powers) (Northern Ireland) Regulations and on the Electoral Law (Northern Ireland) Order.
(Orders each EXEMPTED BUSINESS for 1½ hours)

Divisions are expected and your attendance at 10.00 p.m. and until the

Business is concluded is essential unless you have registered a firm pair.

On TUESDAY, 15th May, the House will meet at 2.30 p.m.

Ten Minute Rule Bill: Employed Persons (Safety). (Mr. E. Wainwright)

Supply (20th allotted day): There will be a debate on Rolls Royce, which will arise on an Opposition Motion.

Important divisions will take place and your attendance at 6.30 p.m.

for 7.00 p.m. is essential.

AFTERWARDS, a debate on School Building Costs, which will also arise on an Opposition Motion.

Important divisions will take place and your attendance at 9.30 p.m.

for 10.00 p.m. is essential.

Bahamas Independence Bill: 2nd Reading.

Land Compensation Bill: Lords Amendments.

Divisions may take place and your continued attendance until the Business is

concluded is particularly requested unless you have registered a pair.

NOTE: A Motion to suspend the Ten o'clock Rule for the Bahamas Independence Bill and for the Lords Amendments to the Land Compensation Bill will be moved at 10 p.m.

On WEDNESDAY, 16th May, the House will meet at 2.30 p.m.

Ten Minute Rule Bill: Age Level of Employment. (Mr. E. Milne)

Fair Trading Bill: Remaining Stages. (1st day)

Divisions will take place and your attendance at 3.30 p.m. and until the

Business is concluded is essential unless you have registered a firm pair.

NOTE: A Motion to suspend the Ten o'clock Rule for this Bill will be moved at 10 p.m.

𝕷𝖔𝖓𝖉𝖔𝖓 𝕭𝖔𝖗𝖔𝖚𝖌𝖍 𝖔𝖋 𝕽𝖎𝖈𝖍𝖒𝖔𝖓𝖉 𝖚𝖕𝖔𝖓 𝕿𝖍𝖆𝖒𝖊𝖘
BYELAWS

Relating to Pleasure Grounds and Open Spaces in the Borough

Byelaws made under Section 164 of the Public Health Act, 1875, Section 15 of the Open Spaces Act, 1906 and Sections 12 and 15 of the Open Spaces Act, 1906 by the Mayor and Burgesses of the London Borough of Richmond upon Thames acting by the Council at a meeting of the Council held on the tenth day of December 1985 with respect to pleasure grounds.

1. Throughout these byelaws the expression "the Council" means the Mayor and Burgesses of the London Borough of Richmond upon Thames, acting by the Council, and the expression "the ground" means, except where inconsistent or imcompatible with the context, each of the open spaces and pleasure grounds set out in the First Schedule to these byelaws and as identified on Map No.PRM1 sealed by the Council on the tenth day of December 1985 and deposited in the Town Clerk's Office.

2. An act by a person for the time being duly authorised by the Council for any purpose in connection with the management, maintenance, improvement or regulation of the ground and acting in the proper execution of that purpose or a person duly authorised by such a person and acting in the proper execution of such authority or a person acting in the legal exercise of some right in, over or affecting the ground shall not be deemed an offence against these byelaws.

3. A person shall not in the ground
    (i) climb any wall or fence in or enclosing the ground, or any tree, or any barrier, railing, post, or other erection;
    (ii) without reasonable excuse remove or displace any wall or fence in or enclosing the ground, or any barrier, railing, post, seat, board, plate or tablet, or any part of any erection or ornament, or any implement provided for use in the laying out or maintenance of the ground.

4. A person shall not, except in pursuance of a lawful agreement with the Council or otherwise in the exercise of any lawful right or privilege, bring

1

Notice of Election

LONDON BOROUGH OF RICHMOND UPON THAMES

ELECTION OF A COUNCILLOR

for the HEATHFIELD WARD OF THE BOROUGH

A poll for the Election of a Councillor for the Heathfield Ward will be held on Thursday, 4th February 1988, between the hours of 8 a.m. and 9 p.m. The particulars of each candidate remaining validly nominated and the names of the persons who signed the nomination papers of candidates are as follows:

WARD	Candidates (surname first)	Home address	Description	Names of the persons who signed the nomination papers
HEATHFIELD	FREITAG Geoffrey John	17 Cobbett Road, Twickenham	Labour	David C. Davidson, Stephen J. Guichard, Edith M. Davidson, Susan Guichard, Howard Davies, Dorothy W. Davies, Mary Dodd, Walter F. Dodd, Gemma M. Cooper, Patricia M. Hunt.
	HYWEL-DAVIES Jeremy Robin	36 St. James's Avenue, Hampton Hill, Middx. TW12 1HH	Green Party	G. D. King, J. C. O'Leary, N. Zakrzewski, John Vine, V. A. Eley, F. J. Roberts, S. Arber, L. M. Pugh, R. Pugh, P. J. Sullivan.
	NARAIN Lisette	154 Percy Road, Twickenham	Liberal Alliance	Margaret E. Letch, Rosaleen M. Maddalena, Richard G. Maddalena, Dennis Maddalena, Jane M. Maddalena, Peter E. Gibbard, Michael L. Jones, Brenda M. E. Jones, William H. T. Satchwill, Mary J. Satchwill.
	WRIGHT Thomas Henry	140 Edgar Road, Hounslow, Middx. TW4 5QP	The Conservative Party Candidate	T. E. Haywood, W. K. Haywood, Joan W. Williams, V. M. Amey, B. Penson, A. J. Penson, M. Lock, Thomas F. G. Lock, Elizabeth Wright, M. Wright.

The polling districts for this election (the roads therein being those shown in the appropriate sections of the Register of Electors published on 15th February 1987), the situation of the polling stations to be used on this occasion and descriptions of the voters entitled to vote there are as follows:

Polling District Letters	Situation of Polling Place	Number of Polling Station	Description of Voters entitled to vote at each Polling Station (Electors' numbers on register)
AA	Heathfield Nursery Unit, Powder Mill Lane, Twickenham	T1	1 - 1729
	as above	T2	1730 - 3613
AB	Heathfield Branch Library, Percy Road, Twickenham	T3	1 - 1591
AC	The Community Centre, Edgar Road, Hounslow	T4	1 - 1500
AD	Rivermeads Hall, Staines Road, Twickenham	T5	1 - 742

22nd January, 1988

YORK HOUSE, TWICKENHAM.

Michael Honey,

Returning Officer.

Printed by E. H. Baker & Co. Ltd., 86 Lower Mortlake Road, Richmond, Surrey TW9 2JH, Ref. 82683, and published by Michael Honey, Returning Officer, York House, Twickenham.

Ballot Paper

VOTE FOR ONE CANDIDATE ONLY

1	**BATCHELOR** (David Stephen Batchelor, of 29 Shaftesbury Way, Twickenham, TW2 5RN, Green Party Candidate.)	
2	**JESSEL** (Toby Francis Henry Jessel, of Old Court House, Hampton Court Road, East Molesey, Surrey. The Conservative Party Candidate.)	
3	**VAZ** (Valerie Carol Marian Vaz, of 18 Elthorne Park Road, Hanwell, London, W7, The Labour Party Candidate.)	
4	**WALLER** (John Waller, of 101 Strawberry Vale, Twickenham, TW1 4SJ, Liberal/SDP Alliance.)	

Counterfoil

This is a printers' proof of an actual ballot paper used in the Parliamentary election on 11th June, 1987. The ballot papers themselves would be numbered consecutively and, in order to preserve the integrity of the ballot, cannot be inspected after an election without a court order

Prime Ministers of Great Britain

Sir Robert Walpole
(Whig)
1721 - 1741

Earl of Wilmington
(Whig)
1742 - 1743

Henry Pelham
(Whig)
1743 - 1754

Duke of Newcastle
(Whig)
1754 - 1756

Duke of Devonshire
(Whig)
1756 - 1757

Duke of Newcastle
(Whig)
1757 - 1762

Earl of Bute
(Tory)
1762 -1763

George Grenville
(Whig)
1763 - 1765

Marquess of Rockingham
(Whig)
1765 - 1766

Earl of Chatham
(Whig)
1766 - 1767

Duke of Grafton
(Whig)
1767 -1770

Lord North
(Tory)
1770 - 1782

Marquess of Rockingham
(Whig)
1782

Earl of Shelburne
(Whig)
1782 -1783

Duke of Portland
(Tory)
1783

William Pitt
(Tory)
1783 - 1801

Henry Addington
(Tory)
1801 - 1804

William Pitt
(Tory)
1804 - 1806

Lord Grenville
(Whig)
1806 - 1807

Duke of Portland
(Tory)
1807 - 1809

Spencer Perceval
(Tory)
1809 - 1812

Earl of Liverpool
(Tory)
1812 - 1827

George Canning
(Tory)
1827

Viscount Goderich
(Tory)
1827 - 1828

Duke of Wellington
(Tory)
1828 - 1830

Earl Grey
(Whig)
1830 - 1834

Prime Ministers of Great Britain (continued)

Viscount Melbourne
(Whig)
1834

Duke of Wellington
(Tory)
1834

Sir Robert Peel
(Tory)
1834 - 1835

Viscount Melbourne
(Whig)
1835 - 1841

Sir Robert Peel
(Tory)
1841 - 1846

Lord John Russell
(Whig)
1846 - 1852

Earl of Derby
(Conservative)
1852

Earl of Aberdeen
(Conservative)
1852 - 1855

Viscount Palmerston
(Liberal)
1855 - 1858

Earl of Derby
(Conservative)
1858

Viscount Palmerston
(Liberal)
1858 - 1865

Earl Russell
(Liberal)
1865 - 1866

Earl of Derby
(Conservative)
1866 -1868

Benjamin Disraeli
(Conservative)
1868

W E Gladstone
(Liberal)
1868 - 1874

Benjamin Disraeli
(Conservative)
1874 - 1880

W E Gladstone
(Liberal)
1880 - 1885

Marquess of Salisbury
(Conservative)
1885 - 1886

W E Gladstone
(Liberal)
1886

Marquess of Salisbury
(Conservative)
1886 - 1892

W E Gladstone
(Liberal)
1892 - 1894

Earl of Rosebery
(Liberal)
1894 - 1895

Marquess of Salisbury
(Conservative)
1895 - 1902

A J Balfour
(Conservative)
1902 - 1905

Sir Henry Campbell-Bannerman
(Liberal)
1905 - 1908

H H Asquith
(Liberal)
1908 - 1916

Prime Ministers of Great Britain (continued)

David Lloyd George
(Liberal)
1916 - 1922

A Bonar Law
(Conservative)
1922 - 1923

Stanley Baldwin
(Conservative)
1923 - 1924

J Ramsay MacDonald
(Labour)
1924

Stanley Baldwin
(Conservative)
1924 - 1929

J Ramsay MacDonald
(Labour)
1929 - 1931

J Ramsay MacDonald
(Coalition)
1931 - 1935

Stanley Baldwin
(Conservative)
1935 - 1937

Neville Chamberlain
(Conservative)
1937 - 1940

Winston S Churchill
(Conservative)
1940 - 1945

Clement Attlee
(Labour)
1945 - 1951

Sir Winston Churchill
(Conservative)
1951 - 1955

Sir Anthony Eden
(Conservative)
1955 - 1957

Harold Macmillan
(Conservative)
1957 - 1963

Sir Alec Douglas-Home
(Conservative)
1963 - 1964

Harold Wilson
(Labour)
1964 - 1970

Edward Heath
(Conservative)
1970 - 1974

Harold Wilson
(Labour)
1974 - 1976

James Callaghan
(Labour)
1976 - 1979

Margaret Thatcher
(Conservative)
1979 - 1990

John Major
(Conservative)
1990 - 1997

Tony Blair
(Labour)
1997 -

Presidents of the United States of America

George Washington
(Federalist)
1789 - 1797

John Adams
(Federalist)
1797 - 1801

Thomas Jefferson
(Democrat-Republican)
1801 - 1809

James Madison
(Democrat-Republican)
1809 - 1817

James Monroe
(Democrat-Republican)
1817 - 1825

John Quincy Adams
(Democrat-Republican)
1825 - 1829

Andrew Jackson
(Democrat)
1829 - 1837

Martin Van Buren
(Democrat)
1837 - 1841

William Harrison
(Whig)
1841

John Tyler
(Whig)
1841 - 1845

James Polk
(Democrat)
1845 - 1849

Zachary Taylor
(Whig)
1849 - 1850

Millard Fillmore
(Whig)
1850 - 1853

Franklin Pierce
(Democrat)
1853 - 1857

James Buchanan
(Democrat)
1857 - 1861

Abraham Lincoln
(Republican)
1861 - 1865

Andrew Johnson
(Republican)
1865 - 1869

Ulysses S Grant
(Republican)
1869 - 1877

Rutherford Hayes
(Republican)
1877 - 1881

James Garfield
(Republican)
1881

Chester Arthur
(Republican)
1881 - 1885

Grover Cleveland
(Democrat)
1885 - 1889

Benjamin Harrison
(Republican)
1889 - 1893

Grover Cleveland
(Democrat)
1893 - 1897

William McKinley
(Republican)
1897 - 1901

Theodore Roosevelt
(Republican)
1901 - 1909

Presidents of the United States of America (continued)

William H Taft
(Republican)
1909 - 1913

Woodrow Wilson
(Democrat)
1913 - 1921

Warren Harding
(Republican)
1921 - 1923

Calvin Coolidge
(Republican)
1923 - 1929

Herbert Hoover
(Republican)
1929 - 1933

Franklin D Roosevelt
(Democrat)
1933 - 1945

Harry S Truman
(Democrat)
1945 - 1953

Dwight D Eisenhower
(Republican)
1953 - 1961

John F Kennedy
(Democrat)
1961 - 1963

Lyndon B Johnson
(Democrat)
1963 - 1969

Richard M Nixon
(Republican)
1969 - 1974

Gerald Ford
(Republican)
1974 - 1977

Jimmy Carter
(Democrat)
1977 - 1981

Ronald Reagan
(Republican)
1981 - 1989

George Bush
(Republican)
1989 - 1993

William Clinton
(Democrat)
1993 -

Kings and Queens of England from 1066

House of Normandy

William I
1066 - 1087
William II
1087 - 1100
Henry I
1100 - 1135
Stephen
1135 - 1154

House of Plantagenet

Henry II
1154 - 1189
Richard I
1189 - 1199
John
1199 - 1216
Henry III
1216 - 1272
Edward I
1272 - 1307
Edward II
1307 - 1327
Edward III
1327 - 1377
Richard II
1377 - 1399

House of Lancaster

Henry IV
1399 - 1413
Henry V
1413 - 1422
Henry VI
1422 - 1461

House of York

Edward IV
1461 - 1483
Edward V
1483
Richard III
1483 - 1485

House of Tudor

Henry VII
1485 - 1509
Henry VIII
1509 - 1547
Edward VI
1547 - 1553
Mary I
1553 - 1558
Elizabeth I
1558 - 1603

House of Stuart

James I
1603 - 1625
Charles I
1625 - 1649
The Commonwealth
1649 - 1659
Charles II
1660 - 1685
James II
1685 - 1688
Mary II & William III
1689 - 1694
William III
1694 - 1702
Anne
1702 - 1714

Kings and Queens of England from 1066 (continued)

House of Hanover

George I
1714 - 1727
George II
1727 - 1760
George III
1760 - 1820
George IV
1820 - 1830
William IV
1830 - 1837
Victoria
1837 - 1901

House of Saxe-Coburg

Edward VII
1901 - 1910

House of Windsor

George V
1910 - 1936
Edward VIII
1936
George VI
1936 - 1952
Elizabeth II
1952 -

THE UNITED KINGDOM

Members of the Cabinet

Prime Minister, First Lord of the Treasury, Minister for the Civil Service
Deputy Prime Minister and Secretary of State for the Environment, Transport
  and the Regions
Lord Chancellor
Secretary of State for Foreign and Commonwealth Affairs
Chancellor of the Exchequer
Secretary of State for the Home Department
President of the Council and Leader of the House of Commons
Secretary of State for Defence
Secretary of State for Wales
Secretary of State for Social Security & Minister for Women
Secretary of State for Northern Ireland
Secretary of State for Scotland
Secretary of State for the Environment
Secretary of State for Health
Secretary of State for International Development
Secretary of State for National Heritage
Secretary of State for Education and Employment
President of the Board of Trade and Secretary of State for Trade and Industry
Minister for Transport
Chancellor of the Duchy of Lancaster
Minister of Agriculture, Fisheries and Food
Chief Secretary to the Treasury
Lord Privy Seal and Leader of the House of Lords
Minister without Portfolio
Law Officers
Attorney General
Lord Advocate
Solicitor General
Solicitor General for Scotland

THE UNITED STATES OF AMERICA

Members of the Cabinet

The President of the United States
The Vice-President of the United States
Secretary of State
Secretary of the Treasury
Secretary of Defense
Secretary of Commerce
Attorney-General
Secretary of the Interior
Secretary of Agriculture
Secretary of Labor
Secretary of Health and Human Services
Secretary of Housing and Urban Development
Secretary of Transportation
Secretary of Energy
Secretary of Education
Secretary of Veterans' Affairs
Ambassador to the United Nations
US Trade Representative
Administrator, Environmental Protection Agency
Director, Office of Management and Budget
National Security Adviser
White House Chief of Staff

A BRITISH GOVERNMENT DEPARTMENT

The Department of Trade and Industry

Minister
President of the Board of Trade, Secretary of State for Trade and Industry
    Private Secretary; Parliamentary Private Secretary
    Special Advisers
Ministers of State
Minister for Trade
    Private Secretary
Minister for Science, Energy and Industry
    Private Secretary
Minister for Trade and Competitiveness in Europe
    Private Secretary
Parliamentary Under-Secretaries of State
Competition and Consumer Affairs
    Private Secretary
Small Firms, Trade and Industry
    Private Secretary
Chairman: British Overseas Trade Board
    Private Secretary
Officials
Permanent Secretary
    Private Secretary
Directorates
Trade Policy Command - Director General, Directors
Export Promotion Command - Director General, Directors
Industry Command - Director General, Directors
Energy Command - Director General, Directors
Regional and SME Command - Director General, Directors
Corporate and Consumer Affairs Command - Director General, Directors
Legal Services Command - Solicitor and Director General, Directors
Resources and Services Command - Director General, Directors
Office of Science and Technology
    Chief Scientific Adviser to the Government
Central Functions and the Ministerial Organisation
    Chief Economic Adviser
    Chief Adviser on Statistics